Anonymous

The Consolidation Act and Other Acts

Relating to the Government of the City and Country of San Francisco

Anonymous

The Consolidation Act and Other Acts
Relating to the Government of the City and Country of San Francisco

ISBN/EAN: 9783744669542

Printed in Europe, USA, Canada, Australia, Japan

Cover: Foto ©Suzi / pixelio.de

More available books at **www.hansebooks.com**

THE

CONSOLIDATION ACT

AND

OTHER ACTS

Relating to the Government

OF THE

City and County of San Francisco.

COMPILED BY A. E. T. WORLEY,

Of the San Francisco Bar.

SAN FRANCISCO:
PRINTED BY WM. M. HINTON & CO., 536 CLAY ST.
1887.

Consolidation Act.

PREFATORY NOTE.

This compilation includes all amendments made to the Acts contained in it, including the session of the Legislature of 1877-8.

There are also added the laws passed by subsequent Legislatures up to and including 1885, which have special reference to San Francisco.

The figures next beneath the number of each Supplement refer to the year and page of the session laws containing the Act which follows; and the figures following the year, in the date of the passage of any Act, or amendment to an Act, throughout this compilation, refer to the page of the volume of laws of the year specified, and such reference indicates the first page of the Act.

CONSOLIDATION ACT.

LAWS OF 1856, PAGE 145.

AN ACT

TO REPEAL THE SEVERAL CHARTERS OF THE CITY OF SAN
FRANCISCO, TO ESTABLISH THE BOUNDARIES OF THE CITY
AND COUNTY OF SAN FRANCISCO, AND TO CONSOLIDATE
THE GOVERNMENT THEREOF.

[Approved April 19, 1856.]

---

*The People of the State of California, represented in Senate and Assembly, do
enact as follows:*

ARTICLE I.

SECTION 1. The corporation, or body politic and corporate, now existing
and known as the City of San Francisco, shall remain and continue to be a
body politic and corporate, in name and in fact, by the name of the City and
County of San Francisco, and by that name shall have perpetual succession,
may sue and defend in all courts and places, and in all matters and proceedings whatever, and may have and may use a common seal, and the same may
alter at pleasure, and may purchase, receive, hold and enjoy real and personal
property, and sell, convey, mortgage and dispose of the same for the common
benefit. The boundaries of the City and County of San Francisco shall be
as follows: [Here follows the boundary lines as then described, but which
have since been changed.]

The present boundaries are thus defined in Section 3950 of the Political Code:

Beginning at the southwest corner, being northwest corner of San Mateo, in Pacific Ocean, on the extension of northern line of Township Three South, of Mount Diablo base; thence northerly along the Pacific Coast, to its point of intersection with westerly extension of low water line on northern side of the entrance to San Francisco Bay, being southwest corner of Marin and northwest corner of San Francisco; thence easterly, through Point Bonita and Point Caballo, to the most southeastern point of Angel Island, all on the line of Marin, as established in Section 3957; thence northerly, along the easterly line of Marin, to the northwest point of Golden Rock (also known as Red Rock), being a common corner of Marin, Contra Costa and San Francisco; thence due southeast four and one-half miles, more or less, to a point distant three statute miles from the natural high-water mark on the eastern shore of San Francisco Bay, being a common corner of Contra Costa, Alameda and San Francisco; thence southeasterly, in a direct line, to a point three miles from said eastern shore, and on the line first named (considered as extending across said bay); and thence west along said first named line to the place of beginning. The islands known as the Farallones shall be attached to and be a part of said city and county.[1]

Provided, however, that all rights and liabilities of the corporation heretofore and now known as the City of San Francisco shall survive to, and continue against, the corporations continued by this act. [By an amendment passed April 18, 1857, page 209, the following was added to the section:] The district or districts of said city and county, bordering upon the southern line thereof, as heretofore established, shall be extended to the southern line of said city and county as established in this Act.

Sec. 2. The public buildings, lands, and property, all rights of property and rights of action, and all moneys, revenues and income, belonging or appertaining either to the corporation of the City of San Francisco or to the County of San Francisco, are hereby declared to be vested in, and to appertain to, the said City and County of San Francisco; and the moneys in the treasury of said city, and in the treasury of said County of San Francisco, and all the revenues and income from whatsoever source arising, including delinquent taxes upon persons and property appertaining to the said City or to the said County, shall be handed over, paid and received into the treasury of the City and County of San Francisco as a part of the General Fund; or where

---

[1] By Section 3953 of the Political Code, as amended March 30, 1874, the western boundary of Alameda county is now made to pass five hundred feet westerly from the western extremity of the Central Pacific Railroad Company's wharf as it now is; provided that no part of Yerba Buena island shall be placed outside of the City and County of San Francisco, and the westerly boundary of the county line of Alameda shall not come within two thousand five hundred feet of any part of said island.

the said moneys, revenues and income, or any part thereof, have been heretofore and still remain set apart and dedicated by lawful authority to the use of a Special Fund, the necessity and objects of which still continue, the same shall continue to be received, held, and disbursed for the same use, unless it is otherwise provided in this or some other Act.

SEC. 3. The records, books, and papers, in the custody of the said City Treasurer, shall be handed over to and received into the custody of the Treasurer of the said City and County, and all other books, records and papers of the said corporation shall be delivered and received into the custody of the Clerk of the Board of Supervisors of said City and County, and shall not be withheld under any claim of a lien thereon for arrears of salary, fees, services or advances, nor under any other pretense whatsoever. Suits and actions may be brought and maintained in the name of the City and County of San Francisco for the recovery of any property, money or thing belonging thereto, or the enforcement of any rights of, or contracts with, said City and County. And from any judgment rendered against the said City and County in any court, an appeal may be taken by the said City and County, where such appeal is allowed by law, without the giving of any appeal bond or undertaking, on complying with the other requisites prescribed by law.

SEC. 4. All the existing provisions of law defining the powers and duties of county officers, excepting those relating to Supervisors and Boards of Supervisors, so far as the same are not repealed nor altered by the provisions of this Act, shall be considered as applicable to officers of the said City and County of San Francisco, acting or elected under this Act. Provision shall be made from the revenues of the said City and County for the payment of the legal indebtedness of the former city corporation and of the County of San Francisco. The taxes which may be levied and collected under the provisions of this Act, shall be uniform throughout the said City and County of San Francisco; but in case it should hereafter be found necessary, for the purpose of providing for the said city indebtedness, to increase taxation beyond the rate of the County tax levied upon property in said County of San Francisco during the year one thousand eight hundred and fifty-five, such increased taxation, over and above the rate aforesaid, shall be levied and assessed exclusively upon the real and personal property situated within the limits defined in the second section of the Act entitled "An Act to re-incorporate the City of San Francisco," passed May fifth, one thousand eight hundred and fifty-five,[2] and not upon such property situated without those limits.

---

[2] Laws 1855, p. 251. Section 2 of this Act thus defined the boundary line of the city: "On the south by a line drawn parallel with Clay street, two and a half miles distant from the center of Portsmouth Square; on the west by a line drawn parallel with Kearny street, two miles distant from the center of Portsmouth Square; its boundaries on the north and east shall be the same with those of the county of San Francisco."

SEC. 5. Immediately after the passage of this Act, the present City Attorney, Surveyor-General and C. K. Garrison shall proceed to lay off the said City and County into twelve convenient districts, equal in population as near as conveniently may be, giving a distinct name to each district, the boundaries of which they shall accurately define by reference to public streets, roads or other permanent monuments, and shall cause a map to be made representing the said districts, with their names and boundaries so fixed. The act of said officers establishing said districts, signed by them, or a majority of them, shall be recorded in the office of the County Recorder of said City and County, and the original be deposited in the office of the County Clerk, and the map shall be deposited with the said County Surveyor. Each of said districts shall constitute an election precinct.[3]

SEC. 6. [*Amended by Act of April 18, 1857, 209, which was superseded by Acts of April 29, 1857, 345;[4] April 22, 1861, 214; May 3, 1861, 291; May 2, 1862, 475; which latter three were superseded or repealed by Act of April 2, 1866; 1865-6, 718; post, Supplement XXIX. Provisions of Act of April 18, 1857, as to election of Inspector and Judges of Elections, superseded by secs. 1142 to 1150, inclusive, Political Code, and Act of March 18, 1878, Supplement, also sec. 4109 of Political Code; and as to election of Justices of the Peace, by Act of March 26, 1866; 1865-6, 423; Supplement XXVII; and by sec. 6 of Act of April 2, 1866, ub. sup. Office of Constable abolished by Act of Feb. 10, 1870; sec. 12, 1869-70, 56. See sec. 12 of portion of Act at end of Supplement XXIX.*]

SEC. 7. By the term "qualification of officers," as used in this Act, is to be understood their having taken the oath of office, given the official bond, where it is required by law, and complied with all the requisites prescribed by the statutes of this State, to entitle and qualify them to exercise the functions of their offices.

SEC. 8. The Sheriff, County Clerk, County Recorder, Treasurer, District Attorney, Auditor, Tax Collector, Superintendent of Public Streets and Highways, Surveyor, Harbor Master,[5] and Clerk of the Board of Supervisors of

---

[3] Districts changed to wards by Act of April 2, 1863; 1865 6, 718, Section 1; post, Supplement XXIX. See also Chap. CCLII, Laws 1877-8, p. 299, by which the Board of Election Commissioners is established, with power to divide the city into election precincts; also Political Code, Sections 1127 to 1132, inclusive.

[4] The portion of this Act relating to supplying a vacancy in the office of School Director, re-enacted by Section 13 of Act of April 27, 1863, 601, Supplement XIII; and that as to vacancy in the office of Supervisor is as follows: "And all vacancies in the office of Supervisor, * * * where the term of the office will not expire at the next ensuing general election, shall be then filled by an election, in the proper district, for the unexpired term; and for the interval between the happening of any such vacancy and the general election next ensuing, any vacancy in the office of Supervisor shall be filled by appointment by the President of the Board of Supervisors, by and with the advice and consent of a majority of the Supervisors then in office. * * * But no such appointment shall be valid, unless the appointee be at the time of his appointment an elector of the district wherein the vacancy occurred."

[5] Office of Harbor Master extinct by Act of March 30, 1874; 1873-4, 910.

said City and County, shall keep public offices, which shall be kept open for the transaction of business every day in the year, except Sundays, Christmas, New Year's, Fourth of July, Thanksgiving, the twenty-second of February, and on any days during which a general election shall be held, between the hours of nine o'clock A. M. and four o'clock P. M. [*Amended, May 14, 1861, 375.*]

SEC. 9. Whenever vacancies occur in any elective office of the said City and County, and provision is not otherwise made in this or some other Act for filling the same until the next election, the Board of Supervisors shall appoint a person to discharge the duties of such office until the next election, when the vacancy shall be filled by election for the term, excepting vacancies in the office of Dock Masters, which vacancies shall be filled by appointments by the Governor.[7] All persons so appointed shall, before entering upon their duties, take the oath of office and give bond as required by law. But in an action or proceeding where the Sheriff of said City and County is a party, or is interested, or otherwise incapacitated to execute the orders or process therein, the same shall be executed by a suitable person, residing in said City and County, to be appointed by the Court, and denominated an " Elisor," who shall give such security as the Court in its discretion may require, and shall execute the process and orders in the same manner as the Sheriff is required to execute similar process and orders in other cases.[8]

SEC. 10. [*Relating to compensation of certain officers. Amended March 28, 1859, 141. Superseded by Sec. 6 of Act of March 26, 1866; 1865–6, 423; Supplement XXVI, and by provisions of Act of May 17, 1861, 554; Supplement VII; and of Act of January 25, 1870; 1869–70, 23; Supplement XLI.*]

SEC. 11. [*Repealed, with the exception of the following provisions, by Act of May 17, 1861, 554; Supplement VII.*]   *   *   *   *   *   *   *

He [*the Clerk of the Board of Supervisors*] shall also be entitled to receive from the parties at whose instance the service may be performed (the City and County excepted), twenty-five cents for administering an oath, twenty-five cents per folio of one hundred words for writing out affidavits, and sixteen cents per folio for certified copies of any records, papers or documents in his custody.[9] [As amended by Sec. 4 of Act April 18, 1857; 1857, 212.]
*   *   *   *   *   *   *   *

The District Attorney   *   *   not being relieved from the obligation to attend personally in said Court [*Police Court*], whenever business of importance shall require his assistance.   *   *   *   No compensation shall be allowed to Supervisors [*allowed $100 per month, Act March 30, 1868; 1867–8, 702; Supplement XL*] or School Directors, and no fees or compensa-

---

[7] Dock Master's office abolished after January 1, 1858, by Act March 26, 1857, 100, Section 16.

[8] Coroner to act as Elisor in such case. Act of March 16, 1872; 1871 2, 403.

Payable into Special Fee Fund. Supplement VII, Section 2.

tion to be paid out of the City and County Treasury, other than those expressly allowed in this Act, shall be allowed or received by any officer of said City and County, or of any district; nor shall any allowance or provision be made for them, or any of them, at the public expense, beyond the fixed compensation aforesaid, under the name of office rent*, fuel, lights, stationery, contingencies, or otherwise, except that the necessary and proper books, stationery and official blanks may, at the discretion of the Board of Supervisors, be purchased and supplied for the Police Court, Court of Sessions,[10] Grand Juries and officers [offices] of the County Clerk, County Recorder, Auditor, Treasurer, Assessor, Superintendent of Streets and Highways and the Board of Supervisors, the expense whereof, when the amount in each particular case shall have been previously authorized and fixed by the Board of Supervisors, may be paid out of the General Fund, upon demands upon the treasury, duly audited as provided in this Act; *provided*, that the total amount of expenditures for all of the aforesaid books, stationery and official blanks shall not exceed the sum of twenty-five hundred dollars in any one year. [*Amended April* 18, 1857, 209.]

SEC. 12. Neither the Board of Supervisors, the Board of Education, nor any officer of the said City and County, or of any district, shall have any power to contract any debt or liability, in any form whatsoever, against the said City and County; nor shall the people or taxpayers, or any property therein, ever be liable to be assessed for, or on account of, any debt or liability hereafter contracted, or supposed or attempted to be contracted, in contravention of this section.

SEC. 13. [*Provision as to first election, obsolete; as to commencement of term of office, changed by Act of March* 7, 1881, *amending Sect.* 4109 *of Political Code.*]

SEC. 14. All officers of the said City and County must, before they can enter upon their official duties, give bond as required by law. The bonds and sureties of such officers must be approved by the County Judge,† Auditor and President of the Board of Supervisors. Where the amount of such official bond is not fixed by law, it shall be fixed by the Board of Supervisors. No banker residing or doing business in said City and County,

---

*By the Act of January 30, 1864; 1863-4, 42; it is provided:

SECTION 3. From and after the 1st day of June, 1864, and after the purchase aforesaid, it shall not be lawful to pay out of the treasury of the City and County of San Francisco, or out of any public funds thereof, any money for rent of rooms or offices for Judges' chambers, the City and County Attorney, the Board of Education, the Board of Delegates of the Fire Department, or for any other officer or officers of the said City and County; provided, that this section shall not impair any contract now existing.

[Sections 1 and 2 provide for purchasing and repairing a building adjoining the City Hall. Obsolete.]

[10] Court of Sessions abolished by amendments to Constitution of 1862.

†Now Judge of the Superior Court by Act of April 3, 1880; 1880, 115.

nor any such banker's partner, clerk, employee, agent, attorney, father, son or brother, shall be received as surety for the Treasurer, President of the Board of Supervisors, Sheriff, Auditor, nor any officer having the collection, custody or disbursement of money. No person can be admitted as surety on any such bond, unless he be worth, in fixed property, including mortgages, situated in said City and County, the amount of his undertaking, over and above all sums for which he is already liable or in any manner bound, whether as principal, indorser, or security, and whether such prior obligation or liability be conditional or absolute, liquidated or unliquidated, certain or contingent, due or to become due. All persons offered as sureties on official bonds may be examined on oath touching their qualifications. The official bond of the Auditor shall be filed and kept in the office of the Clerk of said City and County. All other official bonds shall be filed and kept in the office of the Auditor. [*   *   *As to officers continued in office, obsolete.] [Amended March 28, 1859, 141.]

ARTICLE II.

PUBLIC ORDER AND POLICE.

SEC. 15. The Department of Police of said City and County shall be under the direction of the Chief of Police, in subjection to the laws of this State, and the rules and regulations, not in conflict therewith, which may be established by competent authority, under the powers granted in this Act. In the suppression of any riot, public tumult, disturbances of the public peace, or organized resistance against the laws, or public authorities in the lawful exercise of their functions, he shall have all the powers that now are, or hereafter may be, conferred upon Sheriffs by the laws of this State, and his lawful orders shall be promptly executed by all Police Officers, Watchmen and Constables in the said City and County; and every citizen shall also lend him aid, when required, for the arrest of offenders and maintenance of public order.

SEC. 16. The Chief of Police shall keep a public office, which shall be open, and at which he, or in case of his necessary absence, a Captain of Police, or Police Officer, by him designated for that purpose, shall be in attendance, at all hours, day and night. In case of his necessary absence from his office, it shall be made known to the Police Officer in attendance where he can be found, if needed, and he shall not absent himself from the City and County without urgent necessity, and leave obtained, in writing, from the President of the Board of Supervisors, Police Judge and County Judge, or two of them, who shall, at the time of granting the same, appoint a person to act during his absence, with all his powers, duties and obligations. If

such absence from the City and County be on any other than business immediately connected with his office, he shall lose his salary for the time of such
absence, of which account shall be taken by the Police Judge.

SEC. 17. The Chief of Police shall designate one or more out of the
number of Police officers to attend constantly upon the Police Judge's Court,
to execute the orders and process of the said Court; he may order to be
arrested and to be taken before the Police Judge, any person guilty of a
breach of the peace or a violation of the general regulations established by
the Board of Supervisors under the authority granted in this Act; he shall
supervise and direct the Police force of said City and County, and shall observe and cause to be observed the provisions of this Act, and the regulations
established by the Board of Supervisors in relation thereto; he shall see
that the lawful orders and process issued by the Police Judge's Court are
promptly executed; and shall exercise such other powers connected with his
office, as head of Police, as may be prescribed in the general regulations
adopted by the Board of Supervisors.

SEC. 18. The Chief of Police shall acquaint himself with all the statutes
and laws in force in that State defining public offenses and nuisances, and
regulating criminal proceedings, and shall procure and keep in his office the
Statutes of this State and of the United States, and all necessary elementary
works on that subject; he shall give information and advice touching said
laws, gratuitously, to all Police Officers and Magistrates asking it.

SEC. 19. [*Amended April* 18, 1857, 209; *April* 27, 1863, 739].[11] * * *
A Clerk shall be appointed [for the Police Judge's Court] by the Board of
Supervisors, with a salary of *two hundred dollars per month* [*Amended by Act
of May* 17, 1861, 554, 555; *Supplement VII*]; who shall give bond as required by law, and hold his office during the pleasure of the said Board.
[*The remaining portion of the section is repealed by the Act of January* 27,
1864; *1863-4, 30, Supplement XVI.* By the Act of March 7, 1881, an additional Clerk is appointed for Police Court No 2.]

SEC. 20. Proceedings in the Police Judge's Court shall be conducted in
conformity with the laws regulating proceedings in the Recorders' Courts.
The said Court shall be open daily, Sundays excepted.[12] * * *

SEC. 21. The Clerk of the Police Judge's Court shall keep a record of its
proceedings, issue all process ordered by said Court, receive and pay weekly
into the treasury of the City and County all fines imposed by said Court,[13]

---

[11] By this Act the Police Judge's Court is declared not to be a Court of Record. See also Sections
33 and 34 of the Code of Civil Procedure.

[12] Remainder of section superseded by Act of December 9, 1865; 1865-6, 1; Supplement XXI.
See also Penal Code, Sections 1426 to 1470, inclusive.

[13] Fines and forfeitures not exceeding eight hundred dollars in any one month, imposed for
drunkenness, shall be paid to officers of Home for Care of Inebriates. Act of March 17, 1876; 1875-6,
325; Supplement LXXVII.

and render to the County Auditor, monthly, and before any amount can be paid him on account of salary, an exact and detailed account, upon oath, accompanied with an exhibition of said record, of all fines imposed and moneys collected since his last account rendered. He shall prepare bonds, justify and accept bail, when the amount has been fixed by the Police Judge, in cases not exceeding one thousand dollars, and he shall fix, justify and accept bail after arrest, in the absence of the Police Judge, in all cases not amounting to a felony, in the same manner and to the same effect as though the same had been fixed by the Police Judge. The said Clerk shall remain at the court-room of said Court, in the City Hall, during the hours named in Section eight of the Act of which this is amendatory, and during such reasonable hours thereafter as may be necessary for the purpose of discharging his said duties. [*Amended May* 18, 1861, 544.]

SEC. 22. All fines imposed by the Police Judge's Court, Court of Sessions[14] of said City and County, or any Justices' Court, shall be paid into the treasury thereof, as part of the Police Fund;[15] in cases where, for any offense, the said courts are authorized to impose a fine or imprisonment in the county jail or both, they may, instead thereof, sentence the offender to be employed in labor upon the public works of said City and County, for a period of time equal to the term of imprisonment which might be legally imposed, and may, in case of imposing a fine, embrace as a part of the sentence, that in default of payment of such fine, the offender shall be employed to labor on said public works at one dollar a day till the fine imposed is satisfied. By the public works, as used in this Act, is understood the construction, or repair, or cleaning, of any street, road, dock, wharf, public square, park, building, or other works whatsoever, which is authorized to be done by and for the use of the said City and County, and the expense of which is not to be borne exclusively by the individuals or property particularly benefited thereby.

SEC. 23. The Chief of Police, in conjunction with the President of the Board of Supervisors and the Police Judge,[16] the concurrence of two of them being necessary to a choice, shall appoint four Captains of Police,[17] each from a different district, and as many Police Officers, not exceeding *one hundred and fifty* [*Amendment March* 23, 1872; 1871-2, 512; *Supplement L VII*], [*Further amended April* 1, 1878; 1877-8, 879] as the Board of Supervisors shall determine to be necessary. Thereof an equal number in proportion to population, as near as may be, shall be selected from each district that

14 See note 10, ante. Court of Sessions abolished.

15 See note 13, ante.

16 See note 19, post.

17 One additional allowed by Act of April 1, 1875. Laws 1877 8, p. 879. Police officers now appointed by Commissioners under Act of April 1, 1878.

shall be situated, wholly or partly, within the limits specified in section second of the Act now repealed, entitled "An Act to re-incorporate the City of San Francisco," passed May sixth [fifth], one thousand eight hundred and fifty-five."[18]

SEC. 24. No person can be appointed Captain of Police or Police Officer, unless he be a citizen of the United States and of this State, and a resident and qualified voter of the City and County; and, in case of each Police Officer, a resident of the district from which he is chosen, and also, before his appointment, shall produce to the said President of the Board of Supervisors, Chief of Police and Police Judge, a certificate signed by at least twelve freeholders and qualified voters of the said City and County, who, in case of application for appointment of a Police Officer, must also be residents of the district from which he is to be appointed, stating that they have been personally and well acquainted with the applicant for one year or more next preceding the application, and that he is of good repute for honesty and sobriety, and they believe him to be, in all respects, competent and fit for the office. All the certificates so produced shall be carefully preserved in the office of Chief of Police.

SEC. 25. Police Captains and Officers may be suspended from office by the Chief of Police, and, with the concurrence of the President of the Board of Supervisors and Police Judge, removed from office for official negligence, inefficiency, or misconduct, under such general rules and regulations, not contrary to law, as may have been established by the Board of Supervisors; they shall receive from the treasury of said City and County, payable out of the Police Fund, such compensation as may be fixed by the Board of Supervisors, not exceeding one thousand eight hundred dollars a year, each, for Captains, and one thousand two hundred dollars a year, each, for Officers. *

SEC. 26. Neither the Chief of Police, Captains, or any officer of Police, shall follow any other profession or calling, become bail for any person charged with any offense whatever, receive any present or reward for official services rendered, or to be rendered, unless with the knowledge and approbation of a majority of the Police Commissioners, to wit: the Police Judge, President of the Board of Supervisors, and Chief of Police of the City and County of San Francisco[19]—such approbation to be given in writing; nor be allowed pay for any period during which they shall absent themselves from

---

[18] Laws, 1855, p. 251; "Section 2. The City of San Francisco shall be bounded as follows: On the south by a line drawn parallel with Clay street, two and a half miles distant from the center of Portsmouth Square; on the west by a line drawn parallel with Kearny street, two miles distant from the center of Portsmouth Square; its boundaries on the north and east shall be the same with those of the County of San Francisco." * * *

* For authority to increase salaries of police force, see Supplement X, sub. 16, post.

[19] Board of Police Commissioners, composed as provided by Act of April 1, 1878.

public duty, unless such absence necessarily result from indisposition or disability occasioned by injuries suffered while in the discharge of official duty. Police Officers in subjection to the orders of the respective Captains, and all under the general direction of the Chief of Police, shall be prompt and vigilant in the detection of crime, the arrest of public offenders, the suppression of all riots, frays, duels and disturbances of the public peace, the execution of process from the Police Judge's Court, in causing the abatement of public nuisances, the removal of unlawful obstructions from the public streets, and the enforcement of the laws and regulations of the Police. [*Amended March* 24, 1859, 131.]

SEC. 27.   In case of great public emergency or danger, the Chief of Police may appoint an additional number of Policemen, of approved character for honesty and sobriety, who shall have the same powers as other Police Officers for twenty-four hours only, but without pay. The Chief of Police, Captains, and every officer of the permanent force, shall provide themselves · with a uniform and badge of office, to be prescribed by regulations of the Board of Supervisors, which shall be worn by them upon all occasions, with such exceptions as may be permitted by the Chief of Police in the performance of detective duty.

SEC. 28.   Charges of oppression or official misconduct, when presented by any citizen of said City and County, against any Police Captain or Officer, and verified on oath, setting forth the specific acts complained of, shall be received and attentively considered and determined by the Police Judge, President of the Board of Supervisors, and Chief of Police, giving to the accused due notice, and an impartial hearing in defense.* The Chief of Police, Police Judge, and all other officers now acting or hereafter to be elected or appointed under the provisions of this Act, may be accused, tried, and removed from office in the mode prescribed by the laws of this State for the removal of civil officers otherwise than by impeachment.

SEC. 29.   The Board of Supervisors shall, from time to time, establish a convenient number of Police Stations; determine within what districts the Police Officers and Captains shall usually be distributed and employed; designate the prisons to be used for the reception of all persons arrested or convicted and sentenced for public offenses, in cases not provided for by law; [and] appoint, during the pleasure of the Board, the keeper of such prisons.

ARTICLE III.

PUBLIC INSTRUCTION.

[SECS. 30 *to* 35, *inclusive, repealed by Act of April* 27, 1863, 601; *post Supplement XIII, which supersedes this article.*]

---

* Now Police Commissioners by Act of April 1, 1878; Statutes 1877-8, 870.

ARTICLE IV.

PUBLIC STREETS AND HIGHWAYS.

[SECS. 36 *to* 64, *inclusive, repealed, see post, Supplement LXIII, which is a substitute for this Article. See also Acts* 1883, 32; 1885, 147.]

ARTICLE V.

SUPERVISORS.

SEC. 65.   The Supervisors in their respective districts, shall vigilantly observe the conduct of all public officers, and take notice of the fidelity and exactitude, or the want thereof, with which they execute their duties and obligations, especially in the collection, custody, administration, and disbursement of public funds and property; for which purpose the books, records, and official papers, of all officers and magistrates of such districts shall, at all convenient times, be open to their inspection.   They shall take care that the books and records of all officers in their districts are kept in legal and proper form.   They shall have power, and it shall be their duty, every month, to examine the accounts of any officer of their respective districts, having the collection and custody of public funds, to examine and count over the moneys remaining in the hands of such officers, and shall note any discrepancy or defalcation that may be discovered, or reasonably suspected, and report the same forthwith, together with any willful official negligence or misconduct on the part of any such officer, to the President of the Board of Supervisors.

SEC. 66.   At every regular session of the Board of Supervisors, before proceeding to other business, each member shall be called upon to report, orally, upon the matters specified in the preceding section; to give information of the condition of his district, in regard to public schools, streets, roads, and highways, health, police, industry, and population, and to suggest any defects he may have noticed in the laws and regulations, or the administration thereof, and the means of remedying them.

SEC. 67.   The Supervisors shall meet within five days after each annual election, and also on the first Monday of January, April, July and October, of each year, and at such other times as specially required by law; or they may for urgent reasons, be specially convoked by the President of the Board of Supervisors.   A majority of all the Supervisors to be elected in the several districts shall constitute a quorum to do business; and no regulation, resolution, ordinance, or order of the Board, can pass without the concurrence of a majority of all the members elected,[20] but a smaller number may adjourn from day to day.   All the sessions, acts and resolutions of the Board

---

[20] Seven votes necessary.   Act March 30, 1868; 1867-8, 702; Supplement XL.

shall be public. The President of the Board of Supervisors, elected by the City and County at large, shall preside at all the sessions of the Board, without the right to vote. In his absence, during any session, the Board shall appoint a President *pro tempore*, who shall, however, have the same vote as other members. The Board of Supervisors shall be the judge of the election returns, and qualifications of its own members, and shall order and provide for holding elections in the proper districts, to fill vacancies which may happen or exist more than six months previous to the next general election; at which general election such office shall be filled by election for the full term of two years.[21] The Board of Supervisors shall determine the rules of its proceedings, keep a record of its acts and resolutions, and allow the same to be published; and the yeas and nays on any question shall, at the request of any member, be entered on its journals. The Board of Supervisors shall appoint a clerk, with a salary of *one hundred and seventy-five dollars per month*. [*Amended April* 26, 1862, 466. *Amended April* 26, 1878, 556.[22]], to hold office during the pleasure of the Board, who shall be *ex officio* Clerk of the Board of Equalization, without any additional salary as such, *except as provided in section eleven*. [*Repealed.* ·*See ante, Sec.* 11], and shall be required to take the constitutional oath of office, and give bond for the faithful discharge of the duties of his office. He shall have power to administer such oaths and affirmations as may be required by law or the regulations, or the orders of the Board, relating to any demands upon the Treasury, or other business connected with the government of the City and County; and shall also have power to certify and authenticate copies of all records, papers, and documents in his official custody. The powers of the Board of Supervisors are those granted in this Act, and they are prohibited to exercise any others. [*Amended April* 18, 1857, 209.]

SEC. 68. It shall be the duty of the President of the Board of Supervisors vigilantly to observe the official conduct of each Supervisor in his district, and of all public officers of the City and County, and take note of the fidelity and exactitude, or the want thereof, with which they execute their duties and obligations, especially in the collection, custody, administration and disbursement of the public funds and property; for which purpose the books, records and official papers of all officers and magistrates of said City and County, shall at all convenient times be open to his inspection. He shall take especial care to see that the books and records of all such officers are kept in legal and proper form; and any official defalcation, or willful neglect of duty, or official misconduct, which he may have discovered, or which shall have been reported to him by any Supervisor, shall, at the earliest opportunity, be laid before the Grand Jury, in order that the officer in de-

---

[21] See note 4, ante.

[22] Board of Supervisors authorized to increase salary, by Act of March 30, 1872; 1871 2, 735; Supplement LX.

fault may be proceeded against according to law. Every ordinance or resolution of the Board of Supervisors, providing for any specific improvement, the granting of any privilege, or involving the lease or other appropriation of public property, or the expenditure of public moneys (except
for sums less than five hundred dollars), or laying tax or assessment, and
every ordinance or resolution imposing a new duty or penalty, shall, after
its introduction in the Board, be published, with the ayes and nays, in some
city daily newspaper, at least five successive days before final action by the
Board upon the same; and every such ordinance, after the same shall pass
the Board, shall, before it takes effect, be presented to the President of the
Board for his approval. If he approves, he shall sign it; if not, he shall
return it within ten days, to the Board, with his objections in writing. The
Board shall then enter the objections on the journals, and publish them in
some city newspaper. If at any stated meeting thereafter two-thirds of all
the members elected to the Board vote for such ordinance or resolution, it
shall then, despite the objections of the President, become valid.[23] Should
any such ordinance or resolution not be returned by the President, within
ten days after he receives it, it shall become valid the same as if it had received his signature.

SEC. 69. All contracts for building[24] and printing to be done for the said
City and County, and ordinary supplies for subsistence of prisoners, must
be given by the Board of Supervisors to the lowest bidder offering adequate
security, after due public notice published for not less than five days, in at
least two newspapers in said City and County. *All contracts for subsistence of prisoners must be given out annually at a fixed price per day, not exceeding twenty-five cents per diem, for each person connected with the prison*
[*Amended April 26, 1862, 466*]; and the advertisements for proposals to be
published as aforesaid by the Board of Supervisors, shall specify each article that will be required, the quality thereof, the quantity for each person,
and the existing and probable number of prisoners to be supplied. All articles of food supplied for prisoners must be of a sound and wholesome
quality, and subject to the inspection and approval of the keeper of the
prison, and also of the President of the Board of Supervisors and Police
Judge of said City and County, all of which must be expressed in the contract therefor to be entered into.

SEC. 70. The Board of Supervisors shall have power to hear and determine
appeals from the executive officers of said City and County, in the cases
provided in this act; and in all cases of an appeal taken to the Board of Supervisors, or Board of Education, from the order or decision made by any

---

[23] Nine votes necessary. Section 2, Act of March 30, 1868; 1867-8, 702; Supplement XL.

[24] Declared to be inapplicable to the Board of Education of the City and County of San Francisco
and to the property, real and personal, of the School Department, by Section 8 of Act of April 26,
1858, 341. And see Section 1, Sub. 10, Act of April 1, 1872, 946; Supplement LXIV.

other officer or officers, such officer or officers shall furnish the Board with a statement of his or their reasons for the order or decision so appealed from, and the party appealing shall be heard briefly, but without the observance of any technical or other formalities, not necessary, in the discretion of the Board, to a just decision, which shall, after ascertaining the true state of the case, be given without delay.

Sec. 71. *First.* On or before the first Monday of May,[25] annually, the Board of Supervisors of said City and County shall levy the amount of taxes for State, City and County purposes, required by law to be levied upon all property not exempt from taxation, said amount to be such as the said Board may deem sufficient to provide for the payment of all demands upon the treasury thereof, authorized by law to be paid out of the same; *provided,* that such taxation, exclusive of the State tax, and any and all special taxes now, or which hereafter may be, authorized by law, shall not in the aggregate exceed the rate now allowed by said Act of which this is amendatory—to wit: two dollars and thirty-five cents upon each one hundred dollars' valuation of the property to be assessed; *provided, further,* that the said Board of Supervisors shall, in making the said levy of said taxes, apportion and divide the taxes so levied and to be collected and applied to the several specific funds known as the Corporation Debt Fund, General Fund, School Fund, Street Light Fund, and Street Department Fund, according to the estimate of said Board of the necessities of the said Funds, except that the rate for the School Fund shall not exceed thirty-five cents[26] on each one hundred dollars' valuation of property; and *provided, further,* that the said Board shall authorize the disbursement of said money for the purposes hereinafter mentioned; and at the close of each fiscal year the said Board shall direct the Treasurer to transfer all surplus moneys of all funds, excepting the School Fund, after liquidating or providing for all outstanding demands upon said funds, to the General Fund; but no money shall be transferred from either of the said funds to another; nor used in paying any demands upon such other fund, until all the indebtedness arising in any fiscal year and payable out of said funds so raised for said fiscal year shall have been paid and discharged.

Second. The Corporation Debt Fund shall be applied to and used for the payment of demands authorized under the fourth, fifth, sixth, eighth and tenth subdivisions of section ninety-five of the Act of which this is amendatory, and the several other acts amendatory thereof, and of section seven of an Act entitled an Act to provide for the funding and payment of the outstanding unfunded claims against the City of San Francisco and against the County of San Francisco, as they existed prior to the first day of July, A. D.

---

[25] On fourth Monday of June fix rate of City and County taxes. See Section 4, Act of March 18, 1874, 477; Supplement XCVII. Also see Section 3714, Pol. Code.

[26] The aggregate shall not exceed thirty-five dollars for each pupil who shall have attended and been taught the preceding year; Section 4, Act of April 1, 1872, 846; Supplement LXIV.

eighteen hundred and [fifty-six, approved April twentieth, A. D. eighteen hundred and] fifty-eight.

Third. The General Fund shall be applied and used for the payment of all sums authorized by law to be paid out of the General Fund, and not otherwise provided for in this Act.

Fourth. The School Fund shall be applied and used for the payment of all sums authorized by law to be paid out of the School Fund.

Fifth. The Street Light fund shall be applied and used in payment for lighting the streets of the city, and for the repair of lamps and posts in pursuance of any existing or future contract of the said City and County.

Sixth. The Street Department Fund shall be applied and used for repairing, improving all streets, lanes and the crossings thereof, which shall have been accepted by the said Board of Supervisors; for cleaning streets, lanes, crossings and sewers;* for all street work in front of, or assessable upon, property belonging to the said City and County, except school lots already payable out of [the] School Fund;[27] for all street work on the water front of said City and County not by law assessable upon private property; for all work authorized by the said Board upon the recommendation cf the Superintendent of Streets and Highways, as immediately essential for the safety of life, limb or property, or necessary for public health, or which cannot be by law assessed upon private property, and for such other objects, relating to streets and highways, as shall be directed by law to be paid therefrom. All moneys received from licenses on vehicles, from the income from street railroads, from fines and penalties for violation of any law or ordinance regulating vehicles or the public streets, shall be paid into the Street Department Fund. [*Amended, March* 26, 1866; 1865-6, 436.] ‡

SEC. 72. The said Board of Supervisors shall also constitute a Board of Equalization for said City and County, and as such shall have the powers conferred by the general laws regulating the assessment and collection of taxes, when not inconsistent with the provisions of this Act. Appointments of officers or public agents required by existing statutes, not repealed by this Act, to be made on the nomination of the Mayor, and confirmation by the Common Council of the City of San Francisco, shall, after this Act takes effect, be made in like manner on the nomination of the President of the Board of Supervisors and a confirmation by said Board.

SEC. 73. It shall be the duty of the Auditor, the Superintendent of Common Schools, the Superintendent of Public Streets and Highways, Chief of

---

*See Act April 3, 1876; 1875 6. 795; Supplement LXXXIII; in connection with this.

Also Act of December 21, 1877; 1887 8, 4; also Act of March 27, 1878; 1878, 544.

[27] Expense of improvements in front of school lots payable from same fund as other street work. Act March 30, 1868; 1867 8, 558; Supplement XXXIX, Section 2.

‡See Act April 3, 1876; 1875-6, 795; Supplement LXXXIII; in connection with this. ●
See Supplement X, Section 7.

Police and Chief Engineer of the Fire Department of said City and County, to report to the Board of Supervisors on the first Monday in February* of each year the condition of their respective departments, embracing all their operations and expenditures during the preceding year, and recommending such improvements in them as they may deem necessary. The Auditor shall also present to the Board of Supervsiors at each quarterly session, and must also publish the same, a statement of the exact condition of the finances of said City and County, which must show the receipts into, and disbursements made from the treasury during the preceding quarter, the amount of money on hand, and the amount of audited demands outstanding. Immediately after the first Monday in February the Board of Supervisors shall make up and publish an abstract from these several reports and other sources of the operations, expenditures and condition of all departments of government of the said City and County.

SEC. 74. [*As amended May* 18, 1861, 544.] The Board of Supervisors shall further have power, by regulation or order:

First. [*Superseded by Sec. 1, Sub. 1, Act of April* 25, 1863, 540; *Supplement XII.*]

Second. To provide for the security, custody and administration of all property of said City and County, without any power to sell or encumber the same, or lease any part thereof for more than three years; except, however, that such personal property belonging to the fire, street, or other departments, as they deem unsuited to the uses and purposes for which the same was designed, or so much worn and dilapidated as not to be worth repairing, may be sold or exchanged, by order or resolution.[26]   *   *   *   *   *

[*The portion of this subdivision as thus amended, relating to appointment of a City and County Attorney by the Board of Supervisors, repealed by Act of March* 25, 1862, 98; *Supplement VIII.*]

Third. [*Superseded by Act of April* 25, 1863, 540; *Sec.* 1, *Sub.* 2; *Supplement XII.*]

Fourth. To provide for cases omitted in this Act, and in conformity with the principles adopted in it for opening, altering, extending, constructing repairing, or otherwise improving of public streets and highways, at the expense of the property benefited thereby, without any recourse, in any event, upon the City and County, or the public treasury, for any portion of the expense of such works, or any delinquency of the property-holders or owners.[29]

Fifth. Providing for lighting the streets. [*Amended April* 26, 1862, 466.]

Sixth. To regulate market-houses and market-places.

---

* As the fiscal year now ends June 30, reports of departments are now required to be presented in July.

[26] Inapplicable to property of School Department. See Act April 26, 1858, cited note 24, ante.

[29] In connection with this subdivision see Act April 25, 1863, 560; Supplement XII.

Seventh. [*Superseded by Act of April* 24, 1863, 406.]

Eighth. To provide for inclosing, improving and regulating all public grounds of the City and County, at an expense not to exceed two thousand dollars per annum.

Ninth. To prohibit the erection of wooden buildings, or structures, within any fixed limits where the streets have been established and graded, or ordered to be graded; to regulate the sale, storage and use of gunpowder, or other explosive or combustible materials and substances, and make all needful regulations for protection against fire.*

Tenth. To make such regulations concerning the erection and use of buildings as may be necessary for the safety of the inhabitants.

Eleventh. To determine the fines, forfeitures and penalties that shall be incurred for the breach of regulations established by the said Board of Supervisors, and also for a violation of the provisions of this Act, where no penalty is affixed thereto, or provided by law, but no penalty to be imposed shall exceed the amount of one thousand dollars, or six months' imprisonment, or both; and every violation of any lawful order, or regulation, or ordinance of the Board of Supervisors of the City and County of San Francisco is hereby declared a misdemeanor or public offense, and all prosecutions for the same shall be in the name of the people of the State of California.

Twelfth. To regulate and provide for the employment of prisoners sentenced to labor on the public works of said City and County.

Thirteenth. To license and regulate hackney coaches, carriages and other public vehicles, and to fix the rates to be charged for the transportation of persons, baggage and property therein; and also to license and regulate porters employed in conveying baggage for persons arriving in and departing from said City and County, and to prohibit the exercise of those employments without such licenses. [*The greater part of this subdivision is superseded by Sec.* 1, *Sub.* 4, *Act of April* 25, 1863, 540; *post, Supplement XI.*]

Fourteenth. [*Repealed and substance re-enacted by Act of March* 30, 1872; 1871-2, 763; *post, Supplement LXI.*]

Fifteenth. [*Amended by Sec.* 1, *Sub.* 3, *Act of April* 25, 1863, 540; *post, Supplement XI.*]

Sixteenth. To provide for the erection of a workhouse, house of refuge, or house of correction, and for the regulation and government of the same.[31]

Seventeenth. To direct and control the Fire Department of said City and County, in conformity with the laws.

Eighteenth. To fix the fees and charges to be collected by the Surveyor of

---

*See Supplement LXVIII.

[31] See Act of April 1, 1872; 1871-2, 878; Supplement LXV; and Act of March 31, 1876; 1875-6, 632; Supplement LXXXII. And Act of April 1, 1878.

said City and County for certificates of surveys for buildings, or other purposes, and by tho Superintendent of Streets and Highways, and any and all other municipal officers, where their fees are not otherwise fixed by law.

Nineteenth. To provide, by regulation, where it may be necessary, for carrying the provisions of this Act into effect.

Twentieth. To provide for the care and maintenance of the indigent sick of said City and County; but not to incur any expense therefor exceeding the sum of three thousand dollars a month.[32]

Twenty-first. To provide for the construction and repair of hydrants, fireplugs, cisterns and pumps in the streets, for public security and convenience.

Twenty-second. [*Repealed by Act of April* 26, 1862, 466; *Supplement IX.*]

Twenty-third. To provide ways and means for the prosecution of the claims, in the name of the City of San Francisco, to the public lands, now pending for the same.

Twenty-fourth. To permit the laying down of railroad tracks, and the running of cars thereon, along any street, or portion of street, for the sole purpose of excavating and filling in a street, or portion of a street, or adjoining lots, and for such limited time as may bo necessary for the purposes aforesaid, and no longer.†

ARTICLE VI.

FINANCE AND REVENUE.

SEC. 75. All fines, penalties and forfeitures, imposed for offenses committed within the said City and County, shall be received by the Clerk or Magistrate of the respective Court, and paid into the Treasury thereof, as a part of the Police Fund;[33] forty per cent. of all poll taxes collected in said City and County, or any other proportion of such poll taxes which may be hereafter assigned to said City and County, by law, shall also be paid and received into the treasury thereof, as a part of the Police Fund.[34] All demands payable out of said fund may, in case there be not sufficient money in the treasury arising from the sources specified in this section, be paid out of the General Fund of said City and County.

SEC. 76. The School Fund of said City and County shall consist[35] of all moneys received from the State School Fund; all moneys arising from taxes

---

[32] See Act March 10, 1866; 1865-6, 214; Supplement XXV.

†See Civil Code, Sections 407 to 511, inclusive; also Act March 26, 1878, Subdivision 9; Section 1, 1878, p. 556.

[33] See note 13, ante.

[34] Poll tax to go to State School Fund. Constitution of 1879, Section 12, Art. XIII.

[35] See note 34, ante.

upon property which shall be levied each year for that use, by the Board of Supervisors, and which shall in no case exceed the rate of thirty-five cents[36] on each hundred dollars' valuation of all property, real and personal, liable to be assessed. The General Fund consists of all moneys in the treasury not designated and set apart by law to a specified use, and of the overplus of any Special Fund remaining after the satisfaction of all demands upon it. The Surplus Fund consists of any moneys belonging to the General Fund remaining in the treasury after the satisfaction of all demands due and payable, which are specified in the first fourteen subdivisions in section ninety-five. The fiscal year shall be the same as that of the State.

SEC. 77.   *   *   *   *   *   *   *   *

And in default of such payment before the time when the Tax Collector may be authorized by law to seize and sell the property therefor, the said Tax Collector shall proceed to collect said taxes, together with his legal fees, by seizure and sale of the property liable, in the mode prescribed by law for the collection of such State and County taxes.   *   *   *   *   *   *

[*Omitted portions, as to payment of taxes to Treasurer, superseded by provisions of Revenue Law.*]

SEC. 78.   The Tax Collector, upon the final settlement to be made by him as such Tax Collector, according to the requirements of the law, shall be charged with, and shall pay into the hands of the Treasurer, the full amount of all taxes by him collected and not previously paid over, without any deduction of commissions, fees or otherwise; he shall also be charged with and be deemed debtor to the treasury, for the full amount of all taxes due upon the delinquent list delivered to him for collection; unless it be made to appear that it was out of his power to collect the same by levy and sale of any property liable to be seized and sold therefor; if the impossibility to collect any portion of such delinquent taxes have resulted from any irregularity or defect in the assessment, then the Assessor whose duty it was to make the assessment, shall be liable and be deemed debtor to the treasury for the amount remaining uncollected for that cause.

SEC. 79.   The Treasurer of said City and County shall receive and safely keep in a secure fire-proof vault, to be prepared for the purpose, all moneys belonging to, or which shall be paid into, the treasury, and shall not loan, use or deposit the same, or any part thereof, with any banker or other person, nor pay out any part of said moneys, except upon demands authorized by this Act, and after they have been duly audited; he shall keep the key of said vault, and not suffer the same to be opened except in his presence. At the closing up of the same, each day, he shall take an account and enter in the proper book the exact amount of money on hand, and at the end of every month shall make and publish a statement of all receipts into, and payments

---

[36] See note 26, ante.

from, the treasury, and on what account. If he violate any of the provisions of this section he shall be considered a defaulter, and shall be deemed guilty of a misdemeanor in office, and be liable to removal, and shall be proceeded against accordingly; if he loan or deposit said moneys, or any part thereof, contrary to the provisions of this section, or apply the same to his own use, or the use of any other person, in any manner whatsoever, or suffer the same to go out of his personal custody, except in payment of audited demands upon the treasury, he shall be deemed guilty of a felony, and, on conviction thereof, shall suffer imprisonment in the State Prison for a period of not less than three or more than ten years.

SEC. 80. The Treasurer shall keep the moneys belonging to each fund separate and distinct, and shall, in no case, pay demands chargeable against one fund out of moneys belonging to another, except as otherwise provided in this Act, without an express order of the Board of Supervisors, which can only be made at or after the third regular session, held during the fiscal year, by a vote of two-thirds. The said Treasurer shall give his personal attendance at his public office during the office hours fixed in this Act; and if he absent himself therefrom, except on account of sickness or urgent necessity, during such office hours, he shall lose his salary for the entire day on which he was absent.

SEC. 81. [*Repealed by Act of March* 28, 1859, 141.]

SEC. 82. No payment can be made from the treasury or out of the public funds of said City and County, unless the same be specifically authorized by this Act, nor unless the demand which is paid be duly audited, as in this Act provided, and that must appear upon the face of it. No demand upon the treasury shall be allowed by the Auditor in favor of any person or officer in any manner indebted thereto, without first deducting the amount of such indebtedness, nor to any person or officer having the collection, custody or disbursement of public funds, unless his account has been duly presented, passed, approved and allowed, as required in this Act; nor in favor of any officer who shall have neglected to make his official returns or his reports, in writing, in the manner and at the time required by law, or by the regulations established by the Board of Supervisors; nor to any officer who shall have neglected or refused to comply with any of the provisions of this or any other Act of the Legislature regulating the duties of such officer, on being required in writing to comply therewith, by the President of the Board of Supervisors, or the Supervisor of the respective district; nor in favor of any officer for the time he shall have absented himself without lawful cause, from the duties of his office during the office hours prescribed in this Act, and the Auditor may examine any officer, receiving a salary from the treasury, on oath touching such absence.

SEC. 83. The term "audited," as used in this Act with reference to demands upon the treasury, is to be understood their having been presented to, and passed upon, by every officer and Board of officers, and finally allowed as required by law; and this must appear upon the face of the paper representing the demand, or else it is not audited. The term "law or laws," as used in this Act, is never to be understood as applicable to any regulation of the Board of Education, or of the Board of Supervisors, *   * [obsolete.] but only applicable to the constitution and the laws made or adopted by the Legislature in pursuance thereof.

SEC. 84. Every demand upon the treasury, except the salary of the Auditor, and including [the] salary of the Treasurer, must, before it can be paid, be presented to the Auditor of the City and County to be allowed, who shall satisfy himself whether the money is legally due and remains unpaid, and whether the payment thereof from the treasury of the City and County is authorized by law, and out of what fund. If he allow it he shall indorse upon it the word "allowed," with the name of the fund out of which it is payable, with the date of such allowance, and sign his name thereto; but the allowance or approval of the Auditor, or of the Board of Supervisors, or any other Board, or officer, of any demand, which upon the face of it appears not to have been expressly made by law payable out of the treasury or fund to be charged therewith, shall afford no warrant to the Treasurer or other disbursing officer for paying the same. No demand can be approved, allowed, audited, or paid, unless it specify each several item, date and value composing it, and refer to the law by title, date and section authorizing the same.

SEC. 85. The demand of the Auditor for his monthly salary shall be audited and allowed by the President of the Board of Supervisors. All other monthly demands on account of salaries fixed by law, and made payable out of the Treasury of said City and County, may be allowed by the Auditor without any previous approval. All demands payable out of the School Fund must, before they can be allowed by the Auditor or paid, be previously approved by the Board of Education, or by the President thereof, and Superintendent of Common Schools, acting under the express authorization of said Board.* Demands for teachers' wages or other expenses appertaining to any school, cannot be approved, allowed or audited, to an amount exceeding the share of school money which such school will be entitled to have apportioned to it during the current fiscal year. Demands for monthly pay of Police Captains and Officers must, before they can be allowed by the Auditor or paid, first be approved by the Police Judge and Chief of Police,† or if they refuse or cannot agree, then by the Board of Supervisors. All other lawful demands payable out of the treasury, or any public funds of said City and County, and not hereinbefore in this section specified, must, before they can be allowed by the Auditor, or in any manner be recognized or paid, be first approved by the Board of Supervisors; or, if the demand be under two hun-

---

*See Section 7, Act April, 1872, p. 846, Supplemen LXIV.

†Amended by Act of April 1, 1878.

dred dollars, by the President and two members thereof, appointed by the Board for that purpose, with power to act under and subject to its instructions and regulations during recess of the said Board. The Auditor must number and keep a record of all demands on the treasury allowed by him, showing the number, date, amount and name of the original and present holder; on what account allowed, out of what fund payable, and if previously approved, by what officer, officers or Board it has been so approved; and it shall be deemed a misdemeanor in office for the Auditor to deliver any demand with his allowance thereon, until this requisite shall have been complied with. [*Amended April* 18, 1857, 209.]

SEC. 86. The President of the Board of Supervisors, Auditor, Chief of Police, President of the Board of Education, and each Supervisor shall have power to administer oaths and affirmations concerning any demand on the treasury, or otherwise relating to their official duties. Every officer who shall approve, allow, or pay any demand on the treasury not authorized by this Act, *shall be liable to the City and County,* individually and on his official bond, for the amount of the demand so illegally approved, allowed or paid. Every citizen shall have the right to inspect the books of the Auditor, Treasurer, and Clerk of the Board of Supervisors, at any time during business hours. Copies or extracts from said books, duly certified, shall be given by the officer having the same in his custody, to any citizen demanding the same, and paying or tendering sixteen cents per folio of one hundred words for such copies or extracts. [*Amended April* 18, 1857, 209.]

SEC. 87. The Auditor is the head of the Finance Department of the City and County, and as such is required to be constantly acquainted with the exact condition of the treasury, and every lawful demand upon it. He shall keep a public office, and give his personal attendance there daily during the office hours fixed in this Act, and shall not be permitted to follow or engage in any other occupation, office, or calling, while he holds said office; if he absents himself from his office during such office hours, except on indispensable official business or urgent necessity, he shall lose his salary for the day, and it shall be a part of his official duty to keep account of the times and occasions when he shall be so absent from duty.[37]

SEC. 88. Every lawful demand upon the treasury duly audited, as in this Act required, shall in all cases be paid on presentation and canceled, and the proper entry thereof be made if there be sufficient money in the treasury

---

[37] The Act of April 3, 1876; 1875-6, 852, provides as follows:
"SECTION 1. The clerk of the Auditor of the City and County of San Francisco shall be known and designated as, and exercise the powers of, Deputy Auditor of said City and County, in case of the illness or absence of the Auditor, in the auditing and signing of lawful demands upon the treasury of said City and County, when the same have been approved and allowed by the proper officers and Board of officers in accordance with law, and in administering oaths or affirmations in all matters in connection with demands upon the treasury, or reports required by law to be filed in the office of the Auditor of said City and County."

belonging to the fund out of which it is payable; but if there be not sufficient money belonging to said fund to pay such demand, then it shall be registered in a book to be kept by the Treasurer for that purpose, showing its number, when presented, date, amount, name of the original holder, and on what account allowed, and out of what fund payable; and being so registered, shall be returned to the party presenting it, with an endorsement of the word "registered," dated and signed by the Treasurer."

SEC. 89. Whenever any audited demand has been presented to the Treasurer and not paid, and it be made known to the President of the Board of Supervisors, he shall proceed immediately to investigate the cause of such non-payment; and if it be ascertained that the demand has been illegally and fraudulently approved or allowed, he shall cause the officer guilty of such illegal and fraudulent approval or allowance to be proceeded against for misconduct in office. If he ascertain that the demand has been duly audited, and that the Treasurer has funds applicable to the payment thereof, which, without reasonable grounds for doubt as to the legality of such payment, he refuses to apply thereto, he shall proceed against him as a defaulter; if it be ascertained that the demand was not paid for want of funds, then he shall cause the Sheriff or Tax Collector, or other officer or person or persons, who ought to have collected or to have paid the money into the treasury, if they have been grossly negligent therein, to be proceeded against according to law and without any delay.

SEC. 90. The salaries, fees, and compensation of all officers, including policemen and employees of all classes, and all teachers in common schools, or others, employed at fixed wages, shall be payable monthly; and any demand whatsoever upon the treasury, hereafter accruing, shall not be paid, but shall be forever barred by limitation of time, unless the same be presented for payment, properly audited, within one month after such demand became due and payable; or, if it be a demand which has to be passed and approved by the Board of Supervisors or Board of Education, then within one month after the regular session of the proper Board, held next after the demand accrued, or unless the Board of Supervisors shall, within six months after the demand accrued as aforesaid, on a careful investigation of the facts, certify that the same is in all respects just and legal, and that the presentation of it, as above required, was not in the power either of the original party interested or his agent, or the present holder, in which case it shall be barred in the same manner, unless presented for payment within twenty days thereafter. †

SEC. 91. The Treasurer, for money received into the treasury, and all other offices, [officers] of said City and County receiving money from the

---

*Modified by Acts of February 25, 1878, 111; and March 18, 1878, 333 (One-Twelfth Act).
†See State Constitution of 1879, Art. XI, Section 18.

Treasurer for disbursement, shall give receipt for all moneys by them received, which receipt shall be presented to, and countersigned, by the Auditor. The Auditor, before countersigning any such receipt, shall number it, and make an entry in a book of record, to be kept in his office for that purpose, of the number, date, and amount, by whom and in whose favor given, and on what account. No such receipt shall be valid as evidence in favor of the person or officer receiving it, till presented to the Auditor and countersigned as aforesaid; and any person or officer using, or offering to use, such receipt as evidence, in favor of such person or officer, of the payment specified in it, without being first countersigned as above required, shall forfeit to the said City and County double the amount of money specified in such receipt.

SEC. 92. If any person feel aggrieved by the decision of the Auditor, or other proper officer or officers of said City and County, except the Board of Education, in the rejection of, or refusal to approve or allow any demand upon the treasury presented by such person, he may appeal, and have the same passed upon by the Board of Supervisors, whose decision thereon shall be final; and if the said Board shall approve and allow the demand, it shall afterward be presented to the Auditor, and entered in the proper book in like manner as other demands allowed by him, and an indorsement must be made, of its having been so entered, before it can be paid; *provided*, that from the decision of the President of the Board of Education and Superintendent of Common Schools refusing or not agreeing to allow any demand payable out of the School Fund, the appeal shall be taken to the Board of Education, whose decision thereon shall be final.

SEC. 93. In all cases of such appeals to the Board of Supervisors or the Board of Education, the opinion of the District Attorney thereon shall be required in writing, read and filed; and upon such appeal, and in all other cases, upon the approval or allowance of any demand upon the treasury or School Fund, the vote shall be taken by yeas and nays, and entered upon the records.

SEC. 94. The President of the Board of Supervisors, in conjunction with the County Judge* and Auditor of said City and County, shall, every month, examine the books of the Treasurer, and other officers of said City and County having the collection and custody of public funds, and shall be permitted, and it shall be their duty, to see and count over all the moneys remaining in the hands of such Treasurer or other officer. If they ascertain *clearly* that such Treasurer, or other officer, is a defaulter, they shall forthwith take possession of all funds, books, and papers, belonging to such officer, and appoint a person to fill the same, until the said defaulting officer can be proceeded against according to law, which shall be done without delay. The person so appointed shall give bond and take the oath of office, in the same

_____

*Under the present judicial system one of the Judges of the Superior Court. Act of February 14, 1880, 2; and Act of April 3, 1880, 115.

manner as was required of the officer whose place he is appointed to fill. If the Treasurer, or other officer so charged as a defaulter, be acquitted thereof, he shall resume his duties.

SEC. 95. [*As amended April* 18, 1857, 209.] Payments of demands on the treasury of said City and County may be made for the following objects, and none others:

First—Out of the Police Fund, the fixed salaries of Police Captains and officers, Chief of Police, Police Judge and Clerk of the Police Court.

Second. Out of the School Fund, the salaries or wages of teachers in the common schools, rents, repairs, building, and furnishing of school-houses, as provided by law.

Third. Out of the General Fund, the fixed salaries or compensation of the Assessor and his deputies, * * * and other officers of said City and County, and of officers of the Fire Department, and the legal fees of jurors and witnesses in criminal cases, when the same by law are payable out of the county treasury.

Fourth to tenth, inclusive. [*Obsolete. Bonds redeemed.*]

Eleventh. Out of the Police Fund, bills for the subsisting of prisoners previously authorized by the Board of Supervisors, as in this Act provided, and duly audited, which bills must minutely specify each several item composing the demand.

Twelfth. [*Obsolete.*]

Thirteenth. Out of the General Fund, bills duly audited for expenditures in the care and maintenance of the indigent sick of the City and County, previously authorized by the Board of Supervisors, and not exceeding the amount in this Act limited for that purpose.

Fourteenth. Out of the General Fund, * * * * * the expense legally incurred for books, stationery, and official blanks, as authorized by section eleven of this Act, and the necessary expense of constructing a fire-proof vault, to be prepared for the Treasurer's office, as required by section seventy-nine of this Act; also, expenditures not exceeding *three thousand dollars* (*amended April* 26, 1862, 466; *sec.* 1, *sub.* 10, *Supplement LX; and by Act of March* 30, 1878; *sec.* 1] during any one month, for objects of urgent necessity other than those heretofore specified in this section, when the amount thereof in each particular case shall have been previously authorized and fixed by the Board of Supervisors, in the lawful exercise of their powers. [*Portion of this subdivision relating to expenditures for maintenance of Fire Department repealed by sec.* 8, *Act of March* 2, 1866; 1865–5, 138; *see post, Supplement XXIV. Further amended by Acts of March* 26 *and March* 28, 1878; *see also Supplement X.*]

Fifteenth. Out of the Surplus Fund, expenditures previously authorized by the Board of Supervisors, in the lawful exercise of their powers, for objects other than those specified in the preceding fourteen subdivisions of this section, may be paid out of the Surplus Fund, as specified in sections ninety-seven and ninety-eight, but not otherwise. At the end of each fiscal year and after every lawful demand on the treasury then due and payable, or to accrue for that year, shall have been actually paid, taken up and cancelled, and record thereof made in the proper books, or cash in the treasury shall have been set apart and reserved, equal to the amount of said demands that may then be outstanding, or to accrue for that year, and a surplus of money shall still remain in the treasury, then, and in such case, but not otherwise, the Board of Supervisors may, out of such Surplus Fund, and from no other source whatever, make appropriations for the various objects embraced within their lawful powers, other than those specified in the first fourteen subdivisions of this section, and may, in case the revenue of the year then next ensuing will, in their opinion, be amply sufficient to satisfy all demands upon the General Fund and Police Fund, set apart and reserve the moneys so appropriated, to be expended from time to time, during such succeeding year, subject, however, to the provisions of section ninety-six. Every contract whereby any money is to be paid out of the treasury for other objects than those specified in the first fourteen subdivisions of this section, shall be null and void as against the City and County, if made before such Surplus Fund exists in the treasury, and unless it be in writing, with a printed copy of sections ninety-five, ninety-six, ninety-seven and ninety-eight of this Act attached to it, and in such case, the officer or officers executing the same in behalf of the City and County, in contravention of this provision, shall alone be liable in his or their individual capacity, to the other contracting party, for the fulfillment of such contract.

SEC. 96. The demands specified in the first fourteen subdivisions of section ninety-five, shall be paid out of any moneys in the treasury, in preference to any and all other demands whatsoever; and in case of any deficiency of funds for the payment of any of the said demands, when presented, then all such demands, being presented and registered by the Treasurer, as in this Act required, shall be paid out of any moneys afterwards coming into the said treasury, applicable thereto, in the order in which the same are registered.

SEC. 97. The Board of Supervisers, Board of Education, and each and every officer of the said City and County, being absolutely prohibited to contract any debt or liability, in any form, against the said City and County hereafter, the powers of the Board of Supervisors, enumerated in this Act, so far as the exercise thereof may involve the expenditure of money otherwise than for the objects and demands referred to in the preceding section, shall be deemed to extend only to authorizing the appropriation and application of any surplus moneys remaining in the treasury, during any one fiscal year, to the objects specified in such enumeration of powers, after the demands mentioned in the first fourteen subdivisions of section ninety-five, due and payable during such fiscal year, shall have been paid, and the several Sinking Funds shall have been provided and reserved for the redemption of said bonds and certificates of stock, to the amount hereinbefore specified.

SEC. 98. If any expenditures, not authorized by this Act, be incurred, they can never be paid out of the treasury, nor shall they be deemed to constitute, or lay the foundation of, any claim, demand, or liability, legal, equitable, or otherwise, against the said City and County. If expenditures be incurred, which are authorized by this Act to be paid out of the surplus funds in the treasury, but not for the preferred objects specified in section ninety-six, such expenditures can only be paid out of such surplus funds and revenues strictly appertaining to the fiscal year in which such expenditures have been ordered, or the contracts therefor entered into, and cannot be carried forward and paid out of any revenues accruing and receivable into the treasury for any subsequent year; nor shall any demand for, or arising out of, any such expenditure, contract, or consideration, be deemed to be a legal nor [or] equitable claim or liability against the said City and County, or the treasury thereof, or the taxable property or taxpayers, otherwise than as in this section provided; and no demand preferred against the said City and County, or the treasury thereof, which is not legally obligatory under the provisions of this Act, can be recognized, assumed, or legalized, so as to give it any validity, or authorize the payment thereof.

SEC. 99. The following Acts and Laws are hereby repealed:

The Act entitled "An Act to re-incorporate the City of San Francisco," passed May 5, one thousand eight hundred and fifty-five.

The Act explanatory thereof, passed May 7, one thousand eight hundred and fifty-five.

The Act entitled "An Act to re-incorporate the City of San Francisco," passed April 15, one thousand eight hundred and fifty-one; and the Act entitled "An Act to incorporate the City of San Francisco," passed April 15, one thousand eight hundred and fifty.

The eighth section of the Act, passed April 25th, one thousand eight hundred and fifty-one, entitled "An Act dividing the State into Counties, and establishing the seats of justice therein."

The Act entitled "An Act to create a Board of Supervisors for the County of San Francisco, and define their duties," passed April 29, one thousand eight hundred and fifty-one.

The twenty-eighth section of the Act, passed March 26th, one thousand eight hundred and fifty-one, entitled "An Act concerning County Recorders," so far as it relates to San Francisco County.

All laws and parts of laws defining the powers and duties of Supervisors, or Boards of Supervisors, are declared inapplicable to the said City and County of San Francisco, except such as are expressly referred to in and made applicable thereto by the provisions of this Act; also all laws and parts of laws, so far as they conflict with the provisions of this Act.

SCHEDULE.

SECTIONS 1 *to* 8, *inclusive.* [*Obsolete.*]

SEC. 9. [*Repealed by Sec.* 17, *Act of April* 18, 1857, 222.]

SEC. 10. This Act, excepting this section, and section five of article first, only, shall take effect on and after the 1st day of July next; and, in the meantime, the existing municipal government, or officers of the City of San Francisco, or the Board of Supervisors, or other officers, of the County of San Francisco, shall not have power to contract any debt or liability against the said City, or against the said County. But this prohibition, or anything contained in the existing charter of said city, shall not be construed to prevent the appropriation or payment out of the treasury of any moneys actually existing therein, to the various objects and purposes as authorized by law, or the drawing of any warrant or order therefor. This section and section five of article first of this Act shall take effect immediately after its passage.

Supplementary Acts.

SUPPLEMENTARY ACTS.

An Act to define the Powers and Duties of the Board of Supervisors of the City and County of San Francisco in Certain Cases.

[Approved April 10, 1857.]

The People of the State of California, represented in Senate and Assembly, do enact as follows:

SECTION 1. The Board of Supervisors of the City and County of San Francisco shall have power to appoint a committee, consisting of three members of said Board, to be denominated the "Finance Committee," and to fill all vacancies which may happen in said committee by new appointments, from time to time. Said committee, in addition to the ordinary duties of the Finance Committee of said Board, shall have the power as hereinafter specified.

SEC. 2. The Clerk of the Board of Supervisors shall be Clerk of the Finance Committee, after the expiration of six months from the passage of this Act. * * * [*Remainder of section obsolete.*]

SEC. 3. The Clerk of said committee shall keep a record of its proceedings, with the names of witnesses examined, and a substantial account of the evidence taken. It shall be the duty of the Sheriff, or any Constable, or Policeman of said City and County, to execute the lawful process and orders of the said committee. The said committee may visit any of the public offices when and as often as they think proper, and make their examinations and investigations therein without hindrance. In the exercise of its functions, the concurrence of two members of the committee shall be deemed sufficient.

SECS. 4 and 5. [*Obsolete.*]

SEC. 6. The said committee shall hereafter, as often as may be required by the Board of Supervisors, investigate the transactions and accounts of all officers having the collection, custody or disbursement of public money, or having the power to approve, allow, or audit demands on the treasury, and report thereon to the Board of Supervisors, and for the purpose, shall continue to have and exercise all the powers granted in this Act. But nothing in this Act contained shall be construed to relieve the Auditor, President of the Board of Supervisors, or other officers, from any of the duties and obligations now imposed on them by law.

SEC. 7. The said committee and the Clerk shall have free access to any records, books, and papers in all public offices. And said committee shall have the same power as courts of record, to administer oaths and affirmations, to examine witnesses, and compel their attendance before them by subpœna, and attachment for contempt in case of their refusal to appear or to testify when lawfully required, and shall have the like power to punish as for contempt, any officer, ex-officer, or other person, who shall refuse or neglect, when required in writing by said committee, to exhibit any official records, books, or papers in his custody, or to explain the same, or any official transaction of his own or of any other officer, so far as he may be able.

SEC. 8. If, from the examination made by the Finance Committee, in pursuance of the powers granted by this Act, it shall appear that a misdemeanor in office, or a defalcation, has been committed by any officer of said City and County, whose accounts and transactions they are authorized to examine as aforesaid, said committee shall immediately report the same to the President of the Board of Supervisors, who shall immediately cause said report to be published, in at least two daily newspapers published in the City of San Francisco, for the period of three days.

SUPPLEMENT II.

1858, 166.

An Act to establish the Industrial School Department of the City and County of San Francisco.

[Approved April 15, 1858.]

The People of the State of California, represented in Senate and Assembly, do enact as follows:

[*Section* 1 *to Sec.* 5, *both inclusive, obsolete. See Note* 38, *below, and Supplement LVIII,* post.[38]]

SEC. 6.   The [Board of Supervisors] shall have the control, management, and direction of all the affairs and business of the department, except so far as provision is otherwise made by law; and especially, they shall have power to receive donations and bequests, and to accept, purchase and hold real estate, which shall constitute a permanent fund, the interest of which only shall be applied in payment of the current expenses of the department; but the principal sum thereof, except in case of real estate, shall be invested in the bonds of the City of San Francisco, or of the State of California, or in mortgages upon real estate within said City and County, unless the testator or donors shall otherwise direct.   The [Board of Supervisors] shall also, especially, have power to accept from the parents or guardian of any child the surrender of such child during minority; and all the rights of parents or guardians to keep, control, educate, employ, indenture or discharge such child shall vest in the [Board of Supervisors.]

SEC. 7.   The purposes of said department are hereby declared to be, solely, the detention, management, reformation, education and maintenance of such children as shall be committed or surrendered thereto; and no portion of the funds, whether furnished by members of the department, or by the City and County of San Francisco, or the State of California, or from any other source whatsoever, shall be used, or allowed to be used, for any other purpose whatsoever, excepting such portion thereof as may be required in purchasing the land, and in erecting, improving, enlarging or furnishing the buildings and structures necessary to said department, and in supplying and managing the industry of the school.   *   *   *   And no member of the [Board of Supervisors]   *   *   *   shall   *   *   *   directly or indirectly

-----

[38] Powers and duties of the Board of Managers vested in the Board of Supervisors by Section 2, Act of March 23, 1872; 1871-2, 544; Supplement LVIII.

be interested in any contract connected with the management of the department.

SEC. 8. The [Board of Supervisors] may make, alter, and amend such by-laws as they may deem proper for the orderly and economical management of the concerns of the department, and they shall see that strict discipline is maintained in the Industrial School; they shall provide employment or the inmates, indenture, procure them to be adopted, or discharge them, as is hereinafter provided; they shall appoint a Superintendent, Deputy Superintendent, Matron, Teachers, and such other employees as they may require, and shall fix their salaries; they shall prescribe the duties of the Superintendent, Deputy Superintendent, Matron, Teachers, and other employees, not inconsistent with this Act, and may remove such officers at pleasure, and appoint others in their places. The Superintendent and Deputy Superintendent shall give such official bonds as may be required by the Board.

SEC. 9. For the care and maintenance of the children, and the salaries of the Superintendent, Teachers and other officers of said school, and for other purposes connected with said school, the Auditor of said City and County is hereby authorized and required to audit the demands of the [Board of Supervisors] for an amount not exceeding three thousand dollars per month; and the Treasurer of said City and County is hereby authorized and required to pay the sum so allowed and audited out of the General Fund of the City and County of San Francisco, not exceeding, in all, the said sum of three thousand dollars per month.[39] [Amended, March 28, 1868; 1867-8, 505.]

SEC. 10. The [Board of Supervisors] shall have power to receive and detain in said Industrial School such children, under the age of eighteen years, as may be thereto committed by the Police Judge [County Court or Municipal Criminal Court[40]] of said City and County, as vagrants, living an

---

[39] Current expenses shall not exceed four thousand five hundred dollars per month, to be audited and paid as other claims against the city. Sec. 2, Act of March 23, 1872, 544; Supplement LVIII.

[40] The Act of February 15, 1864; 1863-4, 75; supplementary to the Industrial School Act, provides that:

Section 1. The duties, powers, and jurisdiction which, by the provisions of the Act entitled "An Act to establish the Industrial School Department of the City and County of San Francisco," approved April fifteenth, A. D. eighteen hundred and fifty-eight, are enjoined upon or vested in the Court of Sessions of said City and County, are hereby conferred upon and vested in the County Court, except those mentioned in section twelve of said Act, which are enjoined upon and vested in the County Judge of said City and County.

Sec. 2. The [Board of Supervisors] *   *   shall have power, in their discretion, to grant any children placed under their control and custody leave of absence from said school for such time as to said Board shall seem proper.

Sec. 3. This Act shall take effect and be in force from and after its passage.

The Act of April 1, 1872; 1871-2, 906; supplementary to the foregoing supplemental Act, provides that:

Section 1. The duties, powers and jurisdiction which, by the provisions of an Act entitled "An Act supplementary to an Act entitled 'An Act to establish the Industrial School Department of the City and County of San Francisco,' approved April fifteenth, A. D. eighteen hundred and fifty-eight,"

idle or dissolute life, or who shall be duly convicted of any crime or misdemeanor, or who, upon being tried before such Police Judge [County Court
or Municipal Criminal Court] for any crime or misdemeanor, shall be found
to be under fourteen years of age, and to have done an act which, if done
by a person of full age, would be a crime or misdemeanor; and the said
[Board of Supervisors] shall have power to place the said children committed to their custody, during the minority of said children, to such employments, and cause them to be instructed in such branches of useful knowledge
as may be suitable to their years and capacity; and they shall have power,
in their discretion, to bind out the said children, with their consent, as
apprentices, during their minority, to such persons, and at such places, to
learn such proper trades and employments as in their judgment will be most
conducive to their reformation and amendment, and will tend to the future
benefit and advantage of such children. And the said Police Judge, and
the said [County Court and Municipal Criminal Court], and either of them, are
hereby authorized and empowered to commit all offenders duly convicted, under eighteen years of age, to said Industrial School, in all cases where the said
Police Judge, and the said [County Court* and Municipal Criminal Court*],
or either of them, shall deem such commitment to be more suitable than the
punishment now authorized by law. And if, upon any trial before said Police
Judge [County Court or Municipal Criminal Court], it shall appear that the
person on trial is under the age of fourteen years, and that such child has done
an act which, if done by a person of full age, would warrant a conviction of
the crime or misdemeanor charged; then, and in that case, the said Police
Judge, and the said [County Court and Municipal Criminal Court], and
either of them, shall have power to commit said child to the said Industrial
School. And the said Police Judge, and the said [County Court and Municipal Criminal Court], or either of them, on the application of the President of the Board of Supervisors, or of any member of said Board, or of
any three citizens, shall have power, upon the hearing of the matter, and
upon proof to the satisfaction of said Police Judge, and said [County Court
and Municipal Criminal Court], or either of them, to sentence to said Industrial School any child under eighteen years of age, who lives an idle or
dissolute life, whose parents are dead, or, if living, from drunkenness, or
other vices or causes, neglect to provide any suitable employment, or exer-

---

approved February fifteenth, eighteen hundred and sixty four, are conferred upon and vested in the
County Court of the City and County of San Francisco, are hereby also conferred upon and vested
in the Municipal Criminal Court of the City and County of San Francisco; but this Act shall not be
construed to divest the County Court of such duties, powers and jurisdiction.
   Sec. 2. This Act shall take effect and be in force from and after its passage.

   Powers of County Court and Municipal Court transferred to Superior Court, Act of February 4,
1880; 1880 2.

   * Now Superior Court.

cise any salutary control over such child; and the children thus committed
shall be kept, governed, and disposed of as herein provided; and no child
shall be reclaimed or taken from said school by his or her parents, or any
other person or persons, without leave of the Court or Judge by whom such
child was committed. And whenever, upon the trial of any person before
the Police Judge [*County Court or Municipal Criminal Court] of said City
and County, said person shall be duly convicted of the crime or misdemeanor charged, and it shall appear that such person is under the age of eighteen years; or when on such trial it shall appear that such person has done
an act which, if done by a person of full age, would warrant a conviction of
the crime or misdemeanor charged, and that such person is under fourteen
years of age; then, in that case, the said Police Judge, and the said [*County
Court and Municipal Criminal Court], or either of them, may, in their
discretion, sentence such person to be confined in the correctional department of said Industrial school for any term not exceeding six months; and
such person so sentenced shall be restrained of his or her personal liberty,
and shall be kept in a ward to be provided therefor separately from the body
of said school, during the term of such correction, before being admitted to
the general privileges of the school.[41]

Sec. 11.   All commitments shall be directed to the Superintendent of the
Industrial School, or any of his deputies, and said Superintendent and his
deputies shall be charged by such commitment with the detention and custody
of the children committed to the school, and with the execution of all orders
and process of any court respecting such children, and shall have the same
power, under and by virtue of such commitment, order, or process of court,
or a surrender accepted by the [Board of Supervisors], as the Sheriff of the

---

[41] Section 2 of the Act of March 8, 1860, is incorporated in the text in Sec. 11; and Sec. 3 of said
Act is amended by the Act of February 15, 1864; 1863-4, 76; amendatory thereof and supplementary
thereto. The last mentioned Act is as follows:
Section 1.   Section three of said Act is hereby amended so as to read as follows:
''Sec. 3.   Any person who shall aid, assist, or encourage any child to run away, who has been
committed or surrendered, or who has been indentured by the [Board of Supervisors], or shall harbor
or conceal any such child, knowing of such commitment, surrender or indenture, shall be deemed
guilty of a misdemeanor, and on conviction thereof shall be fined in a sum not exceeding three
hundred dollars, and imprisoned for a term not exceeding thirty days.   And any child who may be
absent on leave of absence, or who may be bound as an apprentice under this Act, or the Act to
which this is an amendment, and shall escape from the person under whose care he or she is placed,
or to whom he or she is bound, shall be considered a fugitive from said school, and may be arrested
and returned to said School by the Superintendent or other officer of said school, or by any Sheriff
or Police Officer in this State, and the necessary expense of such arrest shall be allowed by the said
Board of Supervisors] * * ; and the Auditor of said City and County shall audit the same,
and such expense shall be paid from the General Fund by the Treasurer of said City and County.''
Sec. 2.   [Executed.]
Sec. 3.   This Act shall take effect and be in force from and after its passage.
See Sec. 1388 of the Penal Code, March 15, 1883, in reference to the powers of Courts in certain
cases with regard to minors.
*Now Superior Court

County has or might have under commitments, orders, or process of court directed to him. [*Amended March 8, 1860, 73.*]

SEC. 12. The said Police Judge, [County Court and Municipal Criminal Court], or either of them, upon the application of the [Board of Supervisors] and upon their certificate that it is expedient to do so, shall have power to discharge any child committed to said Industrial School, and who is not bound out as an apprentice, or adopted. And the said Police Judge, [County Court and Municipal Criminal Court], or either of them, may, in like manner, discharge such child, upon the application, in writing, of the parents or guardian of such child; and, after ten days' notice, in writing, to the [Board of Supervisors], if, upon the hearing of the application, said Judge, or Court, shall consider that such discharge is expedient.

SEC. 13. The * * * Superintendent and Deputy Superintendents of the Industrial School Department, are hereby declared to be public officers, and subject to all the laws of this State relating to misdemeanor, malfeasance, and misfeasance in office.

SEC. 14. All laws, and parts of laws, in conflict with the provisions of this Act, are hereby declared to be inapplicable to the City and County of San Francisco; and this Act, and all the provisions thereof, shall be subject to the right of the Legislature to alter, repeal, or modify the same at any time.

SUPPLEMENT III.

1885, 235.

An Act to confer further powers upon the Board of Supervisors and Auditor and Treasurer of the City and County of San Francisco, and to authorize them to perform certain acts therein mentioned.

[Approved April 23, 1858.]

The People of the State of California, represented in Senate and Assembly do enact as follows:

SECTION 1. The Board of Supervisors of the City and County of San Francisco have further powers conferred upon them as follows:[42]

---

[42] The Subdivisions omitted, and not annotated, relate to relief of individuals, or the powers therein contained have been executed or have been superseded or repealed.

First. To order paid any final judgment against said City and County, out of the Surplus Fund.

Second to Thirteenth inclusive.   *   *   *   *   *   *

Fourteenth. To order constructed a common pound for estrays, and to provide for the taking up and impounding of all animals running at large within the streets of said City and County, north of Johnson street and east of Larkin street; *provided*, the cost of the construction of said pound shall not exceed five hundred dollars, which sum, or so much thereof as may be necessary, may be paid out of the General Fund by order of said Board of Supervisors. The said Board shall have power to make all needful rules and regulations necessary for the proper management and control of said pound, and may appoint one or more Pound Keepers, who shall be paid out of the fines imposed and collected of the owners of any animals impounded, and from no other source.[43]

Fifteenth to Nineteenth inclusive.   *   *   *   *   *

Twentieth. To ordain, procure and use, a common seal, to be used at pleasure, as the official seal of the said City and County of San Francisco; the cost of which seal shall not exceed fifty dollars, to be paid out of the General Fund, by order of said Board of Supervisors.

Twenty-first.   *   *   *   *   *   *   *

Twenty-second. To have power to appoint an Assistant Prosecuting District Attorney, who shall hold said office during the pleasure of said Board. The said Assistant shall also be the Prosecuting Attorney for the Police Court of said City and County, and shall receive a salary as such Assistant and Prosecuting Police Attorney, of *two hundred and fifty dollars per month*, [*Amended, Act April 26, 1862, 466; Supplement IX*], payable monthly out of the General Fund, which shall be in full for all services rendered for said City and County, or for either of them.[44]

Twenty-third. The said Board of Supervisors may make all needful rules and police regulations for the safety and well ordering of all omnibus lines in the City and County of San Francisco.

Twenty-fourth to Twenty-sixth inclusive.   *   *   *

SEC. 2. The Auditor of said City and County is hereby authorized to audit, and the Treasurer of the same is hereby authorized to pay, any and all sums that may be allowed and ordered paid by said Board of Supervisors, by authority of this Act.   •

---

[43] Jurisdiction of the Board of Supervisors extended over the whole City and County of San Francisco, or any limited portion thereof, as in their discretion they may prescribe by order, by Act of May 14, 1861, 369.

[44] By Act of April 3, 1876; 1875-6, 856; the Prosecuting Attorney is authorized to appoint a clerk, who shall perform such duties as may be required of him by said Prosecuting Attorney, and who shall receive a salary of one hundred and twenty-five dollars per month, payable in the same manner and out of the same fund as the salary of the Prosecuting Attorney.

By Act of March 7, 1881, 74; the Board of Supervisors is empowered to appoint like officials for Police Judge's Court No. 2.

SUPPLEMENT IV.

1860, 272.

An Act supplementary to an Act entitled " An Act to confer further powers upon the Board of Supervisors and Auditor and Treasurer of the City and County of San Francisco, and to authorize them to perform certain acts therein mentioned," approved April twenty-third, one thousand eight hundred and fifty-eight.

[Approved April 27, 1860.]

The People of the State of California, represented in Senate and Assembly, do enact as follows:

SECTION 1. The Board of Supervisors of the City and County of San Francisco, have hereby further powers conferred upon them, as follows:[45]

First. To allow and order paid out of the General Fund, not exceeding the sum of six thousand dollars in any one fiscal year, for repairs and improvements of streets fronting upon the water front of the City, as defined by an Act entitled "An Act to provide for the disposition of certain property of the State of California," passed March twenty-sixth, one thousand eight hundred and fifty-one. (See sec. 2,525 Political Code, April 3, 1876.)

Second. To allow and order paid out of the General Fund, not exceeding the sum of twelve thousand dollars in any one fiscal year, for repairs to, and improvements upon, streets and sewers in front of property belonging to the City, other than those mentioned in the previous subdivision of this section. * * * * * * ⁷ * * *

Third to Fifth, inclusive. * * * * * * * *

Sixth. To allow and order paid out of the General Fund, such sums as are now due, or may become due, for burying the indigent dead.

Seventh. To allow and order paid out of the General Fund, such sums as are now due, or may become due, for expenses of conveying insane persons to the State Hospital, at Stockton.*

Eighth. * * * * * * * *

Ninth. To allow and order paid out of the General Fund, a sum not to exceed one hundred and fifty dollars per month, to be expended at the instance of the President of the Board of Supervisors, for contingent expenses other than those heretofore provided for, and of which he shall make a quarterly report to the Board.

---

⁴⁵ The portions omitted are obsolete, superseded by later legislation, or are matters of private interest.

*Expenses now paid by State. Sec. 2221 of Pol. Code.

Tenth to Sixteenth, inclusive.   *   *   *   *   *   *

Seventeenth.   *   *   Also, to allow and order paid out of the General Fund, such sums as are now due, or may become due, to the physicians of the City and County Hospitals.

SEC. 2.   This Act to take effect and be in force from and after its passage.

SUPPLEMENT V.

1861, 94.

An Act in relation to the Burning of Bricks in the City and County of San Francisco.

[Approved April 5, 1861.]

The People of the State of California, represented in Senate and Assembly, do enact as follows:

SECTION 1.   From and after the passage of this Act the Board of Supervisors of the City and County of San Francisco shall have full power and authority to fix limits in said City and County, within which the burning of bricks shall be prohibited, and to make such rules and regulations in relation to the burning of bricks in any part of said City and County as they may deem advisable.

SEC. 2.   The Act entitled an Act to prohibit the Burning of Bricks within certain limits in the City and County of San Francisco, approved March thirteen, eighteen hundred and sixty, is hereby repealed.

SUPPLEMENT VI.

1861, 478.

An Act supplementary to an Act approved April twenty-seventh, eighteen hundred and sixty, entitled an Act supplementary to an Act entitled an Act to confer further powers upon the Board of Supervisors and Auditor and Treasurer of the City and County of San Francisco, and to authorize them to perform certain Acts therein mentioned, approved April twenty-third, eighteen hundred and fifty-eight.

[Approved May 17, 1861.]

The People of the State of California, represented in Senate and Assembly, do enact as follows :

SECTION 1. The Board of Supervisors of the City and County of San Francisco have hereby further powers conferred upon them, as follows :[46]

SEC. 2. * * * * * * * * *

SEC. 3. To allow and ordered paid out of the General Fund, for the fiscal year of eighteen hundred and sixty and eighteen hundred and sixty-one, not exceeding the sum of ten hundred dollars, for compiling and publishing the laws and ordinances relating to the City and County of San Francisco ; and for any fiscal year thereafter a further sum, not exceeding three hundred dollars, for the same purpose.

SEC. 4. * * * * * * * * *

SEC. 5. To allow and order paid out of the General Fund, not exceeding the sum of five thousand dollars in any one fiscal year, for the employment of special counsel.

SEC. 6. * * * * * * * * *

---

[46] The portions omitted are obsolete, or have been superseded by later legislation.

SUPPLEMENT VII.

1861, 554.

An Act to fix and regulate the Fees and Salaries of Officials in the City and County of San Francisco.

Approved May 17, 1861.

The People of the State of California, represented in Senate and Assembly, do enact as follows :

SECTION 1.   Salaries shall be allowed and paid to the following officers of the City and County of San Francisco as in this Act provided, and not otherwise, and shall be in full compensation for all official services required of them by law :

[*To Associate Justices of the Court of Sessions, etc. Court of Sessions abolished by Amendment of 1862 to Constitution.*]

To the District Attorney, *five* thousand dollars per annum. [*Amended, March 28, 1872 ; 1871-2, 653 ; Political Code, sec. 4330.*]

To the Clerk of the District Attorney, seventy-five dollars per month.[48]

To the Police Judge, four thousand dollars per annum.

To the Clerk of the Police Court, two hundred dollars per month.

To the Prosecuting Attorney for the Police Court, two hundred *and fifty* dollars per month. [*Amended April 26, 1862, 466, sec. 3; Supplement IX.*]

To two Interpreters and Translators of foreign languages, to be appointed by the County Judge,* Police Judge, and President of the Board of Supervisors, if they deem them necessary, one hundred dollars each per month, subject, however, to be reduced by an order of the Board of Supervisors, if in their opinion such reduction is proper.[49]†

To the City and County Attorney, *five* thousand dollars per annum. [*Amended March 25, 1862, 98 ; Supplement VIII.*]

To the Clerk of the City and County Attorney. [*Superseded by Act of March 4, 1872; 1871-2, 232; Supplement LIII.*]

To the County Clerk, four thousand dollars per annum.

[*Clause relating to salaries of Deputies of the Twelfth and Fourth District, County and Probate Courts, superseded by sec. 1, Act of Feb. 5, 1872; 1871-2, 76; Suplement LII. See also Statutes 1880, 104.*]

---

* Now a Judge of the Superior Court.

† Additional Intepreter allowed by Act of March 8, 1876 ; 1876, 153.

[48] Board of Supervisors may increase to §125. See Act of April 4, 1863, 168; Supplement X. And by Act of March 25, 1874; 1873-4, 602; the District Attorney is authorized and empowered to appoint one clerk in addition to the one now allowed him by law, and at his pleasure to remove him, who shall be entitled to receive a salary of one hundred and fifty dollars a month, payable as the salary of the District Attorney is now made payable by law.

[49] Board of Supervisors authorized to increase salaries to §125, by Act of April 27, 1863, 763.

To the Sheriff, eight thousand dollars per annum.

To one Under Sheriff, two hundred dollars per month.

To three Deputy Sheriffs, each one hundred and fifty dollars per month.

To three Deputy Sheriffs, each one hundred and twenty-five dollars per month.[50]

To four Deputies acting as Jail Keepers, each one hundred and twenty-five dollars per month.[51]

The Book-keeper of the Sheriff of the City and County of San Francisco shall receive a salary of two hundred and fifty dollars per month. [*Amended April 4, 1870; 1869-70, 696.*]

[*Clause relating to salary and fees of Coroner superseded by sec. 30, Act of March 16, 1872; 1871-2, 403; Supplement LV.*]

To the Mayor, three thousand dollars per annum.

To the City and County Surveyor, five hundred dollars per annum, which shall be in lieu of all fees or other charges for official services, which would otherwise be a City and County charge, and he shall charge and collect, for services rendered individuals, such fees as may be prescribed and allowed by the Board of Supervisors.

The Assessor shall receive, for all services required of him by law, a salary at the rate of four thousand dollars per annum, which salary shall be in full for all services required of him, and for all contingent expenses of his office, except necessary books; and he shall devote his whole time, during office hours, to the business of his office, and shall keep his office open to the public during the same hours provided by law for the City and County Auditor. * * * [*The remainder of this clause is repealed by the Act of January 25, 1870; 1869-70, 23; Supplement XL.*]*

[*Clause relating to salary of the Clerk of the Board of Supervisors superseded by Sec. 2, Act of April 26, 1862, 466; Supplement IX. See also Act of March 30, 1873; 1871-2, 735; Supplement LX, and Act of Mar. 26, 1878; 1877-8, 556.*]

To two Porters, not to exceed seventy-five dollars each per month.

To the Auditor, four thousand dollars per annum.

To one Clerk of the Auditor of said City and County, two hundred and fifty dollars per month. [*Amended, Act March 4, 1870; 1869-70, 122.*]

To the Tax Collector, four thousand dollars per annum.[52] * * *

---

[50] Board of Supervisors authorized to increase their salaries to $150, by Act of April 4, 1864, 1863 4, 502; sec. 1, sub. 15; Supplement XX.

[51] Board of Supervisors authorized to allow Sheriff to appoint two additional deputies to act as Jail Keepers, who shall, before entering upon their duties, give the same bonds required of other Jail Keepers, and shall be subject to the same duties and penalties as provided by law, and who shall each receive a salary not exceeding one hundred and twenty-five dollars per month, payable as the salaries of other Deputy Sheriffs are paid. Act of April 1, 1872; 1871-2, 904. The Sheriff allowed to appoint not to exceed sixteen Deputy Jail Keepers at a salary not to exceed $125 per month. Act of March 20, 1878; 1878, 355.

* Assessors allowed fifteen per cent. on collection of Poll Taxes. Sec. 3862 of Pol. Code.

[52] That portion of this clause omitted which relates to deputies and clerks of Tax Collector is repealed by provisions of Act March 25, 1868; 1867-8, 202; Supplement XXXIV.

He shall be allowed one Auctioneer, to conduct tax sales, whose compensation for sales of real estate delinquent for taxes, in any one year, shall not exceed the sum of two hundred dollars. All fees, commissions, percentages, and other compensation of whatever nature or kind, heretofore allowed by law, or which may hereafter be allowed by law, as the compensation of the Tax Collector of said City and County, for the collection of State and County taxes, shall be paid into the Special Fee Fund. [*Amended, April 10, 186 , 239.*]

To the Treasurer, four thousand dollars per annum.

To one Deputy of the Treasurer of said City and County, two hundred and fifty dollars per month, and to one additional Deputy, one hundred and seventy-five dollars per month. [*Amended, by Act of March 4, 1870; 1869-70 122.*]

To the County Recorder, four thousand dollars per annum.

The Chief Deputy of the Recorder of the City and County of San Francisco shall receive a salary of two hundred and fifty dollars per month.[53] [*Amended by Act of April 4, 1870; 1869-70, 696.*]

The Recorder may also employ as many Deputy Clerks as he may deem necessary to duly perform the duties of his office, and they shall be paid at the rate of twelve cents per folio of one hundred words for all matters either registered or copied by them respectively. The Recorder, or his Chief Deputy, when any papers are presented for registration, or to be copied, shall write on the margin of each paper so presented, the number of folios paid for; and shall in his monthly return to the Treasurer, certify under oath the number of folios copied or registered by each one of said Deputy Clerks; and such certificate of the Recorder or his Chief Deputy, shall be conclusive evidence to authorize the Auditor to audit such certified accounts of such Deputy Clerks, monthly.

To one Porter, or Watchman, for the Recorder's office, not to exceed seventy-five dollars per month.

To the Harbor Master. [*Office extinct; Act of March 36, 1874; 1873-4, 910; Supplement LXIX.*]

To the Superintendent of Common Schools, four thousand dollars per annum.

[*Salary of the Secretary of the Board of Education. Provided for by sec. 2, Act of April 2, 1870, 1869-70, 670 ; post, note 68.*]

To the Superintendent of Public Streets and Highways, four thousand dollars per annum.

---

[53] By Sub 17, Sec. 1 of the Act of April 4, 1863, 168; Supplement X; the Supervisors are authorized to allow a salary to an additional deputy for the Recorder; and by that of March 26, 1868; 1867-8, 348; the Recorder is allowed, "in addition to the number of deputies now provided by statute, one additional deputy—said additional deputy to have all the powers appertaining to the deputies now provided by law. The salary of said deputy shall be one hundred and fifty dollars per month."

[*Clause relating to Deputies of the Superintendent of Streets and Highways, and their salaries, superseded by sec.* 21, *Act of April of* 1, 1872 ; 1871-2, 804; *Supplement LXIII. Act of March* 2, 1878; 1878, 139.

FIRE DEPARTMENT.

[*Superseded by the following Acts : As to salary of Chief Engineer, by sec.* 6, *Act of March* 2, 1866, *Amended April* 1, 1872; 1871-2, 855; *Supplement XXIV, post: As to Assistant Engineers and Clerk, by sec.* 13, *Act of March* 30, 1874; 1873-4, 942; *Supplement LXX, post: And as to salaries of Bell Ringers, by sub.* 19, *sec.* 1, *Act of April* 4, 1864 ; 1863-4, 502 ; *Supplement XX, post: Act reorganizing Fire Department, March* 28, 1878; 1877-8, 685.

POLICE DEPARTMENT.

To the Chief of Police, four thousand dollars per annum.

To four Captains of Police, one hundred and twenty-five dollars per month, each.[54] [Increased to five, Act. 1, 1878; 1878, 879.]

To Policemen, not exceeding forty, the number to be determined from time to time by order of the Board of Supervisors, one hundred dollars[54] per month each ; *provided*, that one of the same detailed for Clerk in the office, of Chief of Police, to be appointed by him, shall receive one hundred and twenty-five dollars per month.[54]   *   *   *   (Obsolete.)

SEC. 2. The several officers named in this Act, who are entitled to charge and collect or receive any. fees, commissions, percentages, or other compensation, of whatever nature or kind, allowed by law for services rendered by them or their deputies in their several official capacities, or for the performance of duties appertaining to said offices, shall collect and safely keep the same, and on each Monday they shall pay the total amount by them received to the Treasurer of said City and County, who shall set apart the same as a Special Fee Fund, for the payment of the respective salaries of the several officers entitled to charge and collect fees, commissions, or other compensation. And the salaries of all other officers shall be paid out of the General Fund ; *provided*, that the Assessor, so far as relates to the collection of poll tax, and the City and County Surveyor, shall be exempt from the provisions of this section. It shall be and is hereby made the duty of all such officers, who are entitled to charge and collect or receive fees, commissions, or other compensation for their official services, to keep a book or books, in which shall be entered by items the amount received for all official services performed by them or their deputies, showing the date and nature of such services, and the amount received therefor, which book or books shall, at all

---

[54] Board of Supervisors authorized to increase the salary of each member of the police force twenty-five dollars per month; Act of April 4, 1863, 168, sec. 1, sub. 16 ; Supplement X. post. [Increase allowed to 400, Act April 1, 1878 ; 1878, 871.

office hours, be open to the inspection of the Board of Supervisors or any citizen; and each of said officers shall, at the expiration of each month, make out and verify by oath and file with the Auditor, a full and accurate transcript from his said book or books, of the entries for the preceding month.

SEC. 3. It shall be the duty of the Treasurer of said City and County to receive, receipt for, and safely keep all moneys paid over to him under the provisions of this Act, and to make up, on the first day of October, eighteen hundred and sixty-one, and quarterly thereafter, an accurate statement of said Special Fee Fund, showing the actual condition of the same up to such time, when, if any balance remain in said fund, after satisfying all demands payable out of the same, the Treasurer shall transfer such balance to the General Fund ; but should such Special Fee Fund be insufficient to satisfy all of the demands payable therefrom, then the Treasurer shall, at the request of the holder, register such unpaid demands against, and pay the same in their order of registration out of the General Fund, as in other cases.

SEC. 4. All demands upon the treasury, allowed by this Act, shall, before they are authorized to be paid, be duly audited, as in other cases of demands lawfully payable out of the treasury. The several salaries named shall be payble monthly by the Treasurer, upon the audit of the County Auditor, who is hereby directed to audit the salaries herein provided for.

SEC. 5. The Board of Supervisors may, from time to time, authorize the appointment of such additional deputies from any of the various City and County offices, and for such period of time as in their judgment may be necessary for the proper and faithful discharge of the duties of such office. Deputies appointed under the provisions of this section shall receive not to exceed one hundred and fifty dollars per month, each ; but in no case shall the aggregate pay of such Deputies exceed three thousand dollars per annum.

SEC. 6. The fees receivable by the several officers named in this Act, shall be payable in advance.

SEC. 7. [*Repealed by Act of March 24,* 1868 ; 1867-8, 267 ; *Supplement XXXIII.*]

SEC. 8. For a willful neglect, or refusal to comply with any of the provisions of this Act, by any officer or officers herein named, he or they shall be deemed guilty of felony, and on conviction thereof in the Court * * *, be subject to a fine not to exceed five thousand dollars, and a forfeiture of office, or to imprisonment in the State Prison not less than one nor more than three years, or to both such fine and imprisonment ; *provided*, that nothing herein shall be held to release such officer from the obligation to give the official bond required by law, or from any civil responsibility arising from his official duties.

SEC. 9. All requisitions for books, blanks and stationery, for any of the officers named in this Act, shall be made by such officers, respectively, upon the Board of Supervisors, stating the amount and description thereof, and that the same are essential and necessary for the use of such office, which statement shall be verified by the oath of such officer, and upon their approval thereof, the said Board shall order the cost of the same paid out of the Special Fee Fund.

SEC. 10. [*Superseded by Act of March* 2, 1872; 1871-2, 219.

SEC. 11. This Act shall take effect on and after the first day of July, eighteen hundred and sixty-one, at which time the Act entitled an Act concerning the Offices of County Clerk, Sheriff and County Recorder of the City and County of San Francisco, approved March seventh, eighteen hundred and fifty-nine, shall be, and the same is hereby, repealed. All Acts and parts of Acts in conflict with the provisions of this Act, so far as they affect this Act, are hereby declared inoperative and void, from and after the first day of July, eighteen hundred and sixty-one.

SUPPLEMENT VIII.

1862, 98.

Providing for an Attorney and Counsellor in and for the City and County of San Francisco.

[Approved March 25, 1862.]

The People of the State of California, represented in Senate and Assembly, do enact as follows:

SECTION 1. There shall be elected, hereafter, for the City and County of San Francisco, by the qualified electors thereof, on the third Tuesday of May, eighteen hundred and sixty-two,[56] and every two years thereafter, one Attorney and Counsellor, learned in the law, who shall hold his office for two years, and until his successor shall have been duly elected and qualified, and shall be paid, by said City and County, a salary of five thousand dollars per annum, to be audited and paid monthly, in the same manner as the salary of the County Judge is by law audited and paid. Said Attorney and Counsellor shall perform such duties as Attorney and Counsellor in and for the said City and County as the Board of Supervisors of said City and County shall from time to time prescribe. [*Amended, April* 27, 1863, 771.]

SEC. 2. [*Obsolete.*]*

---

[56] Time of election changed. See sec. 4109 Pol Code.

* Assistant allowed for street cases by sec. 25 of Act April 1, 1872; 1872, 804.

SEC. 3. All other Acts, or parts of Acts, providing for the appointment of City and County Attorney, for said City and County of San Francisco, and payment of salary thereof, and all Acts inconsistent or in conflict with this Act, are hereby repealed.

SEC. 4. This Act shall take effect immediately after its passage.

SUPPLEMENT IX.

1862, 466.

An Act to Confer Further Powers upon the Board of Supervisors of the City and County of San Francisco.

[Approved April 26, 1862.]

The People of the State of California, represented in Senate and Assembly, do enact as follows:

SECTION 1. The Board of Supervisors of the City and County of San Francisco have hereby further powers conferred upon them as follows.[57]
First to Thirteenth, inclusive.   *   *   *   *   *   *
Fourteenth. To exclude, by order, prostitutes from certain limits, in the discretion of said Board.
Fifteenth to Nineteenth, inclusive.   *   *   *   *   *   *

SEC. 2.[58]   *   *   *   *   *   *   *   *   *

SEC. 3. The salary of the Prosecuting Attorney of the Police Court is hereby fixed at two hundred and fifty dollars per month.

SEC. 4. [*Repealed by Act of April 4, 1870 ; 1869-70, 696.*]

SEC. 5.   *   *   *   *   *   *   *   *   *

SEC. 6. Section sixty-nine of the Consolidation Act is so amended as to read—that all contracts for subsistence of prisoners must be given out annually, at a fixed price per day not exceeding twenty-five cents per diem for each person connected with the prison, instead of quarterly, as provided.

SEC. 7. Said Board of Supervisors are hereby authorized to order paid, out of the General Fund, any deficiency that may occur in the Street Light Fund, for lighting the public streets.

---

[57] The portions omitted are obsolete, or matters of private moment, or are superseded.

[58] Board of Supervisors may increase to $250 per month ; sub. 12, sec. 1, Act of March 30, 1872 : 1871-2, 735 ; Supplement LX, post.

SEC. 8. [*Amends sub. 5, sec. 74, of the " Consolidation Act," ante, and repeals sub. 22, of the same section.*]

SEC. 9. * * * * * * * * *

SEC. 10. The amounts which, by this Act, are authorized to be paid, shall be the entire amounts to be paid for the respective purposes herein mentioned, except when otherwise expressly provided in this Act.

— - -

S U P P L E M E N T   X.

1863, 168.

An Act to confer Additional Powers upon the Board of Supervisors of the City and County of San Francisco, and upon the Auditor and Treasurer thereof, and to authorize the Appropriations or Money by said Board.

[Approved April 4, 1863.]

The People of the State of California, represented in Senate and Assembly, do enact as follows :

SECTION 1. The Board of Supervisors of the City and County of San Francisco are hereby authorized and empowered to appropriate, allow, and order paid, the sums of money, and to exercise the powers following :[59]

First to Third, inclusive. * * * * * *

Fourth. To allow and order paid out of the General Fund a sum not to exceed three thousand dollars in any year, for the celebration, in said City and County, of the anniversary of our National Independence.

Fifth. Obsolete.

Sixth.

Seventh. [*See sec. 8, Supplement XXIV, post. See also sub. 6 of sec. 1 of Act of March 26, 1878; 1878, 556.*

Eighth to Twelfth inclusive. * * * * * *

Thirteenth. To allow and order paid out of the General Fund, * * * not to exceed the sum of six thousand dollars for any one year, for the support of the Small-pox Hospital of said City and County.

Fourteenth. To allow and order paid out of the General Fund,[60] * *

---

[59] The subdivisions omittted are on matters of private interest, or are absolute.

[60] As to salary of Clerk of Auditor repealed by Act of March 4, 1870 ; 1869-70, 122 ; salary fixed at $250 per month. As to salary of Clerk of the City and County Attorney repealed by Act of March 4, 1872 ; 1871-2, 232 ; Supplement LIII, post.

*   •   *   *   *   *   *   *   to the Clerk of
the District Attorney of said City and County, the sum of one hundred and
twenty-five dollars per month; and to the Clerk of the Treasurer of said City
and County, the sum of one hundred and twenty-five dollars per month.[61] *

Fifteenth.   *   *   *   *   *   *   *   *

Sixteenth. To increase the salary of each member of the Police force of
said City and County twenty-five dollars per month, and to diminish the
same again at pleasure to the present salary of said Police force ; which said
increase of salary, if made, shall be paid as the salaries of the Police force
are now paid, and out of the same fund.

Seventeenth. To allow and order paid out of the General Fund, the sum of
one hundred and fifty dollars per month, as a salary for an additional deputy
in the office of the Recorder of the said City and County.

Eighteenth to Nineteenth.   *   *   *   *   *   *

Twentieth.   *   *   *   *   *   *   *   *

Twenty-first to Twenty-ninth, inclusive.   *   *   *   *   *   *

SEC. 2. The Auditor of said City and County is hereby directed and empowered to audit and allow, as aforesaid, and the Treasurer thereof to pay,
as aforesaid, all sums of money that may be allowed or ordered to be paid
under the provisions hereof.

SEC. 3. The amounts which by this Act are authorized to be paid, shall
be the only amounts, to be paid for the respective purposes for which they
are authorized to be paid under the provisions hereof, except when otherwise
expressly provided in this Act, and excepting an allowance of two thousand
dollars per annum heretofore provided by law for enclosing, improving and
regulating all public grounds in said City and County. [This latter clause is
superseded by subsequent statutes.]

SEC. 4. All Acts and parts of Acts inconsistent herewith are hereby repealed.

SEC. 5. This Act shall take effect and be in force from and after its passage.

---

[61] Superseded as to salary of Clerk of the Mayor; Act of April 1, 1878, which fixes same at §250.
As to salary of Clerk of the Board of Supervisors, superseded by Act of March 26, 1878.

SUPPLEMENT XI.

1863, 540.

An Act to confer further powers upon the Board of Supervisors of the City and County of San Francisco.

[Approved April 25, 1863.]

The People of the State of California, represented in Senate and Assembly, do enact as follows :

SECTION 1. The Board of Supervisors of the City and County of San Francisco shall have power, by regulation or order :

First. To regulate the Police and Police force of said City and County, and to prescribe their powers and duties.

Second. To authorize and direct the summary abatement of nuisances; to make all regulations which may be necessary or expedient for the preservation of the public health and the prevention of contagious diseases; to provide, by regulation, for the prevention and summary removal of all nuisances and obstructions in the streets, alleys, highways, and public grounds of said City and County; and to prevent or regulate the running at large of dogs, and to authorize the destruction of the same when at large contrary to ordinances. *

Third. To prohibit and suppress or exclude from certain limits, all houses of ill-fame, prostitution and gaming; to prohibit and suppress, or exclude from certain limits, or to regulate all occupations, houses, places, pastimes, amusements, exhibitions and practices, which are against good morals, contrary to public order and decency, or dangerous to the public safety.

Fourth. To license and regulate hackney coaches, and other public passenger vehicles, and to fix the rates to be charged for the transportation of persons, baggage, and property, or either, therein; and to license and regulate all vehicles used for the conveyance of merchandise, earth and ballast, or either ; and also, to license and regulate persons and parties employed in conveying baggage, property, and merchandise, or either, to and from any of the wharfs, slips, bulkheads, or railroad stations within the limits of the City and County of San Francisco;[62]   "   *   to fix and establish the amount of every license paid into the City and County Treasury for City and County purposes, at such rate as said Board shall determine, not exceeding the amount fixed by law ; and, *provided*, said Board shall have no power

---

* The Police powers of the Board have been greatly enlarged by the State Constitution of 1879· See sec. 11 of Art. XI.

[62] Provisions as to License Collectors superseded by Sec. 4, Act of March 30, 1872; 1871-2, 736 Supplement LXI, post.; and Act of March 23, 1878; 1878, 412.

to entirely abolish any license fixed by law, or to reduce the proportion of each license collected, which by law is paid into the City and County Treasury for State purposes.

Fifth. To provide for the summary removal and disposition of any or all vehicles found during certain hours of the day and night, to be designated by said Board, in the streets, highways and public squares of said City and County, or such of them as said Board may designate; and, in addition to all other remedies, to provide, by regulation, for the sale or other disposition of said vehicles so found in said streets, highways or public squares, as aforesaid.

Sixth. To require, by ordinance, all contractors for street work, or other persons lawfully undertaking to improve, grade, or alter streets or public highways in the City and County of San Francisco, to erect fences or other suitable barriers to protect the public from damage, loss or accident, by reason of such grading, alteration, or improvement, and to determine and prescribe the fines and penalties that shall be incurred for breach of such regulations and ordinances as may be passed by virtue hereof.

Seventh. To designate one of their number, who shall, in absence of the Mayor, or during his inability from any cause, perform the duties required by law of the Mayor of said City and County.

Eighth and Ninth.[63]   *   *   *   *   *   *

Tenth. To provide for the safe keeping and disposition of all lost, stolen, or unclaimed property of every kind, which may be in the possession or under the control of the Chief of Police of said City and County, or which may hereafter come into the possession of the Police of said City and County.

SEC. 2. Subdivisions first, third and fifteenth of section seventy-four of an Act entitled an Act amendatory of an Act entitled an Act to repeal the several Charters of the City of San Francisco, to establish the boundaries of the City and County of San Francisco, and to consolidate the government thereof, approved the nineteenth day of April, eighteen hundred and fifty-six, and of an Act amendatory and supplementary thereof, approved the eighteenth day of April, eighteen hundred and fifty-seven, and of an Act amendatory thereof, approved the twenty-eighth day of March, eighteen hundred and fifty-nine, and supplementary to said Acts, are hereby repealed.

SEC. 3. This Act shall take effect and be in force from and after its passage.

----

[63] For the relief of certain persons.

SUPPLEMENT XII.

1863, 560.

An Act to confer further Powers upon the Board of Supervisors of the City and County of San Francisco.

[Approved April 25, 1863.]

The People of the State of California, represented in Senate and Assembly, do enact as follows :

SECTION 1. That the Board of Supervisors of the City and County of San Francisco shall have full power and authority to provide, by order, for laying out, opening, extending, widening, straightening, or closing up, in whole or in part, any street, square, lane, or alley, within the bounds of said City, which, in their opinion, the public welfare or convenience may require; to provide for ascertaining whether any and what amount in value of damage will be caused thereby, and what amount of benefit will thereby accrue to the owner or possessor of any ground or improvements within said City and County, for which such owner or possessor ought to be compensated, or ought to pay a compensation; and to provide for assessing and levying, either generally on the whole assessable property within said City, or specially on the property of persons benefited, the whole or any part of the damages and expenses which they shall ascertain will be incurred in locating, opening, extending, widening, straightening, or closing up the whole or any part of any street, square, lane, or alley, in said City and County; to provide for granting appeals to the *County Court of the City and County of San Francisco, from the decisions of any Commissioners, or other persons, appointed in virtue of any ordinance, to ascertain the damage which will be caused or the benefit which will accrue to the owners or possessors of ground or improvements, by locating, opening, extending, widening, straightening, or closing up, in whole or in part, any street, square, lane, or alley, within said City and County, and for securing to every such owner and possessor the right, on application within a reasonable time, to have decided by a jury trial, whether any damage has been caused or any benefit has accrued to them, and to what amount; to provide for collecting and paying over the amount of compensation adjudged to each person entitled, and to enact and pass all orders from time to time which shall be deemed necessary and proper to exercise the powers and effect the objects above specified; *provided, nevertheless,* that before the Board of Supervisors of the City and County of San

---

*Now Superior Court, by Acts of February 4, 1880; 1880-1; and Act of April 3, 1880; 1880, 115.

Francisco proceed to execute any of the powers vested in them by this Act,
at least thirty days' notice shall be given of any application which may be
made for the passage of any order, by advertisement in at least two of the
daily newspapers of the City and County of San Francisco having the largest
circulation; *provided, further*, that whenever any street or part of any street
in the said City and County, occupied or used by the track of any railroad
company, shall require to be altered or widened for the convenience of public
travel, and proceedings for the altering or widening the same shall have been
taken under the provisions of this Act, it shall be lawful for the Commissioners
appointed as in this Act provided, and whose duty it may be, to make a just
and equitable assessment of the whole amount of costs, damages, and expenses,
of such altering or widening, among the owners of all the lands and real estate
intended to be benefited thereby, to assess such portion of said costs, damages,
and expenses, upon the corporation or company owning or using said railroad
track as shall to them seem equitable and just, and such assessment shall be
a lien upon any property of said corporation or company in the said City and
County, and may also be enforced in the same manner as the assessment upon
such owners of lands and real estate intended to be benefited thereby.

SEC. 2. That before any Commissioners appointed by any order to be
passed in virtue of this Act shall proceed to the performance of their duty,
they shall give notice in at least two of the daily newspapers published in the
City of San Francisco having the largest circulation, of the object of the
order under which they propose to act, at least ten days before the time of
their first meeting to execute the same.

SEC. 3. That upon the return of any assessment to be made under any
ordinance to be passed in virtue of this Act, the Clerk of the Board of Supervisors of the City and County of San Francisco shall cause a copy of said
assessment to be published for ten days, in at least two daily newspapers of
said City and County having the largest circulation.

SEC. 4. That the time within which any appeal is to be made from any
assessment shall be computed from and after the expiration of the ten days
mentioned in the preceding section.

SEC. 5. All the expenses resulting from locating, opening, extending,
widening, straightening, or closing up, in whole or in part, any street, square,
lane, or alley, within said City and County of San Francisco, shall be paid
out of the moneys derived from the assessments upon the property benefited
by such locating, opening, extending, widening, straightening, or closing up,
in whole or in part, any street, square, lane, or alley, within said City and
County; and the City and County of San Francisco shall not be liable for any
expense caused by the same.

SEC. 6. This Act shall take effect and be in force from and after its
passage.

SUPPLEMENT XIII.

1863, 601.

An Act to establish and define the powers and duties of the Board of Education of the City and County of San Francisco and to repeal former Acts regulating the same, and to confer further powers upon the Auditor and Treasurer of said City and County.

[Approved April 27, 1863.]

The People of the State of California, represented in Senate and Assembly, do enact as follows :

OF THE ORGANIZATION OF THE BOARD.

SECTION 1. The Board of Education of the City and County of San Fran. cisco shall consist of the School Directors elected for the several election districts of said City and County.[64] The said Board shall organize annually, on the first Tuesday in July,[65] by electing a President from among its members, and shall hold meetings monthly thereafter, and at such other times as the Board may determine. A majority of all the members elect shall constitute a quorum to transact business, but a smaller number may adjourn from time to time. The Board may determine the rules of its proceedings. Its sessions shall be public, and its records shall be open to public inspection.

OF THE POWERS AND DUTIES OF THE BOARD.

SEC. 2. [*Amended, March* 12, 1864; 1863-4, 162.] The Board of Education, shall have sole power:

First.[66]   *   *   *   *   To establish School Districts, and to fix and alter the boundaries thereof.

Second. To establish Experimental and Normal Schools, either separately or in connection with the State Normal School.

Third.   *   *   *   *   *   *   *   *   *

And to employ and pay such mechanics and laborers as may be necessary to carry into effect the powers and duties of the Board; and to withhold, for good and sufficient cause, the whole or any part of the salary or wages of any person or persons employed as aforesaid.

---

[64] Elected from the City and County at large without reference to their residence; sec. 19, Act of April 1, 1872; Supplement LXIV, post; which see in connection with this Act generally.

[65] First Monday after the 1st day of January. See sec. 4109, Pol. Code.

[66] Portions omitted are re-enacted or superseded. See Acts of April 1, 1872; Supplement LXIV; and April 3, 1876; Supplement XC.

Fourth.   *   *   *   *   *   *   *   *

Fifth. To provide for the School Department of said City and County, fuel, lights, water, blanks, blank books, books, printing, stationery, and such other articles, materials, or supplies as may be necessary and appropriate for use in the schools or in the office of the Superintendent, and to incur incidental expenses not exceeding twenty-five hundred dollars per annum.

Sixth. To build, alter, repair, rent and provide school houses, and furnish them with proper school furniture, apparatus, and school appliances, and to insure any and all school property.

Seventh.   *   *   *   *   *   *   *   *

Eighth. To receive, purchase, lease, and hold in fee, in trust for the City and County of San Francisco, any and all real estate, and to hold in trust any personal property that may have been acquired, or may hereafter be acquired, for the use and benefit of the Public Schools of said City and County; *provided*, the lots to be purchased under the provisions of this section do not exceed ten in number; and all conveyances heretofore made to the said Board of Education are hereby legalized and declared valid, and the property therein conveyed vested in said Board in trust as aforesaid.

. *Ninth.* [*Authorizes sale of certain lots. Repealed by Sec. 3, Act March 30, 1868; 1867–8, 558; Supplement XXXIX.*][67]

Tenth. Superseded by Act of March 30, 1868; 1868, 558, Sec. 1; Supplement XXXIX.

Eleventh. To sue for any and all lots, lands and property belonging to or claimed by the said School Department, and to prosecute and defend all actions, at law or in equity, necessary to recover and maintain the full enjoyment and possession of said lots, lands and property, and to employ and pay counsel in such cases; *provided*, the amount of fees paid to such counsel shall not exceed one thousand dollars in any one year; and further to do any and all lawful acts necessary thereto.

Twelfth.   *   *   .   *   *   *   *   *

Thirteenth. To establish regulations for the just and equal disbursement of all moneys belonging to the Public School Fund.

Fourteenth.   *   *   .   *   *   *   *   *

Fifteenth.   *   *   *   *   *   *   *   *

Sixteenth and Seventeenth.   *   *   *   *   *   *

Eighteenth. And, generally, to do and perform such other acts as may be necessary and proper to carry into force and effect the powers conferred on said Board.

---

[67] Sec. 7 of "An Act to provide Funds for the School Department of San Francisco," approved March 17, 1866; 1865-6, 302; provides as follows: "In case any school lots are hereafter sold in said City and County, at least one-half of the proceeds of such sale shall be reserved and set apart for the redemption of bonds issued under this Act and former Acts, until all such bonds, now outstanding or hereafter issued for school purposes are paid, or sufficient money received and set apart for their final redemption and payment."

Sec. 3. The President of the Board of Education shall have power to administer oaths and affirmations concerning any demand upon the treasury payable out of the School Fund, or other matters relating to his official duties.

Sec. 4. At the last regular session of the Board, in September, December, March and June, of each year, before proceeding to other business, each Director shall be called on to report the condition of the school or schools in his district, and the circumstances and wants of the inhabitants thereof, in respect to education, and to suggest any defect he may have noted and improvement he would recommend in the school regulations. The reports to be made in December and June shall be in writing.

Sec. 5. Before giving out any contract or incurring any liability to mechanics or laborers, or for expenditures authorized by section two, subdivisions three, five, and six, respectively, to any amount exceeding two hundred dollars, the Board of Education shall cause notice to be published for five days, inviting sealed proposals for the object contemplated. All proposals offered shall be delivered to the Superintendent of Public Schools, and said Board shall, in open session, open, examine, and publicly declare the same, and award the contract to the lowest responsible bidder; *provided*, said Board may reject any and all bids, should they deem it for the public good, and also, the bid of any party who may have proved delinquent or unfaithful in any former contract with said City and County or said Board, and cause a republication of the notice for proposals as above specified. [*Amended, March 12, 1864; 1863-4, 162.*].

Sec. 6. No School Director or Superintendent shall be interested in any contract pertaining in any manner to the School Department of said City and County. All contracts in violation of this section are declared void, and any Director or Superintendent violating or aiding in the violation of the provisions of this section shall be deemed guilty of a misdemeanor.*

Secs. 7 and 8. [*Examination of teachers and granting of certificates. Superseded, Secs. 1787 to 1794, inclusive, of the Political Code.*]

OF THE SUPERINTENDENT.

Sec. 9. The Superintendent of Public Schools of the City and County of San Francisco is hereby declared and constituted *ex-officio* a member of the Board of Education, without the right to vote.

Sec. 10. The said Superintendent is hereby authorized to appoint a Clerk, subject to the approval of the Board of Education, who shall act as Secretary of the Board, and who shall be paid a salary, to be fixed by the said Board, not to exceed the sum of *two hundred* dollars per month. *Amended sec. 2,*

*See also Secs. 1876 and 1879 of the Political Code.

note 68, below.] The said Clerk shall be subject to removal at the pleasure of the Superintendent, and shall perform such duties as may be required of him by the Board or the Superintendent.[68]

SEC. 11.   The Superintendent shall report to the Board of Education annually, on or before the twentieth day of June, and at such other times as they require, all matters pertaining to the expenditures, income, and condition and progress of the Public Schools of said City and County, during the preceding year, with such recommendations as he may deem proper.

SEC. 12.   It shall be the duty of the Superintendent   *   *   * to observe, and cause to be observed, such general rules for the regulation, government and instruction of the schools, not inconsistent with the laws of the State, as may be established by the Board of Education; to attend the sessions of the Board, and inform them at each session of the condition of the Public Schools, School Houses, School Funds, and other matters connected therewith, and to recommend such measures as he may deem necessary for the advancement of education in the City and County.   He shall acquaint himself with all the laws, rules and regulations governing the Public Schools in the said City and County, and the judicial decisions thereon, and give advice on subjects connected with the Public Schools, gratuitously, to officers, teachers, pupils, and their parents and guardians.*

SEC. 13.   Any vacancy in the office of School Director shall be filled by appointment by the Superintendent, by and with the consent of a majority of the School Directors then in office; and such appointees shall hold office, respectively, until the municipal election next ensuing, and the election and qualification of their successors in office.   But no such appointment shall be valid, unless the appointee be, at the time of his appointment, an elector of the district wherein the vacancy occured.[69]

SEC. 14.   In case of a vacancy in the office of Superintendent, the Board of Education may appoint a person to fill the vacancy until the regular election then next following, when the office shall be filled by election of the people.

---

[68] "An Act to establish and define the Powers and Duties of the Secretary of the Board of Education of the City and County of San Francisco," approved April 2, 1870; 1869 70, 670; provides:

Section 1.   The Secretary of the Board of Education of said City and County of San Francisco shall have power to administer oaths and affirmations concerning any demand upon the treasury payable out of the School Fund, or other matters brought before the School Department for investigation.

Sec. 2.   The said Secretary shall be paid a salary, to be fixed by the Board of Education, not to exceed the sum of two hundred dollars per month, in lieu of any salary now paid, payable in the same manner and out of the same fund as the Superintendent of Common Schools for the City and County of San Francisco is paid.

Sec. 3.   This Act shall take effect immediately.

See also Pol. Code, Secs.. 1542 to 1553, inclusive

[69] See Sec. 19, Act of April 1, 1872; Supplement LXIV, post.

OF THE SCHOOL FUND.

Sec. 15. The School Fund of the City and County of San Francisco shall consist of all moneys received from the State School Fund; of all moneys arising from taxes which shall be levied annually by the Board of Supervisors of said City and County for school purposes; of all moneys arising from the sale, rent or exchange of any school property; and of such other moneys as may, from any source whatever, be paid into said School Fund; which fund shall be kept separate and distinct from all other moneys, and shall only be used for school purposes under the provisions of this Act, and for the payment of the interest and redemption of the principal of the school bonds, according to law. No fees or commissions shall be allowed or paid for assessing, collecting, keeping or disbursing any school moneys; and if, at the end of any fiscal year, any surplus remains in the School Fund, such surplus money shall be carried forward to the School Fund of the next fiscal year, and shall not be, for any purpose whatever, diverted or withdrawn from said fund, except under the provisions of this Act.

Sec. 16. The said School Fund shall be used and applied by said Board of Education for the following purposes, to wit:

First. For the payment of the salaries or wages of teachers, janitors, school census marshals, and other persons who may be employed by the said Board.

Second. For the erection, alteration, repair, rent, and furnishing of school-houses.

Third. For the expense of Model and Normal Schools.*

Fourth. For the purchase-money or rent of any real or personal property purchased or leased by said Board.

Fifth. For the insurance of all school property.

Sixth. For the payment of interest due on school bonds, and for the redemption of the same.

Seventh. For the discharge of all legal incumbrances now existing on any school property.

Eighth. For lighting school-rooms and the office and rooms of the Superintendent and the Board of Education.

Ninth. For supplying the schools with fuel, water, apparatus, blanks, blank-books, and necessary school appliances, together with books for indigent children.

Tenth. For supplying books, printing, and stationery for the use of the Superintendent and Board of Education, and for the incidental expenses of the Board and Department.

Eleventh.   *.   *   *   *   *   *   *   *

---

*Modified by Sec. 6 of Art. IX of the State Constitution of 1879.

Twelfth. For grading, fencing, and improving school lots, and for grading, sewering, planking or paving, and repairing streets, and constructing and repairing sidewalks in front thereof.

SEC. 17. All claims payable out of the School Fund (excepting the coupons for interest and the School Bonds) shall be filed with the Secretary of the Board, and after they shall have been approved by a majority of all the members elect of the Board, upon a call of yeas and nays (which shall be recorded), they shall be signed by the President of the Board and the Superintendent of Public Schools, and be sent to the City and County Auditor. Every demand shall have endorsed upon it a certificate of its approval by the Board, showing the date thereof and the law authorizing the same by title, date, and section. All demands for teachers' salaries shall be payable monthly.

SEC. 18. Demands on the School Fund may be audited and approved in the usual manner, although there shall not at the time be money in the treasury for the payment of the same; *provided*, that no demand on said fund shall be paid out of, or become a charge against, the School Fund of any subsequent fiscal year ; and *further provided*, that the entire expenditures of the said School Department for all purposes shall not in any fiscal year exceed the revenues thereof for the same year.*

SEC. 19. The City and County Auditor shall state, by indorsement upon every claim or demand audited on the School Fund, the particular money or fund out of which the same is payable, and that it is payable from no other source.

SEC. 20. Audited bills of the current fiscal year, for wages or salaries of the teachers in the Public Schools, shall be receivable for school taxes due upon real estate.

SEC. 21. All demands authorized by this Act shall be audited and approved in the usual manner, and the Auditor and Treasurer of said City and County are respectively authorized and required to audit and pay the same when so ordered paid and approved by the said Board ; *provided*, that the said Board shall not have power to contract any debt or liability in any form whatsoever against the said City and County in contravention of this Act.

SEC. 22. The teachers in the Industrial School in said City and County shall be exempt from the provisions of this Act.

SEC. 23. This Act shall take effect and be in force from and after its passage; and all laws and parts of laws, so far as they are inconsistent with or a repetition of the provisions of this Act, are hereby repealed.

By Sect. 7 of Art. IX of the Constitution, County Superintendents and County Boards of Education have control of the examination of teachers and the granting of certificates within their jurisdictions.

---

* Modified by Acts of Feb. 25, 1878 and March 18, 1873.

SUPPLEMENT XIV.

1863. 730.

An Act to authorize the Board of Supervisors of the City and County of San Francisco to grant the right to lay down Gas Pipes in the Streets of said City and County, subject to certain restrictions and requirements.

[Approved April 27. 1863.]*

The People of the State of California, represented in Senate and Assembly, do enact as follows :

SECTION 1. The Board of Supervisors of the City and County of San Francisco are hereby authorized to grant the right to lay down gas pipes in and through the streets of the City and County of San Francisco, and through said pipes to supply gas for the use of said City and County and the inhabitants thereof, for the term of fifty years, subject to the provisions of this Act.

SEC. 2. In consideration of the rights thus granted by said Board to any grantees, said grantees, their associates or assigns, within ten months, shall commence and prosecute the work in good faith, and within two years from the date of the grant thus made shall have erected the necessary buildings and apparatus for the manufacture of at least fifty thousand cubic feet of gas in each twenty-four hours, and shall have laid down at least two miles of main gas pipe through the public streets of the City and County of San Francisco, and supply gas through the same; within four years from the date of the grant thus made, the said grantees, and their associates and assigns, shall have laid down three additional miles of street main pipes, and shall at all times thereafter during the continuance of the franchise privileges thus granted, supply gas through the same for the use of the City and County of San Francisco and their inhabitants; *provided,* that said grantees shall not charge more than five dollars for each one thousand cubic feet of gas.

SEC. 3. Said streets or ways in which said pipes may be laid shall be placed in the same good order and condition as they were at the time of being disturbed, at the cost of said grantees, associates or assigns, subject to the approval of the Superintendent of Streets and Highways, and to his satisfaction.

---

*Practically obsolete by the operation of Sec. 19 of Art. XI of the State Constitution.

5

SEC. 4. If, under the privileges granted by authority of this Act, any injury shall be done to any water pipes, gas pipes, sewers, or drains, belong_ ing to other parties, the amount of said injury, including losses of water or gas, shall be assessed by the Superintendent of Public Streets and Highways, and paid by the parties causing such injury, their associates and assigns; and the assessment of said Superintendent of Streets and Highways shall be final and conclusive as to the amount of damages to be paid.

SEC. 5. Under the provisions of this Act, such grantees and their asso- ciates and assigns shall not erect any work or apparatus for the manufacture of gas within the district bounded on the north by Francisco street, on the west by Larkin and Ninth streets, and on the south by Brannan street; pro- vided, that nothing in this Act shall authorize the grantees herein named, or their associates or assigns, to build or maintain any works or erections which shall be a nuisance.

SEC. 6. For the faithful performance of the terms of any such grant, on the part of the grantees, their associates and assigns, they shall execute, within twenty days from the date of such grant, a bond to the Treasurer of the City and County of San Francisco, in the sum of thirty thousand dol- lars, with two or more sureties, to be approved by the County Judge of said City and County, and shall file the same in the office of said Treasurer, and upon the forfeiture of said bonds, it shall be the duty of the Attorney of said City and County to bring an action for the amount thereof, and upon recovery to have the amount of said bond, with costs of suit, paid into the treasury of said City and County; and in case said bond shall not be executed, approved and filed, as provided in this Act, or in case of the non-performance of any of the terms and conditions of this Act, or of any grant made under this Act, by such grantees, and their associates or assigns, required to be performed, their franchises thus granted shall utterly cease and determine; provided, that no franchise or privilege shall be claimed or held under any grant made by authority of this Act, unless entirely new buildings and furnaces for the man- ufacture of gas shall be erected, and new main gas pipes for the conveyance of the gas shall be laid down, wholly unconnected with any gas building now standing, or gas pipes which are now or may be hereafter laid down by any other gas company, and unless said building and main pipes be kept and maintained entirely unconnected with any gas building heretofore erected, or main gas pipes laid down heretofore, or which may be hereafter erected or laid down by any other gas company; and, provided, that any violation or infringement of the provisions of this proviso shall work a forfeiture of all rights, franchises and immunities herein granted, and such franchises, rights and immunities shall, ipso facto, cease and determine, all the said property and rights shall vest in the City, and it shall be and is hereby made the duty of the City and County of San Francisco to commence and prosecute pro- ceedings for the enforcement thereof.

SUPPLEMENT XV.

1863, 765.

___

An Act to provide for the Appointment of a Weigher of Coal in and for the City and County of San Francisco, California.

[Approved April 27, 1863.]

The People of the State of California, represented in Senate and Assembly, do enact as follows:

SECTION 1. The Board of Supervisors of the City and County of San Francisco are hereby authorized to appoint a Weigher of Coal in and for the City and County of San Francisco, who shall reside in said place, and continue in office for the term of two years from the date of his appointment, and until his successor is appointed and qualified.

SEC. 2. Said Weigher, before entering upon the duties of his office, shall take and subscribe the oath of office, and give bonds, in the sum of ten thousand dollars, for the faithful discharge of his duties, which oath shall be administered by the County Judge, and said bond acknowledged before him and approved, or before some other competent officer, the oath and bond to be filed in the office of the Auditor of said City and County.

SEC. 3. When requested to do so by any person interested in knowing the weight of any coal, it shall be the duty of said Weigher to weigh all coal brought to his scales to be weighed; and, unless some other price be agreed upon by said Weigher and the person or persons making such request, he may charge and collect ten cents per ton for such service.

SEC. 4. Said Weigher shall have and maintain, at suitable places, such number of scales as he may deem necessary; but this Act shall not be so construed as to enable said Weigher to create any liability against said City and County.

SEC. 5. This Act shall take effect from and after its passage.

SUPPLEMENT XVI.

1863-4, 30.

An Act to prescribe the Jurisdiction of the Police Judge's Court of the City and County of San Francisco.[70]

[Approved January 27, 1864.]

The People of the State of California, represented in Senate and Assembly, do enact as follows:

SECTION 1. The Police Judge's Court of the City and County of San Francisco shall have jurisdiction:*

First. Of an action or proceeding for the violation of any ordinance of the City and County of San Francisco.

Second. Of proceedings respecting vagrants and disorderly persons.

SEC. 2. The said court shall have jurisdiction cf the following public offenses, committed in the said City and County:

First. Petit larceny; receiving stolen property, when the amount involved does not exceed fifty dollars.

Second. Assault and battery, not charged to have been committed upon a public officer in the discharge of his duties, or with intent to kill.

Third. Breaches of the peace, riots, affrays, committing willful injury to property, and all misdemeanors punishable by fine not exceeding one thousand dollars, or by imprisonment not exceeding one year, or by both such fine and imprisonment.

Fourth. Said Court or Judge shall have jurisdiction of proceedings for security to keep the peace; and also, throughout said City and County, the same powers and jurisdiction in other criminal actions, cases, and proceedings as are now or hereafter may be conferred by law upon Justices of the Peace or Justices' Courts.

The Justices of the Peace within the limits of the City and County of San Francisco shall not have power to try and decide any cases of the classes mentioned in this section, [*Amended, Feb.* 13, 1872; 1871-2, 84.[71]]

SEC. 3. The Judge of said Court shall also have power to hear cases for examination, and may commit and hold the offender to bail for trial in the

---

[70] By Sec. 2541, Political Code, as amended Feb. 28, 1886, the Police Judge's Court is given jurisdiction of misdemeanors arising under the Article concerning State Harbor Commissioners.

[71] Sec. 2 of the Act of Feb. 13, 1872; 1871-2, 84; provides that: "The said Judge may punish contempts in the same manner and to the same extent as District Judges; and the laws concerning contempts applicable to District Courts and Judges, shall be applicable to said Police Court and Judge."

proper court, and may try, condemn, or acquit, and carry his judgment into execution, as the case may require according to law, and shall have power to issue warrants of arrest, subpœnas, and all other process necessary to the full and proper exercise of his power and jurisdiction. All fines imposed by the Police Judge not exceeding twenty dollars, exclusive of costs, shall be final and without appeal.*

SEC. 4. This Act shall take effect and be in force from and after its passage

SUPPLEMENT XVII.

1863-4, 195.

An Act to re-district the City and County of San Francisco.

[Approved March 21, 1864.]

*The People of the State of California, represented in Senate and Assembly
do enact as follows:*

SECTION 1. The lines and boundaries of the different election districts[72] in the City and County of San Francisco are hereby fixed and defined as follows:

The First District shall be bounded by Washington street on the south, Kearny street on the west, and the bay of San Francisco on the north and east.

The Second District shall be bounded by Kearny street on the east, Vallejo street on the south, Larkin street on the west, and the Bay of San Francisco on the north.

The Third District shall be bounded by Washington street on the north, Kearny street on the west, California street on the south, and Market street and the Bay of San Francisco on the east.

---

*See also Pol. Code, secs. 4424 to 4432, inclusive.
Extended to Police Court No. 2 by Act of March 7, 1881.
[72] Changed to Wards by Act of April 2, 1866; 1865-6, 718; Supplement XXIX.

The Fourth District shall be bounded by Vallejo street on the north, Kearny street on the east, Washington street on the south, and Larkin street on the west.

The Fifth District shall be bounded by California street on the north, Kearny street on the west, and Market street on the south and east.

The Sixth District shall be bounded by Kearny street on the east, Pine street on the south, Larkin street on the west, and Washington street on the north.

The Seventh District shall be bounded by Harrison street on the south, Second street on the west, Market street on the north, and the Bay of San Francisco on the east.

The Eighth District shall be bounded by Kearny street on the east, Market street on the south, Larkin street on the west, and Pine street on the north.

The Ninth District shall be bounded by Harrison street on the north, Seventh street on the west, and the Bay of San Francisco on the south and east.

The Tenth District shall be bounded by Market street on the north, Seventh street on the west, Harrison street on the south, and Second street on the east.

The Eleventh District shall be bounded by Seventh [street] on the east, by Market street and Ridley street in a direct line to the Pacific ocean on the north, by the Pacific Ocean on the west, and by the line of San Mateo County and the Bay of San Francisco to the line of Seventh street, on the south and east.

The Twelfth District shall be bounded by Larkin street on the east, by Market street and Ridley street in a direct line to the Pacific Ocean on the south, and by the Pacific Ocean and the Bay of San Francisco on the west and north.

SEC. 2. All the Islands in the Bay of San Francisco or in the Pacific Ocean, within the limits of said City and County, shall for all election purposes, be included in the First District.

SECS. 3 *and* 4. [*Obsolete.*]

SEC. 5. All Acts and parts of Acts in conflict with the provisions of this Act are hereby repealed.

SEC. 6. This Act shall take effect and be in force from and after its passage.

---

*See also sec. 1466, Penal Code.

SUPPLEMENT XVIII.

1863-4, 446.

An Act to establish Police Regulations for the Harbor of the City and County of San Francisco, and to authorize and empower the Board of Supervisors to regulate the same.

[Approved April 4, 1864.]

The People of the State of California, represented in Senate and Assembly, do enact as follows:

SECTION 1. No person shall board or attempt to board any vessel arriving in the harbor of the City and County of San Francisco, before said vessel has been made fast to the wharf, without obtaining leave from the Master or person having charge of said vessel, or permission, in writing, from the owner or owners, or the agent thereof, or having boarded said vessel, shall shall refuse or neglect to leave the same upon request of the Master or other person in charge thereof, under the penalty prescribed in the next succeeding section of this Act.[73]

SEC. 2. Any person violating section one of this Act shall be deemed guilty of a misdemeanor, and upon conviction thereof before the Police Judge's Court of said City and County, shall be punished for each offence by a fine not exceeding one hundred dollars, or imprisonment in the County Jail of the City and County of San Francisco for a term not exceeding fifty days, or both, in the discretion of the Judge of said Police Judge's Court, which Court shall have jurisdiction in such cases.

SEC. 3. The provisions of the last two foregoing sections shall not apply to any Pilot or public officer visiting a vessel in discharge of his duty.

SEC. 4. No person shall entice or persuade nor attempt to entice or persuade any member of the crew of any vessel arriving in said harbor, or any vessel in said harbor, to leave or desert said vessel before the expiration of his term of service in such vessel. Any person guilty of so doing shall be

---

[73] By Sec. 2159 of the Political Code, every pilot in charge of a vessel arriving in the port or harbor of San Francisco * * must prevent all persons (except officers of the State or Federal Governments, owners or consignees of the vessel or cargo, and persons admitted on the express order of the Master) from boarding such vessel until she has been safely moored. To enforce the provisions of this section, and other police regulations for the harbor, every pilot in charge of a vessel entering the harbor of San Francisco is authorized and empowered to arrest every one who, in opposition to the Master's orders, persists in boarding such vessel, or who, having boarded her, refuses to leave on the command of such Master, or pilot; when so arrested, he must be immediately brought before the Police Judge's Court, or admitted to bail, as provided in the Penal Code.

deemed guilty of a misdemeanor, and upon conviction thereof shall be subject to the penalty prescribed in section two of this Act.

SEC. 5. No person shall knowingly and willfully persuade or aid any
person who shall have shipped on any vessel for a voyage from said port,
and received any advance wages therefor, to desert or willfully neglect to
proceed on such voyage. Any person guilty of so doing shall be deemed
guilty of a misdemeanor, and upon conviction thereof before the Police
Judge's Court of said City and County shall be punished for each offence by
a fine not exceeding one hundred dollars, or imprisonment in the County
Jail of the City and County of San Francisco for a term not exceeding fifty
days, or both, in the discretion of the Judge of said Police Judge's Court,
which Court shall have jurisdiction in such cases.

SEC. 6. Any person offending against any provision of this Act may be
arrested, with or without warrant, as provided in other cases of misdemeanor,
by any officer qualified to serve criminal process in the said City and County
of San Francisco; *provided*, the person so arrested shall be forthwith brought
before said Police Judge's Court or admitted to bail, as in other cases of
misdemeanor committed in said City and County of San Francisco.

SEC. 7. The word "Harbor," as used in this Act, shall be held to mean
and include all the waters of the Bay of San Francisco within the limits of
the said City and County of San Francisco; and the word "vessel" as used
in this Act, shall be held to mean and include all vessels propelled by steam
or sails plying or bound on a voyage between the said port of San Francisco
and any other port in this State, or other State of the United States, or in
any foreign country.

SEC. 8. The Board of Supervisors of said City and County of San Francisco shall cause this Act to be printed in cheap pamphlet form, and it shall
be the duty of each and every Branch Pilot of the Port of San Francisco to
obtain from the Clerk of the Board of Supervisors of said City and County
a reasonable supply of said pamphlets, and to deliver one copy of the same
to the Master or person in charge of each and every vessel boarded by him
as a Pilot, whether the said Pilot is employed to bring such vessel into said
port or not.

SEC. 9. Any Branch Pilot refusing or neglecting to perform the requirements set forth in the last preceding section shall be deemed guilty of a misdemeanor, and shall, upon conviction thereof before the Police Judge's Court
of said City and County be fined in the sum of ten dollars, or be imprisoned
in the County Jail for the term of twenty-five days, or both, in the discretion of the Judge of said Police Judge's Court, which said Court is hereby
given jurisdiction in such cases.

SUPPLEMENT XIX.

1863–4, 474.

An Act to authorize the Sheriff of San Francisco County to appoint a Matron for the County Jail, and other matters relating thereto.

[Approved April 4, 1864.]

The People of the State of California, represented in Senate and Assembly do enact as follows :

SECTION 1. The Sheriff of the County of San Francisco is hereby authorized and empowered to appoint a Matron and Assistant Matron for the County Jail of said County, who shall have charge of the Female Department of said Jail, under such regulations as said Sheriff may deem requisite, not inconsistent with the laws of this State regulating the management of said Jail. Said Matron and Assistant Matron so appointed, before entering upon their duties, shall give the same bonds and be subject to the same penalties as are required of Deputy Sheriffs or Jail Keepers, conditioned for the faithful performance of their duties as required by law.

SEC. 2. The Board of Supervisors of the City and County of San Francisco, if they deem such Matrons necessary for the public good, shall order paid out of the General Fund of the City and County of San Francisco, as compensation for the services of said Matron and Assistant Matron, a sum not exceeding one hundred dollars per month, to be divided between such Matron and Assistant as said Board of Supervisors may direct, which shall be in full for such services.

SEC. 3. This Act shall take effect and be in force from and after its passage.

SUPPLEMENT XX.

1863-4, 502.

An Act to confer additional powers upon the Board of Supervisors of the City and County of San Francisco, and upon the Auditor and Treasurer thereof, and to authorize the appropriations of Money by said Board.

[Approved April 4, 1864.]

The People of the State of California, represented in Senate and Assembly, do enact as follows:

SECTION 1. The Board of Supervisors of the City and County of San Francisco are hereby authorized and empowered to appropriate, allow, and order paid the sums of money, and to exercise the powers, following:[74]

First to Fourth.   *   *   *   *   *   *   *   *

Fifth. To allow and order paid from the General Fund a sum not to exceed five hundred dollars per annum, for deficiency in salary of the Poundkeeper in said City and County.

Sixth and Seventh.   *   *   *   *   *   *   *

Eighth. To allow and order paid out of the General Fund, to the Clerk of the Mayor of said City and County, the sum of one hundred and fifty dollars per month, in lieu of the present salary allowed by law to said Clerk.*

Ninth[75] and Tenth.   *   *   *   *   *   *

Eleventh. To increase the Police force of said City and County, as from time to time may be deemed necessary by the said Board of Supervisors, to not exceed one hundred members, [76] including the number now allowed by law, a portion of which increase may constitute a Harbor Police in and for the said City and County, and to allow and order paid out of the General Fund the salaries of said additional Police force, not to exceed the sum of one hundred and twenty-five dollars per month, or any less sum which they may deem proper for each member of said additional Police force.

Twelfth. To authorise and empower the Police Commissioners of said City and County to appoint and to regulate local Policemen, whenever in their judgment the necessities of said City and County require it; *provided,* that no money shall be paid out of the treasury of the said City and County to said local Policemen. [Appointment of Special Police modified by Act of April 1, 1878.]

---

[74] The subdivisions omitted relate to matters of private concern, or the subject matter has been executed.

[75] Relates to City and County Hospital buildings. Obsolete.

[76] May be increased to four hundred members. Act of April 1, 1878.

* Increased to $250 by Act of Apr. 1, 1878; 1877-8, 1023.

Thirteenth. To appoint an additional Assistant Porter for the City Hall of said City and County, after the same shall be enlarged, and to allow and order paid out of the General Fund a salary to him not exceeding the sum of seventy-five dollars per month.

Fourteenth. To allow and order paid out of the General Fund, to the Porter of the City Hall of said City and County, a sum not to exceed ninety dollars per month, in lieu of the salary now allowed to him by law.

Fifteenth. To allow and order paid out of the General Fund in lieu of their present salary, the sum of one hundred and fifty dollars per month to three Deputies of the Sheriff of said City and County, which Deputies now receive one hundred and twenty-five dollars per month.

Sixteenth and Seventeenth. ⁕   ⁕   ⁕   ⁕   ⁎   ⁕   ⁒

Eighteenth. [*Provides for a Fire and Alarm Telegraph. Executed.*]

Nineteenth. To appoint, when deemed necessary by said Board during the erection or upon the completion of said system of fire alarm and police telegraphs, one Superintendent for said telegraphs, and three Assistants therefor, in lieu of the Bell Ringers now employed for the watch tower of the City Hall of said City and County; and to allow and order paid out of the General Fund, when by said Board deemed necessary, one hundred and fifty dollars per month, as salary to said Superintendent,   and to allow and order paid in the same manner and out of the same fund[77] as now provided for by law for payment of the aforesaid Bell Ringers, a sum not to exceed one hundred dollars per month each to said Assistants as salary.[78]   ⁕   ⁎

Twentieth to Twenty-fourth, inclusive.   ⁕   ⁕   ⁕   ⁕   ⁕

Twenty-fifth.   ⁕   ⁕   ⁕   ⁕   ⁕   ⁕   ⁕   ⁒

Twenty-sixth. To allow and order paid out of the General Fund a sum not to exceed three hundred dollars per annum, for medical attendance upon the inmates of the Industrial School in said City and County.

Twenty-seventh.   ⁕   ⁕   ⁕   ⁕   ⁕   ⁕   ⁕   ⁕

Twenty-eighth. To allow and order paid to the Interpreter of the German language for the Police and County Courts, to be appointed by the County Judge,† Police Judge, and President of the Board of Supervisors, one hundred and twenty-five dollars per month, to be paid from the General Fund.

SEC. 2. The Auditor of said City and County is hereby directed and empowered to audit and allow as aforesaid, and the Treasurer thereof to pay as aforesaid, all sums of money that may be allowed or ordered to be paid under the provisions hereof.

SEC. 3. The amounts which by this Act are authorized to be paid, shall be the only amounts to be paid for the respective purposes for which they are authorized to be paid under the provisions hereof, except when otherwise

---

⁷⁷ General Fund. See Act of May 17, 1861, 534, sec. 2; Supplement VII.

⁷⁸ Three "operators" allowed, at salary of $125 per month each, by sub. 2, sec. 1, Act March 14, 1868; 1867 8, 160; Supplement XXX.

⁕ Salary of Superintendent now fixed by Supervisors. Act of March 26, 1875; 1877 8, 557.

† The duties now devolve on a Judge of the Superior Court.

expressly provided in this Act, and excepting an allowance of two thousand dollars per annum heretofore provided by law for inclosing, improving and regulating all public grounds in said City and County. And said Board of' Supervisors is hereby authorized and empowered to direct and have executed the work, building, services and improvements hereinbefore mentioned and provided to be paid for.

Sec. 4. All Acts and parts of Acts inconsistent herewith are hereby repealed.

Sec. 5. This Act shall take effect and be in force from and after its passage.

SUPPLEMENT XXI.

1865-6, 1.

An Act respecting the Police Court of the City and County of San Francisco.

[Approved December 9, 1865.]

The People of the State of California, represented in Senate and Assembly, do enact as follows:

Section 1. Any Justice of the Peace of the City and County of San Francisco, who may be designated in writing by the Mayor or President of the Board of Supervisors for the purpose, shall have power to preside in and hold the Police Judge's Court of said City and County, in case of the temporary absence of the Police Judge, or his inability to act from any cause; and during such temporary absence or disability, the Justice so designated shall act as Police Judge, and shall have and exercise all the powers, jurisdiction, and authority which are or may be by law conferred upon said Court or Judge.

Sec. 2. In case of a vacancy in the office of Police Judge, the Board of Supervisors of said City and County shall have power to appoint some suitable person, who is a resident and legal voter thereof, to fill the vacancy, who shall take the constitutional oath of office and enter upon his duties immediately. The person so appointed shall hold office until a Police Judge shall be elected at the next judicial election, and qualified according to law.

Sec. 3. All laws, so far as they conflict with the provisions of this Act, are hereby repealed.

Sec. 4. This Act shall take effect and be in force from and after its passage.

SUPPLEMENT XXII.

1865-6, 79.

An Act to provide for the Prevention of Conflagrations and the Protection of Property saved from Fire in the City and County of San Francisco.

[Approved February 14, 1866.]

The People of the State of California, represented in Senate and Assembly, do enact as follows:

SECTION 1. It shall be lawful for the association known as the Board of Fire Underwriters, in the City and County of San Francisco, to nominate, and, with the approval of the Board of Police Commissioners, to appoint, a public officer to be known as the Fire Marshal, who shall hold his office during the pleasure of the said Board of Fire Underwriters. Before entering upon the duties of his office, he shall take and subscribe the oath of office before the County Judge, and execute a bond to the State of California in the sum of five thousand dollars, conditional for the faithful discharge of his duties, with two sureties, to be approved by the County Judge; and his salary shall be fixed from time to time and paid by said Board of Underwriters. Any person aggrieved by any misconduct of said officer or of his deputy, hereinafter provided for, may bring an action in his own name on such official bond to recover any damages sustained by him. Said bond shall be deposited with the County Clerk of said City and County, subject to the order of the County Judge. And in case of the sickness, absence, or inability of the said Fire Marshal, the said Fire Marshal, with the consent of said Board of Underwriters and Police Commissioners, is hereby authorized and empowered to appoint any competent person to act for and in his stead during such sickness, absence, or inability; and such person so appointed shall have all the powers and authority conferred by this Act upon said Fire Marshal. [*Amended, March 24, 1868; 1867-8, 280.*]

SEC. 2. It shall be the duty of said officer to attend at all fires that may occur in said City and County, with a badge of office conspicuously displayed, upon which his official title shall be legibly printed; and he shall take charge of and protect all property of every kind and description, during such fires, which may be imperiled thereby, and safely keep the same in his possession or under his control, until satisfactory proof of ownership be made thereto, and shall, as far as practicable, prevent property from being injured at such fire, and regulate and direct, when in his opinion it is necessary or expedient, the removal of goods, merchandise, and other property, to a place of safety. He shall and is hereby authorized and empowered to exercise the functions of a peace officer of said City and County. Any person or persons who shall willfully hinder or obstruct said officer in the lawful discharge or performance of any of the duties of his office, shall be deemed guilty of a misdemeanor, and on conviction thereof shall be punished by imprisonment in the County Jail for not more than three months, or by a fine not exceeding five hundred dollars; *provided, however*, that nothing herein contained shall be so construed as to authorize said Fire Marshal to interfere in any manner with the proper discharge of the lawful duties and authority of the Chief and Assistant Engineers of the Fire Department of said City and County.

SEC. 3. It shall be the duty of the Fire Marshal to institute investigations into the causes of such fires as occur in said City and County, and for this purpose he shall have power to issue subpœnas and administer oaths, and compel the attendance of witnesses before him, by attachment or otherwise. All subpœnas issued by him shall be in such form as he may prescribe, and shall be directed to and served by any police officer or by any peace officer of said City and County. Any witness who refuses to attend or testify, in obedence to such subpœna, shall be deemed guilty of contempt, and be punishable by him as in cases of contempt in Justices' Courts in civil cases; *provided*, that said officer shall not have jurisdiction to try any person charged with commission of a crime for the purpose of inflicting punishment therefor, but shall make a written report of the testimony to the District Attorney or Assistant District Attorney, and institute criminal prosecutions in all cases in which there appears to him to be reasonable and probable cause for believing that a fire has been caused by design.

SEC. 4. It shall be the duty of said Fire Marshal to aid in the enforcement of the fire ordinances of said City and County, and for this purpose he is duly authorized to visit and examine all buildings in process of erection or undergoing repairs, and to institute prosecution for all violations of the ordinances of said City and County which relate to the erection, alterations, or repairs of buildings, and the prevention of fires. He shall exercise such additional powers as may be conferred upon him by the ordinances of said City and County, to enable him fully to carry out the object and purposes of this Act and the prevention of fires.

SEC. 5. Any person who saves from fire, or from a building endangered by fire, any property, and who willfully neglects for two days to give notice to the Fire Marshal, or to the owner of such property, of his possession thereof, shall be deemed guilty of grand or petit larceny, as the case may be, according to the value of said property; and any person who shall be guilty of false swearing in any investigation under this Act, shall be deemed guilty of perjury, and upon conviction thereof shall be punished therefor as in other cases of perjury.

SEC. 6. No person shall be entitled to any property in the hands of the Fire Marshal, saved from fire, until satisfactory proof of ownership be made, and until the actual expenses incurred by said officer for the preservation and keeping of the same shall be paid to him by the owner or claimant of said property; and in case of dispute as to the amount of such expenses, said dispute to be determined by the Police Judge of said City and County.

Sec. 7. It shall be lawful for said Board of Underwriters at any time to remove said Fire Marshal, and to fill any vacancy in said office caused by such removal, or by resignation, death, or absence from the city, in the same manner as provided in section first of this Act.

Sec. 8. The said Fire Marshal is hereby authorized and empowered to appoint one or more persons during the time of fire for the purpose of saving and protecting property at said fire, and until it shall be delivered to the owner or claimants thereof; and the said person or persons so appointed shall have, during such period, the authority and power of a policeman of said City and County, and shall be known as the Fire Marshal's Police; and each of such persons shall wear, when in the discharge of his duty, conspicuously displayed on his person, such badge or device as said Fire Marshal shall designate.

Sec. 9. The said Fire Marshal is hereby duly authorized and empowered to hold and sell, or cause to be sold at public auction, all property in his possession saved from a fire or fires, for which no owner can be found, after advertising the same in two daily newspapers published in said City and County for the period of thirty days; provided, however, that [if] upon application by said Marshal to the County Judge, it shall appear that such property is perishable, said Judge may order said Marshal to make sale thereof upon such notice as in the opinion of said Judge may be reasonable. The proceeds of all such sales, together with an account thereof, after deducting all expenses, shall be by him deposited with the Treasurer of said City and County, to be held by said Treasurer subject to the claim of the owner of such property. Said Fire Marshal shall, from time to time, file with the County Clerk of said City and County, under oath, a statement and description of all property in his possession or under his control and sold by him, together with the amount of money by him deposited with the Treasurer of said City and County.

Sec. 10. The Act entitled an Act to provide for the prevention of conflagrations and the protection of property saved from fire in the City and County of San Francisco, approved April first, eighteen hundred and sixty-four, is hereby repealed; provided, that any officer appointed under that Act shall be continued in office under this Act until his successor in office be appointed.

Sec. 11. This Act shall take effect from and after its passage; and all laws and parts of laws in conflict herewith are hereby repealed, so far as they conflict herewith.

SUPPLEMENT XXIII.

1865–6, 82.

An Act to confer additional powers upon the Board of Supervisors of the City and County of San Francisco, and upon the Auditor and Treasurer thereof, and to authorize certain appropriations of money by said Board.

[Approved February 14, 1866.]

The People of the State of California, represented in Senate and Assembly, do enact as follows:

SECTION 1. The Board of Supervisors of the City and County of San Francisco are hereby authorized and empowered to appropriate, allow and order paid the sums of money and to exercise the powers following:

First. To authorize the Clerk of the Board of Supervisors to appoint a Deputy or Assistant Clerk, to be approved by said Board, whose salary shall be fixed by the said Board[79]   *   *   *   payable out of the General Fund; said Deputy, when required by the Board, to act as Sergeant-at-Arms at its meetings, without additional compensation therefor.[80]

Second. [*Repealed by Act of April* 1, 1872; 1871–2, 901; *Supplement LXVI, post.*]

Third. To   *   *   *   appoint a competent person to repair and keep in order said fire alarm and police telegraph, at a salary not to exceed one hundred dollars per month, payable out of the General Fund.[81]

Fourth.   *   *   *   *   *   *   +   *   *

Fifth. [*Repealed. Sec. 3007 Political Code, Supplement XCI.*]

Sixth. [*Authorizes payment of various sums heretofore allowed in excess of statutory allowances.*]

Seventh.   *   *   *   *   *   +   *   *   *

Eighth. All acts and parts of acts inconsistent herewith are hereby repealed.

---

[79] Board of Supervisors authorized to pay one hundred and fifty dollars per month; sub. 12, sec. 1, Act of March 30, 1872; Supplement LX, post.

[80] Board of Supervisors authorized to appoint Sergeant-at-Arms at salary of $100 per month; sub-7, sec. 1, Act of March 30, 1872; Supplement LX, post.

[81] Superintendent of telegraph to appoint a repairer. Act of March 11, 1868; 1367–8, 160; Supplement XXX.

SUPPLEMENT XXIV.

1865-6, 138.

An Act to establish a Paid Fire Department for the City and County of San Francisco.

[Approved March 2, 1866.]

The People of the State of California, represented in Senate and Assembly, do enact as follows :

SECTION 1. [*Superseded by Act March* 28, 1878; 1878, 685.]

SEC. 2. [*Obsolete.*]

SECS. 3, 4 and 5. [*Obsolete, or superseded by Act of March* 30, 1874; *Supplement LXX, post.*]

SEC. 6. [*Superseded by Sec.* 2 *of Act of March* 28, 1878.]

SEC. 7. [*Portion superseded by sec.* 7, *Act of March* 30, 1874; *Supplement LXX, post; remainder, obsolete.*]

SEC. 8. The Board of Supervisors of said City and County are hereby authorized to appropriate, allow, and order paid, annually, out of the General Fund of said City and County, the salaries hereinbefore specified and allowed, and salaries at similar rates to the several officers and men of any additional companies created as aforesaid; also, the sum of forty thousand dollars per annum for running expenses, horse feed, repairs to apparatus, and other expenses of the said Department; also, a sum not exceeding twenty-five thousand dollars annually, for the purchase of horses and apparatus; also, a sum not exceeding twenty-five thousand dollars annually, in lieu of the amount now allowed by law, for the construction and erection of hydrants and cisterns; and the Board of Supervisors shall have power to advertise for proposals, and make contracts for the construction of said cisterns and the erection of said hydrants, and they are hereby empowered to locate the same. [*Amended, April* 1, 1872; 1871-2, 855. *Amended by Act of March* 26, 1878; 1877-8, 556.

SEC. 9. [*Re-enacted, sec.* 12, *Act of March* 30, 1874; *Supplement LXX, post.*]

SEC. 10. The only engines which shall be purchased by the City and used by the Fire Department shall be steam fire-engines, of the best pattern and manufacture. [*Remainder of sec. re-enacted by sec.* 1. *Act of March* 30, 1874; *Supplement LXX, post, which see.*]

6

SEC. 11.   Any person who may have been an active fireman in the Fire Department of said City and County for three years and six months immediately preceding the time when this Act shall take effect, shall be entitled to enjoy all the privileges and immunities now enjoyed by exempt firemen in said City and County under the existing laws of this State.   Any such person shall, upon application and proper proof of such service, receive a certificate to that effect, from the person or persons now issuing such certificates, and in the same form as exempt firemen in said City and County are now entitled to receive such certificate.

SEC. 12.   [*Obsolete.*]

SEC. 13.   [*Repealed, Act April* 2, 1866; 1865-6, 866, *sec.* 4.]

SUPPLEMENT XXV.

1865-6, 214.

An Act to establish and maintain an Almshouse and Hospital in the City and County of San Francisco.

[Approved March 10, 1866.]

The People of the State of California, represented in Senate and Assembly, do enact as follows :

SECTION 1.   The Board of Supervisors of the City and County of San Francisco are hereby authorized and empowered to establish and maintain an Almshouse and Hospital, and for that purpose to set apart and appropriate land belonging to said City and County, or to purchase land, not exceeding eighty acres, as said Board may deem necessary in said City and County, and erect thereon one or more buildings, suitable for almshouse and hospital purposes, and they may from time to time add to and enlarge such buildings as necessity may require.

SEC. 2.   For the purpose of procuring or purchasing and improving land and erecting buildings thereon, as provided in the preceding section, said Supervisors are hereby authorized to appropriate and order paid so much as may be necessary of the appropriation now authorized by law to be expended for purchasing land, or erecting or enlarging buildings for hospital purposes, or for both; also, to expend, in addition thereto, a sum not to exceed twenty thousand dollars for furnishing the same.

SEC. 3.   Said Board of Supervisors may by ordinance make such rules and regulations, not inconsistent with the provisions of this Act, for the government and management of said almshouse, and for the admission, discharge and employment of the inmates thereof, as to them shall seem proper. [*Amended, March* 28, 1867; 1867-8, 427.' *Amended by Act of Mar.* 26, 1878. 1877-8, 556.]

Sec. 4. Said Board shall also have power to appoint for duty at the Almshouse a Superintendent, Matron, Resident Physician, and such assistants and employees as they may from time to time deem necessary;[83] *provided*, they shall not at any time pay more than the following sums as salary to the various employees:

To the Superintendent, one hundred and fifty dollars per month.

To the Matron, fifty dollars per month.

To the Resident Physician, one hundred and twenty-five dollars per month.

To the Cook, sixty dollars per month.

To the Chief Farmer, fifty dollars per month.

To the Principal Teamster, fifty dollars per month.

And to each and every other employee, not to exceed thirty dollars per month each, except nurses, when necessary, may be employed at a salary not to exceed fifty dollars per month. [*Amended, March* 28, 1868; 1867-8, 427.]

Sec. 5. [*Expenditures for persons in Almshouse and Hospital.*[84]]

Sec. 6. Contracts for the support of the inmates of said Almshouse and Hospital shall be given out in the manner now prescribed by law for the support of the inmates of the City and County Hospital.

Sec. 7. The Mayor of said City and County, the Resident Physician of said Almshouse and Hospital, and the Chairman of the Hospital Committee, respectively, and they alone, shall have power to admit inmates to said Almshouse and Hospital, under such restrictions as are provided in section three of this Act.

Sec. 8. The Mayor, when authorized by the Board of Supervisors, shall have power to sell the buildings and land now occupied for hospital purposes, and to that end is hereby authorized to execute, sign, seal and deliver good and sufficient deed or deeds therefor, to such person or persons and for such sum or sums as said Board may prescribe; and he shall pay the proceeds of such sale or sales into the City and County Treasury to the credit of the General Fund.[85]

---

[83] Appointing power vested in Board of Health by sec. 3000, Political Code, as amended March 23, 1874; Supplement XCI, post. As to salaries, see sec. 3010, same Supplement. See also Act of March 30, 1874, Supplement XCII.

[84] By sub. 13, sec. 1, Act of March 30, 1872; Supplement LX, post; this expenditure is increased t.$12,000. Further increased to $15,000 monthly,by Act of March 16, 1878; 1878, 289.

[85] See in connection with this section sub. 13, sec. 1, Act of March 30, 1872; Supplement LX.
*Power to provide for placing money in Treasury for articles manufactured at, or sold from, institution; Act of March 26, 1878, sec. 1, sub. 10.

SEC. 9. The Auditor of 'said City and County is hereby directed to audit and the Treasurer thereof to pay out of the General Fund such sums as the Supervisors may allow and order paid under the provisions of this Act.

SEC. 10.   This Act shall take effect immediately.

SUPPLEMENT XXVI.

1865-6, 423.

An Act to organize and regulate the Justices' Court in the City and County of San Francisco.*

[Approved March 20, 1866.]

The People of the State of California, represented in Senate and Assembly, do enact as follows :

SECTION 1. There shall be, in and for the City and County of San Francisco, one Justices' Court, which shall have the powers and jurisdiction now prescribed and conferred by law upon Justices of the Peace and Justices' Courts in said City and County. All actions, suits and proceedings whereof Justices of the Peace and Justices' Courts in said City and County have jurisdiction shall be commenced, entitled, and prosecuted in said Court. The said Court shall be always open, non-judicial days excepted, and causes therein may be tried before the presiding Justice, before any one of the Justices before whom the original process may be made returnable or to whom the cause may be assigned or transferred for trial, or before any three Justices of the Peace constituting the Court in bank as hereinafter provided; but the Court in bank shall have exclusive power to hear and determine all applications for new trials. In case of sickness or other disability or necessary absence of a Justice of the Peace (on the return of a summons or at the time appointed for trial) to whom a cause has been assigned, the presiding Justice shall re-assign the cause to some other Justice, who shall proceed with the trial and disposition of said cause in the same manner as if originally assigned to him. For the organization of said Court, Justices of the Peace and a Justices' Clerk shall be respectively elected and appointed, and the Sheriff of the City and County of San Francisco ex-officio shall be an officer of said Court as hereinafter provided. [*Amended, March* 30, 187L; 1871-2, 758.]

---

*This Act must be read in connection with Code of Civil Procedure, secs. 85 to 98, inclusive; and Code of Civil Procedure, secs. 110 to 115, inclusive.

SEC. 2. There shall be, for the City and County of San Francisco, five Justices of the Peace, to be elected by the City and County at large, at the time, in the manner, and for the term as now prescribed by law for the election of such Justices.*

SEC. 3. The Board of Supervisors shall biennially appoint one of the Justices of the Peace to be presiding Justice, who, as such, shall hold office for two years and until his successor shall in the same manner be appointed, and any one of the other Justices may attend, preside, and act as presiding Justice during the temporary absence or disability of the Justice so appointed. The Board of Supervisors shall also appoint a Justices' Clerk, on the written nomination and recommendation of said Justices, or a majority of them, who shall hold office for two years, and until his successor is appointed and qualified. The Clerk shall take the constitutional oath of office, and give bond with at least two sufficient sureties, to be approved in the same manner as the official bond of other officers of the City and County of San Francisco, in the sum of ten thousand dollars, payable to the City and County of San Francisco, conditioned for the faithful discharge of the duties of his office, and well and truly to account for and pay into the Treasury of said City and County, as required by law, all moneys by him collected or received and by law designated for that use. A new or additional bond may be required by the Mayor, Auditor, and County Judge,† or any two of them, whenever they may deem it necessary, and on failure to furnish such new and additional bond within three days after it shall be required, the office shall become vacant. The Justices' Clerk shall have authority to administer oaths and take and certify affidavits in any action, suit, or proceeding in said Justices' Court, and to appoint a Deputy Clerk, for whose acts he shall be reponsible on his official bond, the said Deputy Clerk to hold office during the pleasure of said Clerk. [Amended, March 30, 1872; 1871-2, 758.]

SEC. 4. [Appointment of Constables. Office of Constable abolished, sec. 12. Act of February 10, 1870; 1869-70, 56]

SEC. 5. § The Board of Supervisors shall provide in some convenient locality in said City and County, a suitable building, with rooms for the Clerk's office, Court room, and separate rooms for offices or chambers for each of the Justices of the Peace (the presiding Justice excepted), for the transaction of their official business, and shall also provide suitable furniture therefor; or if said Board should deem it necessary and expedient, offices or chambers for the Justices may be provided and assigned for them in different buildings and places. At the Clerk's office, the presiding Justice and Justices' Clerk shall be in attendance daily, non-judicial days excepted, from the hour of

---

*See sec. 4100, Pol. Code.
†Now a Judge of the Superior Court.
§See sec. 83 of the Code of Civil Procedure.

nine A. M. until five P. M., and at such other convenient hours as may be required by urgent official business; and the other Justices aforesaid shall be in attendance at their respective offices or chambers, for the dispatch of official business, daily, from the hour of nine A. M., until five P. M. Unless otherwise ordered by the Board of Supervisors, leave of temporary absence may be granted by the Mayor to the Clerk or any of the Justices, when such absence will not materially prejudice or delay official business; but absence for more than two hours in a day, or for more than four days in one month, shall be charged with a proportionate deduction of salary.[66]

SEC. 6. All legal process of every kind which the Justices of the Peace of said City and County, or any of them, are or may be authorized to issue, for the issuance or service of which any fee is or may be allowed by law, shall be issued by the said Clerk upon the order of the presiding Justice, or upon the order of one of the said Justices of the Peace, except as hereinafter provided; and the fees for issuance and service of all such process, and all other fees which now are allowed by law for any official services of Justices, Sheriff or Justices' Clerk, shall be exacted or paid in advance into the hands of said Clerk, and by him, daily or weekly, as the Board of Supervisors may require, and before his salary shall be allowed, accounted for in detail, under oath, and paid into the treasury of the City and County, as part of the Special Fee Fund; *provided*, that such payment in advance shall not be exacted from parties who, upon proving to the satisfaction of the presiding Justice, by their own affidavit or other evidence, setting forth the facts and circumstances of their demand, that they have a good cause of action, and that they are not of sufficient pecuniary ability to pay the legal fees in advance, shall be admitted by such Justice to sue either *in forma pauperis*, or without such prepayment. [*Amended February* 10, 1870; 1869-70, 56.]

SEC. 7. After this Act shall take effect, it shall not be lawful for any Justice of the Peace, or the Sheriff of the City and County of San Francisco, to collect or receive any fee or compensation whatever (other than the salary in this Act allowed out of the treasury) for any official services performed in the service or execution of process issued out of the Justices' Court of the City and County of San Francisco; but all fees or moneys legally chargeable for such services shall be paid into the hands of the Justices' Clerk, as aforesaid; and no judgment shall be rendered in the said Justices' Court, or in any action before said Justices, or any of them, until the fees allowed therefor, and all fees for previous services, which are destined to be paid into the treasury, shall have been paid as in this Act provided, except in case of poor

---

[66] By Act of March 30, 1868; 1867 8, 679; it is provided that: "The Justices of the Peace of the City and County of San Francisco are authorized and empowered to appoint a Janitor for their court-rooms, at a salary not exceeding seventy-five dollars per month, and his salary shall be allowed by the Auditor of the City and County of San Francisco, and be paid in the same manner that the Justices are paid, out of the Special Fee Fund."

persons, as provided for in the preceding section. [*Amended February* 10, 1870; 1869-70, 56.]

SEC. 8. All actions and proceedings commenced after this Act takes effect, in the City and County of San Francisco, whereof the Justices of the Peace have jurisdiction, shall be entitled "In Justices' Court of the City and County of San Francisco," and shall be commenced in said Court as hereinbefore provided, and the original process shall be returnable, and the parties required to appear before the presiding Justice at the aforesaid Justices' Court room, or before one of the other Justices of the Peace, by the presiding Justice to be designated; but all complaints, answers, and other pleadings and papers required to be filed, shall be filed, and a record of all such actions and proceeding shall be made and kept in the Clerk's office aforesaid; and the presiding Justice, and each of the other Justices, shall have power to hear, try and determine any action so commenced, and which shall be made returnable before him, and to make any necessary and proper orders therein. The presiding Justice shall also have power, in his discretion, on hearing the wishes and objections of the parties, to assign any cause returnable before him after issue joined therein, and in the cases provided for in the next section to transfer the cause returnable before any other Justice, for trial before some other Justice of the Peace, or before three Justices, who shall in such case sit together in the Justices' Court room, and constitute the Court in bank; and the presiding Justice may in like manner assign any contested motion, application, or issue in law arising in any cause returnable before him, for hearing before any other Justice, or before the Court in bank as aforesaid; and the said Court, Justice or Justices to whom any cause, motion, application, or issue shall be so as aforesaid assigned or transferred, shall have full power, jurisdiction, and authority to hear, try, and determine the same accordingly.

SEC. 9. If at the time of setting or assigning for trial any cause or matter returnable or pending before the presiding Justice, either party shall object to any one of the Justices on the ground that he is a material witness for such party, or that he cannot have a fair trial before such Justice, or on any other valid ground, the presiding Justice, in case such objection is substantiated in the maner prescribed by section five hundred and eighty-two of the Civil Practice Act, shall allow such objection, and not assign the case for trial or any matter or motion therein for hearing, before the Justice so objected to, but may assign the same to be tried or heard before some other Justice; and if at the time of joining issue in a cause returnable before any other Justice, objection shall be made to having the cause tried before such Justice, on the ground that such Justice is a material witness for either party, or on the ground of the interest, prejudice, or bias of such Justice, and such objection be substantiated in the manner aforesaid, then the Justice before whom the cause is pending shall suspend proceedings therein, and the presiding Justice, on motion and production before him of the same affidavits and proofs, shall order the transfer of the action for trial before some other Justice by him to be designated, which shall accordingly be done on the terms and in the manner prescribed in the aforesaid section of the Civil Practice Act.

Sec. 10.   Cases which by the provisions of section five hundred and eighty-one of the Civil Practice Act are required to be certified to the District Court, by reason of involving the question of title or possession of real property, or the legality of any tax, impost, assessment, toll, or municipal fine, shall be so certified by the presiding Justice and Justices' Clerk ; and for that purpose, if such question shall arise on the trial while the case is pending before one of the other Justices, such Justice shall certify the same, in the manner in said section of the Civil Practice Act provided, to the presiding Justice.   All transcripts of judgments to be filed in the County Clerk's office or County Recorder's office shall be given and certified from the Justices' register and be signed by the Clerk and Presiding Justice.

Sec. 11.   Applications for new trial shall be made to the presiding Justice ; and the affidavits, motion therefor, and other papers required to be filed, shall be filed with the Justices' Clerk.   The motion shall be heard and determined by the Court in bank.   Appeals from judgments rendered in said Justices' Court may be taken and perfected in the manner now prescribed by law. The notice of appeal, and all papers required to be filed to perfect it, shall be filed with the Justices' Clerk.   The statement on appeal shall be settled, when necessary, before the Justice who tried the cause, or before one of the Justices, if tried in bank.   The sureties on appeal, when required to justify, may justify before any one of the Justices.   The transcript and papers on appeal shall be made out, certified and returned to the County Court in the form prescribed by the Civil Practice Act, by the Justices' Clerk, verified also by the presiding Justice.

Sec. 12.   The presiding Justice, whenever in his judgment the prompt dispatch of business shall demand it, may require the aid of one of the Justices of the Peace in the discharge either of his own duties, or those of the Justices' Clerk (the collection of fees, accounting for and paying the same into the treasury excepted), and each of the Justices when so required shall for the purpose have the same power and authority as the presiding Justice or Clerk in whose aid he shall act ; and any one of the Justices, when required as aforesaid, may act as Justices' Clerk pro tempore during the temporary absence or disability of the said Clerk, with the same powers, duties and responsibilities.

Sec. 13.   In a suitable book, strongly bound, the Justices' Clerk shall keep a permanent record of all actions, proceedings and judgments commenced, had or rendered in said Justices' Court ; which book shall be a public record, and be known as the "Justices Register," for which purpose the said Clerk shall give personal attendance, and keep minutes of all proceedings had, either before the presiding Justice or the Justices in bank ; and such proceedings as may take place before the other Justices in cases returnable before them, or which may be assigned or transferred to them for trial or hearing, shall be entered in the dockets of such Justices ; and minutes of proceedings shall be kept by such Justices, and be certified and returned, together with all pleadings and papers in the cause, to the presiding Justice, who shall cause the same to be filed and the proper entries to be made in the cause in the Justices' Register.

SEC. 14. The Board of Supervisors, whenever they shall deem it necessary, may, by an order duly passed and entered in the records of said Board, establish one other Justices' Court, to be held at such place in the City and County as the public convenience may require, which shall not be within one mile and a half of the Justices' Court room in this Act provided for ; and the said Board shall, by a similar order, designate one of the Justices of the Peace to hold such additional Court. The Justice so designated, and in case of his temporary absence, any other Justice of the Peace, shall have power to hold the said Court, and for that purpose shall have power to issue process, make all necessary orders, and exercise all the power, authority, and jurisdiction now conferred by law upon Justices of the Peace, and shall be governed in his proceedings in all respects by the laws regulating proceedings in Justices' Courts, but shall not be entitled to receive to his own use any fees or compensation for official services other than his salary as fixed by this Act.

SEC. 15. All fees for issuance and service of process in such additional Court, and all other fees which now are or hereafter may be allowed by law for any official services of the Justice, or Sheriff or his deputy, in any cause or proceeding commenced or pending therein, shall be by said Justice exacted in advance (except in case of poor persons, provided for in section six), and be paid into his hands, and be by him, weekly or monthly, as the Board of Supervisors may require, and before his salary shall be allowed, accounted for with the City and County Auditor, in detail, under oath, and in such form as the Auditor shall prescribe, and be paid into the treasury of said City and County as part of the Special Fee Fund. [Amended February 10, 1870; 1869-70, 56.]

SEC. 16. The Justices' Court organized by this Act, and the additional Justices' Court which may be established by the Board of Supervisors under authority thereof, and the Justices of the Peace aforesaid, shall be governed in their proceedings by the provisions of the Civil Practice Act regulating proceedings in civil cases in Justices' Courts, and by the provisions of law relating to any special cases and proceedings whereof jurisdiction is or may be conferred upon such Justice and Justices' Courts, so far as such provisions are not repealed, altered, or modified by those of this Act, and the same are or can be made applicable in the several cases arising before them.

SEC. 17. All actions and proceedings pending and undetermined before any of the Justices of the Peace of the City and County of San Francisco at the time this Act takes effect shall be proceeded in, heard, and determined before the same Justices, and execution shall be issued thereon, and other proceedings therein, whether before or after judgment, whether on appeal or otherwise, shall be taken and had before said Justices in the same manner as if this Act had not been passed; but all suits and proceedings commenced after this Act takes effect shall be commenced, entitled, and prosecuted in the Justices' Court, or the additional Justices' Court, as in this Act provided.

SEC. 18. The County Court of the City and County of San Francisco shall have power to make rules, not inconsistent with the Constitution and laws, for the government of the Justices' Courts therein, and the government of the officers thereof; but such rules shall not be in force until thirty days after their publication, and no rule shall be made imposing any tax or charge on any legal proceeding, or giving an allowance to any Justice or officer for services. [*Superseded by sec. 95 of the Code of Civil Procedure.*]

SEC. 19. The Justices of the Peace and Justices' Clerk and Justices' Clerk's deputy shall receive for their official services the following salaries, and no other compensation, payable monthly out of the City and County Treasury, and out of the Special Fee Fund, after being first allowed and audited as other similar demands are by law required to be allowed and audited; to the Presiding Justice, three thousand dollars per annum;* to the Justices' Clerk and each of the Justices of the Peace (the Presiding Justice excepted), twenty-four hundred dollars each per annum; and to the Justices' Clerk's deputy, the sum of twelve hundred dollars per annum. [*Amended, March 30, 1872; 1871-2, 758.*]

SEC. 20. It shall not be lawful for any Justice of the Peace, the Justices' Clerk, or the Sheriff or any of his deputies, of the City and County of San Francisco to appear or advocate, or in any manner act as attorney, counsel or agent, for any party or person in any cause, or in relation to any demand, account or claim pending, or to be sued or prosecuted before said Justices or any of them, or which may be within their jurisdiction. A violation of the provisions of this section shall be deemed a misdemeanor in office. [*Amended, February 10, 1870; 1869-70, 56.*]

SEC. 21. No person other than an attorney at law, duly admitted and licensed to practice in courts of records, shall be permitted to appear as attorney or agent for any party in any cause or proceeding before said Justices, or any of them, unless he produces a sufficient power of attorney to that effect, duly executed and acknowledged before one of said Justices, or before some other officer authorized by law to take acknowledgment of deeds; which power of attorney, or a true copy thereof duly certified by one of the Justices aforesaid (who, on inspection of the original, shall attest to its genuineness), shall be filed among the papers in such cause or proceeding.

SEC. 22. [*Obsolete.*]

---

*Reduced by sec. 97 of the Code of Civil Procedure to $2,700.

SEC. 23. This Act shall take effect and be in force from and after the first day of January, A. D. eighteen hundred and sixty-eight; *provided*, that at the general election next preceding that date there shall be elected for the City and County of San Francisco five Justices of the Peace, as provided for in section two of this Act, to succeed the present Justices after the expiration of the term for which they were elected; and thereafter, also, the Justices of the Peace in and for said City and County shall be elected at the general election; and all laws, so far as they require Justices of the Peace in and for said City and County to be elected at the special judicial election, are hereby repealed.

[*Sections one to seven, inclusive, of "An Act amendatory of and supplementary to an Act entitled an Act to organize and regulate the Justices' Court in the City and County of San Francisco, approved March 26, 1866," approved February 10, 1870; 1869-70, 56, are incorporated in the next preceding Act as amendments thereto. The remaining sections of said Act are subjoined:*

SEC. 8. The Sheriff of the City and County of San Francisco shall be the officer of said Court, and, in addition to the deputies now allowed by law, may appoint three deputies, whose duty it shall be to assist said Sheriff in serving and executing all the processes, writs and orders of the said Justices' Court. Said deputies shall receive a salary of one hundred and twenty-five dollars per month each, payable monthly out of the City and County Treasury, and out of the Special Fee Fund, after having been first allowed and audited as other demands are by law required to be audited and allowed.

SEC. 9. It shall be the duty of the said Sheriff to serve and execute, or cause to be served and executed, each and every process, writ or order that may be issued by the Justices' Court in and for the City and County of San Francisco. One of said deputies shall remain in attendance during the session of said Court as the Court may direct.

SEC. 10. It shall be the duty of the Board of Supervisors of the City and County of San Francisco to provide and furnish a suitable office for said deputies, convenient to said Justices' Court, where one of said deputies shall remain during the sessions of said Justices' Court, and at such other times as said Court may order and direct, for the purpose of attending to such duties as may be imposed on said Sheriff or said deputies as herein provided. The said Sheriff shall be liable, on his official bond, for the faithful performance of all duties required of him or his said deputies, under the provisions of this Act.

SEC. 11. Subpœnas for witnesses may be issued by said Justices' Clerk without a Justice's order.

SEC. 12. The office of Constable, so far as the City and County of San Francisco is concerned, is hereby abolished.

SEC. 13.   All Acts and parts of Acts, so far as they are in conflict with this Act, are hereby repealed.

SEC. 14.   This Act shall take effect immediately.   •

SUPPLEMENT XXVII.

1865–6, 520.

An Act granting power to the Board of Supervisors of the City and County of San Francisco to order certain Street Work to be done as therein specified.

[Approved March 31, 1866.]

The People of the State of California, represented in Senate and Assembly, do enact as follows:

SECTION 1.   Whenever street work or grading of any street or part thereof may be deemed necessary by the Board of Supervisors of the City and County of San Francisco, on a portion of any street in front of any lot owned or possessed by the Government of the United States, said Board shall have power to order the whole or any portion of such street in front of any such lot to be graded, paved, planked, or repaired, any law to the contrary notwithstanding.[66]

SEC. 2.   This Act shall take effect from and after its passage.

------

[66] "An Act to provide for the Payment of Assessments against the Property of the Government of the United States for Street Improvements in the City and County of San Francisco," approved March 13, 1868; 1867 8, 148: provides:

Section 1.   The Board of Supervisors of the City and County of San Francisco are hereby authorized to allow, the Auditor of said City and County to audit, and the Treasurer to pay, out of the Street Department Fund, all claims not heretofore paid for assessments that have been made, or that may hereafter be made, pursuant to law, against the property of the Government of the United States for street improvements in the said City and County; provided, the Government of the United States shall by its officers refuse to make such payment.

Sec. 2.   This Act shall take effect and be in force from and after its passage.

SUPPLEMENT XXVIII.

1865-6, 624.

An Act concerning the office of Sheriff of the City and County of San Francisco.

[Approved March 31, 1866.]

The People of the State of California, represented in Senate and Assembly, do enact as follows:

Section 1. The Sheriff of the City and County of San Francisco may appoint a deputy to act as Bailiff for the Fifteenth District Court of said City and County. Said deputy shall receive a salary of one hundred and fifty dollars monthly, which salary is to be audited and paid in the same manner as the salaries of other deputies of said Sheriff.

Sec. 2. The appointment of Deputy Sheriff for the Fifteenth District Court of said City and County heretofore made by the Sheriff of said City and County under authority of an order of the Judge of said Court, and of an ordinance of the Board of Supervisors of said City and County, is hereby declared a valid and legal appointment; *provided,* that this ratification shall not be so construed as to allow the appointment of two Deputy Sheriffs for said Court.

Sec. 3. All Acts or parts of Acts in conflict with this Act are hereby repealed.

Sec. 4. This Act shall take effect and be in force from and after its passage.

SUPPLEMENT XXIX.

1865-6, 718.

An Act to change the time for holding Municipal Elections in the City and County of San Francisco, and to define the official terms of certain officers therein mentioned.

[Approved April 2, 1866.]

The People of the State of California, represented in Senate and Assembly, do enact as follows:

Section 1. There shall be elected hereafter for the City and County of San Francisco, by the qualified electors thereof, at the times hereinafter mentioned, and in the manner prescribed by law for the election of State and County Officers, one Mayor, who shall be *ex officio* President of the Board* of Supervisors ; **Police Judge, an Attorney and Counsellor,   *   *   * District Attorney, Sheriff, County Clerk, Recorder, Treasurer, Auditor, Tax Collector, Assessor, Coroner, Public Administrator, Surveyor, Superintend" ent of Common Schools, Superintendent of Public Streets, Highways and Squares,§   *   *   §9.   There shall be elected in each of the twelve pres_ ent election districts of said City and County, which shall hereafter constitute municipal districts and be designated and known in law as wards, by the qualified electors thereof, one Supervisor and one School Director.90

Sec. 2. [*Obsolete.*]

Sec. 3. All elections for City and County Officers, except as provided in section two of this Act, shall be held in said City and County on the days prescribed by law for holding the general elections throughout the State, except in the years when no general election is provided for by law, when elections for City and County Officers shall be held on the first Wednesday of September of said years.

Sec. 4. At the first election to be held under this Act on the first Wednesday of September, eighteen hundred and sixty-six, and at the election held every second year thereafter, there shall be elected an Attorney and Counsellor for said City and County, an Auditor, a Tax Collector, a Public Administrator, a Superintendent of Public Streets, Highways and Squares, a Chief of Police, a Superintendent of Common Schools,(a) and one Fire Commissioner,91 and for each of the First, Third, Fifth, Seventh, Ninth, and Eleventh Wards, one Supervisor and one School Director, who shall respectively hold their offices for the term of two years from and after the first Monday of December next subsequent to their election and until their successors are elected and qualified, and the present incumbents of the respective offices named in this Act shall hold their offices until their successors are elected and qualified. [*Amended March* 30, 1872 ; 1871–2, 729.] [Time of election changed by Section 4109 of Pol. Code.]

---

89 Office of Harbor Master extinct, sec. 3, Act of March 30, 1874; 1873–4, 910; Supplement LXIX. State Harbor Commissioners appointed by Governor, sec. 2520, Political Code, February 28, 1876.

90 As to residence and mode of election of Supervisors and School Directors, see sec. 3, Act of March 30, 1872; 1871–2, 729; Addendum at end of this Act.

91 The term of office of the County Judge is fixed at four years, to commence the 1st day of January next succeeding his election. Constitution, as amended 1862, Article VI, sec 7. The first term under the amended Constitution commenced January 1, 1864. By sec. 43 of the Act of April 20, 1863, p. 333, the term of office of the Probate Judge is fixed at four years, to commence the 1st day of January next after his election. The first term of office of the Probate Judge commenced January 1, 1864; and see Const. ut sup. cit. The Act of April 22, 1861, 214, provided that the Police Judge should hold office for two years, commencing the 1st day of July next succeeding his election, but that Act is expressly repealed by this.

§ Superseded by Act of March 23, 1878.

* Repealed by Constitution.

(a) Superseded so far as Superintendent of Common Schools, by sec. 3, Art. IX of Constitution.

Sec. 5.   At the second election held under this Act, on the day of the general election held in the year eighteen hundred and sixty-seven, and at the election held every second year thereafter, there shall be elected a Mayor, who shall be *ex officio* President of the Board of Supervisors ; a District Attorney, a Sheriff, a County Clerk, a Recorder, a Treasurer, an Assessor,[2] a Coroner, a Surveyor,   *   *   *   and in each of the Second, Fourth, Sixth, Eighth, Tenth and Twelfth Wards, one Supervisor and one School Director, who shall hold their offices for the term of two years from and after the first Monday of September subsequent to their election, and until their successors are elected and qualified. [Time of election changed by Section 4109 of Pol. Code.

Sec. 6.   In and for the City and County at large, at the general election in the year eighteen hundred and sixty-seven, and at the general election every two years thereafter, there shall be chosen by the qualified electors of said City and County five Justices of the Peace, to hold office for the term now prescribed by law ; and all laws are repealed which require or authorize Justices to be elected at a special judicial election. [Time of election changed by Section 4109 of Pol. Code.]

Sec. 7.   [*Superseded by sec.* 2520, *Political Code; see note* 89, *ante, second paragraph.*]

Sec. 8.   [*Obsolete.*]

Sec. 9.   It is hereby made the duty of the Mayor to issue his proclamation by publication in not less than three daily newspapers published in said City and County, at least ten days previous to the day in each year on which the election is to be held under this Act, calling upon the qualified voters in said City and County to meet in their respective districts for the purpose of electing such officers as are provided for in this Act, reciting in such proclamation the different officers to be elected at such election. [Superseded by Act of March 18, 1878; 1877–8, 299.]

Sec. 10.   [*Obsolete.*]

Sec. 11.   An Act entitled an Act to change the time for holding municipal elections in the City and County of San Francisco, and to define the official terms of certain officers therein mentioned, approved April twenty-second, eighteen hundred and sixty-one, and all Acts and parts of Acts inconsistent with the provisions of this Act are hereby repealed.

Sec. 12.   This Act shall take effect and be in force from and after its passage.

---

[2] By sec. 4109, Political Code, as amended Dec. 22, 1873; Amendments to th Codes, 1873–4, 173; the Assessor must be elected and hold office for the term of four years.

[*The following is the only portion of the Act of March 30, 1872; 1871-2, 729; now in force which is not incorporated in the foregoing Act.*]

SEC. 3. The Supervisors of each ward shall be a resident and qualified elector thereof, and shall be designated as the Supervisor of the ward from which he is elected. The School Directors may be elected from the resident and qualified electors of the City and County without reference to the location of their residence. The Supervisors and School Directors shall be elected by a plurality of all the votes cast at said elections in the City and County of San Francisco.

SUPPLEMENT XXX.

1867-8, 160.

An Act to confer additional powers upon the Board of Supervisors of the City and County of San Francisco, and upon the Auditor and Treasurer thereof, and to authorize certain appropriations of money by said Board.

[Approved March 14, 1868.]

The People of the State of California, represented in Senate and Assembly, do enact as follows :

SECTION 1. The Board of Supervisors of the City and County of San Francisco are hereby authorized and empowered to appropriate, allow and order paid, the several sums of money hereinafter mentioned, and to exercise the following powers, to wit :

First.[93]   *   *   *   *   *   *   *   ,   *

Second. To authorize the Superintendent of the Fire Alarm and Police Telegraph to appoint three operators, to be approved by the Board of Supervisors, at a salary of one hundred and twenty-five dollars per month, in lieu of the salary now allowed them by law; also one repairer, at a salary of one hundred dollars per month.

Third.[94]   *   *   *   *   *   *   *   *   *

Fourth. [*Deputy of Superintendent of Streets. Repealed, Act, April 4, 1870; 1869-70, 874.*]

Fifth to Seventh, inclusive. [*Executed.*]

Eighth. [*Private.*]

---

[93] Superseded by sub. 12, sec. 1, Act of March 30, 1872; Supplement LX, post.

[94] Repealed by sec. 6, Act of March 30, 1872; Supplement LXI, post.

Ninth. To pay out of the General Fund, a sum not exceeding eight thousand dollars per annum for advertising and election printing.*

SEC. 2. [*Authorizes payment of various sums heretofore allowed by Supervisors in excess of allowance provided by law. Executed.*]

SEC. 3. This Act shall take effect immediately.

SUPPLEMENT XXXI.

1867–8, 204.

An Act Concerning Railroad Companies in the City and County of San Francisco.

[Approved March 21, 1868.]

The People of the State of California, represented in Senate and Assembly, do enact as follows :

SECTION 1. The Board of Supervisors of the City and County of San Francisco shall have, and is hereby granted, the power and authority to restrict all railroad companies, in laying down their tracks along the streets of said City and County, to a space of not more than ten feet on each side of the center of such street or streets; and for a violation of such restriction, the said Board is hereby granted the power to prescribe and enforce such penalties as they may deem just and proper. [See also Sec. 498 of Civil Code.]

SEC. 2. This Act shall take effect from and after its passage.

SUPPLEMENT XXXII.

1867–8, 220.

An Act in relation to the office of Sheriff in the City and County of San Francisco.

[Approved March 20, 1868.]

The People of the State of California, represented in Senate and Assembly, do enact as follows :

SECTION 1. In addition to the deputies now allowed by law, the Sheriff of the City and County of San Francisco may appoint one deputy, and in

---

* Increased to $15,000 by Act of March 30, 1875; 1878, 829.

7

assistant bookkeeper, to act as Deputy Sheriff. Said deputy shall receive salary of one hundred and fifty dollars per month, and the assistant book-keeper shall receive a salary of one hundred dollars per month.

SEC. 2.   The Sheriff of said City and County shall have power and author-ity to appoint and remove two of the porters allowed by law, and now ap-pointed by the Supervisors, to take charge and perform duties about the court and other rooms of the City Hall of said City and County.

SEC. 3.   The salaries and moneys provided to be paid by this Act shall be paid by the Treasurer of the City and County of San Francisco, out of the Special Fee Fund of said City and County, upon the audit of the City and County Auditor, who is hereby directed to audit the salaries and moneys hereby provided.

SEC. 4.   [*Amended by sec. 3 of Act of March* 28, 1878.]

SEC. 5.   All Acts and parts of Acts, so far as they may be in conflict here-with, are hereby repealed.

SEC. 6.   This Act shall take effect from and after its passage.

SUPPLEMENT XXXIII.

1867-8, 267.

An Act concerning the Sheriff's advertising of the City and County of San Francisco.

[Approved March 24, 1868.]

The People of the State of California, represented in Senate and Assembly, do enact as follows :

SECTION 1.   The Board of Supervisors of the City and County of San Francisco shall include the official advertising of the Sheriff of the City and County of San Francisco in their advertisement for proposals to do the City and County official printing, and shall award the same to the lowest respon-sible bidder publishing a newspaper of general circulation in said City and County; *provided*, said award shall be made to the lowest responsible bid in the aggregate for the whole of said City and County official printing and · Sheriff's advertising; *provided*, also, that if any contract now exists for doing said Sheriff's advertising which shall expire before the usual time fixed by said Board of Supervisors for letting or awarding the City and County official printing, then said Sheriff shall advertise for proposals to do his official ad-vertising from the expiration of such contract to such time as the same shall be awarded, under the provisions of this Act, by the said Board of Supervisors; and he shall award the same for said time to the lowest responsible bidder proposing to advertise the same in a newspaper of general circulation in said City and County.

SEC. 2. All Acts and parts of Acts in conflict with the provisions of this Act are hereby repealed.

SEC. 3. This Act shall take effect immediately.

SUPPLEMENT XXXIV.

1867-8, 292.

An Act to authorize the Tax Collector of the City and County of San Francisco to appoint certain deputies and clerks in lieu of those now allowed by law.

[Approved March 25, 1868.]

The People of the State of California, represented in Senate and Assembly, do enact as follows:

SECTION 1. The Tax Collector of said City and County shall be allowed, in lieu of the deputies and clerks now allowed by law, one Chief Deputy [and] one Cash Deputy, each at a monthly salary of two hundred dollars; three General Deputies, each at a monthly salary of one hundred and fifty dollars; also, extra clerks at salaries at the rate of one hundred and fifty dollars per month each, for the time actually employed; *provided*, said Tax Collector shall not be allowed exceeding twelve thousand dollars for salaries of all such deputies and clerks during any one fiscal year.[95]

SEC. 2. The Auditor of said City and County is hereby directed to audit and the Treasurer to pay, in United States coin, out of the General Fund of said City and County, the several salaries herein provided for, all demands therefor to be first approved and certified as correct by the said Tax Collector.

SEC. 3. The clerks herein provided for shall not have power to receipt for moneys or administer oaths in matters appertaining to said office.

SEC. 4. This Act shall take effect and be in force from and after its passage; and all Acts and parts of Acts conflicting with the provisions of this Act are hereby repealed.

[95] See sub. 10 sec. 1, Act of March 30, 1872; Supplement LX, post.

SUPPLEMENT XXXV.

1867-8, 379.

An Act to confirm a certain order passed by the Board of Supervisors of the City and County of San Francisco.

[Approved March 27, 1868.]

The People of the State of California, represented in Senate and Assembly, do enact as follows:

SECTION 1. Whereas the Board of Supervisors of the City and County of San Francisco passed an order, numbered eight hundred, which said order was approved by the Mayor and President of the Board of Supervisors, on January fourteenth, eighteen hundred and sixty-eight, and which is as follows:

" Order No. 800.—An order for the settlement and quieting titles to land in the City and County of San Francisco, situate above high water mark of the Bay of San Francisco and the Pacific Ocean, and without the corporate limits of the City of San Francisco.

" The People of the City and County of San Francisco do ordain as follows:

" SECTION 1. Immediately after the passage of this order, the Board of Supervisors shall proceed to devise and adopt a plan for the subdivision into blocks and lots of all the lands not reserved to the United States, situated on the peninsula of San Francisco, and within the present corporate limits of said City and County, and above the natural ordinary high water mark of the Bay of San Francisco and the Pacific Ocean, as the same existed on the seventh day of July, eighteen hundred and forty-six, and without the corporate limits of the City of San Francisco, as defined in the Act to re-incorporate the said City, passed by the Legislature of California on the fifteenth day of April, eighteen hundred and fifty-one, so far as said Board may deem such subdi-vision necessary; and to select and set apart for public uses such lots and portions of said land as said Board may deem necessary, subject to the limita-tions and provisions hereinafter in this order contained.

" SEC. 2. After the adoption of the plan provided for in section one of this order, the Board of Supervisors shall cause to be made a map of said lands, according to said plan. Such map shall show the streets and public highways, the blocks formed by the intersection of the streets and public highways, and the lots into which said blocks shall be subdivided, and upon such map shall be designated the lots and portions of land set apart for public uses, and the particular use for which each lot or portion of land shall have been set apart.

"Sec. 3. Upon the completion of the map provided for by section two of this order, it shall be deposited for public inspection in the office of the Clerk of the Board of Supervisors, and there remain for a period of thirty days; and notice shall be published in three of the daily papers during the whole time that said map shall so remain in said office.

"Sec. 4. Any person having or claiming any interest in any portion of said lands, under and by virtue of any of the provisions of this order, may at any time before the completion of said map, or while the same shall remain in the office of the Clerk of the Board of Supervisors for public inspection, present to the Committee on Outside Lands, hereinafter in this order provided for, a description and diagram of the lands in which he shall so claim an interest, and have the same delineated on said map; but no claim shall be delineated upon said map by said committee unless all taxes shall have been paid thereon for five fiscal years preceding the year beginning July first, eighteen hundred and sixty-six.

"Sec. 5. After the said map shall have remained in the office of the Clerk of the Board of Supervisors for the said period of thirty days, as provided in section three of this order, the Board of Supervisors may examine the objections, if any, made thereto, and may make such alterations in the location or designation of any lots or portions of land set apart for public uses as may be necessary to obviate any objection which the said Board shall deem just and proper.

"Sec. 6. As soon as the alterations provided for in section five of this order shall have been made and delineated on said map, the said map shall become and be the official map of said lands; and the portions of land thereon designated as public streets and highways, and the tract or portion of land set apart and designated on said map as a public park, and the tract or portion of land set apart and designated thereon as a cemetery, and lots for a Hospital, City Hall, County Jail, Public Schools, Fire Department, City Library, or other public purposes, shall be deemed absolutely dedicated as such.

"Sec. 7. No lot set apart for public use, other than for a park, plaza, cemetery or public square, or for the erection thereon of a City Hall or buildings for a City Library, Hospital, County Jail or an Asylum, shall exceed in extent two fifty vara lots; and no tract or portion of land set apart for a plaza or public square shall exceed in extent four whole blocks, formed by the intersection of the main streets of the plan; and the tract or portion of land set apart for a cemetery shall not be less in extent than two hundred acres; and the tract or portion of land set apart for a public park shall not be less than one thousand acres.

"Sec. 8. No person shall be entitled to receive compensation for any lot or portion of land set apart for public use, unless his claim shall have been delineated on the map hereinbefore in this order provided for, nor until all conflicting claims to such lot or portion of land shall have been finally determined; and no person shall be entitled to receive compensation for any portion of land included in any street or highway.

"Sec. 9. All that portion of the land described in section one of this order which lies south of a line drawn due south, eighty-one degrees and thirty-five minutes east, magnetic, through Seal Rock, and west of a line easterly not less than two hundred feet from ordinary high water mark, is hereby reserved and set apart for public use as a public highway.

"Sec. 10. After the committee hereinafter provided for in section thirteen shall have made their final report upon the said map and reservations, and the report shall be ratified by the Board of Supervisors, it shall be the further duty of the said committee to make a just appraisement of the lands reserved for public uses other than for streets and highways, and to make a just and equitable assessment of the value of the lands so reserved, ratably and equitably upon and to each piece and parcel of land delineated on said map, according to the appraised value of said lands (exclusive of the lands reserved for public streets and highways). They shall make their report in duplicate, under their hands or the hands of a majority of them; one copy of which said report shall be filed in the office of the Clerk of the Board of ' Supervisors and the other copy of said report shall be filed in the office of the City and County Recorder; *provided*, that no member of such committee shall act in making such appraisements or assessments who shall be interested in any of the lands to be affected; and in case any member of said committee shall be so interested, the Board of Supervisors shall appoint some other member to act in his place in making said appraisements and assessments. The said committee shall be sworn to faithfully discharge their duties.

"Sec. 11. Upon the payment to the County Treasurer of the City and County of San Francisco of the amount assessed by the committee provided for in section thirteen of this order, upon the lands as provided for in section ten of this order, the City and County of San Francisco hereby relinquishes and grants all the right, title and claim which the said City and County now has or may hereafter acquire as the successor of the Pueblo of San Francisco, or as the grantee or the patentee of the United States, in and to the lands hereinbefore in this order described, and not excepted or reserved, or intended to be excepted or reserved, by any of the preceding sections or provisions of this order, and which may not be set apart for public use under any of the preceding sections and provisions, and upon which shall be paid, previous to the first day of April, eighteen hundred and sixty-eight, all taxes which have been assessed thereon during the five fiscal years preceding the year beginning July first, eighteen hundred and sixty-six, unto the person, or to the heirs and assigns of persons, who were, on the eighth day of March, eighteen hundred and sixty-six, in the actual bona fide possession thereof, by themselves or their tenants, or, having been ousted from such possession be fore or since said day, have recovered or may recover the same by legal process. And it is hereby declared to be the intent and object of this section to pass the right, title and claim of the said City and County in and to every tract or portion of said land delineated on said map, except the portions that are or may be reserved as aforesaid, possessed by one person, unto the possessor thereof in severalty; and every separate tract or portion thereof, except the portions that are or may be reserved as aforesaid, possessed by more than one person, jointly or in common, unto the possessors thereof, jointly or in common.

"SEC. 12. The grants and relinquishments by this order made shall be subject to the selections, reservations and conditions hereinbefore in this order made and provided for.

"SEC. 13. A committee of five members of the Board of Supervisors shall be chosen by said Board, whose duty it shall be to prepare and report to the Board the plan provided for in section two of this order, to supervise the making of the map provided for in section three, to select, set apart and designate the lots and portions of land hereinbefore provided to be set apart for public use, and generally to superintend the carrying out of the provisions of this order; all the acts of said committee to be subject to the approval of the Board of Supervisors.

"SEC. 14. The committee aforesaid shall receive a reasonable compensation for their services, to be determined by the County Judge.

"SEC. 15. Whenever a survey shall be required to determine the boundaries of any claim or portion of any claim, whether ordered by the committee or requested by the claimants, the expenses of such survey shall be borne by such claimants; and no survey shall be received by the committee except it shall have been made by the City and County Surveyor, or a surveyor designated by the committee; and the amount of compensation for such survey shall be fixed by the committee at a reasonable rate, not to exceed the ordinary charges for such services.

"SEC. 16. The Board of Supervisors shall provide by order for the distribution and payment to those entitled thereto of the moneys assessed for the cost of reservations, and which shall have been paid to the City and County Treasurer, under the provisions of section eleven of this order.

"SEC. 17. Nothing in this order contained shall have the effect to annul or invalidate any action or proceeding heretofore had or commenced under the orders which are by this order repealed; and it shall not be necessary to do anew, under this order, anything therein provided for which is also provided for in the orders aforesaid, and which has been done under and in pursuance of the provisions of said orders, and have been ratified by the Board of Supervisors; and all proceedings commenced under said orders, relating to maps and surveys not yet completed, shall be continued and completed under this order.

. " Sec. 18. Order seven hundred and thirty-three, and all orders and parts of orders and resolutions, so far as they conflict with the provisions of this order, are hereby repealed.

" Sec. 19. This order is subject in all its parts to ratification by the Legislature, for which application shall be made by the Board of Supervisors."

Be it therefore enacted, that the within and before recited order be and the same is hereby ratified and confirmed; and all proceedings heretofore had, and which have taken place or shall hereafter take place under its provisions, are ratified and confirmed in all respects; provided, that after the Board of Supervisors shall have set apart a tract of land for a cemetery, as provided in said order, and shall have set apart a tract of land for a public park, as therein provided, the said Board may, if in their judgment the same would be better for the public health or convenience, by a vote of at least ten members, and with the approval of the Mayor, exchange such lands so set apart for cemetery purposes for other lands, not less than two hundred acres in extent, to be used as a cemetery; and they may also exchange said lands so set apart for a pubic park for other lands for the purposes of a public park, and not of less extent than one thousand acres; but no person in actual possession of any of the lands mentioned in the first section of said order on the said eighth day of March, eighteen hundred and sixty-six, and on which five years' taxes shall have been paid, as provided in such order, shall be dispossessed of any of said lands under any order heretofore or hereafter made by said Board of Supervisors for the reservation of any of said lands for public uses, except for streets, until compensation shall have been actually made to such person, as provided in said Order Number Eight Hundred; and until such compensation shall have been made such person shall be allowed to continue in possession of such lands so possessed by them.

Sec. 2. This Act shall take effect from and after its passage.

— —.

SUPPLEMENT XXXVI.

1867–8, 410.

———

An Act further to provide for the ratification and confirmation of a certain Order passed by the Board of Supervisors of the City and County of San Francisco, and to modify certain provisions of the same.

[Approved March 27, 1868.]

The People of the State of California, represented in Senate and Assembly, do enact as follows:

Section 1. Nothing in the provisions of a certain order passed by the Board of Supervisors of the City and County of San Francisco, numbered eight hundred, and entitled "An Order for the settlement and quieting titles to land in the City and County of San Francisco, situate above high water mark of the Bay of San Francisco and the Pacific Ocean, and without the corporate limits of the City of San Francisco," nor in the provisions of any Act confirming or purporting to confirm the same, shall authorize the said Board to exchange any lands set apart and reserved, or to be set apart and reserved, for a cemetery or a park, nor to deprive the said Board of the power of taking immediate possession of any lands hereafter reserved for public use under the provisions of said Order Number Eight Hundred, or by virtue of the terms of an Act of Congress approved March eighth, eighteen hundred and sixty-six, entitled an Act to quiet the title to certain lands within the corporate limits of the City of San Francisco.

SEC. 2. Whenever the report of appraisement mentioned in section ten of said Order Number Eight Hundred shall have been made and filed, as therein provided, it shall be the duty of the City and County Recorder to make out, certify and deliver to the Tax Collector of said City and County a copy of the same, which copy shall be deemed and held to have the same force, effect and validity, in regard to the sums therein assessed, as an assessment roll duly approved by said Board of Equalization in regard to State and County taxes. The said Tax Collector shall proceed to collect the said several sums of money assessed in said report in the same manner as State and County taxes are collected by him in said City and County; and all the provisions of the various Acts relating to the collection of the public revenue in said City and County not inconsistent with the provisions of said Order Number Eight Hundred, nor the provisions of this Act, shall apply to the collection of the sums of money so assessed as aforesaid.

SEC. 3. This Act shall take effect from and after its passage.

_____

SUPPLEMENT XXXVII.

1867-8, 458.

___

An Act to provide funds to be applied to building a Hospital in the City and County of San Francisco.

[Approved March 28, 1868.]

The People of the State of California, represented in Senate and Assembly, do enact as follows:

SECTION 1. The Mayor, Auditor, and Treasurer of the City and County of San Francisco, by and with the consent of the Board of Supervisors of said

City and County first obtained by ordinance, are hereby authorized and empowered to issue from time to time, as may be directed by the said Board of Supervisors and as may be necessary for the purposes herein named, bonds not exceeding in the aggregate the sum of two hundred and fifty thousand dollars.

Sec. 2. Said bonds shall be issued in such manner and at such times, not inconsistent with the foregoing section, and made payable in the City and County of San Francisco, at the office of the Treasurer of said City and County, both principal and interest, at such times, not exceeding twenty years from the time of their issuance, as the Board of Supervisors may prescribe by ordinance. The interest on said bonds shall not exceed seven per cent. per annum, and shall be paid semi-annually; and both principal and interest shall be payable in United States gold coin.

Sec. 3. The said bonds shall be signed by the Mayor, Auditor, and Treasurer of the City and County of San Francisco, and shall be known as the " Hospital Fund Bonds of the City and County of San Francisco."

Sec. 4. Said bonds shall have coupons attached to them for the semiannual interest which may accrue upon them, signed by the Auditor of said City and County; and the faith and credit of the said City and County of San Francisco are hereby pledged for the redemption of the same and for the payment of the principal and interest thereof.

Sec. 5. Whenever said bonds or any portion of them are issued, the Treasurer and Auditor of said City and County are hereby authorized and empowered to sell the same to the highest bidder therefor, after having first advertised the same for three successive weeks in three daily newspapers published in said City and County. All moneys derived from the issue and sale of said bonds shall be appropriated and used for the purpose of building and furnishing a hospital, and for improving and inclosing said hospital grounds in the City and County of San Francisco; the location, style, and material thereof; the construction, the furnishing, and all contracts and plans relating thereto, to be determined by said Board of Supervisors, and in all cases to be approved before the adoption or ratification of the same by the Mayor, Auditor, and Treasurer of said City and County. But no bonds authorized to be issued by this Act shall be sold for a less sum than seventy-five cents in gold coin on the dollar, par value. [*Amended February* 2, 1872; 1871-2, 64.]

Sec. 6. To secure the payment of the principal and interest of said bonds, the Board of Supervisors of the said City and County of San Francisco shall, when deemed necessary by them, for the purpose in this section provided, levy an annual tax upon all the taxable property in the said City and County of San Francisco; and a sufficient sum or sums shall be raised by such annual levies to pay the principal of said bonds when the same shall become due. And it shall be the duty of the Treasurer of said City and County to set apart annually, out of the moneys coming into the treasury to the credit of the Hospital Fund, raised by said annual tax, a sum sufficient to pay the semi-annual interest on said bonds, and also to provide a Sinking Fund sufficient for the redemption of the same at maturity.

SEC. 7. This Act shall take effect and be in force from and after its passage.

SUPPLEMENT XXXVIII.

1867-8, 463.

An Act to authorize the Board of Supervisors of the City and County of San Francisco to modify and change the grade of streets in said City and County.

[Approved March 28, 1868.]

The People of the State of California, represented in Senate and Assembly, do enact as follows:

SECTION 1. The Board of Supervisors of the City and County of San Francisco are hereby authorized and empowered, upon petition of the owners of three-fourths of the property to be affected thereby[96]—said property to be ascertained and indicated by said Board of Supervisors in the manner provided in the first subdivision of section two of this Act—to change and modify the grade of any street or avenue, or of any part of any street or avenue, in said City and County, as is hereinafter provided.

SEC. 2. The grade of any street or avenue, or portion of any street or avenue, the grade of which has been fixed by ordinance, shall not be altered or changed, except upon an adjustment of the benefits and damages; and the proceedings shall be as follows:

First. The Board of Supervisors, upon the receipt of a petition in conformity with the provisions of section one of this Act, shall publish in the official newspaper of said City and County a notice of their intention to make such

---

[96] The Act of April 2, 1870; 1369 70, 650; provides as follows: "The Mayor of the City and County of San Francisco is hereby authorized and empowered, on behalf and in the name of the City and County of San Francisco, to petition the Board of Supervisors of said City and County to order the change of the official grade of any street or streets, where such change may affect any public square or other lot of land belonging to said City and County; and such petition shall have the same effect as if the same were signed by or in behalf of the owners of any property not belonging to said City and County."

[change]. Said notice shall be published for thirty days, and shall describe the proposed change, and designate the limits within which the lots of land to be benefited shall be assessed to pay any damages that may be awarded by reason of the change.

Second. Within twenty days after the first publication of said notice, any person claiming that he or she would sustain damage by reason of such change shall file a petition with the County Clerk, addressed to the County Court,* setting forth the fact of his or her ownership, the description and situation of his or her property, its market value, and the amount of damage, over and above all benefits, which he or she would sustain by reason of the proposed change, if completed, asking the appointment of Commissioners to assess such damage; which petition shall be verified by the oath of the petitioner, or his or her agent.

Third. On the filing of such petition, the said County Court* shall take jurisdiction of the proceedings, and the County Clerk shall immediately give notice thereof to the President of the Board of Supervisors.

Fourth. At the expiration of the time of publication of said notice, and at the time indicated by said notice, or at such other time to which it may be continued, the County Court* shall appoint three citizens, who are freeholders in said City and County, and competent judges of the value of real estate therein, and not interested in said proceedings, as Commissioners, to assess the benefits and damages to each separate lot of land within the limits designated in the notice.

Fifth. The Commissioners shall be sworn by the County Judge,* to make the assessments of benefits and damages, to the best of their judgment and ability, without fear or favor, and that they have no interest in the controversy, nor in any of the land within the limits designated, which oath shall be filed with the County Clerk as part of the proceedings. A copy thereof, and of the order of appointment, certified by the Clerk, may be delivered to said Commissioners as their authority.

Sixth. Said Commissioners shall visit and inspect the premises to be assessed and the premises for which damages are claimed, with a committee from their body, appointed for that purpose by the Board of Supervisors.

Seventh. Said Commissioners shall have power, and it is hereby made their duty, to examine, under oath, which any one of them is hereby authorized to administer, any witnesses produced before them by any party, touching the matters to be investigated, and such other witnesses as they may deem necessary to fully acquaint themselves with the actual amount of benefits and damages which will result to the respective parties interested in the proposed change.

Eighth. Said Commissioners, having determined the damage which will be sustained by each petitioner, over and above all benefits by the comple-

---

tion of the proposed change, shall proceed to assess the whole amount thereof, together with the costs, charges and expenses of the proceedings, including the compensation to the Commissioners for their services, to be taxed and allowed by the County Judge, ratably, upon the several lots of land benefited within the limits designated in said notice, so that the same shall be distributed according to the benefits produced by such change as nearly as possible.

Ninth. Said Commissioners shall make their report in writing, and shall subscribe the same and file it with the County Clerk. In their said report they shall describe each piece of property which will sustain damage, stating the amount of the damages which it will sustain over and above all benefits; and they shall also give a brief description of each lot benefited within the designated limits, the name of the owner, if known, and the amount of benefit assessed against the same. In case the three Commissioners do not agree, the award agreed upon by any two of them shall be sufficient. On the filing of said report, the County Clerk shall notify the Board of Supervisors, in writing, of the fact, and thereupon the said Board shall by ordinance confirm or reject said report. If they confirm it, the grades of the streets shall be changed as contemplated, and the Clerk of the Board of Supervisors shall notify the County Court* that the Board have confirmed the report. The County Court shall thereupon enter up judgment against each lot assessed for benefits, describing the same as accurately as can conveniently be done. Upon which judgment an order of sale may issue by order of the Court, commanding the Sheriff of said City and County to collect the amount therein mentioned by sale of the lot assessed in the mode prescribed by law for the sale of real estate, the proceeds to be paid by the Sheriff to the Treasurer of the City and County of San Francisco, who shall place the same to the credit of the Street Department Fund; and the same shall be paid, and the Treasurer of said City and County shall pay the amount collected for damages into the County Court,* which shall hold, invest and distribute the same in the same manner as provided in section nineteen of an Act entitled an Act to declare and regulate the power of the Board of Supervisors of the City and County of San Francisco to take private lands for certain public improvements and to prescribe the manner of its execution, approved April fourth, eighteen hundred and sixty-four. All such judgments shall be in favor of the City and County of San Francisco, and shall be a lien upon the lot until the same is paid; but no sale shall be made nor execution issue until the *County Court shall determine that said work has been completed.

Sec. 3. Before entering up judgment, the Court shall fix a day for hearing parties who may feel aggrieved by reason of any of the proceedings; but no objection shall be considered except such as are specifically set forth in

---

*Now Superior Court.

writing by the parties; and all errors, omissions and irregularities not specifically set forth shall be deemed to be waived. Any party dissatisfied may, within thirty days after judgment against him or his lot, or the order to pay the damages assessed, appeal to the Supreme Court to review the matter complained of, and the appeal shall be taken in the manner and with the same effect as prescribed in, and in all respects be in conformity to, an Act to declare and regulate the power of the Board of Supervisors of the City and County of San Francisco to take private lands for certain public improvements and to prescribe the manner of its execution, approved April fourth, eighteen hundred and sixty-four; and all subsequent proceedings shall be in conformity therewith and with the same effect.

SEC. 4. All Acts and proceedings under this law shall be liberally construed, and the judgments and proceedings of the County Court* shall be construed like judgments and proceedings of ⸴courts of general jurisdiction.

SEC. 5. The Sheriff shall collect fees for the execution, in case an execution issues, as in other cases; but each party may pay to the Treasurer the amount of the judgment against him, and the Treasurer's receipt being produced to the County Court,* satisfaction of the judgment shall be entered by the Clerk. The Clerk shall not charge any fees for the proceedings unless execution issues, in which case he shall be authorized to charge five dollars for each execution, to be collected by the Sheriff on the execution.

SEC. 6. This Act shall take effect from and after its passage.

SUPPLEMENT XXXIX.

1867-8, 558.

An Act to provide additional revenue for the School Department of the City and County of San Francisco, and to change the time and manner of electing the Superintendent of Public Schools of said City and County.

[Approved March 30, 1868.]

The People of the State of California, represented in Senate and Assembly, do enact as follows:

SECTION 1. [*Provides for levy of certain taxes. Obsolete.*]

SEC. 2. The Board of Supervisors of the City and County of San Francisco are hereby authorized and required, to pay for the improvement of all

----
†Now Superior Court, ante.

streets in front of school property in the same manner and from the same fund from which other street improvements in front of public property are paid.

SEC. 3. It shall not be lawful for the Board of Education or the Board of Supervisors of the City and County of San Francisco to dispose of any real estate belonging to the School Department, except fifty-vara lot three hundred and one, and the lot on which the colored school-house is located, on Broadway, between Powell and Mason streets, which lots the Board of Education, with the consent of a majority of the Board of Supervisors, are hereby authorized to sell at public auction, after giving thirty days' notice in some public newspaper in said City and County; *provided*, that one-half of the proceeds of such sale shall be placed to the credit of the School Fund to pay any deficit in the School Fund of the fiscal year eighteen hundred and sixty-seven and sixty-eight.

SEC. 4. It shall be the duty of the Committee on Finance and Auditing of the Board of Education, during the month of July every year, to make an annual estimate of all revenue and disbursements of the School Department for the current fiscal year, specifying separately the amount of funds necessary to defray the different items of expenditures for the first and last half year; and in no case shall it be lawful for the said Board to exceed, during the first half year, the estimated item of expenditures for that period, or in the entire year, the revenues collected for school purposes. All surplus or unexpended funds of any half year shall be available for expenditures of the following half year.   The Auditor and Treasurer shall conform strictly to the provisions of this section.

SEC. 5. [*Relates to election of Superintendent of Common Schools; Superseded by Sec.* 4109 *Pol. Code.*]

SEC. 6. All laws and parts of laws in conflict with the provisions of this Act, for the purposes of this Act, are hereby repealed.

SEC. 7. This Act shall take effect on and after its passage.

S U P P L E M E N T   X L.
1867-8, 702.

An Act relating to the Board of Supervisors of the City and County of San Francisco, and more particularly defining its powers and duties.

[Approved March 30, 1868.]

The People of the State of California, represented in Senate and Assembly, do enact as follows:

SECTION 1. Each member of the Board of Supervisors of the City and County of San Francisco, excepting the Mayor, *ex-officio* President of said

Board, shall, after the passage of this Act, be allowed a salary during the time he is in office of one hundred dollars a month; and the Auditor of said City and County is hereby directed to audit and the Treasurer to pay such salaries, monthly, out of the General Fund.

SEC. 2. The votes of seven members constituting the Board of Supervisors shall be necessary to pass any ordinance, order, or resolution; but in the event of a veto by the Mayor, then nine votes shall be necessary to pass any ordinance, order or resolution over such veto, otherwise such ordinance, order or resolution shall be of no validity.

SEC. 3. If a member of said Board of Supervisors shall hereafter absent himself from the State, or shall neglect to attend the meetings of said Board, for a period of ninety days, his office may be declared vacant by the Board and a successor may be appointed for the unexpired term, as provided in other cases.

SEC. 4. This Act shall be construed so as to harmonize with existing laws in regard to the powers and duties of the said Board of Supervisors; and all such laws shall continue in full force except so far as they may be inconsistent or in conflict with the provisions of this Act, and only so far as they are inconsistent or in conflict with this Act they are hereby repealed.

SEC. 5. This Act shall take effect immediately.

SUPPLEMENT XLI.

1869-70, 23.

An Act to authorize the Assessor of the City and County of San Francisco to appoint deputies.

[Approved January 25, 1870.]

The People of the State of California, represented in Senate and Assembly, do enact as follows:

SECTION 1. The Assessor of the City and County of San Francisco shall be allowed to assist him in making his assessments, in lieu of the deputies now provided by law, as follows: For the office, one chief deputy, seven office deputies, one head draughtsman, one assistant draughtsman. For the field, one chief deputy and seven under deputies, [*As amended by Act of March 6, 1878; 1878. 173.*]

SEC. 2. Four of the office deputies shall be paid at the rate of one hundred and fifty dollars per month each, and shall be employed and paid only from the first day of February until the assessment roll is finally completed and handed over to the Auditor.

SEC. 3. The seven under field deputies shall be paid at the rate of one hundred and fifty dollars per month each. The term for which such deputies shall be paid shall not exceed an average of six months each, namely, from the first day of February until the first day of March of each year, and from the first day of August until the first day of January of each year. [*As amended by Act of March 6, 1878.*]

SEC. 4. The chief office deputy, chief field deputy, head draughtsman, assistant draughtsman, and three under office deputies, may be employed the entire year.

SEC. 5. The chief office deputy, chief field deputy and head draughtsman shall be paid two hundred dollars per month each; the under office deputies and assistant draughtsman, one hundred and fifty dollars per mouth each.

SEC. 6. The Auditor of the said City and County is hereby directed to audit, and the Treasurer of said City and County to pay out of the General Fund, the salaries herein provided for.

SEC. 7. All Acts and parts of Acts, so far as they conflict with the provisions of this Act, are hereby repealed.

SEC. 8. This Act shall take effect and be in force from and after its passage.

—

SUPPLEMENT XLII.

1869-70, 221.

———

An Act to confer additional powers upon the Board of Supervisors of the City and County of San Francisco, and upon the Auditor and Treasurer thereof, and authorize appropriations by said Board.

[Approved March 9, 1870.]

The People of the State of California, represented in Senate and Assembly, do enact as follows :

SECTION 1. [*Obsolete.*]

SEC. 2. The Board of Supervisors are hereby authorized and directed to procure a strongly-built covered spring wagon, capable of seating twelve

8

persons, also two horses and harness, etc., to be used under the direction of said Sheriff, and exclusively in the transportation of prisoners and insane persons.

SEC. 3. The Sheriff of the City and County of San Francisco is hereby authorized to appoint a suitable person to drive and take charge and care of the two horses, wagon, etc., named in section two of this Act, who shall receive a salary of seventy-five dollars per month, payable out of the General Fund of said City and County.

SEC. 4. The Board of Supervisors are hereby authorized and directed to allow and order paid out of the General Fund, fifty ($50) dollars per month, to the Sheriff, which shall be in full satisfaction for the keeping and maintaining of the horses named in section two of this Act.

SEC. 5. This Act shall take effect immediately.

SUPPLEMENT XLIII.

1869-70, 240.

An Act to confer additional powers upon the Board of Supervisors of the City and County of San Francisco, and upon the Auditor and Treasurer thereof, and to authorize certain appropriations of money by said Board.

[Approved March 9, 1870.]

The People of the State of California, represented in Senate and Assembly, do enact as follows :

SECTION 1. The Board of Supervisors of the City and County of San Francisco are hereby authorized and empowered to appropriate, allow and order paid out of the General Fund, the several sums of money hereinafter mentioned, and to exercise the following powers, to wit :

First. To appoint a Janitor for the City Hall, at a salary of seventy-five dollars per month.

Second. To appoint four Gardeners to take charge of Portsmouth, Washington, Union and Columbia Squares, at a salary of seventy-five dollars per month each.

Third and Fourth. [*Appointment and salaries of Health Inspectors and Clerk of Board of Health. Superseded by secs. 3009, 3010, Political Code; Supplement XCI.*]

Fifth. [*Expenditure for persons in Hospital and Almshouse. Superseded by sub.* 18, *sec.* 1, *Act of March* 30, 1872; *Supplement LX.*]

Sixth and Seventh. [*Executed.*]

Eighth. [*Superseded by subs.* 1 *and* 2, *sec.* 1, *Act of March* 30, 1872; *Supplement LX.*]

SEC. 2. [*Authorizes payment of certain sums heretofore allowed, in excess of allowance provided by law.*]

SEC. 3. This Act shall take effect immediately.

SUPPLEMENT XLIV.

1869–70, 353.

An Act to expedite the settlement of land titles in the City and County of San Francisco, and to ratify and confirm the acts and proceedings of certain of the authorities thereof.

[Approved March 14, 1870.]

The People of the State of California, represented in Senate and Assembly, do enact as follows:

SECTION 1. Upon receiving a petition from any person or persons, claiming that they, by themselves, their tenants or the persons through whom they claim or derive possession, have been, from and including the eighth day of March, Anno Domini eighteen hundred and sixty-six (1866), and still are, in the possession of any of the lands without the corporate limits of the City of San Francisco, as defined in an Act to re-incorporate said city, passed by the Legislature of the State of California on the fifteenth day of April, Anno Domini eighteen hundred and fifty-one (1851), and described in the decree of Justice Field, of the United States Circuit Court, confirming the claim of the City and County of San Francisco, entered November second, Anno Domini eighteen hundred and sixty-four (1864), in the Circuit Court of the United States for the Northern District of the State of California, and that they, or the persons through whom they claim or derive possession, have paid to the Tax Collector of the City and County of San Francisco the amount assessed by the Outside Land Committee upon the land described in said petition, to pay for land reserved for public use, pro-

vided for in section ten (10) of Order Eight Hundred (800), and also paid
the taxes mentioned in section four (4) of said order, and all the taxes
levied on said lands for State and municipal purposes now due and remaining unpaid; or, upon receiving a petition from any person or persons, setting forth that said petitioners, by themselves, their tenants, or the persons
through whom they claim or derive possession, were, on or before the first
(1st) day of January, Anno Domini eighteen hundred and fifty-five (1855),
to and including the twentieth (20th) day of June, Anno Domini eighteen
hundred and fifty-five (1855), and still are, in possession of the land described in said petition, embraced within the corporate limits of the City of
San Francisco, and above high water mark, as defined in the Act to incorporate said city, passed by the Legislature of the State of California, on the
fifteenth (15th) day of April, Anno Domini eighteen hundred and fifty-one
(1851); and such petition in either case setting forth that such lands have
not been sold, leased, dedicated, reserved or conveyed by authority of the
said City and County of San Francisco, or the United States, to any one, or
for any purpose, and asking for a grant from said City and County, the
Board of Supervisors shall proceed to act thereon as hereinafter provided.
This petition shall be verified by the oath or affirmation of the party in
whose behalf the petition is presented, or by some one acting as his agent,
and conversant with the facts detailed in the petition.

SEC. 2. All petitions mentioned in the first section of this Act shall be
referred to the Committee on Outside Lands. The Clerk of the Board of
Supervisors shall be the Clerk of the Outside Land Committee. The party
presenting the said petition may appear before said Clerk and make proof,
verbal and documentary, of the truth of the matters alleged in his petition.
Copies of the documentary evidence shall be filed with said Clerk, and the
oral testimony shall be reduced to writing by said Clerk and subscribed by
the witness. The proofs of the petitioner being closed, the said Committee
shall proceed to consider the same, and shall make such report and recommendation thereon as to them shall seem just and proper in the premises.
The said Committee shall file with the Clerk of the Board of Supervisors
the testimony taken as aforesaid, together with the report of the said Committee, and said report shall be submitted to the Board of Supervisors for
their approval, and if, in their judgment, the claim of the petitioner is well
founded, they shall, by an order entered in their minutes, adjudge and award
a grant of such lands to the petitioner or petitioners therefor, less the
amount reserved for public use. The said Board shall thereupon give public
notice of their award by notice, published at least once a week for three
successive weeks, in some daily newspaper published in the City and County
of San Francisco, which notice shall specify the name of the applicant, the
date and filing of his petition, and the tract of land awarded, by a good and
sufficient description thereof ; proof of publication of such notice shall be
made in the manner now or hereafter required by law for the proof of publication in civil process. The Clerk of the said committee shall be allowed

compensation, for taking the oath or affirmation of witnesses, twenty-five cents; and for reducing the testimony to writing, twenty cents a folio, which shall be in full for all services rendered by him as Clerk of said committee. The compensation herein allowed to the Clerk of said Committee shall be paid to said Clerk by the party presenting the petition.

SEC. 3. Upon receiving proof of the publication of the notice provided for in the second section hereof, and the payment of all necessary expenses for deeds, the Mayor of the City and County of San Francisco is hereby authorized and empowered to execute, acknowledge and deliver to the party or parties presenting the aforesaid petition, a deed of conveyance of the tract or lot of land as aforesaid, adjudged and awarded to the petitioner, and attach thereto the corporate seal of the City and County of San Francisco; *provided*, the petitioner or petitioners shall, before receiving a deed as aforesaid, be required to quitclaim and peaceably deliver the possession of all land claimed by said petitioner or petitioners, reserved by the Commissioners acting under Ordinance Eight Hundred and Twenty-two (822), and all those lands reserved by the Committee of the Board of Outside Lands for the use and benefit of the City and County of San Francisco; *provided, however,* that in case a suit shall be pending between the petitioner and some third person, involving the right of possession of the tract, or some portion thereof, petitioned for, and such third person shall file with the Clerk of the Board of Supervisors a copy of the complaint filed in such action, before the deed shall have been executed and delivered to the petitioner, and also competent proof that such third persons, or the persons through whom they claim or derive possession, have paid the taxes and assessments mentioned in the first section of this Act, then and in that case the deed shall be withheld until such suit shall be finally determined; and there shall thereafter be executed a deed of conveyance of so much of the tract of land as shall be involved in the said suit, to the party in whose favor the said suit shall be finally determined as aforesaid; *provided, further,* that the expenses hereinafter provided for shall be paid before such conveyance shall be delivered.

SEC. 4. Upon the filing of a petition, as hereinbefore provided, the petitioner shall deposit with the Clerk of the Board of Supervisors a sum of money sufficient to pay for the publication of the notice hereinbefore provided, and other expenses incident to the granting of the prayer of the petitioner. But the Clerk shall not receive on file any petition that shall not be in conformity with the provisions of this Act.

SEC. 5. A conveyance executed and delivered in pursuance of the provisions of this Act shall operate as an acknowledgment on the part of the said City and County, that the title to the land therein described has passed under and by virtue of said Order Number Eight Hundred (800), or of said Ordinance Number Eight Hundred and Twenty-two (822), as the case may be, and also under and by virtue of the several Acts of Congress and the

Legislature ratifying said order and ordinance, or under the authority of which the same have been passed; and such conveyance shall likewise operate to grant, convey, remise and release to the party, his heirs and assigns, named therein, the lands in such conveyance described, and all the estate and interest, present and future, of the said City and County of San Francisco, in and to such lands. But no such conveyance shall in any event be held to import a warranty or covenant of title on the part of, or to bind said City and County, or any officer thereof.

SEC. 6. All orders and parts of orders of the Board of Supervisors of the City and County of San Francisco, conflicting with order Eight Hundred and Sixty-six (866), are hereby repealed, but such repeal shall not invalidate any of the proceedings instituted under the order of which Order Eight Hundred and Sixty-six (866) is amendatory, and such proceedings may be continued under the provisions of said Order Eight Hundred and Sixty-six (866). Whenever such proceedings have been completed, and the Committee on Outside Lands of said Board of Supervisors, or a majority of them, have executed and delivered a deed or deeds, the person or persons to whom such deed or deeds were executed, may obtain from the Mayor, at his or their own expense, a deed of the same land, executed by him and sealed with the corporate seal of the City and County of San Francisco, without further petition, proof, award or notice; and the Mayor is hereby authorized and empowered to execute such deeds. Any and all such deeds shall have the like force and effect as the conveyances mentioned in section five of this Act; *provided*, that if any grantee in any deed executed by such committee has heretofore sold or conveyed any land included in such deed, or his, her or their interest in such land, by writing recorded in the office of the City and County Recorder of the City and County of San Francisco, the deed executed by the Mayor, and sealed with the aforesaid corporate seal, shall be, as to the lands so sold or conveyed, for, and inure to the benefit of such purchaser or purchasers, grantee or grantees, and their heirs, and the deed executed by the Mayor shall expressly so state.

SEC. 7. Whereas, divers co-owners and tenants in common of certain tracts of land situate in the City and County of San Francisco, and within the limits described in Order Number Eight Hundred (800) of said Board of Supervisors, who are or claim to be in possession thereof as such owners and tenants in common, under and in accordance with the terms and provisions of said Order Number Eight Hundred (800), and as such alleged co-owners and tenants in common, have had said tracts of land delineated by metes and bounds, and as entireties, upon the map mentioned and provided for in said Order Number Eight Hundred (800), and have also severally paid their proportionate share of the taxes upon said tracts of land for the five fiscal years preceding the year beginning July first (1st), eighteen hundred and sixty-six (1866), and all subsequent taxes due thereon, and have filed with said Board their petition, claiming said land under and in accordance with the terms and provisions of said order and Order Number Seven Hundred and Forty-eight (748) of said Board; now, therefore, it shall be lawful for any such alleged co-owners or tenants in common of lands situate within the limits described by said Order Number Eight Hundred (800), or one or more thereof, or his or their successor or successors in interest, who shall have performed the acts and conditions aforesaid, to pay, as such co-owners or tenants in common, his or their proportionate share of the amount of any and all taxes or assessments now levied and due, or which may hereafter (at any time prior to the delivery of a deed from the City and County of San Francisco, for his or their undivided interest in said lands) be levied and become due upon the tract or tracts of land, wherein he or they hold as such co-owners or tenants in common; and to facilitate the payment of such proportionate shares, the Tax Collector is hereby authorized to divide into smaller parcels any tract of land claimed by co-owners, owners in severalty or tenants in common, and to apportion to each subdivision the ratable proportion, value considered, of the assessment made to the whole tract so divided, and after the payment of the apportioned assessment upon any one of such subdivisions, no valid objection shall be made by any party to the acts of the Tax Collector in respect to such division, and the apportioned assessment shall become as valid and binding upon the respective subdivisions to which they have been so apportioned, as if no division had been made by said Tax Collector.

SEC. 8. All of the acts and proceedings of the Tax Collector of the City and County of San Francisco, taken or done by him in pursuance of or under the authority of any order or resolution of the Board of Supervisors of said City and County, or in pursuance of or under the authority of any Act of the Legislature of the State of California, in reference to the collection of the taxes or assessments upon what are commonly designated as the outside lands of the said City and County, are hereby ratified and confirmed, and declared to be legal, valid and binding, both upon the lands embraced within the purview of any such Act of the Legislature of this State, or order or resolution of said Board of Supervisors of said City and County.

SEC. 9. And whereas, certain lands, known as outside lands of the City and County of San Francisco, have been advertised for sale by the Tax Collector of said City and County, for the non-payment of taxes or assessments levied thereon, known as the outside land tax, which sale has been postponed from time to time by said Tax Collector; and whereas, some of the parties claiming to be the owners of portions of said lands refuse or neglect to pay the taxes so levied as aforesaid, and have enjoined the said Tax Collector from proceeding with said sale; now, therefore, be it enacted, that all the pieces or parcels of land so advertised by the said Tax Collector as aforesaid, on which assessments heretofore levied have not been already paid, or shall not be paid to said Tax Collector within thirty days from and after the passage of this Act, shall be sold by said Tax Collector for gold coin of the United States, as hereinafter provided. Said sales may be adjourned from time to time by said Tax Collector, not exceeding in all sixty days, and may take place at such place in said City and County as the said Tax Collector may designate. The time during which any injunction may be in force restraining the said Tax Collector or other officer of said City and County from proceeding with said sale shall not be computed as any part of the periods limited and fixed within which he may perform the acts and duties herein defined, but shall be excluded therefrom. The said Tax Collector may retain in his custody so much of the proceeds arising from said sale as shall be necessary to liquidate and pay off the appraisements for reserved lands as heretofore made, pursuant to Order Number Eight Hundred, and all such proper and necessary costs as he may be at in conducting said sale and the collection of such assessments, and the overplus thereof he shall pay over to the Treasurer of the said City and County; and said Treasurer shall carry the amount so paid to him to the credit of the General Fund of said City and County. The amount so retained by the said Tax Collector shall be paid over by him to the parties entitled thereto under section eleven of Order Number Eight Hundred, in discharge of the appraisements for reserved lands; and within thirty days from and after he shall have received a sum from assessments equal to the total amount of appraisements for reserved lands, over and above the expenses and costs of making collections, he shall settle and pay off in full the appraisements made as aforesaid; *provided, however,* when there are conflicting claimants for particular appraisements, said Tax Collector shall not be obliged to make payment in such cases until such conflicting claims shall be determined, amicably or otherwise; and the said Tax Collector is hereby authorized, from time to time, to make make distribution on account of said appraisements for reserved lands, pro rata, as often as he shall have on hand fifty per cent. or less thereof.

SEC. 10.   Said Tax Collector shall issue to each successful purchaser a receipt, in duplicate, for the amount bid and paid by him, which receipt shall also contain a brief description of the premises sold, and upon its face entitle the bidder, or his assigns, to a deed of conveyance of the premises therein described, at the expiration of twelve months from the date of the sale, unless there shall be a redemption of the premises as hereinafter provided.

SEC. 11.   Said lands shall be sold subject to redemption, and such redemption may be made at any time within twelve months from the date of sale, upon paying to the said Tax Collector the amount bid therefor, together with twenty-five per cent. thereon and in addition thereto; and the party redeeming shall also pay such expenses of advertising and other expenses as the said Tax Collector may have incurred in and about the particular tract from the sale of which redemption is sought to be effected; *provided,* that all lands sold for assessment prior to the passage of this Act shall have the same right of redemption as provided for in section eleven of this Act.

SEC. 12.   The Tax Collector, after the expiration of twelve months from the date of sale, in which there has been no redemption, shall make a conveyance of the premises sold to the purchaser thereof, or his assigns; and where there has been a redemption, he may make conveyance thereof to the redemptioner. In cases of redemption, the Tax Collector shall pay over to the holders of receipts the amount bid, together with the sum paid by the redemptioner, in addition to the bid.

SEC. 13. This Act shall take effect and be in force from and after its passage.

SUPPLEMENT XLV.

1869-70, 528.

An Act to establish a Municipal Criminal Court in the City and County of San Francisco.

[Approved March 31, 1870.]

The People of the State of California, represented in Senate and Assembly, do enact as follows:

SECTIONS 1 to 8. *Superseded by the Superior Court.*

SEC. 9. The Sheriff of the City and County of San Francisco shall be the Sheriff of the said Municipal Criminal Court, and shall execute, either in person or by deputy, such of the process of said Court as may be required to be executed by a Sheriff, and shall be amenable to said Court by proceedings, as for contempt, on his failure to execute such process. And said Sheriff is hereby authorized to appoint a deputy, in addition to those now appointed by him, who shall act as Bailiff or Deputy Sheriff of said Court, and who shall receive a salary of one hundred and fifty dollars per month, to be paid in the same manner as the salaries of the other deputies of said Sheriff are paid.

SECS. 10 to 15. [*Obsolete.*]

SEC. 16. The District Attorney in and for the said City and County may, by written certificate, signed by himself, appoint an Assistant District Attorney, and at his pleasure remove him; who, during the time he is acting as such assistant, shall be entitled to receive a salary of three hundred dollars a month, payable as the salary of the District Attorney is now made payable by the law. It shall be the duty of such Assistant District Attorney to assist the District Attorney in the performance of any official duty enjoined upon the latter by law, and to do and perform such other duties in the prosecution of criminal actions in the Court herein established, in any of the Courts of said City and County, as the said District Attorney may order or direct.

Sec. 17.   This Act shall take effect and be in force in thirty days after its passage.

SUPPLEMENT XLVI.

1869-70, 579.

An Act to regulate the distribution of the Police Fund of the City and County of San Francisco.

[Approved April 1, 1870.]

The People of the State of California, represented in Senate and Assembly, do enact as follows :

SECTION 1.   One-half of all the fines, penalties and forfeitures imposed for offences committed within the said City and County, and now paid into the treasury thereof as a part of the Police Fund, by the Clerk of the Police Judge's Court, shall be paid to the Treasurer of the San Francisco Benevolent Association; *provided*, that such payment shall not diminish the amount now authorized by law to be paid out of said fines, penalties and forfeitures to other associations, or to the School Fund of said City and County; and *provided, further*, that the sum so paid to the Treasurer of the San Francisco Benevolent Association under the provisions of this Act shall not in any event exceed the sum of five thousand dollars per annum.

SEC. 2.   All laws and parts of laws inconsistent herewith are hereby repealed, so far as they relate to said Police Fund.

SEC. 3.   This Act shall take effect from and after its passage.

SUPPLEMENT XLVII.

1869-70, 585.

An Act relating to the Home of the Inebriate of San Francisco and to prescribe the powers and duties of the Board of Managers and the officers thereof.

[Approved April 1, 1870.]

The People of the State of California, represented in Senate and Assembly, do enact as follows:

SECTION 1.   The Home for the care of the Inebriate of San Francisco shall always be kept open for the reception and care of inebriates, both male and female, of every nationality and sect, free of charge for their support, care or medical attendance while they necessarily remain therein; *provided*, the Superintendent of said home may require, on the admission of any such person, a permit from at least one of the Board of Managers of said home, unless such person is committed to said home as provided in the next section of this Act.

SEC. 2. Any Police Judge or magistrate of the City and County of San Francisco is hereby empowered to commit any person whom he shall convict of habitual intemperance to said home, for a term not exceeding six months; *provided*, the Board of Managers of said home may release, by a two-third vote of said Board of Managers, any person so convicted or otherwise placed in said home before his or her sentence shall expire.*

SEC. 3. The said Board of Managers are hereby empowered to receive and to detain in said home, under such restrictions and discipline as they shall deem proper, such persons as may be thereto committed or otherwise placed in said home; *provided*, any Court of competent jurisdiction may inquire, by writ of habeas corpus, into such detention or discipline, and release any person therefrom.

SEC. 4. The said Board of Managers shall have power to make by-laws and rules for the government of its body, officers and employees; to elect, discharge and pay such officers and employees as may be necessary to manage and carry on said home; and to prescribe rules and regulations for the government and management of the inmates and officers of said home.

SEC. 5. The Board of Managers of said home shall elect from their number a President, Vice-President, Treasurer and Secretary, and prescribe their respective duties and responsibilities.

SEC. 6. Any person having been an officer of said Board, or of said home, or an employee or inmate thereof, who shall, after his or her term of office ceases, or employment expires, or has been discharged, retains in his or her possession or control any of the property of said home, or the books or the papers of said Board, or seal thereof, shall be guilty of a misdemeanor, and upon conviction thereof shall be fined not less than five dollars and not to exceed five hundred dollars, or imprisonment in the County Jail not to exceed six months, or both such fine and imprisonment.

SEC. 7. The title to the lot set apart by the Board of Supervisors of San Francisco, or a committee of said Board, to and for the corporation known as the "Home for the Care of the Inebriate," is hereby confirmed to said coporation; and the title of said City and County in and to said lot is vested in said corporation forever.

SEC. 8. All Acts and parts of Acts in conflict with the provisions of this Act are hereby repealed.

---

*Is this power not repealed by Act VII of the Constitution of 1879?

Sec. 9. This Act shall take effect immediately after its passage. [*See also Act of Mar.* 17, 1876; 1876, 325; *Supplement*].

SUPPLEMENT XLVIII.

1869-70, 653.

An Act further to define the powers and duties of the Sheriff of the City and County of San Francisco.

[Approved April 2, 1870.]

The People of the State of California, represented in Senate and Assembly, do enact as follows:

Section 1. The Sheriff of the City and County of San Francisco is authorized and empowered to exact in advance, and to receive any and all fees that are now allowed by law for services under and by virtue of any process, order or proceeding issued or had in the Justices' Court of the City and County of San Francisco, and all such fees shall be accounted for by said Sheriff, and paid by him to the Treasurer of said City and County, as now provided by law for other fees allowed to the Sheriff of said City and County.

Sec. 2. It shall not be lawful for the Clerk of said Justices' Court to demand or receive any fees for the service of any process or order, nor for any service to be rendered by said Sheriff.

Sec. 3. All Acts or parts of Acts, so far as the same are in conflict with the provisions of this Act, are hereby repealed.

Sec. 4. This Act shall take effect immediately after its passage.

SUPPLEMENT XLIX.

1869-70, 674.

An Act to define the powers of Justices of the Peace within the City County of San Francisco in criminal cases.

[Approved April 2, 1870.]

The People of the State of California, represented in Senate and Assembly, do enact as follows:

Section 1. The Justices of the Peace within the limits of the City and

County of San Francisco shall have power and it shall be lawful for them to hear complaints and issue warrants in all criminal cases, and transfer the same to the Police Court of said City and County for trial or examination, by an indorsement of said transfer upon the warrant ; but nothing in this Act shall be so construed as to deny to the said Police Court of said City and County the power to try and decide certain criminal cases as now provided by law.

SEC. 2. All Acts or parts of Acts, so far as they are in conflict with this Act, are repealed.

SUPPLEMENT L.

1869-70, 802.

An Act to provide for the improvement of public parks in the City of San Francisco.

[Approved April 4, 1870.]

The People of the State of California, represented in Senate and Assembly, do enact as follows :

SECTION 1. The lands designated upon a map of the outside lands of the City and County of San Francisco, made in pursuance of Order Number Eight Hundred, by the word " Park," to wit: Extending from Stanyan street on the east to the Pacific Ocean, is hereby designated, and shall be known as the " Golden Gate Park;" and the other parcel of land fronting on Haight street, and also marked " Park," is hereby designated and shall be known as " Buena Vista Park ; " and also the land marked on said map " Avenue," extending from Baker street westward until it crosses Stanyan street, shall be and remain public parks of said City and County, and shall be improved as such by the Commissioners hereinafter mentioned and their successors.

SEC. 2. The said parks and avenues shall be under the exclusive control and management of a Board of three Commissioners, who are hereby designated as " Park Commissioners."* Two members shall constitute a quorum for the transaction of business; but no money shall be expended or contract entered into authorizing the expenditure of money without the approval of the Mayor of said City and a majority of said Board.

SEC. 3. The Governor of the State of California is hereby authorized and

---

* Jurisdiction extended, by Act of April 1, 1878, to Point Lobos road; Act of 1878, 967.

directed, within thirty days after the passage of this Act, to appoint three Commissioners, who shall hold their offices for four years, and who shall receive no compensation for their services. In case of a vacancy, the same shall be filled by the remaining members of the Board for the residue of the term then vacant; and all vacancies occasioned by expiration of terms of office, or neglect or incapacity of qualification, shall be filled by the Governor aforesaid. Each of said Commissioners shall be a freeholder and resident of said City and County.

SEC. 4. The said Board shall have the full and exclusive power to govern, manage and direct the said parks and avenues; to lay out, regulate and improve the same; to pass ordinances for the regulation and government of the same; to appoint such engineers, surveyors, clerks and other officers, as may be necessary; to prescribe and define their respective duties and authority;. to fix the amount of their compensation, and to have the management of the funds provided for the improvement thereof.

SEC. 5. It shall be a felony for any Commissioner, directly or indirectly, to be interested in any contract or work of any kind whatever connected with either of said parks or avenue; and it shall be the duty of any Commissioner or other person who may have any knowledge or information of the violation of this provision, forthwith to report the same to the Governor, who shall hear the allegations in regard thereto; and if, after such hearing, he shall be satisfied of the truth thereof, he shall immediately remove such Commissioner thus offending. The Governor shall issue a commission to each of the Commissioners appointed by him, who shall, within twenty days after the receipt thereof, take and subscribe the oath of office prescribed by law.

SEC. 6. The said Board shall semi-annually, and on the second Monday in January in each year, make to the Legislature of the State, and to the Board of Supervisors of said City and County annually, and on the second Monday of January in each year, a full report of their proceedings and a detailed statement of all their receipts and expenditures.

SEC. 7. It shall be lawful for the said Commissioners to let any portion of said grounds from time to time, until the same shall be required for the improvement of said parks; but no lease shall extend beyond three years from the date thereof. All moneys realized thereby shall be devoted to the improvement of said parks and avenue.

SEC. 8. During the year next ensuing their appointment, the said Commissioners may expend upon said parks and avenue the sum of one hundred thousand dollars and no more ; and during the second year the sum of seventy-five thousand dollars ; and annually thereafter, for the next three years, the sum of fifty thousand dollars per annum.

SEC. 9. The said Commissioners shall, from time to time, create and issue bonds, which shall be countersigned by the Mayor of said City and County, with the corporate seal affixed, in sums of not less than three hundred dollars nor more than one thousand dollars, which bonds shall not exceed in the aggregate the sum of two hundred and twenty-five thousand dollars, and shall be payable twenty-five years from their date, and may sell or dispose of the same at not less than ninety per cent. of their par value, to create a fund to be called " Park Improvement Fund." Such bond, and the interest thereon, shall be paid in gold coin. Said interest shall be paid semi-annually at the office of the Treasurer of said City and County, and said bonds shall bear interest at a rate not exceeding six per cent per annum. The said parks and avenues are hereby pledged as security for the redemption of said bonds. Any balance of the appropriations made for any one year may be expended in any succeding year. It shall be lawful for the holder or holders of any bond or bonds heretofore issued under the provisions of the Act to which this Act is amendatory and supplemental, to surrender such bond or bonds, with the unpaid coupons thereon, to the Auditor of said City and County; and upon such surrender being made, bonds of like denominations to those surrendered, payable as herein provided, with coupons attached bearing interest at six per cent per annum, shall be issued and delivered to the person or persons making the surrender aforesaid; and the Auditor shall, in the presence of the Mayor, cancel all bonds and coupons so surrendered in exchange for others as herein provided. [*Amended March* 30, 1872 ; 1871-2, 706.]

SEC. 10. The Park Commissioners shall sell the bonds from time to time, as the money arising therefrom shall be needed for the prosecution of improvements on said parks, and all moneys arising from sales of bonds shall be paid into the Treasury of the City and County to the credit of a fund to be known as the "Park Improvement Fund," and shall only be drawn therefrom upon the order of said Park Commissioners, or a majority of them, audited by the Auditor of said City and County. [*Amended March* 30, 1872; 1871-2, 706.]

SEC. 11. For the payment of the interest of the said bonds, the Board of Supervisors of said City and County shall order and cause to be raised, by tax on the estate, real and personal, subject to taxation according to law, within said City and County, and to be collected in addition to the ordinary taxes, yearly and every year, sufficient money to pay the interest annually accruing on the bonds then issued.

SEC. 12. The moneys raised by sales of such bonds shall be deposited with some one or more of the savings or banking institutions in said City and County, and such institution, bank or banks, with which the same may be deposited, shall allow interest upon such deposits, as may be agreed upon with said Board, and shall open and keep an account with said Board. No moneys shall be drawn from said fund except upon a warrant signed by a majority of the Commissioners and the Mayor.

SEC. 13. It shall be lawful for said Board of Commissioners to pass such ordinances as they may deem necessary for the regulation, use and government of said parks and avenue, not inconsistent with the laws of the State of California. Said ordinances shall, within five days after their passage, be published for ten days, Sundays excepted, in a daily newspaper published in said City and County, to be selected by said Commissioners.

SEC. 14. All persons offending against such ordinances shall be deemed guilty of a misdemeanor, and be punished on conviction in the Police Court of said City and County.

SEC. 15. This Act shall take effect immediately.

[*The following is the remaining portion of the Act of March* 30, 1872; 1871-2, 706; *besides that incorporated in the foregoing Act:*]

SEC. 3. In order to render said avenues and parks of easy access to the citizens of San Francisco, the said Commissioners are hereby authorized and empowered to draw from the said " Park Improvement Fund " not exceeding the sum of twenty thousand dollars, and expend the same on such of the public streets of the said City leading to said avenues and parks as in the judgment of said Commissioners shall best subserve the public convenience; but the said Commissioners shall not expend any moneys as in this section contemplated unless the property holders along the line of the streets thus designated and selected by the Commissioners shall unite with the said Commissioners and contribute an amount equal to that proposed to be expended by the Commissioners, and place the same in the said " The Park Improvement Fund," the whole to be laid out under the direction and supervision of the said Commissioners.

SEC. 4. This Act shall take effect from and after its passage.   ●

SUPPLEMENT LI.

1871-2, 58.

An Act in relation to the office of the County Clerk of the City and County of San Francisco.

[Approved February 2, 1872.]

The People of the State of California, represented in Senate and Assembly, do enact as follows:

SECTION 1. The County Clerk of the City and County of San Francisco shall keep open his office, and all offices attached to the various Courts of which he is the Clerk, within said City and County, for the transaction of business, every day in the year, except Sunday, New Year's Day, Twenty-second of February, Fourth of July, Thanksgiving, Christmas Day, and on the days on which the general and the special judicial elections are held, from nine o'clock in the forenoon to the hour of four o'clock in the afternoon.

SEC. 2. He shall take charge of and safely keep, or dispose of according to law, all books, papers, and records which are or may be filed or deposited in his office, and of all the Courts of which he is Clerk; and he shall not allow any paper, files, or records to leave his custody except when required by the Judges of the Courts; to be used by them, or either of them.

SEC. 3. No Judge or other officer of any Court shall make any order for the delivery by the County Clerk of said City and County of any paper, files, or records in his custody; nor shall the Courts or Judges thereof have any power to make orders for the delivery of any certificate of incorporation, bonds, or other papers filed with the said County Clerk. When any of said papers are required for evidence in any of the Courts within said County the County Clerk or his deputies shall produce the same, under subpœna or order of the Court, or furnish certified copies of the same, on application, on payment to said Clerk for said copies, at the rate of ten cents per folio for each one hundred words, which shall be allowed said Clerk, to be used and disbursed by him for copying as aforesaid.

SEC. 4. Neither the County Clerk nor any of his deputies shall be required to attend as witnesses, in their official capacities, outside of the City and County of San Francisco, unless his expenses be paid, at the rate of ten cents per mile to and from the place he may be required, and five dollars per day for each day's attendance.

SEC. 5. All Acts and parts of Acts so far as they conflict with this Act, are hereby repealed.

SEC. 6. This Act shall take effect immediately.

SUPPLEMENT LII.

1871-2, 76.

An Act concerning the office of County Clerk in and for the City and County of San Francisco.

[Approved February 5, 1872.]

The People of the State of California, represented in Senate and Assembly, do enact as follows:

SECTION 1. The County Clerk of the City and County of San Francisco may appoint Deputies as follows: For the District Court of the Fourth Ju-

9

dicial District, in and for said City and County, one Register Clerk, who shall receive a salary of one hundred and seventy-five ($175) dollars per month; one Court Room Clerk, who shall receive a salary of one hundred and seventy-five ($175) dollars per month, and two Assistant Register Clerks, who shall receive a salary of one hundred and fifty ($150) dollars per month each. For the District Court of the Twelfth Judicial District, in and for said City and County, one Register Clerk, who shall receive a salary of one hundred and seventy-five ($175) dollars per month; one Court Room Clerk, who shall receive a salary of one hundred and seventy-five ($175) dollars per month, and two Assistant Register Clerks, who shall receive a salary of one hundred and fifty ($150) dollars per month each. For the District Court of the Fifteenth Judicial District, in and for said City and County, one Register Clerk, who shall receive a salary of one hundred and seventy-five ($175) dollars per month; one Court Room Clerk, who shall receive a salary of one hundred and seventy-five ($175) dollars per month, and two Assistant Register Clerks, who shall receive a salary of one hundred and fifty ($150) dollars per month each. For Probate Court, in and for said City and County, one Court Room Clerk, who shall receive a salary of one hundred and seventy-five ($175) dollars per month; one Register Clerk and two Record Clerks, who shall receive a salary of one hundred and fifty ($150) dollars per month each. For County Court, in and for said City and County, one Court Room Clerk, who shall receive a salary of one hundred and seventy-five ($175) dollars per month; one Register Clerk and one Assistant Register Clerk, who shall receive a salary of one hundred and fifty ($150) dollars per month each. For Municipal Court, in and for said City and County, one Court Room Clerk, who shall receive a salary of one hundred and seventy-five dollars per month; one Register Clerk, who shall receive a salary of one hundred and fifty ($150) dollars per month; *provided*, that the Deputies appointed by virtue of this Act shall be in lieu of all those heretofore authorized to be appointed by said County Clerk, and all Acts or parts of Acts conflicting with this Act, or providing for the appointment of other Deputies not named in this Act, are hereby repealed.

SEC. 2. The salaries provided for in section one of this Act shall be audited and paid in the same manner as the salaries of Deputy Clerks in said City and County of San Francisco have been audited and paid heretofore.

SEC. 3. The County Clerk of said City and County is hereby authorized to employ as many Copyists (not to exceed three in number) as may be necessary to perform the duties of his office, who shall severally be paid such reasonable compensation as their services may be worth, not to exceed six cents a folio of one hundred words, for the matter copied or recorded by them respectively; *provided*, the amount paid to such copyists in any one month shall not exceed three hundred ($300) dollars.

SEC. 4. The County Clerk shall certify monthly, on the demands of said Copyists, the number of folios copied by each one of said Copyists, and such certificate of said Clerk shall be conclusive and sufficient evidence to authorize and require the Auditor of said City and County to audit severally the accounts of said Copyists, monthly, and the payment of such demands by the County Treasurer, out of the Special Fee Fund, as is provided for the payment of other officers of said City and County.

SEC. 5. The following Acts and parts of Acts are hereby repealed: An Act entitled "An Act concerning the office of the County Clerk of the City and County of San Francisco," approved May fifteenth, eighteen hundred and sixty-two; an Act entitled "An Act concerning the office of County Clerk of the City and County of San Francisco," approved March second, eighteen hundred and sixty-four; an Act entitled "An Act concerning the office of County Clerk of the City and County of San Francisco," approved February twentieth, eighteen hundred and sixty-eight; an Act entitled "An Act concerning the office of County Clerk of the City and County of San Francisco," approved March thirty-first, eighteen hundred and seventy.

SEC. 6. This Act shall take effect immediately.

[*This Act is continued in force by Act of Feb.* 13, 1880; 1880, 13, *and amended by Act of April* 2, 1880; 1880, 104.]

SUPPLEMENT LIII.

1871-2, 232.

An Act supplementary to an Act entitled "An Act providing for an Attorney and Counselor in and for the City and County of San Francisco," approved March twenty-fifth, eighteen hundred and sixty-two.

[Approved March 4, 1872.]

The People of the State of California, represented in Senate and Assembly, do enact as follows:

SECTION 1. The City and County Attorney of the City and County of San Francisco shall keep in his office well bound books of registry, in which shall be entered and made a register of all actions in which said City and County Attorney may appear. Each outgoing City and County Attorney shall deliver such books of registry and all other property of said City and County in his possession to his successor in office, who shall give him duplicate receipts therefor, one to be filed in the office of the Auditor of said City and County and one to be retained by such outgoing officer. The Board of Supervisors of said City and County are hereby empowered and required to provide complete sets of the statutes of this State and of the reports of the Supreme Court of this State, for use in the office of the City and County Attorney, and the Auditor of said City and County is hereby required to audit the claims therefor, and the Treasurer of said City and County to pay the same out of the General Fund of said City and County. There shall be two Clerks in the office of said City and County Attorney, one of whom shall receive a salary of one hundred and fifty dollars per month and the other a salary of seventy-five dollars per month, and the Board of Supervisors of said City and County are hereby authorized and required to allow and order the said salaries paid monthly out of the General Fund.

SEC. 2. The Clerks allowed by this Act shall be in lieu of all others allowed by law to the City and County Attorney, and no other persons shall receive pay from the Treasurer of the City and County for services rendered to said City and County Attorney.

SEC. 3. All Acts or parts of Acts conflicting with this Act are hereby repealed.

SUPPLEMENT LIV.

1871–2, 301.

An Act creating the Nineteenth and Twentieth Judicial Districts, and defining the Third, Fourth, Twelfth and Fifteenth Judicial Districts.

[Approved March 8, 1872.]

The People of the State of California, represented in Senate and Assembly, do enact as follows:

SECTIONS 1 to 9, *inclusive.* [*Obsolete.*]

SEC. 10. The County Clerk of the City and County of San Francisco shall be *ex-officio* Clerk of the District Court of the Third Judicial District in and for said City and County, and also *ex-officio* Clerk of the District Court of the Nineteenth Judicial District, and is hereby authorized to appoint one Register Clerk and one Court-room Clerk for each of said Courts, each of whom shall receive a salary of one hundred and seventy-five dollars per month; also, one additional Copying Clerk,* who shall receive a salary of one hundred and fifty dollars per month. Such salaries shall be paid in the same manner as the salaries of other Deputies of said County Clerk.

SEC. 11.   The Sheriff of said City and County of San Francisco is hereby authorized to appoint two Deputies, in addition to those now appointed by him, who shall act as Bailiffs or Deputy Sheriffs of said Third and Nineteenth District Courts in and for the City and County of San Francisco, who shall each receive a salary of one hundred and fifty dollars per month, to be paid in the same manner as other Deputies of said Sheriff are paid.

[*Secs.* 12 *and* 13 *relate to the Twentieth Judicial District exclusively.*]

SEC. 14.   [*Obsolete.*]

SEC. 15.   [*Obsolete.*]

SEC. 16.   This Act shall take effect immediately.

—

SUPPLEMENT LV.

1871-2, 403.

An Act in Relation to Coroners in the City and County of San Francisco.

[Approved March 16, 1872.]

The People of the State of California, represented in Senate and Assembly, do enact as follows :

SECTION 1.   Every person elected or appointed to the office of Coroner, before he shall enter upon the duties of such office, shall take the constitutional oath of office, and give an official bond in the sum of five hundred dollars.

SEC. 2.   The duties of Coroner shall be: First, to hold inquests upon the bodies of persons slain, or who shall have committed suicide, or been found dead under such circumstances as to lead to a suspicion of crime committed, within the county in which such Coroner resides; second, to issue process for the arrest of one charged upon inquest with murder or manslaughter; to hold nquest on the body of every prisoner who dies in jail; and it shall be the duty of the Jailor, whenever a prisoner dies in his custody, to send for the Coroner who has jurisdiction, who shall hold inquest upon the body of such prisoner.   The duties of Coroners upon inquests shall not be delegated.

---

* Modified as to copying clerks by Act of April 2, 1880; 1880, 104.

SEC. 3. Whenever any Coroner shall receive notice that any person has been slain, or has committed suicide, or has died suddenly, or has been found dead under circumstances such as to require an inquisition, it shall be his duty to go to the place where such person shall be, or if the body shall have been interred, shall cause it to be disinterred, and shall forthwith summon not less than nine or more than fifteen persons to serve as jurors, to appear before him forthwith, at such place as he shall appoint, and make inquisition concerning such death. He shall summon none but persons duly qualified by law to serve as jurors, and no such person shall be exempt, except at the discretion of the Coroner. No person shall be summoned who is related to the deceased, or to any person who may be suspected or charged with the killing ; nor shall any one be summoned who is known to be prejudiced for or against him, but the jurors who are selected and appear shall not be challenged by any party. [*Amended, March 23, 1876; 1875-6, 397.*]

SEC. 4. Every person summoned as a juror who shall fail to appear without having a reasonable excuse, shall forfeit a sum not exceeding the sum of two hundred dollars, to be recovered by the Coroner, in the name of the people of the State, before any Justice of the Peace in the proper township, and when collected to be paid into the County Treasury for the use of the county.

SEC. 5. When six or more of the jurors attend they shall be sworn by the Coroner and charged by him to inquire how and in what manner and when and where such person came to his death, and who such person was, and into all the circumstances attending such death, and to make a true inquisition according to the evidence offered to them or arising from the inspection of the body.

SEC. 6. There shall be but one inquest upon a body, unless that taken be set aside by the Court ; and there shall be but one inquest held upon several bodies of persons who were killed by the same cause and who died at the same time. Whenever it shall appear that an error in the identity of the body has been made by the jury, it shall be discretionary with the Coroner to call another inquest upon the body without reference to the Court, and a memorandum of the error shall be entered upon the erroneous inquisition.

SEC. 7. After the jury has been sworn and charged by the Coroner, they shall go together with the Coroner to view and examine the body of the deceased person. They shall not proceed upon the inquest until they have so viewed the body. After the jury have viewed the body they may retire to any convenient place to hear the testimony of witnesses and deliberate upon their verdict. For this end the Coroner may adjourn the inquest from time to time, as may be necessary.

SEC. 8. The Coroner may issue subpoenas for witnesses, returnable forthwith or at such time and place as he may appoint therein, which may be served by any competent person by reading the same to the witness or informing him or her of the contents thereof, and such witness shall not be entitled to any fee for attendance. Every person served with such subpœna shall be liable to the same penalties for disobedience thereto, and his attendance may be enforced in like manner as in case of subpœnas issued by a Justice of the Peace.

SEC. 9. The Coroner shall summon and examine as witnesses every person who, in his opinion or that of the jury, has any knowledge of the facts, and he may summon a surgeon or physician to inspect the body and to give a professional opinion as to the cause of death; and if it shall be necessary, the Coroner may cause a post mortem examination or chemical analysis to be made, and the expense of such examination or analysis shall be a county charge, to be fixed by the Board of Supervisors.

SEC. 10. Witnesses produced shall be sworn by the Coroner, and the whole of the testimony shall be reduced to writing by the Coroner, or under his direction, and signed by the witnesses in the presence of the jury, and each deposition shall have a jurat attached. The jury, after hearing all the testimony offered before them, shall retire as jurors in other cases and deliberate upon their verdict, suffering no one, not even the Coroner, to mingle with them in their deliberations; but they may, as in the case of jurors in the Courts of law, take the opinion of the Coroner upon any question of law that may arise upon the investigation.

SEC. 11. The Coroner may call upon the District Attorney to assist him in the examination of witnesses, and the jurors may put any proper question to the witness, but the party suspected or charged with the crime shall have no right to produce witnesses on the inquest, or to cross-examine those produced on behalf of the people by himself or counsel; nor shall it be necessary that he be present during the examination. But it shall be the duty of the Coroner to examine any witness who he may have reason to believe may know anything concerning the matter pertinent to the inquiry, and to put to any witness any proper and pertinent question that such person may desire. Such party suspected or charged, however, may be attended by counsel on the inquest to advise with him as to his rights in answering any question that may be put to him when under examination. If the party accused of the crime be present at the inquest, and is then charged with the crime, or the testimony tends to criminate him, and he is called upon by the Coroner to testify, it is the duty of the Coroner first to inform the accused that he is at liberty to refuse to answer any question that he may put to him, otherwise his answer on such examination cannot be read in evidence against him when on trial for the offense. But if such person is not under arrest or charged with the crime, his answer may be given in evidence against him on his subsequent trial for the crime charged, though the Coroner may not have so advised him of his rights. The jury must hear all the evidence offered before them, whether it be in favor of or against any party suspected of the killing.

SEC. 12. Upon the investigation the Coroner's jury shall not be limited in their inquiry like a jury upon the trial of one charged with the crime; their duty shall be to determine if a crime has or has not been committed; and if a crime has been committed, who perpetrated or caused the same to be perpetrated, and all the circumstances attending it; and any proper testimony tending in any degree to throw light upon the subject may be properly given. Matters of opinion, except of professional witnesses, or hearsay evidence, shall not be permitted.

SEC. 13. When the jury shall have agreed upon a verdict they shall reduce their inquisition to writing, which writing shall show before what Coroner the same was taken, and that the same was taken upon the oath of good and lawful men of the county, who were first duly sworn; and it must also show by whom and when the same was executed. They shall also find and certify how or in what manner and when and where the person so dead came to his death, and all the circumstances attending such death; and if a crime has been committed in the case, who were guilty thereof, either as principal or accessory, and in what manner. The jury shall not be required to find who were accessories after the fact—only those before the fact. If the person who is found dead is unknown, or the person who caused the death is unknown, the jury shall so find; and they shall find, if the fact so appears before them, whether the killing was accidental or suicide, murder or manslaughter, excusable or justifiable homicide; and if the manner of the death is unknown, they shall so state. Such inquisitions shall be signed by such jurors, and the Coroner shall certify the fact that the inquest was held, and indorse under the verdict his approval or non-approval of the same.

SEC. 14. It shall not be necessary that the jury should be kept together until they have agreed upon a verdict. If there shall appear any irreconcilable opinion as to any material fact concerning which they are to make inquest, the jurors agreeing may find accordingly, and two or more inquisitions may be presented.

SEC. 15. If the jury find that any murder or manslaughter has been committed, the Coroner shall bind over the witnesses against the accused to appear and testify at the next Court or Grand Jury, or before any Court at which an indictment for such offense can be found and triable that shall be held in the county, and obey all orders of said Court in the premises. Such recognizance shall be in writing, and shall be subscribed by the parties to be bound thereby. Said recognizances shall be made payable to the people of the State of California. The amount of the same shall be fixed by the Coroner, County Judge,* or by the District Attorney, and approved by the County Judge* or any of the Judges of a Court of record; and in case of their refusal to sign such recognizance, the Coroner shall have power to commit such witness as in the case of examination of criminals by a magistrate.

---

* Superseded by the Superior Court Act of April 3, 1880; 1880, 115.

Sec. 16. The testimony of all witnesses examined before a Coroner's jury, together with the inquisition of the jury, and all recognizances taken by such Coroner, shall be returned by him forthwith to the County Clerk of his County.

Sec. 17. The Coroner shall have the same power on all investigations or inquests as are allowed by law to Judges of Courts of record in this State to preserve order in the matter of investigations before him; and for any disrespect shown towards him or contempt of his authority in his investigations by any juror, witness, or other persons, he shall have power to issue an order for the arrest of said person or persons, and forthwith to have said person or persons brought before the Police Judge or County Judge* of his county, to be punished according to law.

Sec. 18. Any juror, witness or other person summoned as juror, witness or any other person who may be in attendance on any official investigation who shall use any disrespectful language toward said Coroner, or behave disrespectfully towards said Coroner in his presence, shall be declared guilty of contempt, and shall be liable to pay a fine not to exceed one hundred dollars, or be imprisoned in the County Jail of said County not to exceed sixty days ; said imprisonment to be enforced by any of the magistrates named in the preceding sections, upon the warrant of the Coroner, as provided for in the last section.

Sec. 19. If the Coroner's jury find that any murder or manslaughter has been committed, and the person charged with such offense be not in custody, the Coroner shall have power to issue process for the arrest of the person charged. The warrant of arrest must be under the hand of the Coroner, and must recite the finding of the jury upon the inquest, and be directed to the Sheriff, or to any Constable, Marshal, or Policeman of the County, and commanding the officer to whom it shall be directed forthwith to take the person accused of having committed such offense, and to bring him before a committing magistrate, to be dealt with according to law. The warrant of the Coroner shall be served in the same manner and in the same places as criminal process issued by a Justice of the Peace in any County of the State, without indorsement by a magistrate of such County.

Sec. 20. When the inquest shall be held by the Coroner, and there shall be no friends to take charge of the body of the deceased, it shall be the duty of the Coroner, after the same has been viewed by him and the jury, to see that it is properly buried, and for that purpose, he shall immediately give notice to the person or firm having the contract for the burial of the indigent dead, for the burial of the body, and it shall be buried by him, under the provisions of said contract. [Amended, March 30, 1874; 1873-4, 908.]

---

* Superseded by the Superior Court Act of April 3, 1880; 1880, 115.

SEC. 21.   It shall be the duty of the Coroner to take charge of all money and other valuable things which may be found with or upon the bodies of persons on whom inquests shall be held, when there is no other persons legally entitled to take charge of the same; and he shall forthwith make out and enter in a book to be kept in his office, open to public inspection, a full a[n]d complete inventory of all money, and every article or thing of value found with or upon said deceased, and he shall also make an entry in said book, of any note or memorandum found upon said deceased, that may tend, in any way, in the future, to identify said person.   Said Coroner shall, within thirty *days after the holding of such inquest, deliver over to the Treasurer of said City and County, all such money or valuable things which have not been claimed by legal representatives of the deceased or the Public Administrator. Said Coroner shall also keep in his office another book, open to public inspection, in which he shall enter a full description of every article and thing, and all money found with or upon the bodies of deceased persons, or belonging to said deceased persons, that may come into his possession, before he delivers up, or permits the same to go out of his possession; and no money, article, thing, or property of any nature or kind, shall be delivered to any person, until the same shall have been entered in such book as aforesaid, and signed in the presence of said Coroner, by the person receiving the same.   [*Amended, March* 30, 1874; 1873-4, 908.]

SEC. 22.   For a failure on the part of the Coroner to perform such duty required by the last section, or any of the duties required by this Act, he shall be deemed guilty of a misdemeanor, and on conviction thereof, shall be punished by a fine not exceeding five thousand dollars, or imprisonment in the County Jail not to exceed one year, and shall be liable on his official bond for any and all moneys, chattels, and property which shall be found on said deceased, and which shall or may come into his possession belonging to said deceased; the same to be recovered in the name of any party who may be entitled to recover the same in any Court having jurisdiction thereof.

SEC. 23.   Upon the delivery of money so found to the Treasurer, he shall place it to the credit of the County.   If other property, and perishable in its nature, he shall, within thirty days, sell the same at public auction, upon reasonable public notice, and shall in like manner place the proceeds to the credit of the County.   Other property shall only be sold upon the order of the County Judge.   If the said money or property in the treasury be demanded within six years by the legal representatives of the deceased, the Treasurer shall, upon legal showing, after deducting the fees and expenses of the Coroner and of the County in relation to the matter, pay the balance thereof to such legal representative.

SEC. 24.   Before auditing and allowing the accounts of the Coroner, the Supervisors of the County shall require a statement from him, in writing,

---

containing an inventory of all money and other valuables found with or upon all persons upon whom inquests shall have been held, and the manner in which the same has been disposed of, verified by the oath or affirmation of the Coroner making the same that such statement is in all respects just and true, and that the money and other articles mentioned therein have been delivered to the Treasurer of the County, or to the legal representatives of such person or persons.

SEC. 25. The Coroner shall perform the duties of Sheriff in all cases when the Sheriff is interested or otherwise incapacitated from serving. Whenever the Coroner acts as Sheriff he shall possess the powers and perform all the duties of the Sheriff, and shall be entitled to the same fees as are allowed by law to the Sheriff for similar services.

SEC. 26. If the office of Coroner be vacant, or he be absent or unable to attend, the duties of his office may be performed by any Justice of the Peace of the County, with the like authority and subject to the same obligations and penalties as the Coroner.

SEC. 27. The Coroner of the City and County of San Francisco, in addition to the duties imposed by this Act upon every Coroner, shall keep a record of all inquests held by him, with a copy of all testimony and the inquisition of the juries in full; and in case of loss of the original records, the same shall be admissible in evidence with like effect as the original would have been.

SEC. 28. The Coroner of said City and County shall be authorized to appoint two clerks, who shall be sworn to act as First and Second Deputy Coroners in all matters, except those duties on inquests which have been forbidden to be delegated by this Act. The salary of the clerk sworn to act as First Deputy Coroner shall not exceed one hundred and fifty dollars per month, and the salary of the clerk sworn to act as Second Deputy Coroner one hundred and twenty-five dollars per month, which shall be paid from the Special Fee Fund of the said City and County. The Coroner of said City and County shall be authorized to appoint a Messenger, whose duty it shall be to have charge of the dead wagon, keep in order the morgue, and perform such other duties as are required by the Coroner or his deputies in connection with the duties of his office. He shall receive a salary not to exceed seventy-five dollars per month, to be paid in like manner as that of the Coroner's clerks. [*Amended, March 23, 1876; 1875–6, 397.*]

SEC. 29. The Board of Supervisors of the City and County of San Francisco are hereby authorized to provide a suitable office and jury room, and dead house or morgue, with the furniture necessary to enable the Coroner to efficiently discharge the duties of his office, and to make the necessary appropriation therefor. They are further authorized to audit and pay, for the necessary expenses of maintaining the morgue and offices attached, such sum as may be necessary, not to exceed seventy-five dollars per month, to be paid out of the General Fund.

SEC. 30.   The Coroner of the City and County of San Francisco shall receive no fees for any services rendered by him, but he shall in lieu thereof receive a salary of four thousand dollars per annum, payable in like manner as other county officers within said County, to be audited by the Auditor and paid out of the same fund provided for in the City and County Treasury as in the cases of other officers in said City and County.

SEC. 31.   All Acts or parts of Acts in conflict with the provisions of this Act, so far as they so far conflict, are hereby repealed.   This Act shall apply only to the City and County of San Francisco.

SEC. 32.   This Act shall be in force from and after its passage.

————

[*The foregoing must be read in connection with secs. 4285 to 4291, inclusive, of the Pol. Code.   See also Act of April 8, 1872; 1872, 81.*]

——————————— '

SUPPLEMENT LVI.

1871-2, 511.

———

An Act to confirm Order Number One Thousand [and] Four, passed by the Board of Supervisors of the City and County of San Francisco.

[Approved March 23, 1872.]

The People of the State of California, represented in Senate and Assembly, do enact as follows :

SECTION 1.   Whereas, the Board of Supervisors of the City and County of San Francisco passed an order, numbered one thousand and four, which said order was approved by the Mayor and President of the Board of Supervisors, on August seventh, eighteen hundred and seventy-one, and which is as follows: " Order Number One Thousand and Four, amendatory of Order Number One Thousand and Two, requiring property owners to fence lots, to prevent the sand from drifting or being blown into or upon streets that are planked, paved, or macadamized; the People of the City and County of San Francisco do ordain as follows:

Section 1. Sections one and two of Order Number One Thousand and Two are hereby amended so as to read as follows:

Section 1. All persons shall prevent sand or dirt from drifting, or being blown or otherwise moved from all lots owned by them, into or deposited upon any paved, planked, or macadamized street of the City and County of San Francisco.

SEC. 2. All persons owning or having the control of any premises fronting on streets that are paved, planked, or macadamized, situated in said City and County, shall, within five days after notice from the Superintendent of Public Streets and Highways, requiring him or them so to do, and without expense to the City and County, so construct fences or bulkheads around the premises or lots owned by them as to prevent sand or dirt from drifting, or being blown, or falling from such lots or premises, into or upon any planked, paved, or macadamized street, or upon the sidewalks thereof.

SEC. 3. Any person who shall violate any of the provisions of this order shall be deemed guilty of a misdemeanor, and upon conviction thereof shall be punished by a fine of not more than one hundred dollars, or by imprisonment in the County Jail not more than fifty days.

SEC. 4. All Orders or parts of Orders, conflicting with the provisions of this Order, are hereby repealed.["] The within and before recited Order be and the same is hereby ratified and confirmed; and all proceedings heretofore had, and which have taken place, or shall hereafter take place under its provisions, are ratified and confirmed in all respects.

SEC. 5. This Act shall take effect from and after its passage.

SUPPLEMENT LVII.

1871-2, 512.

--- ---

An Act to increase and regulate the Police force of the City and County of San Francisco.

[Approved March 23, 1872.]

The People of the]State of California, represented in Senate and Assembly, do enact as follows:

SECTION 1. [*Obsolete.*] The salaries of the additional officers hereby authorized shall be of the same amount, not exceeding one hundred and twenty-five dollars per month, and shall be paid in the same manner and at the same time as other members of the said Police force are now or shall hereafter be paid. The Chief of Police of said City and County may detail a regular Police officer to act as his Clerk, who shall receive the same salary as the Property Clerk of the Police Department. The Captain of the Harbor Police shall receive the same salary as is now or may hereafter be paid to Police Captains.

SEC. 2. No member of the Police force of the City and County of San Francisco shall be allowed to interfere in politics on the day of election, or at any other time, while employed on said Police force; nor shall be removed from office for political or partisan causes, reasons or purposes.

SEC. 3. This Act shall take effect and be in force from and after its passage.

SUPPLEMENT LVIII.

1871-2, 544.

An Act to transfer to the Board of Supervisors of the City and County of San Francisco the management, control and direction of the affairs of the Industrial School Department of said City and County.

[Approved March 23, 1872.]

The People of the State of California, represented in Senate and Assembly, do enact as follows:

SECTION 1. The President of the Board of Managers of the Industrial School of the City and County of San Francisco is hereby authorized and directed to grant, convey, and deliver to the Board of Supervisors of the City and County of San Francisco all and singular the property, both real and personal, now in the possession or under the control of said department, as created under and by virtue of an act of the Legislature of the State of California, entitled, "An Act to establish the Industrial School Department of the City and County of San Francisco," approved April fifteenth, eighteen hundred and fifty-eight, and the Acts supplementary thereto and amendatory thereof, and he is hereby authorized and directed to make, execute, and deliver to said City and County of San Francisco, all and singular such deeds and instruments in writing, as the act and deed of said department, as may be necessary to carry the provisions of this section into effect.

SEC. 2. From and after the passage of this Act, all and singular the powers and duties now vested in the Board of Managers of said Industrial

School, shall be vested in the Board of Supervisors of the said City and County of San Francisco. Said Board of Supervisors shall exercise all the duties and possess all the rights now vested in the Board of Managers of the Industrial School Department, and all present indebtedness and liabilities of said Industrial School Department, and future expenditures and disbursements on account of the same, shall be presented, audited, and paid in the same manner as is now provided by law for the presentment, auditing, and payment of other claims against said City and County of San Francisco; *provided*, that the current expenses of such Industrial School shall only be audited and paid to the extent of four thousand five hundred dollars ($4,500) per month.

SEC. 3. The purposes and objects of said Industrial School shall hereafter be the same as are now provided by law for the Industrial School Department of the City and County of San Francisco; *provided*, that persons who may be convicted of offenses mentioned in section ten of the Act entitled " An Act to establish the Industrial School Department of the City and County of San Francisco," approved April fifteenth, eighteen hundred and fifty-eight, in counties other than San Francisco, may be committed by the proper authorities of such counties to the Industrial School of the City and County of San Francisco, on the approval of the Supervisors of the County in which such persons are committed to said Industrial School, upon payment to the City and County of San Francisco by such counties of the sum of fifteen ($15) dollars, gold coin, per month for each month that such persons and each of them shall be inmates of said Industrial School.

SEC. 4. All Acts and parts of Acts inconsistent with the provisions of this Act are hereby repealed.

SEC. 5. This Act shall take effect immediately.

SUPPLEMENT LIX.

1871-2, 735.

An Act to confer additional powers upon the Board of Supervisors of the City and County of San Francisco, and upon the Auditor and Treasurer thereof, and to authorize certain appropriations of money by said Board.

[Approved March 30, 1872.]

The People of the State of California, represented in Senate and Assembly, do enact as follows:

SECTION 1. The Board of Supervisors of the City and County of San Francisco are hereby authorized and empowered to appropriate, allow, and order paid out of the General Fund, the several sums of money hereinafter mentioned, and to exercise the following powers, to wit:

First. *

Second. To expend such sums as may be hereafter annually levied for improving the City Cemetery.

Third. To expend a sum not to exceed ten thousand dollars per annum for extending and repairing the Fire Alarm and Police Telegraph. [*As amended by Act of Mar.* 26, 1878; 1877-8, 556.]

Fourth. [*Obsolete.*]

Fifth. [*Obsolete.*]

Sixth. To appoint a gardener for Jefferson Square, at a salary not to exceed seventy-five dollars per month.

Seventh. To appoint a Sergeant-at-Arms, who shall have the same power as is conferred upon police officers, to attend meetings of the Board, serve notices, subpœnas, and perform such other duties as may be required, at a salary not to exceed one hundred dollars per month.

Eighth. To pay for fuel furnished to and used in public buildings.

Ninth. To pay rent for Harbor Police office a sum not to exceed fifty dollars per mouth.

Tenth. To authorize the employment of such extra clerks as may be required by the Tax Collector in his office from time to time, at a salary not to exceed one hundred and fifty dollars per month each.

Eleventh. To appoint a night watchman for public buildings, at a salary not to exceed ninety dollars per month.

Twelfth. To pay * * * * to the Deputy Clerk of said Board of Supervisors a salary not to exceed one hundred and fifty dollars per month.

Thirteenth. To dedicate and appropriate the Hospital grounds and buildings on Francisco street for the purposes of a Corporation Yard, and to make provision for the storage and safe keeping of all materials used in the repair of public streets and highways, and of all apparatus, material, and hose belonging to and not in use by the Fire Department; and also to provide for the storage of all supplies, of whatever nature or kind, that may in the judgment of said Board be deemed necessary for the use of any or all departments and offices of the city government.†

Fourteenth.

Fifteenth.   *   *   *   *   *   *   *   *   *

---

* Amended by new Section added to Political Code, to be designated as Section 3035. Act of March 9, 1878.

† In part superseded by Sec. 18 of Act of Mar. 28, 1878; 1877 8, 685.

Sixteenth. [*Obsolete.*]

Seventeenth. [*Superseded by sub.* 1 *of sec.* 1, *of Act of March* 16, 1878; 1878, 280.]

Eighteenth.

Nineteenth.

Twentieth. To allow and order paid out of the General Fund such sums as they deem absolutely necessary for extra assistance in the offices of Assessor, Tax Collector and Auditor.

Sec. 2. This Act shall take effect from and after its passage.*

SUPPLEMENT LXI.

1871-2, 736.

An Act to facilitate and increase the collection of State and County and Municipal licenses in the City and County of San Francisco.

[Approved March 30, 1872.]

The People of the State of California, represented in Senate and Assembly, do enact as follows:

Section 1. If any person or persons, whether as principal or principals, agent or agents, clerk or clerks, employee or employees, or any firm or any member of any firm or corporation shall be engaged in carrying on, pursuing, or transacting, within the limits of the City and County of San Francisco, any business, trade, or profession, occupation or employment, which now is or shall hereafter be by law required to be licensed, without having first obtained and procured the license therefor so required by the laws of this State, or by the lawful orders of the Board of Supervisors of said City and County, or shall, after five days' notice in writing, refuse, neglect, omit, or fail to comply with any requirement or requirements, provision or provisions of the laws of this State or orders of the said Board of Supervisors requiring such person or persons, firm or corporation to procure a license, he, she, or they, or either of them, as the case may be, shall be deemed guilty of a misdemeanor, and on conviction thereof, shall be punished by a fine of not less than one hundred dollars, or by imprisonment for a period not exceeding thirty days, in case the fine is not paid.

---

* In part superseded by Sec. 13 of Act of March 28, 1878; 1878, 635.

10

Sec. 2. The Collector of Licenses, Chief Deputy Collector of Licenses, and Assistant Deputy Collectors of Licenses of said City and County are hereby authorized, empowered, and required to collect all State and county licenses provided for and required by law to be collected within the limits of said City and County, in addition to the municipal licenses now required to be collected or which shall hereafter be required to be collected by them or either of them; and it shall be the duty of said Collector of Licenses, Deputy Collector of Licenses, and Assistant Collectors of Licenses to attend to the collection of licenses, and examine all places of business and persons liable to pay licenses, and see that licenses are taken out and paid for. They shall each have and exercise, in the performance of their official duties, the same powers as Police officers in serving process or summons and in making arrests; also, shall each have and exercise the power to administer such oaths and affirmations as shall be necessary in the discharge and exercise of their official duties; and they and each of them are hereby empowered to enter any place of business for which a license by law is provided and required, free of charge, at their pleasure, and to demand the exhibition of any license for the current time, from any person, or firm, or corporation engaged or employed in the transaction of any business for which a license is by law rendered necessary; and if such person, or firm, or corporation, or either of them, shall be unable, or refuse, or neglect, or fail to then and there exhibit such license, he, she, or they, as the case may be, shall be deemed guilty of a misdemeanor, and on conviction thereof shall be punished as provided by section one of this Act for punishment upon conviction of a misdemeanor.

Sec. 3. The Board of Supervisors of the City and County of San Francisco shall have power, by ordinance, to license and regulate all such callings, trades, and employments as the public good may require to be licensed and regulated, and as are not prohibited by law, and shall have power to make all needful rules and regulations to govern the official conduct and duties of the Collector of Licenses, Deputy Collector of Licenses, and the Assistant Collectors of Licenses, who shall each hold office during the pleasure of the power appointing them[101] (and who shall pursue no other calling or business), and to alter and amend the same from time to time in such manner as they may deem proper and for the public good, and to fix the amounts of the bonds to be required from the Collector of Licenses and Deputy Collector of Licenses and Assistant Collectors of Licenses. The Auditor of said City and County is hereby authorized and required to deliver, from time to time, to the Collector of Licenses as many of such municipal licenses as may be required; also, to deliver from time to time to said Collector of Licenses for collection, such State and County licenses as may be required and such as he shall have received from the Controller of the State, and to sign the same and charge them to the Collector of Licenses

---

[101] Collector of Licenses to be appointed biennially; sec. 3, Act of April 3, 1876; Supplement LXXXVIII.

receiving them, specifying in the charge the amounts thereof named in such licenses, respectively, and the class of licenses, taking receipts therefor; and said Collector shall proceed to collect the same, signing the same in lieu of the County Treasurer; and he shall daily pay to the Treasurer of the said City and County all moneys so collected for licenses sold, or by him received as fees; and shall, under oath, at least once in each calendar month, and oftener when required so to do by the Auditor, make to the Auditor a report of all such licenses sold and on hand and of all amounts so paid to the County Treasurer in the same manner and upon the same conditions as by law the County Treasurer heretofore has been required to make return thereof to the County Auditor, and shall at such time exhibit to the Auditor all unsold licenses in his hands and the Treasurer's receipts for all moneys paid into the Treasury; and all licenses so signed by the license Collector or Deputy License Collector shall be as valid as if signed by the County Treasurer. All fees so paid to him shall be placed to the credit of the Special Fee Fund by the said Treasurer.

Sec. 4. It is hereby made the duty of the Mayor, the Auditor, and the Treasurer of said City and County, and they are hereby authorized and empowered to appoint, subject to confirmation by the Board of Supervisors of said City and County, one person as Collector of Licenses for the City and County of San Francisco, who shall receive a monthly salary of two hundred dollars, payable monthly; and the said Collector of Licenses is hereby authorized and empowered to appoint one Deputy Collector of Licenses, who shall be paid a monthly salary of one hundred and fifty dollars, payable monthly, and three[102] Assistant Collectors of Licenses, who shall be paid each a monthly salary of one hundred and twenty-five dollars, payable monthly. Such License Collector and deputies shall hold office during the pleasure of the Board of Supervisors.[103] All salaries herein provided for shall be paid from the General Fund in the same manner as the salaries of other City and County officers are paid. The Assistant Collectors of Licenses and the Deputy Collector of Licenses shall, under the direction and instruction of the Collector of Licenses, observing the form and rules and regulations prescribed by said Collector and Board of Supervisors, make to the said Collector daily reports of duty performed and daily payments of money received for licenses and fees; and at the close of each month, and oftener when required by the Collector of Licenses, each shall make oath to the Auditor that he has so paid over to the Collector of Licenses all such moneys, and a failure so to do shall be a cause for removal from office.

Sec. 5. The Police Commissioners of the City and County of San Fran-

---

[102] Number of Assistant Collectors may be increased not to exceed twelve. Sec. 2, Act of April 3, 1876; Supplement LXXXVIII.
[103] Collector of Licenses appointed biennially. Sec. 3, Act of April 3 1876; Supplement LXXXVIII. As to tenure of office of Deputy and Assistants, see sec. 2, same Act.

cisco are hereby authorized and empowered to revoke any licenses provided to be collected under the provisions of this Act, upon the conviction in the Police Judge's Court of any person of disorderly or improper conduct, or any offense upon the premises of any person holding a license, or upon the conviction of the person holding said license of any offense which in the judgment of said Commissioners ought to disqualify such person from holding such license.

SEC. 6. It shall be the duty of the County Treasurer to deliver to the Collector of Licenses, immediately upon this Act taking effect, all papers, books, materials, and other property appertaining and belonging to the License Department. And all Acts or parts of Acts requiring the County Treasurer to collect licenses in the City and County of San Francisco, and all other Acts or parts of Acts, so far as they conflict with this Act, are hereby repealed; *provided*, that nothing in this Act contained shall curtail the clerical force in the office of the Treasurer of the City and County of San Francisco during the term of office of the present incumbent.

SEC. 7. This Act shall take effect and be in force on and after the twentieth day subsequent to its passage.

SUPPLEMENT LXII.

1871-2, 764.

An Act to prevent hunting and shooting on private grounds in the City and County of San Francisco.

[Approved March 30, 1872.]

The People of the State of California, represented in Senate and Assembly, dv enact as follows:

SECTION 1. It shall not be lawful for any person or persons to enter any inclosure belonging to or occupied by another, in the City and County of San Francisco, for the purpose of hunting or to shoot, kill, or destroy any kind of game, without having first obtained permission from the owner or agent of such inclosure.

SEC. 2. Any person who shall violate the provisions of this Act shall be deemed guilty of a misdemeanor, and shall be punished upon conviction by a fine of not less than twenty-five dollars nor more than one hundred dollars, or imprisonment in the County Jail not to exceed sixty days, or by both such fine and imprisonment, and jurisdiction of such offenses is hereby vested in the Police Judge's Court in said City and County.

[See also Act of March 23, 1876; 1876, 408.]

SUPPLEMENT LXIII.

1871-2, 804.

An Act repealing Article Fourth of an Act entitled " An Act to repeal the several charters of the City of San Francisco, to establish the boundaries of the City and County of San Francisco, and io consolidate the government thereof," approved the nineteenth day of April, eighteen hundred and fifty-six, and all Acts and parts of Acts amendatory thereof and supplementary thereto, and substituting this Act for said Article Four.

[Approved April 1, 1872.]

The People of the State of California, represented in Senate and Assembly, do enact as follows:

ARTICLE IV.

SECTION 1. All the streets, lanes, alleys, places, or courts as laid down on the map now in the office of the City and County Surveyor of the City and County of San Francisco, which was made official by the Board of Supervisors of said City and County as per order number six hundred and eighty-four, January thirtieth, eighteen hundred and sixty-six, signed by George C. Potter and Thaddeus R. Brooks, and on the map now in the office of the said City and County Surveyor, which was made official by the said Board of Supervisors as per order number nine hundred and sixty-six, October twenty-fifth, eighteen hundred and seventy, and all other streets, lanes, alleys, places, or courts now dedicated or open to public use, are hereby declared to be open public streets, lanes, alleys, places, or courts for the purpose of this law; and the said Board of Supervisors are hereby invested with jurisdiction to order any of the work mentioned in section three of this Act to be done on any of said streets, lanes, alleys, places, or courts when the grade and width of said streets, lanes, alleys, places, or courts have been officially established; and for the purposes of this Act the grade of all intermediate or intersecting streets, lanes, alleys, places, or courts in any one block shall conform to the grades as established of the crossings of the main streets.

SEC. 2. All streets, lanes, alleys, places, or courts now open, or which may hereafter be open to public use, shall be deemed and held to be open public streets, lanes, alleys, places, or courts for the purposes of this Act, and the Board of Supervisors shall have the same jurisdiction to order work to be done thereon as is conferred upon them by section one of this Act.

SEC. 3. The Board of Supervisors are hereby authorized and empowered to order the whole or any portion of the said streets, lanes, alleys, places, or courts graded or regraded to the official grade, planked or replanked, paved or repaved, macadamized or remacadamized, piled or repiled, capped or re-capped, and to order sidewalks, sewers, cesspools, manholes, culverts, curb-ing, and crosswalks to be constructed, and to order any other work to be done which shall be necessary to make and complete the whole or any portion of said streets, lanes, alleys, places, or courts, and they may order any of the said work to be improved. The work provided for in this Act shall not be deemed to be "specific improvements" within the meaning of section sixty-eight, Article V of Chapter one hundred and twenty-five of the Act en-titled an Act to repeal the several charters of the City and County of San Francisco, and to establish the boundaries of the City and County of San Francisco, and to consolidate the Government thereof, approved April nine-teenth, eighteen hundred and fifty-six, nor shall the ordinances or resolutions passed by the Board of Supervisors under the provisions of this Act be deemed to be such ordinances or resolutions as are mentioned in said section sixty-eight.

SEC. 4. The Board of Supervisors may order any work authorized by sec-tion three of this Act to be done, after notice of their intention so to do in the form of a resolution describing the work, and signed by the Clerk of said Board of Supervisors, has been published for the period of ten days in the paper doing the printing under this law, and also in two daily news-papers, one of which newspapers shall be published as a morning edition and one as an evening edition, printed and published in said City and County, for ten days, Sundays and non-judicial days excepted; *provided*, that no such notice shall be given or order made for the grading of any street men-tioned in section three of this Act unless the majority of the frontage of the lots and land fronting on the work proposed to be done, and described in said resolution, or which is to be made liable for such grading, except public property, shall have been represented by the owners thereof, or by their agents, in a petition to the said Board of Supervisors, stating that they are the owners and in possession or agents of the lots named in the petition; and also requesting that such improvements or street work shall be done; and for any other character of street improvements the Board of Supervisors shall

have power, without petition of the property owners, to give the notice prescribed in this section to be published in the manner hereinbefore provided,
and to order the said work to be done. All owners of lands or lots, or portions of lots, who may feel aggrieved or have objection to the ordering of the
work described in said notice, or who may have objections to any of the subsequent proceedings of the said Board of Supervisors in relation to the work
mentioned in such notices of intention, or may have any objections to any of
the acts of the Superintendent of Public Streets, Highways and Squares of
the City and County of San Francisco, in the discharge of any of the obligations or duties imposed upon him by virtue of his office, shall file with the
Clerk of the said Board of Supervisors a petition or remonstrance, wherein
they shall set forth in what respect they feel aggrieved, or the acts or proceedings to which they object, which petition or remonstrance shall be passed
upon by said Board of Supervisors, and their decisions thereon shall be final
and conclusive; but said Board of Supervisors shall not order the work described in said notices to be done unless all objections and protests that may
have been presented and filed as aforesaid shall have been by them disposed
of. Should the owners or agents of more than one-half in frontage of the lots
and lands fronting on the work proposed to be done, and designated in said
notice or resolution, or liable to be assessed for work, file with the Clerk of
the Board of Supervisors written objections against any grading described in
said notice, at any time before the expiration of the publication of said notice
of intention, and his publication thereof as hereinbefore provided, then and
thereupon the said Board of Supervisors shall be barred from proceeding further for the period of six months; and the said Board of Supervisors shall not
renew the notice of intention for doing any grading so protested against
within six months, unless the owners or agents of a majority of the frontage
of the lots and lands fronting on said grading, or liable to be assessed therefor as aforesaid, shall petition anew for the work to be done. At the expiration of any notice of intention the Board of Supervisors shall be deemed to
have acquired jurisdiction to order any work to be done which is authorized
by section three of this Act, except as hereinbefore provided; and it is further
provided, that where any public street shall have been graded, or graded and
macadamized, or graded and paved for the distance of two or more blocks
upon each side thereof of any one or more blocks or crossing of a street
which is not improved, it shall be the duty of the Board of Supervisors, upon
the recommendation of the Superintendent of Public Streets, Highways and
Squares, to order the notice provided in this section to be given without the
petition provided first aforesaid; and if the owners of three-fourths of the
frontage of the lands and lots fronting on said portions of said streets to be
graded or improved shall, within the time prescribed in said notice, file written objections to the improvement of the said street, the Board of Supervisors shall duly consider said objections before ordering said work; and if said
Board of Supervisors shall decide and declare by an entry in the minutes of
said Board of Supervisors that the objections so made are not good, thereup-

on the Board of Supervisors shall be deemed to have acquired jurisdiction to order any such street work to be done that is prescribed in said notice and in section three of this Act; *provided* further, that when one-half or more of the grading, planking, macadamizing, paving, sidewalking, or sewering of any one street lying between two main street crossings, has been already performed, the Board of Supervisors may order the remainder of such grading, planking, macadamizing, paving, sidewalking, or sewering to be done, notwithstanding the objections of any or all of the property owners.

SEC. 5. The owners of more than one-half in frontage of lots and lands fronting on any street, lane, alley, place, or court, mentioned in sections one and two of this Act, or their duly authorized agents, may petition the said Board of Supervisors to order any of the work mentioned in section three of this Act to be done; and the said Board of Supervisors may order the work mentioned in said petition to be done, after notice of their intention so to do has been published, as provided in section four of this Act. No order or permission shall be given to grade, or pile and cap, any street, lane, alley, place or court, in the first instance, or any portion thereof, without extending and completing the same throughout the whole width of such street, lane, alley, place, or court. When any such work has heretofore been done, or when any such work shall hereafter be done, in violation of this section, neither the lots, or portions of lots, in front of which such work has been or may be done hereafter, nor the owners thereof, shall be exempt from assessments made for the payment of the work afterward done to complete said street, lane, alley, place, or court to its full width, as provided in section eight of this Act.

SEC. 6. Before the awarding of any contract by the Board of Supervisors for doing any work authorized by section three of this Act, the Clerk of the Board of Supervisors shall cause notice to be conspicuously posted in the office of the Superintendent of Public Streets, Highways and Squares, and also publish for five days, inviting sealed proposals for the work contemtemplated, which notice shall specify the time within which said work is to be performed, and shall contain specifications, to be furnished by said Superintendent of Public Streets, Highways and Squares, substantially in the manner now adopted by the said Clerk of said Board of Supervisors; and all notices, resolutions, and orders required to be posted or published under the provisions of this law shall be posted or published, or both posted and published, as the law may require, by said Clerk, as a matter of course, and without any special direction or authority from said Board of Supervisors. Prior to the publication of the notice hereinbefore provided, the Superintendent of Public Streets, Highways and Squares shall furnish specifications for the performance of any and all street work ordered by the Board of Supervisors, and authorized by section three of this Act, in which specifications shall be given, and the time within which the contract must be completed. All proposals shall be delivered to the Clerk of the Board of

Supervisors, and said Board of Supervisors shall, in open session, open, examine, and publicly declare the same, and shall award said work to the lowest responsible bidder, and all bids shall be for a price payable in gold coin of the United States; *provided*, said Board of Supervisors may reject any and all bids, should they deem it for the public good, and also may reject the bid of any party who may be proved delinquent or unfaithful in any former contract with said City and County; and if all bids shall be rejected, the said Board of Supervisors shall direct the Clerk of said Board of Supervisors to again post said notice, and publish the same, as in the first instance. All proposals shall be accompanied with a check, payable at sight, on a bank or banking house in said City and County, duly certified, for the sum of five hundred dollars United States gold coin, payable to the order of the Clerk of the Board of Supervisors, and to be approved by him. And if the bidder to whom the contract is awarded shall for ten days thereafter fail or neglect to enter into a contract, as hereinafter provided, and to commence said work within five days thereafter, it shall be the duty of said Superintendent of Public Streets, Highways and Squares to certify such failure on the part of said bidder to the Clerk of the Board of Supervisors, who shall thereupon draw the money due on said check and pay it over to the Treasurer of the City and County of San Francisco, to be by him placed to the credit of the Street Department Fund. It is further *provided*, that all persons, owners included, who shall fail to enter into any contract as herein provided, or to complete the contracts entered into, are hereby prohibited from bidding a second time for the same work; and in case of owners, they are hereby prohibited from electing to take the same work a second time, and from entering into any contract concerning the same. Notice of such award shall be published for three days (Sundays and non-judicial days excepted), and within five days after the first publication of such award the owners of a majority of the frontage of lots and lands liable to be assessed for said work, or their agents, and who shall make oath that they are such owners, or the agents of such owners, may elect to do the said work, and enter into a written contract to do the whole work at the price for which the same is awarded, upon giving the bond as hereinafter provided; and they shall commence said work within fifteen days from the first publication last above mentioned, and shall prosecute it diligently and continuously, and complete it within the time limited in the contract, or within any extended time ; but should the said contractor, or the property owners, fail to prosecute the same diligently or continuously in the judgment of said Superintendent of Public Streets, Highways and Squares, or complete it within the time prescribed in the contract, or within such extended time, then it shall be the duty of said Superintendent of Public Streets, Highways and Squares to report the same to the Board of Supervisors, who shall, without further petition on behalf of the property owners, order the Clerk of the Board of Supervisors to advertise for bids, as in the first instance, and relet the contract in the manner hereinbefore provided; and it is further *provided*, that all contractors for street work shall, at the time of entering into said contract, execute a bond, payable to the City and County of San Francisco, with two or more sureties, in the sum of not less than one thousand dollars, and in such additional amount as may be fixed by said Superintendent of Public Streets, Highways and Squares, conditioned for the faithful perfor mance of said contract; and said sureties shall justify in double the amount of the penalty fixed in said bond, such sureties to justify before said Superintendent of Public Streets, Highways and Squares, or his deputy, and the qualifications and responsibility of such sureties shall be the same as are now prescribed for sureties on the official bonds of the officers of said City and County of San Francisco; and it is further *provided*, that all contractors for street work, at the time of entering into contract, and giving the bond as hereinbefore provided, shall, in addition, execute a proper bond with two good and sufficient sureties, who must be freeholders of said City and County of San Francisco, in the sum of five hundred dollars (said sureties to justify in double the amount), conditioned that in case of the non-fulfillment of the contract, said sum shall be sued for and collected as liquidated damages to said City and County of San Francisco for such failure and neglect; and it shall be the duty of the City and County Attorney to sue for and collect said sum in any Court of competent jurisdiction, and pay the same into the City and County Treasury, to the credit of the Street Department Fund.

SEC. 7   The Superintendent of Public Streets, Highways and Squares is hereby authorized, in his official capacity, to enter into all written contracts, and to receipt all bonds authorized by this Act, and to do any other acts, either express or implied, that pertain to the street department under this Act; and said Superintendent of Public Streets, Highways and Squares shall fix the time for the commencement and completion of the work under all contracts entered into by him, and may extend the time so fixed from time to time, under the direction of the Board of Supervisors; and it shall be the duty of the Superintendent of Public Streets, Highways and Squares, on the execution of a contract to perform street work, or on the passage of a resolution by the Board of Supervisors directing an extension of time to be granted to complete a contract, to cause the same to be recorded in the office of the County Recorder of the City and County of San Francisco; and in issuing a certificate of an extension of time to be recorded, to specify in the same the number of the resolution of the Board of Supervisors, the date thereof, and the number of days granted for completion of the contract, a general description of the work, with the date of indorsement of said extension upon the original contract; and prior to the execution of a contract, and prior to granting or indorsing upon a contract as aforesaid any extension of time, to collect from said contractor or his assigns the sum of three dollars for each contract, and the sum of fifty cents for each and every extension of time.   And the County Recorder of the City and County of San Francisco shall cause books of record to be prepared, to be entitled Record

of Street Contracts, in which all contracts for the performance of street
. work, and all extensions of time granted by the Board of Supervisors, as
certified to by the Superintendent of Public Streets, Highways and Squares,
shall be recorded, said books to be properly arranged and indexed, so as to
facilitate reference thereto; and for each contract so recorded, said County
Recorder of the City and County of San Francisco shall charge and collect
the sum of three dollars, and for each extension of time the sum of fifty
cents; and in all cases where said Superintendent of Streets, Highways and
Squares, under the direction of said Board of Supervisors, has extended the
time for the performance of contracts, the same shall be held to have been
legally extended. The work provided for in section three of this Act must
in all cases be done under the direction and to the satisfaction of the Superintendent of Public Streets, Highways and Squares, and the materials used
shall be such as are required by the said Superintendent of Public Streets,
Highways and Squares, and all contracts made therefor must contain this
condition, and also express notice that in no case (except when it is otherwise provided in this Act) will the City and County of San Francisco be
liable for any portion of the expense, nor for any delinquency of persons or
property assessed. The assessment and apportionment of the expenses of
all such work in the mode herein provided shall be made by the said Superintendent of Public Streets, Highways and Squares.

SEC. 8. *Subdivision One.* The expenses incurred for any work authorized
by section three of this Act shall be assessed upon the lots and lands fronting thereon, except as hereinbefore specially provided, each lot or portion
of lot being separately assessed in proportion to its frontage, at a rate per
front foot sufficient to cover the total expense of the work.

Subdivision Two. The expense of all improvements (except such as done
by contractors under the provisions of section fourteen of this Act), until
the streets, street crossings, lanes, alleys, places, or courts are formally accepted as provided in section twenty-one of this Act, shall be assessed upon
the lots and lands as provided in this section, according to the nature and
character of the work; and after such acceptance, the expense of all work
thereafter done thereon shall be paid by said City and County of San Francisco out of the Street Department Fund.

Subdivision Three. The expenses of work done on main street crossings,
except such as are provided for in subdivision eight of this section, shall be
assessed upon the four quarter blocks adjoining and cornering on the crossings; and each lot or part of lot in such quarter blocks fronting on such
main street shall be separately assessed, according to its proportion of frontage on the said main street.

Subdivision Four. Where a street terminates at right angles in another
main street, the expense of the work done on one-half the width of the
street opposite the termination shall be assessed upon the lots in each of the
two quarter blocks adjoining and cornering on the same, according to the

frontage of such lots on said main streets, and the expense of the other half of the width of the said street upon the lots fronting on the latter half of the street opposite such termination.

Subdivision Five. Where any small or subdivision street crosses a main street, the expense of all work done on said crossing shall be assessed on all the lots or portions of lots half way on said small streets to the next crossing or intersection or the end of said small or subdivision street, if it does not meet another.

Subdivision Six. The expense of work done on the small or subdivision street crossings shall be assessed on the lots fronting upon such small streets, on each side thereof in all directions half way to the next street, place, or court, on either side respectively, or to the end of such street, if it does not meet another.

Subdivision Seven. When a small street, lane, alley, place, or court terminates in another street, lane, alley, place, or court, the expense of the work done on one-half of the width of the street, lane, alley, place or court opposite the termination shall be assessed upon the lots fronting on such small street, lane, alley, place, or court so terminating according to its frontage thereon, half way on each side respectively, to the next street, lane, alley, place, or court, or to the end of such street, lane, alley, place, or court, if it does not meet another, and the other half of the width upon the lots fronting such termination.

Subdivision Eight. The maps now in the office of the Superintendent of Public Streets, Highways and Squares, showing the street crossings or spaces formed or made by the junction or intersection of other streets with Market street, other than at right angles; also showing other street crossings adjoining fractional or irregular blocks (all of which crossings or spaces are colored on said maps and numbered from three to one hundred and fifty, inclusive), and heretofore certified by said Superintendent of Public Streets, Highways and Squares—one adopted by a resolution of the Board of Supervisors (number fifteen hundred and seventy-eight), approved on the sixteenth day of December, eighteen hundred and sixty-one, and the other adopted by a resolution of the said Board of Supervisors (number three thousand two hundred and eighty-four), approved on the twenty-first day of March, eighteen hundred and sixty four, which resolutions are copied on the face of said maps respectively, shall be deemed and held to be official maps for the purposes of this Act, and the same are hereby approved. And the expenses incurred for the work done on the said crossings or spaces formed by the junction or intersection of East street with Market street, and of other streets with Market street, and not squarely in front of, and not properly assessable to lots fronting on such streets, and for the work done on said other street crossings and spaces, all of which are colored on said maps, shall be assessed on the contiguous, adjacent, and neighboring irregular or quarter blocks or lots of land which are of the same color as the crossings or spaces, and which have a number thereon corresponding with the number of the crossing or space on which the work has been done.

Subdivision Nine. In all the streets constituting the water front of the City and County of San Francisco, or bounded on one side by the property of said City and County of San Francisco, or crossings cornering thereon or on the water front, the expense of the work done on that portion of said streets, from the center line thereof to the said water front, or to such property of the City and County of San Francisco bounded thereon, and one-fourth of their crossings, shall be provided for by the said City and County of San Francisco; but no contract for any such work will be given out except to the lowest responsible bidder after an observance of all the formalities required by this Act.

Subdivision Ten. When any work mentioned in section three of this Act (sewers, manholes, cesspools, culverts, crosswalks, crossings, curbings, grading, piling and capping excepted) is done on one side of the center line of said streets, lanes, alleys, places or courts, the lots or portions of lots fronting on that side only in front of which said work is done shall be assessed to cover the expenses of said work according to the provisions of this section.

Subdivision Eleven. The assessment made to cover the expenses of grading, mentioned in the proviso in section four of this Act, shall be assessed upon all the lands, lots and portions of lots fronting on either side of said street, lying and being between the said main street crossings in the manner provided in subdivision one of this section. Before any work is done under a contract to complete the grading of a partially graded street, lane, alley, place or court, under the provisions of section four of this Act, the City and County Surveyor shall ascertain as near as possible the number of cubic yards of grading done previous to the letting of the contract in front of each lot or parcel of land fronting upon the work, or any street crossing under contract, and also ascertain the number of cubic yards of grading necessary to complete the grading included in the contract, and certify such estimates to the Superintendent of Public Streets, Highways and Squares before the completion of the work included in the contract. And when any owner of a lot or lots fronting on said partially graded street, lane, or alley, place, or court, or any part liable to be assessed for the work under contract, has graded a part of the same, and desires credit for grading done by him previous to the publication of the notice of intention, he shall apply to and receive from the City and County Surveyor a certificate of the amount of grading done by him or those under whom he claims or deraigns title, for which he is entitled to credit, which certificate shal be recorded in the office of the Superintendent of Public Streets, Highways and Squares (in a book to be kept for that purpose, properly indexed, so that reference may be easily had thereto) previous to the completion of the grading under contract. And for all grading done prior to the passage of this Act, the owner of a lot or lots desiring credits shall file in the office of the Superintendent of Public Streets, Highways and

Squares a certificate of the City and County Surveyor when the work was performed, showing the number of cubic yards of grading done by him or those under whom he claims or deraigns title, which certificate shall be filed and recorded in the office of said Superintendent of Public Streets, Highways and Squares, and shall entitle the party named, or his successor in interest, to credit on the assessment for the amount specified; *provided*, no party shall be entitled to any credit in excess of his assessment; *provided*, however, that he shall not be allowed any credits at any time for any embankment made above or excavation made below the official grade; but the costs of removing such embankment or filling in such excavations shall always be charged exclusively to the owner or owners of the lot or lots of land fronting thereon, in addition to the pro rata rate which may be assessed to them. If the credit for grading, so certified as aforesaid in cubic yards or measurement, equals the proportional amount of grading which such owner would be obliged to do if no grading had been done on such street, lane, alley, place, or court, then such owner and his lot or lots shall be exempted from assessment for the remaining work; and if the grading done by such owner is less than his proportional share, then the work required to be done in front of his lot or lots, according to the original profile of the land previous to any grading thereon, shall be included in the assessment, and the work certified as aforesaid to have been done by him at his own expense, shall be credited to him at the contract rate; *provided*, that in making the assessment to cover the expense of any work mentioned in this section, the said Superintendent of Public Streets, Highways and Squares may deviate from its provisions and assess such lots and lands fronting on any street, lane, alley, place or court, as he may decide liable to assessment for said work, which decision may be appealed from as hereinafter provided.

Subdivision Twelve. Section one of an Act entitled an Act amendatory of and supplementary to an Act to provide revenue for the support of the Government of this State, approved April twenty-ninth, eighteen hundred and fifty-seven, approved April nineteenth, eighteen hundred and fifty-nine, shall not be applicable to the provisions of this section, but the property therein mentioned shall be subject to the provisions of this Act, and to be assessed for the work done under the provisions of this section.

SEC. 9. After the contractor of any street work has fulfilled his contract to the satisfaction of the Superintendent of Public Streets, Highways and Squares, the said Superintendent of Public Streets, Highways and Squares shall make an assessment to cover the sum due for the work performed and specified in such contract, including incidental expenses (if any), in conformity with the provisions of this Act, and according to the character of the work done, which assessment shall briefly refer to the contract, the work contracted for and performed, and shall allow [show] the amount to be paid therefor, together with the incidental expenses (if any), the rate per front foot assessed, the amount of each assessment, the name of the owner of each lot or portion of lot, if known to the Superintendent of Public Streets, Highways and Squares. If unknown, the word "unknown" shall be written opposite the number of the lot (but an assessment made to a person not the owner shall not render such assessment illegal), and the amount assessed thereon, the number of each lot or portion of lot assessed; and shall have attached thereto a diagram, exhibiting each street or street crossing, lane, alley, place or court on which any work has been done, and showing the relative location of each distinct lot or portion of lot to the work done, numbered to correspond with the numbers in the assessment, and showing the number of feet frontage assessed for said work and contracted for and performed, and such assessment shall in all cases be payable in gold coin of the United States.

Sec. 10. To said assessment shall be attached a warrant, which shall be signed by the Superintendent of Public Streets, Highways and Squares and countersigned by the Auditor of said City and County of San Francisco, who, before countersigning it, shall examine the contract, the steps taken previous thereto, and the record of assessments, and must be satisfied that the proceedings have been legal and fair. The said warrant shall be substantially in the following form:

"Form of Warrant.—By virtue hereof, I, (name of Superintendent), Superintendent of Public Streets, Highways and Squares of the City and County of San Francisco, in the State of California, by virtue of the authority vested in me as said Superintendent of Public Streets, Highways and Squares, do authorize and empower (name of contractor), (his or their) agents or assigns, to demand and receive the several assessments upon the assessment and diagram hereto attached, and this shall be (his or their) warrant for the same.

"San Francisco, (date), eighteen hundred and—— .

"(Name of Superintendent),
" Superintendent of Public Streets, Highways and Squares.

" Countersigned by :
"(Name of Auditor),

"Auditor of the City and County of San Francisco."

Said warrant, assessment, and diagram shall be immediately recorded in the office of the Superintendent of Public Streets, Highways and Squares, and, when certified and so recorded, the several amounts assessed shall be a lien upon the lands, lots, or portions of lots assessed, respectively, for the period of two years from the date of said recording, unless sooner discharged; and, when suit is commenced within said two years, said lien shall continue for six months after the final determination of said suit; and all assessment liens heretofore created shall continue in full force for two years from the date of the recording of said warrant, assessment, and diagram, respectively;

and when suits have been or shall hereafter be commenced within said two years from the date of said recording, said liens shall continue and be in force until the end of six months from the final determination of said suits, respectively; and from and after the date of said recording of any warrant, assessment, and diagram, all persons mentioned in section twelve of this Act shall be deemed to have notice of the contents of the record thereof. After said warrant, assessment, and diagram are recorded, the same shall be delivered to the contractor, or his agents or assigns, on demand, but not until after the payment to the said Superintendent of Public Streets, Highways and Squares of the incidental expenses not previously paid by the contractor or his assigns; and, by virtue of said warrant, said contractor, or his agents or assigns, shall be authorized to demand and receive the amount of the several assessments made to cover the sum due for the work specified in such contract and assessment.

SEC. 11. The contractor or his assigns, or some person in his or their behalf, shall call upon the person assessed or their agents, if they can conveniently be found, and demand payment of the amount assessed to each. If any payment be made, the contractor, his assigns, or some person in his or their behalf, shall receipt the same upon the assessment, in presence of the person making such payment, and shall also give a separate receipt, if demanded. Whenever the persons so assessed, or their agents, cannot conveniently be found, or whenever the name of the owner of the lot is stated as "Unknown" on the assessment, then the said contractor or his assigns, or some person in his or their behalf, shall publicly demand payment on the premises assessed. The warrant shall be returned to the Superintendent of Public Streets, Highways and Squares within ten days after its date, with a return indorsed thereon, signed by the contractor or his assigns, or some person in his or their behalf, verified upon oath, stating the nature and character of the demand, and whether any of the assessments remain unpaid, in whole or in part, and the amount thereof. Thereupon the Superintendent of Public Streets, Highways and Squares shall record the return so made in the margin of the record of the warrant and assessment, and also the original contract referred to therein, if it has not already been recorded, at full length, in a book to be kept for that purpose in his office, and shall sign the record. The said Superintendent of Public Streets, Highways and Squares is authorized at any time to receive the amounts due upon any assessment list and warrant issued by him, and give a good and sufficient discharge therefor; *provided*, that no such payment so made after suit has been commenced, without the consent of the plaintiff in the action, shall operate as a complete discharge of the lien until the costs in the action shall be refunded to the plaintiff, and he may release any assessment upon the books in his office on the production to him of the receipts of the party or his assigns, to whom the assessment and warrant was issued. And if any contractor shall fail to return his warrant within the time and in the form provided in this section, he shall thenceforth have no lien upon the property assessed; *provided*, however, that in case any warrant is lost, upon proof of such loss a duplicate can be issued upon which a return may be made with the same effect as if the original had been so returned. After the return of the assessment and warrant as aforesaid, all amounts remaining due thereon shall draw interest at the rate of one per cent. per month until paid.

SEC. 12. The owner, contractor or his assigns, and all persons, whether named in the assessment or not, feeling aggrieved by any of the acts or determinations of the said Superintendent of Public Streets, Highways and Squares, in relation to the acceptance of work or to the assessment, or to any act, proceeding, matter or thing done, suffered or committed by him, shall, within fifteen days after the issuance of said assessment as provided, appeal to said Board of Supervisors as provided in this section, by briefly stating their objections in writing, and filing the same with the Clerk of said Board of Supervisors. Notice of the time and place of hearing, briefly referring to the subject matters of appeal and to the acts or determination objected to or complained of, shall be published for five days, Sundays and non-judicial days excepted. The said Board of Supervisors, on appeal, may correct, alter or modify said assessment as to them shall seem just, and may annul the same, and may order a new assessment to be made in the manner by them directed; and may make any order or decision in relation to any contract or the performance thereof, or in relation to any of the acts of the contractor or the said Superintendent of Public Streets, Highways and Squares, prior to the date of the hearing of said appeal. And all the decisions and determinations of said Board of Supervisors shall be final and conclusive upon all parties entitled to an appeal. The said warrant, assessment and diagram shall be held prima facie evidence of the regularity and correctness of the assessment, and of the prior preceedings and acts of the said Superintendent of Public Streets, Highways and Squares, and of the regularity of all the acts and proceedings of the Board of Supervisors upon which said warrant, assessment and diagram are based. After jurisdiction to order any work has been obtained, no irregularity in any of the subsequent proceedings shall render any assessment illegal.

SEC. 13. At any time after the period of fifteen days from the day of the date of the warrant as hereinbefore provided, or if an appeal is taken to the Board of Supervisors, as is provided in section twelve of this Act, any time after five days from the decision of said Board of Supervisors, or after the return of the warrant or assessment after the same may have been corrected, altered, or modified, as provided in section twelve of this Act (but not less than fifteen days from the date of the warrant), the contractor or his assigns may sue, in his own name, the owner of the land, lot, or portions of lots assessed, on the day of the date of the recording of the warrant, assessment, and diagram, or on any day thereafter during the continuance of the lien of said assessment, and recover the amount of any assessment remaining due and unpaid, with interest thereon, as hereinbefore provided; and in all cases

11

of recovery under the provisions of this Act, the plaintiff shall recover the sum of fifteen dollars in addition to the taxable costs, as attorney's fees, provided he shall waive the percentage on recovery as provided by law. Suit may be brought in any Court in said City and County of San Francisco; and in case any one or more of the items in the assessment or assessments are against owners thereof who cannot with due diligence be found, the service in each of such actions may be had either in manner as is now prescribed by the Civil Practice Act of this State, or in manner as is prescribed by an Act of the Legislature of the State of California, entitled "An Act supplementary to an Act entitled an Act in relation to suits brought for the collection of delinquent taxes, approved May twelfth, eighteen hundred and sixty-two, approved March twenty-fourth, eighteen hundred and sixty-four," and the remedies therein provided are cumulative. The Court in which such suit shall be commenced shall have power to adjudge and decree a lien against the premises assessed, and to order such premises to be sold on execution or decree, as in other cases of the sale of real estate by the process of said Courts; and on appeal the appellate Court shall be vested with the same power to adjudge and decree a lien, and to order to be sold such premises on execution or decree, as is conferred on the Court from which an appeal is taken. Such premises, if sold, may be redeemed as in other cases. In bringing an action to recover street assessments the complaint need not show any of the proceedings prior to the issuance of the assessment, diagram, and certificate; but it shall be held legally sufficient if it shows the title of the Court in which the action is brought [by?] the parties plaintiff and defendant, the date of the issuance of the assessment, the date of the recording thereof, the book and page where recorded, a general statement of the work done, a description of the lot or lots sought to be charged with the assessments, the amount assessed thereon, that the same remains unpaid, and the proper prayer for relief. In all suits brought to recover street assessments the proceedings therein shall be general and regulated by the provisions of this Act, and also, when not in conflict herewith, by the Civil Practice Act of this State; but no defense shall be interposed except:

First—Want of jurisdiction to order work;

Second—That the assessment has been paid;

Third—Fraud in the assessment, or in any of the acts or proceedings prior thereto, setting out the facts showing such fraud.

It is hereby expressly provided that nothing but gold and silver coin of the United States shall be received in payment of street assessments, and the judgment or decree in every case shall be made payable in and entered for gold coin.

SEC. 14. The Superintendent of Public Streets, Highways and Squares may require, at his option, by notice in writing, to be delivered to them personally or left on the premises, the owners, tenants or occupants of lots or portions of lots liable to be assessed for work done under the provisions of this Act, to improve forthwith any of the work mentioned in section three of this Act in front of the property of which he is the owner, tenant or occupant, to the center of the street or otherwise, as the case may require, or to remove all filth, sand, earth or dirt from the street in front of his premises; and by a like notice, to be served personally upon the president or any officer of a railroad corporation or company or to be left at the office of said corporation or company, to require such corporation or company to improve forthwith any work mentioned in this Act which said corporation or company are required by law to do and perform, said notice to specify what improvement is required or work is to be done. After the expiration of five days the said Superintendent of Public Streets, Highways and Squares shall be deemed to have acquired jurisdiction to contract for the doing of the work, or making the improvements, or the removing of the filth, sand, earth or dirt required by said notice. If such improvement or work of cleaning be not commenced within five days after notice given, as aforesaid, and diligently, and without interruption, prosecuted to completion, the said Superintendent of Public Streets, Highways and Squares may enter into a contract with any suitable person to make said improvement, or to do said cleaning, at the expense of the owner, tenant or occupant, or railroad corporation or company, as the case may be, at a reasonable price, to be determined by said Superintendent of Public Streets, Highways and Squares; and such owner, tenant or occupant, or railroad corporation or company, shall be liable to pay the same. After the certificate referred to in section fifteen shall have been recorded in the office of [the Superintendent of] Public Streets, Highways and Squares, the sum contracted to be paid shall be a lien, the same as provided in section ten of this Act, and also a lien upon the franchise and property of said corporation or company, and may be enforced in the same manner as other assessments.

SEC. 15. If the expense of such improvements or removing such sand, earth, dirt or filth, after the completion thereof, be not paid to the contractor so employed, or his agent or assignee, on demand, the said contractor or his assigns shall have the right to sue the owner, tenant or occupant, or railroad corporation or company, under the provisions of this Act, for the amount contracted to be paid, and the certificate of the Superintendent of Public Streets, Highways and Squares that the work has been properly done, and that the charges for the same are reasonable and just, shall be prima facie evidence of the amount claimed for said work and of the right of the contractor to recover the same in such action.

SEC. 16. In addition, and as cumulative to the remedies above given, the Board of Supervisors shall have power, by ordinance, to prescribe the penalties that shall be incurred by any owner, tenant, occupant, or railroad corporation or company neglecting or refusing to make improvements or remove sand, earth, dirt or filth, as provided for in section fourteen of this Act, which fines and penalties shall be recovered for the use of the City and

County of San Francisco, by prosecution in the name of the people of the State of California, in the Police Judge's Court of the City and County of San Francisco, which shall have jurisdiction in all such cases. All fines collected hereunder shall be paid into the Treasury of the City and County of San Francisco, to the credit of the Street Department Fund, at least once in each week.

SEC. 17. The person owning the fee, or the person in the possession of lands, lots, or portions of lots, or buildings, under claim of ownership, or exercising acts of ownership over the same for himself, or as the administrator or guardian of the owner, or the person in whom on the day the action commenced appears the legal title to the land by deeds recorded in the Recorder's office in the City and County of San Francisco, shall be regarded, treated, and deemed to be the owner (for the purposes of this law), according to the intent and meaning of that word as used in this Act; and in case of property leased, possession by a tenant or lessee holding and occupying under an owner shall be deemed to be in possession by such owner.

SEC. 18. The records kept by the Superintendent of Public Streets, Highways and Squares, in conformity with the provisions of this Act, and signed by him, shall have the same force and effect as other public records, and such records or copies thereof, duly certified by said Superintendent of Public Streets, Highways and Squares, may be used in evidence with the same force and effect as the original assessments, diagrams, and warrants. The said records shall, during all office hours, be open to the inspection of any citizen wishing to examine them, free of charge.

SEC. 19. Notices in writing, which are required to be given by the Superintendent of Public Streets, Highways and Squares, under the provisions of this Act, may be served by any police officer, and the fact of such service shall be verified by the oath of the person making it, taken before the Superintendent (who is hereby authorized to administer oaths), Police Judge, or any Judge, or Justice of the Peace; or such notices, whether verbal or written, may be delivered by the Superintendent of Public Streets, Highways and Squares himself, or any of his deputies. The Superintendent of Public Streets, Highways and Squares shall keep a record of the fact of giving such notices and proof of service.

SEC. 20. When any street or portion of a street has been or shall hereafter be constructed to the satisfaction of the Committee on Streets, Wharves, Grades and Public Squares of the Board of Supervisors, and the said Superintendent of Public Streets, Highways and Squares, and shall have a brick sewer or cement pipe constructed therein, under such regulations as said · Board of Supervisors shall adopt, the same shall be accepted by the said Board of Supervisors, and thereafter shall be kept open and improved by the said City and County, the expense thereof, together with all work done in front of City property, to be paid out of the Street Department Fund; *provided*, that the Board of Supervisors shall not accept any portion of the street less than the entire width of the roadway (including the curbing and one block in length, or one entire crossing); and *provided* further that the Board of Supervisors, may, partially or conditionally, accept any street or portion of a street without a sewer or pipe therein, as above stated, if a sewer or pipe therein shall be deemed by them unnecessary; but the lots of land previously assessable for the cost of construction of a sewer or pipe shall still remain and be assessable for such cost, and for the cost of repair and restoration of the street damaged in the said construction, when a sewer or pipe shall be deemed necessary, the same as if no partial or conditional acceptance had ever been had. The said Superintendent of Public Streets, Highways and Squares shall keep in his office a register of all accepted streets, the same to be indexed so that reference may be easily had thereto.*

SEC. 21. The said Superintendent of Public Streets, Highways and Squares shall keep a public office, in some convenient place to be designated by the Board of Supervisors, and his office shall be kept open as in this Act required. He shall not, during his continuance in office, follow any other profession or calling, but shall be required to devote himself exclusively to the duties of his office. He shall be allowed not more than sixteen deputies, to be by him appointed from time to time; three of said deputies shall receive a salary of two hundred dollars per month each, and six of said deputies shall receive a salary of hundred and fifty dollars per month each, and seven of said deputies shall receive a salary of hundred and twenty-five dollars per month each. It shall be lawful for the said deputies to perform all or any of the duties conferred by this Act upon the Superintendent of Public Streets, Highways and Squares, under the direction of said Superintendent of Public Streets, Highways and Squares, except the acceptance or approval of work done. The Superintendent of Public Streets, Highways and Squares, or his deputies, shall superintend and direct the cleaning of all the public streets and the cleaning of all sewers in the public streets; and the expense of the same shall be paid out of the Street Department Fund, in the same manner provided for the improvement of streets that have been finally accepted, as in this Act provided. [*As amended by Act of March 2, 1878; 1878, 139*].

SEC. 22. It shall be the duty of said Superintendent of Public Streets, Highways and Squares to see that the laws, orders and regulations relative to the public streets and highways are carried into execution, and that the penalties therefor are rigidly enforced, as may be prescribed by the Board of Supervisors. It is required that he shall keep himself informed of the condition of all public streets and highways, and also of all public buildings,

---

*The condition of acceptance of streets was modified by Act of April 1, 1878; 1878, 959.

parks, lots, and grounds of the said City and County, as may be prescribed by the said Board of Supervisors. He shall, before entering upon the duties of his office, give bonds to the City and County, in such sums as may be fixed by the said Board of Supervisors, conditioned for the faithful discharge of the duties of his office; and should such Superintendent of Public Streets, Highways and Squares fail to see that the laws, orders, and regulations relating to public streets and highways are carried into execution, after notice from any citizen of a violation thereof, the said Superintendent of Public Streets, Highways and Squares and his sureties shall be liable upon his official bond to any person injured in his person or property in consequence of said official neglect.

SEC. 23. No recourse shall be had against said City and County for damage to person or property suffered or sustained by or by reason of the defective condition of any street or public highway of said City and County, whether originally existing or occasioned by construction, excavation, or embankment, or want of repair of said street or public highway, and whether such damage be occasioned by accident on such street or public highway, or by falling from or upon the same; but if any person while carefully using any street or public highway of said City and County, graded or in course of being graded, or carefully using any other street or public highway leading into or crossing the same, be injured, killed, lost or destroyed, or any horses, animals, or other property be lost, injured, or destroyed through any defect in said street or public highway, graded or in course of being graded as aforesaid, or by reason of any excavation or embankment in or of the same, or by falling from or upon such embankment or excavation, then the person or persons upon whom the law may impose the duty either to repair such defect or to guard the public from the excavation, embankment, or grading aforesaid, and also the officer or officers through whose official neglect such defect remained unrepaired, or said excavation or embankment remained unguarded as aforesaid, shall be jointly and severally liable to the person or persons injured for the damages sustained.*

SEC. 24. The City and County Surveyor shall be the proper officer to do the surveying and other work which may be necessary to be done under sections one and two of this Act, and to survey, measure, and estimate the work done under contracts for grading streets; and every certificate of work done, given by him, signed in his official character, shall be prima facie evidence in all Courts in this State of the truth of its contents. He shall also keep a record of all surveys made under the provisions of section one of this Act as in other cases. The Superintendent of Public Streets, Highways and Squares shall measure and determine any other work which may be done under the provisions of this Act.

---

* Is this section amended by the Street Law of 1885 ?

Second. The words "improve," "improved," and "improvements," as used in this Act, shall include all necessary repairs of all work mentioned in section three of this Act, and also the reconstruction of all or any portion of said work.

Third. The term "main street," as used in this Act, means such street; or streets as bound a block; the term "street" shall include crossing.

Fourth. The word "block" shall mean the blocks which are known or designated as such on the map and books of the Assessor of said City and County of San Francisco.

Fifth. The term "incidental expenses" shall mean the expense for work done by the City and County Surveyor under the provisions of this Act; also, the expense of printing, measuring, and advertising the work done under contracts for grading.

Sixth. The publication of notices required by the provisions of this Act shall be published daily (Sundays and non-judicial days excepted) in the newspaper doing the printing by contract for the said City and County of San Francisco.

Seventh. The word "paved," within the meaning of this Act, shall be held to mean and embrace pavement of stone, iron, wood, or other materials which the Board of Supervisors shall by ordinance adopt, whether patented or not.

SEC. 25. All assessments hereafter to be made, to cover the expense of work provided for by contracts awarded prior to the passage of this Act, shall be assessed by the Superintendent of Public Streets, Highways and Squares in manner as is provided by the law in relation to assessments in force at the time said work was awarded. The office of the Assistant City and County Attorney is hereby abolished, and the City and County Attorney is hereby substituted for such officer, for the purposes of the prosecution and collection of the assessments issued under the provisions of the Act approved April fourth, eighteen hundred and seventy, and is invested with the same authority to commence suits, and prosecute and continue all suits now pending; *provided*, that any contractor or his assigns, for whose benefit any such assessment may have been made, may at his or their option collect the same, in which event the City and County of San Francisco shall be liable and responsible for no part or portion of such assessment. Any assessment, diagram, and certificate in the possession of the Superintendent of Public Streets, Highways and Squares, or of the Tax Collector, or of the City and County Attorney, made in pursuance of the Act approved April fourth, eighteen hundred and seventy, shall, on demand of the contractor named therein, or his assigns, be delivered to him or them, as the case may be, and thereupon all moneys which have been collected on account of said assessment shall be paid to the City and County Treasurer, as provided by the Act approved

April fourth, eighteen hundred and seventy, and by the Treasurer paid over
to the parties entitled thereto; such delivery of the assessment, diagram, and
certificate, or either, shall terminate the liability of the City and County of
San Francisco in the matter involved therein; and the reception of the assessment, diagram, and certificate, or either, shall be held to be a waiver on the
part of the said contractor, or his assigns, of any claims whatever thereunder
against said City and County. Immediately upon such delivery, the said
contractor and his assigns shall be fully empowered to collect such assessment in the manner herein provided for the collection of assessments made,
or to be made, under the provisions of this Act. The Mayor, by and with
the consent of the Board of Supervisors, is hereby empowered to allow the
City and County Attorney such assistance as may be necessary for the purposes of this section, at an expense not exceeding two hundred and fifty dollars per month, payable out of the General Fund.

SEC. 26. The Superintendent of Public Streets, Highways and Squares,
and his deputies, shall take charge of and superintend the construction or
improvement of each and every sewer, and of piling and capping, and of repiling and recapping, paving and repaving, macadamizing and remacadamizing, and all other street work and improvements; and it shall be their duty
to see that the contract made for the doing of said work is strictly fulfilled in
every respect. It shall be the duty of the Superintendent of Public Streets,
Highways and Squares, or any of his deputies, to enter upon a record book,
to be kept in the office of said Superintendent of Public Streets, Highways
and Squares for public inspection, entries under appropriate headings, showing how often, at what time, and by whom the work has been inspected, and
in what manner the same is being performed; and on the completion of said
work, and prior to the issuance of the assessment therefor, if the work has
been performed and completed in accordance with the terms of the contract
and specification, an entry certifying to the same, signed by the aforesaid
Superintendent of Public Streets, Highways and Squares, or any of said
deputies, who have had charge of and superintended the work performed.

SEC. 27. Article four, embracing sections from thirty-six to sixty-four inclusive, of an Act entitled "An Act to repeal the several charters of the City
of San Francisco and to establish the boundaries of the City and County of
San Francisco and to consolidate the government thereof," approved April
nineteenth, eighteen hundred and fifty-six, and sections three, four, five, six,
seven, eight, nine, ten, eleven, twelve, thirteen and fourteen of an Act entitled
"An Act amendatory to an Act entitled an Act to repeal the several charters of
the City of San Francisco, to establish the boundaries of the City and County
of San Francisco, and to consolidate the government thereof," approved
April nineteenth, eighteen hundred and fifty-six, approved March twenty-
eighth, eighteen hundred and fifty-nine, and sections two, three, four, five,
six, seven, eight, nine, ten, eleven, twelve, thirteen, sixteen and seventeen of
an Act entitled "An Act amendatory of an Act entitled an Act to repeal the

several charters of the City of San Francisco, and to establish the boundaries of the City and County of San Francisco, and to consolidate the government thereof," approved April nineteenth, eighteen hundred and fifty-
six; and of an Act amendatory and supplementary thereof, approved the
eigteenth day of April, eighteen hundred and fifty-seven; and of an Act amendatory thereof, approved the twenty-eighth day of March, eighteen hundred
and fifty-nine; and supplementary to said Acts, approved May the eighteenth,
eighteen hundred and sixty-one; and an Act amendatory of Article fourth
of an Act entitled an Act to repeal the several charters of the City of San
Francisco, to establish the boundaries of the City and County of San Francisco, and to consolidate the government thereof, approved the nineteenth
day of April, eighteen hundred and fifty-six, repealing sections thirty-six to
sixty-four inclusive, and Acts and parts of Acts amendatory and supplementary thereof, and substituting this Act for said Article fourth, approved April
twenty-fifth, eighteen hundred and sixty-two; and an Act to amend an Act
entitled an Act amendatory of Article fourth of an Act entitled an Act to repeal the several charters of the City and County of San Francisco, to establish the boundaries of the City and County of San Francisco, and to consolidate the government thereof, approved the nineteenth day of April, eighteen
hundred and fifty-six, repealing sections thirty-six to sixty-four inclusive; and
Acts and parts of Acts amendatory and supplementary thereof, and substituting this Act for said Article four, approved April twenty-fifth, eighteen
hundred and sixty-two, approved March thirty-first, eighteen hundred and
sixty-six; and an Act to amend an Act entitled an Act amendatory of Article
fourth of an Act entitled an Act to repeal the several charters of the City of
San Francisco, to establish the boundaries of the City and County of San
Francisco, and to consolidate the government thereof, approved the nineteenth day of April eighteen hundred and fifty-six, repealing sections thirty-
six to sixty-four inclusive, and Acts and parts of Acts amendatory and supplementary thereof, and substituting this Act for said Article four, approved the
twenty-fifth day of April, eighteen hundred and sixty-two, approved March
twenty-six, eighteen hundred and sixty-eight; and an Act entitled an Act to
amend sections one, two, nine, ten, and seventeen of an Act entitled an Act
amendatory of Article fourth of an Act entitled an Act to repeal the several
charters of the City of San Francisco, to establish the boundaries of the City
and County of San Francisco, and to consolidate the government thereof, approved the nineteenth day of April, eighteen hundred and fifty-six, repealing
sections thirty-six to sixty-four inclusive, and Acts and parts of Acts amendatory and supplementary thereof, and substituting this Act for said Article
four, approved April twenty-fifth, eighteen hundred and sixty-two; and to
amend sections one and five of said Act amendatory of the Act aforesaid, approved April twenty-fifth, eighteen hundred and sixty-three; and to amend
section two of an Act amendatory of the Act first mentioned atoresaid, approved March thirty-first, eighteen hundred and sixty-six; and to amend sec-

tions one, three and four of an Act amendatory of the Act first mentioned aforesaid, approved March twenty-sixth, eighteen hundred and sixty-eight, being the original sections one, two, four, six, nine, ten, eleven, twelve, thirteen, seventeen, and twenty-one of the Act mentioned first aforesaid; and to repeal an Act for paving the streets in the City and County of San Francisco, approved March fourteenth, eighteen hundred and sixty-eight, approved April fourth, eighteen hundred and seventy; and also an Act entitled an Act to provide for paving the streets in the City and County of San Francisco, approved April second, eighteen hundred and sixty-six; all and singular, and all Acts and parts of Acts in conflict with this Act are hereby repealed; and this Act shall be deemed to be substituted in place of said Article four, and as amendatory of the Act first above recited in this section, and held as a part thereof; and all advertisements being published at the date of the passage of this Act shall be published for the respective periods provided by the law in force at the time the publication may have been commenced.

SEC. 28.   This Act shall be liberally construed to carry out the intentions and purposes of this Act, and shall not be construed so as to affect any contracts heretofore awarded or assessments issued.

SEC. 29.   This Act shall be a public act and take effect from and after its passage. *

[*The following section of the Act of April* 25, 1863, 525, *seems to be unrepealed:*]

SEC. 10.   The Board of Supervisors, upon receiving a petition for that purpose from the owners of a majority of the property on any one or more blocks, estimating the property by the front foot, in that portion of the City and County of San Francisco lying west of Larkin street and southwest of Ninth street, may order the grading or other improvement of such street or streets, in accordance with the prayers of the petitioners, and without reference to the official width or grade of such street or streets, and in the same manner as other street improvements provided for in this Act; *provided*, that no street shall be raised above or cut below the official grade.

The Supreme Court of the State, Dep. 2, in McDonald v. Patterson, 54 Cal. 245, decided that Sec. 19 of Art. XI of the Constitution, as adopted in 1873, is not a provision which requires legislation; and the provisions of the Act of April 1, 1872, relating to street improvements in San Francisco, which authorize the Superintendent of Streets to execute contracts for such improvements, in advance of the levy and collection of the assessment, are inconsistent with the section referred to, and ceased to be operative on the 1st day of January, 1880. This decision was affirmed by the Supreme Court in bank in Donahue v. Graham, 61 Cal. 276, Justices McKinstry and Sharpstein dissenting.

SUPPLEMENT LXIV.

1871-2, 846.

An Act to provide for the support of the common schools of the City and County of San Francisco, and to define the powers and duties of the Board of Education thereof.

[Approved April 1, 1872.]

The People of the State of California, represented in Senate and Assembly, do enact as follows :

SECTION 1. The Board of Education of the City and County of San Francisco shall have power:

First. To maintain public schools as now organized in said City and County, and to establish additional ones as required, and to consolidate and discontinue schools, as shall be deemed best for the public interest.[104]

Second. To establish experimental and normal schools for the education and training of teachers.

Third. To employ and dismiss teachers, janitors, and School Census Marshals, and to fix, alter, allow and order paid their salaries or compensation, and to withhold, for good and sufficient cause, the whole or any part of the salary or wages of any person or persons employed as aforesaid.

Fourth. To make, establish and enforce all necessary and proper rules and regulations, not contrary to law, for the government and efficiency of the public schools within said City and County, the teachers thereof and pupils therein, and for carrying into effect the laws relating to education. Also, to establish and regulate the grade of schools, and determine the course of studies and the mode of instruction to be used in said schools.

Fifth. To issue a subpœna, duly attested by the President and Clerk of said Board, directed to any person whose attendance shall be required before said Board, or any committee thereof, as a witness on the examination

---

[104] The Act of March 30, 1874; 1873-4, 828; provides as follows:

"SECTION 1. The Board of Education of the City and County of San Francisco shall establish and maintain common schools, in said City and County, in which shall be taught the German and French languages in conjunction with studies in the English language. The number of such schools shall be not less than two grammar and two primary schools. They shall be designated as cosmopolitan schools, and shall be subject to such rules and regulations as shall be prescribed by said Board of Education."

of any charges against any employee of said Board for violation of any of the rules or regulations thereof, requiring such person to attend before said Board, or a committee thereof, at a time and place to be therein named, to testify in relation to such charges; and if such person shall refuse or neglect to obey such subpœna, or refuse to testify when so required, he or she shall be deemed guilty of a misdemeanor, and shall be punished, on conviction thereof, by a fine of not less than ten dollars nor more than one hundred dollars, or by imprisonment in the County Jail for not less than ten days nor more than thirty days.

Sixth. To provide for the School Department of said City and County, fuel, lights, water, blanks, blank books, printing, stationery, and such other articles, materials or supplies as may be necessary or required for use in the schools, either by the pupils or teachers.

Seventh. To make rules of order and by-laws for the government of the Board, its members and committees, and general regulations, to secure proper economy and accountability in the expenditure of school moneys.

Eighth. To use and control such building or buildings as shall be necessary for the uses of the Board and its committees, and for storing supplies.

Ninth. To dispose of such personal property used in the schools or in other buildings under the charge of the Board as shall be no longer required for use therein, and all moneys realized by the sale of any such property shall be paid into the City treasury for the same purposes as the money received under the fifth section of this Act.

Tenth. To build, alter, repair, rent and provide school-houses and furnish them with proper school furniture, apparatus, and school appliances, and to insure any and all school property.

Eleventh. To lease, for a term not exceeding ten years, any unoccupied property of the School Department not required for school purposes.

Twelfth. To examine and allow, in whole or in part, every demand payable out of the School Fund, or to reject any such demand for good cause, of which the said Board shall be the sole judge.

Thirteenth. To prohibit any child under six years of age from attending the public schools. "

SEC. 2. It shall be the duty of the Board of Education of the City and County of San Francisco:

First. To furnish all necessary supplies, or make regulations for furnishing supplies, for the several schools under their care; but when such sup-

---

' See also Section 1617 Pol. Code.

plies are furnished by the Board of Education they shall be obtained by contract, proposals for which shall bo advertised for the period of at least two
weeks.

Second. To make and transmit, between the fifteenth day of January and
the first day of February in each year, to the State Superintendent of Public
Instruction and to the Board of Supervisors of the City and County of San
Francisco, a report in writing, bearing date on the thirty-first day of December next preceding, stating the whole number of schools within their jurisdiction, the length of time they shall have been kept open, the number of
pupils taught in each school, the whole amount of money drawn from the
treasury for the purposes of education during the year ending at the date of
the report, distinguishing the amounts received from the General Fund of
the State, and from all other and what sources, the manner in which such
moneys shall have been expended, and such other information as the State
Superintendent of Public Instruction may from time to time require in relation to public school education in the City and County of San Francisco.
And the report which said Board of Education is hereby required to make
shall be held and taken to be a full compliance with every law requiring
a report from said Board relative to the schools in said City or any matter
connected therewith.

Third. To provide evening schools for those whose ages or vocations are
such as to prevent attendance at the day schools established by law, in such
school houses or other buildings used for school purposes, and in such other
places in said city as said Board may from time to time deem expedient; and
also a normal school or schools for the instruction of those who desire to become teachers, which school shall be attended by such of the teachers in the
public schools as the Board of Education by general regulations shall direct,
under penalty of forfeiture of their situations as teachers for failure to attend
said normal school as required, which forfeiture shall be declared by the
Board of Education.

Fourth. To require the principal teachers of each school to enter in books,
to be furnished by the Board, the names, ages, and residences of the pupils
attending the school, the name of the parent or guardian of each pupil, the
days on which the pupils shall have respectively attended, and the aggregate
attendance of each during the year; also, the days on which each school shall
have been visited by the City Superintendent of Schools, or his assistant, and
the members of the Board of Education, or any of them; which entries shall
be verified by the oath or affirmation of the principal teacher in such school;
also, to require the principal teacher of each school, prior to the first day of
January of each year, to make to said Board of Education a report in writing,
bearing date the thirty-first day of December, which report shall state the
whole number of scholars over six and under twenty-one years of age, who
shall have been taught free of expense to such scholars in their schools dur-

ing the year ending with the date of the report, which number shall be ascertained by adding to the number of children on the register at the commencement of the year the number admitted during the year, not having previously attended any public school during that year; also, the average number that has actually attended such school during the year, to be ascertained by keeping an exact account of the number of pupils present at each session, or half day of the school, which, being added together and divided by four hundred and thirty, or, if less than a year, by the number of school sessions, shall be considered the average attendance, which average shall be sworn or affirmed to by the principal teacher of the school; also, a particular account of the state of the school, and of the property and affairs of the school, and the titles of all books used, with such other information as the Board of Education shall require.

Fifth. To provide, by general rules and regulations, a proper classification of studies, scholars, and salaries, in such manner that the system of instruction pursued in the public schools, and the salaries paid to teachers, shall be as nearly as practicable uniform throughout the city.

SEC. 3. It shall be the duty of the Superintendent of Common Schools of the City and County of San Francisco:

First. To visit and examine every school under the charge of the Board of Education as often as once in every six months, to inquire into all matters relating to the government, course of instruction, books, studies, discipline, and conduct of such schools, and the condition of the school houses and the schools generally, and to counsel with and advise the teachers in relation to their duties, the proper studies, discipline, and conduct of the pupils, the course of instruction to be pursued, and the books of elementary instruction to be used, and to examine, ascertain and report to the Board of Education whether the provisions or [of] the Act in relation to religious sectarian teaching and books have been violated in any of the schools, and to make a monthly report to the Board of Education, stating which of the schools have been visited by him, and adding such comments in respect to the matters here specified as he may deem advisable.

Second. To make annually to the State Superintendent of Public Instruction, at such times as said officer may direct, a report in writing, containing a statement of the whole number of schools within said City and County, and a certified copy of the reports of the Board of Education to the Supervisors of the City and County of San Francisco, with such additional information as the State Superintendent of Public Instruction may require.*

SECS. 4, 5, and 6. [*Relate to estimating necessary annual expenses of schools*

See also Sections 1543 to 1553, inclusive, Political Code.

and collecting tax therefor. Superseded by sec. 1, *Act of April* 3, 1876; *Supplement XC.* |

SEC. 7. All moneys received or collected on account of public education in the City and County of San Francisco shall be deposited in the City Treasury, and be known as the School Fund. Payments from said Fund shall only be made by the Treasurer of said City and County upon drafts drawn on him by the Board of Education, signed by the President and the Superintendent of Common Schools, and countersigned by the Auditor of said City and County; and all drafts shall be made payable to the person or persons entitled to receive the same.

SEC. 8. If the school moneys received and collected shall, during any year, exceed the necessary and legal expenses of the public schools, the Board of Education shall authorize the payment only of such sum or sums as shall be sufficient to provide for such expenses, and any deficiency in the sums so received and collected to meet the necessary and legal expenses of public education in the said schools shall be supplied by the Board of Supervisors of said City and County; and they are hereby authorized and directed to raise, by loan or otherwise, in anticipation of the annual tax, such sum or sums as shall be necessary to meet such deficiency; and the Board of Education shall in all such cases certify to the Board of Supervisors the cause of such deficiency, and that the same was unavoidable, and unless such certificate shall be made, the said Board of Supervisors may refuse to meet such deficiency; but the Board of Education shall not be authorized to call upon the Board of Supervisors in any year for any money or moneys for the purpose of purchasing sites, building, altering, repairing, or fitting up school houses, in excess of the estimates for these purposes, in pursuance of section seventh of this Act, except in cases of destruction of or injury to the buildings by fire or other unforeseen calamity.

SEC. 9. The Board of Education of the City and County of San Francisco are hereby authorized to establish in some central locality of said city a school, to which shall be admitted only those pupils who shall have been found, upon satisfactory examination and trial, too depraved to be permitted to associate longer with the pupils of other schools; but such pupil or pupils may be restored to any school under charge of said Board, upon satisfactory evidence of thorough reformation of conduct.

SEC. 10. The Clerk of the Board of Education shall have charge of the rooms, books, papers and documents of the Board, and shall, in addition to his duties as Secretary of the Board, perform such other clerical duties as may be required by its members or committees.

SEC. 11. In all cases where the erection of a building, fitting up thereof, and the fitting up of any hired building, or repairing any building belonging to the department, shall exceed the sum of two hundred dollars, the same shall be done by contract awarded to the lowest responsible bidder, proposals for which contract shall be advertised for two weeks previous to deciding upon the estimates thereon; but the Board of Education may reject any or all proposals, should they deem such action for the public good.

SEC. 12. Whenever, owing to any nuisance in the immediate vicinity of any school, or other unfavorable circumstances, or to the small attendance of pupils, or other sufficient reason, it shall appear to the Board of Education necessary and proper to discontinue such school, they may, after thirty days' notice given to the Board of Supervisors of their intention to abandon the building and site, for school purposes, withdraw entirely from the control of said property, which shall then be used or disposed of as a part of the general property of the City and County. In the event of the same being sold, the proceeds shall go into the School Fund of the City and County of San Francisco; but nothing herein shall be so construed as to authorize the sale of any such building or lot.

SEC. 13. Every person in the employ of the Board of Education, and every officer or teacher of a school who shall willfully sign a false report to the Board of Education shall, for each offense, forfeit the sum of twenty-five dollars, and shall be deemed guilty of a misdemeanor; and every such person or officer who shall willfully misapply any of the public funds committed to his care shall be deemed guilty of embezzlement.

SEC. 14. No school shall receive any portion of the school moneys in which the religious doctrines or tenets of any particular Christian or other religious sect shall be taught, inculcated or practiced, or in which any book or books containing compositions favorable or prejudicial to the particular doctrines or tenets of any particular Christian or other religious sect is used.

SEC. 15. The following shall be substantially the form of oath or affirmation to be made by the teacher:

"A. B., of the City and County of San Francisco, teacher of —— school, being duly sworn (or affirmed), declares and says, that to the best of his (or her) knowledge and belief the average number of children, actually residents of the City and County of San Francisco, between the ages of six and twenty-one years, who attended said school from the —— day of —— to the first day of January, ——, was ——; said average having been obtained by adding together the number of pupils present each half day, and dividing the sum by four hundred and thirty (or by the total number of half school days during the year)."

SEC. 16. The Clerk of the Board of Education is hereby authorized to administer oaths and take affidavits in all matters appertaining to the schools in the City and County of San Francisco.

SEC. 17. No person receiving a salary from the Board of Education shall be interested in any contract, payments under which are to be made in whole or in part of the moneys derived from the School Fund, or raised by taxation for the support of public schools.

SEC. 18. The public schools in the City and County of San Francisco shall be classified as High, Grammar, Primary, Evening and Normal Schools.

SEC. 19. The members of the Board of Education of the City and County of San Francisco shall be elected by vote of the electors of the entire City and County, and from the City and County at large, without reference to their residence.

SEC. 20. The Mayor, Auditor and Treasurer of the City and County of San Francisco are hereby authorized and required to issue school bonds from time to time in such sums as may be required for school purposes, not to exceed in the aggregate the sum of one hundred thousand dollars. Such bonds shall be signed by the Mayor, Auditor and Treasurer of said City and County, and shall be payable in ten years from the first day of June, one thousand eight hundred and seventy-two. Such bonds shall draw interest at the rate of seven per centum per annum from the date of their issuance, which interest shall be payable semi-annually, on the first days of June and December, in the City and County of San Francisco. The coupons attached to said bonds shall be signed by the said Treasurer.*

SEC. 21. The principal and interest of the said bonds shall be payable in gold coin of the United States of America, and the faith and credit of the City and County of San Francisco are hereby pledged for the redemption of said bonds and the payment of the principal and interest in said gold coin of the United States of America as set forth in this Act.

SEC. 22. As soon as said bonds are issued the Treasurer of said City and County is hereby authorized and empowered to sell the same to the highest bidder therefor for cash in gold coin of the United States (after having first advertised the same for four weeks in two daily newspapers published in said City and County), and the proceeds thereof shall be immediately placed in the Treasury of said City and County, and constituted a part of the School Fund. From the proceeds thus obtained and paid into the Treasury the Board of Education of the City and County of San Francisco, are hereby authorized to liquidate any unpaid bills or claims in the current expenses of the public Schools of said City and County for the year ending the thirtieth day of June, one thousand eight hundred and seventy-one; *provided*, said bills or claims do not exceed in the aggregate the sum of twenty thousand dollars; and the balance of such proceeds, or so much thereof as may be necessary, shall be used for the sole purpose of meeting any deficiency that may arise in

---

* See Section 13 of Article XI of State Constitutio

12

the current expenses of the schools for the year ending the thirtieth day of June, eighteen hundred and seventy-two. But no portion of the proceeds of this fund shall be used in the purchase of sites for the erection or repairs of school buildings, nor in the fitting up of the same; and any balance then remaining on hand shall be carried forward and form a part of the available funds for school purposes for the following year; *provided*, the Mayor, Auditor and the Treasurer may reject any and all bids for said bonds as the public good may require.

SEC. 23. To secure the payment of the principal and interest of said bonds it shall be the duty of the Board of Supervisors of the City and County of San Francisco to raise yearly by taxation, in the same manner as other City and County taxes are levied and collected, a sum sufficient to pay the semi-annual interest on said bonds, and also to provide a Sinking Fund for the redemption of the same at maturity, as directed in section twenty-four of this Act.

SEC. 24. Whenever and as often as there shall be funds in the Treasury of said City and County, to the credit of the Sinking Fund provided in section twenty-three of this Act, amounting to ten thousand dollars, it shall be the duty of the Treasurer of said City and County to advertise from time to time for thirty days, in two daily newspapers published in said City and County of San Francisco, for proposals to surrender said bonds upon the best terms, not exceeding their par value, and report the same to the Commissioners of the Sinking Fund, who shall immediately thereafter order paid the amount necessary to redeem the bonds so offered, and shall issue demands therefor in the usual form. The Auditor of said City and County is authorized and required to audit, and the Treasurer to pay the same out of the Sinking Fund in his hands, set apart therefor; and if such proposal to surrender bonds do not equal the amount of such Sinking Fund, then the Commissioners of the Sinking Fund shall have power to loan any balance remaining thereof, upon the security of any bonds of the City or of the City and County of San Francisco, or of the State of California, or of securities of the United States, at the best rates of interest obtainable therefor, such interest, when paid, to be entered by the Treasurer to the credit of the Sinking Fund for the redemption of said bonds.

SEC. 25. The money required hereafter to meet the interest and create the Sinking Fund for the bonds issued under the Act of the seventeenth of March, eighteen hundred and sixty-six, also for the bonds issued under the Act of the nineteenth of February, eighteen hundred and seventy, shall be raised in the like manner as is provided for in section twenty-three of this Act, and the Sinking Fund applied in the like manner provided for in section twenty-four of this Act.

SEC. 26. All Acts and parts of Acts passed prior to the first day of March, eighteen hundred and seventy-two, so far as inconsistent with the provisions of this Act, are hereby repealed.

SEC. 27. This Act shall take effect and be in force from and after its passage.

SUPPLEMENT LXV.

1871-2, 878.

An Act to provide funds to be applied to building a House of Correction in the City and County of San Francisco, and to authorize the Construction of such House of Correction.

[Approved April 1, 1872.]

The People of the State of California, represented in Senate and Assembly, do enact as follows:

SECTION 1. The Mayor, Auditor and Treasurer of the City and County of San Francisco, by and with the consent of the Board of Supervisors of said City and County first obtained by ordinance, are hereby authorized and empowered to issue from time to time, as may be directed by the said Board of Supervisors and as may be necessary for the purposes herein named, bonds not exceeding in the aggregate the sum of one hundred and fifty thousand dollars.

SEC. 2. Said Bonds shall be issued in such manner and at such times not inconsistent with the foregoing section, and made payable in the City and County of San Francisco, at the office of the Treasurer of said City and County, both principal and interest, at such times, not exceeding twenty years from the time of their issuance, as the Board of Supervisors may prescribe by ordinance. The interest on said bonds shall not exceed seven per cent. per annum, and shall be paid semi-annually; and both principal and interest shall be payable in United States gold coin.

SEC. 3. The said bonds shall be signed by the Mayor, Auditor and Treasurer of the City and County of San Francisco, and shall be known as the "House of Correction Fund Bonds of the City and County of San Francisco."

SEC. 4. Said Bonds shall have coupons attached to them for the semi-annual interest which may accrue upon them, signed by the Auditor of said City and County; and the faith and credit of the said City and County of San Francisco are hereby pledged for the redemption of the same and for the payment of the principal and interest thereof.

SEC. 5. Whenever said bonds or any portion of them are issued, the Treasurer and Auditor of said City and County are hereby authorized and empowered to sell the same to the highest bidder thereof, after having first advertised the same for three consecutive weeks in three daily papers published in said City and County. All money derived from the issue and sale of said bonds shall be appropriated and used for the sole purpose of building and furnishing a House of Correction upon any property of the City and County of San Francisco, to be selected by the Board of Supervisors and approved by the Mayor, south of Twenty-sixth street or west of new Cemetery Avenue, in the City and County of San Francisco; the style and material thereof, the construction, and all contracts and plans relating thereto to be determined by said Board of Supervisors, and in all cases to be approved before the adoption or ratification of the same by the Mayor, Auditor and Treasurer of said City and County. But no bonds authorized to be issued by this Act shall be sold for a less sum than ninety cents in gold coin on the dollar, par value. Said House of Correction shall be used for the safe keeping of such persons as shall be sentenced to be punished for crime by the Criminal Courts of the City and County of San Francisco, and are now and who would be confined in the County Jail.

SEC. 6. To secure the payment of the principal and interest of said bonds, the Board of Supervisors of the said City and County of San Francisco shall, when deemed necessary by them for the purpose in this section provided, levy an annual tax upon all the taxable property in the said City and County of San Francisco; and a sufficient sum or sums shall be raised by such annual levies to pay the principal of said bonds when the same shall become due. And it shall be the duty of the Treasurer of said City and County to set apart annually out of the moneys coming into the Treasury to the credit of the House of Correction Fund, raised by said annual tax, a sum sufficient to pay the semi-annual interest on said bonds, and also to provide a Sinking Fund sufficient for the redemption of the same at maturity.

SEC. 7. This Act shall take effect and be in force from and after its passage.

SUPPLEMENT LXVI.

1871–2, 901.

An Act to provide for the repair and improvement of roads and highways in the City and County of San Francisco.

[Approved April 1, 1872.]

The People of the State of California, represented in Senate and Assembly, do enact as follows:

SECTION 1. The Board of Supervisors of the City and County of San Francisco is hereby authorized and empowered to repair and improve the public roads within the said City and County, outside the charter line of eighteen hundred and fifty-one.

SEC. 2. It shall be the duty of the Superintendent of Public Streets and Highways to carefully examine all the public roads in said City and County, and report the condition of the same, from time to time, to the Board of Supervisors; *provided*, that from the month of November to May of each year, such report shall be made on the first Monday of each month; and said report shall specify the kind of repairs and the portion or portions of the road or roads in which they are required, together with an estimate of the cost.

SEC. 3. Upon presentation to the Board of Supervisors of the report and estimate of the said Superintendent of Public Streets and Highways, as herein provided, the said Board of Supervisors shall direct the Clerk of said Board to advertise, inviting sealed proposals for doing the work required, and shall award the contract for doing said work to the lowest responsible bidder, the proceedings in relation hereto to be the same as is provided by law for the letting of contracts for the improvement of streets and highways in said City and County; *provided*, that the amount of all appropriations authorized by this Act shall not exceed ten thousand dollars for any one fiscal year.

SEC. 4. For the purpose of this Act, public roads and highways shall include all roads that have been open to the public, and used as public highways long enough to evince their utility and necessity, but shall not include any road or highway when, in the judgment of the Board of Supervisors, the same should be kept in order by the owners of the property fronting on said road or highway.

SEC. 5. Whenever any improvement or repairs require to be made to any public road or highway, for which, in the judgment of the Board of Supervisors, the owners of the property fronting thereon should be assessed to defray the cost of the same, then and in that case the Board of Supervisors shall acquire jurisdiction, and shall have power to proceed in the same manner as is now provided by law for the improvement of streets within said City and County; and all provisions of law in relation to the improvement of streets within said City and County, and for the making and collection of the assessment for the cost of the work performed, shall apply to the collection of the sums of money so assessed as aforesaid.

SEC. 6. The Superintendent of Public Streets and Highways is hereby authorized and it is made his duty to superintend all repairs made on public roads and highways, and, when authorized by the Board of Supervisors, to purchase all necessary timber, plank or other material for the construction and repair of bridges, and to hire at just and reasonable rates all necessary labor, tools or implements for grading or otherwise improving such roads and highways.*

---

* See also Section 2 of Act of December 21, 1877; 1877-8, 4.

Sec. 7.   An Act entitled "An Act to create certain road districts in the City and County of San Francisco and to provide for the repair and improvement of roads therein," approved May twentieth, eighteen hundred and sixty-one, and all Acts or parts of Acts conflicting with any of the provisions of this Act, or authorizing any expenditure upon public roads or highways within the City and County of San Francisco, other than is provided in this Act, are hereby repealed.

Sec. 8.   This Act shall take effect from and after its passage.

SUPPLEMENT LXVII.

1873-4, 271.

An Act in relation to the Industrial School Department of the City and County of San Francisco.

[Approved March 4, 1874.]

The People of the State of California, represented in Senate and Assembly, do enact as follows:

SECTION 1.   All Acts and parts of Acts, relating to the Industrial School Department of the City and County of San Francisco, which were in force on the thirty-first day of December, eighteen hundred and seventy-two, are hereby declared to be and the same are in full force.

Sec. 2.   Any person duly convicted of a crime and duly committed to the Industrial School of said City and County, shall there remain until he arrives at the age of twenty-one years, unless sooner discharged according to law, or unless a shorter term shall be prescribed in the order of commitment.

Sec. 3.   If any person who has been duly convicted of a crime, and is called for sentence, shall state to the Court or Judge that he is under the age of eighteen years, and shall thereupon be committed to said Industrial School, such statement shall be recited in the order of commitment, and shall, as against such person, be conclusive as to his age in all questions relating to his connection with said school.

Sec. 4.   If any person committed to said Industrial School, upon conviction of a crime, shall escape therefrom, and be thereafter arrested, he shall be brought before the Court or Judge by whom he was so committed, and the said Court or Judge may recommit him to said school, or may punish him by fine or imprisonment, or both, as might have been originally done upon such conviction; but this section shall not apply in case of conviction of a crime committed prior to the passage of this Act.

SEC. 5. It shall be the duty of every Sheriff and police officer to arrest any person who has been committed to said Industrial School upon conviction of a crime, and has escaped therefrom, and to bring him before the Court or Judge by whom he was so committed, that he may be dealt with as provided in the next preceding section.

SEC. 6. This Act shall take effect from and after its passage.

·

SUPPLEMENT LXVIII.

1873-4, 333.

An Act concerning certain Public Reservations of the City and County of San Francisco.

[Approved March 11, 1874.]

The People of the State of California, represented in Senate and Assembly, do enact as follows :

SECTION 1. So much of the land situated around the sheet of water known as "Mountain Lake," marked "Park" on the official map of the outside lands of the City and County of San Francisco, as lies within the official survey of the lands confirmed by Acts of Congress and the decisions of the Federal Courts confirming said lands to said City and County, shall be hereafter known as "Mountain Lake Park." Also, that strip of land bounded west by the Pacific Ocean, referred to in the first section of an Act of the Legislature of this State, approved March twenty-seventh, eighteen hundred and sixty-eight, entitled "An Act to confirm a certain order passed by the Board of Supervisors of the City and County of San Francisco," which is particularly described in the ninth section of the order confirmed by said last mentioned Act, and which, on said official map, is designated as "Great Highway," shall be hereafter known and designated by such name. All the provisions of an Act entitled "An Act to provide for the improvement of public parks in the City of San Francisco," approved April fourth, eighteen hundred and seventy, and also all the provisions of an Act amendatory of and supplemental to the same, approved March thirtieth, eighteen hundred and seventy-two, so far as the same may be applicable, shall apply to all and singular the lands in this section described, and also to the lands referred to in section two of this Act.

SEC. 2. The Park Commissioners, appointed or elected, or to be appointed or elected, under and by virtue of said Acts of April fourth, eighteen hundred and seventy, and March thirtieth, eighteen hundred and seventy-two, are hereby authorized to purchase, or if unable to purchase at what they may deem a reasonable price, to condemn and appropriate to the public use, lands suitable for a reservoir for irrigation, connected with the improvements upon said park.

SEC. 3. For the purpose of condemning and appropriating land for a reservoir, the said Park Commissioners shall have and enjoy all powers and privileges that are by law accorded to water companies in general, or to any particular water company or companies, and shall exercise that power in the manner and form now provided, or hereafter to be provided in cases of condemnation and appropriation of land by such water companies. In like manner the said Commissioners may proceed to obtain all necessary rights of way for flumes, pipes, and other contrivances for conveying water to and from said reservoir. And all rights and privileges which are now or hereafter may be granted by the State, or by said City and County, to any water company, to use the public streets or highways for laying pipes, erecting gates, hydrants and other appliances needful for the conveyance and control of water, are hereby granted to the said Park Commissioners, but subject to the same conditions, regulations and restrictions.

SEC. 4. [*Obsolete.*]

SEC. 5. The principal and interest of the said bonds shall be payable in gold coin of the United States of America. The faith and credit of the City and County of San Francisco are hereby pledged for the redemption of said bonds and the payment of said principal and interest in said gold coin.

SEC. 6. All and singular the parks, avenue, highway, and reservoir, described or referred to in said Acts of April fourth, eighteen hundred and seventy, and March thirtieth, eighteen hundred and seventy-two, and in this Act, are hereby pledged, and shall be deemed mortgaged as security for the redemption of said bonds, and of all bonds hitherto created and issued by said Commissioners.

SEC. 7. As soon as said bonds are prepared, the Treasurer of said City and County may, and if requested by said Park Commissioners, shall sell, from time to time, so many thereof as the said Commissioners direct, to the highest bidder therefor, for cash, in gold coin of the United States of America, after having first advertised the same for four weeks, in two daily papers in said City and County, and two weeks in two daily newspapers of general circulation in the City of New York; but said bonds shall not be sold or disposed at less than ninety per cent. of their par value, and the proceeds thereof shall be immediately placed in the treasury of said City and County, and credited to the Park Improvement Fund; *provided*, the Mayor, Auditor, and Treasurer may reject any and all bids for said bonds.

Sec. 8.   The Board of Supervisors of the City and County of San Francisco are hereby authorized and required to levy upon all taxable property within said City and County, a special tax, for the purpose of meeting said interest, and of providing for the gradual or ultimate redemption of said bonds.   Said tax shall be levied annually, and shall be assessed and collected in the same manner and at the same time as other city taxes.   All moneys received from this tax shall be placed to the credit of the Park Interest and Sinking Fund.

Sec. 9.   Whenever after A. D. eighteen hundred and eighty-four, there shall be in the Park Interest and Sinking Fund a balance of at least ten thousand dollars over and above what may be necessary for the payment of said interest, said Treasurer shall endeavor to redeem outstanding bonds, by advertising for proposals.   Said Treasurer, Mayor, and Auditor shall meet and consider all proposals, and they, or a majority of them, shall accept or reject; but no proposal shall be accepted for a higher rate than par.   Whenever any proposal shall be accepted, the usual notice and demand shall be given and made; the amount due on the proposal so accepted shall be audited and paid, and the redeemed bonds with their coupons canceled.   Should no proposal be accepted or made, the amount of said balance shall, according as said Mayor, Auditor, and Treasurer, or a majority of them, shall deem best, be paid over to the Park Improvement Fund, or invested in securities of the said City and County, of this State, or of the United States.

Sec. 10.   The Park Commissioners are hereby prohibited from contracting any debt or debts, liability or liabilities, which, together with existing liabilities, shall exceed the amount of money that may be realized from the sale of the bonds provided for in this Act.   Any violation of this provision shall be a misdemeanor, and shall be punished as provided by law; and all contracts made or debts contracted in violation of this section shall be void.

Sec. 11.   This Act shall take effect immediately.

SUPPLEMENT LXIX.

1873-4, 910.

_____

An Act concerning the State Harbor Commissioners, and for other purposes.

[Approved March 30, 1874.]

The People of the State of California, represented in Senate and Assembly, do enact as follows :

SECTION 1.   The Harbor of San Francisco is hereby placed under the control of the Board of State Harbor Commissioners, and they are authorized to regulate the position of ships, their moorings and anchorage, and generally to make rules and regulations concerning them, with power to enforce the same as fully as that formerly used and exercised by the Harbormaster of the City and County of San Francisco.

SEC. 2.   The Commissioners shall keep the routes of the ferry boats, passing in and out of said harbor, free and open at all times, so that ferry boats can conveniently make their trips without impediment on the part of vessels at anchor, or other obstacles.

SEC. 3.   [*Obsolete.*]

SEC. 4.   At the end of the term of office of the present Harbormaster of San Francisco, either by lapse of time, resignation or otherwise, the State Harbor Commissioners shall require said duties to be performed by the Chief Wharfinger, or other executive officer of said Board, as they may deem most advantageous to the public interests, but no special office shall be created for that purpose alone.

SEC. 5.   This Act shall take effect and be in effect and in force from and after its passage.

SUPPLEMENT LXX.

1873–4, 942.

An Act providing for a paid fire department in the City and County of San Francisco.

[Approved March 30, 1874.]

The People of the State of California, represented in Senate and Assembly, do enact as follows :

SECTION 1. The fire department of the City and County of San Francisco shall consist of such engine, hook and ladder and hose companies, as shall be recommended by the Board of Fire Commissioners, and be determined by the Board of Supervisors of said City and County, with the approval of the Mayor, to be necessary to afford protection against fire; *provided*, that as auxiliary thereto, patent fire extinguishers may also be purchased and employed, if, in the judgment of said Board, deemed advisable; *provided*, that no hand engines shall hereafter be purchased for the use of said department; but those now in possession of said City and County may be used in such localities and under such regulations as the Board of Fire Commissioners, with the approval of the Board of Supervisors, may prescribe.

SECS. 2 and 3. [*Amended by Act of March 28, 1878; 1878, 685.*]

SEC. 4. The companies composing said fire department shall be furnished with all the horses, hose, hooks, ladders, apparatus and appurtenances, necessary and proper, in the opinion of the Board of Fire Commissioners and Board of Supervisors, to place said department in the most effective condition for service; and should it hereafter, in the judgment of said Board of Supervisors and Board of Fire Commissioners, be deemed advisable and necessary to organize and establish any company or companies to operate and manage any patent fire extinguisher, or appliance for extinguishing fire, that may be purchased for the use and more effectual working of said fire department, said company or companies shall be organized, officered and manned as said Boards may, by regulation or order, direct. Volunteer companies may be organized for outside districts of said City and County, upon the recommendation of the Board of Fire Commissioners, and approval of the Board of Supervisors, and when so organized, they shall be under the provisions of this Article, and subject to such rules and regulations as the Board of Fire Commissioners may prescribe; but none of the members thereof, except the steward of the company, shall receive any salary, which salary shall be fixed by the Board of Supervisors, upon the application of the Board of Fire Commissioners.

SEC. 5.   [*Amended by section 5 of Act of March* 28, 1878, *ante.*]

SEC. 6.   All the paid members of said fire department, except the veterinary surgeon, foreman, assistant foreman, company clerks, hosemen, hook and ladder men, and stewards of volunteer companies, shall give their undivided attention to their respective duties; but the foreman, assistant foreman, company clerks, hosemen, hook and ladder men, and stewards of volunteer companies, shall perform such duties as may be prescribed from time to time by said Board of Fire Commissioners, and ordered to be executed by the Chief Engineer.

SEC. 7.   The Board of Supervisors of said City and County shall have power to contract for and locate all cisterns, hydrants, engine, hose, and hook and ladder houses required; to contract for and furnish all supplies; to direct and control all alterations and repairs; and to [?] all orders for the government and control of said fire department, as they shall deem for the best interest thereof.   And said Board of Fire Commissioners shall have power to prescribe the duties of the officers and members of said fire department, and to adopt rules and regulations for the management and discipline thereof; *provided*, that such rules and regulations shall first be approved by said Board of Supervisors.   And said Board of Supervisors are authorized and required to provide and furnish, for the use of said Board of Fire Commissioners, a suitable room or rooms in some of the public buildings of said City and County, to serve as an office for their meetings and the transaction of business relating to said fire department, in which their clerk shall be in attendance daily, during office hours.   The Chief and Assistant Engineers of said Department shall also make it their headquarters daily, during office hours, when not otherwise engaged in official duties.

SEC. 8.   [*Obsolete.*]

SEC. 9.   Said Board of Fire Commissioners shall supervise and control said fire department, its officers and members, subject to the laws governing the same, and shall see that the officers and members thereof faithfully discharge their duties, and that the laws, orders and regulations relating thereto are carried into operation and effect. They shall not, nor shall either of them, or the Chief or Assistant Engineers of said fire department, be interested in any contract pertaining in any manner to said department, or in the sale or furnishing of apparatus or supplies for the same; and all contracts in violation of this section are declared void, and any of said persons violating the

provisions of this section, shall be deemed guilty of felony, and, upon conviction, may be punished accordingly.

SEC. 10.   [*Amended by section 9, of Act of March* 28, 1878.]

SECS. 11, 12 and 13, *are superseded by Act of March* 28, 1878.

SEC. 12.   [*Obsolete.*]

SEC. 13.   [*Obsolete.*]

SEC. 14.   This Act shall take effect and be in force from and after its passage.

SUPPLEMENT LXXI.

1875-6, 54.

---

*An Act to establish and maintain a training-ship in the City and
County of San Francisco.*

[Approved February 15, 1876.]

*The People of the State of California, represented in Senate and Assembly,
do enact as follows:*

SEC. 1.   The Board of Supervisors of the City and County of San Francisco is hereby authorized to procure a ship, of suitable size and tonnage,
with all the necessary tackle, furniture, and equipments, provided said ship
can be obtained without expense to said City and County, on board of which
to instruct boys in practical seamanship and navigation, to be called a training ship.   Said ship shall cruise at least fifteen days in each month, in order
that the pupils may acquire a thorough knowledge of nautical evolutions by
experience and practice.   When not engaged in cruising she shall be anchored
in the Bay of San Francisco, within the corporate limits of said City and
County.   Said Board shall supply said ship with all the materials and implements necessary to give to said boys a proper and efficient nautical education;
and the said Board is hereby authorized to apply to the United States Government for the use of a vessel and supplies for the purpose above mentioned, and to accept therefrom any vessel, together with its necessary tackle,
furniture, and equipments, which the said Government may assign to said
City and County, to be used for the purposes contemplated by this Act; and

to accept the service of any officers or men which said Government may detail for services on board any such vessel, and upon such terms and conditions, consistent with the provisions of this Act, as the said Government may prescribe.

SEC. 2. Said training-ship shall be under the general management of the Board of Supervisors of the City and County of San Francisco, who shall appoint as one of their standing committees a committee of three of their members, to be called the "Training-ship Committee," who shall, subject to the approval of the said Board of Supervisors, prescribe terms and conditions of service; *provided*, that no boys shall be received on board of said ship as punishment, or in commutation of punishment for crime; *and further provided*, that all boys received on board such ship shall be examined by a competent physician and prove to be in sound bodily health, and shall not be under fourteen or over eighteen years of age. Said committee shall, under the directions of said Board of Supervisors, adopt rules and regulations for the government of said boys, and appoint all necessary instructors and employees, and fix their compensation; and shall require the Principal or Superintendent to furnish to said Board quarterly reports of the number of pupils, their character, progress, and such other matters as said Board shall direct.

SEC. 3. Said Board is hereby authorized and empowered to indenture or transfer from the training-ship, after any semi-annual examination, and with his consent, and that of his parents or guardian, any boy thereon, to any merchant ship or vessel of the United States, for service thereon, upon such terms and conditions as said Board shall prescribe, consistent with the original enlistment of said boys.

SEC. 4. Any person who shall aid any boy in escaping or deserting from said training-ship shall be guilty of a misdemeanor, and be punished by fine not exceeding one thousand dollars, or imprisonment in the County Jail for a term not exceeding one year, or by both such fine and imprisonment.

SEC. 5. [*Amended by Act of March* 13, 1878; 1878, 233.]

SEC. 6. The ship known as the training-ship shall be exempt from all charges for pilotage when going into or out of any port of this State. When the commander of said ship applies for the services of a pilot, said pilot refusing the same free of charge, the power appointing said pilot may revoke his license.

SEC. 7. An Act entitled "An Act to establish and maintain a training-ship or ships in the City and County of San Francisco," approved March sixteenth, eighteen hundred and seventy-four, and all Acts or parts of Acts, so far as the same may be inconsistent with the provisions of this Act, are hereby repealed.

SEC. 8. This Act shall take effect from and after its passage, and the

Board of Supervisors of said City and County is hereby authorized to accept the ship "Jamestown," or any vessel substituted therefor, from the Government of the United States, if fully equipped for the purposes indicated in this Act.

SUPPLEMENT LXXIV.

1875-6, 82.

An Act to establish water rates in the City and County of San Francisco.

[Approved March 1, 1876.]

The People of the State of California, represented in Senate and Assembly, do enact as follows:

SECTION 1. [*Obsolete.*]

SEC. 2. [*Obsolete.*]

SEC. 3. [*Obsolete.*]

SEC. 4. [*Obsolete.*]

SEC. 5. [*Obsolete.*]

SEC. 6. [*Obsolete.*]

SEC. 7. The Board of Supervisors of the City and County of San Francisco are hereby fully authorized and empowered to determine and establish, by order or resolution, the size of the pipes or mains to be laid down in the streets, highways, public squares, and parks of said City and County, and to regulate the pressure and amount of water to be kept flowing in and through said pipes and mains at all times, and to fix and determine the fine to be imposed, not exceeding five hundred dollars, for any violation of the provisions of this section, at the suit of the City and County of San Francisco, to be collected in any court of competent jurisdiction; and every day's failure to maintain a proper supply of water to meet the public requirements shall be deemed a new offense and punished accordingly; and all fines collected for a violation of the provisions of this Act, and of the orders passed by the Board of Supervisors to carry out its provisions, shall be paid into the City and County treasury.

Sec. 8. [*Obsolete.*]

Sec. 9. This Act shall take effect and be in force from and after its passage; and all Acts or parts of Acts conflicting with the provisions of this Act are hereby repealed.

[*The Act of April 3, 1876; 1875-6, 760; is both amendatory of and supplementary to the foregoing; the amendments are incorporated therein, the supplementary portions are given below:*]

Sec. 2. [*Obsolete.*]

Sec. 3. The Board of Supervisors of said City and County are hereby empowered, by ordinance, to provide regulations to prevent waste, by consumers, of the waters supplied for their use, as hereinbefore mentioned; and any violation of the provisions of such ordinance is hereby declared to be a misdemeanor punishable by such penalty as may be prescribed by said Board of Supervisors.

Sec. 4. The provisions of the Act to which this Act is amendatory and supplementary, and this Act, shall be applicable to all corporations engaged in, or which may hereafter engage in the business of supplying water to the inhabitants of the City and County of San Francisco.

Sec. 5. This Act shall take effect immediately.

S U P P L E M E N T   L X X V.

1875-6, 153.   *

An Act to authorize the appointment of an additional Interpreter for the Criminal Courts of the City and County of San Francisco.

[Approved March 8, 1876.]

The People of the State of California, represented in Senate and Assembly, do ordain as follows:

Section 1. The Police Judge and County Judge* and Mayor of the City and County of San Francisco shall have power to appoint an additional In-

---

* Now Judge of Superior Court. Act of April 30, 1880; 1880, 115.

terpreter for the Criminal Courts of said City and County, of the Portuguese, Italian and Sclavonian languages.

Sec. 2. The salary of such interpreter shall be of the same amount, not exceeding one hundred and twenty-five dollars per month, and shall be paid in the same manner, and at the same time, as the other Interpreters of said Courts are now or shall hereafter be paid.

Sec. 3. This Act shall take effect and be in force from and after its passage.

SUPPLEMENT LXXVI.

1875-6, 310.

An Act to confer additional powers upon the Board of Supervisors of the City and County of San Francisco, and upon the Auditor and Treasurer thereof, and to authorize certain appropriations of money by said Board.

[Approved March 16, 1876.]

The People of the State of California, represented in Senate and Assembly, do enact as follows:

Section 1. The Board of Supervisors of the City and County of San Francisco is hereby authorized and empowered to appropriate, allow and order paid out of the General Fund, the sum of ten thousand dollars, for preparing a comprehensive and intelligent system of sewerage for that portion of the City and County of San Francisco where the grades have been established, and for making surveys, and preparing a map showing the size and materials of all sewers constructed and to be constructed by order of the Board of Supervisors, and for reporting upon the mode adopted to secure ventilation of sewers, with plans and rules as to the construction and connection of private sewers with the public sewers, etc.

Sec. 2. This Act shall take effect and be in force from and after its passage.

13

SUPPLEMENT LXXVII.

1875-6, 325.

An Act to provide for the care and maintenance of inebriates and certain insane persons in the City and County of San Francisco.

[Approved March 17, 1876.]

The People of the State of California, represented in Senate and Assembly, do enact as follows:

SECTION 1. The fines and forfeitures, not exceeding eight hundred dollars in the aggregate, in any one month, imposed and collected by the Police Judge's Court, in and for the City and County of San Francisco, from persons arrested for being drunk or under the influence of liquor, shall be, by the Clerk of said Police Judge's Court, immediately paid to the President, Secretary, and Treasurer, or a majority of them, of the Home for the Care of Inebriates, of said City and County, for the support and maintenance of said Home for the Care of Inebriates, and the construction and improvement of a building for said Home for the Care of Inebriates; and the said President, Secretary, and Treasurer, and each of them, shall give a good and sufficient bond in the sum of ten thousand dollars, with two or more sufficient sureties, to be approved by the County Judge* of said City and County, for the faithful management and disbursement of the moneys received by them under the provisions of this Act; and the said President, Secretary, and Treasurer shall, semi-annually, and as often as they may be required by the Board of Supervisors of said City and County, report, under oath, to said Board, a detailed Statement of all their receipts and disbursements of said moneys; and neither the President, Secretary, Treasurer, nor any Trustee of said Home shall be entitled to or receive any fee, salary, emolument, or reward of any kind whatsoever, for any services rendered by them or either of them as such officers.

SEC. 2. The Clerk of said Police Judge's Court shall take from the President, Secretary, and Treasurer aforesaid, or a majority of them, a receipt in duplicate for all money paid to them under the provisions of this Act, one of

---

Now Judge of Superior Court.

which he shall file in the said Police Judge's Court, and the other with the Clerk of the Board of Supervisors of said City and County.

Sec. 3. All persons in said City and County charged with being insane, and pending their examination, or found to be insane and en route for a State Insane Asylum, shall be placed in said Home, and shall be cared for by the officers thereof while in said Home, without charge to said City and County.

Sec. 4. All Acts and parts of Acts in conflict with the provisions of this Act are hereby repealed, and an Act entitled "An Act to confer further powers upon the Board of Supervisors of the City and County of San Francisco," approved April twenty-fifth, eighteen hundred and sixty-three, is hereby repealed.

Sec. 5. This Act shall take effect immediately.

SUPPLEMENT LXXVIII.

1875-6, 360.

_____

An Act in relation to the manufacture of acids and explosive chemicals in the City and County of San Francisco, and for other purposes.

[Approved March 20, 1876.]

The People of the State of California, represented in Senate and Assembly, do enact as follows:

Section 1. From and after the passage of this Act, the Board of Supervisors of the City and County of San Francisco shall have full power and authority to fix limits in said City and County, within which the manufacture of gunpowder, giant powder, dynamite, nitro-glycerine, or other combustible or explosive chemicals, and the maintenance of acid works, shall be prohibited; and to make such rules and regulations in relation to the manufacture and transportation of such substances and the maintenance of acid works in any part of said City and County as they may deem proper and advisable.

Sec. 2. This Act shall take effect immediately.

SUPPLEMENT LXXIX.

1875-6, 461.

*An Act to provide for the completion of the building in the City
and County of San Francisco known as the New City
Hall.*

[Approved March 24, 1876.]

*The People of the State of California, represented in Senate and Assembly, do
enact as follows :*

SECTION 1. The Mayor, City and County Attorney, and Auditor of the
City and County of San Francisco, and their successors in office, are hereby
authorized to act as a Board to be known as the Board of New City Hall
Commissioners for the City and County of San Francisco. And the said
Board are hereby authorized, empowered, and directed to take possession of
the premises bounded by Larkin Street on the west, McAllister Street on the
north, and Park Avenue on the South and Southeast, and the improvements
thereon, and to proceed with the construction of the building on said premises known as the New City Hall, according to the plans heretofore adopted
for a permanent building, as contemplated by "An Act of the Legislature of
the State of California to provide for the erection of a City Hall in the City
and County of San Francisco," approved April fourth, eighteen hundred and
seventy. And the Board of Supervisors of the City and County of San
Francisco are hereby authorized, empowered, and directed to turn over and
deliver to the Board of New City Hall Commissioners, all and singular, the
site, superstructure, and material of said City Hall, as well as all the plans,
specifications, books, papers, contract rights, privileges, machinery, tools
and appliances, and property of every description and nature belonging to
the same.

SEC. 2. Before entering upon the discharge of their duties, the said Commissioners shall take and subscribe, before an officer authorized to administer oaths, the oath of office; and shall each give a bond in the sum of ten
thousand dollars, with two good and sufficient sureties, to be approved by
the Judge of the Municipal Court of the City and County of San Francisco,
conditioned for the faithful discharge of the duties as herein prescribed; and
the said oaths of office and bonds shall be filed in the office of the County
Treasurer of the City and County of San Francisco.

SEC. 3. As soon as said Commissioners are qualified as herein provided, they shall proceed to organize the Board. The Mayor shall be President of the Board, and keep a record of its proceedings until a Secretary is duly appointed and qualified. The Board shall appoint a Secretary, in the manner herein provided, who shall take the oath of office, and give a bond, conditioned for the faithful discharge of his duties, in the sum of five thousand dollars, with two good and sufficient sureties, to be approved by the Judge of the Municipal Court* of the City and County of San Francisco; which bond shall be filed in the office of the County Treasurer of said City and County. The Secretary shall hold office at the pleasure of the Board.

SEC. 4. As soon after the organization of the Board as the Commissioners may deem expedient, they shall proceed to appoint an Architect and a Superintendent of Works, who shall hold their respective offices at the pleasure of the Board. The Architect and Superintendent of Works shall each take and subscribe the oath of office, and each shall give a bond; the Architect in the sum of twenty-five thousand dollars, and the Superintendent of Works in the sum of twenty thousand dollars, with two good and sufficient sureties, to be approved by the Judge of the Municipal Court, conditioned for the faithful discharge of their respective duties. The Superintendent of Works shall be a master builder, and have been a resident of the City and County of San Francisco for at least five years.

SEC. 5. It shall be the duty of the Secretary to take charge of and safely keep the books, papers and records of the Board of Commissioners, to attend all meetings of the Board, and keep full and correct minutes of their proceedings, to keep an accurate account of the receipts and disbursements of the Commission, keep an accurate account with each officer, clerk, contractor, and employee, and perform such other services as are herein provided, and such as may be required of him by the Board of Commissioners. He shall keep his office open every day (Sundays and holidays excepted), from eight o'clock A. M. until five o'clock P. M.

SEC. 6. It shall be the duty of the Architect, under the direction and control of the Commissioners, to draw specifications of the work to be done, to make the necessary drawings for the same, to judge of the quality and durability of the materials that may be furnished for the construction of the said City Hall, and to take special care that all work be done in a good, substantial, and workmanlike manner, and in accordance with the specifications.

SEC. 7. It shall be the duty of the Superintendent of Works, herein authorized to be appointed, when work is being done upon said building, or materials to be used in the construction are being furnished, to be in constant attendance at the said building to see that the work is done in a good, and substantial, and workmanlike manner, and that the materials used are of the

---

* Now Superior Court.

description and quality called for by the specifications. All work upon the said building shall be done under the immediate supervision of the Superintendent of Works, and all materials used in its construction shall also be furnished under his immediate supervision. He shall also perform such other and further duties connected with the construction of said City Hall as shall be required of him by the Board of Commissioners hereby created.

SEC. 8. The salary of each Commissioner shall be one hundred dollars per month. The salary of the Secretary shall be two hundred dollars per month. The salary of the Architect shall be two hundred and fifty dollars per month. The salary of the Superintendent shall be two hundred and fifty dollars per month. The salaries herein provided shall be in full compensation for all services rendered under this Act, and no other or greater compensation shall at any time be allowed or paid to either of the officers herein named. [*As amended Mar.* 20, 1878; 1878, 382.]

SEC. 9. All meetings of the Board shall be held in the room in which the meetings of the Board of Supervisors of the City and County of San Francisco are held, and shall be public; and the records and proceedings of the Board shall be open to the inspection of the public at any time during office hours.

SEC. 10. The Board shall appoint officers, award contracts, allow claims, and authorize the expenditure of money, by resolutions entered in the minutes of the Board. All resolutions appointing an officer, awarding a contract, allowing a claim, or authorizing the expenditure of money, after its introduction, and before it is finally acted upon by the Board, shall be published for at least five successive days (Sundays and holidays excepted), in at least two daily newspapers, published in the City and County of San Francisco, of general circulation. At any time after the first and before the last publication of a resolution, as herein provided, any citizen may protest in writing against the adoption of such resolution by the Board, and the Board shall consider and dispose of such protest before acting upon the resolution. All resolutions shall be voted upon by ayes and nays, which shall be entered in the minutes of the Board.

SEC. 11. In the event that the Board of Supervisors of the City and County of San Francisco shall deem it expedient to continue the construction of the New City Hall in the mode and manner prescribed by this Act, they are hereby authorized and empowered to express such judgment by resolution or order, in such form as they may deem proper.. And for the purpose of raising the money necessary to complete said building, the said Board of Supervisors are hereby authorized and empowered to levy and collect annually, for the fiscal year commencing July first, eighteen hundred and seventy-six, and ending June thirtieth, eighteen hundred and seventy-seven, and each and every fiscal year thereafter, during the four fiscal years next ensuing, in the same manner and at the same times as other taxes in said City and County are levied and collected, an ad valorem property tax, on real and personal property within said City and County, of fifteen cents on each one hundred dollars of value, as shown by the assessment roll of said City and County for the current fiscal year.

SEC. 12. The money arising from the tax hereby authorized to be levied and collected shall be kept by the City and County Treasurer in a fund to be known as the "New City Hall Fund," and out of which said fund all claims for work, labor, and materials used in the construction of said building, and the salaries of the Commissioners, the Secretary, the Architect, the Superintendent of Works, and others employed in and about the construction of said building, and necessary office expenses of the Board of Commissioners, shall be paid. All claims against the said fund shall be allowed by the Board of Commissioners, by resolution entered upon the minutes, before the Auditor shall be authorized to audit the same, and in no case shall any portion of said fund be used or expended for any other purpose than that herein indicated, nor shall any part of the cost of the construction of said building be paid out of any other or different fund; nor shall any lien for work, labor, or material at any time attach to the said building, nor the land upon which the same is located, in any manner whatever. The Board of Commissioners, in each fiscal year, may make contracts and expend in the construction of said building a sum equal to the estimated receipts of the fund during the current fiscal year, but no larger or greater sum.

SEC. 13. The first moneys coming into the fund hereby authorized to be created shall be applied by the said Board of Commissioners to completing, so that it may be immediately occupied, that part of the said City Hall which is intended to be used as the Hall of Records, or office of the City and County Recorder, and other moneys coming into the said fund shall be expended as far as practicable, without increasing the cost of the work, in completing, from time to time, other parts of the said building; and the parts so completed shall be used for the purposes for which they were constructed, as soon as they are ready for occupancy.

SEC. 14. When work is to be done upon said building, or materials to be furnished, it shall be the duty of the Board of Commissioners to advertise, for at least thirty days, in the official paper, and in the morning and the evening newspapers published in said City and County, having the largest circulation, for sealed proposals for doing said work or furnishing said material, or for doing both said work and furnishing said material, as they may deem best. The said work and materials shall be of the best quality. The advertisement shall contain a general description of the work to be done and the materials to be furnished, the time within which the same is to be done or furnished, and may refer to plans and specifications for such other details as may be necessary to give a correct understanding regarding the work or materials. The advertisement shall also state the day and an hour on said

day within which bids will be received. At the time named in the advertisement the Board shall assemble and remain in session for at least one
hour, and all bids shall be delivered to the Board whilst it is in session, and
within the hour named in the advertisement. No bids not so delivered to
the Board shall be considered. All bids called for by the advertisement
shall be on blanks to be furnished by the Secretary of the Board; each bid,
as it is received, shall be numbered and marked " Filed " by the President.
At the expiration of the hour stated in the advertisement within which bids
will be received, the Board shall proceed to open the bids in the presence of
the bidders, and an abstract of each shall be recorded in the minutes of the
Board by the Secretary. Before adjourning, the Commissioners shall compare the bids with the record made by the Secretary, and fix the day and
hour for a meeting of the Board to consider the bids and award the contract.
An abstract of said bids, showing the name of each bidder, the price at which
work, labor, or materials is offered by each, and such other things as may be
necessary to show or explain the offer, shall be made by the Secretary, and
published for five days in a daily newspaper published in the City and County
of San Francisco, of general circulation. At the expiration of five days after the
first publication of the abstract, on the day and at the hour fixed by the
Board, the said Board of Commissioners, with the aid and assistance of the
Architect and Superintendent of Works, shall proceed to consider the several bids, and award the contract for doing the work or supplying the materials for which proposals were invited, and for none other, to the lowest
bidder who shall furnish sufficient sureties to guarantee the performance of
the contract; *provided*, the said Board of Commissioners shall have the
right to reject any and all bids when, in their judgment, the public interests
are thereby promoted; *and provided further*, that no contract shall be
awarded, except by the final passage of the resolution awarding said contract by the Board, in the manner herein prescribed. No change or modification in the place or specification shall be made after proposals for doing
work or furnishing materials have been called for; nor shall a contractor be
allowed a claim for work done, or materials furnished, not embraced in his
contract. All contracts shall be in writing, and shall be carefully drawn by
the District Attorney, in and for said City and County, and shall contain
detailed specifications of the work to be done, the manner in which the
same shall be executed, the quality of the material, and the time in which
the same shall be completed, with such penalty for the non-performance of
such contract as the said Board of Commissioners shall deem just and reasonable. Every contract entered into by the said Board, under the provisions of this Act, shall be signed by the Commissioners and by the other
contracting party. All contracts shall be signed in triplicate—one copy of
which, with the plans and specifications of the work to be done, shall be
filed with the Clerk of the Board of Supervisors, and shall at all times, in
office hours, be open to the inspection of the public; one, with the plans
and specifications, shall be kept in the office of the Board, or placed in the

hands of the Architects, and the other copy, with plans and specifications, shall be delivered to the contractor. All bids made, and all contracts entered into for the construction of any portion of the said City Hall, shall contain an express condition that no Chinaman or Mongolian shall be employed in the factory, mill, foundry, workshop, or by the firm, company, or person in doing any of the work bid and contracted for; and a failure to comply with said provision of said contract shall work a forfeiture of said contract.

SEC. 15. The Board of Commissioners may make payments to contractors from time to time, as work progresses or materials are furnished. But until the contract is completed, at no time shall such payment exceed seventy-five per cent. of the value of the labor or materials furnished, which said value shall be ascertained and determined by the Architect and Superintendent of Works, subject to the approval of the Board of Commissioners.

SEC. 16. It shall be the duty of the Board of Commissioners, on the second Monday of July, eighteen hundred and seventy-seven, and on the second Monday of July in each and every year thereafter, to and including the year eighteen hundred and eighty-one, to make out and publish in two of the daily newspapers published in the City and County of San Francisco, a tabular statement, showing as follows, to wit:

First. The receipts of the New City Hall Fund during the fiscal year ending June thirtieth preceding.

Second. The amount to which the said fund is entitled for the same fiscal year, but yet not received.

Third. The amount paid out of the fund during the same fiscal year.

Fourth. The amount due upon contracts awarded during said fiscal year.

Fifth. The amount credited to the fund in each previous fiscal year.

Sixth. The amount paid out of the fund in each previous fiscal year.

Seventh. The estimated amount required to complete the City Hall; and such other matters and things as go to show the condition of the fund and its management, and the progress that has been made in the construction of the said City Hall, together with a list of all contracts that have been awarded under the provisions of this Act.

SEC. 17. When the said City Hall shall be erected and completed, as in this Act provided, the said Commissoners shall turn over to the Board of Supervisors of the City and County of San Francisco, all their books, papers and vouchers, and property of every description, and, at the same time, shall render a full and final account of their transactions, which said account shall be examined by said Board of Supervisors, and if found correct, approved, and thereupon the office of said Commissioners, and their powers and duties, shall cease and determine; *provided*, the sureties on their official bonds shall not be discharged from liability until such accounts shall have been so examined and found correct.

SEC. 18. The Commissioners authorized by this Act shall not, nor shall either of them, or the Architect, the Superintendent of Works, or the Secretary, be interested, directly or indirectly, in any contract for work, labor or materials furnished in the construction of the City Hall; nor shall either of them be allowed to receive any gratuity or advantage from any contractor, laborer or person furnishing labor or materials for the same. A violation of the provisions of this section shall be a felony, and upon conviction thereof, the party so offending shall be punished by a fine not exceeding five thousand dollars, or imprisonment in the State Prison for a period not exceeding five years, or by both fine and imprisonment, in the discretion of the Court.

SEC. 19. Any public officer or employee of the City and County of San Francisco, in any way connected with the construction of the City Hall, who shall willfully aid or assist a bidder for a contract to furnish labor or materials to be used in the construction of said City Hall, to secure the award of a contract at a higher price or rate than another bidder had proposed to contract to do the work or furnish the material, when sealed proposals have been advertised for, or who shall in any way favor one bidder for a contract over another, by giving or withholding information relative to the plans or specifications, or who shall willfully mislead any bidder with regard to the plans and specifications, and any person who shall change or modify the plans or specifications of work or materials, after proposals have been solicited, or shall aid a contractor in obtaining compensation for work and material not embraced in his contract, shall be guilty of a misdemeanor, and upon conviction thereof, shall be punished by imprisonment in the County Jail of the City and County of San Francisco for a period of not less than six months, or by a fine of five hundred dollars, or by fine and imprisonment, at the discretion of the Court.

SEC. 20. Any officer or employee of the City and County of San Francisco, whose duty it is to superintend, supervise, direct, or control a contractor on the said City Hall, who shall willfully or carelessly accept other or different material, or permit other or different material than such that is called for by the specifications to be used in the construction of the City Hall, or who shall permit unskilled or inferior labor to be employed in the construction of the said building, or shall accept on behalf of the City and County work which is not good, substantial, and workmanlike, or who shall knowingly or carelessly certify to the correctness of a claim of a contractor, or other, for work, or labor, or material, for more than such contractor is lawfully entitled, or who shall willfully or carelessly certify that a greater amount of work or labor has been performed than has actually been done, or a larger or greater amount of material, or different material has been furnished than has actually been furnished, with the intention of defrauding, or permitting another to defraud the City and County, or who shall be interested directly or indirectly in any contract for work, labor, or for furnishing material to be used in the construction of said City Hall, shall be guilty of a misdemeanor, and upon conviction thereof, shall be punished by imprisonment in the County Jail of the City and County of San Francisco, for a period of not less than six months, or fined in a sum of not less than five hundred dollars, or by fine and imprisonment, at the discretion of the Court.

Sec. 21. This Act shall take effect from and after its passage.

SUPPLEMENT LXXX.

1875-6, 501.

An Act to authorize the City and County of San Francisco to provide and maintain public water-works for said City and County, and to condemn and purchase private property for that purpose.

[Approved March 27, 1876.]

The People of the State of California, represented in Senate and Assembly, do enact as follows:

[Repealed January 23, 1880.]

SUPPLEMENT LXXXI.

1875-6, 507.

An Act to confer further powers upon the Superintendent of Public Streets, Highways and Squares of the City and County of San Francisco.

[Approved March 28, 1876.]

The People of the State of California, represented in Senate and Assembly, do enact as follows:

SECTION 1. The owners of the majority of front feet in any block of the City and County of San Francisco may, within five days after the award of any contract for paving, sewering, piling, and capping on such block, select and recommend in writing to the Superintendent of Public Streets, Highways and Squares of said City and County, a competent person as Inspector, to superintend the construction or improvement of each and every sewer, and of piling and capping, or repiling and recapping, paving and repaving, and thereupon it shall be the duty of said Superintendent to appoint the person so selected as such Inspector; and the person so selected and appointed shall make oath before the said Superintendent to faithfully perform his duties as such Inspector. In case such owners shall fail or neglect, for the period of five days after the award of any contract, to select or recommend a person as Inspector as aforesaid, the said Superintendent shall appoint a competent person as such Inspector. It shall be the duty of such Inspector to remain on the work continuously during the performance thereof, and to see that the contract for any such work is strictly fulfilled in every respect, and in case of any departure from said contract, it shall be his duty to report the same to the said Superintendent of Public Streets, Highways and Squares. The Inspector shall be allowed, for his time actually employed in the discharge of his duties, compensation not to exceed five dollars per day, to be paid by the contractor before the issuance of the assessment, and included therein as part of the expenses of the improvements therein mentioned.

SEC. 2.   All Acts and parts of Acts in conflict with this Act are hereby repealed.

SEC. 3.   This Act shall take effect from and after its passage.

————·————

SUPPLEMENT LXXXII.

1875-6, 632.

————

An Act to utilize the prison labor and govern the House of Correction of the City and County of San Francisco.

[Approved March 31, 1876.]

The People of the State of California, represented in Senate and Assembly, do enact as follows :

SECTION 1.   The Board of Supervisors of the City and County of San Francisco are hereby empowered to make all necessary arrangements, as hereinafter provided, to utilize the labor of the prisoners committed to the Jail or House of Correction of said City and County, for a term of imprisonment, by the Judges of said City and County.

SEC. 2.   All persons convicted by the Judge of the Police Judge's Court and sentenced to a term in the County Jail or House of Correction, shall be deemed to have been also sentenced to labor during such term, unless said Judge, for good cause, orders otherwise, or for reasons hereinafter provided in this Act.

SEC. 3.   [*Repealed by Act of April 1, 1878; 1878, 953.*]

SEC. 4. The Board of Supervisors of the City and County of San Francisco are hereby intrusted with the government of the House of Correction,
and are hereby empowered to carry out the provisions of this Act, and to see
that they are strictly enforced. They shall, on the passage of this Act, appoint a competent Superintendent for the House of Correction of said City
and County, who shall also be Treasurer of said House of Correction, and
who shall give good and sufficient bonds in a sum, and with sureties to be
approved by said Supervisors, for the faithful discharge of his duties, and to
whom shall be paid a salary to be fixed by them, not to exceed two hundred
dollars per month, paid monthly. Said Superintendent shall only be removed for just and sufficient legal cause, after a fair and impartial investigation of his case by said Supervisors. He shall, immediately after his
appointment, and when authorized by said Supervisors, appoint, subject to
the approval of the Supervisors of said City and County, such subordinates
as may be deemed necessary by the Supervisors, and the pay of such subordinates shall be fixed by said Supervisors, not exceeding one hundred dollars per month to each party so appointed.

SEC. 5. The Superintendent shall manage the general interests of the institution; see that its affairs are conducted in accordance with the requirements of this Act, and of such by-laws as the Board of Supervisors may
from time to time adopt for the orderly and economical management of its
concerns; to see that strict discipline is maintained therein; to provide employment for the inmates; adjust and certify all claims against the institution; and all by-laws made by said Supervisors for the management of said
institution, and not contrary to the laws of this State, shall be binding in all
respects upon said Superintendent, officers, and inmates; and said Superintendent shall each year prepare and submit, under oath, to the Board of Supervisors, a report of the concerns of said institution.

SEC. 6. The Superintendent shall reside at the House of Correction, have
charge of its inmates and property, and be its Treasurer; keep accounts of
all his receipts and expenditures, and of all such property, and account in
such manner as the said Board of Supervisors may require; hold all books
and papers open to their inspection.

SEC. 7. The Board of Supervisors of said City and County shall provide
the House of Correction with yard, of sufficient extent for the convenient
employment of the persons confined therein, and enclosed by fences of sufficient height and strength to prevent escapes, and also to prevent all persons
from without from all access to or communication with any persons confined
therein.

SEC. 8. The Board of Supervisors shall cause to be provided, at the expense of said City and County, suitable material and implements sufficient
to keep at work all persons committed to the House of Correction. Said
Board of Supervisors, from time to time as the Superintendent may require,
shall furnish such raw material, within the yard of said House of Correc-

tion, as may be deemed necessary for the constant occupation of the prisoners.

Sec. 9. The Superintendent shall manage the House of Correction, subject to the rules of the said Board of Supervisors and their written orders, and shall be assisted by such police officers as may be required, and whose service shall be obtained by an order by the Board of Supervisors on the Chief of Police, given at least twenty-four hours in advance. The Superintendent shall keep all prisoners employed in such labor, on the public or other works, as may be included in the sentence of the Judge committing the prisoner; and in case the prisoners are disobedient or disorderly, or do not faithfully perform their task, the officers in charge may put fetters and shackles on them, or confine them in dark and solitary cells, and the officers so punishing shall keep a record of the punishment, showing its cause, mode and degree, and duration of such punishment, and furnish the same to the Superintendent, who shall make monthly report to the Board of Supervisors of such punishment, together with a detailed statement of the workings of the House of Correction. A like record of the conduct of each prisoner shall be kept by the Superintendent, and similarly returned to said Board of Supervisors at the end of each month.

Sec. 10. For each month in which the prisoner appears, by the record provided for in section nine of this Act, to have been obedient, orderly and faithful, three days shall, with the consent of the said Board of Supervisors, be deducted from his term of sentence, and for each month that it shall appear from such record that his conduct has been positively good, and that he has rendered a prompt and cheerful obedience to the rules of the House of Correction, five days shall be deducted from such term.

Sec. 11. The Superintendent shall see that the prisoners are at all times kept at labor on the public works of the City and County of San Francisco at least six hours a day, during six days of the week, when the weather will permit. By the public works, as used in this Act, is understood the construction, or repair, or cleaning of any streets, road, dock, wharf, public square, park, building, cutting away hills, grading, or other work whatever, which is authorized to be done by and for the use of the said City and County, and the expense of which is not to be borne exclusively by individuals or property particularly benefited thereby.

Sec. 12. The Superintendent may, with the consent of the said Board of Supervisors, let out the labor of the prisoners to good and responsible parties, at a sum per day to be determined by the said Board; *provided,* the prisoners so laboring shall be duly and sufficiently secured at all times while at work. No prisoner or prisoners shall be allowed to go from the walls of the prison without a proper and sufficient guard.

Sec. 13. When any contract shall be entered into between the Board of Supervisors and others for the labor of the prisoners, as provided in the last section, the Superintendent shall keep an exact account of all such hired labor, the number of days' work done, and for whom, and the amount collected or due on such work. The said Board of Supervisors are hereby authorized to apply the proceeds of such labor to defraying the expenses of the House of Correction.

SEC. 14. If any prisoner shall abscond, or escape, or depart from the House of Correction without license, the Superintendent shall have power to pursue, retake, and bring him back, and to require all necessary aid for that purpose; the Superintendent may confine him to his work by fetters or shackles, or in such manner as he may judge necessary, or may put him in close confinement until he shall submit to the regulations of the House of Correction, and for every escape each offender shall be holden to labor in the House of Correction for the term of one month, in addition to the time for which he was first committed.

SEC. 15. Male and female prisoners shall be confined and kept separately in the House of Correction.

SEC. 16. The Superintendent shall keep the female prisoners at such work at all times as they are able to perform, and shall provide them with necessary material and means whereby they may be enabled to occupy their time in mending or making clothing, etc., for the public or charitable institutions under the charge of said City and County; or the said Board of Supervisors may, from time to time, when in their judgment it may be beneficial or profitable, hire out the work of such women to the highest bidder, and under like circumstances as are provided for in section thirteen of this Act.

SEC. 17. When any person is committed to said House of Correction and is too sick for immediate work, the Superintendent shall order him or her to be well taken care of, in such comfortable quarters as may be provided in the institution for the care of the sick by said Board of Supervisors. Should the attending physician deem any prisoner too sick to remain in the House of Correction, the Superintendent may order him or her to be sent to the City and County Hospital until cured, when he or she must be retained to serve out his or her unexpired term of imprisonment.

SEC. 18. The Board of Supervisors shall fix the salaries of the Superintendent and the other officers of the House of Correction, and shall certify to the Board of Supervisors, every month, the amount of each officer's salary, and said Board of Supervisors are instructed to order the same paid out of the City and County treasury, as other salaries are paid.

SEC. 19. The provisions of this Act requiring prisoners to labor are made applicable to prisoners who may be confined in the County Jail on commitments from the Police or Municipal Criminal Court, for punishment for misdemeanor. But nothing in this Act shall be so construed as to require labor from such defendants as may be detained in said County Jail or House of Correction to await trial in any court, or who may be committed there for contempt of court, or witnesses in any suit, civil or criminal, or on any civil process.

SEC. 20. The City and County Physician shall be required to visit the House of Correction at regular prescribed times to be fixed by the Board of Supervisors, and without additional salary.

SEC. 21. All Acts and parts of Acts in conflict with this Act are hereby repealed.

SEC. 22. This Act shall take effect and be in force from and after its passage.

SUPPLEMENT LXXXIII.

1875-6, 795.

An Act to confer additional powers upon the Board of Supervisors of the City and County of San Francisco.

[Approved April 3, 1876.]

The People of the State of California, represented in Senate and Assembly, do enact as follows:

SECTION 1. The Board of Supervisors of the City and County of San Francisco are hereby authorized and empowered to have the streets in said City and County kept clean, in the following manner: From the first of October to the first of April, in each year, they may employ not to exceed twenty horses and carts, with drivers, and twenty-five additional men, as scrapers and sweepers; and from the first of April to the first of October, in each year, fifteen horses and carts, with drivers, and twenty additional men, as scrapers and sweepers.

SEC. 2. [*Superseded by section 1 of Act of March 2, 1878; 1878, 139.*]

SEC. 3. The Board of Supervisors are hereby authorized and empowered to employ not to exceed ten men and three horses, carts and men, to clean out and remove all sand and dirt that may accumulate in the public sewers.

SEC. 4. [*Superseded by Act, supra.*]

SEC. 5. All the work specified in this Act shall be done under the supervision of the Street Committee of the Board of Supervisors, and of the Superintendent of Public Streets of the City and County of San Francisco.

SEC. 6. The Board of Supervisors are hereby invested with full power and authority to cause the persons sentenced or committed to the House of Correction to be employed in cleaning the public streets, highways and sewers of said City and County of San Francisco.

SEC. 7. This Act shall take effect immediately.

SUPPLEMENT LXXXIV.

1875-6, 829.

An Act to create a City Criminal Court in and for the City and County of San Francisco, to define its powers and jurisdiction.

[Approved April 3, 1876.]

The People of the State of California, represented in Senate and Assembly, do enact as follows:

[Repealed by Constitution of 1879.]

SUPPLEMENT LXXXV.

1875-6, 854.

An Act to confer additional powers upon the Board of Supervisors of the City and County of San Francisco, and upon the Auditor and Treasurer thereof.

[Approved April 3, 1876.]

The People of the State of California, represented in Senate and Assembly do enact as follows:

SECTION 1. If at the beginning of any month any money remains unexpended in any of the funds set apart for maintaining the municipal government of the City and County of San Francisco, and which might lawfully have been expended the preceding month, such unexpended sum or sums may be carried forward and expended by order of the Board of Supervisors in any succeeding month; *provided*, that said Board of Supervisors shall not hereafter make any contract for any purpose, binding said city for a longer period than two years. *

SEC. 2. This Act shall take effect from and after its passage.

---

* See Act of February 25, 1878; 1877-78, 111.

14

SUPPLEMENT LXXXVI.

1875-6, 858.

An Act to confer additional power on the Board of Supervisors of the City and County of San Francisco.

[Approved April 3, 1876.]

The People of the State of California, represented in Senate and Assembly, do enact as follows:

SECTION 1. The Board of Supervisors of the City and County of San Francisco are hereby authorized and directed to appropriate, from the General Fund of said City and County, the sum of five thousand dollars for the improvement of Hamilton Square of said City and County; also, to allow and order paid, out of the General Fund, the sum of fifteen thousand dollars for the maintenance of the Golden Gate Park, said sum to be expended in such manner as the Board of Park Commissioners may direct.

SEC. 2. The Auditor of said City and County is hereby directed to audit, and the Treasurer of said City and County is hereby directed to pay out of the General Fund of said City and County, upon the order of the Board of Supervisors of said City and County, in accordance with the provisions of section one of this Act.

SEC. 3. This Act shall take effect immediately.

SUPPLEMENT LXXXVII.

1875-6, 859.

An Act to confer further powers upon the Board of Supervisors of the City and County of San Francisco.

[Approved April 3, 1876.]

The People of the State of California, represented in Senate and Assembly, do enact as follows:

SECTION 1. The Board of Supervisors of the City and County of San Francisco are hereby authorized and empowered to appropriate and order to be paid, out of the General Fund of said City and County, the following sums, for the purposes hereinafter named: Ten thousand dollars for grading and otherwise improving Jefferson Square, in said City and County; ten thousand dollars ($10,000) for grading, fencing, and otherwise improving Alta Plaza, in said City and County; five *thousand dollars ($5,000) for fencing and otherwise improving Pioneer Park, on Telegraph Hill, in said City and County; *provided*, that the absolute title to said park shall be first granted to the said City and County by deed of gift; *and provided further*, that no money be appropriated or paid out of any fund for the purchase of said Pioneer Park.

SEC. 2. The Auditor of said City and County is directed to audit, and the Treasurer of said City and County to pay, upon the order of the said Board, the several sums hereinbefore mentioned, for the purposes specified.

SEC. 3. This Act shall take effect from and after its passage.

SUPPLEMENT LXXXVIII.

1875-6, 860.

An Act concerning the office of Collector of Licenses for the City and County of San Francisco.

[Approved April 3, 1876.]

The People of the State of California, represented in Senate and Assembly, do enact as follows:

SECTION 1. The Collector of Licenses, the Deputy Collector of Licenses, and the Assistant Collectors of Licenses of the City and County of San Francisco shall, from and after the first day of the month next succeeding the passage of this Act, receive as salaries, payable out of the General Fund, the following sums, namely: Collector of Licenses, the sum of two hundred dollars per month;* the Deputy Collector of Licenses, one hundred and fifty dollars per month; and the Assistant Deputy Collector, one hundred and twenty-five dollars each, payable in the same manner as the salaries of the other City and County officers are paid.

SEC. 2. From and after the first day of the month next succeeding the

---

* Superseded by Act of March 26, 1878, and fixed at $3,000 per annum,

passage of this Act there shall be as many Assistant Collectors of Licenses for the City and County of San Francisco as the Collector of Licenses, with the advice and consent of the Mayor, Auditor and Treasurer, may deem necessary, not exceeding twelve in number, who, together with the Deputy Collector of Licenses, shall hold their offices by the appointment and during the pleasure of the Collector of Licenses of said City and County.

SEC. 3. Not more than thirty days prior to the first day in July, eighteen hundred and seventy-seven, and biennially thereafter, not more than thirty days prior to the first Monday in July of such biennial year, the Mayor, the Auditor and the Treasurer of the said City and County shall appoint, subject to the confirmation by the Board of Supervisors of said City and County, a suitable person as Collector of Licenses for the City and County of San Francisco, who shall hold office for the term of two years from, on, and after the first Monday in July succeeding his appointment and confirmation, and until his successor shall, in the same manner, be appointed and confirmed, and shall have qualified.

SEC. 4. In case of a vacancy occurring by death or otherwise, in the office of the Collector of Licenses of said City and County, holding his office under the provisions of the last preceding section, the same shall be filled for the remainder of the unexpired term by appointment of the Mayor, Treasurer and Auditor, and confirmation of the Board of Supervisors of said City and County; and in case of the inability of said Collector of Licenses to act, his place shall, in the same manner, be temporarily filled until such disability is removed.

SEC. 5. All Acts and parts of Acts, so far as they are in conflict with this Act, are hereby repealed.

SEC. 6. This Act shall take effect and be in force immediately.

———————

SUPPLEMENT LXXXIX.

1875-6, 861.

————

An Act to provide for the preservation and improvement of Golden Gate Park, in the City and County of San Francisco.

[Approved April 3, 1876.]

The People of the State of California, represented in Senate and Assembly, do enact as follows:

SECTION 1. The Board of Supervisors of the City and County of San

Francisco shall have the power to levy and collect, in the mode prescribed by law for the assessment and collection of taxes, by tax each year, upon all property in said City and County, the sum of one and one-half cents upon each one hundred dollars' valuation of taxable property therein, for the purpose of preserving and improving Golden Gate Park, in said City and County. Said sum of money so raised shall be so disbursed by the Park Commissioners for the purposes in like manner as the moneys heretofore disbursed by said Commissioners.

SEC. 2. The Park Commissioners shall employ one general Superintendent, who shall perform the duties of overseer and managing gardener, and shall receive a salary not to exceed the sum of two hundred dollars per month for his services. The City and County Surveyor shall be *ex officio* the engineer for said park, and perform such engineering work as the Commissioners may require of him. Said Commissioners, in addition to said general Superintendent, may from time to time employ at wages such laborers and other workmen as may be necessary to properly carry on the duties herein provided for, and no others except as provided in this Act. They shall in no year incur any greater liability or disburse moneys beyond the amount raised by the tax provided for in section one for such year. No employees shall be kept by said Commissioners except as herein prescribed.

SEC. 3. This Act shall take effect immediately.

SUPPLEMENT XC.

1875-6, 902.

An Act to authorize the Board of Education of the City and County of San Francisco to provide for the support of the Common Schools of said City and County.

[Approved April 3, 1876.]

The People of the State of California, represented in Senate and Assembly, do enact as follows:

SECTION 1. It shall be the duty of the Board of Education of the City and County of San Francisco, on or before the second Monday of September in each year, to report to the Board of Supervisors of the said City and County an estimate of the amount of money which will be required during the year for the purpose of meeting the current annual expenses of public instruction in said City and County, specifying the amount required for supplies furnished to pupils, for purchasing and procuring sites, for leasing rooms or buildings, or erecting buildings, and for furnishing, fitting up, altering, enlarging, and repairing the buildings and premises under their charge, for the support of schools which shall have been organized by the Board since the last annual apportionment, for salaries of teachers, janitors, clerks, and other employees of the Board, and for such further sum or sums as may be necessary for any of the purposes authorized by this Act; but the aggregate amount so reported shall not exceed the sum of thirty-five dollars for each pupil who shall have actually attended and been taught in the preceding year in the schools entitled to participate in the apportionments. The number of pupils who shall be considered as having attended the schools during any one year shall be ascertained by adding together the number of days' attendance of all the pupils in the common schools during the year, and dividing the same by the number of school days in the year. Said Board of Supervisors are hereby authorized and empowered to levy and cause to be collected, at the time and in the manner of levying State and other City and County taxes, the amount of tax, not to exceed thirty-five dollars per pupil, determined and reported by the Board of Education. The amount so levied and collected by said Board of Supervisors shall not include the amounts annually received from poll-taxes.

SECS. 2, 3, 4. [*Obsolete.*]

SEC. 5. This Act shall be in force from and after its passage.

SUPPLEMENT XCI.

1877-8, 5.

An Act relative to street repairs in the City and County of San Francisco.

[Approved December 21, 1877.]

The People of the State of California, represented in Senate and Assembly, do enact as follows:

SECTION 1. The Superintendent of Public Streets, Highways, and Squares, of the City and County of San Francisco, is hereby authorized to employ, at such compensation as the Board of Supervisors may from time to time fix, not to exceed one hundred men, and not to exceed twenty-five horses and carts, to perform the work of ordinary repairs on accepted public streets and on those parts of the water front of said City and County upon which street work done is not by law assessable upon private property, and to perform all ordinary repairs upon brick and pipe sewers in unaccepted streets in said City and County, and such other work on the public streets, highways, and squares, as the Board of Supervisors may direct.

SEC. 2. Upon the requisition of the Superintendent of Public Streets and Highways, the Board of Supervisors may purchase, or authorize said Superintendent to purchase, from the lowest bidder (offering adequate security), all materials required to be used in such repairs. All moneys expended under this Act shall be allowed and paid out of the Street Department funds.

SEC. 3. The Superintendent of Public Streets, Highways, and Squares, shall take charge of and protect all materials belonging to the Street Department, use it for repairs, or make such disposition of the same as the Board of Supervisors may direct.

SEC. 4. In case of urgent necessity the Board of Supervisors may authorize the employment by the Superintendent of Streets of such additional men, horses, and carts, for the purposes of the work mentioned in this Act, as in the judgment of the Board may be expedient, and all moneys expended under this Act shall be allowed and paid out of the Street Department funds.

SEC. 5. This Act shall take effect from and after its passage.

SUPPLEMENT XCII.

1877–8, 5.

An Act to confer additional powers upon the Board of Supervisors of the City and County of San Francisco, and upon the Auditor and Treasurer thereof, and to authorize certain appropriations of money by said Board.

[Approved December 21, 1877.]

The People of the State of California, represented in Senate and Assembly, do enact as follows:

SEC. 1. [*Authorized Supervisors to appropriate ten thousand dollars for the improvement of Golden Gate Park, the money to be expended by the Park Commissioners.*]

SEC. 2. The Park Commissioners, mentioned in section one of this Act, are hereby authorized to employ a Secretary, at a monthly salary of not exceeding one hundred dollars per month, payable out of the Park Improvement Fund; also to rent an office for the transaction of their business, at an expense of not exceeding fifty dollars per month.

SEC. 3. The Auditor of said City and County is directed to audit, and the Treasurer of said City and County to pay, upon the order of the Board of Supervisors, the several sums hereinbefore mentioned for the purposes specified.

SEC. 4. This Act shall take effect immediately.

SUPPLEMENT XCIII.

1877–8, 18.

———

An Act to limit and fix the rates of fares on street railroads in cities and towns of more than one hundred thousand inhabitants.

[Approved January 1, 1878.]

The People of the State of California, represented in Senate and Assembly, do enact as follows:

SECTION 1. No street railroad in any city or town in this State, with more than one hundred thousand inhabitants, shall be allowed to charge or collect a higher rate of fare than five cents for each passenger per trip of any distance in one direction, either going or coming, along any part of the whole length of the road or its connections.

SEC. 2. Every violation of the provisions of section one of this Act shall subject the owner or owners of the street railroad violating the same to a forfeiture to the person so unlawfully charged, or paying more than is therein allowed to be charged, the sum of two hundred and fifty dollars for each and every instance when such unlawful charge is made or collected, to be recovered by suit in any Court of competent jurisdiction; such causes of action shall be assignable, and the action may be maintained by the assignee in his own name, and several causes of action arising out of unlawful charges or collections from different persons may be vested in the assignee and united in the same action.

SEC. 3. This Act shall be in force from its passage.

SUPPLEMENT XCIV.

1877-8, 23.

An Act to preserve the name of a street in the City of San Francisco.

[Approved January 15, 1578.]

The People of the State of California, represented in Senate and Assembly, do enact as follows:

SECTION 1. The street in San Francisco heretofore known as Dupont Street, and running from Market Street to the bay, shall hereafter be known by that name through the entire length thereof, notwithstanding any attempt by the Board of Supervisors of said city and county to change the same.

SEC. 2. This Act shall take effect immediately.

SUPPLEMENT XCV.

1877-8, 70.

An Act to authorize the District Attorney of the City and County of San Francisco to appoint a Second Assistant District Attorney.

[Approved February 6, 1578.]

The People of the State of California, represented in Senate and Assembly, do enact as follows:

SECTION 1. The District Attorney of the City and County of San Francisco may, in writing, appoint a deputy, who shall, while in office, receive a salary of two hundred and fifty dollars a month, payable as the salary of the District Attorney is now payable by law.

SEC. 2. This Act shall take effect from and after its passage.

SUPPLEMENT XCVI.

1877-8, 83.

An Act supplementary to an Act entitled an Act to provide for the completion of the building in the City and County of San Francisco known as the "New City Hall," approved March twenty-fourth, eighteen hundred and seventy-six.

[Approved February 15, 1878.]

The People of the State of California, represented in Senate and Assembly, do enact as follows :

SECTION 1. Whenever the Board of Commissioners provided for and established by virtue of the Act to which this is supplementary shall have rejected all the bids for doing any specified work or furnishing material pursuant to section fourteen (14) of said Act, said Board may re-advertise, for ten days, for sealed proposals for doing said work or furnishing said material, as often as may be necessary, but without changing the specifications therefor; *provided*, that all other requirements of said Act shall be complied with, and thereupon a legal award may be made and contract entered into for the doing of said work and furnishing of said material.

SEC. 2. The said Board may reject and not further consider the proposal or bid of any person or persons who have failed or may hereafter fail to enter into any contract awarded to them by said Board, or to carry out or perform the same, and to make award of and enter into contracts as though such delinquent person or persons were not bidding.

SECS. 3 and 4. [*Obsolete.*]

SEC. 5. This Act shall take effect immediately.

SUPPLEMENT XCVII.

1877-8, 106.

An Act to amend an Act entitled "An Act to provide for a Police Contingent Fund," approved February twenty-eighth, eighteen hundred and fifty-nine.

[Approved February 25, 1878.]

The People of the State of California, represented in Senate and Assembly, do enact as follows :

SECTION 1. An Act entitled " An Act to provide for a Police Contingent

Fund," approved February twenty-eighth, eighteen hundred and fifty-nine, is hereby amended so as to read as follows:

SECTION. 1. The Board of Supervisors of the City and County of San Francisco shall annually set apart from the General Fund, in the treasury of said city and county, the sum of seven thousand two hundred dollars, to be called the Police Contingent Fund.

SEC. 2. The Police Commissioners of the City and County of San Francisco, or a majority of them, are hereby authorized to allow, out of the Police Contingent Fund of said city and county, any and all orders signed by the Chief of Police of said city and county; *provided*, that the aggregate of said orders shall not exceed the sum of seven thousand two hundred dollars per annum.

SEC. 3. The Auditor of said city and county is hereby authorized to audit, and the Treasurer of said city and county to pay out of the Police Contingent Fund, any and all orders so allowed by the Police Commissioners, not exceeding in the aggregate the sum of seven thousand two hundred dollars per annum.

SEC. 4. At the end of each fiscal year, any sum remaining in the Police Contingent Fund, upon which no order shall have been allowed, shall be returned to the credit of the General Fund.

SUPPLEMENT XCVIII.

1877-8, 111.

An Act to regulate and limit the payment of money out of the treasury of the City and County of San Francisco.

[Approved February 25, 1878.]

The People of the State of California, represented in Senate and Assembly, do enact as follows:

SECTION 1. It shall not be lawful hereafter for the Board of Supervisors of the City and County of San Francisco, or any Committee, officer, or Board having power to authorize or contract liabilities against the treasury of said city and county, to authorize, allow, contract for, pay, or render payable, in the present or future, in any one month, any demand or demands against said treasury, or any of the funds thereof, which shall in the aggregate exceed one twelfth part of the amount allowed by laws existing at the time of such contract, authorization, allowance, payment, or liability, to be expended within the fiscal year of which said month is a part. If at the beginning of any month any money remains unexpended in any of the funds set apart for maintaining the municipal government of the City and County of San Francisco, and which might lawfully have been expended the preceding month, such unexpended sum or sums may be carried forward and expended, by order of the Board of Supervisors, in any succeeding month.

Sec. 2. All contracts, authorizations, allowances, payments, and liabilities to pay, made or attempted to be made in violation of section one of this Act, shall be absolutely void, and shall never be the foundation or basis of a claim against the treasury of said city and county. And all officers of said city and county are charged with notice of the condition of the treasury of said city and county and the extent of the claims against the same.

Sec. 3. It is hereby made the duty of the Superintendent of Public Streets, Highways, and Squares of said city and county to keep an exact account of all street work upon accepted streets, as well as every other expenditure chargeable to or payable out of the Street Department Fund, or expended under the supervision of said Superintendent, in any manner whatsoever, and for that purpose he shall have the power to demand and receive from every other city and county officer detailed statements in writing, when necessary to keep said account; and it is hereby made the duty of any and all officers to furnish said Street Superintendent said statements when demanded. Such account so kept by said Superintendent shall show every contract for street work and authorization of expenditure from their incipiency through the various stages of their progress to completion with the amount to be paid for the same, so far as the same is capable of exact estimation, and when not, a sworn estimate of the probable cost. Said account shall be kept constantly posted up to date, so that it can be known exactly at any time what part or proportion of the monthly sum allowed by this Act and existing laws has been contracted for, paid, or rendered liable to pay in the present and future.

Sec. 4. Whenever at any time the contracts performed or unperformed, lawful claims due or to become due, exceed the amount that can lawfully be expended during any one month, the Superintendent of Streets shall give notice, in writing, to the Auditor and Treasurer of said city and county, and also the Board of Supervisors, by notice in writing, served upon the Clerk of said Board. Notice of the fact that the legal limit of expenditure for the month has been reached, and that no more claims can be lawfully contracted, shall be posted in a conspicuous place in the Street Superintendent's office by said officer, and in the office of the Clerk of the Board of Supervisors by said Clerk.

Sec. 5. Any failure or neglect on the part of the Superintendent of Public Streets and Highways to comply with any of the provisions of this Act shall render him liable personally, and upon his official bond, to any contractor or other persons suffering damage by his said failure or neglect.

SEC. 6. All Supervisors, as well as the Auditor and any other officer authorizing or aiding to authorize, or auditing, or allowing any claim or demand upon or against said treasury, or any fund thereof, in violation of any of the provisions of this Act, shall be liable in person, and upon their several official bonds, to the contractor damaged by such illegal authorization, to the extent of his loss by reason of the non-payment of his claim.

SEC. 7. The Treasurer paying any claim authorized, allowed, or audited in violation of this provision, shall be liable on his official bond to refund the same to the City and County treasury.

SEC. 8. This Act shall take effect and be in force on and after the first day of the month succeeding its passage.

SUPPLEMENT XCIX.

1877-8, 167.

Act to regulate the quality and standard illuminating power, and the price of gas, in all cities within the State of California having a population of one hundred thousand or more.

[Approved March 4, 1878.]

The People of the State of California, represented in Senate and Assembly, do enact as follows:

SECTION 1. That in all cities in the State of California having a population of one hundred thousand or more, the local legislative body thereof, whether known and designated as the Board of Supervisors, or Board of Aldermen, or Common Council, or Board of Trustees, or otherwise, are hereby authorized and required to fix the standard quality and illuminating power of gas to be furnished, and the rate and price for each one thousand cubic feet to be charged therefor, by any person, company, or corporation whose pipes or mains are or shall be laid down in the streets or highways of such city, for the purpose of supplying gas for the use of such city, or for the inhabitants thereof, or for such city and its inhabitants; *provided, however,* that said Board or local authority shall not fix or establish the standard quality and illuminating power of gas in such city at less than sixteen-candle power, or such that five cubic feet of gas per hour so furnished shall give light at least equal to that afforded by the combustion of sixteen standard sperm candles consuming one hundred and twenty grains of sperm each per hour, the burner to be used in making such test to be that best adapted to the economical consumption of gas; *and provided further*, that such Board of Supervisors, or local legislative authority, by whatever name it may be known, shall not fix or establish the rate or price of gas so furnished to such city or its inhabitants at any greater price or rate than three dollars per thousand cubic feet.

SEC. 2. It shall be the duty of the Mayor of each city having the population mentioned in section one of this Act, and such Mayor is hereby required, within thirty days after the passage and approval of this Act, to appoint, subject to the approval of the Board of Supervisors, or other local legislative body aforesaid, a person of competent experience and knowledge of and concerning the proper qualities and illuminating power of gas, and who shall not be directly or indirectly interested in or connected with any person, company, or corporation, engaged in the manufacture or furnishing of illuminating gas in such city, or elsewhere, either to such city or its inhabitants, or any of them, either as a stockholder or otherwise, who shall be known and designated as Gas Inspector of such city, who shall hold his said office for the term of two years, or until his successor shall be appointed and qualified; subject, however, to removal from his said office by the Mayor, with the concurrence of a majority of the Board of Supervisors, or other local legislative board aforesaid, for any one of the following causes, to wit: by reason of any interest in the manufacture or furnishing of gas in such city, whether such interest existed at the date of his appointment or was afterward acquired, or for want of competent knowledge, skill, or experience to enable him to properly discharge the duties of said office, or for any neglect, misconduct or inefficiency in the discharge of the duties of said office, to the prejudice of such city or its inhabitants, or any of them. The person so appointed shall, before he enters upon the duties of said office, and within ten days after his appointment and confirmation, take and subscribe an oath or affirmation before the County Judge* of the county in which such city is situated, that he will faithfully and impartially perform and discharge all the duties required by this Act, and the ordinances or resolutions of said Board passed and adopted under and pursuant to the provisions thereof, as such Gas Inspector of such city, and shall also, within the same time, give bond to the city in and for which he is appointed, in the sum of ten thousand dollars, with sureties to be approved by said Board, conditioned for the faithful performance of the duties of said office, which said oath and bond shall be filed with the Clerk of said Board. Such Gas Inspector shall be entitled to a salary to be fixed and allowed by said Board, which shall be paid monthly out of the General Fund of such city.

SEC. 3. It shall be the duty of such Inspector, immediately upon his appointment and qualification as such officer, as aforesaid, to make a careful examination and inquiry, by inspection, letter, or otherwise, as to the quality and illuminating power of the gas furnished and used in the principal

---

* Now Superior Judge.

cities of the United States, and the prices charged therefor, and also the comparative cost of the manufacture and supply of gas in other cities of the United States, with the cost of the manufacture and supply of the same in the city for which he is such Inspector, and report fully the result of such examination and information to said Board within six months after his appointment and qualification; and upon receiving such reports, said Board shall proceed to fix and establish the quality and standard illuminating power of gas to be used in such city, and the maximum price to be charged therefor; and such standard and price may be changed by said Board from time to time, not oftener than once every year, as increased consumption or other circumstances may in their judgment require.

SEC. 4. After said Board shall have fixed and established the quality and illuminating power, and the price of gas, as hereinbefore, it shall be the duty of such Inspector to examine and inspect, from time to time, at least once every week, without notice to the person, company or corporation furnishing the same, the quality and illuminating power of the gas furnished to such city and the inhabitants thereof, and in case the same shall fall below the standard fixed by said Board, the said Inspector shall forthwith report the same to said Board; and at such other times as he may be requested thereto by the Mayor or any committee of said Board, he shall report to said Board upon any and all matters connected with the manufacture, supply, and consumption of gas coming within the scope of his official duties, and specially upon any subject or subjects, matters or things connected therewith and specified in such request.

SEC. 5. After said Board shall have fixed and established the quality and standard illuminating power of the gas, and the price per thousand cubic feet, as in this Act provided to be charged therefor, it shall be unlawful for any person, company, or corporation to furnish to such city, or any inhabitant thereof, or any person therein, for illuminating purposes, gas of a lower standard or quality, or to charge or receive therefor a higher price than is provided by said Board, under the authority and subject to limitations of this Act; and for every violation of the provisions of this Act, or the provisions of any order, resolution, or ordinance of said Board made in pursuance thereof every such person, company, or corporation shall incur a penalty of not less than one hundred nor more than one thousand dollars, to be recovered in a civil action in the name and for the use of such city, in any Court of competent jurisdiction; and each day upon which such person, company, or corporation shall, without reasonable cause or excuse therefor, furnish gas of a lower quality or standard illuminating power than that fixed by said Board, shall constitute and be considered and held one violation thereof, and each month or shorter period for which said person, company, or corporation shall take an account of gas consumed, and for which they shall charge or receive a price greater than that fixed by said Board, shall be held and regarded as one offense, and any number of such offenses of either class, or both, may be joined in the same action, and the several penalties for the several violations proved or confessed in said action may be united and recovered in the same judgment; and such person, company, or corporation shall also be liable to such city and to any and each person or corporation who shall be injured by any such violation, in double the amount of damages actually sustained.

Sec. 6. All actions for penalties under the provisions of this Act shall be tried by the Court, unless a jury be demanded by either party; and when such action shall be tried by a jury, the jury shall find, as to each violation charged in the complaint, that "the defendant is guilty," or "the defendant is not guilty;" and upon each charge in respect to which the jury has has found the defendant guilty, the Court shall fix the penalty, and render judgment for the aggregate amount of such penalties, together with costs of suit.

Sec. 7. All penalties recovered under this Act shalll be paid into the General Fund of such city.

Sec. 8. This Act shall apply to the City and County of San Francisco, as well as to cities whose municipal government is distinct from the county in which they are located.

Sec. 9. This Act shall take effect immediately.

SUPPLEMENT C.

1877-8, 820.

An Act to define the powers of the Board of Supervisors of the City and County of San Francisco, with reference to contracts.

[Approved March 9, 1878.]

The People of the State of California, represented in Senate and Assembly, do enact as follows:

SECTION. 1. Advertisements published by order of the Board of Supervisors of the City and County of San Francisco, calling for bids, shall be published in three daily papers (including the official paper), for a period not less than five days. All bids shall be received under such guarantees, or deposits of money, and subject to such conditions as the Board of Supervisors may prescribe.

Sec. 2. Contracts shall be awarded to the lowest bidder.

Sec. 3. If, for any cause, the said Board of Supervisors reject the lowest bid, the said Board shall re-advertise for proposals *de novo*.

Sec. 4. This Act to take effect on the sixtieth day after its passage.

SUPPLEMENT CI.

1877-8, 231.

An Act to confer additional powers upon the Board of Supervisors of the City and County of San Francisco.

[Approved March 12, 1878.]

The People of the State of California, represented in Senate and Assembly, do enact as follows:

SECTION 1. The Board of Supervisors of the City and County of San Francisco is hereby authorized and empowered to fill and grade to the official grade, as now or hereafter established by said Board, and macadamize and culvert that portion of Seventh Street, in said City and County, lying between the northerly line of King Street and the southerly line of Santa Clara Street; also the intersection of Santa Clara Street with Pennsylvania Avvenue, and such other portion of Pennsylvania Avenue as to said Board shall seem necessary and useful; also such portion of Santa Clara Street running easterly from Seventh Street as to said Board shall seem necessary and useful for travel and the interest and convenience of the public; said filling, grading, macadamizing, and culverting may be commenced, prosecuted, and completed without unnecessary delay after the passage of this Act, and notwithstanding the protests of any or all the property owners affected thereby, or liable to be assessed therefor.

SEC. 2. The said Board of Supervisors is also hereby authorized and empowered to establish, without unnecessary delay, such an official grade on and for said Seventh Street, between the southerly line of Bryant Street and the southerly line of Santa Clara Street, and also on said Santa Clara Street and Pennsylvania Avenue, and on the streets, alleys, and places intersecting said Seventh and Santa Clara Streets and Pennsylvania Avenue, as to said Board may seem proper, and may grade and improve the same, or any portion thereof, to such official grade, notwithstanding the protests of any or all property owners liable to be assessed therefor.

SEC. 3. The Board of Supervisors may, without any petition whatsoever on the part of any person or persons, commence, prosecute, and complete the work contemplated in sections one and two of this Act, and pass all orders and resolutions, and do all things in connection therewith, as may be neces-

15

sary to commence, prosecute, and speedily complete said work, in such a manner, and with such materials as to said Board shall seem proper; and, for the purpose of carrying out the objects and intentions of this Act, all laws, Acts, and parts of Acts in force at the time of the passage of this Act, not inconsistent therewith, or any of the provisions thereof, regulating or providing for the improvement, grading, and macadamizing of public streets and highways in the city and county of San Francisco, and the levying, assessing, and collection of assessments for the improvement, grading, and macadamizing of such streets and highways are hereby made applicable to this Act.

SEC. 4. The said Board of Supervisors shall demand and receive from the Board of Seventh Street Commissioners of said city and county (which Board of Commissioners was created by an Act of the Legislature of the State of California, entitled an Act to open and establish a public street in the City and County of San Francisco, to be called Seventh Street, to take private lands therefor, and to grade, macadamize, and improve a portion of Seventh Street, and to construct a bridge thereon, approved April third, eighteen hundred and seventy-six) all books, papers, maps, diagrams, and other property and data in the possession of said Board of Commissioners connected with said Seventh Street, and when so received shall use the same for the purposes of this Act in doing said work, so far as the same can be made useful or applicable thereto, and the said Board of Commissioners shall, on demand, deliver all such books, papers, maps, diagrams, property, and data over to said Board of Supervisors.

SEC. 5. The said Board of Supervisors are hereby further authorized and empowered to construct a draw-bridge of such capacity, dimensions, and ma-terials as to said Board shall seem proper, across Channel Street, as laid down upon the latest official map of said city and county, extending from the northerly line of said Channel Street, where Seventh Street intersects the same, to the southerly line of Channel Street, where Seventh Street inter-sects the same, said bridge to be a free, public bridge, and to be suitable for all traveling purposes. And all cost and expenses for constructing and maintaining the same shall be paid out of the General Fund of the treasury of said City and County of San Francisco, and the space required for said bridge is hereby excepted from the operation of sections one, two, three, and four of this Act.

SEC. 6. All Acts and parts of Acts conflicting with the provisions of this Act are hereby repealed.

SEC. 7. This Act shall take effect immediately.

SUPPLEMENT CII.

1877-8, 232.

An Act to establish the grade of Seventh Street between Bryant and Brannan Streets, in the City and County of San Francisco.

The People of the State of California, represented in Senate and Assembly, do enact as follows:

SECTION. 1. The grade of Seventh, on the south line of Bryant Street, shall be established at nine feet above base, and decline therefrom on a uniform grade towards Brannan Street a distance of four hundred and seventy-five feet, at which point it shall be seven feet above base, and from the said point it shall decline uniformly to the north line of Brannan Street as already established, and the grade as established by this Act shall be the official grade of Seventh between Bryant and Brannan Streets until said grade shall be changed as by law provided.

SEC. 2. All Acts or parts of Acts that are in conflict with the provisions of this Act, for the purposes of this Act, are hereby repealed.

SEC. 3. This Act shall be in force and effect from and after its passage.

SUPPLEMENT CIII.

1877-8, 233.

An Act to amend an Act entitled an Act to establish and maintain a training ship in the City and County of San Francisco, approved February fifteenth, eighteen hundred and seventy-six.

[Approved March 13, 1878.]

The People of the State of California, represented in Senate and Assembly, do enact as follows:

SECTION 1. Section five of an Act entitled an Act to establish and maintain a training ship in the City and and County of San Francisco, approved February fifteenth, eighteen hundred and seventy-six, is amended to read as follows: Section 5. The Board of Supervisors of said city and county is hereby authorized and required to direct to be paid out of the General Fund of said city and county, for the support and maintenance of said training ship, a sum not exceeding twenty-five thousand dollars per annum, and an additional sum of twenty-five thousand dollars per annum is hereby appropriated out of the State treasury for the support and maintenance of said training ship, and the State Controller is hereby required to draw his warrant in favor of, and the State Treasurer to pay to the City and County of San Francisco the said sum of twenty-five thousand dollars per annum, for the purposes aforesaid, and the Auditor of said City and County is hereby required to audit all claims passed by said Board in pursuance of the provisions of this Act, and the Treasurer of the said city and county is hereby directed to pay the same.

SEC. 2. The said Board of Supervisors shall provide accommodations on said training ship for not less than two hundred boys at all times, and shall provide officers and instructors sufficient for their government.

SEC. 3. Of the total number of boys provided for by this Act one hundred may be admitted from the City and County of San Francisco and one hundred from the other counties of the State of California, as may be determined by an Advisory Board provided for in the next succeeding section of this Act.

SEC. 4. An Advisory Board, consisting of three members, to serve without compensation, shall be appointed by the Governor of the State, at his earliest convenience after the passage of this Act, to which Board a report shall be made quarterly of the condition and operation of said training ship, by said standing committee of said Board of Supervisors. It shall be the duty of said Advisory Board to inspect said training ship from time to time as may be necessary, and to make such apportionment and such changes in the number of boys apportioned to each county (the County of San Francisco excepted) as may be found necessary to secure to the several counties of the State the full number of boys herein provided for. The population of each county shall form the basis of said apportionment.

SEC. 5. This Act shall take effect and be in force from and after its passage.

SUPPLEMENT CIV.

An Act to ascertain the amount and provide for the payment of damages done to St. Francis' Church property, in the City and County of San Francisco, by changing the grade of Montgomery Avenue in said city and county.

[Approved March 15, 1878.]

The People of the State of California, represented in Senate and Assembly, do enact as follows:

SECTION 1. The City and County of San Francisco shall be liable to the congregation of St. Francis' Church, in said city and county, for all damages to the church building and property of said congregation, by reason of the lowering of the grade of Montgomery Avenue and Vallejo Street, in pursuance of an Act entitled an Act to change and modify the grade and to provide for the grading and regrading of certain portions of Montgomery Avenue, and of certain portions of certain streets intersecting Montgomery Avenue, in the City and County of San Francisco, approved April third, eighteen hundred and seventy-six. Such damages shall be assessed and paid in the manner hereinafter provided.

SEC. 2. The Mayor, the City and County Surveyor, and the Superintendent of Public Streets, Highways and Squares of said city and county are hereby appointed Commissioners to ascertain and assess said damages. As soon as practicable after the passage of this Act the Commissioners shall give notice, for the period of ten days, by publication in some newspaper published in said city and county, of a time and place at which they will meet for the purposes of hearing evidence in regard to the damages. At the time and place specified in the notice, or at some other time and place of which previous notice shall have been given as above provided, the Commissioners, or a majority of them, shall meet and proceed to hear such evidence as may be brought before them, and the hearing may be adjourned from time to time without further notice. All persons interested in the proceedings may appear before the Commissioners and introduce evidence. The Commisioners shall include in their estimate of damages the cost of any changes and alterations made or to be made in or about said building, so far as such changes and alterations may appear to them necessary or proper by reason of the lowering of the grade as aforesaid. In order to enable them to determine the cost of changes and alterations to be afterwards made, they shall be furnished with plans, drawings, and estimates by one or more competent architects.

SEC. 3. After hearing the evidence the Commissioners shall assess and award such damages as they may deem to be just and reasonable, including the cost of changes and alterations as aforesaid, and shall make a written report thereof to the Board of Supervisors of said city and county, stating the amount of the damages and the cost of the proceedings. On receiving said report the Board of Supervisors shall make an order referring to the report and directing the payment of such damages and cost, the amount of which shall be stated in the order. Said order need not be published or approved by the Mayor. A certified copy of said order shall be presented to the Auditor of said city and county, who shall thereupon draw his warrant on the Treasurer for the amount of the damages and cost, as stated in the order. The warrant shall be drawn in favor of Joseph S. Alemany, or some other person authorized to act for and represent said congregation, and shall be paid by the Treasurer, out of the General Fund, in gold coin of the United States.

SEC. 4. The acts to be performed by the Commissioners as aforesaid may be performed by any two of them, and each of the Commissioners shall receive a reasonable compensation for his services, to be fixed by the Board of Supervisors, and paid out of the General Fund, upon the warrant of the Auditor.

SEC. 5. If the changes and alterations in or about said building should require the use of a portion of the sidewalk on Vallejo Street for the erection of steps, platforms, or other like purposes, the right to the use of the same is hereby granted to the extent of six feet in width on the northerly side thereof, in front of said building, such right to continue for the period of twenty years.

SEC. 6. This Act shall take effect and be in force from and after its passage.

SUPPLEMENT CV.

1877-8, 270.

An Act to confer additional powers on the Board of Supervisors of the City and County of San Francisco, to provide for the opening of Army Street, and the condemnation of private property therefor.

[Approved March 16, 1878.]

The People of the State of California, represented in Senate and Assembly, do enact as follows:

SECTION 1. The Board of Supervisors of the City and County of San Francisco are hereby authorized and empowered:

First—To receive and accept from the owners or claimants of the lots and lands lying contiguous to " Precita Creek," from the old San Jose road to the San Bruno road of said city, a deed or deeds of a tract of land, not less than sixty-four feet in width and without abrupt curves or short angles, to be located on a line to be located by and to be satisfactory to said Board of Supervisors, for the construction of a sewer therein and for the purposes of a public street.

Second—The Board of Supervisors are hereby authorized and empowered to acquire (by purchase, for such consideration as to said Board shall seem reasonable,) any of the lots or lands hereinbefore described, for the purposes of said sewer and street, as cannot be acquired by voluntary gift or donation, and to order payment of such considerations out of the General Fund of the treasury of said city and county.

Third—For the purpose of acquiring title to all such portions of said lots and lands as may not be acquired under the provisions of the first and second subdivisions of this section, the said Board of Supervisors are hereby authorized and required to cause the same to be condemned and appropriated to public uses for the purposes of said sewer and street; the Mayor, Assessor, and Surveyor of said city and county are hereby appointed and constitute Commissioners, with power to ascertain and determine the value of the lands and the sums to be paid therefor to the owners thereof: in case of a vacancy in said Commission, by reason of any member thereof being disqualified from acting, or for other cause, the County Judge of said city and county shall fill such vacancy by appointment of some competent and disinterested person. The moneys to be paid for any lands, under the provisions of this Act, must be paid out of the General Fund of the treasury of said city and county. The said proceedings to acquire title to lands, except as herein otherwise provided, must conform to the provisions of the "Act approved April first, eighteen hundred and seventy-two," entitled an Act to open and establish a public street in the City and County of San Francisco, to be called Montgomery Avenue, and take private lands therefor, and to the provisions of any other Act passed at the present session of the Legislature, defining the powers of said Board of Supervisors, which are hereby made applicable to this Act, so far as the same are not inconsistent therewith.

Fourth—The said Board of Supervisors are hereby authorized and required, under such rules and regulations as they may prescribe, to sell at public auction, to the highest and best bidders, all of Serpentine Avenue running from the old San Jose road to the San Bruno road, except such portions thereof as may be required for the purposes of said sewer and street herein provided for. The lands so offered for sale shall first be surveyed and subdivided into lots, conforming as near as may be practicable in form and size to the lots next contiguous thereto. Streets, in conformity to and connecting with the streets laid down upon the official plan of said city, shall be reserved and dedicated to public use. A deed from the Mayor of said city and county, executed to the purchaser of any lot, after full payment therefor shall have been made, shall vest the title of such lot in said purchaser. The proceeds of said sales shall be paid into the General Fund of the treasury of said city and county. The said Commissioners shall receive for their services such compensation as the Board of Supervisors may allow. Whenever the said city and county shall have acquired the lands herein mentioned, for said sewer and street, the said Board of Supervisors are authorized to open and improve said street, and construct said sewer of such material and of such capacity as said Board may determine, and are authorized to appropriate, allow, and order paid out of the General Fund such sums as may be necessary for said purposes, also for all contracts for the necessary surveys.

SEC. 2. All of Serpentine Avenue lying between the old San Jose road and San Bruno road is hereby vacated as a public street or highway.

SEC. 3. This Act shall take effect and be in force from and after its passage.

SUPPLEMENT CVI.

1877-8, 280.

An Act to increase the appropriation for the support of the Hospital and Alms-house in the City and County of San Francisco, etc.

[Approved March 16, 1878.]

The People of the State of California, represented in Senate and Assembly, do enact as follows:

SECTION 1. The Board of Supervisors of the City and County of San Francisco are hereby authorized and empowered to appropriate, allow, and order paid out of the General Fund the several sums of money hereinafter mentioned, to wit:

First. To expend a sum not exceeding fifteen thousand dollars per month for the support, care, and maintenance of such persons as may be admitted to the City and County Hospital and Alms-house, which shall be in lieu of all sums now authorized by law to be expended for such purposes.

Second. [*Obsolete.*]

SEC. 2. This Act shall take effect and be in force from and after its passage.

SUPPLEMENT CVII.

1877–8, 329.

An Act to establish and maintain free public libraries and reading-rooms.

[Approved March 18, 1878.]

The People of the State of California, represented in Senate and Assembly, do enact as follows:

SECTION 1. The Boards of Supervisors of the City and County of San Francisco, and the municipal authorities of the several incorporated cities and towns of this State, are authorized to levy and collect, as in other cases, annually, a tax, not to exceed one mill on the dollar, for the purpose of establishing in such cities and towns, respectively, free public libraries and reading-rooms, and purchasing or leasing such real and personal property, books, journals, and other publications, and erecting such buildings as may be necessary therefor.

SEC. 2. The municipal authorities, respectively (except as hereinafter otherwise provided), in their respective cities and towns, may appoint such Trustees (not exceeding seven), and such other officers and assistants as may be necessary to carry into effect the provisions of this Act; they may declare and fix the terms of office (not exceeding four years) of all such Trustees, officers, and assistants, and, at their pleasure, on the request of a majority of the Trustees, may remove any from office, and fill vacancies; they may fix the salaries of all officers and assistants, except the Trustees, who shall serve without salary or other compensation; and they may make, or may authorize the Trustees to make, such rules and regulations, and by-laws, as may be necessary for the government and protection of such libraries and reading-rooms, and all property belonging thereto, or that may be loaned, devised, bequeathed, or donated to the same.

Sec. 3. All money and revenue collected or received by authority of any-thing herein contained shall be known and designated as the "Librar Fund," and shall be paid into the proper city or town treasury, and there kept separate and apart from other funds, and be drawn therefrom as in other cases provided, but only to be used and applied for the purposes herein authorized.

Sec. 4. All property, real and personal, acquired by purchase, gift, devise, bequest, or otherwise, under the provisions of or for the purposes authorized by this Act, shall vest and be and remain in the proper city or town, respectively, and may be protected, defended, and sued for, by action at law or otherwise, by such cities and towns, respectively, as in other cases.

Sec. 5. The following eleven persons, to wit: Geo. H. Rogers, John S. Hager, Irving M. Scott, Robt. J. Tobin, E. D. Sawyer, John H. Wise, An-drew J. Moulder, Louis Sloss, A. S. Hallidie, C. C. Terrell, Henry George, and their successors, are hereby constituted and appointed, during good behavior, honorary Trustees, without salary, of any library and reading-room, and of the real and personal property thereunto belonging, that may be established or acquired under the provisions of this Act, in and for the City and County of San Francisco. Such Trustees shall meet for business purposes on the first Tuesday of each month, and at such other times as they may appoint, in a place to be provided for the purpose, and six shall constitute a quorum for business. They may appoint one of their number President, and they may also elect a Secretary, who shall keep a record and full minutes, in writing, of all their proceedings. The Secretary may certify to such proceedings, or any part or portion thereof, under his hand, verified by a seal to be adopted and provided by the Trustees for that purpose. Such Trustees, by a majority vote of all their members, to be recorded in the minutes, with ayes and noes, at length, shall have the power:

First—To make and enforce all rules, regulations, and by-laws necessary for the administration, government, and protection of such library, reading-room, and property.

Second—To fill all vacancies that may from any cause occur in the Board of Trustees.

Third—To remove any Trustee who may neglect to attend the meetings of the Board, or who may absent himself from such meetings, or, without the consent of the Board, from the State for three consecutive months.

Fourth—To appoint and define the powers and duties of any and all authorized officers and assistants, and at their pleasure remove the same.

Fifth—To provide memorial tablets and niches to perpetuate the memo-ries of those persons who may make valuable donations to any such library.

Sixth—By and with the consent and approval of the Board of Supervisors of said city and county, expressed by resolution duly passed by that body: To determine the number of officers and assistants to be appointed for such library and reading-room, and to fix the salaries of such officers and assistants, and of the Secretary; to purchase necessary real and personal property; to lease and erect buildings; to order the drawing and payment of money from out of the Library Fund for any expenditure or liability herein authorized; and generally to do all that may be necessary to fully carry into effect the provisions of this Act.

SEC. 6.   The Board of Supervisors of the City and County of San Francisco are authorized and empowered, by a resolution duly passed for that purpose, to grant, donate, or authorize the use of, either in whole or in part, any land, square, or other real estate belonging to said city and county, or dedicated to public use therein, for the purpose of erecting and maintaining thereon a building to be used only for a public library and reading-room in and for said city and county, as in this Act authorized and provided.

SEC. 7.   The proprietors, or other competent authority, of any subscription or other library may, upon such terms and conditions as shall be agreed upon by them and the municipal authorities of any incorporated city or town, except in the City and County of San Francisco, donate and transfer its property, real and personal, to any such city or town for the purpose of establishing and maintaining a public library and reading-room within the meaning of this Act; and as a condition, and in consideration of any such donation, such proprietors may at their option nominate and appoint as honorary Trustees, without salary, a number equal to those appointed or authorized to be appointed by such municipal authorities respectively as in this Act provided. Such honorary Trustees, by a majority vote, may fill all vacancies that may occur in their number, and they respectively shall have an equal voice with the other Trustees in the direction, management, and control of such libraries after such donation and transfer shall be made and accepted.

SEC. 8.   This Act shall take effect immediately.

SUPPLEMENT CVIII.

1877-8, 333.

An Act supplementary to and amendatory of an Act entitled "An Act to regulate and limit the payment of money out of the treasury of the City and County of San Francisco," approved February twenty-sixth, eighteen hundred and seventy-eight.

[Approved March 18, 1878.]

The People of the State of California, represented in Senate and Assembly, do enact as follows:

SECTION 1.   The provisions of an Act entitled "An Act to regulate and limit the payment of money out of the treasury of the City and County of

San Francisco," approved February twenty-sixth, eighteen hundred and seventy-eight, are hereby suspended for and during the months of March, April, and May, A. D. eighteen hundred and seventy-eight, and no longer; *provided*, that any money expended for liabilities created or contracted for during said months of March, April, and May, in excess of what is permitted by said Act, shall be deducted from the amount that may be lawfully expended, or liability created or contracted for during the same fiscal year, in such manner that at the end of such fiscal year there shall be no deficit.

SEC. 2. The provisions of said Act, from and after the first day of June, A. D. eighteen hundred and seventy-eight, shall extend to and include all departments of the municipal government of said city and county, except the New City Hall and Golden Gate Park Commissioners, as to all moneys expended or obligations created or contracted for purposes or against funds that by law are authorized to carry on such departments as running annual expenditures; and the officers, Directors, Commissioners, or others having the power to make such contracts or disbursements, shall be liable to all the duties, obligations, and penalties as to all such funds and contracts and disbursements resting upon the Supervisors and others named in said Act to which this is supplementary.

SEC. 3. In case of any great public calamity or danger, such as earthquakes, conflagrations, pestilence, invasion, insurrection, or other great and unforeseen emergency, the provisions of said Act may be suspended, as to any lawful contract, authorization, or expenditure necessary to avert, mitigate, or relieve such evil; *provided*, that such expenditure, contract, or authorization, shall be passed by the unanimous vote of all the Supervisors, Directors, Commissioners, or other officers, and entered in the journals and approved by the Mayor, the Auditor, and the Treasurer, and the notice of the emergency must be recited in the resolution authorizing such action.

SEC. 4. This Act shall take effect immediately.

SUPPLEMENT CIX.

1877-8, 341.

An Act to ratify and confirm certain orders and resolutions of the Board of Supervisors of the City and County of San Francisco, relative to street work on Montgomery Avenue.

[Approved March 19, 1878.]

The People of the State of California, represented in Senate and Assembly, do enact as follows:

WHEREAS, The City and County of San Francisco has, through its proper officers, from time to time ordered street work on Montgomery Avenue, in said city and county, and has awarded contracts for the same, and doubts existing as to the validity of the orders and resolutions providing for the same, therefore, be it enacted:

SECTION 1. That all orders and resolutions heretofore from time to time passed by the Board of Supervisors of the City and County of San Francisco, in relation to street work done and being done, in whole or in part, on Montgomery Avenue in said city and county, and all contracts and assessments for such street work made by the Superintendent of Public Streets, Highways, and Squares of said city and county, and all other proceedings under and in accordance with the provisions of such orders and resolutions, are hereby made valid, ratified, and confirmed.

SEC. 2. All assessments for street work done on the crossings or spaces formed by the junction or intersection of other streets with said Montgomery Avenue, and all assessments for street work done on the crossings or spaces formed by the junction or intersection of other streets or avenues which form irregular or fractional blocks, and bound the same, and not squarely in front of, and not properly assessable to, lots fronting on such streets, shall be made in conformity with the principles prescribed by law in the matter of making assessments for similar work done on Market Street, in said city and county; *provided*, that nothing herein contained shall be held to create any liability on the City and County of San Francisco, except in case of charges against property belonging to said city and county.

SEC. 3. This Act shall take effect immediately.

S U P P L E M E N T   C X .

1877-8, 355.

An Act in relation to the office of Sheriff of the City and County of San Francisco.

[Approved March 20, 1878.]

The People of the State of California, represented in Senate and Assembly, do enact as follows:

SECTION 1. In addition to the deputies now allowed by law, the Sheriff of the City and County of San Francisco may appoint four deputies—one to act as Bailiff of the Probate Court of said city and county, and wait upon the Grand Jury; one to act as Assistant Bailiff of the Municipal Criminal Court of said city and county; and two to act as office deputies. Said deputies shall receive a salary of one hundred and fifty dollars per month each.

Sec. 2. The authority to appoint Deputy Jail-keepers, in the City and County of San Francisco, not to exceed sixteen in number, shall vest in and be exercised by the Sheriff of said city and county. Said deputies shall receive a salary not to exceed one hundred and twenty-five dollars per month each.

Sec. 3. The said Sheriff shall be allowed the sum of one hundred and fifty dollars per month to defray his expenses for counsel and attorney's fees.

Sec. 4. The salaries and moneys provided to be paid by this Act shall be paid by the Treasurer of the City and County of San Francisco, out of the General Fund of said city and county, upon the audit of the City and County Auditor, who is hereby directed to audit the salaries and moneys hereby provided.

Sec. 5. The said Sheriff may retain, out of the moneys received by him from this State, for the transportation of persons committed to the Asylum for the Insane, and prisoners delivered at the State Prison, the actual expenses incurred by him in the transportation of said persons to said institutions, and shall make a monthly report to the Treasurer of the City and County of San Francisco of all moneys expended and received by him; and if any surplus remain of the moneys so received, over and above the actual expenses incurred, the same shall be paid into said treasury monthly.

Sec. 6. The Deputy Sheriffs acting as Bailiffs in the District Courts shall receive a salary of one hundred and fifty dollars per month.

Sec. 7. All Acts and parts of Acts, so far as they may be in conflict herewith, are hereby repealed.

Sec. 8. This Act shall take effect immediately.

SUPPLEMENT CXI.

1877–8, 442.

An Act to facilitate and equalize the collection of licenses in the City and County of San Francisco.

[Approved March 23, 1878.]

The People of the State of California, represented in Senate and Assembly, do enact as follows:

Section 1. Every person, firm or corporation engaged in carrying on, pursuing, or transacting within the limits of the City and County of San Francisco any business, trade, profession, occupation, or employment hereinafter specified, shall pay licenses as is herein provided.

Sec. 2. Every person, firm, or corporation engaged in the business of buying or selling mining stocks, bonds, State, county, or city stocks, or stocks of incorporated companies, or evidences of indebtedness of private persons or of incorporated companies, on commission or otherwise, shall pay licenses as follows:

First—Those whose aggregate purchases and sales amount to three hundred and fifty thousand dollars and over per quarter, constitute the first class, and shall pay a license of fifty dollars per quarter.

Second—Those whose aggregate purchases and sales amount to two hundred and fifty thousand dollars and less than three hundred and fifty thousand dollars per quarter, constitute the second class, and shall pay a license of forty dollars per quarter.

Third—Those whose aggregate purchases and sales amount to one hundred and fifty thousand dollars and less than two hundred and fifty thousand dollars per quarter, constitute the third class, and shall pay a license of twenty-five dollars per quarter.

Fourth—Those whose aggregate purchases and sales amount to seventy-five thousand dollars and less than one hundred and fifty thousand dollars, constitute the fourth class, and shall pay a license of fifteen dollars per quarter.

Fifth—Those whose aggregate purchases and sales amount to twenty thousand dollars and less than seventy-five thousand dollars per quarter, constitute the fifth class, and shall pay a license of ten dollars per quarter.

Sixth—Those whose aggregate purchases and sales amount to less than twenty thousand dollars per quarter, constitute the sixth class, and shall pay a license of five dollars per quarter.

Seventh—All licenses issued under the provisions of this section [shall] be known and designated as "broker's license."

SEC. 3.   All persons, firms, and corporations engaged in the business of loaning money at interest, receiving deposits, or buying and selling gold and silver coin or currency, or notes or bills of exchange, and gold and silver bullion, shall be divided into three classes, and shall pay licenses as follows:

One—Those whose total receipts shall exceed in the aggregate the sum of two millions of dollars per quarter, shall pay a license of three hundred dollars per quarter.

Two—Those whose total receipts shall exceed in the aggregate the sum of one million of dollars and less than two millions per quarter, shall pay a license of two hundred dollars per quarter.

Three—Those whose total receipts shall be in any amount under one million of dollars per quarter, shall pay a license of one hundred dollars per quarter.

Four—All licenses issued under the provisions of this section shall be known and designated as "banker's license."

SEC. 4.   Every person who, at any fixed place of business, sells any goods, wares, or merchandise, on commission or otherwise (except agricultural or vinicultural, productions of any stock, dairy, or poultry farm of this State, when sold by the producer thereof, and except such as are sold by auctioneers at public sale under license) shall pay licenses as follows:

First—Those whose aggregate sales amount to five hundred thousand dollars and over per quarter, constitute the first class, and shall pay a license of two hundred and fifty dollars per quarter.

Second—Those whose aggregate sales amount to three hundred thousand dollars and less than five hundred thousand dollars per quarter, constitute the second class, and shall pay a license of one hundred and fifty dollars per quarter.

Third—Those whose aggregate sales amount to two hundred thousand dollars and less than three hundred thousand dollars per quarter, constitute the third class, and shall pay a license of one hundred dollars per quarter.

Fourth—Those whose aggregate sales amount to one hundred and twenty-five thousand dollars and less than two hundred thousand dollars per quarter, constitute the fourth class, and shall pay a license of sixty-five dollars per quarter.

Fifth—Those whose aggregate sales amount to seventy-five thousand dollars and less than one hundred and twenty-five thousand dollars per quarter, constitute the fifth class, and shall pay a license of forty dollars per quarter.

Sixth—Those whose aggregate [sales] amount to fifty thousand dollars and less than seventy-five thousand dollars per quarter, constitute the sixth class, and shall pay a license of twenty-five dollars per quarter.

Seventh—Those whose aggregate sales amount to thirty thousand dollars and less than fifty thousand dollars per quarter, constitute the seventh class, and shall pay a license of eighteen dollars per quarter.

Eighth—Those whose aggregate sales amount to twenty thousand dollars and less than thirty thousand dollars per quarter, constitute the eighth class, and shall pay a license of twelve dollars per quarter.

Ninth—Those whose aggregate sales amount to ten thousand dollars and less than twenty thousand dollars per quarter, constitute the ninth class, and shall pay a license of seven dollars per quarter.

Tenth—Those whose aggregate sales amount to five thousand dollars and less than ten thousand dollars per quarter, constitute the tenth class, and shall pay a license of five dollars per quarter.

Eleventh—Those whose aggregate sales amount to fifteen hundred dollars and less than five thousand dollars per quarter, constitute the eleventh class, and shall pay a license of three dollars per quarter.

Twelfth—Those whose aggregate sales amount to six hundred dollars and less than fifteen hundred dollars per quarter, constitute the twelfth class, and shall pay a license of one dollar per quarter.

Thirteenth—Those whose aggregate sales amount to less than six hundred dollars per quarter shall not be required to pay a license; *provided*, that no person shall be entitled to this exemption unless he files with the License Collector, every three months, a sworn statement of the amount of his sales.

All licenses issued under the provisions of this section shall be known and designated as " merchandise license."

SEC. 4. Every person who sells spirituous, or malt, or fermented liquors or wines, in less quantities than one quart, shall be known as a "retail liquor dealer," and shall pay license as follows:

First—Those making sales to the amount of fifteen thousand dollars and over per quarter, shall pay a license of forty dollars per quarter.

Second—Those making sales of less than fifteen thousand dollars per quarter shall pay a license of twenty dollars per quarter; *provided*, that on and after January first, eighteen hundred and seventy-nine, no license as a retail liquor dealer shall be issued by the Collector of Licenses, unless the person desiring the same shall have obtained the written consent of a majority of the Board of Police Commissioners of the City and County of San Francisco to carry on or conduct said business; but in case of refusal of such consent, upon application, said Board of Police Commissioners shall grant the same upon the written recommendation of not less than twelve citizens of San Francisco owning real estate in the block or square in which said business of retail liquor dealer is to be carried on, or in the four blocks or squares bounding the same. All licenses issued under the provisions of this section shall be known and designated as " retail dealer's license."

SEC. 6. Every person who sells cider, sarsaparilla, ginger pop, or soda or mineral water, except from a fountain, in quantities of less than one quart, shall, in addition to the license required to be paid, be subject to the same conditions and provisions contained in the preceding section.

SEC. 7. Every person violating any of the provisions of sections five and six of this Act, or falsely representing himself as being a citizen of San Francisco and owning real estate in the blocks or squares therein specified, shall be guilty of a misdemeanor.

SEC. 8. Auctioneers shall pay licenses as follows:

First—Those whose sales amount to three hundred thousand dollars and over per quarter, shall pay a license of two hundred dollars per quarter.

Second—Those whose sales amount to one hundred and fifty thousand dollars and less than three hundred thousand dollars per quarter, shall pay a license of one hundred dollars per quarter.

Third—Those whose sales amount to seventy-five thousand dollars and less than one hundred and fifty thousand dollars per quarter, shall pay a license of fifty dollars per quarter.

Fourth—Those whose sales amount to thirty thousand dollars and less than seventy-five thousand dollars per quarter, shall pay a license of twenty-five dollars per quarter.

Fifth—Those whose sales amount to fifteen thousand dollars and less than thirty thousand dollars per quarter, shall pay a license of ten dollars per quarter.

16

Sixth—Those whose sales amount to fifteen thousand dollars per quarter, shall pay a license of five dollars per quarter.

Seventh—All licenses issued under the provisions of this section shall be known and designated as "auctioneer's license."

SEC. 9.   All keepers or owners of livery stables shall pay licenses as follows:

First—Those whose gross receipts from the hiring of horses and carriages amount to four thosand dollars and over per quarter, shall pay a license of seven dollars per quarter.

Second—Those whose gross receipts from the hiring of carriages and horses amount to less than four thousand per quarter, shall pay a license of three dollars per quarter.

Third—All licenses issued under the provisions of this section shall be known and designated as "livery stable license."

SEC. 10.   In all cases where the amount of license to be paid by any person, firm, or corporation is based upon or regulated by the amount of sales effected or business transacted, such person, firm or corporation shall render a sworn statement to the License Collector of the total amount of sales made or business done by them respectively during the three months next preceding the expiration of the last license, which statement shall determine the amount for which such license shall be renewed.

SEC. 11.   Every proprietor or lessee of any theatre, concert hall, or of any place of amusement, entertainment, or exhibition, shall pay licenses according to the seating capacity of such theatre, concert hall, or other place of amusement, entertainment, or exhibition.   One seat is twenty-two inches.

First—Those seating nine hundred and seventy-five persons, or more, shall pay a license, if issued for one year, three hundred dollars per annum; if for three months, one hundred dollars per quarter; if for one month, fifty dollars per month; if for one day, four dollars per day.

Second—Those seating less than nine hundred and seventy-five persons shall pay a license, for one year, of two hundred dollars; for three months, seventy-five dollars; for one month, forty dollars; for one day, four dollars.

Third—All licenses issued under the provisions of this section shall be known and designated as "theater license."

SEC. 12.   All Acts and parts of Acts in conflict with this Act are hereby repealed.

SEC. 13.   This Act shall take effect immediately.

SUPPLEMENT CXII.

1877–8, 544.

An Act to authorize and facilitate the repairing of streets and sewers in the City and County of San Francisco, in case of urgent necessity.

[Approved March 27, 1878.]

The People of the State of California, represented in Senate and Assembly, do enact as follows:

SECTION 1. In case of urgent necessity, the Superintendent of Public Streets, Highways, and Squares is hereby authorized and required to repair any of the public streets, sewers, or crossings cornering thereon, either by contract or otherwise; and the expense of the same shall be paid out of the Street Department Fund, in the same manner as provided by law for the improvement of streets that have been finally accepted; *provided, however,* that all repairs shall be made to be in uniformity with the work to be repaired, and that the repairs between two main streets shall not exceed the sum of one hundred dollars, and the repairs of any crossing shall not exceed the sum of fifty dollars; *provided,* the sum so expended shall not exceed the sum of one thousand dollars in any one month.

SEC. 2. All Acts and parts of Acts in conflict with the provisions of this Act are hereby repealed, except the provisions of an Act entitled "An Act to regulate and limit the payment of money out of the treasury of the City and County of San Francisco, approved February twenty-sixth, A. D. eighteen hundred and seventy-eight;" and also of an Act supplementary and amendatory thereto, approved March eighteenth, eighteen hundred and seventy-eight.

SEC. 3. This Act shall take effect immediately.

SUPPLEMENT CXIII.

1877-8, 556.

An Act to confer additional powers upon and to authorize certain appropriation of money by the Board of Supervisors of the City and County of San Francisco.

[Approved March 26, 1878.]

The People of the State of California, represented in Senate and Assembly, do enact as follows:

SECTION 1. The Board of Supervisors of the City and County of San Francisco are hereby authorized and empowered to appropriate, allow, and order paid the several sums of money hereinafter mentioned, and to exercise the following powers, to wit:

First—[*Obsolete.*]

Second—[*Obsolete.*]

Third—[*Obsolete.*]

Fourth—To allow and order paid out of the Special Fee Fund to the Collector of Licenses a salary not to exceed three thousand ($3,000) dollars per annum.

Fifth—To allow and order paid out of the Special Fee Fund to the Clerk of the Board of Supervisors a salary not to exceed three thousand six hundred ($3,600) dollars per annum.

Sixth—To appropriate a sum not to exceed eighty thousand ($80,000) dollars, annually, for running expenses, horse feed, repairs to apparatus, and for the construction and erection of cisterns and hydrants, and for the erection and repair of buildings, and other expenses of the Fire Department, in lieu of the amount now allowed.

Seventh—To appropriate, annually, a sum not to exceed thirty thousand ($30,000) dollars for the purchase of horses and apparatus for the Fire Department, in lieu of the amount now allowed.

Eighth—To appropriate annually a sum not to exceed ten thousand ($10,000) dollars for extending and repairing the fire and alarm and police telegraph, in lieu of the amount now allowed.

Ninth—To grant to street railroad companies the right to use steam to propel cars over such roads, or parts of roads, in the suburbs of the city and county, as in the discretion of the Board may be proper and for the public convenience, under such restrictions as contained in those portions of the Civil Code applicable to street railroads; *provided*, that such privileges shall only be granted to ronds operated west of the east line of Larkin Street and west of the east line of Ninth Street.

Tenth—To provide for placing all moneys received and paid into the treasury for articles manufactured at, or produce sold from the Industrial School, House of Correction, Hospital, and Alms-house, to the credit of their respective funds, to be used solely for the purposes of those institutions.

Eleventh—[*Obsolete.*]   *   *   *   *   *   *   *

The salary of the Superintendent of said Fire Alarm and Police Telegraph shall be fixed and determined by the Board of Supervisors of said City and County of San Francisco.

SEC. 2.   This Act shall take effect and be in force from and after its passage.

SUPPLEMENT CXIV.

1877-8, 579.

An Act to establish and maintain a Free Dispensary in the City and County of San Francisco.

[Approved March 27, 1878.]

The People of the State of California, represented in Senate and Assembly, do enact as follows :

SECTION 1.   The Board of Supervisors of the City and County of San Francisco are hereby authorized and empowered to appropriate the sum of twenty-five hundred dollars per annum, payable out of the Urgent Necessity Fund of the said city and county, said sum of money to be used for the purchase of medicines to be dispensed gratuitously to the indigent sick not inmates of public institutions.

SEC. 2.   The Auditor of the City and County of San Francisco is hereby directed and authorized to audit and allow, out of the Urgent Necessity Fund, the sum named in preceding section, and to issue his warrants therefor in favor of the President of the Board of Health of the City of San Francisco, the amount to be drawn quarterly; the said sums to be appropriated as the Board of Health of the City of San Francisco may, in their judgment, direct, for the purpose of establishing one Free Medical Dispensary, of each established system of medicine, in said city.

SEC. 3.   The Board of Supervisors are also authorized, should they deem it expedient, to furnish medicine to the indigent sick of the Magdalen Asylum, the same to be furnished at the City and County Hospital of said city.

SEC. 4.   This Act shall take effect and be in force from and after its passage.

SUPPLEMENT CXV.

1877-8, 630.

An Act to ratify and confirm resolution number eleven thousand nine hundred, new series, of the Board of Supervisors of the City and County of San Francisco.

[Approved March 29, 1878.]

The People of the State of California, represented in Senate and Assembly, do enact as follows:

SECTION 1. Resolution number eleven thousand nine hundred (new series) of the Board of Supervisors of the City and County of San Francisco, vacating Florida, York, Hampshire, and Jersey Streets, from Twenty to Twenty-first Streets, Columbia Street from Twenty-first to Butte Street, and Shasta Street from Potrero Avenue to Harrison Street, and opening in lieu thereof Alabama Street, from Twenty-first Street to Butte Street, and Columbia Street, Bryant Avenue, York and Hampshire Streets, from Twenty-first to Twenty Streets, is hereby ratified and confirmed, and said streets vacated are hereby declared to be severally vacated, and said streets opened are hereby declared to be opened in accordance with the terms of said resolution.

SEC. 2. This Act shall take effect immediately.

SUPPLEMENT CXVI.

1877-8, 630.   •

An Act providing for the payment of certain salaries out of the "Special Fee Fund" of the City and County of San Francisco.

[Approved March 29, 1878.]

The People of the State of California, represented in Senate and Assembly, do enact as follows:

SECTION 1. The salaries of such Clerks as are now employed in the different departments of the government of the City and County of San Francisco, under authority of the Board of Supervisors of said City and County, and not otherwise provided for by law, and which are now paid out of the "Urgent Necessity Fund," may hereafter be allowed by said Board and be audited and paid out of the " Special Fee Fund " of said City and County.

SEC. 2. This Act shall take effect from and after its passage.

SUPPLEMENT CXVII.

1877-8, 682.

An Act to close an unused street in San Francisco.

[Approved March 23, 1878.]

The People of the State of California, represented in Senate and Assembly, do enact as follows :

SECTION 1. The street projected and delineated on the map of the City and County of San Francisco, through the middle of Block No. 74, Western Addition, bounded by Van Ness Avenue, Grove, Franklin, and Hayes Streets, and on said map designated as Ivy Avenue, never having been open or used through said block, is hereby closed and vacated, so far as it purports to extend through the same.

SEC. 2. This Act shall take effect immediately.

SUPPLEMENT CXVIII.

1877-8, 685.

An Act to provide for reorganizing and better regulating the paid fire department of the City and County of San Francisco.

[Approved March 23, 1878.]

The People of the State of California, represented in Senate and Assembly, do enact as follows:

SECTION 1. There shall be a Board of Fire Commissioners of the City and County of San Francisco, consisting of five persons of good character and standing, three of whom shall be appointed by the Board of Supervisors of the City and County of San Francisco, one by the Judge of the Municipal Criminal Court of said City and County, and one by the Judge of the County Court of said county; *provided*, that no appointment shall be made until the expiration of the term of office of the several members of the present Board of Fire Commissioners, except to fill vacancies. The Board of Supervisors, the Judge of the Municipal Criminal Court, and the Judge of the County Court, hereinbefore mentioned, shall each appoint one Commissioner to fill the vacancies occurring on the first Monday in December, A. D. eighteen hundred and seventy-nine, which Commissioners shall serve for the term of four years; and thereafter the vacancies occurring, by expiration of term of office, in December, A. D. eighteen hundred and eighty-one, shall be filled by appointment of two Commissioners by the Board of Supervisors of said City and County to serve for the term of four years, and thereafter the appointment of Commissioners shall be in the manner hereinbefore mentioned. They shall be citizens of the United States, and who shall have been residents of said City and County for at least two years previous to their appointment as such Commissioners; and the persons so appointed shall, before entering upon their duties as such Commissioners, give a bond each in the sum of five thousand dollars, to be approved and filed in the same manner as the bonds of other City and County officers, and they shall hold their office for the term of four years from and after the date of their appointment, and until their successors are appointed and qualified. And in the event of any one or more of said Commissioners neglecting or refusing to perform the duties of their office, or in the event of a vacancy or vacancies occurring in said Board of Fire Commissioners from any cause other than the expiration of their term of office, the Board of Supervisors shall appoint some suitable person or persons to fill such vacancy or vacancies; *provided*, that if any vacancy shall occur by resignation, or otherwise, of any Commissioner appointed, as provided in this Act, such vacancy shall be filled by the same power which made the original appointment, and the person or persons so appointed to fill such vacancy or vacancies shall be appointed to fill the same for the unexpired term; *and provided further*, that all appointments by the Board of Supervisors of said city and county, under this Act, shall be made in open session, by viva voce vote, entered in the journals of said Board, and no appointments made otherwise shall be valid. No member of said Board of Fire Commissioners shall be eligible to any elective office during his incumbence of the office of Fire Commissioner.

SEC. 2. The officers of the fire department of said city and county shall be: The Fire Commissioners, to be appointed as aforesaid, without salary; one Chief Engineer, whose salary shall be two hundred and fifty dollars per month; one Assistant Chief Engineer, at a salary of two hundred dollars per month, and four Assistant Engineers, whose salaries shall be one hundred and fifty dollars per month each. All salaries shall be paid monthly.

SEC. 3. The members and employes of said fire department shall be: One Superintendent of Steam Fire Engines, at a salary of one hundred and fifty dollars per month; one Assistant Superintendent of Steam Fire Engines, at a salary of one hundred and forty dollars per month; one Clerk and Storekeeper for the Corporation Yard, at a salary of one hundred and twenty-five dollars per month; one Corporation Yard Drayman, at a salary of ninety dollars per month; one Night Watchman for the Corporation Yard, at a salary of seventy-five dollars per month; two Hydrantmen, at a salary of ninety dollars per month each; a Veterinary Surgeon, at a salary of sixty dollars per month; a Foreman of each company, at a salary of forty-five dollars per month; one Engineer for each steam fire engine, at a salary of one hundred and forty dollars per month; one substitute Engineer and Machinist, at a salary of one hundred and forty dollars per month; one Driver for each company, at a salary of ninety dollars per month; one Fireman for each steam engine company, at a salary of ninety dollars per month; one Carpenter, at a salary of one hundred dollars per month; one Tillerman for each hook and ladder company, at a salary of ninety dollars per month; one Steward for each hose company, at a salary of eighty dollars per month; each Hoseman and each Hook and Ladderman shall receive a salary of thirty-five dollars per month; and one Janitor and Messenger, at a salary of seventy-five dollars per month; one Clerk, at a salary of one hundred and fifty dollars per month.

SEC. 4. All paid members of said fire department, except the Veterinary Surgeon, Foreman, Assistant Foreman, Company Clerks, Hosemen, Hook and Laddermen, and Stewards of volunteer companies, shall give their undivided attention to their respective duties; but the Foreman, Assistant Foreman, Company Clerks, Hosemen, Hook and Laddermen, and Stewards of volunteer companies, shall perform such duties as may be prescribed, from time to time, by said Board of Fire Commissioners, and ordered to be executed by the Chief Engineer.

SEC. 5. The Chief Engineer, the Assistant Chief Engineer, the Assistant Engineers, the Clerk, and all members and employes of the fire department shall be appointed by the Fire Commissioners, and retain their positions during good behavior. No officer, member, or employe of said fire department shall be removed for political reasons.

SEC. 6. The fire department of the City and County of San Francisco shall consist of such engine, hook and ladder, and hose companies, as shall be recommended by the Board of Fire Commissioners, and be determined by the Board of Supervisors of said city and county, with the approval of the Mayor, to be necessary to afford protection against fire; *provided*, that, as auxiliary thereto, patent fire extinguishers may also be purchased and employed if, in the judgment of said Board, deemed advisable; *provided*, that no hand engine shall hereafter be purchased for the use of said department, but those now in possession of said city and county may be used in such localities and under such regulations as the Board of Fire Commissioners, with the approval of the Board of Supervisors, may prescribe. The companies of said department shall be organized as follows: Each steam fire engine company shall consist of one Foreman, one Engineer, one Driver, one Fireman, and eight Horsemen, one of whom shall act as Assistant Foreman, and one as Clerk. Each hook and ladder company shall consist of one Foreman, one Driver, one Tillerman, and twelve Hook and Laddermen, one of whom shall act as Assistant Foreman, and one as Clerk. Each hose company shall consist of one Foreman, one Driver, one Steward, and six Hosemen, one of whom shall act as Assistant Foreman, and one as Clerk.

SEC. 7. The Board of Supervisors of said city and county shall have power to contract and provide for all cisterns, hydrants, apparatus, supplies, engine, hose, and hook and ladder houses, and all alterations and repairs required, and said Board of Fire Commissioners shall supervise all contracts awarded and work done for the said fire department, and shall see that all contracts awarded and work done are faithfully performed. They shall have power to prescribe the duties of the officers, members and employes of said fire department, and to adopt rules and regulations for the management and discipline thereof; and a majority of them shall certify to the correctness of all claims and demands before the same shall be paid. And said Board of Supervisors are authorized and required to provide and furnish, for the use of said Board of Fire Commissioners, a suitable room or rooms, in some of the public buildings of said city and county, to serve as an office for their meetings and the transaction of business relating to said fire department, in which their Clerk, Janitor, and Messenger shall be in attendance, daily, during office hours. The Chief, Assistant Chief Engineer, and Assistant Engineers of said department shall also make it their headquarters, daily, during office hours, when not otherwise engaged in official duties. And said Board of Supervisors shall furnish the Chief Engineer, and also the Assistant Chief Engineer, with a horse and buggy, and shall provide for the keeping of the same.

SEC. 8. Said Board of Fire Commissioners shall supervise and control said fire department, its officers, members, and employes, subject to the laws governing the same, and shall see that the officers, members and employes thereof faithfully discharge their duties, and that the laws, orders, and regulations relating thereto are carried into operation and effect. They shall not, nor shall either of them, or the Chief, or Assistant Chief Engineer, or Assistant Engineers, of said fire department, be interested in any contract pertaining in any manner to said department, or in the sale, furnishing of apparatus, or supplies for the same; and all contracts in violation of this section are declared void, and any of said persons violating the provisions of this section shall be deemed guilty of a misdemeanor, and upon conviction may be punished accordingly.

SEC. 9. The Chief Engineer shall be the executive officer of said fire department, and it shall be his duty (and that of the Assistant Chief Engineer, and Assistant Engineers) to see that the laws, orders, rules, and regulations concerning the same are carried into effect; and also to attend to such duties as Fire Wardens as may be required, and to see that all laws, orders, and regulations, established in said city and county to secure protection against fire, are enforced. It shall also be his duty to enforce the rules and regulations, made from time to time, to secure discipline in said fire department; and he shall have power to suspend any subordinate officer, member, or employe, for a violation of the same, and shall forthwith report, in writing, with his reasons therefor, to the Board of Fire Commissioners for their action. He shall diligently observe the condition of the apparatus and working of said department, and shall report in writing, at least once in each week, to the said Board of Fire Commissioners, upon the same, and make such recommendations and suggestions respecting it, and for securing its greater efficiency, as he may deem proper; and in the absence or inability of the Chief Engineer to act, the Assistant Chief Engineer shall assume the duties of said office of Chief Engineer.

Sec. 10. The person elected as Clerk by said Board of Fire Commissioners shall, before entering upon the discharge of his duties, execute a bond, with two or more sureties, in the penal sum of twelve thousand dollars, for the faithful discharge of his duties, which shall be approved by said Board of Fire Commissioners and the Mayor of said city and county, and when so approved shall be filed in the office of the Auditor. The amount of said bond may be increased from time to time, when directed by the Board of Supervisors, should they deem it necessary for the public good. Said Clerk shall attend daily, during office hours, at the office of the Board of Fire Commissioners (which shall be the office of the Chief, Assistant Chief Engineer, and Assistant Engineers), shall perform the duties of Clerk to said Board and Chief Engineer, and perform such other duties as from time to time said Board may prescribe. The Clerk and Storekeeper for the Corporation Yard shall, before entering upon his duties, furnish a bond, in the sum of ten thousand dollars, in the same manner and form as above provided in regard to the Clerk of the Board of Fire Commissioners.

Sec. 11. The Mayor of said city and county, upon the recommendation of the Board of Fire Commissioners, is hereby authorized to sell, at private or public sale, from time to time, with the approval of the Board of Supervisors, any or all of the engines, hose carriages, engine houses, lots on which such houses stand, or parts of lots (or to exchange any of said lots when, in their judgment, demanded by the public good), or other property which shall not be required for the use of the department, and to execute, acknowledge and deliver good and sufficient deeds or bills of sale for the same, paying the proceeds of such sales into the county treasury to the credit of the Fire Department Fund.

Sec. 12. The Board of Supervisors of said city and county are hereby authorized to appropriate, allow, and order paid, annually, out of the General Fund of said city and county, the salaries hereinbefore specified and allowed, and salaries at similar rates to the several officers and men of any additional companies created as aforesaid. And the Board of Supervisors are required to appropriate, allow, and order paid, out of the General Fund, the sum of fifteen thousand dollars (for the year eighteen hundred and seventy-eight only), ten thousand dollars of said sum to be used in the erection of two new engine houses (said houses not to exceed the sum of five thousand dollars each), and the remaining five thousand dollars to be applied to repairs of the engine houses now in use by the said department.

SEC. 13.   Whenever any member of the paid fire department of the City and County of San Francisco shall become disabled by reason of injuries received at any fire, so as to be unable to perform his duties, the Board of Supervisors, upon the recommendation of the Board of Fire Commissioners of said city and county, are hereby authorized and empowered to allow said disabled man a sum not exceeding fifty dollars per month, not to exceed three months, payable out of the General Fund of said city and county, in the same manner and form as other payments are made out of said fund.

SEC. 14.   The Chief Engineer shall have power to appoint one member of each company to act as Assistant Foreman, also one member to act as Clerk to each company, said Clerk to receive five dollars per month extra pay.

SEC. 15.   The Fire Commissioners shall organize said Board on the first Monday in December of each and every year, by selecting one of their number as President, and they shall meet at least once in each month, publicly, at their office, to transact the business of said fire department, and, in addition to the stated meeting, they shall meet twice in each month for the purpose of investigating charges against officers, members, and employes of said department, for violating any of the rules and regulations thereof.   No person shall be eligible to any position in said department who is not a citizen of the United States, nor a resident of said city and county for at least two years, nor under twenty-one years of age at the time of his appointment.

SEC. 16.   In all investigations for violations of the rules and regulations of the fire department, the President of the Board of Fire Commissioners shall have power to issue subpœnas and administer oaths, and compel the attendance of witnesses before him, by attachment or otherwise.   All subpœnas issued by him shall be in such form as he may prescribe, and shall be served by any police officer, or by any peace officer of said city and county. Any witness who refuses to attend or testify in obedience to such subpœna shall be deemed guilty of contempt, and be punishable by him as in cases of contempt in Justices' Courts in civil cases.

SEC. 17.   No officer, member, or employe of the fire department shall be dismissed except for cause, nor until after a trial.   The accused shall be furnished with a written copy of the charges against him, at least five days previous to the day of trial; and he shall have an opportunity to examine witnesses in his behalf, and all witnesses shall be examined under oath, and all trials shall be public.

SEC. 18.   The Board of Supervisors of said city and county is hereby authorized and empowered to establish and maintain, at the Corporation

Yard, a workshop for making repairs and improvements upon the apparatus of the fire department; such workshop and such repairs and improvements to be under the supervision of the Board of Fire Commissioners, and said Board of Supervisors shall allow and order paid, out of the Fire Department Fund, all the expenses of such workshop, repairs, and improvements; *provided*, that the Board of Supervisors shall have power to limit the expenditures under this section to such an amount as they in their discretion think necessary.

Sec. 19. No person belonging to the fire department of said city and county shall hold more than one position in said department, nor any other position under the municipal government of San Francisco, or Federal Government, to which there is a salary attached, except that the Clerk of engine, hose, and hook and ladder companies shall have five dollars per month extra for acting as Clerk, as hereinbefore provided.

Sec. 20. All Acts and parts of Acts in conflict with the provisions of this Act, relating to a paid fire department in the City and County of San Francisco, are hereby repealed.

Sec. 21. No member of said Board of Fire Commissioners shall, during his term of office, be a member of any party convention, the purpose of which is to nominate candidates for political office. Nor shall the officers, members, or employes of said fire department take any part whatever in any partisan convention held for the purposes of a political party, nor shall any member of the said Board of Fire Commissioners, directly or indirectly, attempt to control or influence the action of any member of said fire department, or any employe thereof, in any primary or general election. No member of the fire department shall levy, collect, or pay any amount of money as an assessment or contribution for political purposes. Any violation of the provisions of this section shall be deemed a misdemeanor.   •

Sec. 22. This Act shall take effect and be in force from and after its passage.

SUPPLEMENT CXIX.

1877-8, 829.

An Act to confer further powers upon the Board of Supervisors of the City and County of San Francisco.

[Approved March 30, 1878.]

The People of the State of California, represented in Senate and Assembly, do enact as follows:

Section 1. The Board of Supervisors of the City and County of San

Francisco are hereby authorized and empowered to exercise the powers following:

First—To expend and order paid out of the General Fund, not to exceed three thousand dollars per month, for objects of urgent necessity not otherwise provided for by statute, in lieu of the amount now allowed by law.

Second—To order paid out of the General Fund not to exceed twenty thousand dollars in any one fiscal year hereafter, for furniture and for repairs to public buildings, in lieu of the amount now allowed by law.

Third—To order paid out of the General Fund not to exceed fifteen thousand dollars in any one fiscal year hereafter, for advertising expenses of said city and county, in lieu of the amount now allowed by law.

SEC. 2. This Act shall take effect and be in force from and after its passage.

SUPPLEMENT CXX.

1877-8, 829.

An Act to provide for the improvement of Van Ness Avenue, in the City and County of San Francisco.

[Approved March 30, 1878.]

The People of the State of California, represented in Senate and Assembly, do enact as follows :

SECTION 1. The Board of Supervisors of the City and County of San Francisco shall have power to declare, by ordinance, that the roadway of Van Ness Avenue, between Market and Pacific streets, in said city and county, shall be fifty-five feet in width, and shall be laid out in the middle of said street, twenty-seven and one-half feet on each side of the center line thereof, with a gutter on each side of said roadway, and a curb on the outer line thereof, corresponding with the official grade of said street, and that the sidewalks, on each side of said portion of Van Ness Avenue, shall be thirty-five feet in width, during the pleasure of said Board.

SEC. 2. The said Board of Supervisors shall have power, whenever a petition therefor shall be presented to it by the owners of a majority of the frontage of the lots fronting upon any block in said portion of Van Ness Avenue, to authorize said block to be improved, by planting trees, shrubbery, and grass upon the outer seventeen feet of each of the sidewalks upon said block, whenever the width of said sidewalks shall have been fixed as defined in section one of this Act. The said improvements shall be made in accordance with plans that may be adopted and prescribed by said Board of Supervisors, and whenever the said Board of Supervisors shall have adopted such plans, and shall have authorized the improvement of any block in said portion of Van Ness Avenue, the said Board shall have power to provide, by ordinance, for the protection and preservation of said improvements, and for compelling the same to be made and preserved, and for preventing the injury or destruction of the same, and for prohibiting those portions of said street that may be so improved from being traveled upon by vehicles, animals, or persons, and to prescribe a penalty to be imposed for any violation of said ordinance.

SEC. 3. Whenever any block in said portion of Van Ness Avenue shall have been improved under the provision of this Act, the said Board of Supervisors shall not thereafter cause any sidewalk to be constructed upon the said space of seventeen feet so improved, but the sidewalks upon said block that shall be thereafter constructed shall be constructed with a width of eighteen feet, and shall have a curb and gutter at their outer edge, aside from the curbs and gutters at the outer edges of the roadway, and thereafter the space of seventeen feet upon said block, between the outer edge of the roadway and the outer edge of said sidewalk, improved as aforesaid, shall be and remain an open space, for the purposes of a park, during the pleasure of the said Board of Supervisors. .

SEC. 4. Whenever the said Board of Supervisors shall have passed any order for the improvement of any block in said portion of Van Ness Avenue, as is provided by this Act, the owners of the property fronting on said block shall, within sixty days thereafter, cause the said improvements to be made in front of the lots and lands respectively owned by them. In case the owner of any lot fronting upon said street, within the block so ordered to be improved, shall neglect, for the space of sixty days after the passage of said order, to cause the said improvements to be made, the Superintendent of Public Streets, Highways, and Squares of said city and county shall thereafter, by a notice in writing, to be delivered to said owner personally, or if said owner shall not reside upon said lot, to be left upon said lot, require the said owner forthwith to cause said improvements to be made; and if the said owner shall neglect, for the space of ten days thereafter, to cause the said improvements to be commenced, and thereafter to be prosecuted [with] reasonable diligence, the said Superintendent may enter into a contract, in writing, with any suitable person to make said improvement at the expense of said owner, at a reasonable price, to be determined by said Superintendent, and such owner shall be liable to pay the same; and upon the completion of the said contract to the satisfaction of the said Superintendent, who shall thereupon issue his certificate to that effect, stating therein the amount due upon said contract. The said contractor shall cause the said contract and certificate to be recorded in the office of the County Recorder in and for the City and County of San Francisco, and shall thereafter have a lien upon the said lot of land in front of which he has made the said improvement, for the amount specified in said certificate, until the same shall be paid, which said lien may be enforced in the mode provided by law for the foreclosure of mortgages or other liens.

SEC. 5. Order number one thousand three hundred and thirteen, adopted by the Board of Supervisors of the City and County of San Francisco, September thirteenth, A.D. eighteen hundred and seventy-six, is hereby confirmed and made valid; *provided, however,* that nothing is hereby intended to prevent the said Board of Supervisors from amending or repealing the said order, and that the said order shall only remain in force during the pleasure of the said Board.

SEC. 6. This Act shall take effect from and after its passage.

<hr>

SUPPLEMENT CXXI.

1877-8, 849.

<hr>

An Act concerning the macadamizing, etc., of Tyler Street, from Market to Devisadero Street, and to prohibit the laying down of railroad tracks thereon.

[Approved March 30, 1878.]

The People of the State of California, represented in Senate and Assembly, do enact as follows :

SECTION 1. The Board of Supervisors of the City and County of San Francisco are hereby authorized and empowered to have the roadway of Tyler Street, from Market Street to Devisadero Street, in said city and county, macadamized, curbed with stone curbs, and stone crosswalks laid on the cross streets, sidewalks constructed thereon where not already constructed, and the sidewalks thereon reconstructed, and sewers to be constructed in said street where not already constructed. The roadway of said Tyler Street is to be excavated to a sufficient depth to permit the making a bed for said macadam to rest upon, one foot in depth, composed of good hard rock, free from dirt; said rock to be well broken and rolled down before the macadam is placed thereon. After said road bed shall have been so prepared, there shall be placed thereon the best quality of either basalt, blue gneiss, trap rock, or granite, as per sample to be furnished by the Street Superintendent of said city and county. Said rock is to be broken to an egg size before brought on the work. The bottom of the gutter-ways to be eight inches below the top of the curbs, and to be paved with basalt blocks for two and a half feet from the curbs, and the roadway to have a crown to the center of not less than six inches above the top of the curbs; it is then to be well rolled down; it is then to be covered to the depth of two inches with said rock, finely broken; after the work is done, it is again to be rolled down. The macadam is to be twelve inches in depth at the center, and six inches in thickness at the sides, after rolling the same. The curbs and crosswalks are to be of the best California stone, clear, and of the best quality, and are to be constructed in accordance with plans on file in the office of the Superintendent of Public Streets and Highways. The sewer and sidewalks are to be constructed in conformity to plans and specifications to be furnished by said Superintendent. All surplus material is to be be removed, and the work is to be done in a good and workmanlike manner, under the direction and to the satisfaction of said Superintendent. The mode and manner of letting said work, and of making and collecting the assessment to be issued for the cost of said work, shall be the same as is now in force in said city and county in relation to street work, being Article Four of the Consolidation Act.

SEC. 2. When the roadway of said portion of Tyler Street shall have been constructed, as provided aforesaid, the same shall be accepted by the Board of Supervisors, subject to such other provisions as are provided by section twenty, of Chapter Five Hundred and Sixty-two, of the Session Laws of April first, eighteen hundred and seventy-one and two, approved April first, 1872, and thereafter the same shall be kept repaired and sprinkled at the expense of said city and county.

SEC. 3. The said Board of Supervisors are hereby prohibited from granting any right or franchise to lay railroad tracks upon or over said street, lengthwise of the same, between the points named.

SEC. 4. Said Board of Supervisors are authorized to have shade trees planted along said Tyler Street, under such regulations as said Board may adopt, and thereafter have the same protected.

SEC. 5. This Act to take effect from and after its passage.

17

An Act to enable the Board of Supervisors of the City and County of San Francisco to increase the police force of said city and county, and provide for the appointment, regulation, and payment thereof.

[Approved April 1, 1878.]

The People of the State of California, represented in Senate and Assembly, do enact as follows :

SECTION 1. The Board of Supervisors of the City and County of San Francisco shall have power to increase the police force of said city and county, and to reorganize the same in the following manner. In addition to the force of one hundred and fifty, now allowed by law, said Board may increase the same by not to exceed two hundred and fifty, making not more than four hundred in all, to be appointed and governed in the manner provided for the appointment and regulation of the police force of said city and county.

SEC. 2. The compensation of the two hundred and fifty (250) police officers provided for by this Act, or such part thereof as said Board of Supervis' ors shall allow, shall not exceed one hundred and two ($102) dollars per month each, and the compensation of the police officers in office at the time of the passage of this Act shall continue at the amount or rate established by the Act or Acts under which they have been appointed, until the first day of January, A.D. eighteen hundred and seventy-nine, when and upon which day their pay shall be graded and fixed by the Board of Commissioners provided to be appointed by this Act. The police officers now in office shall be known as the " old police," and those appointed by virtue of this Act shall be known as the " new police." Police officers hereafter appointed to fill vacancies upon the " old police," shall receive the same pay with the " new police," subject to the condition that the Treasurer of said city and county shall retain from the pay of each police officer the sum of two dollars per month, to be paid into a fund to be known as " The Police Life and Health Insurance Fund," which said fund shall be administered as is provided in sections nine to thirteen, inclusive, of this Act.

SEC. 3. The system of "special police" officers, as heretofore practiced in said city and county, is hereby abolished and prohibited, and no special officer shall be appointed, except as herein provided for. It shall be lawful for the Police Commissioners to appoint a special officer when the same is petitioned for by any persons, firms, or corporations, to be named in the warrant of appointment, to do a special service, to be paid by such persons, firms, or corporations so petitioning. Any special officer asking for, soliciting, demanding, collecting, or receiving, or causing others to do so for his benefit, any money, or other valuable thing, upon pretense of guarding or protection of the persons, or property of the persons, from whom the same shall be asked, demanded, solicited, collected, or received, except the persons, firms, or corporations so petitioning for his said appointment, and named in said warrant, shall be guilty of a misdemeanor, and on conviction punished accordingly, and shall be dismissed from the service; *provided*, that this section shall not take effect until ninety days after its passage.

SEC. 4. No special police officer shall ever be appointed in that portion of said city and county known as the Chinese quarter, the boundaries of which shall be established from time to time by the Police Commissioners. It shall be the duty of the Chief of Police to change the police officers of the regular force stationed in the Chinese quarter, and to substitute others in their places, so that the whole force, in their turn, shall regularly be assigned for duty in said quarter, in regular and continuous rotation.

SEC. 5. The police officers now in office shall continue to be paid in the manner and out of the fund the same as before the passage of this Act. The members of the "new police" force shall be paid in the following manner: Each police officer of said new police shall have issued to him monthly, by the Auditor, a demand on the Treasurer, showing the amount due him for his salary for such month. Said demand, on presentation to the Treasurer of said city and county, shall be by him registered, in order of its issuance, in a book to be kept by him for the purpose, and shall, from the date of such registration, bear interest at the rate of six per cent. per annum until paid. Both interest and principal shall be paid in United States gold coin, in the manner herein provided for.

SEC. 6. The Board of Supervisors of said city and county shall include, in the tax levy for the fiscal year commencing on the first day of July, A.D. one thousand eight hundred and seventy-eight, a sum and rate sufficient to pay all such registered demands on the treasury, with said interest, and also for the future payment of the salaries of said "new police," and from the time money comes into the treasury sufficient to pay off all of said registered demands; then and from such time forth said "new police" shall be paid in cash in the same manner as the old police are paid. [*Amended April* 1, 1878.]

SEC. 7. The Judge of the Fifteenth Judicial District of the State of California, the Judge of the Twelfth Judicial District of the State of California, and the Judge of the Fourth Judicial District of the State of California, or so many of them as shall act, are hereby empowered and required to meet together within ten days after the passage of this Act, or as soon thereafter as is practicable, and as often as shall be necessary, and to choose three citizens of said city and county, householders of good repute, without respect to their politics, who, together with the Chief of Police, shall constitute the Board of Police Commissioners for said city and county. Said four Commissioners shall be vested with all the powers, and subject to all the duties and liabilities of, and shall supersede the Board of Police Commissioners provided for in section seven of an Act entitled an Act to create a City Criminal Court in and for the City and County of San Francisco, and to define its powers and jurisdiction, approved April third, A. D. eighteen hundred and seventy-six, which section of said Act, and all Acts and parts of Acts in conflict with or inconsistent with this Act, are hereby repealed. The Police Commissioners appointed under this Act shall choose, from their own number, a President of the Board, whose salary shall be two hundred and fifty dollars per month, and the other Commissioners so appointed shall receive one hundred dollars per month each, to be paid in like manner with other official salaries in said city and county. All vacancies shall be filled by the aforesaid Judges making the appointments; *provided*, that from and after the official term of the present Chief of Police said office shall cease to be elective, and shall be filled by the Commissioners, whose appointment is herein provided for, at a salary of four thousand dollars per annum. No member of said Board of Police Commissioners, appointed as herein provided for, shall be eligible to any other office during his incumbency of the office of Police Commissioner, nor for one year thereafter. No member of said Board of Police Commissioners shall, during his term of office, be a member of any party convention the purpose of which is to nominate candidates for office. Nor shall the officers, members, or employes of said police department take any part whatever in any partisan convention, held for the purpose of a political party, nor shall any member of the said Board of Police Commissioners, directly or indirectly, attempt to influence or control the action of any member of said police department, or any employe thereof, in any primary or general election. Any violation of the provisions of this section shall be deemed a misdemeanor, and, on conviction, punished accordingly.

SEC. 8.   The entire police force of said city and county shall be and continue subject to all laws and regulations in force before the passage of this Act, and not inconsistent or in conflict herewith.

SEC. 9.   That the Mayor, Auditor, and Treasurer of the City and County of San Francisco shall constitute a Board, known as " The Police Life and Health Insurance Board."

SEC. 10.   The said Board shall, from time to time, as in their judgment may be best, invest the moneys of " The Police Life and Health Insurance Fund " in such of the following securities as shall seem the most safe and profitable, namely: The bonds of the City and County of San Francisco; the bonds of the State of California; the bonds of the United States of America;

nd the securities shall be held by said Treasurer, subject to the order of said Board, and the said Treasurer shall have no power to deposit, pledge, or in any way part with the possession of said securities, or the evidence thereof, except on the order of said Board.

SEC. 11. Upon the death of any member of the said police force, after the first day of June, eighteen hundred and seventy-eight, there shall be paid by the Treasurer, out of said "Life and Health Insurance Fund," to the legal representative of said police officer, the sum of one thousand dollars. In case any police officer shall resign, from bad health or bodily infirmity, there shall be paid to him from said fund the amount of the principal sum which he shall have contributed thereto. In case of dismissal of any police officer for mere incompetency, not coupled with any offense against the laws of the State, such officer shall be paid from said fund such amount as the Board may award, not exceeding one-half of the sum he may have contributed to said fund. Any officer dismissed for gross neglect or violation of duty, or upon conviction of any misdemeanor or felony, shall forfeit all claim upon said fund.

SEC. 12. In case such fund shall not be sufficient to pay the demand upon it, such demand shall be registered and paid in the order of its registry out of the funds as received.

SEC. 13. The said Mayor, Auditor, and Treasurer shall receive no compensation for their services as members of said Board, nor shall the said Treasurer receive any compensation as Treasurer and custodian of said funds.

SEC. 14. In addition to the Captains of Police now allowed by law, the Commissioners shall appoint one Captain, who shall be known as the Captain of the Harbor Police, and shall receive the same salary as other Captains of the police.

SEC. 15. The Police Commissioners appointed under this Act shall hold their meetings in the office of the Chief of Police, or in such other convenient place as the Board of Supervisors shall designate, and the Clerk of the Chief of Police shall act as the Clerk of said Board of Commissioners.

SEC. 16. This Act shall take effect immediately.

SUPPLEMENT CXXIII.

1877-8, 931.

An Act to confer further powers on the Board of Supervisors of the City and County of San Francisco, and to establish the grade of Vallejo Street, in said city and county.

[Approved April 1, 1878.]

The People of the State of California, represented in Senate and Assembly, do enact as follows:

SECTION 1.   The grade of Vallejo Street, from the westerly line of Taylor Street to the easterly line of Jones Street, shall be a direct line.

SEC. 2.   All Acts or parts of Acts, so far as they are in conflict with this Act, are hereby repealed.

SUPPLEMENT CXXIV.

1877-8, 931.

An Act to authorize the Board of Supervisors of the City and County of San Francisco to order Bay Street graded, and to change its grade.

[Approved April 1, 1878.]

The People of the State of California, represented in Senate and Assembly, do enact as follows:

SECTION 1.   The Board of Supervisors of the City and County of San Francisco are hereby authorized and empowered to order graded the whole or any part of Bay Street, in said city and county, from the east line of Larkin Street to east line of the Military Reservation known as the "Presidio Reservation," without receiving any petition from any person therefor;

provided, that the Board of Supervisors shall have said grading, between the east side of Larkin Street and Fillmore Street, graded either as a whole or in subdivisions, at their discretion; *and provided further*, that they shall have said grading, between Fillmore Street and the east line of the Presidio Reservation, graded either as a whole or in subdivisions, at their discretion.

SEC. 2. The grade of the crossing of Bay and Polk Streets is hereby fixed and established at eighty feet above base, instead of seventy feet; and the grade of the crossing of Bay Street and Van Ness Avenue is hereby fixed at seventy-five feet above base, instead of sixty-five feet; and the grade of the crossing of Bay and Gough Streets is hereby fixed and established at sixty feet above base, instead of fifty-six feet; and the grade of the crossing of Bay and Octavia Streets is hereby fixed and established at forty-five feet above base, instead of thirty feet; and the grade of the crossing of Bay and Laguna Streets is hereby fixed and established at thirty feet above base, instead of twenty-one feet.

SEC. 3. All Acts and parts of Acts in conflict with the provisions of this Act, so far only as they are inconsistent herewith, are hereby repealed.

SEC. 4. This Act shall take effect immediately.

SUPPLEMENT CXXV.

1877–8, 944.

An Act creating the Twenty-third Judicial District, and defining the Third and Twelfth Judicial Districts.

[Approved April 1, 1878.]

The People of the State of California, represented in Senate and Assembly, do enact as follows:

[SECS. 1 *to* 6, *inclusive, obsolete.*]

SEC. 7. The County Clerk of the City and County of San Francisco shall be ex-officio Clerk of the District Court of the Twenty-third Judicial District, in and for said city and county, and the Register Clerk, Court-room Clerk and Copying Clerk, heretofore appointed by the County Clerk of the City and County of San Francisco, as the Clerks of the Third Judicial District Court, shall be transferred as the Clerks of the said Twenty-third Judicial District Court. The salaries of such Clerks to remain the same.

SEC. 8. And the Bailiff heretofore appointed by the Sheriff of the City and County of San Francisco, to act as Bailiff or Deputy Sheriff of said Third Judicial District Court, shall be transferred as the Bailiff of the said Twenty-third Judicial District Court; the salary of said Deputy Sheriff or Bailiff to remain the same.

[*The remainder of this Act is obsolete.*]

SUPPLEMENT CXXVI.

1877-8, 947.

*An Act to create a new Court in the City and County of San Fran-
cisco, to be designated as the Municipal Court of Appeals of
the City and County of San Francisco.*

[Approved April 1, 1878.]

*The People of the State of California, represented in Senate and Assembly, do
enact as follows:*

[SECS. 1 *to* 6, *inclusive, obsolete.*]

SEC. 7.   The Sheriff and County Clerk of the said city and county shall,
respectively, be the Sheriff and Clerk of said Court, and shall provide the
same with deputies, the same as are provided for the County Court, and at
the same salaries, paid in the same way, out of the General Fund.

[*The remainder of the Act is obsolete.*]

SUPPLEMENT   CXXVII.

1877-8, 953.

*An Act in relation to the House of Correction of the City and
County of San Francisco.*

[Approved April 1, 1878.]

*The People of the State of California, represented in Senate and Assembly,
do enact as follows:*

SECTION 1.   The Board of Supervisors of the City and County of San
Francisco are hereby authorized to maintain and support in said city and
county the institution now existing therein, and known as the House of Correction, and to make additions thereto as the same may be required, and
also to make all proper rules and regulations for the discipline, management,
and employment of persons committed to the House of Correction by any
Court of said city and county.

SEC. 2.   In making rules and regulations, as provided in the preceding section, the Board of Supervisors shall endeavor, as far as possible, to prevent crime, reform prisoners, and make the House of Correction self-supporting.

SEC. 3. All persons appearing for sentence in the Police Judge's Court, the City Criminal Court, or the Municipal Criminal Court, of the City and County of San Francisco, who might be sentenced to imprisonment in the County Jail, or in the State Prison, may, instead thereof, be by the proper Court sentenced to imprisonment in the House of Correction, in said city and county, subject, however, to the provisions of the next section; and no person shall be sentenced to imprisonment in the House of Correction except under the provisions of this Act.

SEC. 4. No person shall be sentenced to imprisonment in the House of Correction for a shorter or a longer term than that for which he might be sentenced in the County Jail, or in the State Prison, and in no case whatever for a shorter term than three years. No person who might be sentenced to imprisonment in the State Prison shall be sentenced to imprisonment in the House of Correction, if he is more than twenty-five years of age, if he has been once before convicted of a felony, or twice before convicted of petit larceny, nor unless, in the opinion of the Court, imprisonment in the House of Correction will be more for his interest than imprisonment in the State Prison, and equally for the interest of the public. The fact of a previous conviction may be found by the Court upon evidence introduced at the time of sentence.

SEC. 5. Persons imprisoned in the House of Correction may be put to work on the public works and other property of the City and County of San Francisco, or may be employed at any other work, as the Board of Supervisors of said city and county may direct. And the said Board of Supervisors may, so far as a due regard to economy will permit, provide for the learning of trades by persons whose terms of imprisonment in said House of Correction are of sufficient length, and who have the capacity requisite therefor, and will work industriously thereat.

SEC. 6. The Superintendent shall give his personal attention to the duties of his office, and shall reside at the House of Correction, and the Board of Supervisors shall provide therein room and board for him, and for the subordinates whose presence may be required in and about said house.

SEC. 7. The third section of an Act entitled "An Act to utilize the prison labor and govern the House of Correction of the City and County of San Francisco," approved March thirty-first, eighteen hundred and seventy-six, and all Acts and parts of Acts, so far as they are inconsistent with this Act, are hereby repealed; provided, that all offenses committed before this Act takes effect shall be inquired of, prosecuted, and punished in the same manner as if this Act had not been passed.

SEC. 8. Every person who shall, at the time of the passage of this Act, be confined in the House of Correction under or by virtue of a sentence of imprisonment in the County Jail, may remain in the House of Correction till his term of imprisonment shall expire, and, so far as relates to him, the House of Correction shall be deemed to be the County Jail, and he shall be in the charge and keeping of the Superintendent, who shall have the same power over him as the Sheriff might exercise if he was in fact in the County Jail. While any such person shall be in charge of the Superintendent, as above provided, the Sheriff shall be under no responsibility in regard to him; but nothing herein shall prevent the Sheriff from removing at any time any such person from the House of Correction to the County Jail. Nothing in this Act shall be construed to abolish or in any way interfere with the government or control of the County or Branch County Jails of said city and county by the Sheriff of said city and county.

SEC. 9.   This Act shall take effect in 30 days from and after its passage.

SUPPLEMENT CXXVIII.

1877-8, 957.

An Act to relieve the necessities of the San Francisco School Department.

[Approved April 1, 1878.]

WHEREAS, The Board of Supervisors of the City and County of San Francisco, in pursuance of an Act of the Legislature, approved March 30th, 1874, lease the Lincoln School lot, fronting on Market Street, for the term of 20 years, the total income of which lease will be five hundred and thirty-six thousand and one hundred dollars, and there was issued against the said sum two hundred thousand dollars in twenty years six per cent. bonds, the total sum of which, including interest, will be four hundred and forty thousand dollars, thus leaving a balance of ninety-six thousand one hundred dollars; therefore,

The People of the State of California, represented in Senate and Assembly, do enact as follows:

SECTION 1.   The Mayor, Auditor, and Treasurer of the City and County of San Francisco are hereby authorized and required to issue school bonds for school purposes in the total sum of forty-three thousand five hundred dollars. Said bonds shall be payable in twenty years from the first day of

May, one thousand eight hundred and seventy-eight, and shall bear interest at the rate of six per cent. per annum, which interest shall be payable on the first day of July and January, in the City and County of San Francisco. Said bonds shall be signed by the Mayor, Auditor, and Treasurer of said city and county, and the coupons attached to said bonds shall be signed by said Treasurer.

SEC. 2. The principal and interest of the said bonds shall be payable in gold coin of the United States of America, and the faith and credit of the City and County of San Francisco are hereby pledged for the redemption of said bonds and the payment of the principal and interest, in said gold coin of the United States of America, as set forth in this Act.

SEC. 3. As soon as the said bonds are issued, the Mayor, Auditor, and Treasurer of the City and County of San Francisco are hereby authorized if there is any money in the several sinking funds under their control, to deposit the said bonds in the treasury of the City and County of San Francisco, and take therefrom in lieu thereof a sum, in gold coin, equal to the face value of the bonds so deposited, and if there is not sufficient money in said fund, or if at any time there should be a need for the money so withdrawn from the said funds, then the Mayor, Auditor, and Treasurer are authorized to sell the remainder or the whole of said bonds to replace the money so taken out of the funds. Upon sale of said bonds for the purposes herein named, notice of such proposed sale shall be given by publication in two daily newspapers published in said city, for the period of not less than thirty days. Such notice shall specify the total amount of the bonds to be disposed of, the rate of interest which they draw, and the time for redemption thereof, at the time fixed and specified in said notice. All sealed proposals therefor shall be opened by said named officers, or a majority of them, and the sale awarded to the highest bidder, in U. S. gold coin; *provided*, that said highest bid amount to ninety-nine per cent. of the nominal or par value of said bonds.

SEC. 4. The money obtained from the disposal of the bonds, as provided for in Section 3 of this Act, shall be a special fund, under the control of the Board of Education of the City and County of San Francisco, for the sole purpose of purchasing school lots within that portion of San Francisco bounded as follows: Howard Street on the north, Townsend Street on the south, Sixth Street on the west, and Fourth Street on the east.

SEC. 5. The principal and interest of said bonds shall be paid, when due, by the Treasurer of the City and County of San Francisco, from moneys received from the lease of the school lot on the corner of Market and Fifth Streets, in said city and county, as provided for in an Act of the Legislature approved March 30th, eighteen hundred and seventy-four; and if at any time, through default in payment of rent or from other causes, said special fund shall be found insufficient to meet said interest or principal, it shall become the duty of the Board of Supervisors to pay the same out of the General Fund, and to levy a tax sufficient to meet the deficiency.

SEC. 6.   All Acts and parts of Acts, so far as they are inconsistent with the provisions of this Act, are, for the purposes of this Act, are hereby repealed.

SEC. 7.   This Act shall take effect from and after its passage.

SUPPLEMENT CXXIX.

1877–8, 959.

An Act to confer additional powers on the Board of Supervisors of the City and County of San Francisco in relation to accepted streets.

[Approved April 1, 1878.]

The People of the State of California, represented in Senate and Assembly, do enact as follows:

SECTION 1.   The Board of Supervisors of the City and County of San Francisco are hereby authorized and empowered to suspend from the benefits of acceptance any portion of a street where the owner of the property fronting thereon shall hereafter fail to pay the assessments for the improvements which form the basis for acceptance by the corporate authorities.

SEC. 2.   The Superintendent of Streets shall keep a thorough record in his office and list all property where the owner shall evade payment for the improvements which form the basis for acceptance, and he shall make a careful record of the same in a book or books kept for that purpose, showing correctly the portion of frontage in each block where the owners have paid their assessments, and the portion where payments have been evaded.

SEC. 3.   The said Superintendent of Streets shall also keep a careful record of all expenditures hereafter made for repairs and renewals upon accepted streets, charging to each block separately the amount expended thereon, and in every block containing one or more lots hereby suspended for the benefits of acceptance, he shall charge up to each its due proportion per front foot of the whole cost, and the same shall become at once a valid lien upon the realty, and bear interest at the rate of ten per cent. per annum till liquidated by full payment into the city treasury; *provided*, that at the expiration of one year from the date of the expenditures, if the same is not paid, the same shall be marked "delinquent," and a list thereof shall be certified to the Tax Collector of the City and County of San Francisco, and said Tax Collector shall thereupon advertise the said property for sale to pay said delinquent assessment and interest due thereon, and the costs and charges of advertising the same, and six months thereafter shall execute a deed therefor, provided the said property shall not be redeemed; and if redeemed, fifty per cent. shall be added as a redemption fee therefor. Said certificate of sale and deed shall be in manner and form as the certificates and deeds provided to be executed by the Tax Collector on the sale of property for delinquent taxes, and shall be conclusive evidence of the validity of the assessment and of all prior proceedings, and shall be subject to be declared invalid by proof only that the assessment for which the property was sold had been paid prior to the date of sale.

SEC. 4. Any piece of property which shall be suspended from the benefits of acceptance through the operations of this law, may, at any time, be restored to its lost privileges, and the street in front of it accepted, by payment to the contractor who did the work the amount of the assessment against such lot for the improvement of which it was suspended, and upon filing a receipt therefor in the office of the Superintendent of Public Streets and Highways. It may also be restored by payment of such sum into the Treasury of the City and County of San Francisco. All payments and collections of money under this Act shall be placed in a special fund, to be designated as the "Special Street Fund." And each payment or collection must be entered in a book to be kept by the Treasurer for that purpose, showing the amount collected, a description of the lot, with the date of the contract and assessment for the non-payment of which said lot was suspended, and the name of the contractor doing the work, as shown by the books of the Street Commissioner. The contractor who did the work in front of any lot suspended for non-payment of his assessment, or his assigns, shall be entitled to receive from the Treasurer all moneys paid into the treasury, either voluntarily or by the lot owner, or collected under the provisions of section three of this Act, from time to time, as the same shall be paid into the treasury, up to the amount due him on said invalid assessment, and when he has been fully paid said lot shall be released from its disabilities, and the street in front thereof shall be accepted. Nothing in this law contained shall be construed so as to give any person a claim against said city and county for any money, unless the same shall have been first collected and paid into the treasury, in accordance with the provisions of this Act, and to the extent of such payment only. No lot shall be liable to pay any sum beyond the amount of the assessment for work done to place the same in condition to make the same an accepted street.

SEC. 5. It shall in future be lawful for the city authorities to accept any portion of a street, for future maintenance by the city, where it is clearly shown to their satisfaction that all the requisite improvements have been paid for by the owners of the property fronting thereon; but no portion of a street shall hereafter be accepted while the bills remain unpaid for the improvements which form the basis for acceptance.

SEC. 6. All laws and parts of laws in conflict with the provisions of this Act are hereby repealed.

SEC. 7. This Act shall take effect from and after its passage.

SUPPLEMENT CXXX.

1877-8, 961.

An Act to confer additional powers on the Board of Supervisors of the City and County of San Francisco.

[Approved April 1, 1878.]

The People of the State of California, represented in Senate and Assembly, do enact as follows:

SECTION 1. That portion of Elm Street or Avenue extending from Polk Street towards Larkin Street, through only a portion of Block No. Six, Western Addition, in the City and County of San Francisco, which has not been used by the public as a thoroughfare, may be closed by the Board of Supervisors of the said city and county, on petition of the majority of the owners of all the land fronting on said portion of Elm Street or Avenue.

SEC. 2. This Act shall take effect immediately.

SUPPLEMENT CXXXI.

1877-8, 962.

An Act supplemental to an Act entitled "An Act to legalize the assessment of taxes in the City and County of San Francisco, and to ratify and confirm a resolution of the Board of Supervisors of the City and County of San Francisco," approved March 19th, 1878.

[Approved April 1, 1878.]

The People of the State of California, represented in Senate and Assembly, do enact as follows:

SECTION 1. It is hereby provided that all suits that may be brought under the provisions of the Act to which this Act is supplemental, whether for State, and city, and county taxes, or either, may be brought in the name of the City and County of San Francisco, and no want of description or indescription, or uncertainty, or ambiguity of description of the property assessed upon the assessment rolls of said years, in said Act mentioned, or either of them, if it can be ascertained or proved by the testimony of the Assessor of the City and County of San Francisco, or otherwise, what property is intended, shall invalidate the assessment, but the same shall be sufficient and be considered valid, both in law and equity.

SEC. 2. This Act shall take effect and be in force from and after its passage.

SUPPLEMENT CXXXII.

1877-8, 1023.

An Act to fix the salary of the Clerk of the Mayor of the City and County of San Francisco, and to provide for the payment thereof.

[Approved April 1, 1878.]

The People of the State of California, represented in Senate and Assembly, do enact as follows:

SECTION 1. The salary of the Mayor's Clerk of the City and County of

San Francisco shall, from and after the passage of this Act, be fixed at two hundred and fifty dollars per month, in lieu of all other compensation, and shall be paid in the same manner that other official salaries are paid in said city and county.

Sec. 2.   This Act shall take effect and be in force from and after its passage.

SUPPLEMENT CXXXIII.

1877-8, 966.

An Act to change the grades of certain streets in the City and County of San Francisco.

[Approved April 1, 1878.]

The People of the State of California, represented in Senate and Assembly, do enact as follows:

SECTION 1.   The Board of Supervisors of the City and County of San Francisco is hereby authorized and empowered, without the petition of property owners therefor, to establish the following grades: The grade of the crossing of Franklin and Green Streets at ninety-four feet above base, instead of seventy-four feet above; the grade of the crossing of Franklin and Lombard Streets at sixty-four feet above base, instead of fifty feet above; the crossing of Van Ness Avenue and Green Streets at one hundred and five feet above base, instead of ninety feet above; the crossing of Van Ness Avenue and Greenwich Street at one hundred feet above base, instead of ninety feet above; the crossing of Van Ness Avenue and Lombard Street at ninety-five feet above base, instead of eighty feet above; the crossing of Polk and Greenwich Streets at one hundred and sixty feet above base, instead of one hundred and forty feet above.

SEC. 2.   The grades of said several streets intermediate the main street crossings herein named and contiguous thereto shall conform to the grades as herein established.

SEC. 3.   This Act shall take effect on the first day of July, eighteen hundred and seventy-eight.

SUPPLEMENT CXXXIV.

1877–8, 967.

An Act to extend the jurisdiction of the Park Commissioners over a certain highway in the City and County of San Francisco.

[Approved April 1, 1878.]

The People of the State of California, represented in Senate and Assembly, do enact as follows:

SECTION 1. Order number one thousand four hundred and sixteen of the Board of Supervisors of the City and County of San Francisco, approved December seventh, one thousand eight hundred and seventy-seven, is hereby ratified and confirmed, and the road therein mentioned, commencing at Central Avenue and extending to the Pacific Ocean, and purchased under said order, together with the personal property purchased with said road, is hereby placed under the control and management of the Park Commissioners having charge of Golden Gate Park, who shall have all the powers, and be subject to the same duties respecting said road, as if the same had been originally part of said park, and all Acts relating to said park, so far as the same may be applicable, are hereby extended to said road.

SEC. 2. The said Board of Supervisors are hereby authorized and directed to include in their tax levy for the coming fiscal year, an amount sufficient to make the payment provided to be made in section one of said order, with interest thereon from the date of the approval of said order, which taxes under said levy shall be levied as other municipal taxes, and paid into the General Fund, and disbursed in discharge of said indebtedness.

SEC. 3. This Act shall take effect and be in force from and after its passage.

18

GENERAL LAWS AND SAN FRANCISCO STATUTES.

The following statutes passed since the adoption of the Constitution of 1879 have special reference to the City and County of San Francisco:

SUPPLEMENT CXXXV.

1860, 1.

An Act to repeal an Act entitled an Act to authorize the City and County of San Francisco to provide and maintain public water-works for said city and county, and to condemn and purchase private property for that purpose, approved March twenty-seventh, eighteen hundred and seventy-six.

[Approved January 22, 1880.]

The People of the State of California, represented in Senate and Assembly, do enact as follows:

SECTION 1. The Act entitled an Act to authorize the City and County of San Francisco to provide and maintain public water-works for said city and county, and to condemn and purchase private property for that purpose, approved April 27th, A.D. one thousand, eight hundred and seventy-six, is hereby repealed.

SEC. 2. This Act shall take effect and be in force from and after its passage.

SUPPLEMENT CXXXVI.

1880, 2.

An Act to transfer the records, papers, and business of the Courts existing on the 31st day of December, 1879, to the Courts now existing therein.

[Approved February 4, 1880.]

The People of the State of California, represented in Senate and Assembly, do enact as follows:

SEC. 1. [*Relates to the Supreme Court.*]

SEC. 2. The Superior Court of each county in this State shall, for all purposes, be considered the successor of the District, County and Probate

Courts thereof, and, in the City and County of San Francisco, of the Municipal Criminal Court and Municipal Court of Appeals, and shall be deemed to have succeeded to all the unfinished business of said Courts. The Superior Courts shall hear, determine, or otherwise dispose of, all causes and proceedings which were pending on the first day of January, eighteen hundred and eighty, in the said Courts superseded by them, and every motion or proceeding then pending or thereafter made or taken in such causes and proceedings, and of which said Courts would have had jurisdiction had they not been abolished; and also, all appeals taken or perfected, before or after said day, from all orders or judgments of Justices' and Police Courts which by law are declared to be appealable. From and after the first day of January, eighteen hundred and eighty, the Superior Courts shall have the custody of all the records, books, and papers of the said Courts superseded by them, and shall have jurisdiction thereof, and of the judgments, orders, and process of said Courts; and shall enforce the same and issue process thereon in like manner, and with the same effect, as if they had in the first instance been filed, commenced, rendered, made, or issued in or by the Superior Court. The Superior Court of the City and County of San Francisco shall have jurisdiction of, and shall try and dispose of, all indictments for misdemeanor pending in the City Criminal Court of said city and county, on the first day of January, eighteen hundred and eighty; and such indictments, and all papers and records relating thereto, shall be transferred to the said Superior Court and become records thereof. Any application, motion, or proceeding, set by the District, County, or Probate Court of any county, or by the Judge thereof, to be heard by such Court or Judge after the first day of January, eighteen hundred and eighty, may be heard in the Superior Court of such county, upon the same notice that was required to authorize the hearing thereof in such District, County, or Probate Court, or by the Judge thereof. Any process issued out of any District, County, or Probate Court of this State before the first day of January, eighteen hundred and eighty, may be served, or the service thereof completed, after said day, in the same manner, and with like effect, as if such Courts had not been abolished; *provided*, that such process shall be returned to the Superior Court of the county in which it was issued, and any appearance or answer required by such process shall be made or filed in such Court.

SEC. 3.   All prosecutions which were transferred or certified for trial to the City Criminal Court of the City and County of San Francisco, by the Police Court, thereof, and were pending or undetermined on the first day of January, eighteen hundred and eighty, shall be tried and disposed of in the said Police Court; and all the papers, pleadings, and records relating to such prosecutions shall be transferred to, and deposited with said Police Court, and become records and papers thereof.

SEC. 4.   This Act takes effect immediately.

SUPPLEMENT CXXXVII.

1880, 4.

An Act to continue in force school teachers' certificates, State educational diplomas, and life diplomas.

[Approved February 5, 1880.]

The People of the State of California, represented in Senate and Assembly, do enact as follows:

SECTION 1. All teachers' City, City and County, County, and State certificates, State Educational diplomas, Life diplomas, and all other teachers' certificates and diplomas issued in the State of California, under and in pursuance of the laws thereof, on or before the 31st day of December, 1879, shall be and the same are hereby continued in full force and effect, and shall be deemed valid for all purposes, and to the full extent of time that the same were and were intended respectively to be under the said laws, on and before the said 31st day of December, A.D. 1879.

SEC. 2. This Act shall take effect from and after its passage.

SUPPLEMENT CXXXVIII.

1880, 5.

An Act in relation to certain deputies and assistants of County Clerks.

[Approved February 13, 1880.]

The People of the State of California, represented in Senate and Assembly, do enact as follows :

SECTION 1. In all cases in which by statutes in force on the thirty-first day of December, eighteen hundred and seventy-nine, the County Clerk of any county, or city and county, is authorized to appoint deputies or assistants, to whom duties are assigned by such statutes, in, or in connection with any of the Courts which were abolished by the Constitution, the Clerk may assign to such deputies or assistants duties in, or in connection with the Superior Court of his county, or city and county, and they shall be entitled to the same compensation as is provided in said statutes, and the same shall be audited and paid at the same time and in the same manner and from the same source as is provided therein.

Sec. 2. This Act shall take effect immediately.

SUPPLEMENT CXXXIX.

1880, 8.

An Act in relation to the currency of the United States.

[Approved March 12, 1880.]

The People of the State of California, represented in Senate and Assembly, do enact as follows:

Section 1. All legal tender notes heretofore issued, or which may hereafter be issued by the Government of the United States of America, as legal tender notes, shall be received at par in payment for all taxes due or to become due to this State, or to any county or municipal corporation thereof, and such notes shall be a legal tender for all debts, dues, and demands between citizens of this State.

Sec. 2. All Acts, and the provisions of any Acts or parts of Acts conflicting with this Act, are hereby repealed.

Sec. 3. This Act shall take effect and be in force from and after its passage.

SUPPLEMENT CXL.

1880, 8.

An Act to repeal an Act entitled "An Act for the appointment of Inspector of Stationary Steam Boilers and Steam Tanks, and for the better security of life and property in the City and County of San Francisco," approved March twenty-seventh, eighteen hundred and seventy-six.

[Approved March 12, 1880.]

The People of the State of California, represented in Senate and Assembly, do enact as follows:

Section 1. An Act entitled "An Act for the appointment of Inspector of

Stationary Steam Boilers and Steam Tanks, and for the better security of life and property in the City and County of San Francisco," approved March twenty-seventh, eighteen hundred and seventy-six, is hereby repealed.

Sec. 2. This Act shall take effect and be in force from and after its passage.

SUPPLEMENT CXLI.

1880, 18.

An Act to repeal an Act entitled "An Act to compel the County Clerk of the City and County of San Francisco to keep open his office upon all election days," approved March seventh, eighteen hundred and seventy-six.

[Approved March 31, 1880.]

The People of the State of California, represented in Senate and Assembly, do enact as follows:

SECTION 1. An Act entitled "An Act to compel the County Clerk of the City and County of San Francisco to keep open his office upon all election days," approved March seventh, eighteen hundred and seventy-six, is hereby repealed.

Sec. 2. This Act shall take effect and be in force from and after its passage.

SUPPLEMENT CXLII.

1880, 20.

An Act in relation to certain Deputies, Assistants and Copyists of County Clerks.

[Approved April 2, 1880.]

The People of the State of California, represented in Senate and Assembly, do enact as follows:

SECTION 1. In all cases in which, by statutes in force on the thirty-first day of December, eighteen hundred and seventy-nine, the County Clerk of any city and county having over one hundred thousand inhabitants, is authorized to appoint deputies, assistants, and copyists, in, or in connection with the Courts which are abolished by the Constitution now in force, the County Clerk may appoint four competent persons as such deputies, assistants, and copyists for each Superior Court; and where by law such Superior Court is entitled to more than one Judge, he may appoint four competent persons as such deputies, assistants, and copyists for each additional Judge; and such deputies, assistants, and copyists, so appointed, shall be entitled to the same compensation as is provided in said statutes, and the same shall be audited and paid at the same time and manner and from the same source as is provided therein. He may also appoint such additional number of copyists as the business of his office shall, in his discretion, from time to time, require (provided, said number shall not exceed, at any one time, three copyists for each Judge of the Superior Court), at a compensation not to exceed three dollars per day each, for the days of actual service rendered; such additional copyists shall be paid at the same time and manner as is provided for such deputies, assistants, and copyists.

Sec. 2. This Act shall take effect immediately.

SUPPLEMENT CXLIII,

1880, 22.

———

An Act to provide for the removal of Chinese, whose presence is dangerous to the well being of communities, outside the limits of cities and towns in the State of California.

[Approved April 3, 1880.]

The People of the State of California, represented in Senate and Assembly, do enact as follows:

SECTION 1. The Board of Trustees or other legislative authority of any incorporated city or town, and the Board of Supervisors of any incorporated city and county, are hereby granted the power, and it is hereby made their duty, to pass and enforce any and all acts, or ordinances, or resolutions necessary to cause the removal without the limits of such cities and towns, or city and county, of any Chinese now within or hereafter to come within such limits; provided, that they may set apart certain prescribed portions of the limits of such cities, or towns, or city and county, for the location therein of such Chinese.

SEC. 2.   This Act shall take effect and be in force from and after its passage.

SUPPLEMENT   CXLIV.

1880, 23.

An Act to confer upon the Superior Court of each county and the Judge thereof the powers heretofore possessed by the District, County, and Probate Courts of such county, and the Judges thereof.

[Approved April 3, 1880.]

The People of the State of California, represented in Senate and Assembly, do enact as follows:

SECTION 1.   In all cases in which, on the first day of January, one thousand, eight hundred and eighty, any authority or jurisdiction was by law vested in the County or Probate Court of any county, or in the Judge thereof, or in any District Court of such county, or in the Judge thereof, such jurisdiction and authority shall hereafter, while such law continues in force, be vested in and exercised by the Superior Court of such county, or by a Judge thereof.

SEC. 2.   If any Judge of the Superior Court of any county was the Judge of the County, Probate, or District Court, in and for said county, on the first day of January, eighteen hundred and eighty, and any cause, proceeding, or motion, wholly or partially tried before him, remains undecided, the Superior Court, when presided over by him, may resume the consideration or trial of such cause, proceeding or motion, at the stage where it was suspended in such Probate, County, or District Court, and may complete such trial or hearing, or determine such cause, motion, or proceeding, as if the same had first been brought or made in such Superior Court.

SEC. 3.   This Act shall take effect immediately.

SUPPLEMENT CXLV.

1880, 61.

An Act to confer power upon Supervisors of cities and counties containing more than one hundred thousand inhabitants, to extend and complete all main intercepting sewers heretofore partially constructed.

[Approved April 15, 1880.]

The People of the State of California, represented in Senate and Assembly, do enact as follows:

SECTION 1. The Supervisors of any city and county in this State containing a population of more than one hundred thousand inhabitants, shall have power, and it shall be the duty of said Supervisors, to promote the sanitary condition of such city and county, to complete all main intercepting sewers heretofore constructed, or partially constructed, at the expense of such city and county, and to extend the same to a suitable and proper outlet, deemed necessary for sanitary purposes in the judgment of said Supervisors, the expense thereof to be chargeable to and to be paid out of the General Fund of the treasury of such city and county. The said work to be performed under the charge and supervision of an experienced engineer, to be appointed by said Board or Boards. The expense of said work is not to exceed one hundred and fifty thousand dollars.

SEC. 2. This Act shall take effect and be in force from and after its passage.

SUPPLEMENT CXLVI.

1880, 76.

An Act to repeal an Act conferring further powers upon the Board of Supervisors of the City and County of San Francisco, approved April first, eighteen hundred and seventy-eight.

[Approved April 15, 1880.]

The People of the State of California, represented in Senate and Assembly, do enact as follows:

SECTION 1. That an Act conferring further powers upon the Board o

Supervisors of the City and County of San Francisco, approved April first, eighteen hundred and seventy-eight, is hereby repealed.

SEC. 2.   This Act shall take effect immediately.

SUPPLEMENT CXLVII.

1880, 101.

An Act to empower consolidated cities and counties of over one hundred thousand inhabitants, to make alterations to county prisons and County Jails, for sanitary purposes.

[Approved April 16, 1880.]

The People of the State of California, represented in Senate and Assembly, do enact as follows:

SECTION 1.   The Board or Boards of Supervisors, or the Municipal Council, or other governing bodies of consolidated cities and counties having a population of over one hundred thousand inhabitants, are hereby empowered to enlarge, construct additional cells in and make necessary alterations to county prisons and County Jails in said cities and counties, wherever the same are required for sanitary reasons, and to allow and order paid all expenditures therefor out of the General Fund of said cities and counties.

SEC. 2.   This Act shall take effect and be in force from and after its passage.

SUPPLEMENT CXLVIII.

1880, 106.

An Act providing for the appointment of an additional Notary Public for the City and County of San Francisco, for the accommodation of the inhabitants of said city and county residing at the Presidio.

[Approved April 16, 1880.]

The People of the State of California, represented in Senate and Assembly, do enact as follows:

SECTION 1.   The Governor is authorized to appoint and commission one additional Notary Public for the City and County of San Francisco, who shall keep an office for the transaction of business in that portion of the city and county known as the Presidio.

SEC. 2.   This Act shall take effect from and after its passage.

SUPPLEMENT CXLIX.

1880, 114.

An Act to empower consolidated cities and counties of over one hundred thousand inhabitants to pay out of the General Fund demands for rent of court-rooms and chambers for Superior Courts, and of Police Stations, and for salaries of Janitors.

[Approved April 16, 1880.]

The People of the State of California, represented in Senate and Assembly, do enact as follows:

SECTION 1. The Board or Boards of Supervisors, or the Municipal Council, or other governing bodies of consolidated cities and counties having a population of over one hundred thousand inhabitants, are hereby empowered to allow and order paid out of the General Fund of said cities and counties, all amounts required to pay for rent of Court-rooms and chambers for the Superior Courts, rents of Police stations, and salaries of all porters, engineers, and firemen, employed in public buildings and offices in said cities and counties.

SEC. 2. This Act shall take effect and be in force from and after its passage.

SUPPLEMENT CL.

1880, 231.

An Act to establish free public libraries and reading rooms.

[Approved April 26, 1880.]

The People of the State of California, represented in Senate and Assembly, do enact as follows:

SECTION 1. For the purposes of this Act cities of this State are classified as follows:

1. Cities of less than one hundred thousand population.
2. Cities of more than one hundred thousand population.

SEC. 2. The municipal authorities of any incorporated city of this State are authorized and empowered by a resolution duly passed for that purpose to levy and collect, as in other cases, annually, a tax not to exceed one mill on the dollar for the purpose of establishing and maintaining in such city free public libraries and reading rooms, and purchasing such books, journals, and other publications, purchasing and leasing such real and personal property, and erecting such buildings as may be necessary therefor.

Sec. 3. All money and revenue paid, collected, or received by authority of anything herein contained, whether by taxation, gift, devise, bequest, or otherwise, shall belong to and be known and designated as the " Library Fund," and shall be paid into the proper city treasury, and there kept separate and apart from other funds, and be drawn therefrom as hereinafter provided, but only to be used and applied t) the purposes herein authorized.

Sec. 4. All property, real and personal, acquired by purchase, gift, devise, bequest, or otherwise, under the provisions of or for any purpose authorized by this Act, shall vest, be, and remain in the proper city, and may be protected, defended, and sued for by action at law, or otherwise, in the name of such city as in other cases.

Sec. 5. In a city of less than one hundred thousand population five Trustees shall be elected at the same time and in the same manner as the other town officers are elected. They shall hold office the same length of time to carry into effect the provisions of this Act.

Sec. 6. In a city of more than one hundred thousand population the Mayor or chief executive officer, during his continuance in office, and eleven citizens thereof, to be appointed by the Governor of this State, shall constitute the first Board of Trustees of any library or reading room established or acquired in such city under this Act.

Sec. 7. The office of Trustee shall be honorary, without salary or other compensation, and shall continue during good behavior; but for good cause a Trustee may be removed from office by proceedings in the Superior Court in behalf of the proper city in manner provided for the removal from office of other city officers.

Sec. 8. The Trustees of any library or reading room established or acquired by authority of this Act, shall take charge of the same and of all real and personal property thereunto belonging, or that may be acquired by loan, purchase, gift, devise, or otherwise. They shall meet for business purposes on the first Tuesday of each month, and at such other times as they may appoint, at a place to be provided for the purpose, and a majority of all their number shall constitute a quorum for business. They may appoint one of their number to act as President of their Board, and may elect a Librarian. They shall also elect a Secretary, who shall keep a full statement and account of all property, money receipts and expenditures, and a record and full minutes in writing of all their proceedings. The Secretary may certify to such proceedings, or any part or portion thereof under his hand, verified by an official seal adopted and provided by the Trustees for that purpose.

Sec. 9. Such Trustees, by a majority vote of all their members, to be recorded in the minutes with the ayes and noes at length, shall have power:

First—To make and enforce all rules, regulations, and by-laws necessary for the administration, government, and protection of such library and reading room, and all property belonging thereto, or that may be loaned, devised, bequeathed, or donated to the same.

Second—To exercise and administer any trust declared or created for such library or reading room, and to provide memorial tablets and niches to perpetuate the memories of those persons who may make valuable donations thereto.

Third—To remove any Trustee who may neglect to attend the meetings of the Board of Trustees, or who may absent himself from such meetings, or without the consent of the Board from the State for three consecutive months; and to fill all vacancies that may from any cause occur in the Board.

Fourth—To define the powers and describe the duties of any and all officers, determine the number, and elect all necessary subordinate officers and assistants, and at their pleasure remove any officer or assistant.

Fifth—To purchase necessary books, journals, publications, and other personal property.

Sixth—To order the drawing and payment, upon properly authenticated vouchers, duly certified by the President and Secretary, of money from out of the Library Fund for any liability or expenditure herein authorized; and generally to do all that may be necessary to fully carry into effect the provisions of this Act.

Seventh—To fix the salaries of the Librarian, Secretary, and other subordinate officers and assistants, and by and with the consent and approval of the legislative or other proper authority of the proper city, expressed by resolution duly passed, to purchase said real estate, erect and equip such buildings as may be necessary for such library and reading room.

SEC. 10. The orders and demands of the Trustees of any such library or reading room of any city, when duly made and authenticated, as above provided, shall be verified and audited by the auditing officer, and paid by the Treasurer of such city out of the Library Fund properly belonging thereto, of which full entry and record shall be kept as in other cases.

SEC. 11. The Trustees of such library or reading room, on or before the first Monday of July of each year, shall make an annual report to the municipal authorities of their city, giving the condition of their trust, with full statements of all property and money received, whence derived, how used and expended; the number of books, journals, and other publications on hand, the number added by purchase, gift, or otherwise, during each year, the number lost or missing, the number and character of those loaned, and such other statistics, information, and suggestions as may be of general interest. A financial report showing all receipts and disbursements of money shall also be made by the Secretary of the Board of Trustees, duly verified by his oath.

SEC. 12. The proper municipal authorities of any city wherein a public library or reading room may be established, shall have power to pass ordinances for the protection of the same and all property thereto belonging, and for imposing penalties for the punishment of persons committing injury to such library or reading room, or the property or books thereof, or for failure to return any book or other property belonging thereto. They shall also have power, by a resolution duly passed for such purpose, to grant, donate, or authorize the use of either, in whole or in part, any land, square, or real estate belonging to such city or town, or dedicated to public use therein, for the purpose of erecting and maintaining a building to be used only for a public library and reading room as herein authorized.

SEC. 13.   The words "city" or "cities" wherever used in this Act are intended to and shall include all incorporated cities and towns, and cities and counties with consolidated government, and shall be construed accordingly.

SEC. 14.   An Act entitled "An Act to establish and maintain free public libraries and reading rooms," approved March the eighteenth, eighteen hundred and seventy-eight, is hereby repealed.   All libraries and reading rooms heretofore established by authority of the last mentioned Act in any city or town, or city and county, and all property, real and personal, thereto belonging, shall be turned over to the charge, custody, and administration of such Trust es as may be continued or appointed therein respectively under the provisions of this Act, with like powers and liabilities as if such library had been established under this Act.

SEC. 15.   This Act shall take effect on the first day of May, A.D. eighteen hundred and eighty.

SUPPLEMENT CLI.

1881, 2.

An Act to authorize the several counties, cities and counties, cities, and towns of this State, and the officers and Boards of officers thereof, to receive property by gift, bequest, and devise, and to hold, manage, and dispose of such property and the income and increase thereof.

[Approved February 10, 1881.]

The People of the State of California, represented in Senate and Assembly, do enact as follows:

SECTION 1.   The Boards of Common Council, Supervisors, Trustees, houses of legislation, or other legislative bodies of the several counties, cities and counties, cities, and towns of this State, are hereby authorized to accept or reject, as they may deem advisable, any gift, bequest, or devise heretofore or that may be hereafter made to or in favor of the counties, cities and counties, cities, or towns represented by them respectively, or to or in favor of any of the officers or Boards of officers thereof, in their official capacity, or to or in their favor in trust for any lawful public purpose.

SEC. 2. The several counties, cities and counties, cities, and towns of this State, and the several officers and Boards of officers thereof, in their official capacity, are hereby authorized to receive property by gift, bequest, and devise, and to hold and dispose of the same, and the income and increase thereof, to and for such lawful uses and purposes as have been or may hereafter be prescribed in the terms of such gift, bequest, or devise. In the event of any such gift, bequest, or devise having been, or being hereafter made, unaccompanied by any provision prescribing or limiting the uses or purposes to which the property received thereunder, or the income or increase thereof shall be put, such uses and purposes may be prescribed and regulated by the Common Council, Board of Supervisors, Board of Trustees, houses of legislation, or other legislative body of the proper county, city and county, city, or town. Such legislative bodies may make such regulations concerning the mode and manner of carrying into effect the purposes as aforesaid, and devoting the property so received, and the income and increase thereof, to the uses aforesaid, in their respective counties, cities and counties, cities, and towns, as may necessary.

SUPPLEMENT CLII.

1881, 54.

An Act to enable the Board of Supervisors, Town Council, Board of Aldermen, or other legislative body of any city and county, city, or town, to obtain data and information, from any corporation, company, or person supplying water to such city and county, city, or town, requiring such Boards, Town Council, or other legislative body to perform the duties prescribed by section one, of article fourteen of the Constitution, and prescribing penalties for the non-performance of such duties.

[Approved March 7, 1881.]

The People of the State of California, represented in Senate and Assembly, do enact as follows:

SECTION. 1. The Board of Supervisors, Town Council, Board of Aldermen, or other legislative body of any city and county, city, or town, are

hereby authorized and empowered, and it is made their official duty, to
annually fix the rates that shall be charged and collected by any person,
company, association, or corporation for water furnished to any such city and
county, or city, or town, or the inhabitants thereof. Such rates shall be fixed
at a regular or special session of such Board or other legislative body, held
during the month of February of each year, and shall take effect on the first
day of July thereafter, and shall continue in full force and effect for the term
of one year and no longer.

SEC. 2. The Board of Supervisors, Town Council, Board of Aldermen, or
other legislative body of any city and county, city, or town, are hereby
authorized, and it is hereby made their duty, at least thirty days prior to the
fifteenth day of January of each year, to require, by ordinance or otherwise,
any corporatio , company, or person supplying water to such city and
county, city or town, or to the inhabitants thereof, to furnish to such Board,
or other governing body, in the month of January in each year, a detailed
statement, verified by the oath of the President and Secretary of such
corporation or company, or of such person, as the case may be, showing the
name of each water-rate payer, his or her place of residence, and the amount
paid for water by each of such water-rate payers, during the year preceding
the date of such statement, and also showing all revenue derived from all
sources, and an itemized statement of expenditures made for supplying water
during said time.

SEC. 3. Accompanying the first statement made as prescribed in section
two of this Act, every such corporation, company, or person shall furnish a
detailed statement, verified in like manner as the statement mentioned in
section two hereof, showing the amount of money actually expended annually,
since commencing business, in the purchase, construction, and maintenance,
respectively, of the property necessary to the carrying on of 'its business,
and also the gross cash receipts annually, for the same period, from all
sources.

SEC. 4. Every corporation, company, or person who shall refuse or neglect to furnish the statements mentioned in sections two and three of this
Act, or either of them, or who shall furnish any false statement in relation
thereto, within thirty days after having been required or requested to furnish
the same as prescribed in sections one, two, and three of this Act, shall be
deemed guilty of a misdemeanor.

SEC. 5. Upon receiving the statements provided for in sections two and
three of this Act, the Board of Supervisors, Town Council, Board of Aldermen, or other legislative body, shall cause a copy thereof to be made and
filed in the office of the County Recorder of such city and county, or of the
county wherein such city or town is situated.

SEC. 6. Rates for the furnishing of water shall be equal and uniform.
There shall be no discriminations made between persons, or between persons
and corporations, or as to the use of water for private and domestic, and

public or municipal purposes; *provided*, that nothing herein shall be so construed as to allow any person, company, association, or corporation, to charge any person, corporation, or association, anything for water furnished them when, by any present law, such water is free.

Sec. 7. Any person, company, association, or corporation charging, or attempting to collect from the persons, corporations, or municipalities using water, any sum in excess of the rate fixed as hereinbefore designated, shall, upon the complaint of said Board of Supervisors, Town Council, Board of Aldermen, or other legislative body thereof, or of any water-rate payer, and upon conviction before any Court of competent jurisdiction, shall forfeit the franchises and waterworks of such person, company, association, or corporation to the city and county, city or town, wherein the said water is furnished and used.

Sec. 8. Any Board of Supervisors, or other legislative body of any city and county, city, or town which shall fail or refuse to perform any of the duties prescribed by this Act, at the time and in the manner hereinbefore specified, shall be deemed guilty of malfeasance in office, and upon conviction thereof, at the suit of any interested party, in any Court of competent jurisdiction, shall be removed from office.

Sec. 9. This Act shall take effect and be in force from and after the date of its passage.

SUPPLEMENT CLIII.

1881, 75.

———

An Act to create an additional Police Judge's Court for the City and County of San Francisco, to define its powers and jurisdiction.

[Approved March 7, 1881.]

The People of the State of California, represented in Senate and Assembly, do enact as follows:

Section 1. There is hereby created and established in and for the City and County of San Francisco an additional Police Judge's Court, to be known and designated as the "Police Judge's Court No. 2," which Court shall have concurrent jurisdiction of all preliminary examinations of persons charged with felony, and of all misdemeanors and violations of city and county ordinances, and all other offenses of which the Police Judge's Court of said city and county now has jurisdiction.

Sec. 2. There shall be, as far as practicable, an equal distribution of

19

cases between the said Courts, which cases shall be alternately set down for trial to each Court, in the order in which the warrants are issued.

SEC. 3. The mode of examination, trial, and procedure in the Police Judge's Court No. 2 shall, in all cases, be governed by the same rules prescribed by law for other Police Courts in similar cases.

SEC. 4. A Judge of the Police Judge's Court No. 2 shall be elected at the same time and in a like manner as the Police Judge of the Police Judge's Court of said city and county, and whose term of office shall be the same. The Governor of the State of California shall, within thirty days after the passage of this Act, appoint some suitable person as Judge of the Police Judge's Court No. 2, who shall hold such office until his successor has been elected and qualified. The compensation of the Judge of the Police Judge's Court No. 2 shall be four thousand dollars per annum, payable in the same manner as the salary of the Police Judge of said city and county is now paid.

SEC. 5. The said Police Judge's Court No. 2 shall hold its session in the City and County of San Francisco, in such central and convenient place as shall be provided for that purpose by the Board of Supervisors. The said Board of Supervisors shall also, within thirty days after the passage of this Act, elect some suitable person as Prosecuting Attorney of the said Police Judge's Court No. 2, at the same salary per annum as is now paid to the Prosecuting Attorney of the Police Judge's Court of said city and county. And said Board of Supervisors shall elect a Clerk of Court, at a salary of one thousand eight hundred dollars per annum, payable in the same manner as the salaries of the Judge and Clerk of the Police Judge's Court of said city and county are now paid.

SEC. 6. The Judge of the Police Judge's Court No. 2 shall be a conservator of the peace in said city and county, and may exercise all the powers conferred by law upon the Police Judge as magistrate.

SEC. 7. The Judge of said Court shall appoint a suitable person to act as Bailiff of said Court, who shall receive a like compensation for such services as is now paid to the Bailiff of the Police [Judge's Court for said city and county.

SEC 8. This Act shall take effect and be in force from and after its passage.

SUPPLEMENT CLIV.

1883, 24.

— ·· —

An Act to provide for the classification of municipal corporations.

[Approved March 2, 1883.]

The People of the State of California, represented in Senate and Assembly, do enact as follows:

SECTION 1. All municipal corporations within the State are hereby classified as follows: Those having a population of more than one hundred thousand shall constitute the first class; those having a population of more than thirty thousand, and not exceeding one hundred thousand, shall constitute the second class; those having a population of more than fifteen thousand, and not exceeding thirty thousand, shall constitute the third class; those having a population of more than ten thousand, and not exceeding fifteen thousand, shall constitute the fourth class; those having a population of more than three thousand, and not exceeding ten thousand, shall constitute the fifth class; those having a population of not exceeding three thousand, shall constitute the sixth class.

SEC. 2. The census taken under the direction of the Congress of the United States, in the year eighteen hundred and eighty, and every ten years thereafter, shall be the basis upon which the respective populations of said municipal corporations shall be determined, unless a direct enumeration of the inhabitants thereof be made, as in this Act provided, in which case such direct enumeration shall constitute such basis.

SEC. 3. The Council, Board of Trustees, or other legislative body of any municipal corporation, may, at any time, cause an enumeration of the inhabitants thereof to be made, and in such manner and under such regulations as such body may by ordinance direct. If upon such enumeration it shall appear that such municipal corporation contains a sufficient number of inhabitants to entitle it to reorganize under a higher or lower class, the Common Council, Trustees, or other legislative body, shall, upon receiving a petition therefor signed by not less than one-fifth of the qualified electors thereof, submit to the electors of such city or town, at the next general election to be held therein, the question whether such city or town shall reorganize under the laws relating to municipal corporations of the class to which such city or town may belong. And thereupon such proceedings shall be had and election held as provided in the general law for the organization, incorporation, and government of municipal corporations. If a majority of the votes cast at such election shall be in favor of such reorganization, thereafter such officers shall be elected as are or may be at the time prescribed by law for municipal corporations of the class having the population under which such reorganization is had, and from and after the qualification of such officers, such corporation shall belong to such class.

SUPPLEMENT CLV.

1883, 35.

An Act to provide for the improvement of streets, lanes, alleys, courts, places, and sidewalks, and the construction of sewers within municipalities.

[Approved March 6, 1883.]

The People of the State of California, represented in Senate and Assembly, do enact as follows:

PART I.

SECTION 1. No public work or improvement of any description whatsoever shall be done or made within any municipality organized and existing for municipal purposes, or hereafter organized, in, upon, or about the streets thereof, the cost or expense of which is made chargeable or may be assessed upon private property by special assessment, except as in this Act provided.

SEC. 2. Whenever the public interest or convenience may require, the City Council is hereby authorized and empowered to order the whole or any portion of the streets, sidewalks, lanes, alleys, courts, or places of any such city graded or regraded to the official grade, planked or replanked, paved or repaved, macadamized or remacadamized, graveled or regraveled, piled or repiled, capped or recapped, and to order sidewalks, sewers, manholes, culverts, curbing, and crosswalks to be constructed therein, and to order any other work to be done which shall be necessary to make and complete the whole or any portion of said streets, sidewalks, lanes, alleys, courts, or places.

SEC. 3. Before ordering any work done, or improvement made, which is authorized by section two of this Act, the City Council shall pass a resolution declaring its intention so to do, describing the work and specifying the exterior boundaries of the district of lands to be affected or benefited by said work or improvement, and to be assessed to pay the costs and expenses thereof. The Street Superintendent shall thereupon cause to be conspicuously posted along the line of said contemplated work or improvement, at not more than three hundred feet in distance apart, but not less than three in all, notices of the passage of said resolutions. Said notice shall be headed "Notice of street work," in letters of not less than one inch in length, and shall, in legible characters, state the fact of passage of the resolution, its date, and, briefly, the work or improvement proposed, and refer to the resolution for further particulars. He shall also cause a notice, similar in substance, to be published for a period of fifteen days in one or more daily newspaper published and circulated in said city, and designated by said City Council, or by two successive insertions in a weekly newspaper so published, circulated, and designated. The owners of one-half or more of the frontage of the property fronting on said proposed work or improvement may make a written objection to the same within ten days after the expiration of the time of the publication of said notice, which objection shall be delivered to the Clerk of the City Council, who shall indorse thereon the date of its reception by him, and such objection, so delivered and indorsed, shall be a bar for six months to the doing of said work or making said improvement, except that when the work or improvement proposed to be done is the construction of sewers, manholes, culverts, crosswalks, and sidewalks, the Clerk shall lay said objection before said City Council, which shall, at its next meeting, fix a time for hearing said objection, not less than one week thereafter. The City Clerk shall thereupon notify the persons making such objection, by depositing a notice thereof in the Post Office of said city, postage prepaid, addressed to each objector. At the time specified, said City Council shall hear the objections urged, and pass upon the same, and its decision shall be final and conclusive; *provided*, that when any street or highway shall have been sewered its entire length, and not more than two blocks of said street remain ungraded, said City Council may order the grading, curbing, and macadamizing or graveling of that part of said street, or highway, so remaining ungraded, not exceeding two blocks; and said work of grading, curbing, macadamizing, graveling, culverting, crosswalking, and sidewalking said street or highway for said two blocks and less, shall not be stayed or prevented by any written or other objection, unless such Council shall deem proper; *provided, also*, that if one half or more, in width or in length, of any street lying and being between two main street crossings, has been already improved as aforesaid, said Council may order the remainder improved, notwithstanding such objections of property owners whose property is affected or benefited thereby, and to be assessed to pay the cost and expense thereof. Objections to the extent of the district of lands to be affected or benefited by said work or improvement, and to be assessed to pay the costs and expenses thereof, may be made by interested parties within the time allowed for other objections; but the City Council may, in its discretion, overrule all such objections, and if sustained after hearing, to be had as in this section above provided in case of other objections, all proceedings shall be stopped; but proceedings may be immediately again commenced by giving the notice of intention to do said work or make said improvement; if such objection is overruled by the City Council, the proceedings shall continue the same as if such objection had not been made. At the expiration of the time prescribed during which objection to said work or improvement may be made, if no objection shall have been made, or if an objection shall have been made, and said Council, after hearing, shall have overruled the same, the City Council shall be deemed to have acquired jurisdiction to order any of the work to be done, or improvements to be made, which is authorized by section two of this Act. Before passing any resolution for the construction of said improvements, plans and specifications, and careful estimates of the costs and expenses thereof shall be furnished to said City Council by the City Engineer of such city.

SEC. 4.   Before giving out any contracts by the City Council for doing any work authorized by section two of this Act, the City Council shall cause notice to be published for at least five days in one or more daily newspapers, published and circulated in said city, or by at least one insertion in a weekly or semi-weekly newspaper, so published and circulated, and to be conspicuously posted for five days on or near the Council-room door of said Council, inviting sealed proposals for the work contemplated.   All proposals offered shall be accompanied by a check payable to the order of the Mayor, certified by a responsible bank, in an amount equal to at least ten per cent. of the amount named in the estimate of the City Engineer, and shall be delivered to the Clerk of said City Council; and said Council shall, in open session, open, examine, and publicly declare the same; *provided, however,* that no proposal shall be considered unless accompanied by such check satisfactory to the Council; and thereafter, but not later than its next regular meeting, said Council may reject the bid of any party who has been delinquent and unfaithful in any former contract with the municipality, and shall reject all bids other than the lowest regular bid of any responsible bidder, and shall thereupon return to the proper parties the respective checks corresponding to such bids so rejected. But the check accompanying such lowest regular proposal or bid shall be held by the City Treasurer of such city, and said proposal or bid itself shall be held by said Council, to be disposed of as hereinafter provided.   Upon ascertaining the amount specified in such lowest regular and responsible bid, said Council shall compare the same with the estimate of the cost and expenses theretofore furnished by said City Engineer for said work so bid upon; and if such sum specified in such bid shall be less than or greater than the estimate of said City Engineer, then said City Council shall refer said bid and said estimate to said City Engineer for revision, and if, upon revision, said estimate shall correspond in amount with amount specified in such bid, such revised estimate, increased by the incidental expenses of such proposed work, which incidental expenses shall be determined by said Council, shall be and become the estimated costs and expenses of said proposed work; *provided, however*, that in all cases the said Council shall have power, in its discretion, to reject any and all bids, and to readvertise for proposals, as in the first instance, but without readvertising the resolution of intention, and thereafter the same proceedings shall be had as if the rejected bids had not been presented. After proposals have been received, examined, and declared, and after the said Council shall have ascertained the whole costs and expenses of the work, as provided in this section, the said Council shall direct the City Engineer to make a diagram of the property affected or benefited by said proposed work, as described in the resolution of intention therefor, and to be assessed to pay the expenses thereof. Said diagram shall show each separate lot, piece, or parcel of land, the area in square feet of each of such lots, pieces, or parcels of land, and the relative location of the same to the work proposed to be done, all within the limits of the assessment district; and when said diagram shall have been approved by said Council, the Clerk shall, at the time of such approval, certify the fact and date thereof. Immediately thereafter, said diagram shall be delivered to the Superintendent of Streets, together with a statement of the final estimated costs and expenses of such proposed work, fixed as above provided.

SEC. 5. Upon receipt of such diagram and statement, said Superintendent of Streets shall proceed to estimate upon the lands, pieces of land, lots, and portions of lots within said assessment district, as shown by said diagram, the benefits to arise from such proposed work, and to be received by each such lot, portion of lot, piece, or subdivision of land, and shall thereupon assess upon and against said lands in said assessment district the total amount of the costs and expenses of such proposed work, and in so doing shall assess said total sum upon the several pieces, parcels, lots, portions of lots, and subdivisions of land in said assessment district benefited thereby, to wit: upon each respectively in proportion to the estimated benefits to be received by each of said several lots, portions of lots, pieces, parcels, or subdivisions of land as theretofore determined by him, as above provided; *provided further*, that no assessment shall be levied on any property which, together with all assessments for street improvements that may have been levied upon the same property during the next preceding year, will amount to a sum greater than fifty per cent. of the value at which said property was assessed upon the last preceding assessment roll of said city.

SEC. 6. Within five days after the receipt by him of said diagram and statement, unless further time be granted by said Council therefor, said Superintendent of Streets shall make out and complete an assessment list, which shall show and exhibit in separate columns, first, the name of the owner of each separate lot, piece, parcel, or subdivision of land separately assessed, if known to him, and if the name of the owner be unknown to him, the word "unknown" shall be written opposite the number of each such subdivision of land; second, the assessment number of each separate subdivision of land separately assessed; third, a brief description by lot and block, or otherwise, of each such subdivision of land, which, in connection with the diagram hereinbefore and hereinafter mentioned, shall be sufficient for the identification and location of each such subdivisions of land; fourth, the estimated benefits to each such subdivision of land; fifth, the amount assessed separately to each such subdivision; and sixth, a list of all separate lots, pieces, parcels, or subdivisions of land, if any, which are not benefited by said work or improvement. To the assessment list thus completed, said Superintendent of Streets shall attach said diagram, showing the relative location of each of said subdivisions of land to the work proposed to be done; each of which subdivisions of land shall be by him numbered on said diagram to correspond, each respectively, with its assessment number as shown on said assessment list, and said assessment list and said diagram thus attached shall constitute and be known as the "assessment roll;" said assessment roll, when completed, shall be by said Superintendent of Streets filed with the City Clerk.

SEC. 7.   Upon receiving said assessment roll, said City Clerk shall forthwith give notice, by publication for at least five days in one or more daily newspapers published and circulated in such city, or by at least one insertion in a weekly newspaper so published and circulated, that said assessment roll is on file in his office, the date of the filing of the same, and that the same is open for public inspection.   The owners of land in said assessment district, whether named or not in said assessment roll, and all other persons directly interested in any property affected by the assessments set forth in said assessment roll, feeling aggrieved by any act or determination of the said Council or said Superintendent of Streets, in relation to said assessments or assessment roll, or having or making any objections to the legality of said assessments or assessment roll, or other act, or determination, or proceeding of said Council or Superintendent of Streets, shall, within ten days after first publication of such notice, appeal to said Council by briefly stating their objections in writing, and filing the same with the Clerk of said Council.   After the expiration of the time above provided for filing such objections, the said Council shall, if any such objections have been filed, fix the time for hearing the same, and shall order the said City Clerk to give notice of the time and place of the hearing of the said objections so filed; and said notice shall be posted by the City Clerk in three of the most public places in said City at least five days prior to the day of such hearing.   Upon the hearing of such appeal or appeals, the said City Council shall have power to approve and confirm said assessment roll, or to refer the same back to the said Superintendent of Streets, with directions to alter or modify the same in the particulars specified by the Council in the resolution referring back the same; and in case of such reference back to him, the said Superintendent of Streets shall thereupon proceed to make the alterations and modifications specified in the said resolution of reference of said Council.   The alterations and modifications aforesaid having been made, the assessment roll shall be again submitted to the said Council, and if the Council, upon examination, shall find that the alterations and modifications have been made according to the directions contained in said resolution of reference, the said Council shall adopt and confirm the same; but if the said Superintendent of Streets shall have neglected or failed to make the said alterations and modifications, the Council shall again refer the said assessment roll back to the said Superintendent of Streets, and so on until the original resolution of alteration and modification shall have been complied with by said Superintendent of Streets, and then the said Council shall adopt and confirm said assessment roll. Said City Council, at a meeting subsequent to the expiration of eleven days from and after the first publication by said Clerk of said notice that said assessment roll has been filed with him and is open for public inspection, shall adopt and confirm said assessment roll, in case no appeal shall have been taken, as above provided for in this section. The adoption and confirmation of said assessment roll, as aforesaid, shall be final and conclusive upon all persons entitled to an appeal under the provisions of this section, as to all errors, informalities, or irregularities which said Council might have remedied or avoided.

SEC. 8. No assessment shall be held invalid except upon appeal to the City Council, as provided in the preceding section, because of any error, informality, or other defect in any of the proceedings prior to the assessment, or in the assessment itself, when notice of the intention of the City Council to order the work to be done for which the assessment is made has been published in such newspaper or newspapers of such municipality for the length of time hereinbefore prescribed therefor before the passage of the resolution ordering the work to be done.

SEC. 9. Upon the adoption and confirmation of the assessment roll as hereinbefore provided, the City Clerk shall endorse thereon his certificate, to the effect that said assessment roll has been adopted and confirmed by the City Council, and shall also give the date of its adoption and confirmation. Said Clerk shall then deliver said assessment roll to the Superintendent of Streets of such city.

SEC. 10. The Superintendent of Streets shall thereupon give notice by publication for ten days in one or more daily newspapers published and circulated in such city, or by two successive insertions in a weekly newspaper so published and circulated, that he has received said assessment roll, and that all sums levied and assessed in said assessment roll are due and payable immediately, and that the payment of said sums is to be made to him within thirty days from the date of the first publication of said notice. Said notice shall also contain a statement that all assessments not paid before the expiration of said thirty days will be declared to be delinquent, and that thereafter the sum of five per cent. upon the amount of each delinquent assessment, together with the cost of advertising each delinquent assessment, will be added thereto. When payment of any assessment is made to said Super-

intendent of Streets, he shall write the word " Paid," and the date of payment, opposite the respective assessment so paid, and the names of persons
by or for whom said assessment is paid, and shall, if so required, give a receipt therefor.   On the expiration of said thirty days all assessments then
unpaid shall be and become delinquent, and said Superintendent of Streets
shall certify such fact at the foot of said assessment roll, and shall add said
five per cent. to the amount of each assessment so delinquent.   The said
Superintendent of Streets shall, within five days from the date of said delinquency, proceed to advertise and collect the various sums delinquent, and
the whole thereof, including the cost of advertising, which last shall not exceed the sum of fifty cents for each lot, piece, or parcel of land separately
assessed, by the sale of the assessed property in the same manner as is or
may be provided for the collection of State or county taxes; and after the
date of said delinquency, and before the time of such sale herein provided
for, no assessment shall be received unless at the same time the five per
cent. added thereto as aforesaid, together with the cost of advertising then
already incurred, shall be paid therewith.   The said five per cent., when
collected, shall be paid into the General Fund of the city.   Said list of delinquent assessments shall be published daily for five days in one or more
daily newspapers published and circulated in such city, or by at least one
insertion in a weekly newspaper so published and circulated, before the day
of sale of such delinquent assessments.   Said time of sale must not be less
than seven nor more than ten days from the date of the first publication of
said delinquent assessment list, and the place must be in or in front of the
office of said Superintendent of Streets.   All property sold shall be subject
to redemption in the same time and manner as in sales for delinquent State
and county taxes; and the Superintendent of Streets may collect for each
certificate fifty cents, and for each deed one dollar.   All fees collected by
said Superintendent of Streets shall be paid into the General Fund of such
city.   All provisions of the law in reference to the sale and redemption of
property for delinquent State and county taxes in force at any given time
shall also then, so far as the same are not in conflict with the provisions of
this Act, be applicable to the sale and redemption of property for delinquent
assessments hereunder, including the issuance of certificates and execution
of deeds.   Before the day of sale for such delinquent assessments the Superintendent of Streets shall, from time to time, pay over to the City Treasurer
all moneys collected and received by him on account of any such assessments.   The City Treasurer shall, upon receipt thereof, place the same in a
separate fund, designating such fund by the name of the street, lane, alley,
court, or place, for the improvement of which the assessment was made.
And whenever sufficient money shall have been received by said Treasurer on
account of any such assessment, to pay the said estimated costs and expenses
of such work and improvement for the payment of which said assessment
was levied and collected, said Treasurer shall report that fact to said Council.

SEC. 11. Upon receiving such notice from said Treasurer, said Council shall order the Treasurer to pay the incidental expenses to the persons entitled thereto, and shall proceed to and shall award the contract for the work and improvement, to pay the costs and expenses of which said moneys shall have been so collected, to that person who shall have theretofore presented the lowest regular responsible bid therefor, as hereinafter provided. If the bidder to whom the contract is thus awarded fails, neglects, or refuses to enter into a contract to perform said work and improvement as hereinafter provided, then the certified check accompanying his bid and the amount therein mentioned shall be declared to be forfeited to said city, and shall be collected by said city and be paid into the fund into which has already been paid said moneys so collected on said assessment. All persons, owners included, who shall fail to enter into contract as herein provided, are hereby prohibited from bidding a second time for the same work. Notice of such awards shall be published for five days in the same manner as hereinbefore provided for the publication of proposals for such work. The owners of the major part of said area in square feet of lots and lands assessed for said work shall not be required to present sealed proposals, but may, nevertheless, within said five days after the first publication of notice of said award, elect to take said work, and enter into a written contract to do the whole work at the pr ce at which the same may have been awarded. Should the said owners fail to elect to take said work, and to enter into a written contract therefor within said five days, or to commence the work within ten days after the first publication of said award, and to prosecute the same with diligence to completion, it shall be the duty of the Superintendent of Streets to enter into a contract with the original bidder to whom the contract was awarded, and at the prices the same may have been awarded him; but if said original bidder neglects, for fifteen days after the first publication of notice of award, to enter into the contract, then the City Council shall again advertise for proposals as in the first instance, and award the contract for said work to the then lowest regular responsible bidder. If the owners or contractor who may have taken said contract do not complete the same within the time limited in the contract, or within such further time as the City Council may give them, the said Superintendent of Streets shall contract for the completion of the unfinished portion of said work, according to the terms of the original contract therefor, and the costs and expenses so incurred in prosecuting and completing such unfinished work shall be paid out of the moneys theretofore collected to pay for the costs and expenses of such work and improvements, and not otherwise. All contractors, contracting owners included, shall, at the time of executing the contract for such work, execute a bond to the satisfaction of the City Council, which bond shall be twenty-five per cent. of the amount of the contract price, with two or more sureties, and payable to such city in such sums as the said City Council shall deem adequate, conditioned for the faithful performance of the contract; and the sureties shall justify,

before any officer competent to administer an oath, in double the amount
mentioned in said bond, over and above all statutory exemptions.

SEC. 12. The Superintendent of Streets is hereby authorized, in his official capacity, to make all written contracts and receive all bonds authorized
by this Act, and to do any other act, either express or implied, that pertains
to the Street Department under this Act, and he shall fix the time for the
commencement and for the completion of the work, under all contracts
entered into by him, which work shall be prosecuted with diligence from
day to day thereafter, to completion, and he may extend the times so fixed
from time to time, under the direction of the City Council. The work provided for in section two of this Act must in all cases be done under the
direction and to the satisfaction of the Superintendent of Streets, and the
materials used shall be such as are required by said Superintendent of
Streets, and all contracts made therefor must contain a provision to that
effect, and also express notice that in no case, except where it is otherwise
provided in this Act, will the city or any officer thereof be liable for any portion of the expense, nor for any delinquency of persons or property assessed.

SEC. 13. Whenever any contract shall have been completed, the contractors shall notify the Superintendent of Streets, who shall notify said
City Council that said work and improvement, and the contract therefor,
have been completed. Thereupon said City Council shall direct the City
Clerk to give notice by publication for five days, in one or more daily newspapers published and circulated in such city, that said work and improvement, and the contract therefor, have been completed, and that it will hear
objections to the manner in which said work has been done on the day
therein named, from any or all persons directly interested in said work.

SEC. 14. At the time and place fixed for said hearing of said objections,
said Council shall proceed to hear all parties present and desiring to be
heard concerning the manner in which said work shall have been done. And
whenever said Council shall ascertain that said work and improvement have
been completed in all respects according to the terms of the contract therefor, they shall, by resolution, accept such work and improvement, and direct
said Superintendent of Streets to issue to said contractor, a certificate that
said work has been completed according to contract. All acts and determinations of said City Council to be heard under the provision of this and the
next preceding section shall be final and conclusive upon all persons entitled to be heard.

SEC. 15. Whenever any work or improvement shall have been so accepted
the said City Council shall, by resolution, direct the City Treasurer to pay
out of the appropriate fund, at the expiration of fifteen days from the passage of such resolution, to the contractor who shall have so completed said
work and improvement, the amount to which he is entitled under the terms
of his contract; *provided, however*, that such payment by the Treasurer shall

be made subject to the following provision, to wit: That any person or persons who have performed labor upon, or furnished materials for the construction of said work or improvement, may file, within said fifteen days, with the City Treasurer, any written claim or claims he or they may make, on account of such labor performed, or materials furnished; and, at the expiration of said fifteen days, said City Treasurer shall pay to said contractor the amount specified in said last named resolution, less the aggregate amount of all such claims, if any, filed in accordance with the provisions of this section. Should any money be retained by said Treasurer on account of such claim or claims, he shall pay over the amount of each claim only upon the order therefor of said contractor, indorsed by the claimant thereof, or upon the order therefor of any Court of competent jurisdiction.

SEC. 16. And when all moneys required to be paid by the said City Treasurer under the last preceding section shall have been by him paid, as required in said section, if there is any money remaining in the fund out of which said payments shall have been made as aforesaid, it shall be the duty of said Treasurer immediately to report the amount of said remaining moneys to said Council. Thereupon it shall be the duty of said Council to empower and direct said Treasurer to distribute and repay such remaining moneys, and in the proportion of the amounts of the original assessments, to the persons by or for whom said original assessments were paid, or to their legal representatives; and it shall be the duty of said Treasurer, in each instance of such repayment, to require, receive, and file away a receipt for said proportionate amount from said persons, or their legal representatives; and in no case shall a contractor who has failed to fulfill the terms and conditions of his contract be entitled to receive any portion of the contract price therefor, and he shall be deemed to have forfeited all right to recover or receive any compensation whatever under said contract.

SEC. 17. Whenever any portion of any street, lane, alley, court, or place in said city, improved, or any sidewalk constructed thereon according to law, shall be out of repair and in condition to endanger persons or property passing thereon, or in condition to interfere with the public convenience in the use thereof, it shall be the duty of the said Superintendent of Streets to require, by notice in writing, to be delivered to them personally, or left on the premises, the owners or occupants of lots, or portions of lots, fronting on said portion of said street, lane, alley, court, or place, or of said portion of said walk so out of repair, as aforesaid, to repair forthwith said portion of said street, lane, alley, court, or place to the center thereof, or said sidewalk in front of the property of which he is the owner, or tenant, or occupant; and said Superintendent of Streets shall specify in said notice what repairs are required to be made. After the expiration of three days from the date of the service of said notice, the Superintendent of Streets shall be deemed to have acquired jurisdiction to contract for the making of the repairs required by said notice. If said repairs be not commenced within three days after notice given as aforesaid, and diligently and without interruption prosecuted to completion, the said Superintendent of Streets may, under authority from said City Council, make such repairs or enter into a contract with any suitable person, at the expense of the owner, tenant, or occupant, at a reasonable price, to be determined by said Superintendent of Streets, and such owner, tenant, or occupant shall be liable to pay the same. Upon the completion of said repairs by said contractors as aforesaid to the satisfaction of said Superintendent of Streets, said Superintendent of Streets shall make and deliver to said contractor a certificate to the effect that said repairs have been properly made by said contractor, and that the charges for the same are reasonable and just, and that he, said Superintendent, has accepted the same.

SEC. 18. If the expenses of the work and material for such improvements, after the completion thereof, and the delivery to said contractor of said certificate, be not paid to the contractor so employed, or his agent, or assignee, on demand, the said contractor, or his assignee, shall have the right to sue such owner, tenant, or occupant, for the amount contracted to be paid; and said certificate of the Superintendent of Streets shall be prima facie evidence of the amount claimed for said work and materials, and of the right of the contractor to recover for the same in such action.

SEC. 19. In addition, and as cumulative to the remedies above given, the City Council shall have power, by resolution or ordinance, to prescribe the penalties that shall be incurred by any owner or person liable, or neglecting, or refusing to make repairs when required, as provided in section seventeen of this Act, which fines and penalties shall be recovered for the use of the city by prosecution in the name of the people of the State of California, in the Court having jurisdiction thereof, and may be applied, if deemed expedient by the said Council, in the payment of the expenses of any such repairs not otherwise provided for.

SEC. 20. The records kept by the Superintendent of Streets of said city in conformity with the provisions of this Act, and signed by him, shall have the same force and effect as other public records, and copies therefrom, certified by him, may be used in evidence with the same effect as the originals. The same record shall, during all office hours, be open to the inspection of any citizen wishing to examine them.

SEC. 21. Notices in writing, which are required to be given by the Superintendent of Streets under the provisions of this Act, may be served by any person, with the permission of the Superintendent of Streets, and the fact of such service shall be verified by the oath of the person making it, taken before the Superintendent of Streets, or other person authorized to administer oaths; or such notices may be served by the said Superintendent of Streets himself. The Superintendent of Streets shall keep a record of the fact of giving such notices, when delivered by himself personally, and also of the notices and proof of service when delivered by any other person.

SEC. 22. The Superintendent of Streets shall superintend and direct the cleaning of all sewers, and the expense of the same shall be paid out of the Street or Sewer Fund of such city.

SEC. 23. If in consequence of any graded street or public highway improved under the provisions of this Act, being out of repair and in condition to endanger persons or property passing thereon, any person while carefully using said street or public highway, and exercising ordinary care to avoid the danger, suffer damage to his person or property, through any such defect therein, no recourse for damages thus suffered shall be had against such city; but if such defect in the street or public highway shall have existed for the period of twenty-four hours or more after notice thereof to the said Superintendent of Streets, then the person or persons or whom the law may have imposed the obligations to repair such defect in the street or public highway, and also the officer or officers through whose official negligence such defect remain unrepaired, shall be jointly and severally liable to the party injured for the damage sustained.

SEC. 24. The City Council of such city shall have full power and authority to construct sewers and manholes, culverts with crosswalks, or culverts or crosswalks, or sidewalks, or any portion of any sidewalk, upon or in any street, lane, alley, court, or place in such city, of such materials, in such a manner, and upon such terms as it may deem proper. None of the work or improvements described in this section shall be stayed or prevented by any written or any other remonstrance or objection, unless such Council deems proper.

SEC. 25. The City Council may, in its discretion, repair and water streets that shall have been graded, curbed, and planked, paved or macadamized, and may build, repair, and clean sewers, and shall provide a Street Contingent Fund at the same time and in the same manner as other funds are provided, out of which to pay the costs and expenses of making said repairs, and watering said streets, and building, repairing, and cleaning said sewers; but whenever any street requires regrading, recurbing, repiling, repaving, replanking, regraveling or remacadamizing, or require new culverts, or new crosswalks, or new sidewalks, the work shall be advertised and let out by contract, and the costs and expenses thereof shall be assessed upon the property affected or benefited thereby, the same as in the first instance.

SEC. 26. When any street or portion of a street has been or shall hereafter be constructed to the satisfaction of said Superintendent of Streets of such city, under such regulations as said Council shall adopt, the same shall be accepted by said Council, and thereafter shall be kept open and improved by the said city, and the expense thereof shall be paid out of the Street Department Fund; *provided*, that the City Council shall not accept of any portion of a street less than the full width thereof and one block in length, or one entire crossing. The Superintendent of Streets shall keep in his office a register of all accepted streets, the same to be indexed so that reference may be easily had thereto.

PART II.

SEC. 27. Whenever the City Council deem it necessary to construct a receiving sewer, then the said Council may, in its discretion, determine to construct said sewer, and assess the cost and expenses thereof upon the property to be affected or benefited thereby, as provided in part one hereof, or said Council may determine to construct said sewer and pay therefor out of the Street Contingent Fund.

SEC. 28. If at any time the City Council shall deem it necessary to incur any indebtedness for the construction of receiving sewers, in excess of the money in the Street Contingent Fund applicable to the construction of such sewers, they shall give notice of a special election by the qualified electors of the city, to be held to determine whether such indebtedness shall be incurred. Such notice shall specify the amount of indebtedness proposed to be incurred, the route and general character of the sewer or sewers to be constructed, and the amount of money necessary to be raised annually by taxation for an Interest and Sinking Fund as hereinafter provided. Such notice shall be published for at least three weeks in some newspaper published in such city, and no other question or matter shall be submitted to the electors at such election. If, upon a canvass of the vote cast at such election, it appear that not less than two-thirds of all the qualified electors voting at such election shall have voted in favor of incurring such indebtedness, it shall be the duty of the City Council to pass an ordinance providing for the mode of creating such indebtedness, and of paying the same; and in such ordinance provision shall be made for the levy and collection of an annual tax upon all the real and personal property subject to taxation within such city sufficient to pay the interest on such indebtedness as it falls due, and also to constitute a Sinking Fund for the payment of the principal thereof within a period of not more than twenty years from the time of contracting the same. It shall be the duty of the City Council in each year thereafter, at the time at which other taxes are levied, to levy a tax sufficient for such purpose, in addition to the taxes authorized to be levied for city purposes. Such tax, when collected, shall be kept in the treasury as a separate fund, to be inviolably appropriated to the payment of the principal and interest of such indebtedness.

SEC. 29. If bonds are issued under the provisions of the last section, said bonds shall be in sums of not less than one hundred dollars nor more than one thousand dollars, shall be signed by the Mayor and Treasurer of the city, and the seal of the city shall be affixed thereto. Coupons for the interest shall be attached to each bond, signed by the Mayor and Treasurer. Said bonds shall bear interest, to be fixed by the City Council, at the rate of not to exceed five per cent. per annum.

SEC. 30. Before the sale of said bonds the Council shall, at a regular meeting, by resolution, declare its intention to sell a specified amount of said bonds, and the day and hour of such sale, and shall cause such resolution to be entered in the minutes, and shall cause notice of such sale to be published for fifteen days in at least one newspaper published in the city in which the bonds are issued, and one published in the City and County of San Francisco, and in any other newspaper in the State, at their discretion. The notice shall state that sealed proposals will be received by the Council for the purchase of the bonds on the day and hour named in the resolution. The Council, at the time appointed, shall open the proposals and award the purchase of the bonds to the highest bidder, but may reject all bids.

Sec. 31. The Council may sell said bonds, at not less than par value, without the notice provided for in the preceding section.

Sec. 32. The proceeds of the sale of the bonds shall be deposited in the city treasury to the account of the Receiving Sewer Fund, but no payment therefrom shall be made, except to pay for the construction of the sewer or sewers for the construction of which the bonds were issued, and upon the certificate of the Superintendent of Streets and the City Engineer, that the work has been done according to contract.

Sec. 33. Whenever said Council shall determine to construct any receiving sewer and pay therefor out of the Street Contingent Fund, or by the issuance of bonds as above provided, then said Council shall cause to be prepared plans and specifications of said work in sections, and shall advertise for twenty days in at least one newspaper published in the city in which the sewer is to be constructed, and one in the City and County of San Francisco, for sealed proposals for constructing said sewer. The work may be let in sections, and must be awarded to the lowest responsible bidder, Council having the right to reject any and all bids. The work shall be done and the materials furnished under the supervision and to the satisfaction of the Superintendent of Streets and the City Engineer.

PART III.

Sec. 34. *First*—The City Engineer shall be the proper officer to do the surveying and other engineering work necessary to be done under this Act, and to survey and measure the work necessary to be done under contracts for grading and macadamizing streets, and to estimate the cost and expenses thereof; and every certificate signed by him in his official character shall be prima facie evidence, in all the Courts in this State, of the truth of its contents. He shall also keep a record of all surveys made under the provisions of this Act, as in other cases. In all those cities where there is no City Engineer, the City Council is hereby authorized and empowered to appoint a suitable person to discharge the duties herein laid down as those of City Engineer; and all the provisions hereof applicable to the City Engineer shall apply to such person so appointed.

20

Second—The words "improve," "improved," and "improvement," as used in this Act, shall include all work mentioned in section two of this Act, and also the reconstruction of all or any portion of said work.

Third—The term "incidental expenses," as used in this Act, shall include the compensation of the City Engineer for work done by him, also the cost of printing and advertising, except the advertising of the delinquent assessment list; also, the compensation of Superintendents of sewers, and of piling and capping.

Fourth—The notices required to be published by the provisions of this Act shall be published in a daily, semi-weekly, or weekly newspaper, to be designated by the Council of such city, as often as the same is issued; *provided, however*, that in case there is no daily, semi-weekly, or weekly newspaper printed and circulated in any such city, then such notices as are herein required to be published in a newspaper shall be posted, and kept posted, for the same length of time as required herein for the publication of the same in a semi-weekly or weekly newspaper, in three of the most public places in such city. Proof of the publication or posting of any notice provided for herein shall be made by affidavit.

Fifth—The word "municipality," and the word "city," as used in this Act, shall be understood and so construed as to include, and is hereby declared to include, all corporations heretofore organized and now existing, and those hereafter organized for municipal purposes.

Sixth—The word "street," as used in this Act, shall be deemed to and is hereby declared to include highways, lanes, alleys, crossings, or intersections, courts, and places.

Seventh—The terms "Street Superintendent" and "Superintendent of Streets," as used in this Act, shall be understood and so construed as to include, and is hereby declared to include, any person or officer whose duty it is, under the law, to have the care or charge of the streets, or the improvement thereof, in any city. In all those cities where there is no Street Superintendent, or Superintendent of Streets, the City Council thereof is hereby authorized and empowered to appoint a suitable person to discharge the duties herein laid down as those of Street Superintendent or Superintendent of Streets; and all the provisions hereof applicable to the Street Superintendent or Superintendent of Streets shall apply to such person so appointed.

Eighth—The term "City Council," is hereby declared to include any body or board which, under the law, is the legislative department of the government of any city.

Ninth—The term "receiving sewer," and "receiving sewers," as used in this Act, shall be construed to mean any and all sewers which are to be used as an outlet for ordinary street sewers, and which are to be used as an outlet for the sewage of a watershed, instead of an outlet for the sewage of the property abutting upon a street.

Tenth—In municipalities in which there is no Mayor, then the duties imposed upon said officer by the provisions of this Act shall be performed by the President of the Board of Trustees, or other chief executive officer of the municipality.

Eleventh—The term " Clerk," and " City Clerk," as used in this Act, is hereby declared to include any person or officer who shall be Clerk of said City Council.

Sec. 35. The Superintendent of Streets shall, when necessary, appoint a suitable person to take charge of and superintend the construction and improvement of each and every sewer constructed or improved under the provisions of this Act, and of piling and capping, whose duty it shall be to see that the contract made for the doing of said work is strictly fulfilled in every respect; and in case of any departure therefrom, to report the same to the Superintendent of Streets. Such person shall be allowed for his time actually employed in the discharge of his duties such compensation as shall be just, but not to exceed four dollars per day. The sum to which the party so employed shall be entitled shall be deemed to be incidental expenses, within the meaning of those words as defined in this Act.

Sec. 36. All Acts and parts of Acts in conflict with any of the provisions of this Act are hereby repealed.

Sec. 37. This Act shall take effect and be in force from and after its passage.

SUPPLEMENT CLIV.

1883, 295.

An Act to authorize cities to erect and maintain drawbridges across navigable streams that flow through or penetrate the boundaries of such cities.

[Approved March 13, 1883.]

The People of the State of California, represented in Senate and Assembly, do enact as follows:

Section 1. It shall be lawful for municipal corporations, and they are hereby authorized by their respective legislative body or bodies, to erect and maintain drawbridges across navigable streams that flow through or penetrate the boundaries of such cities, when the public necessities require it. Such bridges shall in all respects be constructed in accordance with the provisions of Section 2,875 of the Political Code.

SUPPLEMENT CLV.

1883, 366.

———

An Act entitled an Act to grant to Boards of Health in cities and cities and counties, the power to regulate the plumbing and drainage of buildings.

[Approved March 15, 1883.]

The People of the State of California, represented in Senate and Assembly, do enact as follows:

SECTION 1.   Every master or journeyman plumber, carrying on his trade shall, under such rules and regulations as the Board of Health of such county, or city and county, shall prescribe, register his name and address at the Health Office of such county, or city and county; and, after the said date, it shall not be lawful for any person to carry on the trade of plumbing in any county, or city and county, unless his name and address be registered as above provided.

SEC. 2.   A list of the registered plumbers shall be published in the yearly report of the Health Office.

SEC. 3.   The drainage and plumbing of all buildings, both public and private, hereafter erected in any county, or city and county, shall be executed in accordance with plans previously approved, in writing, by the Board of Health of said county, or city and county; suitable drawings and description of the said drainage and plumbing shall, in each case, be submitted and placed on file in the Health Office.   The said Board of Health are also authorized to receive and place on file drawings and descriptions of the drainage and plumbing of buildings erected prior to the passage of this Act.

SEC. 4.   The Boards of Supervisors, or other city or county officials, whose duty it is to make appointments for the Board of Health of such county, or city and county, shall make the necessary apportionments and shall insert the same in the yearly tax levy, to provide for carrying out the provisions of this Act.

SEC. 5.   Any court of record in said county, or city and county, or any Judge or Justice thereof, shall have power at any time after the service of notice of the violation of any of the provisions of this Act, and upon the affidavit of the Health Officer, or a member of the Board of Health of such county, or city and county, to restrain by injunction order the further violation named in this Act, or of any work upon or about the building or premises upon which the said violation exists, and no undertaking shall be required as a condition to the granting or issuing of such injunction, or by reason thereof.

SEC. 6. Any person violating any of the provisions of this Act shall be deemed guilty of a misdemeanor.

SEC. 7. This Act shall take effect immediately.

SUPPLEMENT CLVI.

1885, 12.

An Act to grant to Boards of Health or Health Officers, in cities, and cities and counties, the power to regulate the plumbing and drainage of buildings, and to provide for the registration of plumbers.

[Approved March 3, 1885.]

The People of the State of California, represented in Senate and Assembly, do enact as follows:

SECTION 1. Every master or journeyman plumber carrying on his trade shall, under such rules and regulations as the Board of Health of a city, or city and county, shall prescribe, register his name and address at the Health Office of such city, or city and county; and after the establishment of such rules and regulations it shall not be lawful for any person to carry on the trade in any city, or city and county, unless his name and address be registered as above provided.

SEC. 2. A list of the registered plumbers shall be published in the yearly report of the Health Officer or Board of Health.

SEC. 3. The drainage and plumbing of all buildings, both public and private, hereafter erected in any city, or city and county, shall be executed in accordance with plans previously approved in writing by the Board of Health of said city, or city and county; and suitable drawings and description of the said drainage and plumbing shall, in each case, be submitted to the Board of Health, and placed on file in the Health Office. The said Board of Health is also authorized to receive and place on file drawings and descriptions of the drainage and plumbing of buildings erected prior to the passage of this Act.

SEC. 4. The Board of Supervisors, or other city, or city and county, officials, whose duty it is to make appropriations and tax levies for general purposes of such city, or city and county, shall make the necessary appropriations and tax levies, and shall insert the same in the yearly tax levy, to provide for carrying out the provisions of this Act. Such appropriations and levy shall be made at the same time, and in the same manner, as appropriations and tax levies are made for other city, or city and county, purposes.

SEC. 5. In any city, or city and county, where there is, under existing laws, a HealthOfficer, but no Board of Health, such HealthOfficer shall perform all the duties required by this Act of the Board of Health until a Board of Health shall be created, and in any city, or city and county, where there is no Health Officer, nor Board of Health, the Board of Supervisors, or City Council, or other municipal legislative Board or body, shall create a Board of Health, who shall perform all the duties required by this Act of the Board of Health or Health Officer.

SEC. 6. Any Superior Court, or Judge thereof, shall have power to restrain by injunction the continuance of work to be done upon or about buildings or premises where the provisions of this Act have not been complied with, and no undertaking shall be required as a condition to the granting or issuing of such injunction, or by reason thereof.

SEC. 7. Any person violating any of the provisions of this Act shall be deemed guilty of a misdemeanor, and, upon conviction, shall be punished accordingly.

SEC. 8. This Act shall take effect immediately.

SUPPLEMENT CLVII.

1885, 25.

An Act to provide for the construction and maintenance of a public morgue in the City and County of San Francisco.

[Approved March 5, 1885.]

The People of the State of California, represented in Senate and Assembly, do enact as follows:

SECTION 1. The Board of Supervisors of the City and County of San Francisco are hereby authorized to appropriate the surplus of money accumulated from the disinterment fund, for the purpose of erecting a Morgue in the City and County of San Francisco.

SEC. 2. The building so erected shall be known as " The Public Morgue" of San Francisco, and the title to the same shall be vested in the said city and county, absolutely and forever. The said Morgue shall contain offices for the Coroner, suitable rooms for holding inquests and autopsies upon the dead, and all the appliances necessary to enable the Coroner to discharge the duties of his office in an efficient manner.

SEC. 3. The said Board of Supervisors are hereby authorized and required to advertise for proposals for the construction, furnishing, and finishing of said Morgue, and to cause the said work to be commenced and completed in a prompt and efficient manner.

SEC. 4. The said Board of Supervisors are hereby authorized to use and appropriate so much of the public fund called the " Disinterment Fund," in the treasury of San Francisco, as will be necessary for the erection, furnishing, and finishing of said Public Morgue.

SEC. 5. The said Board of Supervisors is hereby authorized and required to pay out of the General Fund such sums as may be necessary, per month, for the maintenance of the Morgue and offices attached to the Morgue, and the Auditor of said city and county is required to audit, and the Treasurer shall pay said accounts out of the General Fund.

SEC. 6. This Act shall be in force from and after its passage.

SUPPLEMENT CLVIII.

1885, 38.

An Act authorizing the Commissioners of any public park in this State, and especially the Park Commissioners of Golden Gate Park, in San Francisco, to accept donations and bequests in aid of the improvement and embellishment of their respective parks, and to invest the funds derived therefrom.

[Approved March 9, 1885.]

The People of the State of California, represented in Senate and Assembly, do enact as follows :

SECTION 1. The Commissioners in any public park in this State, and especially the Park Commissioners of Golden Gate Park, in the City and County of San Francisco, are hereby authorized and empowered to accept and receive donations and aid from individuals and corporations, and to receive legacies and bequests by the last wills and testaments of deceased persons, and especially to receive aid and contributions from that certain corporation organized and incorporated under the laws of the State of California, known as the Park Aid Improvement Company, and the moneys derived and to be derived therefrom shall be and are hereby recognized as a portion of the public funds belonging to said Park Commissioners, and applicable under the direction of the said Park Commissioners to the purposes of preserving and embellishing the parks under their respective management and control.

SEC. 2.   If the funds derived as aforesaid shall, at any time, exceed in amount the sum necessary for immediate expenditure on the said park grounds, or if, in the judgment of the said Park Commissioners, it should be advisable to invest the same and make the same productive, the said Park Commissioners are hereby authorized to invest the same, or any portion thereof, in interest-bearing bonds of the Government of the United States, or of the State of California, and to use the interest and income thereof for the purposes aforesaid, with the like power to sell and dispose of the said bonds if, in their discretion, the principal thereof shall be necessary for the purposes aforesaid.

SEC. 3.   This Act shall take effect and be in force immediately.

SUPPLEMENT CLIX.

1885, 108.

An Act to authorize the appointment of an interpreter of the Italian language and dialects, in criminal proceedings, in cities and counties of over one hundred thousand inhabitants.

[Approved March 12, 1885.]

The People of the State of California, represented in Senate and Assembly, do enact as follows:

SECTION 1.   In all cities and cities and counties of over one hundred thousand inhabitants, where an interpreter of the Italian language is necessary, it shall the duty of the Mayor and Police Judge of such city, or city and county, and of the Superior Judge of said city and county, or of the county in which said city is situated, or where there are more Judges than one, then it shall be the duty of the presiding judge of said Superior Court, and the Mayor and Police Judge, to appoint an interpreter of the Italian language, who shall be an Italian, and who must also be able to interpret the Italian dialects into the English language, to be employed in criminal proceedings, when necessary, in said cities, or cities and counties.

SEC. 2. The said interpreter shall receive a salary of fifteen hundred dollars per annum, which shall be paid out of the General Fund of such city, or city and county.

SEC. 3. This Act shall not repeal any Act heretofore made and now in force for the appointment of interpreters, except so much of any Act which may conflict with this Act in the appointment of Italian interpreters.

SEC. 4. This Act shall take effect and be in force from and after its passage.

SUPPLEMENT CLX.

1885, 147.

An Act to provide for work upon streets, lanes, alleys, courts, places, and sidewalks, and for the construction of sewers within municipalities.

[Approved March 18, 1885.]

The People of the State of California, represented in Senate and Assembly, do enact as follows:

PART I.

SECTION 1. All streets, lanes, alleys, places, or courts, in the municipalities of this State now open or dedicated, or which may hereafter be opened or dedicated to public use, shall be deemed and held to be open public streets, lanes, alleys, places, or courts, for the purposes of this Act, and the City Council of each municipality is hereby empowered to establish and change the grades of said streets, lanes, alleys, places, or courts, and fix the width thereof, and is hereby invested with jurisdiction to order to be done thereon any of the work mentioned in section two of this Act, under the proceedings hereinafter described.

SEC. 2. Whenever the public interest or convenience may require, the City Council is hereby authorized and empowered to order the whole or any portion of the streets, lanes, alleys, courts, or places of any such city graded or regraded to the official grade, planked or replanked, paved or repaved, macadamized or remacadamized, graveled or regraveled, piled or repiled, capped or recapped, and to order sidewalks, sewers, manholes, culverts,

curbing, and crosswalks to be constructed therein, and to order any
other work to be done which shall be necessary to complete the whole or
any portion of said streets, sidewalks, lanes, alleys, courts, or places, and
it may order any of the said work to be improved.

SEC. 3. Before ordering any work done, or improvements made, which
is authorized by section two of this Act, the City Council shall pass a resolution of intention so to do, and describing the work. The Street Superintendent shall thereupon cause to be conspicuously posted along the line of
said contemplated work or improvement, at not more than three hundred
feet in distance apart, but not less than three in all, or when the work to
be done is the improvement of an entire crossing in front of each quarter
block liable to be assessed, notices of the passage of said resolution. Said
notice shall be headed " Notice of Street Work," in letters of not less than
one inch in length, and shall, in legible characters, state the fact of the passage of the resolution, its date, and briefly, the work or improvement proposed, and refer to the resolution for further particulars. He shall also
cause a notice, similar in substance, to be published for a period of five
days in one or more daily newspapers published and circulated in said city,
and designated by said City Council, or by one insertion in a weekly newspaper so published, circulated, and designated. The owners of one half or
more of the frontage of the property fronting on said proposed work or
improvement, where the same is for one block or more, may make a
written objection to the same within ten days after the expiration of the
time of the publication of said notice, which objection shall be delivered to the Clerk of the City Council, who shall indorse thereon the date
of its reception by him, and such objection so delivered and indorsed shall
be a bar for six months to any further proceedings in relation to the
the doing of said work or making said improvement, unless the owners of
one half or more of the frontage as aforesaid shall meanwhile petition for
the same to be done. At any time before issuance of the assessment roll,
all owners of lots or lands, liable to assessment therein, who after the first
publication of said resolution of intention may feel aggrieved, or who may
have objections to any of the subsequent proceedings of said Council, in
relation to the performance of the work mentioned in said notice of intention, shall file with the Clerk a petition of remonstrance, wherein they shall
state in what respect they feel aggrieved, or the proceedings to which they
object; such petition or remonstrance shall be passed upon by the said
City Council, and its decisions therein shall be final and conclusive. But
when the work or improvement proposed to be done is the construction of
sewers, manholes, culverts, crosswalks, and sidewalks, and the objection
thereto is signed by the owners of one half or more of the frontage as aforesaid, the said City Council shall, at its next meeting, fix a time for hearing
said objection, not less than one week thereafter. The City Clerk shall
thereupon notify the persons making such objection, by depositing a notice

thereof in the Post Office of said city, postage prepaid, addressed to each objector, or his agent, when he appears for such objector. At the time specified said City Council shall hear the objections urged, and pass upon the same, and its decision shall be final and conclusive, and the said bar for six months to any proceedings shall not be applicable therein. And when not more than two blocks remain ungraded between one or more blocks on each side thereof, which have been graded, said City Council may order that part of said street or highway so remaining ungraded, not exceeding two blocks, to be graded and improved, and the grading or improvement of said two blocks or less shall not be stayed or prevented by any written or other objection, unless such Council shall deem proper. And if one half or more in width or in length, or as to grading, one half or more of the grading work, of any street lying and being between two successive main street crossings, or if a crossing has been already graded or improved as aforesaid, said Council may order the remainder improved, graded or otherwise, notwithstanding such objections of property-owners. At the expiration of ten days after the expiration of the time of the publication, and at the expiration of fifteen days after the posting of any resolution of intention, if no written objection to the work therein described has been delivered as aforesaid by the owners of one-half or more of the frontage of the property fronting on said work or improvement, the City Council shall be deemed to have acquired jurisdiction to order any of the work to be done, or improvement to be made, which is authorized by section two of this Act. Before passing any resolution for the construction of said improvements, plans, and specifications, and careful estimates of the cost and expenses thereof, shall be furnished to said City Council, if required by it, by the City Engineer of said city, and for the work of constructing sewers, specifications shall always be furnished by him. Whenever the estimated or actual cost of any work contemplated or ordered to be done by the City Council, and chargeable under the provisions of this Act against any lot or lots of land, or the owner thereof, shall exceed one half of the assessed value of such lot or lots as borne upon the last assessment roll whereon it was assessed, made for the levying of taxes for municipal purposes, the amount of the cost of said work, exceeding said one half of the assessed value of said lot or lots, shall be paid out of the city treasury, unless the owner of such lot or lots shall, in writing, signed by himself or his authorized agent, consent that the whole expense of said improvement may be made a charge against said lot or lots.

SEC. 4. The owners of more than one-half in frontage of lots and lands fronting on any street, lane, alley, place, or court, or their duly authorized agents, may petition the City Council to order any of the work mentioned in section two of this Act to be done, and the City Council may order the work mentioned in said petition to be done, after notice of its intention so to do has been posted and published as provided in section three of this Act.

SEC. 5. Before the awarding of any contract by the City Council for doing any work authorized by section two of this Act, the City Council shall
cause notice to be posted conspicuously for five days on or near the Council
Chamber door of said Council, inviting sealed proposals for the work contemplated. All proposals offered shall be accompanied by a check payable to
the order of the Mayor of the city, certified by a responsible bank, for an
amount which shall not be less than ten per cent of the aggregate of the proposal; or, if so prescribed by the City Council, by a bond for the said
amount signed by the bidder and by two sureties, who shall justify before
any officer competent to administer an oath, in double the said amount over
and above all statutory exemptions. Said proposals shall be delivered to the
Clerk of the said City Council, and said Council shall, in open session, examine and publicly declare the same; *provided, however*, that no proposal
shall be considered unless accompanied by said check or bond satisfactory to
the Council. The City Council may reject any and all bids, should it deem
this for the public good, and also the bid of any party who has been delinquent and unfaithful in any former contract with the municipality, and shall
reject all bids other than the lowest regular bid of any responsible bidder,
and may award the contract for said work or improvement to the lowest responsible bidder at the prices named in his bid, and shall thereupon return
to the proper parties the respective checks and bonds corresponding to the
bids so rejected. But the check accompanying such accepted proposal or
bids shall be held by the City Clerk of said city until the contract for doing
said work as hereinafter provided has been entered into, either by said
lowest bidder or by the owners of a major part of the frontage, whereupon
said certified check shall be returned to said bidder. But if said bidder fails,
neglects, or refuses to enter into the contract to perform said work or improvement, as hereinafter provided, then the certified check accompanying his bid, and the amount therein mentioned, shall be declared to be
forfeited to said city, and shall be collected by it and paid into its fund for
repairs of streets, and any bond forfeited may be prosecuted and the
amount due thereon collected and paid into said fund. Notice of such
awards of contract shall be posted for five days, in the same manner as
hereinbefore provided for the publication of proposals for said work. The
owners of the major part of the frontage of lots and lands upon the street
whereon said work is to be done, which are liable to be assessed for said
work, or their agents, and who shall make oath that they are such owners or
agents, shall not be required to present sealed proposals, but may within
ten days after the first posting of notice of said award elect to take said
work, and enter into a written contract to do the whole work at the price at
which the same has been awarded. Should the said owners fail to elect
to take said work and to enter into a written contract therefor within said
ten days, or to commence the work within fifteen days after the first
publication of said award, and to prosecute the same with diligence to completion, it shall be the duty of the Superintendent of Streets to enter into a

contract with the original bidder to whom the contract was awarded, and at the prices specified in his bid. But if said original bidder neglects, fails, or refuses for fift' en days after the first posting of notice of the award to enter into the contract, then the City Council shall again advertise for proposals, as in the first instance, and award the contract for said work to the then lowest regular responsible bidder. The bids of all persons and the election of all owners as aforesaid who have failed to enter into contract as herein provided, shall be rejected in any bidding or election subsequent to the first, for the same work. If the owners or contractor who may have taken any contract do not complete the same within the time limited in the contract, or within such further time as the City Council may give them, the Superin. tendent of Streets shall report such delinquency to the City Council, which may relet the unfinished portion of said work, after pursuing the formalities prescribed hereinbefore for the letting of the whole. All contractors, contracting owners included, shall, at the time of executing any contract for street work herein, execute a bond to the satisfaction and approval of the Superintendent of Streets of said city, with two or more sureties, and payab!e to such city, in such sums as the said Mayor shall deem adequate, conditional for the faithful performance of the contract; and the sureties shall justify before any person competent to administer an oath in double the amount mentioned in said bond over and above all statutory exemptions. Before being entitled to a contract the bidder to whom award was made, or the owners who have elected to take the contract, must advance to the Superintendent of Streets for payment by him the cost of publication of the notices required hitherto under the proceedings prescribed in this Act.

SEC. 6. The Superintendent of Streets is hereby authorized, in his official capacity, to make all written contracts, and receive all bonds authorized by this Act, and to do any other act, either express or implied, that pertains to the Street Department under this Act; and he shall fix the time for the commencement, which shall not be more than fifteen days from the date of the contract, and for the completion of the work under all contracts entered into by him, which work shall be prosecuted with diligence from day to day thereafter to completion, and he may extend the time so fixed from time to time, under the direction of the City Council. The work provided for in section two of this Act must, in all cases, be done under the direction and to the satisfaction of the Superintendent of Streets, and the materials used shall comply with the specifications and be to the satisfaction of said Superintendent of Streets, and all contracts made therefor must contain a provision to that effect, and also express notice that, in no case, except where it is otherwise provided in this Act, will the city, or any officer thereof, be liable for any portion of the expense, nor for any delinquency of persons or property assessed. The City Council may, by ordinance, prescribe general rules directing the Superintendent of Streets and the contractor as to the materials to be used, and the mode of executing the work, under all contracts thereafter made. The assessment and apportionment of the expenses of all such work or improvement shall be made by the Superintendent of Streets in the mode herein provided.

SEC. 7. *Subdivision One*—The expenses incurred for any work authorized by section two of this Act, which shall not include such portion of any street as is required by law to be kept in order or repair by any person or company having railroad tracks thereon, shall be assessed upon the lots and lands fronting thereon, except as hereinafter specifically provided; each lot or portion of a lot being separately assessed, in proportion to the front-age, at a rate per front foot sufficient to cover the total expenses of the work. But wherever the said assessment upon any lot or portion of a lot would exceed one-half the valuation of said lot, or portion of a lot, as it was last assessed for municipal taxation, then, unless the owner, or his attorney in fact, shall have previously filed with the Superintendent of Streets a written waiver of the partial exemption herein provided, the assessment and the lien thereof upon said lot or portion of a lot shall be only to the amount of one-half of said last preceding municipal valuation, and the proper remainder of said assessment shall be assessed to the city, and be payable out of the city treasury.

Subdivision Two—The expenses of all improvements, except such as are done by contractors, under the provisions of section thirteen of this Act, until the streets, street crossings, lanes, alleys, places, or courts, are finally accepted, as provided in section twenty of this Act, shall be assessed upon the lots and lands as provided in this section, according to the nature and character of the work; (and after such acceptance, the expense of all work thereafter done thereon shall be paid by said city out of the Street Department Fund).

Subdivision Three—The expense of work done on main street crossing shall be assessed at a uniform rate per front foot of the four quarter blocks ad-joining and cornering upon the crossing, and separately upon the whole of each lot or portion of a lot having any frontage in the quarter blocks fronting on said main streets, but only according to its frontage in said quarter blocks.

Subdivision Four—Where a main street terminates in another main street, the expenses of the work done on one half of the width of the street oppo-site the termination shall be assessed upon the lots in each of the two quar-ter blocks adjoining and cornering on the same, according to the frontage of such lots on said main streets, and the expense of the other half of the width of said street, upon the lot or lots fronting on the latter half of the street opposite such termination.

Subdivision Five—Where any small or subdivision street crosses a main street, the expense of all work done on said crossings shall be assessed on all the lots or portions of lots half way on said small streets to the next crossing or intersection, or to the end of such small or subdivision street, if it does not meet another.

Subdivision Six—The expense of work done on small or subdivision street crossings shall be assessed upon the lots fronting upon such small streets, on each side thereof, in all directions, half way to the next street, place, or court, on either side, respectively, or to the end of such street, if it does not meet another.

Subdivision Seven—Where a small street, lane, alley, place, or court, terminates in another street, lane, alley, place, or court, the expense of the work done on one half of the width of the street, lane, alley, place, or court, opposite the termination, shall be assessed upon the lot or lots fronting on such small street, or lane, alley, place, or court, so terminating, according to its frontage thereon, half way on each side, respectively, to the next street, lane, alley, place, or court, or to the end of such street, lane, alley, place, or court, if it does not meet another; and the other one half of the width upon the lots fronting such termination.

Subdivision Eight—Where any work mentioned in section two of this Act (sewers, manholes, cesspools, culverts, crosswalks, crossings, curbings, grading, curbing, piling, and capping excepted) is done on one side of the center line of said streets, lanes, alleys, places, or courts, the lots or portions of the lots fronting on that side only shall be assessed to cover the expenses of said work, according to the provisions of this section.

Subdivision Nine—Section one of chapter three hundred and twenty-five of the laws of this State entitled an Act amendatory of and supplementary to an Act to provide revenue for the support of the government of this State, approved April twenty-ninth, eighteen hundred and fifty-seven, approved April nineteenth, eighteen hundred and fifty-nine, shall not be applicable to the provisions of this section, but the property herein mentioned shall be subject to the provisions of this Act, and to be assessed for work done under the provisions of this section.

Subdivision Ten—It shall be lawful for the owner or owners of lots or lands fronting upon any street, the width and grade of which have been established by the City Council, to perform at his own expense (after obtaining from the Council permission so to do, but before said Council has passed its resolutions of intention to order grading inclusive of this) any grading upon said street to its full width, and to its grade as then established, and thereupon to procure, at his own expense, a certificate from the City Engineer, setting forth the number of cubic yards of cutting and filling made by him or them in said grading, and the proportions performed by each owner, and that the same is done to the established width and grade of said street, and thereafter to file said certificate with the Superintendent of Streets, which certificate the Superintendent shall record in a book kept for that purpose in his office, properly indexed. Whenever thereafter the City Council orders the grading of said street, or any portion thereof, on which any grading certificated as aforesaid, has been done, the bids and the contract must express the prices by the cubic yard for cutting and filling in grading; and the said owner and his successors in interest shall be entitled to credit on the assessment upon his lots and lands fronting on said street for the grading thereof, to the amount of the cubic yards of cutting and filling set forth in his said certificate, at the prices named in the contract for said cutting and filling, or if the grade meanwhile has been duly altered, only for so much of said certificated work as would be required for grading to the altered grade; *provided, however,* that such owner shall not be entitled to such credit as may be in excess of the assessments for grading upon the lots and lands owned by him and proportionately assessed for the whole of said grading; and the Superintendent of Streets shall include in the assessment for the whole of said grading upon the same grade the number of cubic yards of cutting and filling set forth in any and all certificates so recorded in his office, or for the whole of said grading to the duly altered grade so much of said certificated work as would be required for grading thereto, and shall enter corresponding credits, deducting the same as payments made upon the amounts assessed against the lots and lands owned respectively by said certificated owners and their successors in interest; *provided, however,* that he shall not so include any grading quantities, or credit any sums in excess of the proportionate assessments for the whole of the grading which are made upon any lots and lands fronting upon said street and belonging to any such certificated owners, or their successors in interest.

Subdivision Eleven—The City Council may include in one resolution of intention and order any of the different kinds of work mentioned in section two of this Act, and it may except therefrom any of said work already done upon the grade. The lots and portions of lots fronting upon said excepted work shall not be included in the frontage assessment for the class of work from which the exception is made; *provided,* that this shall not be so construed as to affect the special provisions as to grading contained in subdivision ten of this section.

Sec. 8.   After the contractor of any street work has fulfilled his contract to the satisfaction of the Street Superintendent of the said city, or City Council on appeal, the Street Superintendent shall make an assessment to cover the sum due for the work performed and specified in said contracts (including any incidental expenses), in conformity with the provisions of the preceding section, according to the character of the work done ; or, if any direction and decision shall be given by said Council on appeal, then, in conformity with such direction and decision, which assessment shall briefly refer to the contract, the work contracted for and performed, and shall show the amount to be paid therefor, together with any incidental expenses, the rate per front foot assessed, the amount of each assessment, the name of the owner of each lot, or portion of a lot (if known to the Street Superintendent); if unknown, the word "unknown" shall be written opposite the number of the lot, and the amount assessed thereon, the number of each lot or portion of a lot assessed, and shall have attached thereto a diagram exhibiting each street or street crossing, lane, alley, place, or court, on which any work has been done, and showing the relative location of each distinct lot or portion of a lot to the work done, numbered to correspond with the numbers in the assessments, and showing the number of feet fronting assessed for said work contracted for and performed.

SEC. 9. To said assessment shall be attached a warrant, which shall be signed by the Superintendent of Streets, and countersigned by the Mayor of said city. The said warrant shall be substantially in the following form:

FORM OF THE WARRANT.

" By virtue hereof, I (name of Superintendent of Streets) of the City of ———, County of———, [or City and County of———,] and State of California, by virtue of the authority vested in me as said Superintendent of Streets, do authorize and empower (name of contractor) (his or their) agents or assigns, to demand and receive the several assessments upon the assessment and diagram hereto attached, and this shall be (his or their) warrant for the same.

"(Date.)   (Name of Superintendent of Streets.)

" Countersigned by (name of) Mayor."

Said warrant, assessment, and diagram shall be recorded in the office of said Superintendent of Streets. When so recorded the several amounts assessed shall be a lien upon the lands, lots, or portions of lots assessed, respectively, for the period of two years from the date of said recording, unless sooner discharged; and from and after the date of said recording of any warrant, assessment, and diagram, all persons mentioned in section eleven of this Act shall be deemed to have notice of the contents of the record thereof. After said warrant, assessment, and diagram are recorded, the same shall be delivered to the contractor, or his agent or assigns, on demand, but not until after the payment to the said Superintendent of Streets of the incidental expenses not previously paid by the contractor, or his assigns ; and by virtue of said warrant, said contractor, or his agents or assigns, shall be authorized to demand and receive the amount of the several assessments made to cover the sum due for the work specified in such contracts and assessments.

SEC. 10. The contractor, or his assigns, or some person in his or their behalf, shall call upon the persons assessed, or their agents, if they can conveniently be found, and demand payment of the amount assessed to each. If any payment be made the contractor, his assigns, or some person in his or their behalf, shall receipt the same upon the assessment in presence of the person making such payment, and shall also give a separate receipt if demanded. Whenever the person so assessed, or their agents, cannot conveniently be found, or whenever the name of the owner of the lot is stated as "unknown" on the assessment, then the said contractor, or his assigns, or some person in his or their behalf, shall publicly demand payment on the pre-

21

mises assessed. The warrant shall be returned to the Superintendent of Streets within thirty days after its date, with a return indorsed thereon, signed by the contractor, or his assigns, or some person in his or their behalf, verified upon oath, stating the nature and character of the demand, and whether any of the assessments remain unpaid, in whole or in part, and the amount thereof. Thereupon the Superintendent of Streets shall record the return so made, in the margin of the record of the warrant and assessment, and also the original contract referred to therein, if it has not already been recorded at full length in a book to be kept for that purpose in his office, and shall sign the record. The said Superintendent of Streets is authorized at any time to receive the amount due upon any assessment list and warrant issued by him, and give a good and sufficient discharge therefor ; *provided*, that no such payment so made after suit has been commenced, without the consent of the plaintiff in the action, shall operate as a complete discharge of the lien until the costs in the action shall be refunded to the plaintiff ; and he may release any assessment upon the books of his office, on the payment to him of the amount of the assessment against any lot with interest, or on the production to him of the receipt of the party or his assigns to whom the assessment and warrant were issued; and if any contractor shall fail to return his warrant within the time and in the form provided in this section, he shall thenceforth have no lien upon the property assessed; *provided, however*, that in case any warrant is lost, upon proof of such loss a duplicate can be issued, upon which a return may be made, with the same effect as if the original had been so returned. After the return of the assessment and warrant as aforesaid, all amounts remaining due thereon shall draw interest at the rate of ten per cent. per annum until paid.

SEC. 11. The owners, whether named in the assessment or not, the contractor, or his assigns, and all other persons directly interested in any work provided for in this Act, or in the assessment, feeling aggrieved by any act or determination of the Superintendent of Streets in relation thereto, or, who claim that the work has not been performed according to the contract in a good and substantial manner, or having or making any objection to the correctness or legality of the assessment or other act, determination, or proceedings of the Superintendent of Streets, shall, within thirty days after the date of the warrant, appeal to the City Council, as provided in this section, by briefly stating their objections in writing, and filing the same with the Clerk of said City Council. Notice of the time and place of the hearing, briefly referring to the work contracted to be done, or other subject of appeal, and to the acts, determinations, or proceedings objected to or complained of, shall be published for five days. Upon such appeal, the City Council may remedy and correct any error or informality in the proceedings, and revise and correct any of the acts or determinations of the Superintendent of Streets relative to said work ; may confirm, amend, set aside, alter, modify, or correct the assessment in such manner as to them shall seem just, and require the work to be completed according to the directions of the City Council ; and may instruct and direct the Superintendent of Streets to correct the warrant, assessment, or diagram in any particular, or to make and issue a new warrant, assessment, and diagram, to conform to the decisions of said City Council in relation thereto, at their option. All the decisions and determinations of said City Council, upon notice and hearing as aforesaid, shall be final and conclusive upon all persons entitled to appeal under the provisions of this section, as to all errors, informalities, and irregularities which said City Council might have remedied and avoided ; and no assessment shall be held invalid, except upon appeal to the City Council, as provided in this section, for any error, informality, or other defect in any of the proceedings prior to the assessment, or in the assessment itself, where notice of the intention of the City Council to order the work to be done, for which the assessment is made, has been actually published in any designated newspaper of said city for the length of time prescribed by law, before the passage of the resolution ordering the work to be done.

SEC 12. At any time after the period of thirty-five days from the day of the date of the warrant, as hereinbefore provided, or if any appeal is taken to the City Council, as is provided in section eleven of this Act, at any time after five days from the decision of said Council, or after the return of the warrant or assessment, after the same may have been corrected, altered, or modified, as provided in section eleven of this Act (but not less than thirty-five days from the date of the warrant), the contractor, or his assignee, may sue, in his own name, the owner of the land, lots, or portion of lots assessed, on the day of the date of the recording of the warrant, assessment, and diagram, or on any day thereafter, during the continuance of the lien of said assessment, and recover the amount of any assessment remaining unpaid, with interest thereon, as hereinbefore provided; and in all cases of recovery, under the provisions of this Act, the plaintiff shall recover the sum of fifteen dollars, in addition to the taxable costs, as attorneys' fees, but not any percentage upon said recovery. Suit may be brought in the Superior Court within whose jurisdiction the city is in which said work has been done, and in case any of the assessments are made against lots, portions of lots, or lands, the owners whereof cannot with due diligence be found, the service in each of such actions may be had in such manner as is prescribed in the Codes and laws of this State. The said warrant, assessment, and diagram, with the affidavit of demand and non-payment, shall be held prima facie evidence of the regularity and correctness of the assessment, and of the prior proceedings and acts of the Superintendent of Streets and City Council, upon which said warrant, assessment, and diagram are based, and like evidence of the right of the plaintiff to recover in the action. The Court in which such suit shall be commenced shall have power to adjudge and decree a lien against the premises assessed, and to order such premises to be sold on execution, as in other cases of the sale of real estate by the process of said Courts; and on appeal the appellate Court shall be vested with the same power to adjudge and decree a lien, and to order such premises to be sold on execution or decree, as is conferred on the Court from which an appeal is taken. Such premises, if sold, may be redeemed as in other cases. In all suits, now pending, or hereafter brought, to recover street assessments, the proceedings therein shall be governed and regulated by the provisions of this Act, and also when not in conflict herewith by the Codes of this State. This Act shall be liberally construed to effect the ends of justice.

SEC. 13. Whenever any portion of any street, lane, alley, court, or place is said city, improved, or any sidewalk constructed thereon according to law, shall be out of repair and in condition to endanger persons or property passing thereon, or in condition to interfere with the public convenience in the use thereof, it shall be the duty of the said Superintendent of Streets to require, by notice in writing, to be delivered to them personally, or left on the premises, the owners or occupants of lots, or portions of lots, fronting on said portion of said street, lane, alley, court, or place, or of said portion of said walk so out of repair as aforesaid, to repair forthwith said portion of said street, land, alley, court, or place to the center thereof, or said sidewalk in front of the property of which he is the owner, or tenant, or occupant; and said Superintendent of Streets shall specify in said notice what repairs are required to be made. After the expiration of three days from the date of the service of said notice, the said Superintendent of Streets shall be deemed to have acquired jurisdiction to contract for the making of the repairs required by said notice. If said repairs be not commenced within three days after notice given as aforesaid, and diligently and without interruption prosecuted to completion, the said Superintendent of Streets may, under authority from said City Council, make such repairs, or enter into a contract with any suitable person, at the expense of the owner, tenant, or occupant, at a reasonable price, to be determined by said Superintendent of Streets, and such owner, tenant, or occupant shall be liable to pay the same. Upon the completion of said repairs by said contractors as aforesaid to the satisfaction of said Superintendent of Streets, said Superintendent of Streets shall make and deliver to said contractor a certificate to the effect that said repairs have been properly made by said contractor, and that the charges for the same are reasonable and just, and that he, said Superintendent, has accepted the same.

SEC. 14. If the expenses of the work and material for such improvements, after the completion thereof, and the delivery to said contractor of said certificate, be not paid to the contractor so employed, or his agent or assignee, on demand, the said contractor, or his assignee, shall have the right to sue such owner, tenant, or occupant, for the amount contracted to be paid; and said certificate of the Superintendent of Streets shall be prima facie evidence of the amount claimed for said work and materials, and of the right of the contractor to recover for the same in such action. Said certificate shall be recorded by the said Superintendent of Streets in a book kept by him in his office for that purpose, properly indexed, and the sum contracted to be paid shall be a lien, the same as provided in section nine of this Act, and may be enforced in the same manner.

SEC. 15. In addition, and as cumulative to the remedies above given, the City Council shall have power, by resolution or ordinance, to prescribe the penalties that shall be incurred by any owner or person liable, or neglecting, or refusing to make repairs when required, as required in section (13) thirteen of this Act, which fines and penalties shall be recovered for the use of the city by prosecution in the name of the people of the State of California, in the Court having jurisdiction thereof, and may be applied, if deemed expedient by the said Council, in the payment of the expenses of any such repairs not otherwise provided for.

SEC. 16. The person owning the fee, or the person in whom, on the day the action is commenced, appears the legal title to the lots and lands, by deeds duly recorded in the County Recorder's office of each county, or the person in possession of lands, lots, or portions of lots or buildings under claim, or exercising acts of ownership over the same for himself, or as the executor, administrator, or guardian of the owner, shall be regarded, treated, and deemed to be the "owner" (for the purpose of this law), according to the intent and meaning of that word as used in this Act. And in case of property leased, the possession of the tenant or lessee holding and occupying under such persons shall be deemed to be the possession of such owner.

SEC. 17. Any tenant or lessee of the lands or lots liable may pay the amount assessed against the property of which he is the tenant or lessee under the provision of this Act, or he may pay the price agreed on to be paid under the provision of section thirteen of this Act, either before or after suit brought, together with costs, to the contractor, or his assigns, or he may redeem the property, if sold on execution or decree for the benefit of the owner, within the time prescribed by law, and deduct the amount so paid from the rents due and to become due from him, and for any sums so paid beyond the rents due from him, he shall have a lien upon and may retain possession of the said land and lots until the amount so paid and advanced be satisfied, with legal interest, from accruing rents, or by payment by the owner.

SEC. 18. The records kept by the Superintendent of Streets of said city, in conformity with the provisions of this Act, and signed by him, shall have the same force and effect as other public records, and copies therefrom, duly certified, may be used in evidence with the same effect as the originals. The said records shall, during all office hours, be open to the inspection of any citizen wishing to examine them, free of charge.

SEC. 19. Notices in writing which are required to be given by the Superintendent of Streets, under the provisions of this Act, may be served by any person, with the permission of the Superintendent of Streets, and the fact of such service shall be verified by the oath of the person making it, taken before the Superintendent of Streets (who, for that purpose, is hereby authorized to administer oaths), or other person authorized to administer oaths, or such notices may be delivered by the Superintendent of Streets himself, who must also verify the service thereof, and who shall keep a record of the fact of giving such notices, when delivered by himself personally, and also of the notices and proof of service when delivered by any other person.

SEC. 20. Whenever any street, or portion of a street, has been or shall hereafter be fully constructed to the satisfaction of the Superintendent of Streets and of the City Council, and is in good condition throughout, and a sewer, gas pipes, and water pipes are laid therein, under such regulations as the City Council shall adopt, the same shall be accepted by the City Council, by ordinance, and thereafter shall be kept in repair and improved by the said municipality; the expense thereof, together with the assessment for street work done in front of city property, to be paid out of a fund to be provided by said Council for that purpose; *provided*, that the City Council shall not accept of any portion of the street less than the entire width of the roadway (including the curbing), and one block in length, or one entire crossing; and, *provided further*, that the City Council may partially or conditionally accept any street, or portion of a street, without a sewer, or gas pipes, or water pipes therein, if the ordinance of acceptance expressly states that the Council deems such sewer, or gas pipes, or water pipes, to be then unnecessary, but the lots of land previously or at any time assessable for the cost of constructing a sewer, shall remain and be assessable for such cost, and for the cost of repairs and restoration of the street damaged in the said construction, whenever said Council shall deem a sewer to be necessary, and shall order it to be constructed, the same as if no partial or conditional acceptance had ever been made. The Superintendent of Streets shall keep in his office a register of all streets accepted by the City Council under this section, which register shall be indexed for easy reference thereto.

SEC. 21. The Superintendent of Streets shall keep a public office in some convenient place within the municipality, and such records as may be required by the provisions of this Act. He shall superintend and direct the cleaning of all sewers, and the expense of the same shall be paid out of the Street or Sewer Fund of said city.

SEC. 22. It shall be the duty of the Superintendent of Streets to see that the laws, ordinances, orders, and regulations relating to the public streets and highways be fully carried into execution, and that the penalties thereof are rigidly enforced. He shall keep himself informed of the condition of all the public streets and highways, and also of the public buildings. parks, lots, and grounds of said city, as may be prescribed by the City Council. He shall, before entering upon the duties of his office, give bonds to the municipality, with such sureties and for such sums as may be required by the City Council; and should he fail to see the laws, ordinances, orders, and regulations relative to the public streets or highways carried into execution, after notice from any citizen of a violation thereof, he and his sureties shall be liable upon his official bond to any person injured in his person or property in consequence of said official neglect.

SEC. 23. If, in consequence of any graded street or public highway improved under the provisions of this Act, being out of repair and in condition to endanger persons or property passing thereon, any person while carefully using said street or public highway, and exercising ordinary care to avoid the danger, suffer damage to his person or property, through any such defect therein, no recourse for damages thus suffered shall be had against such city; but if such defect in the street or public highway shall have existed for the period of twenty-four hours or more after notice thereof to the said Superintendent of Streets, then the person or persons on whom the law may have imposed the obligations to repair such defect in the street or public highway, and also the officer or officers through whose official negligence such defect remains unrepaired, shall be jointly and severally liable to the party injured for the damage sustained; *provided*, that said Superintendent has the authority to make said repairs, under the direction of the City Council, at the expense of the city.

SEC. 24. The City Council of such city shall have full power and authority to construct sewers and manholes and provide for the cleaning of the same, culverts with crosswalks, or culverts, or crosswalks, or sidewalks, or any portion of any sidewalk, upon or in any street, lane, alley, court, or place in such city, of such materials, in such a manner, and upon such terms as it may deem proper. None of the work or improvements described in this section shall be stayed or prevented by any written or any other remonstrance or objection, unless such Council deems proper.

SEC. 25. The City Council may, in its discretion, repair and water streets, that shall have been graded, curbed, and planked, paved, or macadamized, and may build, repair, and clean sewers, and shall provide a Street Contingent Fund at the same time and in the same manner as other funds are provided, out of which to pay the costs and expenses of making said repairs, and watering said streets, and building, repairing, and cleaning said sewers; but whenever any unaccepted street or part of a street requires regrading, recurbing, repiling, repaving, replanking, regraveling, or remacadamizing, or requires new culverts, or new crosswalks, or new sidewalks, or new sewers, the work shall be advertised and let out by contract, and the costs and expenses thereof shall be assessed upon the property affected or benefited thereby, the same as in the first instance.

SEC. 26. The City Council may, in its discretion, order that the whole or any part of the cost and expenses of any of the work mentioned in section two of this Act be paid out of the treasury of the municipality from such fund as the Council may designate. Whenever a part of such cost and ex-

penses is so ordered to be paid, the Superintendent of Streets, in making up
the assessment heretofore provided for such cost and expenses, shall first
deduct from the whole cost and expenses such part thereof as has been so
ordered to be paid out of the municipal treasury, and shall assess the remainder of said cost and expenses proportionately upon the lots, parts of lots,
and lands fronting on the streets where said work was done, and in the manner heretofore provided. And whenever the City Council shall order to be
done any of the work mentioned in section two of this Act, it shall be
deemed to exercise its discretion mentioned in this section, and to include
an order for the payment out of its treasury for the excess of any assessment
for said work otherwise chargeable upon any lot, or portion of a lot, over and
above one-half of the valuation of said lot, or portion of a lot, in its last preceding assessment for municipal taxation.

PART II.

SEC. 27. Whenever the City Council deem it necessary to construct a
sewer, then the said Council may, in its discretion, determine to construct
said sewer, and assess the costs and expenses thereof upon the property to
be affected or benefited thereby, in such manner and within such assessment district as it shall prescribe, and the lien therefor upon said property
shall be the same as is provided in section nine of this Act, or said Council
may determine to construct said sewer and pay therefor out of the Street
Contingent Fund.

SEC. 28. If, at any time, the City Council shall deem it necessary to
incur any indebtedness for the construction of sewers, in excess of the
money in the Street Contingent Fund applicable to the construction of such
sewers, they shall give notice of a special election by the qualified electors
of the city, to be held to determine whether such indebtedness shall be incurred. Such notice shall specify the amount of indebtedness proposed to
be incurred, the route and general character of the sewer or sewers to be
constructed, and the amount of money necessary to be raised annually by
taxation for an interest and sinking fund as hereinafter provided. Such
notice shall be published for at least three weeks in some newspaper published in such city, and no other question or matter shall be submitted to
the electors at such election. If, upon a canvass of the votes cast at such
election, it appear that not less than two-thirds of all the qualified electors
voting at such election shall have voted in favor of incurring such indebtedness, it shall be the duty of the City Council to pass an ordinance providing
for the mode of creating such indebtedness, and of paying the same; and in
such ordinance provision shall be made for the levy and collection of an
annual tax upon all the real and personal property subject to taxation,
within such city, sufficient to pay the interest on such indebtedness as it
falls due, and also to constitute a sinking fund for the payment of the prin-

cipal thereof, within a period of not more than twenty years from the time of contracting the same. It shall be the duty of the City Council in each year thereafter, at the time when other taxes are levied, to levy a tax sufficient for such purpose, in addition to the taxes authorized to be levied for city purposes. Such tax, when collected, shall be kept in the treasury as a separate fund, to be inviolably appropriated to the payment of the principal and interest of such indebtedness.

SEC. 29. If bonds are issued under the provisions of the last section, said bonds shall be in sums of not less that one hundred dollars nor more than one thousand dollars, shall be signed by the Mayor and Treasurer of the city, and the seal of the city shall be affixed thereto. Coupons for the interest shall be attached to each bond, signed by the Mayor and Treasurer. Said bonds shall bear interest, to be fixed by the City Council, at the rate of not to exceed five per cent per annum.

SEC. 30. Before the sale of said bonds, the Council shall, at a regular meeting, by resolution, declare its intention to sell a specified amount of said bonds, and the day and hour of such sale, and shall cause such resolution to be entered in the minutes, and shall cause notice of such sale to be published for fifteen days in at least one newspaper published in the city in which the bonds are issued, and one published in the City and County of San Francisco, and in any other newspaper in the State, at their discretion. The notice shall state that sealed proposals will be received by the Council for the purchase of the bonds on the day and hour named in the resolution. The Council, at the time appointed, shall open the proposals and award the purchase of the bonds to the highest bidder, but may reject all bids.

SEC. 31. The Council may sell said bonds, at not less than par value, without the notice provided for in the preceding section.

SEC. 32. The proceeds of the sale of the bonds shall be deposited in the city treasury, to the account of the Sewer Fund, but no payment therefrom shall be made, except to pay for the construction of the sewer or sewers for the construction of which the bonds were issued, and upon the certificate of the Superintendent of Streets and the City Engineer, that the work has been done according to contract.

SEC. 33. Whenever said Council shall determine to construct any sewer, and pay therefor out of the Street Contingent Fund, or by the issuance of bonds, as above provided, then said Council shall cause to be prepared plans and specifications of said work in sections, and shall advertise for twenty days in at least one newspaper published in the city in which the sewer is to be constructed, and one in the City and County of San Francisco, for sealed proposals for constructing said sewer. The work may be let in sections, and must be awarded to the lowest responsible bidder, the Council having the right to reject any and all bids. The work shall be done and the materials furnished under the supervision and to the satisfaction of the Superintendent of Streets and the City Engineer.

PART III.

Sec. 34. *First—*The City Engineer, or where there is no City Engineer, the County or City and County Surveyor, shall be the proper officer to do the surveying and other engineering work necessary to be done under this Act, and to survey and measure the work to be done under contracts for grading and macadamizing streets, and to estimate the cost and expenses thereof; and every certificate signed by him in his official character shall be prima facie evidence, in all Courts in this State, of the truth of its contents. He shall also keep a record of all surveys made under the provisions of this Act, as in other cases. In all those cities where there is no City Engineer, the City Council thereof is hereby authorized and empowered to appoint a suitable person to discharge the duties herein laid down as those of City Engineer, and all the provisions hereof applicable to the City Engineer shall apply to such person so appointed; said City Council is hereby empowered to fix his compensation for said services.

Second—The words "improve," "improved," and "improvement," as used in this Act, shall include all work mentioned in section two of this Act, and also the reconstruction of all or any portion of said work.

Third—The term "incidental expenses," as used in this Act, shall include the compensation of the City Engineer for work done by him; also, the cost of printing and advertising; also, the compensation of Superintendents of Sewers, and of piling and capping.

Fourth—The notices, resolutions, orders, or other matter required to be published by the provisions of this Act, shall be published in a daily, semi-weekly, or weekly newspaper, to be designated by the Council of such city, as often as the same is issued ; *provided, however,* that in case there is no daily, semi-weekly, or weekly newspaper printed and circulated in any such city, then such notices as are herein required to be published in a newspaper shall be posted, and kept posted for the same length of time as required herein for the publication of the same in a semi-weekly or weekly newspaper, in three of the most public places in such city. Proof of the publication or posting of any notice provided for herein shall be made by affidavit of the owner, publisher, or clerk of the newspaper, or of the poster of the notice.

Fifth—The word "municipality," and the word "city," as used in this Act, shall be understood and so construed as to include, and is hereby declared to include, all corporations heretofore organized and now existing, and those hereafter organized, for municipal purposes.

Sixth—The words "paved or repaved," as used in this Act, shall be held to mean and include pavement of stone, iron, wood, or other materials, whether patented or not, which the City Council shall by ordinance adopt.

Seventh—The word "street," as used in this Act, shall be deemed to and is hereby declared to include highways, lanes, alleys, crossings, or intersections, courts, and places; and the term "main street," means such actually opened street or streets as bound a block.

Eighth—The terms "Street Superintendent" and "Superintendent of Streets," as used in this Act, shall be understood and so construed as to include, and are hereby declared to include, any person or officer whose duty it is, under the law, to have the care or charge of the streets, or the improvement thereof, in any city. In all those cities where there is no Street Superintendent, or Superintendent of Streets, the City Council thereof is hereby authorized and empowered to appoint a suitable person to discharge the duties herein laid down as those of Street Superintendent or Superintendent of Streets; and all the provisions hereof applicable to the Street Superintendent, or Superintendent of Streets, shall apply to such person so appointed.

Ninth—The term " City Council" is hereby declared to include any body or Board which, under the law, is the legislative department of the government of any city.

Tenth—In municipalities in which there is no Mayor, then the duties imposed upon said officer by the provisions of this Act shall be performed by the President of the Board of Trustees, or other chief executive officer of the municipality.

Eleventh—The term " Clerk," and "City Clerk," as used in this Act, is hereby declared to include any person or officer who shall be Clerk of said City Council.

Twelfth—The term "quarter blocks," as used in this Act, as to irregular blocks, shall be deemed to include all lots, or portions of lots, having any frontage on each intersecting street, half way from said crossing or intersection to the next main street.

SEC. 35. The Superintendent of Streets shall, when necessary, appoint a suitable person to take charge of and superintend the construction and improvement of each and every sewer constructed or improved under the provisions of this Act, and of piling and capping, whose duty it shall be to see that the contract made for the doing of said work is strictly fulfilled in every respect, and in case of any departure therefrom to report the same to the Superintendent of Streets. Such person shall be allowed for his time, actually employed in the discharge of his duties, such compensation as shall be just, but not to exceed four dollars per day. The sum to which the party so employed shall be entitled shall be deemed to be incidental expenses, within the meaning of those words as defined in this Act.

SEC. 36. The Act entitled " An Act to provide for the improvement of streets, lanes, alleys, courts, places, and sidewalks, and the construction of sewers within municipalities," approved March sixth, eighteen hundred and eighty-three, is hereby repealed ; *provided*, that any work or proceedings commenced thereunder prior to the passage of this Act shall in nowise be affected hereby, but shall in all respects be finished and completed under said Act of March sixth, eighteen hundred and eighty-three, and said repeal shall in nowise affect said work or proceedings.

SEC. 37.   This Act shall take effect and be in force from and after its passage.

SUPPLEMENT CLXI.

ELECTION LAWS.

An Act to regulate the registration of voters and to secure the purity of elections in the City and County of San Francisco.

1877-8, 299.

[Approved March 18, 1878.]

The People of the State of California, represented in Senate and Assembly, do enact as follows:

SECTION 1.   The conduct, management, and control of elections and matters pertaining to elections in the City and County of San Francisco is hereby taken from the Board of Supervisors and vested in a Board of five Commissioners, who shall consist of the Mayor, the Auditor, the Tax Collector, the City and County Attorney, and the City and County Surveyor of said city and county, which Board is hereby invested with all the powers and charged with all the duties as to elections and matters pertaining to elections now vested in said Board of Supervisors.   The Mayor shall be ex-officio President of the Board of Election Commissioners, and the Registrar of Voters hereafter provided for shall be ex-officio Secretary of said Board, and shall give advice and information to said Board when required by them so to do.   Said Board shall meet and organize within twenty days after the passage of this Act, or sooner if practicable.

SEC. 2.   The Board of Election Commissioners shall, as soon after each general election as convenient (not to exceed ninety days), proceed to divide said city and county into election precincts, of which there shall be so many as shall be sufficient to make the number of votes polled at any one election precinct to be not more than three hundred nor less than two hundred, as near as can be ascertained; *provided*, that the first division of said city and county into precincts under this Act shall be made as speedily as the same can be done after the organization of said Board.

SEC. 3.   There shall be a "Registrar of Voters" for the city and county of San Francisco, to be appointed by the Governor of the State of California from among the citizens of said city and county. His salary shall be thirty-six hundred dollars per annum, payable out of the treasury of said city and county as other salaries are paid, and he shall be allowed a clerk, who shall receive a salary of one hundred and fifty dollars per month, payable in the same manner, and such other necessary clerical assistance as shall be found necessary to the discharge of the duties of said office, to be allowed and authorized by the Board of Election Commissioners of said city and county. He shall have a suitable office provided for him by the said Board, and such allowance for stationery, printing, and incidental expenses as shall prove necessary. He shall give an official bond in the sum of ten thousand dollars, with two sureties to be approved by the County Judge, conditioned for the faithful performance of his duty.

SEC. 4. The Registrar of Voters, when appointed and qualified, shall be clothed with all the powers, discharge all the duties, and be liable to all the obligations and official consequences now belonging to, discharged by, or resting upon the County Clerk and Assessor of said city and county, with respect to the registration of voters and other matters pertaining to elections in said city and county, under the provisions of the Political Code of this State, so far as the same are not annulled by this Act. Said County Clerk, upon demand, shall transfer and deliver to said Registrar the Great Register, as well as other registers, records, books, documents, and things belonging or in anywise appertaining to the registration of voters or other election matters in said city and county, and from thenceforward said Clerk and Assessor shall cease to be charged with any registration or election duties, and the same shall rest upon and be discharged by the Registrar.

SEC. 5. Said Registrar shall keep his office open for business every day in the year (Sundays and legal holidays excepted), from nine o'clock A. M. till five o'clock P. M. He shall have the power to administer oaths to election officers and all other persons in the discharge of his duty.

SEC. 6. The Registrar shall constantly inform himself, by examination and inquiry, as to the condition of the precinct registers and the legality of the names therein, or demanding to be placed thereon, and shall see that none but legal voters are registered. Should the Registrar have reason to believe that any name or names upon the precinct register is improperly or illegally there, it shall be his duty forthwith to send a written or printed notice, by postal card or otherwise, to such person, directing the same to his address as found in the Directory, or in case his name is not in the Directory, then to the address of such person opposite the name on the register of the last preceding election at which such name was voted, requiring such person to show cause before the Board of Election Commissioners why said Commissioners shall not cancel said name. If such person fail for five days to appear and establish the legality of such name on the day fixed for the hearing, and on the certificate of the Registrar that notice and publication in accordance herewith has been made, the Board shall inquire into the case, and if it appears to the satisfaction of the Board that such name is improperly upon the precinct register, then said Board shall make and enter an order directing the Registrar to cancel such name or names. But the parties may appear before said Board at the hearing and show cause against said order, and if the Board finds them properly registered, or entitled to registry, an order shall be made accordingly, which shall be final. The Board may designate any one of the Commissioners to hear and determine such matters.

SEC. 7. The Registrar shall keep in his office a list of all deaths occurring in said city and county of adult males, as well as of the deaths of such citizens as may come to his knowledge who may die elsewhere, to be alphabetically arranged for convenience of reference. Also, all removals or changes of residence, so far as he can learn the same, and commitments to prisons and insane asylums, with time and place, as well as such other information as shall be found useful and within his reach. It shall be the duty of all Clerks of Courts, Prison-keepers, Health Officers, and all other public officers and others, to furnish to said Registrar certified statements of such official facts within their knowledge necessary for him to obtain necessary or useful information in and about his said duty on demand.

SEC. 8. The Registrar of Voters, under and subject to the rules of the Board, must take charge of the business of placing the election officers, and at the last moment, when it is too late to call the Board together to fill vacancies, may select and appoint election officers for said purpose. Should any election officer fail to appear at the opening of any election, or at any time during the progress thereof, the officers in attendance may, subject to such rules as the Board of Commissioners shall provide, fill up the same by appointing any competent citizen. Any person refusing to serve, when so appointed, shall be liable to all the pains and penalties of this Act.

SEC. 9. The counting of votes, and all proceedings connected therewith, shall be in public, and citizens shall have free ingress and egress to and from the place where the same is being done.

SEC. 10. It is hereby made the duty of any and all voters in the city and county of San Francisco, persons holding office or employment under the United States, the State of California, or the city and county of San Francisco, or any of its departments, excepted, to serve as Judges, Inspectors, and Clerks, or other officers of election, whenever required to do so under the provisions of this Act.

SEC. 11. It shall be the duty of the Registrar to obtain from the tax list and register of voters of said city and county the names of the resident citizens of said city and county possessing the necessary qualifications to act as Judges, Inspectors, and Clerks of Election, taking care to select persons of good reputation and character, and have the same placed in a book so as readily to refer to the places of residence and the precinct in which they vote. He shall take care that said list shows the names and residences of all taxpayers who reside in said city and county, and who are voters, and shall ascertain, as nearly as he can, the capabilities of such voters to act as election officers. If any of them are incompetent to serve by reason of infirmity and not otherwise, their names may be left off, but the reason must be noted.

SEC. 12. Said Board of Election Commissioners shall select all election officers provided for by law for said city and county, and shall appoint them to their respective places. They shall have the power to make any regulations and rules for the appointment or selections they may deem advisable, so as to secure integrity, impartiality and capacity for the work to be done; and if the list furnished them by the Registrar does not contain a sufficiency of names of respectable and fit persons for election officers, they must take measures to secure the names of proper persons, citizens and voters of said city and county, and to fill up all appointments as herein provided; *provided*, that in selecting election officers the Commissioners shall take care to select as nearly as possible an equal number of persons of opposite political faith and opinions to serve at each precinct.

SEC. 13. Each election officer under this Act shall be entitled to receive for his services the sum of two dollars per day while actually engaged in said work of receiving and counting votes, to be paid out of the treasury of said city and county in the manner now provided by law for the payment of such service, and no more; *provided*, that said Board of Commissioners may, in their discretion, raise the compensation of clerks for tallying, writing and other matters requiring special skill and qualifications, to such sum as they shall find necessary to secure such service, but not to exceed six dollars per day; *provided*, that such increased compensation shall, under no circumstances, be allowed to any Judge or Inspector; *and provided further*, that no person holding any office or employment under the United States, the State of California, of the city and county of San Francisco, or any of its departments, nor any candidate for office, or who shall have been either thereof within ninety days, shall be eligible to or be allowed to serve as an election or registration officer, clerk, or in any manner whatsoever at an election; *provided*, that the members of the Precinct Registration Boards shall receive for their services while acting upon the precinct registers the sum of forty dollars each, in full for such service.

SEC. 14. Each and every person selected by the Board of Election Commissioners shall be notified by the Registrar of Voters of the fact of his appointment. Such notice shall be in writing, or printed, and shall have printed thereon a copy of this section. Such person, on receipt of such notice, shall appear within the time fixed in the notice, but which shall not be less than five days, before the Registrar and any two of the Commissioners, for the purpose of examination, and if found qualified shall, unless excused by said Commissioners by reason of ill-health or other good and sufficient cause, be bound to serve as such officer for the term of one year from the date of his appointment, unless previously excused or dismissed by the Board, and in case of neglect or refusal to comply with the above-mentioned requirements, or to serve or act, shall be liable to a penalty of five hundred dollars, recoverable by civil action in any Court of competent jurisdiction, in the name of said city and county, and when collected shall be paid into the treasury for the benefit of the Election Fund. And a failure on the part of any such person to present himself for examination and to comply with any of the requirements of this Act preliminary to receiving his certificate of appointment within the time prescribed, or to attend on the day of any registration, or revision or examination of registration, or the day of any election during said term, unless prevented by sickness or other sufficient cause (the burden of proof of which shall be upon the delinquent), shall be deemed a refusal within the meaning of this section.

SEC. 15. The registration of electors in the city and county of San Francisco shall hereafter be done by election or voting precincts, each precinct register being kept separate and distinct from all other precincts. The provisions of the Political Code requiring the keeping of a Great Register and ward registers shall no longer be applicable to said city and county. The provisions of said Code as to making and keeping the Great Register and as to the ward registers and the manner of entering the names of electors therein, and the substance and contents of said entries, and the alterations, changes, and cancellation thereof, as well as the proceedings and proof to enable voters to be registered in said Great and Ward Registers, and all other matters relating thereto, so far as the same are not in conflict or inconsistent with the provisions of this Act, are hereby made applicable to the precinct registers of said city and county authorized by this law. And said precinct registers shall be used at all elections in like manner and with like effect that ward registers were used before the passage of this Act; and no person shall vote at any election except he be legally registered upon the precinct register of the precinct in which he is a qualified voter.

SEC. 16. The registration of electors in the precinct registers in the city and county of San Francisco shall take place previous to each general State election as herein provided, and an elector properly enrolled therein, without being again enrolled, may vote at the general election ensuing his registration and at all special elections between said general election and the next general election, but not afterwards until re-registered according to law.

SEC. 17. In addition to the matters required by section one thousand and ninety-six of the Political Code to be entered in the register, the precinct registers in the city and county of San Francisco shall particularize the place of residence of each elector registered, by specifying the name of the street, avenue, or other location of the dwelling of such elector, with the number of such dwelling, if the same has a number, and if not, then with such a description of the place that it can be readily ascertained and identified. If the elector be not the proprietor or head of the house, then it must show that fact, and upon what floor thereof, and what room such elector occupies in such house; all of which facts are to be ascertained from such elector in the manner required by law for proving the qualification of electors to entitle them to be registered. Any person making a false oath with respect to residence, as provided for in this section, shall be deemed guilty of perjury, and on conviction punished accordingly.

SEC. 18. A sufficient quantity of blanks for precinct registers for all the precincts of said city and county shall be prepared by said Registrar of Voters as soon as is practicable after his entry upon office, and as often as required by this Act thereafter, and kept at the office of said Registrar, so that voters may be registered upon application and proper proof according to law. Ninety days before each general election the Registrar shall commence the registration of all voters entitled thereto, who apply with the proper proof. Such voters shall be registered in the precinct registers for the precinct where they are entitled to vote, and not otherwise. Such registration shall continue at the office of the Registrar until the precinct registers are turned over to the Board of Precinct Registration, as is hereinafter provided for, when it shall cease at said office. Such registration shall be made subject to the rules herein provided for the Board of Precinct Registration.

SEC. 19. There shall be a Board of Precinct Registration in each precinct of said city and county, which shall be constituted in the following manner: The Board of Election Commissioners, as soon as is practicable after they shall have divided the city and county into election precincts, as herein before provided for, shall proceed, in the manner provided in section thirteen hereof, to appoint the one original Inspector and the two original Judges of Election provided for in section one thousand one hundred and forty-two of the Political Code for each precinct. Said Inspector and Judges shall serve for one year, unless otherwise ordered by the Commission, and in addition to acting as election officers at all the elections during the year, shall serve as precinct registering officers for enrolling the electors of their respective precincts on the precinct register thereof. All other election officers shall be appointed by the Board of Election Commissioners at such time as shall be necessary before the election.

SEC. 20. Said Boards of Precinct Registration shall meet in the places provided in their respective precincts for such purpose by the Registrar of Voters, commencing five days (not counting Sundays or legal holidays) before the day fixed by this Act for the cessation of the registration of electors in said city and county, and shall sit in open session from nine o'clock A. M. until ten o'clock P. M. of each day until the day of such cessation (Sundays and legal holidays excepted), to receive and act upon applications for registration on the part of the voters of said precinct. They shall organize by electing one of their number chairman. They shall receive the applications for registration of such male residents of their several election precincts as

22

then are, or on the day of election next following the day of making such application would be, entitled to vote therein, and who shall personally present themselves, and such only.

SEC. 21. It shall be the duty of the Registrar of Voters to provide suitable places in each precinct for the sessions of the Board of Precinct Registration. He also shall furnish them with blanks, stationery, and all other matters and things necessary to enable them to conveniently and speedily perform the duties devolving upon them under this Act. He shall also give such Boards his assistance and advice in organizing and conducting the registration of voters and other matters required of them by law, and shall visit said boards while engaged in said duty, and see that said proceedings are conducted according to law, and the registers made in due form. He shall be allowed free access to the precinct registers at all times, and within such reasonable limits as the Board of Election Commissioners shall prescribe; the public shall have access thereto in like manner.

SEC. 22. As soon as the Board of Precinct Registration shall have commenced their sittings for registration in the several precincts, as herein provided for, registration at the office of the Registrar shall cease, and the precinct registers shall be turned over by the Registrar to said respective Boards, who shall go on with the registration of voters at the places provided by law for them in their respective precincts until the time provided by law for registration to cease, when all registration shall stop, except in the cases specially provided for in section twenty-nine of this Act. It shall be the duty of the Board of Precinct Registration, in addition to their other duties, to carefully examine and revise the names of voters upon their several precinct registers, as turned over to them by the Registrar, and to ascertain if such names are the names of legal voters, properly on said precinct register and entitled to vote in said precinct.

SEC. 23. The Board of Precinct Registration shall keep the several precinct registers for such time as shall be necessary, not to exceed three days after the time for registration ceases according to law, during which time they shall hear and determine applications for registration in the excepted cases provided for in section twenty-nine of this Act. [Should be section twenty-eight.] They shall also make diligent examination and inquiry during said period as to the right of the respective voters who have been registered on said precinct register to such registration, and shall in all doubtful cases certify their doubts, with the reason thereof, to the Board of Election Commissioners for further action. All persons who are refused registration by the Registrar or by the Precinct Board can appeal to the Board of Election Commissioners, who shall hear and determine the same in a summary manner, so as not to delay the completion of the registers.

SEC. 24. When the Board of Precinct Registration have completed the examination and inquiry provided for in the preceding section, they shall certify the precinct register, as is hereinafter provided, and deliver the same to the Registrar of Voters. Said delivery shall be made not later than three full days after the cessation of registration as provided by law. They shall at the same time prepare and duly certify a separate and distinct list, showing the names of all persons concerning whose right of registration they are in doubt, together with grounds or reasons for such doubt. Such list and certificate shall be delivered to the Registrar at the same time with the precinct register. Proper blanks shall be prepared and furnished by the Registrar for the purpose of making the return of doubtful names on the registers, and also blank certificates and all other necessary things for said purpose.

SEC. 25. The certificate to be attached to the precinct register shall be substantially in the following form, to wit:

We, the undersigned, Inspectors and Judges of Election forming the Board of Precinct Registration for the ——— Precinct of the ——— Ward, of the City and County of San Francisco, do jointly and severally certify that on the ——— day of ———, 18—, we met and organized as such Board, at the place appointed by law for the holding thereof in said precinct. That the precinct register was delivered to us by ——— ———, Esquire, Registrar of Voters for said city and county, containing at the time of its delivery to us the names of (stating number) voters. That we have examined and inquired into said list to the best of our ability, and have noted all doubtful registration thereon. We also certify that we sat as a Board of Precinct Registration at said place, ———, from the ——— day of ——— till the ——— day of ———, 18—, and have admitted to registration (showing number) citizens, whose names and other matters of qualification will appear upon the foregoing register, and that the whole number of qualified voters upon said register is (number) ———.

Dated, San Francisco, ———, 18—.
    (Signed): ——— ———.
    (Signed): ——— ———.
    (Signed): ——— ———.

SEC. 26. The certificate to be annexed to the list of doubtful names shall be substantially in the following form, to wit:

We, the undersigned, composing the Board of Precinct Registration for the ——— Precinct of the ——— Ward, of the city and county of San Francisco, hereby certify that the accompanying list shows all the names and other matters of qualification of voters upon the precinct register for said precinct about whose right of registration we entertain a reasonable doubt, together with a statement of the cause or grounds for such doubts.

Dated, San Francisco, ———, 18—.
    (Signed): ——— ———.
    (Signed): ——— ———.
    (Signed): ——— ———.

SEC. 27. It shall be the duty of the Registrar to forthwith notify all persons certified as doubtful of said fact, and to cite them before the Board of Election Commissioners, as provided in section six of this Act, in cases where the Registrar has reason to believe persons have been improperly registered, and the same proceedings shall be had as to citation and cancellation as provided for in said section.

SEC. 28. Fifteen days before a general election all registration or enrollment of voters shall cease, and the precinct registers as they stand shall be the precinct registers for said ensuing election, and until the next general election, subject only to changes in the following cases:

I. All that for any reason are illegally on the precinct register shall be canceled.

II. Any name that has been once lawfully on the precinct register so as to entitle the person to vote at said ensuing election, and which has been by fraud, mistake or otherwise improperly removed or canceled, may be restored on proper evidence thereof.

III. Any legal voter who applied in time for enrollment on a precinct register, and through any fault or neglect of the Registrar or Board of Precinct Registration, or for want of time on the last day, he having duly applied on said day, has his name left off, may have the same put on afterward on showing that he applied in time, and that it was through no fault or neglect of his own that it was left off.

Any voter entitled to have his name on the precinct register under the terms of any of the three preceding subdivisions, and no others, may have the same placed upon the supplementary register provided for in the next section, within five days from the time herein provided for the cessation of enrollment on the precinct register. Any person who does not so apply within said time shall not be enrolled on the precinct register for said election; provided, that nothing in this section shall be deemed to prevent any lawful changes, additions and supplements to said precinct registers after the general election and prior to any special election thereafter to be made under the regulations fixed by the Board of Election Commissioners, and to be used at other than general elections.

SEC. 29. As soon as the Registrar shall receive the precinct register from any Board of Precinct Registration, he shall proceed with the greatest diligence to cause said precinct register to be printed, and the same shall be printed and copies of them posted in his office for public inspection within three days. He shall also proceed by means of clerks and other assistants, to be provided by the Board of Election Commissioners, to ascertain by inquiry and examination the correctness of said precinct registers, and to cancel all names not legally thereon, and shall prepare a supplemental list for each precinct showing the cancellations and additions to the regular list made after the publication of the same, which supplemental list shall be printed and posted in like manner five days before the election, after which no changes shall be made; *provided*, that all cancellations and additions to the registers made by the Registrar shall be subject to the approval of the Board of Election Commissioners. In printing precinct registers each letter of the alphabet shall be commenced upon a new or separate page, and blank pages to a sufficient and proper number shall be left with printed headings only so as to allow for such additional names as are authorized by law to be written in by the Registrar supplementary to the printed names.

Sec. 30. Not less than ten days before the day for the sitting of the Board of Precinct Registration, the Registrar shall cause an advertisement to be printed for ten consecutive days in three daily morning and three daily evening (including the official paper) newspapers published in said city and county, giving notice to the voters of said city and county, that the time for the enrollment of voters on the precinct register will expire on a certain day, naming the day, fixed in this Act for the last day of registration, and inviting them to present themselves for registration at the place of the meeting of said Boards, which shall be named, within the time, under penalty of being debarred the privilege of voting at said election. Such notice shall specify the day upon which the precinct registration by the Board of Precinct Registration shall commence, and also the day upon which it is to end.

Sec. 31. Any elector who has been legally registered in the precinct register, provided he has not changed his residence or otherwise lost his right to vote in his precinct, shall not be required to renew such registration until the making up as herein provided of the precinct register for the next ensuing general election, after the election for which such registration was made, but may vote in such precinct at any election taking place before such general election. The precinct registers shall be printed in sufficient numbers to allow for their being used at all elections likely to occur before the next general election after the one then for which the registration is made, and all necessary changes or additional names shall be noted upon the register for each special election thereafter, or added in supplements thereto, conformatory so far as the same is applicable to the provisions of the law governing the making of the general election register. The Board of Election Commissioners are hereby empowered to make rules governing such supplemental registrations for special elections. The Board is also empowered to provide for and regulate all special elections occurring before the making of the first set of precinct registers under this Act, and for such elections the ward registers shall be used in the precincts, subject to such rules and regulations as the Board of Election Commissioners shall establish.

Sec. 32. The Registrar of Voters shall procure rooms or places both for the sitting of the Board of Precinct Registration as well as for polling places, subject to the approval of the Board of Election Commissioners both as to location and cost.

SEC. 33. All provisions for carrying out the registration and election laws in said City and County of San Francisco shall be made by the Board of Election Commissioners, and demands on the Treasury authorized or allowed by them for such purposes shall have the same force and effect as if authorized or allowed by the Board of Supervisors.

SEC. 34. All of the provisions of the Political Code touching the registration and qualifications of voters and the methods of calling, holding, and conducting elections in force in said city and county at the passage of this Act, shall continue in force therein, so far as they are not inconsistent with the provisions hereof.

SEC. 35. This Act takes effect from and after its passage.

. 1883, 58.

An Act to divide the State into Senatorial Districts, and to provide for the election of Senators therein.

[Approved March 8, 1883.]

SECTION 1. The State is hereby divided into forty Senatorial Districts, constituted as follows:

*   *   *   *   *   *   *   *

SEC. 20. That portion of the City and County of San Francisco bounded as follows: Commencing at the intersection of Bryant Street with the waters of the Bay of San Francisco, continuing thence along the center of the following named streets: Bryant to Third, Third to Market, Market to Kearny, Kearny to Sacramento, and Sacramento to the waters of the Bay of San Francisco, thence along the shore of said bay to the place of beginning, shall constitute the Nineteenth Senatorial District.

SEC. 21. All that portion of the City and County of San Francisco bounded as follows: Commencing at the intersection of Green Street with the waters of the Bay of San Francisco, thence along the center of the following named streets: Green to Mason, Mason to Sutter, Sutter to Kearny, Kearny to Sacramento, Sacramento to the Bay of San Francisco, thence along the shore of said bay to the place of beginning, together with all the waters of the Bay of San Francisco and the islands contained therein situated within the boundaries of the City and County of San Francisco, shall constitute the Twentieth Senatorial District.

SEC. 22. All that portion of the City and County of San Francisco bounded as follows: Commencing at the intersection of Hyde Street with the waters of the Bay of San Francisco, thence along the center of the following named streets: Hyde to Sutter, Sutter to Mason, Mason to Green, Green to its intersection with the waters of the Bay of San Francisco, thence along the shore of said bay to the place of beginning, shall constitute the Twenty-first Senatorial District.

SEC. 23. All that portion of the City and County of San Francisco bounded as follows: Commencing at the intersection of Hyde Street with the waters of the Bay of San Francisco, thence along the center of the following named streets: Hyde to Sutter, Sutter to Van Ness, Van Ness to Eddy, Eddy to Devisadero, Devisadero to Turk, Turk to First Avenue, First Avenue to Avenue B, and Avenue B to its intersection with the waters of the Pacific Ocean, thence northerly and easterly along the shore of the Pacific Ocean and the Bay of San Francisco to the place of beginning, together with the islands known as the Farallone Islands, shall constitute the Twenty-second Senatorial District.

SEC. 24. All that portion of the City and County of San Francisco bounded as follows: Commencing at the intersection of the center of Third and Bryant Streets, thence along the center of the following named streets: Bryant to Fifth, Fifth to Market, Market to Mason, Mason to Sutter, Sutter to Kearny, Kearny to Market, Market to Third, Third to the place of beginning, shall constitute the Twenty-third Senatorial District.

SEC. 25. All that portion of the City and County of San Francisco bounded as follows: Commencing at the intersection of the center of Bryant and Fifth Streets, thence along the center of the following named streets: Bryant to Seventh, Seventh to Market, Market to McAllister, McAllister to Leavenworth, Leavenworth to Sutter, Sutter to Mason, Mason to Market, Market to Fifth, and Fifth to the place of beginning, shall constitute the Twenty-fourth Senatorial District.

SEC. 26. All that portion of the City and County of San Francisco bounded as follows: Commencing at the intersection of the center of Bryant and Seventh Streets, continuing thence along the center of the following named streets: Bryant to Eleventh, Eleventh to Market, Market to Van Ness, Van Ness to Sutter, Sutter to Leavenworth, Leavenworth to McAllister, McAllister to Market, Market to Seventh, and Seventh to the place of beginning, shall constitute the Twenty-fifth Senatorial District.

SEC. 27. All that portion of the City and County of San Francisco bounded as follows: Commencing at the intersection of the center of Bryant Street and the waters of the Bay of San Francisco, continuing thence along the center of the following named streets: Bryant to Channel, Channel to Harrison, Harrison to Fourteenth, Fourteenth to Guerrero, Guerrero to Twentieth, Twentieth to Napa, Napa to its intersection with the waters of the Bay of San Francisco, thence along the shore of said bay to the place of beginning, shall constitute the Twenty-sixth Senatorial District.

SEC. 28. All that portion of the City and County of San Francisco bounded as follows: Commencing at the intersection of Avenue B and the waters of the Pacific Ocean, thence along the center of the following named streets: Avenue B to First Avenue, First Avenue to Turk Street, Turk to Devisadero, Devisadero to Eddy, Eddy to Van Ness, Van Ness to Market, Market to Eleventh, Eleventh to Channel, Channel to Harrison, Harrison to Fourteenth, Fourteenth to Guerrero, Guerrero to Eighteenth, thence along Eighteenth Street to its western limit, thence in a direct line westerly to an intersection of the eastern limit of K Street, or Avenue, thence along K to the waters of the Pacific Ocean, thence along the shore of the ocean, in a northerly direction, to the place of beginning, shall constitute the Twenty-seventh Senatorial District.

SEC. 29. All that portion of the City and County of San Francisco bounded as follows: Commencing at the point of intersection of a continuation of the line of K Street and the waters of the Pacific Ocean, continuing thence along the line of K Street, or Avenue, to its eastern limit; thence in a direct line easterly to an intersection of the western limit of Eighteenth street; thence along the center of the following named streets: Eighteenth to Guerrero, Guerrero to Twentieth, Twentieth to Napa, Napa to the waters of the Bay of San Francisco; thence along the shore southerly to its intersection with the boundary line dividing the Counties of San Francisco and San Mateo; thence along said line to its intersection with the waters of the Pacific Ocean; thence northerly along the shore to the place of beginning, shall constitute the Twenty-eighth Senatorial District.

*   *   *   *   *   *   *   *

SEC. 42. At the general election in the year eighteen hundred and eighty-six, there shall be elected forty Senators, one from each Senatorial District. The Senators elected from the odd numbered districts in the year eighteen hundred and eighty-six shall hold office for two years. Their successors shall be elected in the year eighteen hundred and eighty-eight, and every four years thereafter. The Senators elected from the even-numbered districts shall hold office for four years. Their successors shall be elected in the year eighteen hundred and ninety, and every four years thereafter.

SEC. 43. Neither Boards of Supervisors, municipal authorities, or any other officers, shall have power to alter the boundaries of any township, ward, election precinct, or other local subdivision of any county, city, or town, so as to change the boundaries of any Senatorial District as defined in this Act.

SEC. 44. All Acts and parts of Acts in conflict with the provisions of this Act are hereby repealed.

SEC. 45. This Act shall take effect July first, eighteen hundred and eighty-six.

— ––

1883, 85.

–––

An Act to divide the State into Assembly Districts, and to provide for the election of Assemblymen therein.

[Approved March 13, 1883.]

The People of the State of California, represented in Senate and Assembly, do enact as follows:

SECTION 1. The State is hereby divided into eighty Assembly Districts, constituted as follows:

*   *   *   *   *   *   *   –   –

SEC. 30. All that portion of the city and county of San Francisco bounded as follows: Commencing at the point of intersection where the center line of Bryant street intersects the waters of the Bay of San Francisco, continuing thence along the center of the following named streets: Bryant to First, First to Minna, Minna to Second, to Market, Market to Kearny, Kearny to Sacramento, Sacramento to the waters of the Bay of San Francisco, thence along the shore to the place of beginning, shall constitute the Twenty-ninth Assembly District.

SEC. 31. All that portion of the city and county of San Francisco bounded as follows: Commencing at the intersection of the center of Bryant and First streets, continuing thence along the center of the following named streets: Bryant to Third, Third to Market, Market to Second, Second to Minna, Minna to First, and first to the place of beginning, shall constitute the Thirtieth Assembly District.

SEC. 32. All that portion of the city and county of San Francisco bounded as follows: Commencing at the intersection of Sacramento street and the waters of the bay of San Francisco, continuing thence along the center of the following named streets: Sacramento to Kearny, Kearny to Sutter, Sutter to Stockton, Stockton to Pacific, Pacific to the waters of the Bay of San Francisco, thence along the shore of said bay to the place of beginning, together with all the waters of the bay of San Francisco, and the islands contained therein situated within the boundaries of the city and county of San Francisco, shall constitute the Thirty-first Assembly District.

SEC. 33. All that portion of the city and county of San Francisco bounded as follows: Commencing at the intersection of Pacific street and the waters of the bay of San Francisco, continuing thence along the center of the following named streets: Pacific to Stockton, Stockton to Sutter, Sutter to Mason, Mason to Green, Green to the waters of the bay of San Francisco, thence along the shore of said bay of San Francisco to the place of beginning, shall constitute the Thirty-second Assembly District.

SEC. 34. All that portion of the city and county of San Francisco bounded as follows: Commencing at the point of intersection of Green street and the waters of the bay of San Francisco, continuing thence along the center of the following named streets: Green to Mason, Mason to Sutter, Sutter to Jones, Jones to Greenwich, Greenwich to the waters of the bay of San Francisco, thence along the shore of said bay to the place of beginning, shall constitute the Thirty-third Assembly District.

SEC. 35. All that portion of the city and county of San Francisco bounded as follows: Commencing at the intersection of Greenwich street and the waters of the bay of San Francisco, continuing thence along the center of the following named streets: Greenwich to Jones, Jones to Sutter, Sutter to Hyde, Hyde to the waters of the bay of San Francisco, thence along the shore of said bay to the place of beginning, shall constitute the Thirty-fourth Assembly District.

SEC. 36. All that portion of the city and county of San Francisco bounded as follows: Commencing at the intersection of the center of Bryant and Third streets, continuing thence along the center of the following named streets: Bryant to Fourth, Fourth to Market, Market to Stockton, Stockton to Sutter, Sutter to Kearny, Kearny to Market, Market to Third, Third to the place of beginning, shall constitute the Thirty-fifth Assembly District.

SEC. 37. All that portion of the city and county of San Francisco bounded as follows: Commencing at the intersection of Fourth and Bryant streets, thence along the center of the following named streets: Bryant to Fifth, Fifth to Market, Market to Mason, Mason to Sutter, Sutter to Stockton, Stockton to Market, Market to Fourth, and Fourth to the place of beginning, shall constitute the Thirty-sixth Assembly District.

SEC. 38. All that portion of the city and county of San Francisco bounded as follows: Commencing at the intersection of Fifth and Bryant streets, continuing thence along the center of the following named streets: Bryant to Sixth, Sixth to Market, Market to Taylor, Taylor to Sutter, Sutter to Mason, Mason to Market, Market to Fifth, and Fifth to the place of beginning, shall constitute the Thirty-seventh Assembly District.

Sec. 39. All that portion of the city and county of San Francisco bounded as follows: Commencing at the intersection of Sixth and Bryant streets, continuing thence along the center of the following named streets: Bryant to Seventh, Seventh to Market, Market to McAllister, McAllister to Leavenworth, Leavenworth to Sutter, Sutter to Taylor, Taylor to Market, Market to Sixth, and Sixth to the place of beginning, shall constitute the Thirty-eighth Assembly District.

Sec. 40. All that portion of the city and county of San Francisco bounded as follows: Commencing at the intersection of Bryant and Seventh streets, continuing thence along the center of the following named streets: Bryant to Eighth, Eighth to Market, Market to Larkin, Larkin to Sutter, Sutter to Leavenworth, Leavenworth to McAllister, McAllister to Market, Market to Seventh, and Seventh to the place of beginning, shall constitute the Thirty-ninth Assembly District.

Sec. 41. All that portion of the city and county of San Francisco bounded as follows: Commencing at the intersection of Bryant and Eighth streets, continuing thence along the center of the following named streets: Bryant to Eleventh, Eleventh to Market, Market to Van Ness, Van Ness to Sutter, Sutter to Larkin, Larkin to Market, Market to Eighth, and Eighth to the place of beginning, shall constitute the Fortieth Assembly District.

Sec. 42. All that portion of the city and county of San Francisco bounded as follows: Commencing at the intersection of Hyde street with the waters of the bay of San Francisco, continuing thence along the center of Hyde street to the center of California street, thence along the center of California street in a direct line to its intersection with the east line of the City Cemetery; thence northerly in a direct line to the waters of the Pacific ocean; thence along the shore in an easterly direction to the place of beginning, shall constitute the Forty-first Assembly District.

Sec. 43. All that portion of the city and county of San Francisco bounded as follows: Commencing at the intersection of Avenue B and the waters of the Pacific ocean, continuing thence along the center of the following named streets: Avenue B to First avenue, First avenue to Turk street, Turk to Devisadero, Devisadero to Eddy, Eddy to Van Ness, Van Ness to Sutter, Sutter to Hyde, Hyde to California, California to the east line of the City Cemetery; thence northerly in a direct line to the waters of the Pacific ocean; thence along the shore in a westerly and southerly direction to the place of beginning, together with the islands known as the Farallone islands, shall constitute the Forty-second Assembly District.

Sec. 44. All that portion of the city and county of San Francisco bounded as follows: Commencing at the intersection of Avenue B and the waters of the Pacific ocean, continuing thence along the center of the following named streets: Avenue B to First avenue, First avenue to Turk, Turk to Devisadero, Devisadero to Eddy, Eddy to Van Ness, Van Ness to Fell, Fell to Stanyan, Stanyan to D, D to the waters of the Pacific ocean, thence along the shore of said ocean to the place of beginning, shall constitute the Forty-third Assembly District.

Sec. 45. All that portion of the city and county of San Francisco bounded as follows: Commencing at the intersection of Avenue D and the waters of the Pacific ocean, continuing thence along the center of the following named streets: Avenue D to Stanyan, Stanyan to Fell, Fell to Van Ness, Van Ness to Market, Market to Eleventh, Eleventh to Channel, Channel to Harrison, Harrison to Fourteenth, Fourteenth to Guerrero, Guerrero to Eighteenth; thence along Eighteenth to its westerly end; thence in a direct line westerly to an intersection of the eastern limit of K street (or avenue); thence along K to the waters of the Pacific ocean; thence northerly along the shore to the place of beginning, shall constitute the Forty-fourth Assembly District.

Sec. 46. All that portion of the city and county of San Francisco bounded as follows: Commencing at the intersection of Guerrero and Fourteenth streets, continuing thence along the center of the following named streets: Fourteenth to Harrison, Harrison to Channel, Channel to Bryant, Bryant to Seventh, Seventh to Mississippi, Mississippi to Napa, Napa to Twentieth, Twentieth to Guerrero, and Guerrero to the place of beginning, shall constitute the Forty-fifth Assembly District.

Sec. 47. All that portion of the city and county of San Francisco bounded as follows: Commencing at the intersection of Bryant street and the waters of the Bay of San Francisco, continuing thence along the center of the following named streets: Bryant to Seventh, Seventh to Mississippi, Mississippi to Napa, Napa to the waters of the Bay of San Francisco, and thence along the shore of said bay to the place of beginning, shall constitute the Forty-sixth Assembly District.

Sec. 48. All that portion of the city and county of San Francisco bounded as follows: Commencing at the intersection of Napa street and the waters of the Bay of San Francisco, continuing thence along the center of the following named streets: Napa to Howard, Howard to Army, Army to Mission, thence along the county road to its intersection with the boundary line dividing the counties of San Francisco and San Mateo, thence along said boundary line to its intersection with the waters of the Bay of San Francisco, thence along the shore of said bay to the place of beginning, shall constitute the Forty-seventh Assembly District.

Sec. 49. All that portion of the city and county of San Francisco bounded as follows: Commencing at the intersection of K street and the waters of the Pacific ocean; continuing thence along the center of the following named streets: K to its easterly limit, thence in a direct line to the westerly end of Eighteenth, Eighteenth to Guerrero, Guerrero to Twentieth, Twentieth to Howard, Howard to Army, Army to Mission, thence along the county road to its intersection with the boundary line dividing the counties of San Francisco and San Mateo, thence along said line to the waters of the Pacific ocean, thence along the shore of said ocean to the place of beginning, shall constitute the Forty-eighth Assembly District.

*   *   *   *   *   *   *   *

SEC. 82. Each Assembly District shall elect one member of the Assembly, as follows: A member of the Assembly shall be elected in each Assembly District at the general election, to be held in the year eighteen hundred and eighty-four, and every two years thereafter.

SEC. 83. Neither Boards of Supervisors, municipal authorities, or any other officer, shall have power to alter the boundaries of any township, ward, election precinct, or other local subdivision of any county, city, or town, so as to change the boundaries of any Assembly District as defined in this Act.

SEC. 84. All Acts and parts of Acts in conflict with this Act are hereby repealed.

1883, 296.

———

An Act to divide the State of California into Congressional Districts.

[Approved March 13, 1883.]

The People of the State of California, represented in Senate and Assembly, do enact as follows:

SECTION 1. For the purpose of electing Representatives to the Congress of the United States, the State is hereby divided into six Congressional Districts, as follows:

*   *   *   *   *   *   *   *   *

SEC. 5. All that portion of the City and County of San Francisco described as follows, to wit: Commencing at the intersection of Bryant Street with the waters of the Bay of San Francisco, continuing thence along the center of Bryant Street to the center of Seventh Street; thence along the center of Seventh Street to the center of Market Street; thence along the center of Market Street to the center of McAllister Street; thence along the center of McAllister Street to the center of Leavenworth Street; thence along the center of Leavenworth Street to the center of Sutter Street; thence along the center of Sutter Street to the center of Hyde Street; thence along the center of Hyde Street to the center of California Street; thence along the center of California Street to its intersection with the east line of the City Cemetery; thence northerly in a direct line to the waters of the Pacific Ocean; thence along the shore in an easterly direction to the place of beginning, together with all the islands within the boundaries of the City and County of San Francisco, shall comprise the Fourth Congressional District.

SEC. 6. All that portion of the City and County of San Francisco not included in the Fourth Congressional District, together with the Counties of San Mateo, Santa Cruz, and Santa Clara, shall comprise the Fifth Congressional District.

   *   *   *   *   *   *   *   *   *   *   *

SEC. 8. All Acts or parts of Acts in conflict with this Act are hereby repealed.

SEC 9. This Act shall take effect immediately.

———

1877-8, 180.

———

An Act to prevent the Circulation of Bogus Election Tickets and to prevent Frauds upon Voters.

[Approved March 7, 1878.]

The People of the State of California, represented in Senate and Assembly, do enact as follows:

SECTION 1. It shall hereafter be lawful for the State Central or other managing committee of any political party having a State organization, and for the city and county or other managing committee of any municipal or local party, before each election in this State to prepare and adopt, by engraving or otherwise, a ticket vignette, or heading, with an appropriate inscription, to be printed at the top of the ticket of the party, on the inside thereof, as a distinctive and characteristic heading thereto. Such vignette shall not be more than two inches high by four and a half inches wide, and, in addition to the device adopted, shall set forth legibly the fact that the ticket is the regular ticket of the party, with the name thereof. It shall also show the district, ward, or precinct where such ticket may be lawfully voted. Said vignette and inscription shall stand at the head of the ticket, on the inside thereof, and be followed within a space not to exceed one-half of an inch, by the word "For" on the first line thereof, and the names of candidates and offices shall then be printed below in the order and manner provided for in section eleven hundred and ninety-one of the Political Code. The length of the tickets to be used at elections in this State hereafter shall, in case the length of tickets now allowed by law is insufficient to permit of the printing of such vignette, or heading, and have sufficient margin at the top and bottom, and not otherwise, be increased two inches in addition to the length prescribed by section one thousand one hundred and ninety-one of the Political Code, in order to allow space for said vignette and inscription.

SEC. 2. When such vignette and inscription have been adopted and prepared, an impression of the same, followed by the regular ticket of such party, printed so as to constitute a lawful election ballot, and sealed up in an envelope, may be filed with the County Clerk of the county at any time before the opening of the polls on election day. Such ballot shall be kept by said Clerk on deposit, and from the time of such filing it shall be unlawful for any person to imitate, copy, or in any manner counterfeit the same. Any person violating the foregoing provision shall be deemed guilty of a misdemeanor, and on conviction punished accordingly.

SEC. 3. Any person who shall knowingly print, circulate, or distribute, any ticket, or tickets, ballot or voting paper, having therein, or thereon, the vignette, or an imitation of the vignette or inscription, of any ballot or ticket so filed with the County Clerk, but containing the name or names, of any candidate or candidates, other or different from the name or names, candidate or candidates, upon the ballot or ticket of such party, so filed or deposited with said Clerk, shall be deemed guilty of a misdemeanor, and on conviction punished accordingly; *provided*, that nothing in this Act shall be construed to interfere with the right of any elector to erase or insert any name or proposition upon said ticket, if done in writing.

SEC. 4. Hereafter all tickets, in addition to the matters provided for in section eleven hundred and ninety-one of the Political Code, and immediately above the word "For," as specified in said section, shall show the name or number of the district, ward, or precinct where the same is to be used, and if such name or number is not contained in the party vignette (as it must be if one is used), then the same shall be printed in capital letters, so as to take up not more than two inches of space, which in all cases shall be added to the lengths of the ticket as established by said section of the Political Code; *provided*, that the provision of this section shall not be compulsory except in the city and county of San Francisco.

1877-8, 73.

An Act concerning Special Elections.

[Approved February 9, 1878.]

The People of the State of California, represented in Senate and Assembly, do enact as follows: .

SECTION 1. At any special election to be held in any county, except in the City and County of San Francisco, copies of the Great Register of such, county, and in the City and County of San Francisco copies of the ward registers of said city and county, which were printed before and used at the next preceding general election, shall be used.

SEC. 2. Before the day on which said special election is appointed to be held, the Board of Supervisors of the county, except the City and County of San Francisco, must furnish the Board of Election of each precinct in the county at least one copy of the aforesaid printed Great Register; and the Board of Supervisors of the City and County of San Francisco must furnish the Board of Election of each precinct in the county at least one copy of the ward register of the ward in which the precinct is located. If the Board cannot otherwise obtain a sufficient number of copies of the register for the purpose, it must take the copies filed in the office of the County Clerk, in pursuance of section twelve hundred and sixty-eight of the Political Code.

SEC. 3. If the copy of the register which shall be furnished to any preciret shall have been used at a previous election, the letter "V" may be used instead of the word "Voted," as required by section twelve hundred and twenty-eight of the Political Code.

SEC. 4. It shall not be the duty of the Board of Election to post copies of the Great Register, as required by section eleven hundred and forty-nine of the Political Code.

SEC. 5. The voter, when he offers his ballot at a polling place, shall not be required to announce his number on the Great Register, as provided for in section twelve hundred and twenty-five of the Political Code.

SEC. 6. This Act shall take effect immediately.

In addition to the foregoing, the following are general laws and provisions governing elections:

Constitution of the State of California, Art. II, Art. XX, Secs. 2, 10, 11, 12 and 13.

Political Code, Secs. 50, 51, 52, 1071, 1083, 1084, 1094, 1095, 1096, 1097, 1100, 1104, and Chapters V, VI, VII, VIII, IX, X and XI of Title II of Part III.

Revised Statutes of the United States, Secs. 5425, 5426, 5427, 5457, 5428, 5506, 5507, 5511, 5512, 5513 and 5515.

S U P P L E M E N T   C L X I I .

HEALTH AND QUARANTINE REGULATIONS FOR THE CITY AND HARBOR OF SAN FRANCISCO.

POLITICAL CODE, PART III, TITLE VII, CHAPTER III, ART. III.

SEC. 3004. The quarantine grounds of the Bay and harbor of San Francisco are at the anchorage of Saucelito.

SEC. 3005. The Board of Health for the City and County of San Francisco consists of the Mayor of the city and county and four physicians in good standing, residing in the City and County of San Francisco, appointed by the Governor and holding their office for the term of five years.

SEC. 3006. The Mayor is ex-officio President of the Board. The Board must meet monthly, and at such other times as the President may direct. In the absence of the President, the Board may elect a Chairman, who is clothed with the same powers as the President.

SEC. 3007. The Health Officer for the City and County and Port of San Francisco is elected by the Board of Health, and holds office at its pleasure. He must be a graduate of some medical college, in good standing, and must reside within the city limits of San Francisco.

SEC. 3008. Ths Health Officer is the executive officer of the Health Department, and he may, in his discretion, cause the removal to a hospital of any and all persons, within the limits of the City and County of San Francisco, infected with variola.

SEC. 3009. The Board of Health must appoint a Quarantine Officer, who shall be a physician in good standing, a Secretary, one Assistant Secretary,

23

six Health Inspectors, one Market Inspector, and one Messenger, whose duties must be fixed by the Board of Health. They must also appoint one Superintendent Physician, one Resident Physician, one Stewart, one Matron, one Apothecary, two Visiting Physicians, two Visiting Surgeons, as officers of the City and County Hospital in and for the City and County of San Francisco, one each of said Visiting Physicians and Surgeons to be nominated by the Faculty of the Medical Department of the University of California, and one each of said Visiting Physicians and Surgeons to be nominated by the Medical College of the Pacific. Said Board may also appoint one Engineer for the City and County Hospital. They may also appoint one Superintendent, one Resident Physician, one Matron, and such other employees as are now authorized by law to be employed in and for the Almshouse of said city and county. They shall also have power to appoint and prescribe the duties of one City Physician and one Assistant City Physician, who shall be designated as Police Surgeons, and whose duty it shall be to make all autopsies required of them by the Coroner of said city and county. And said Board is also empowered to appoint such employees and such medical attendants as they may deem necessary in the Health Department, and in all the various institutions which are by law placed under their supervision; and the compensation of such employees and medical attendants shall be fixed by the Board of Health. The appointing power aforesaid is vested solely in said Board of Health, and said Board shall have power to prescribe the duties of said appointees, and shall not remove the same without just cause. The heads of departments appointed by the Board of Health, to-wit, the Health Officer, Resident Physician of City and County Hospital, and Superintendent of Alms-house, shall not be removed except by a concurrence of four members of said Board of Health.

SEC. 3010. The following annual salaries are hereby allowed to the officers of the Health Department, and such other officers and employees as are mentioned in the preceding section, viz.: Health Officer, three thousand dollars; Quarantine Officer, eighteen hundred dollars; Secretary, twenty-one hundred dollars; Assistant Secretary, twelve hundred dollars; Health Inspectors, twelve hundred dollars each; Market Inspector, twelve hundred dollars; Messenger, nine hundred dollars; City Physician, eighteen hundred dollars; Assistant City Physician, twelve hundred dollars; all of said salaries, together with the salaries of such other employees of the Health Department as may be appointed by the Board of Health, must be paid in equal monthly installments out of the General Fund of the City and County of San Francisco, in the same manner as the salaries of the other officers of said city and county are paid. There shall be paid to the officers and employees of the City and County Hospital and Alms-house the following annual salaries, viz.: Superintendent Physician, twenty-four hundred dollars; Resident Physician, fifteen hundred dollars; Steward, fifteen hundred dollars; Matron, seven hundred and twenty dollars; one Apothecary, twelve hundred dollars; Visiting

Physicians and Surgeons, twelve hundred dollars each; Engineer, twelve hun dred dollars; Superintendent of Alms-house, twenty-four hundred dollars; Resident Physician of Alms-house, fifteen hundred dollars; Matron of Alms_ house, seven hundred and twenty dollars; and all other medical attendants and employees of said institutions are to be paid such sums as may be authorized by law, and as provided in the preceding section; all to be paid in equal monthly installments out of the Hospital and Alms-house Fund of said City and County of San Francisco; and the Auditor of said City and County is hereby directed to audit the said demands, payable out of the funds afore-said, upon the approval of the same by the said Board of Health, and also to audit all demands for salaries of medical attendants and employees ap-pointed by the Board of Health in accordance with this Chapter, for the amounts authorized to be paid, when the same shall have been approved by said Board; and the Treasurer of said city and county must pay said de-mands out of said funds. The Clerk of the Mayor of the City and County of San Francisco shall not receive any compensation as Clerk of the Board of Health.

Sec. 3011. The Health Officer, in addition to his salary, receives such sums for the necessary expenses of his office as the Board of Health may direct, and the Auditor must audit and the Treasurer pay such sums out of the General Fund. The Board of Supervisors must provide proper offices for the Health Department.

Sec. 3012. The Board of Health have general supervision of all matters appertaining to the sanitary condition of the city and county, including the City and County Hospital, the County Jail, Alms-house, Industrial School, and all public health institutions provided by the City and County of San Francisco, and may adopt such orders and regulations, and appoint or dis-charge such medical attendants and employees, as to them seems best to pro-mote the public welfare; and may appoint as many Health Inspectors as they deem necessary in time of epidemics.

Sec. 3013. Shipmasters bringing vessels into the Harbor of San Fran-cisco, and masters, owners, or consignees having vessels in the harbor which have on board any cases of Asiatic cholera, small-pox, yellow, typhus, or ship fever, must report the same, in writing, to the Quarantine Officer before land-ing any passengers, casting anchor, or coming to any wharf, or as soon there-after as they, or either of them, become aware of the existence of either of the diseases on board of their vessels.

Sec. 3014. No captain or other officer in command of any vessel sailing under a register, arriving at the Port of San Francisco, nor any owner, consignee, agent, or other person having charge of such vessel must, under a penalty of not less than one hundred dollars nor more than one thousand dollars, land, or permit to be landed, any freight, passengers, or other persons from such vessel until he has reported to the Quarantine Officer, presented his bill of health, and received a permit from that officer to land freight, passengers, or other persons.

SEC. 3015. Every pilot who conducts into the Port of San Francisco any vessel subject to quarantine or examination by the Quarantine Officer, must:

1. Bring the vessel no nearer the city than is allowed by law.

2. Prevent any person from leaving, and any communication being made with the vessel under his charge, until the Quarantine Officer has boarded her and given the necessary orders and directions.

3. Be vigilant in preventing any violation of the quarantine laws, and report, without delay, all such violations that come to his knowledge to the Quarantine Officer.

4. Present the master of the vessel with a printed copy of the quarantine laws, unless he has one.

5. If the vessel is subject to quarantine, by reason of infection, place at the mast-head a small yellow flag.

SEC. 3016. Every master of a vessel subject to quarantine or visitation by the Quarantine Officer, arriving in the Port of San Francisco, who refuses or neglects either:

1. To proceed with and anchor his vessel at the place assigned for quarantine, when legally directed so to do; or,

2. To submit his vessel, cargo, and passengers to the Quarantine Officer, and furnish all necessary information to enable that officer to determine what quarantine or other regulations they ought respectively to be subject; or,

3. To report all cases of disease and of deaths occurring on his vessel, and to comply with all the sanitary regulations of the bay and harbor—

Is liable in the sum of five hundred dollars for every such neglect or refusal. [See also Section 376 of Penal Code.]

SEC. 3017. All vessels arriving off the Port of San Francisco from ports which have been legally declared infected ports, and all vessels arriving from ports where there is prevailing at the time of their departure, any contagious, infectious, or pestilential diseases, or vessels with decaying cargoes, or which have unusually foul or offensive holds, are subject to quarantine, and must be, by the master, owner, pilot, or consignee, reported to the Quarantine Officer without delay. No such vessel must cross a right line drawn from Meiggs' wharf to Alcatraz Island until the Quarantine Officer has boarded her and given the order required by law.

SEC. 3018. The Quarantine Officer must board every vessel, subject to quarantine or visitation by him, immediately on her arrival, make such examination and inspection of vessel, books, papers, or cargo, or of persons on board, under oath, as he may judge expedient, and determine whether the vessel should be ordered to quarantine, and if so, the period of quarantine.

SEC. 3019. No captain or other officer in command of any passenger-carrying vessel of more than one hundred and fifty tons burden, nor of any vessel of more than one hundred and fifty tons burden, having passengers on board, nor any owner, consignee, agent, or other person having charge of such vessel or vessels, must, under a penalty of not less than one hundred dollars nor more than one thousand dollars, land, or permit to be landed, any passenger from the vessel until he has presented his bill of health to the Quarantine Officer and received a permit from that officer to land such passenger, except in such case as the Quarantine Officer deems it safe to give the permit before seeing the bill of health.

SEC. 3020. The following fees may be collected by the Quarantine Officer: For giving a permit to land freight or passengers, or both, from any sailing vessel of less than five hundred tons burden, from any port out of this State, two dollars and fifty cents; over five hundred and under one thousand tons burden, five dollars; each additional one thousand tons burden or fraction thereof, an additional two dollars and fifty cents; for steam vessels, propelled in whole or in part by steam, of one thousand tons burden or less, five dollars, and two dollars and fifty cents for each additional one thousand tons burden or fraction thereof; but vessels not propelled in whole or part by steam, sailing to and from any port or ports of the Pacific States, or the United States, or Territories, and whaling vessels entering the harbor of San Francisco, are excepted from the provisions of this section.

SEC. 3021. The Board of Health may enforce compulsory vaccination on passengers in infected ships or coming from infected ports.

SEC. 3022. The Board of Health may provide suitable hospitals, to be situated at or near Saucelito, and furnish and supply the same with nurses and attaches, and remove thereto all persons afflicted with cholera, smallpox, yellow, typhus, or ship fever.

SEC. 3023. The Health Officer must keep a record of all births, deaths and interments occurring in the City and County of San Francisco. Such records, when filed, must be deposited in the office of the County Recorder, and produced when required for public inspection.

SEC. 3024. Physicians and midwives must, on or before the fourth day of each month, make a return to the Health Officer of all births, deaths, and the number of still-born children occurring in their practice during the preceding month. In the absence of such attendants, the parent must make such report within thirty days after the birth of the child. Such returns must be made in accordance with rules adopted, and upon blanks furnished by the Board of Health.

SEC. 3025. No person shall deposit in any cemetery, or inter in the City and County of San Francisco, any human body, without first having obtained and filed with the Health Officer a certificate, signed by a physician, or midwife, or a Coroner, setting forth as near as possible, the name, age, color, sex, place of birth, occupation, date, locality, and the cause of death of the deceased, and obtain from such Health Officer a permit; nor shall any human body be removed or disinterred without the permit of the Health Officer, or by order of the Coroner. Physicians, when deaths occur in their practice, must give the certificate herein mentioned. Hereafter it shall be the duty of the Assistant City Physician, or Police Surgeons, to perform all autopsies which may be required in the Coroner's office of the City and County of San Francisco, all such autopsies being made without charge to the city. It shall be the duty of the Health Officer to see that the dead body of a human being is not allowed to remain in any public receiving vault for a longer period than five days. At the expiration of that time he shall cause the body to be placed in a vault or niche constructed of brick, stone, or iron, and hermetically sealed. It shall also be his duty to require all persons having in charge the digging of graves and burial of the dead to see that the body of no human being who had reached ten years of age shall be interred in a grave less than six feet deep, or if under the age of ten years, the grave to be not less than five feet deep.

SEC. 3026. Superintendents of cemeteries, within the boundaries of the City and County of San Francisco, must return to the Health Officer, on each Monday, the names of all persons interred or deposited within their respective cemeteries for the preceding week.

SEC. 3027. No Superintendent of a cemetery can remove or cause to be removed, disinter or cause to be disinterred, any corpse that has been deposited in the cemetery, without a permit from the Health Officer, or by order of the Coroner.

SEC. 3028. Whenever a nuisance shall exist on the property of any non-resident or any property, the owner or owners of which cannot be found by either Health Inspector, after diligent search, or on the property of any owner or owners, upon whom due notice may have been served, and who shall, for three days, refuse or neglect to abate the same, or on any city property, it shall be the duty of the Board of Health to cause the said nuisance to be at once removed or abated, and to draw upon the General Fund for such sums as may be required for its removal or abatement, not to exceed two hundred dollars; *provided*, that whenever a larger expenditure is found necessary to be made for the removal or suppression of any nuisance, the Board of Supervisors of said city and county shall, upon the written application of the Board of Health, by ordinance, appropriate, allow, and order paid out of the General Fund, such sum or sums as may be necessary for that purpose, and the Auditor shall audit, and the Treasurer shall pay all appropriations of money made in pursuance of this section, in the same manner as is now provided by law for auditing and paying demands upon the treasury; said sum or sums so paid shall become a lien on the property from which said nuisance has been removed or abated in pursuance of this section, and may be recovered by action against such property. And it shall be the duty of the City and County Attorney to foreclose all such liens in the proper Court, in the name of and for the benefit of said city and county, and when the property is sold enough of the proceeds shall be paid into the city and county treasury to satisfy the lien and costs, and the overplus, if any there be, shall be paid to the owner of the property, if he be known, and if not, then into the Court for his use when ascertained. The Board of Health is hereby vested with power to act upon, define, determine, and adjudge what shall constitute a nuisance in said city and county, and to require the same to be abated in a summary manner. Any person who maintains, permits or allows a nuisance to exist upon his or her property or premises, after the same has been determined by said Board to be a nuisance, after notice to remove the same has been served upon such person, is guilty of a misdemeanor, and shall be punished accordingly; and each day of such existence, after notice, shall be deemed a separate and distinct offense, and it is the duty of the Health Officer to prosecute all persons guilty of violating this law by continuous prosecutions until the same is abated and removed.

SEC. 3029. The Health Officer must keep in his office a book in which he must make an entry of all fees collected by him. He must pay all fees collected to the City and County Treasurer weekly, to the credit of the General Fund.

SEC. 3030. The Health officer must execute an official bond, to be approved by the Board of Health, in the sum of ten thousand dollars.

SEC. 3031. Any member of the Board of Health, Health Officer, or Quarantine Officer, or Secretary, or Assistant Secretary of the Health Department, is empowered to administer oaths on business connected with that Department.

SEC. 3032. Whenever any cause of action arises under any of the provisions of this chapter, suit may be maintained therein, in the name of the Health Officer, in any District Court of this State.

SEC. 3033. Whenever it shall be certified to the Board of Health, by the Health Officer, that any building, or part thereof, is unfit for human habitation, by reason of its being so infected with disease as to be likely to cause sickness among the occupants, or by reason of its want of repair has become dangerous to life, said Board may issue an order, and cause the same to be affixed conspicuously on the building, or part thereof, and to be personally served upon the owner, agent or lessee, if the same can be found in this State, requiring all persons therein to vacate such building, for the reasons to be stated therein as aforesaid. Such building, or part thereof, shall, within ten days thereafter be vacated, or within such shorter time, not less than twenty-four hours, as in said notice may be specified; but said Board, if it shall become satisfied that the danger from said house, or part thereof, has ceased to exist, may revoke said order, and it shall thenceforward become inoperative.

SEC. 3034. *One*—Every physician in the city and county shall report to the Health Officer, in writing, every patient he shall have laboring under Asiatic cholera, variola, diphtheria, or scarlatina, immediately thereafter, and report to the same officer every case of death from such disease, immediately after it shall have occurred.

Two—Every household in said city and county shall forthwith report, in writing, to the Health Officer, the name of every person boarding or an inmate at his or her house, whom he or she shall have reason to believe sick of cholera or small-pox, and any deaths occurring at his or her house from such disease.

SEC. 3035. The Board of Health shall have entire charge of the City Cemetery, and shall employ a Superintendent, at a salary of seventy-five dollars per month, the same to be paid as the salaries· of other employees are paid.

*   *   *   *   *   *   *   *   *

SEC. 3084. Whenever, by existing law, or by ordinance of any incorporated city, or city and county, or by ordinance or resolution of the Board of Supervisors of any county, a permit is required from a Board of Health, Health Officer, or other officer or person, before depositing or burial in any cemetery of any human body, such permit shall not be granted without the production and filing with such Board of Health, Health Officer, or other authorized officer or person, a certificate, signed by a physician, or a Coroner, or two reputable citizens, setting forth, as near as possible, the name, age, color, sex, place of birth, occupation, date, locality, and the cause of death of the deceased. And no certificate shall be received, upon which to grant such permit, unless signed by a physician, Coroner, or two reputable citizens, registered as such under his proper signature at the office of such Board of Health, Health Officer, or other authorized officer or person.

The following section of an Act passed March 16, 1876, Statutes 1875–6, p. 305, appears to be still in force:

SECTION 4. No person, master, captain, or conductor in charge of any boat, vessel, railroad car, or public or private conveyance, shall receive for transportation, or shall transport the body of any person who has died within the limits of the City and County of San Francisco, without obtaining a permit for the same from the Health Officer, which permit shall accompany the body to its destination; and no person, master, captain or conductor, as aforesaid, shall bring into or transport through the said city and county, the dead body of any person, unless it be accompanied with a certificate from some proper authority of the place whence it came, stating name, age, sex and cause of death, which certificate shall be filed at the Health Office; provided, that in no case shall the body of any person who died of a contagious disease be brought to the city within one year of the day of death.

SUPPLEMENT CLXIII.

REVENUE AND TAXATION.

STATE CONSTITUTION ART. XIII.

SECTION 1. All property in the State, not exempt under the laws of the United States, shall be taxed in proportion to its value, to be ascertained as provided by law. The word "property," as used in this article and section, is hereby declared to include moneys, credits, bonds, stocks, dues, franchises, and all other matters and things, real, personal, and mixed, capable of private ownership; *provided*, that growing crops, property used exclusively for public schools, and such as may belong to the United States, this State, or to any county or municipal corporation within this State, shall be exempt from taxation. The Legislature may provide, except in case of credits secured by mortgage or trust deed, for a deduction from credits of debts due to bona fide residents of this State

SEC. 2. Land, and the improvements thereon, shall be separately assessed. Cultivated and uncultivated land, of the same quality, and similarly situated, shall be assessed at the same value.   *   *

SEC. 4. A mortgage, deed of trust, contract, or other obligation by which a debt is secured, shall, for the purposes of assessment and taxation, be deemed and treated as an interest in the property affected thereby. Except as to railroad and other quasi-public corporations, in case of debts so secured, the value of the property affected by such mortgage, deed of trust, contract, or obligation, less the value of such security, shall be assessed and taxed to the owner of the property, and the value of such security shall be assessed and taxed to the owner thereof, in the county, city, or district in which the property affected thereby is situate. The taxes so levied shall be a lien upon the property and security, and may be paid by either party to such security; if paid by the owner of the security, the tax so levied upon the property affected thereby shall become a part of the debt so secured; if the owner of the property shall pay the tax so levied on such security, it shall constitute a payment thereon, and to the extent of such payment a full discharge thereof; *provided*, that if any such security or indebtedness shall be paid by any such debtor or debtors, after assessment and before the tax levy, the amount of such levy may likewise be retained by such debtor or debtors, and shall be computed according to the tax levy for the preceding year.

SEC. 5. Every contract hereafter made, by which a debtor is obligated to pay any tax or assessment on money loaned, or on any mortgage, deed of trust, or other lien, shall, as to any interest specified therein, and as to such tax or assessment, be null and void.

SEC. 6. The power of taxation shall never be surrendered or suspended by any grant or contract to which the State shall be a party.

SEC. 7. The Legislature shall have the power to provide, by law, for the payment of all taxes on real property by installments.

SEC. 8. The Legislature shall, by law, require each taxpayer in this State to make and deliver to the County Assessor, annually, a statement, under oath, setting forth specifically all the real and personal property owned by such taxpayer, or in his possession, or under his control, at twelve o'clock meridian on the first Monday of March.

SEC. 9. A State Board of Equalization, consisting of one member from each Congressional District in this State, as the same existed in eighteen hundred and seventy-nine, shall be elected by the qualified electors of their respective districts, at the general election to be held in the year one thousand eight hundred and eighty-six, and at each gubernatorial election thereafter, whose term of office shall be for four years; whose duty it shall be to equalize the valuation of the taxable property in the several counties of the State for the purposes of taxation. The Controller of State shall be ex officio a member of the Board. The Boards of Supervisors of the several counties of the State shall constitute Boards of Equalization for their respective counties, whose duty it shall be to equalize the valuation of the taxable property in the county for the purpose of taxation; *provided*, such State and County Boards of Equalization are hereby authorized and empowered, under such rules of notice as the County Boards may prescribe, as to the county assessments, and under such rules of notice as the State Board may prescribe as to the action of the State Board, to increase or lower the entire assessment roll, or any assessment contained therein, so as to equalize the assessment of the property contained in said assessment roll, and make the assessment conform to the true value in money of the property contained in said roll; *provided*, that no Board of Equalization shall raise any mortgage, deed of trust, contract, or other obligation by which a debt is secured, money, or solvent credits, above its face value. The present State Board of Equalization shall continue in office until their successors, as herein provided for, shall be elected and shall qualify. The Legislature shall have power to redistrict the State into four districts as nearly equal in population as practical, and to provide for the elections of members of said Board of Equalization. [Amendment adopted November 4, 1884.]

SEC. 10. All property, except as hereinafter in this section provided, shall be assessed in the county, city, city and county, town, township, or district in which it is situated, in the manner prescribed by law. The franchise, roadway, roadbed, rails, and rolling stock of all railroads operated in more than one county in this State shall be assessed by the State Board of Equalization, at their actual value, and the same shall be apportioned to the counties, cities and counties, cities, towns, townships, and districts in which such railroads are located, in proportion to the number of miles of railway laid in such counties, cities and counties, cities, towns, townships, and districts.

SEC. 11. Income taxes may be assessed to and collected from persons, corporations, joint-stock associations, or companies resident or doing business in this State, or any one or more of them, in such cases and amounts and in such manner as shall be prescribed by law.

SEC. 12. The Legislature shall provide for the levy and collection of an annual poll tax of not less than two dollars on every male inhabitant of this State, over twenty-one and under sixty years of age, except paupers, idiots, insane persons, and Indians not taxed. Said tax shall be paid into the State School Fund.

SEC. 13. The Legislature shall pass all laws necessary to carry out the provisions of this article.

POLITICAL CODE.

PART III, TITLE IX, CHAPTER I.

PROPERTY LIABLE TO TAXATION.

SEC. 3607. All property in this State, not exempt under the laws of the United States, excepting growing crops, properly used exclusively for public schools, and such as may belong to the United States, this State, or to any county, or municipal corporation within this State, is subject to taxation as in this Code provided; but nothing in this Code shall be construed to require or permit double taxation.

SEC. 3608. Shares of stock in corporations possess no intrinsic value over and above the actual value of the property of the corporation which they stand for and represent, and the assessment and taxation of such shares and also of the corporate property would be double taxation. Therefore, all property belonging to corporations shall be assessed and taxed, but no assessment shall be made of shares of stock, nor shall any holder thereof be taxed therefor.

CHAPTER II.

DEFINITIONS.

SEC. 3617. Whenever the terms mentioned in this section are employed in this Act they are employed in the sense hereafter affixed to them:—

First—The term "property" includes moneys, credits, bonds, stocks, dues, franchises, and all other matters and things, real, personal, and mixed, capable of private ownership.

Second—The term "real estate" includes:

1. The possession of, claim to, ownership of, or right to, the possession of land.

2. All mines, minerals, and quarries in and under the land, all timber belonging to individuals or corporations growing or being on the lands of the United States, and all rights and privileges appertaining thereto.

3. A mortgage, deed of trust, contract, or other obligation by which a debt is secured, when land is pledged for the payment and discharge thereof, shall, for the purpose of assessment and taxation, be deemed and treated as an interest in the land so pledged.

4. Improvements.

Third—The term "improvements" includes:

1. All buildings, structures, fixtures, fences, and improvements erected upon or affixed to the land.

2. All fruit, nut-bearing or ornamental trees and vines not of natural growth.

Fourth—The term "personal property" includes everything which is the subject of ownership not included within the meaning of the term "real estate."

Fifth—The terms "value" and "full cash value" mean the amount at which the property would be taken in payment of a just debt due from a solvent debtor.

Sixth—The term "credits" means those solvent debts, not secured by mortgage or trust deed, owing to the person, firm, corporation, or association assessed. The term "debts" means those unsecured liabilities owing by the person, firm, corporation, or association assessed to bona fide residents of this State, or firms, associations, or corporations doing business therein; but credits, claims, debts, and demands due, owing, or accruing for or on account of money deposited with savings and loan corporations shall, for the purpose of taxation, be deemed, and treated as an interest in the property of such corporation, and shall not be assessed to the creditor or owner thereof.

CHAPTER III.

ASSESSMENT OF PROPERTY.

SEC. 3627. All taxable property must be assessed at its full cash value Land and improvements thereon shall be separately assessed. Cultivated and uncultivated land of the same quality, and similarly situated, shall be assessed at the same value. A mortgage, deed of trust, contract, or other obligation by which a debt is secured, shall, for the purposes of assessment and taxation, be deemed and treated as an interest in the property affected thereby, except as to railroad and other quasi-public corporations. In case of debts so secured, the value of the property affected by such mortgage, deed of trust, contract, or obligation, less the value of such security, shall be assessed and taxed to the owner of the property, and the value of such security shall be assessed and taxed to the owner thereof, in the county, city, or district in which the property affected thereby is situated. The taxes so levied shall be a lien upon the property and security, and may be paid by either party to such security; if paid by the owner of the security, the tax so levied upon the property affected thereby shall become a part of the debt so secured. If the owner of the property shall pay the tax so levied on such security, it shall constitute a payment thereon, and, to the extent of such payment, a full discharge thereof. If any such security or indebtedness shall be paid by any such debtor or debtors after assessment and before the tax levy, the amount of such levy may likewise be retained by such debtor or debtors, and shall be computed according to the tax levy for the preceding year; and every contract by which a debtor is obliged to pay any tax or assessment on money loaned, or on any mortgage, deed of trust, or other lien, shall, as to any interest specified therein, and as to such tax or assessment, be null and void.

SEC. 3628. The franchise, roadway, roadbed, rails, and rolling stock of all railroads operated in more than one county in this State, shall be assessed by the State Board of Equalization as hereinafter provided for. Other franchises, if granted by the authorities of a county, city, or city and county, must be assessed in the county, city, or city and county within which they were granted; if granted by any other authority they must be assessed in the county in which the corporations, firms, or persons owning or holding them have their principal place of business. All other taxable property shall be assessed in the county, city, city and county, town, township, or district in which it is situated. Land shall be assessed in parcels or subdivisions not exceeding six hundred and forty acres each, and tracts of land containing more than six hundred and forty acres, which have been sectionized by the United States Government, shall be assessed by sections or fractions of sections. The Assessor must, between the first Mondays of March and July in each year, ascertain the names of all taxable inhabitants, and all property in his county subject to taxation, except such as is required to be assessed by the State Board of Equalization, and must assess such property to the persons by whom it was owned or claimed, or in whose possession or control it was at twelve o'clock M. of the first Monday of March next preceding; but no mistake in the name of the owner, or supposed owner of real property, shall render the assessment thereof invalid. In assessing solvent credits not secured by mortgage or trust deed, a reduction therefrom shall be made of debts due to bona fide residents of this State.

SEC. 3629. He must exact from each person a statement, under oath, setting forth specifically all the real and personal property owned by such person, or in his possession, or under his control, at twelve o'clock M. on the first Monday in March. Such statement shall be in writing, showing separately:

1. All property belonging to, claimed by, or in the possession or under the control or management of such person.

2. All property belonging to, claimed by, or in the possession or under the control or management of any firm of which such person is a member.

3. All property belonging to, claimed by, or in the possession or under the control or management of any corporation of which such person is President, Secretary, Cashier, or managing agent.

4. The county in which such property is situated, or in which it is liable to taxation, and (if liable to taxation in the county in which the statement is made) also the city, town, township, school district, road district, or other revenue districts in which it is situated.

5. An exact description of all lands in parcels or subdivisions, not exceeding six hundred and forty acres each, and the sections and fractional sections of all tracts of land containing more than six hundred and forty acres, which have been sectionized by the United States Government, improvements and personal property, including all vessels, steamers, and other water craft, and all taxable State, county, city, or other municipal or public bonds, and the taxable bonds of any person, firm, or corporation, and deposits of money, gold dust, or other valuables, and the names of the persons with whom such deposits are made, and the places in which they may be found, all mortgages, deeds of trust, contracts, and other obligations by which a debt is secured and the property in the county affected thereby.

6. All solvent credits, unsecured by deed of trust, mortgage, or other lien on real or personal property, due or owing to such person, or any firm of which he is a member, or due or owing to any corporation of which he is President, Secretary, Cashier, or Managing Agent, deducting from the sum total of such credits such debts only, unsecured by trust deed, mortgage, or other lien on real or personal property, as may be owing by such person, firm, or corporation, to bona fide residents of this State. No debt shall be so deducted unless the statement shows the amount of such debt as

stated under oath in aggregate; *provided*, in case of banks the statement is not required to show the debt in detail, or to whom it is owing; but the Assessor shall have the privilege of examining the books of such banks to verify said statement. Whenever one member of a firm, or one of the proper officers of a corporation, has made a statement showing the property of the firm, or corporation, another member of the firm, or another officer, need not include such property in the statement made by him; but his statement must show the name of the person or officer who made the statement in which such property is included.

SEC. 3630. The Board of Supervisors must furnish the Assessor with "blank forms" of the statements provided for in the preceding section, affixing thereto an affidavit, which must be substantially as follows: " I, —— ——, do swear that I am a resident of the county of (naming it); that the above list contains a full and correct statement of all property subject to taxation which I, or any firm of which I am a member, or any corporation, association, or company of which I am President, Cashier, Secretary, or Managing Agent, owned, claimed, possessed, or controlled at 12 o'clock M. on the first Monday in March last, and which is not already assessed this year; and that I have not in any manner whatsoever transferred or disposed of any property, or placed any property out of said county, or my possession, for the purpose of avoiding any assessment upon the same, or of making this statement; and that the debts therein stated as owing by me are owing to bona fide residents of this State, or to firms or corporations doing business in this State." The affidavit to the statement on behalf of a firm or corporation must state the principal place of business of the firm or corporation, and in other respects must conform, substantially, to the preceding form.

SEC. 3631. The Assessor may fill out the statement at the time he presents it, or he may deliver it to the person and require him, within an appointed time, to return the same to him, properly filled out.

SEC. 3632. Every Assessor shall have power:

First—To require any person found within such Assessor's respective county to make and subscribe an affidavit, giving his name and place of residence.

Second—To subpœna and examine any person in relation to any statement furnished to him, or which discloses property which is assessable in his respective county; and he may exercise this power in any county where the persons whom he desires to examine may be found, but shall have no power to require such persons to appear before him in any other county than that in which the subpœna is served upon them. Every person who shall refuse to furnish the statement hereinbefore required in this chapter, or to make and subscribe such affidavit respecting his name and place of residence, or to appear and testify when requested so to do by the Assessor, as above provided, shall, for each and every refusal, and as often as the same is repeated, forfeit to the people of the State the sum of one hundred dollars, in gold coin of the United States, to be recovered by action brought in their name by the respective Assessor in any Police or Justice's Court. In case such affidavit shall show the residence of the person making the same to be in any county other than that in which it is taken, or the statement shall disclose property in any county other than that in which it is made, the Assessor shall, in the respective case, file the affidavit or statement in his office, and transmit a copy of the same, certified by him, to the Assessor of the county in which such residence or property is therein shown to be. One-half of all moneys recovered by any Assessor under the provisions of this section must by him be paid into the Treasury of his county, and the other half may be retained by the Assessor for his own use.

SEC. 3633. If any person, after demand made by the Assessor, neglects or refuses to give, under oath, the statement herein provided for, or to comply with the other requirements of this title, the Assessor must note the refusal on the assessment book, opposite his name, and must make an estimate of the value of the property of such person; and the value so fixed by the Assessor must not be reduced by the Board of Supervisors.

SEC. 3634. When the Assessor has not received from the owner of a tract of land the statement required by section three thousand six hundred and twenty-nine, or when such statement does not sufficiently describe a tract of land to enable the Assessor to assess the same as required by law, and the owner or his agent, or in case they cannot be found or are unknown, the person in possession thereof, neglects for ten days after demand by the Assessor to furnish said Assessor with such description, the Assessor shall cite such owner, or agent, or person in possession, to appear before the Superior Court of the county wherein such land is situated, within five days after service of such citation, and the said Superior Court shall, upon the day named in such citation, to the exclusion of all other business, proceed to hear the return and answer of the said owner, or agent, or person in possession, to the said citation; and if the Court shall find that the land has not been surveyed or divided into subdivisions of six hundred and forty acres, or less, so that each part or parcel may be described by metes and bounds, then the Court shall, by order duly entered in open Court, direct the County Surveyor to make a survey, and define the boundaries and location of said land by parcels or subdivisions not exceeding six hundred and forty acres each, and deliver the same to the County Assessor. The expense of making such survey and description by the County Surveyor shall be a lien upon the land, and shall, when approved by the said Superior Court, be certified by said Court to the Tax Collector of the county where the land is situated, and be added to the taxes upon said land, and be collected as other taxes are collected.

SEO. 3635. If the owner or claimant of any property, not listed by another person, is absent or unknown, the Assessor must make an estimate of the value of such property.

Sec. 3636. If the name of the absent owner is known to the Assessor, the property must be assessed in his name; if unknown, the property must be assessed to "unknown owners."

Sec. 3637. The Assessor, as soon as he receives a statement of any taxable property situated in another county, must make a copy of such statement for each county in which the same is situated, and transmit the same, by mail or express, to the Assessor of the proper county, who must assess the same as other taxable property therein.

Sec. 3638. All personal property consigned for sale to any person within this State from any place out of this State must be assessed as other property.

Sec. 3639. When a person is assessed as agent, trustee, bailee, guardian, executor, or administrator, his representative designation must be added to his name, and the assessment entered on a separate line from his individual assessment.

Sec. 3641. The property of every firm and corporation must be assessed in the county where the property is situate, and must be assessed in the name of the firm or corporation.

Sec. 3642. The undistributed or unpartitioned property of deceased persons may be assessed to the heirs, guardians, executors, or administrators; and a payment of taxes made by either binds all the parties in interest for their equal proportions.

Sec. 3643. A ferryboat is a vessel traversing across any of the waters of the State, between two constant points, regularly employed for the transfer of passengers and freight, authorized by law so to do, and also any boat employed as a part of the system of a railroad for the transfer of passengers and freight, plying at regular and stated periods between two points. Where ferries connect more than one county, the wharves, storehouses, and all stationary property belonging to or connected with such ferries, must be assessed, and the taxes paid, in the county where located. The value of the franchise, and watercraft, and of all toll bridges connecting more than one county, must be assessed in equal proportions in the counties connected by such ferries or toll bridges.

Sec. 3644. All vessels, except ferryboats, which may be registered, of every class which are by law required to be registered, must be assessed, and the taxes thereon paid, only in the county, or city and county, where the same are registered, enrolled, or licensed.

Sec. 3645. Vessels registered, licensed, or enrolled out of and plying in whole or in part in the waters of this State, the owners of which reside in this State, must be assessed in this State.

Sec. 3646. All boats and small craft not required to be registered, must be assessed in the county where their owner resides.

24

SEC. 3647. Money and property in litigation in possession of a County Treasurer, of a Court, County Clerk, or Receiver, must be assessed to such Treasurer, Clerk, or Receiver, and the taxes be paid thereon under the direction of the Court.

SEC. 3648. Any property willfully concealed, removed, transferred, or misrepresented by the owner or agent thereof, to evade taxation, upon discovery must be assessed at not exceeding ten times its value, and the assessment so made must not be reduced by the Board of Supervisors.

SEC. 3649. Any property discovered by the Assessor to have escaped assessment for the last preceding year, if such property is in the ownership or under the control of the same person who owned or controlled it for such preceding year, may be assessed at double its value.

SEC. 3650. The Assessor must prepare an assessment book, with appropriate headings, alphabetically arranged, unless otherwise directed by the State Board of Equalization, in which must be listed all property within the county, and in which must be specified in separate columns, under the appropriate head:

1. The name of the person to whom the property is assessed.

2. Land, by township, range, section, or fractional section; and when such land is not a congressional division or subdivision, by metes and bounds, or other description sufficient to identify it, giving an estimate of the number of acres (not exceeding in each and every tract, six hundred and forty acres), locality, and the improvements thereon. When any tract of land is situate in two or more school, road, or other revenue district of the county, the part in each township or district must be separately assessed, together with the improvements thereon.

3. City and town lots, naming the city or town, and the number of the lot and block, according to the system of numbering in such city or town, and improvements thereon.

4. All personal property, showing the number, kind, amount, and quality; but a failure to enumerate in detail such personal property, does not invalidate the assessment.

5. The cash value of real estate, other than city or town lots.

6. The cash value of improvements on such real estate.

7. The cash value of city and town lots.

8. The cash value of improvements on city and town lots.

9. The cash value of improvements on real estate assessed to persons other than the owners of the real estate.

10. The cash value of all personal property, exclusive of money.

11. The amount of money.

12. The assessment of the franchise, roadway, roadbed, rails, and rolling stock of any railroad, as apportioned to his county by the State Board of Equalization; and also such other apportionments of such franchises, road-

ways, roadbeds, rails, and rolling stock as may be made by such Board, and furnished to him for the purpose of taxation in any district in his county. Taxable improvements owned by any person, firm, association, or corporation, located upon land exempt from taxation, shall, as to the manner of assessment, be assessed as other real estate upon the assessment roll. No value shall, however, be assessed against the exempt land, nor under any circumstances shall the land be charged with or become responsible for the assessment made against any taxable improvements located thereon.

13. The school, road, and other revenue districts in which each piece of property assessed is situated.

14. The total value of all property.

15. When any property, except that owned by a railroad or other quasi-public corporation, is subject to, or affected by a mortgage, deed of trust, contract or other obligation by which a debt is secured, he must enter, in the proper column, the value of such security, and deduct the same. In entering assessments containing solvent credits subject to deductions, as provided in section three thousand six hundred and twenty-eight of this Code, he must enter, in the proper column, the value of the debts entitled to exemption, and deduct the same. In making the deductions from the total value of property assessed, as above directed, he must enter the remainder in the column provided for the total value of all property for taxation. Each franchise must be entered on the assessment roll without combining the same with other property or the valuation thereof.

16. The figure one (1), in separate columns, opposite the name of every person liable to pay a poll tax.

17. Such other things as the State Board of Equalization may require. The State Board of Equalization may direct the book to be otherwise than alphabetically arranged in any county or city and county of this State.

*　　*　　*　　*　　*　　*　　*　　*　　*　

SEC. 3651. The form of the assessment book shall be as directed by the State Board of Equalization, and in those counties, or cities and counties, for which said Board does not prescribe a different form, it must be substantially as follows:

[In the City and County of San Francisco the form is such as is directed by the State Board of Equalization.]

SEC. 3652. On or before the first Monday in July, in each year, the Assessor must complete his assessment book. He and his deputies must take and subscribe an affidavit in the assessment book, to be substantially as follows: "I, ——, Assessor of (or Deputy Assessor, as the case may be), —— County, do swear that between the first Monday in March and the first Monday in July, eighteen hundred and ——, I have made diligent inquiry and examination to ascertain all the property within the county (or within the subdivision thereof assessed by me, as the case may be), subject to assessment by me, and that the same has been assessed on the assessment

book, equally and uniformly, according to the best of my judgment, information, and belief, at its full cash value; and that I have faithfully complied
with all the duties imposed on the Assessor under the revenue laws; and
that I have not imposed any unjust or double assessment through malice or
ill-will, or otherwise; nor allowed any one to escape a just and equal assessment through favor, or reward, or otherwise." But the failure to take or
subscribe such an affidavit, or any affidavit, will not in any manner affect the
validity of the assessment.

SEC. 3653. The Assessor must, when directed so to do by the Board of
Supervisors, in a map-book make a plan of the various blocks within any
incorporated city or town, and mark thereon in each subdivison the name
of the person to whom it is assessed.

SEC. 3654. As soon as completed, the assessment book, together with the
map-book and statements, must be delivered to the Clerk of the Board of
Supervisors, who must immediately give notice thereof and of the time the
Board will meet to equalize assessments, by publication in a newspaper, if
any is printed in the county; if none, then in such manner as the Board
may direct; and in the meantime the assessment book must remain in his
office for the inspection of all persons interested.

SEC. 3655. On the first Monday in July in each year the Assessor of each
county must transmit to the State Board of Equalization a statement showing:

1. The several kinds of personal property;

2. The average and total value of each kind;

3. The number of live stock, number of bushels of grain, number of gal-
lons of wines or liquors, number of pounds or tons of any article sold by the
pound or ton;

4. When practicable, the separate value of each class of land, specifying
the classes and the number of acres in each.

SEC. 3656. Every Assessor who fails to complete his assessment book, or
who fails to transmit the statement mentioned in the preceding section to
the State Board of Equalization, forfeits the sum of one thousand dollars, to
be recovered on his official bond, for the use of the county.

SEC. 3657. Lands once described on the assessment book need not be
described a second time, but any person claiming the same, and desiring to
be assessed therefor, may have his name inserted with that of the person
to whom such land is assessed.

SEC. 3658. The Board of Supervisors must provide maps for the use of
the Assessor, showing the private lands owned or claimed in the county, and,
if surveyed under authority of the United States, the divisions and subdivisions of the survey; if held under Spanish grants, the exterior boundaries of
such grants and the number of acres claimed. Maps of cities and villages,
or school districts, may in like manner be provided. The cost of making
such maps is a county charge, and must be paid from the County General
Fund.

SEC. 3659.   On or before the first Monday in March in each year, the Surveyor General of the State and the Tide Land Commissioners must make out and transmit to the Assessor of each county where lands or lots he that may have been sold by the State, for which certificates of purchase, patents, or deeds have issued during the year preceding, certified lists of such lands or lots, giving a description thereof by congressional divisions or subdivisions, or lots and blocks, together with the names of the purchasers thereof.

SEC. 3660.   The Assessor and his sureties are liable on his official bonds for all taxes on property within the county, which, through his willful failure or neglect, is unassessed.

SEC. 3661.   The District Attorney must, after the Assessor completes the assessment book for the year, commence an action on the Assessor's bond for the amount of taxes lost from such willful failure or neglect.

SEC. 3662.   On the trial of such action, the value of the property unassessed being shown, judgment for the amount of taxes that should have been collected thereon must be entered.

SEC. 3663.   Water ditches constructed for mining, manufacturing, or irrigation purposes, and wagon or turnpike toll-roads, or telegraph lines, must be assessed the same as real estate by the Assessor of the county, at a rate per mile for that portion of such property as lies within his county.

SEC. 3664.   The President, Secretary, or Managing Agent, or such other officer as the State Board of Equalization may designate, of any corporation, and each person, or association of persons, owning or operating any railroad in more than one county in this State, shall, on or before the first Monday in April of each year, furnish the said Board a statement, signed and sworn to by one of such officers, or by the person or one of the persons forming such association, showing in detail for the year ending on the first Monday in March in each year:—

1.   The whole number of miles of railway in the State; and where the line is partly out of the State, the whole number of miles without the State, and the whole number within the State, owned or operated by such corporation, person, or association.

2.   The value of the roadway, roadbed, and rails of the whole railway, and the value of the same within the State.

3.   The width of the right of way.

4.   The number of each kind of all rolling stock used by such corporation, person, or association in operating the entire railway, including the part without the State.

5.   Number, kind, and value of rolling stock owned and operated in the State.

6.   Number, kind, and value of rolling stock used in the State, but owned by the party making the returns.

7.   Number, kind, and value of rolling stock owned, but used out of the State, either upon divisions of road operated by the party making the returns, or by and upon other railways.

Also, showing in detail for the year preceding the first of January:—

1.   The gross earnings of the entire road.

2.   The gross earnings of the road in the State, and where the railway is let to other operators, how much was derived by the lessor as rental.

3.   The cost of operating the entire, exclusive of Sinking Fund, expenses of land department, and money paid to the United States.

4.   Net income for such year, and amount of dividend declared.

5.   Capital stock authorized.

6.   Capital stock paid in.

7.   Funded debt.

8.   Number of shares authorized.

9.   Number of shares of stock issued.

10.   Any other facts the State Board of Equalization may require.

11.   A description of the road, giving the points of entrance into and the points of exit from each county, with a statement of the number of miles in each county.   When a description of the road shall once have been given no other annual description thereafter is necessary, unless the road shall have been changed.   Whenever the road, or any portion of the road, is advertised to be sold, or is sold, for taxes, either State or county, no other description is necessary than that given by, and the same is conclusive upon, the corporation, person, or association giving the description.   No assessment is invalid on account of a misdescription of the railway or the right of way for the same.   If such statement is not furnished as above provided the assessment made by the State Board of Equalization upon the property of the corporation, person, or association failing to furnish the statement is conclusive and final.   .

SEC. 3665.   The State Board of Equalization must meet at the State Capitol on the first Monday in August, and continue in open session from day to day, Sundays excepted, until the third Monday in August.   At such meeting the Board must assess the franchise, roadway, roadbed, rails, and rolling stock of all railroads operated in more than one county.   Assessment must be made to the corporation, person, or association of persons owning the same, and must be made upon the entire railway within the State, and must include the right of way, bridges, culverts, wharves, and moles upon which the track is laid, and all steamers which are engaged in transporting passengers, freights, and passenger and freight cars across waters which divide the road.   The depots, stations, shops, and buildings erected upon the space covered by the right of way are assessed by the Assessor of the county wherein they are situate.   Within ten days after the third Monday of August, the Board must apportion the total assessment of the franchise, roadway, roadbed, rails, and rolling stock of each railway to the counties, or cities and counties, in which such railway is located, in proportion to the number of miles of railway laid in such counties, and cities and counties. The Board must also, within said time, transmit by mail to the County Auditor of each county, or city and county, to which such apportionment shall have been made, a statement showing the length of the main track of such railway within the county, or city and county, with a description of the whole of the said track within the county, or city and county, including the right of way by metes and bounds or other description sufficient for identification, the assessed value per mile of the same as fixed by a pro rata distribution per mile of the assessed value of the whole franchise, roadway, roadbed, rails, and rolling stock of such railway within the State, 'and the amount apportioned to the county, or city and county. The Auditor must enter the statement on the assessment roll or book of the county, or city and county, and where the county is divided into assessorial townships or districts, then on the roll or book of any township or district he may select, and enter the amount of the assessment apportioned to the county, or city and county, in the column of the assessment book or roll as aforesaid, which shows the total value of all property for taxation either of the county, city and county, or such township or district. On the first Monday in October the Board of Supervisors must make, and cause to be entered in the proper record book, an order stating and declaring the length of main track of the railway assessed by the State Board of Equalization within the county; the assessed value per mile of such railway, the number of miles of track, and the assessed value of such railway lying in each city, town, township, school, and road district, or lesser taxing district in the county, or city and county, through which such railway runs, as fixed by the State Board of Equalization, which shall constitute the assessment value of said property for taxable purposes in such city, town, township, school, road, or other district; and the Clerk of the Board of Supervisors must transmit a copy of each order or equalization to the City Council or Trustees, or other legislative body of incorporated cities or towns, the Trustees of each school district, and the authorized authorities of other taxation districts through which such railway runs. All such railway property shall be taxable upon said assessment, at the same rates, by the same officers, and for the same purposes, as the property of individuals within such city, town, township, school, road, and lesser taxation districts, respectively. If the owner of a railway assessed by the State Board of Equalization is dissatisfied with the assessment made by the Board, such owner may, at the meeting of the Board, under the provision of section three thousand six hundred and ninety-two of the Political Code, between the third Monday in August and the third Monday in September, apply to the Board to have the same corrected in any particular, and the Board may correct and increase or lower the assessment made by it, so as to equalize the same with the assessment of other property in the State. If the Board shall increase or lower any assessment previously made by it, it must make a statement to the County Auditor of the county affected by the change in the assessment, of the change made, and the Auditor must note such change upon the assessment book or roll of the county as directed by the Board.

SEC. 3666. The State Board of Equalization must prepare each year a book, to be called "Record of Assessment of Railways," in which must be entered each assessment made by the Board, either in writing or by both writing and printing. Each assessment so entered must be signed by the Chairman and Clerk. The record of the apportionment of the assessments made by the Board to the counties, and cities and counties, must be made in a separate book, to be called "Record of Apportionment of Railway Assessments." In such last-described book must be entered the names of the railways assessed by the Board, the names of the corporation to which, or the name of the person or association to whom, each railway was assessed, the whole number of miles of the railway in the State, the number of miles thereof in each county, or city and county, the total assessment of the franchise, roadway, roadbed, rails, and rolling stock for the purposes of State taxation, and the amount of the apportionment of such total assessment to each county, and city and county, for county and city and county taxation. Before the third Monday of October of each year the Clerk of the State Board of Equalization must prepare and transmit to the Controller of State duplicates of the "Record of Assessment of Railways," and "Record of Apportionment of Railway Assessments," each certified by the Chairman and Clerk of the Board, and to be known respectively, as "Duplicate Record of Assessment of Railways" and "Duplicate Record of Apportionment of Railway Assessments." In the last-named duplicate two columns must be added, in one of which the Controller must enter the State taxes due the State upon the whole assessment by each corporation, person, or association, and in the other the county, or city and county, taxes due upon the assessment apportioned to each county, or city and county, by each corporation, person, or association. The two duplicates constitute the warrant for the Controller to collect the State and county, and city and county, taxes levied upon such property assessed by the Board, and the amount of the apportionment of the assessment to each county, and city and county, respectively.

SEC. 3667. When the Board of Supervisors of each county, and city and county, to which the State Board of Equalization has apportioned the assessment of railways shall have fixed the rate of county, or city and county, taxation, the Clerk of the Board of Supervisors must forthwith by mail, postage-paid, transmit to the Controller a statement of the rate of taxation levied by the Board of Supervisors for county, or city and county, taxation. If the Clerk fails to transmit such statement, the Controller must obtain the information as to such rate of taxation from other sources. On or before the fourth Monday of October the Controller must compute and enter in separate money columns in the "Duplicate Record of Apportionment of Railway Assessments" the respective sums, in dollars and cents, rejecting fractions of a cent, to be paid by the corporation, person, or association liable therefor·

as the State tax upon the total amount of the assessment, and the county, or city and county, tax upon the apportionment of the assessment to each county, and city and county, of the property assessed to such corporation, person, or association named in said duplicate record.

SEC. 3668. Within ten days after the fourth Monday in October, the Controller must publish a notice for two weeks in one daily newspaper of general circulation at the State capital, and in two daily newspapers of general circulation published in the city of San Francisco, specifying:—

1. That he has received from the State Board of Equalization the "Duplicate Record of Assessments of Railways" and the "Duplicate Record of Apportionment of Railway Assessments."

2. That the taxes are now payable and will be delinquent on the last Monday in December next, at six o'clock P. M., and that unless paid to the State Treasurer at the Capitol prior thereto, five per cent. will be added to the amount thereof. On the last Monday of December of each year, at six o'clock P. M., all of unpaid taxes are delinquent, and thereafter there must be collected by the State Treasurer or other proper officer an addition of five per centum, which sum when collected must be set aside by the Treasurer as a fund with which to pay the contingent expenses of actions against any delinquents, the said expenses to be audited by the Board of Examiners. When any taxes are paid to the State Treasurer by order of the Controller, upon assessments made and apportioned by the State Board of Equalization, the Controller must forthwith notify the Auditor and Treasurer respectively of each county, and city and county, that such taxes have been paid, and of the amount thereof to which each county and city and county interested is entitled. The State's portion of the taxes must be distributed by the Treasurer to each fund entitled thereto, and the portion belonging to the counties, and cities and counties, must be placed in a fund, to be called "Railway Tax Fund," to the credit of each county, and city and county, entitled thereto. When any taxes are placed in the "Railway Tax Fund" to the credit of a county, or city and county, the Controller, at the next settlement with the Controller by the Treasurer of such county, or city and county, must draw and deliver to such Treasurer, his warrant upon the State Treasurer for the amount in the fund to the credit of such county, or city and county.

SEC. 3669. Each corporation, person, or association assessed by the State Board of Equalization must pay to the State Treasurer, upon the order of the Controller, as other moneys are required to be paid into the Treasury, the State and county, and city and county, taxes each year levied upon the property so assessed to it or him by said Board. Any corporation, person, or association, dissatisfied with the assessment made by the Board, upon the payment of the taxes due upon the assessment complained of, and the five per cent. added, if to be added, on or before the first Monday in February, and the filing of notice with the Controller of an intention to begin an action, may, not later than the first Monday of February, bring an action against the

State Treasurer for the recovery of the amount of taxes and percentage so paid to the Treasurer, or any part thereof, and in the complaint may allege any fact tending to show the illegality of the tax, or of the assessment upon which the taxes are levied in whole or in part. A copy of the complaint and of the summons must be served upon the Treasurer within ten days after the complaint has been filed, and the Treasurer has thirty days within which to demur or answer. At the time the Treasurer demurs or answers he may demand that the action be tried in the Superior Court of the county of Sacramento. The Attorney-General must defend the action. The provisions of the Code of Civil Procedure relating to pleadings, proofs, trials, and appeals are applicable to the proceedings herein provided for. If the final judgment be against the Treasurer, upon presentation of a certified copy of such judgment to the Controller he shall draw his warrant upon the State Treasurer, who must pay to the plaintiff the amount of the taxes so declared to have been illegally collected, and the cost of such action, audited by the Board of Examiners, must be paid out of any money in the General Fund of the Treasury, which is hereby appropriated; and the Controller may demand and receive from the county, or city and county. interested the proportion of such costs, or may deduct such proportion from any money then, or to become due to said county, or city and county. Such action must be begun on or before the first Monday in February of the year succeeding the year in which the taxes were levied, and a failure to begin such action is deemed a waive of the rights of action.

Sec. 3670. After the first Monday of February of each year, the Controller must begin an action in the proper court, in the name of the people of the State of California, to collect the delinquent taxes upon the property assessed by the State Board of Equalization; such suit must be for the taxes due the State, and all the counties, and cities and counties, upon property assessed by the Board of Equalization, and appearing delinquent upon the "Duplicate Record of Apportionment of Railway Assessments." The demands for State and county, and city and county, taxes may be united in one action. In such action a complaint in the following form is sufficient:—

(Title of Court.)
The People of the State of California
vs.
(Naming the defendant.)

Plaintiff avers that on the —— day of ——, in the year (naming the year), the State Board of Equalization assessed the franchise, roadway, roadbed, rails, and rolling stock of the defendant at the sum of (naming it) dollars. That the Board apportioned the said assessment as follows: To the county of (naming it) the sum of (naming it) dollars (and so on, naming each county).

That the defendant is indebted to plaintiff for State and county taxes for the year eighteen ——, in the following sums: For State taxes, in the sum of (naming it) dollars; for county taxes of the county of (naming it), in the sum of (naming it) dollars, etc., with five per cent added for non-payment of taxes. Plaintiff demands payment for said several sums, and prays that an attachment may issue in form as prescribed in section five hundred and forty of the Code of Civil Procedure.

(Signed by the Controller or his attorney.)

On the filing of such complaint, the Clerk must issue the writ of attachment prayed for, and such proceedings shall be had as under writs of attachments issued in civil actions; no bond nor affidavit previous to the issuing of the attachment is required. If in such action the plaintiff recover judgment, there shall be included in the judgment as counsel fees, and in case of judgment of taxes after suit brought but before judgment the defendant must pay as counsel fees such sum as the Court may determine to be reasonable and just. Payment of the taxes or the amount of the judgment in the case must be made to the State Treasurer. In such actions the Duplicate Record of Assessments of Railways and the Duplicate Record of Apportionment of Railway Assessments, or a copy of them, certified by the Controller, showing unpaid taxes against any corporation, person, or association for property assessed by the State Board of Equalization, is *prima facie* evidence of the assessment, the property assessed, the delinquency, the amount of the taxes due and unpaid to the State and counties, or cities and counties therein named, and that the corporation, person, or association is indebted to the people of the State of California in the amount of taxes, State and county, and city and county, therein appearing unpaid, and that all the forms of law in relation to the assessment and levy of such taxes have been complied with.

SEC. 3671.   The assessment made by the County Assessor, and that of the State Board of Equalization, as apportioned by the Boards of Supervisors to each city, town, township, school, road, or other district in their respective counties, or cities and counties, shall be the only basis of taxation for the county, or any subdivision thereof, except in incorporated cities and towns, and may also be taken as such basis in incorporated cities and towns when the proper authorities may so elect. All taxes upon townships, road, school, or other local districts shall be collected in the same manner as county taxes.

CHAPTER IV.

EQUALIZATION OF TAXES.

ARTICLE I.

COUNTY BOARDS OF EQUALIZATION.

SEC. 3672.   The Board of Supervisors of each county must meet on the first Monday of July in each year, to examine the assessment book and equalize the assessment of property in the county. It must continue in session for that purpose from time to time until the business of equalization is disposed of, but not later than the fourth Monday in July.

SEC. 3673. The Board has power, after giving notice in such manner as it may, by rule, prescribe, to increase or lower the entire assessment roll, or any assessment contained therein, so as to equalize the assessment of the property contained in said roll, and make the assessment conform to the true value of such property in money.

SEC. 3674. No reduction must be made in the valuation of property, unless the party affected thereby, or his agent, makes and files with the Board a written application therefor, verified by his oath, showing the facts upon which it is claimed such reduction should be made.

SEC. 3675. Before the Board grants the application, or makes any reduction applied for, it must first examine, on oath, the person or the agent making the application, touching the value of the property of such person. No reduction must be made unless such person or the agent making the application attends and answers all questions pertinent to the inquiry.

SEC. 3676. Upon the hearing of the application the Board may subpœna such witnesses, hear and take such evidence in relation to the subject pending, as in its discretion it may deem proper.

SEC. 3677. During the session of the Board the Assessor and deputy whose testimony is needed must be present, and may make any statement, or introduce and examine witnesses on questions before the Board.

SEC. 3678. To assist the Assessor in the performance of his duties, the Recorder must annually transmit to the Assessor, on or before the first Monday in April, a complete abstract of all mortgages, deeds of trust, contracts, and other obligations by which any debt is secured, remaining unsatisfied on the records of his office, not barred by the statute of limitation, at twelve o'clock meridian, on the first Monday in March of said year. Such abstract shall be written under appropriate headings, to embrace all information requisite for the Assessor, in a book or books to be furnished by the Board of Supervisors upon the requisition of the Assessor. Should any such list be found to contain any instrument relating to lands situated in more than one county, it shall the duty of the Assessor to transmit to the State Board of Equalization all information relating thereto; and it shall be the duty of the said Board to attach an apportionment of valuation of such instrument to be assessed in each county, and the Board shall transmit to the Assessor of each county mentioned as affected in said instrument a statement of valuation of assessment to be levied against said instrument in each county. The valuation so set by said Board shall be final, and the Assessor shall accept said valuation and charge said assessment upon said instrument accordingly. Should the said list contain any instrument mortgaging or pledging two or more subdivisions of land, or land assessed in two or more subdivisions, in the same county, township, district, or city, the Assessor shall apportion the amount of assessment to be deducted from each subdivision on account of assessment against said instrument. Any assessment on a mortgage or deed of trust, which has been erroneously taxed to the mortgagee or party loaning the money, when the same has been paid or satisfied prior to the first Monday in March, shall be valid only as against the real estate from the assessment on which a deduction had been previously made. When partial payments have been made on a debt, secured by mortgage or deed of trust, the owner is authorized to make the proper deduction, listing only the balance due on the first Monday in March. When necessary, the Board of Supervisors of each county must provide for the payment of such additional clerical force as may be required to enable the County Recorder to comply with this section.

SEC. 3679. The Board must use the abstract and all other information it may gain from the records of the County Recorder or elsewhere, in equalizing the assessment of the property of the county, and may require the Assessor to enter upon the assessment book any property which has not been assessed; and any assessment made as prescribed in this section has the same force and effect as if made by the Assessor before the delivery of the assessment book to the Clerk of the Board.

SEC. 3081. During the sessions of the Board, it may direct the Assessor to assess any taxable property that has escaped assessment, or to add to the amount, number, or quantity of property when a false or incomplete list has been rendered, and to make and enter new assessments (at the same time canceling previous entries) when any assessment made by him is deemed by the Board so incomplete as to render doubtful the collection of the tax; but the Clerk must notify all persons interested, by letter deposited in the Post Office, or Express, post-paid, and addressed to the person interested, at least ten days before action taken, of the day fixed when the matter will be investigated.

SEC. 3682. The Clerk of the Board must record, in a book to be kept for that purpose, all changes, corrections, and orders made by the Board, and during its session, or as soon as possible after its adjournment, must enter upon the assessment book all changes and corrections made by the Board, and on or before the first Monday of August must deliver the assessment so corrected to the County Auditor, and accompany the same with an affidavit thereto affixed, subscribed by him, as follows:

" I, —— ——, do solemnly swear that, as Clerk of the Board of Supervisors of ———— county, I have kept correct minutes of all the acts of the Board touching alterations in the assessment book; that all alterations agreed to or directed to be made have been made and entered in the book, and that no changes or alterations have been made therein except those authorized."

ARTICLE II.

SEC. 3692. The powers and duties of the State Board of Equalization are as follows:

5. To annually assess the franchise, roadway, roadbed, rails, and rolling stock of all railroads operated in more than one county in this State, at their actual value, on the first Monday in March, at twelve o'clock M., and to apportion such assessment to the counties, and cities and counties, in which such railroads are located, in proportion to the number of miles of railway laid in such counties, and cities and counties, in the manner provided for in section three thousand six hundred and sixty-four of said Code.

6. To equalize the assessment of each mortgage, deed of trust, contract, or other obligation by which a debt is secured, and which affects property situate in two or more counties, and to apportion the assessment thereof to each of said counties.

7. To transmit to the Assessor of each county, or city and county, its apportionment of the assessments made by said Board upon the franchises, roadways, roadbeds, rails, and rolling stock of railroads; and also its apportionment of the assessments made by such Board upon mortgages, deeds of trust, contracts, and other obligations by which debts are secured, in the manner provided for in section three thousand six hundred and sixty-four of said Code.

8. To meet at the State Capitol on the third Monday in August, and remain in session from day to day (Sundays excepted), until the third Monday in September.

9. At such meeting to equalize the valuation of the taxable property of the several counties in this State for the purpose of taxation; and to that end, under such rules of notice to the Clerk of the Board of Supervisors of the county affected thereby as it may prescribe, to increase or lower the entire assessment roll, or any assessment contained therein, so as to equalize the assessment of the property contained in said roll, and make the assessment conform to the true value in money of the property assessed, and to fix the rate of State taxation, and to do the things provided in section three thousand six hundred and ninety three of said Code.

SEC. 3693. When, after a general investigation by the Board, the property is found to be assessed above or below its full cash value, the Board may, without notice, so determine, and must add to or deduct from the valuation :

1. The real estate ;

2. Improvements upon such real estate ;

3. The personal property, except money, such per centum respectively as is sufficient to raise or reduce it to its full cash value.

     ,   *   *   *   *   -   *   *

SEC. 3698.　Whenever the State Board of Equalization is satisfied that the Assessor or a Deputy Assessor of any county has knowingly, fraudulently, or corruptly assessed any property below its actual cash value, it must immediately inform the District Attorney of such county in writing of the facts that may have come to its knowledge, with a request that such Assessor or Deputy Assessor be prosecuted, and the District Attorney must at once comply with such request.

SEC. 3704.　If the Board of Supervisors of any county fails or refuses either —1. To allow the Assessor to appoint a sufficient number of deputies to make the assessment; or, 2. To furnish the proper books or blanks for his use; or, 3. To furnish the Assessor necessary office room;—

Then the State Board of Equalization may, upon the application of the Assessor, make the allowance, or furnish the proper books, blanks or office room ; and all the expense incurred in carrying into effect the provisions of this section must, by the Secretary of the Board, be certified to the Controller, who must, in his next settlement with the County Treasurer of any such county, require such Treasurer to pay the amount out of any funds belonging to such county.

SEC. 3705.　The State Board of Equalization may, by an order entered upon its minutes, and certified to the County Auditor of any county, extend, for not exceeding thirty days, the time fixed in this Title for the performance of any act.

CHAPTER V.

LEVY OF TAXES.

SEC. 3714.　The Board of Supervisors of each county must, on the first Monday of October*, fix the rate of county taxes, designating the number of cents on each hundred dollars of property levied, for each fund, and must levy the State and county taxes upon the taxable property of the county ; *provided*, that it shall not be lawful for any Board of Supervisors of any county in

---

* In San Francisco the fourth Monday in June.　See local Statute, post.

the State to levy, nor shall any tax greater than fifty cents on each one hundred dollars of property be levied and collected in any one year, to pay the bonded indebtedness, or judgment arising therefrom, of this State, or of any county or municipality in this State.

SEC. 3715. The action of the State Board of Equalization, in fixing the rate of taxation for State purposes, is, in the absence of action by the Board of Supervisors, a valid levy of the rate so fixed, and imposes upon the Auditor, Tax Collector, and all other officers charged with the performance of any duties under the Revenue Law, the same obligations as if the Board of Supervisors had made the levy at the proper time.

SEC. 3716. Every tax has the effect of a judgment against the person, and every lien created by this Title has the force and effect of an execution duly levied against all property of the delinquent ; the judgment is not satisfied nor the lien removed until the taxes are paid or the property sold for the payment thereof.

SEC. 3717. Every tax due upon personal property is a lien upon the real property of the owner thereof, from and after twelve o'clock M. of the first Monday in March in each year. [In effect March 22, 1880.]

SEC. 3718. Every tax due upon real property is a lien against the property assessed ; and every tax due upon improvements upon real estate assessed to others than the owner of the real estate, is a lien upon the land and improvements ; which several liens attach as of the first Monday of March in each year.

SEC. 3719. The State Board of Equalization must levy, annually, at the time other State taxes are levied, a tax of such number of cents on each one hundred dollars value of taxable property in the State, as will produce a net sum equal to the amount reported to them by the Controller as being necessary to be raised by an ad valorem tax for school purposes ; and the assessment and collection of said tax shall be performed in the same manner, and at the same time, as other State taxes are assessed and collected.

CHAPTER VI.

DUTIES OF THE AUDITOR IN RELATION TO REVENUE.

SEC. 3727. The County Auditor, as soon as the assessment book is delivered to him by the Clerk of the Board of Supervisors, must proceed to add up the valuations, and enter the total valuation of each kind of property, and the total valuation of all property, on the assessment book. The column of acres must show the total acreage of the county.

Sec. 3728. The Auditor must, on or before the third Monday in August of each year, prepare for the "assessment book" of such year, as corrected by the Board of Supervisors, duplicate statements, showing in separate columns:

1. The total value of all property.
2. The value of real estate.
3. The value of the improvements thereon.
4. The value of personal property, exclusive of money.
5. The amount of money.
6. The number of acres of land.

Sec. 3729. The Auditor must, as soon as such statements are prepared, transmit, by mail or express, one to the Controller of State and one to the State Board of Equalization.

Sec. 3730. As soon as the Auditor receives from the State Board of Equalization a statement of the changes made by the Board in the assessment roll of the county, or in any assessment contained therein, he must make the corresponding changes in the assessment roll, by entering the same in a column provided with a proper heading in the assessment book, counting any fractional sum, when more than fifty cents, as one dollar, and omitting it when less than fifty cents, so that the value of any separate assessment shall contain no fraction of a dollar; but he shall, in all cases, disregard any action of the Board of Supervisors which is prohibited by section three thousand six hundred and thirty-three of this Code.

Sec. 3731. The Auditor must then compute and enter in a separate money column in the assessment book, the respective sums in dollars and cents, rejecting the fractions of a cent, to be paid as a tax on the property therein enumerated, and foot up the column showing the total amount of such taxes, and the columns of total value of property in the county, as corrected under the direction of the State Board of Equalization.

Sec. 3732. On or before the fourth Monday of October, he must deliver a copy of the corrected assessment book, to be styled "duplicate assessment book," to the Tax Collector, with an affidavit attached thereto, and by him subscribed, as follows: "I, —— ——, Auditor of the County of ———, do swear that I received the assessment book of the taxable property of the county from the Clerk of the Board of Supervisors, with his affidavit thereto affixed, and that I have corrected it and made it conform to the requirements of the State Board of Equalization; that I have reckoned the respective sums due as taxes, and have added up the columns of valuations, taxes, and acreage, as required by law, and that the copy to which this affidavit is affixed is a full, true, and correct copy thereof, made in the manner prescribed by law."

Sec. 3733. The original assessment book must remain in the office of the Auditor.

25

SEC. 3734. On delivering the "Duplicate Assessment Book" to the Tax Collector, the Auditor must charge the Tax Collector with the full amount of the taxes levied, except the taxes due upon railway assessments made by the State Board of Equalization, and forthwith transmit by mail to the Controller of State a statement of the amount so charged.

SEC. 3735. The Auditor must verify, by his affidavit attached thereto, all statements made by him under the provisions of this Title.

SEC. 3736. The Auditor, if the "duplicate assessment book" or the delinquent tax list is transferred from one Collector to another, must credit the one and charge the other with the amount then outstanding on the tax list.

SEC. 3737. If the County Auditor fails or neglects to perform the duties prescribed by section three thousand seven hundred and twenty-eight and three thousand seven hundred and twenty-nine of the Political Code, he shall forfeit to the State five hundred dollars, to be recovered by action in the name of the State Board of Equalization.

SEC. 3738. The Board of Supervisors of any county may, in their discretion, dispense with the making or use of any duplicate assessment book mentioned in any part of this Code; and in all cases where said duplicate assessment book is referred to, it shall be lawful to use and consider the original assessment book in all the requirements of every part of this Code referring to the same, and all affidavits, or other statements in reference to said duplicate assessment book, shall be substantially worded to conform to the use of the original assessment book.

CHAPTER VII.

COLLECTION OF PROPERTY TAXES.

SEC. 3746. Within ten days after the receipt of the "duplicate assessment book," the Tax Collector must publish a notice, specifying :

1. That taxes will be delinquent on the last Monday in December next thereafter, at six o'clock P. M., and that unless paid prior thereto five per cent will be added to the amount thereof.

2. The time and place at which payment of taxes may be made.

SEC. 3747. In the City and County of San Francisco, and in the County of Los Angeles, the notice must specify the office of the Collector as the place where taxes may be paid.

SEC. 3748. In other counties the notice must specify a time and place within each township in the county when and where the Collector will attend to receive payment of taxes.

SEC. 3749. The notice in every case must be published for two weeks in some weekly or daily newspaper published in the county, if there is one ; or if there is not, then by posting it in three public places in each township.

SEC. 3750. The Tax Collector must mark the date of the payment of any tax in the assessment book, opposite the name of the person paying.

SEC. 3751. He must give a receipt to the person paying any tax, specifying the amount of the assessment and the tax paid, with a description of the property assessed.

SEC. 3752. The Superior Court must require every administrator or executor to pay out of the funds of the estate all taxes due from such estate ; and no order or decree for the distribution of any property of any decedent among the heirs or devisees must be made until all taxes against the estate are paid.

SEC. 3753. On the first Monday in each month the Tax Collector must settle with the Auditor for all moneys collected for the State or county, and pay the same to the County Treasurer, and on the same day must deliver to and file in the office of the Auditor a statement, under oath, showing :

1. An account of all his transactions and receipts since his last settlement ;

2. That all money collected by him as Tax Collector has been paid.

SEC. 3754. A Tax Collector refusing or neglecting for a period of five days to make the payments and settlements required in this Title, is liable for the full amount of taxes charged upon the assessment roll.

SEC. 3755. The District Attorney must bring suit against the Tax Collector and his sureties for such amount, and in case of neglect, the Controller of State or the Board of Supervisors may require him to do so ; and when the suit is commenced, no credit or allowance must be made to the Collector for the taxes outstanding.

SEC. 3756. On the last Monday in December of each year, at six o'clock P. M., all unpaid taxes are delinquent, and thereafter the Tax Collector must collect for the use of the county an addition of five per cent.

SEC. 3758. On the third Monday in January of each year, in each of the counties other than San Francisco, and on the first Monday in February of each year, in the City and County of San Francisco, the Tax Collector must attend at the office of the Auditor with the duplicate assessment book, and carefully compare the duplicate with the original assessment book, and every item marked "paid" in the former must be marked "paid" in the latter.

SEC. 3759. The Tax Collector must, at the time specified in the preceding section, deliver to the Auditor a complete "delinquent list" of all persons and property then owing taxes.

SEC. 3760. In the list so delivered must be set down in numerical or alphabetical order, all matters and things contained in the assessment book, and relating to delinquent persons or property.

SEC. 3761. The Auditor must carefully compare the list with the assessment book, and if satisfied that it contains a full and true statement of all taxes due and unpaid, he must foot up the total amount of taxes so remaining unpaid, credit the Tax Collector who acted under it therewith, and make a final settlement with him of all taxes charged against him on the assessment book, and must require from him the Treasurer's receipt, or if the Treasurer is the Collector, require from him an immediate account for any existing deficiency.

SEC. 3762. After settlement with the Tax Collector, as prescribed in the preceding section, the Auditor must charge the Tax Collector then acting with the amount of taxes due on the delinquent tax list, with the five per cent. added thereto, and within three days thereafter deliver the list, duly certified, to such Tax Collector.

SEC. 3763. Within ten days after the final settlement, the Auditor must transmit, by mail or express, a statement to the Controller of State, in such form as he requires, of each kind of property assessed and delinquent, and the total amount of delinquent taxes.

SEC. 3764. On or before the first Monday in February of each year, the Tax Collector in each of the counties other than San Francisco, and on or before the first Monday in March of each year in the City and County of San Francisco the Tax Collector of said city and county must publish the delinquent list, which must contain the names of the persons and a description of the property delinquent, and the amount of taxes and costs due, opposite each name and description, with the taxes due on personal property added to taxes on real estate, where the real estate is liable therefor, or the several taxes are due from the same person. The expense of the publication to be a charge against the county.

SEC. 3765. The Tax Collector must append and publish with the delinquent list a notice that unless the taxes delinquent, together with the costs and percentage, are paid, the real property upon which such taxes are a lien will be sold at public auction.

SEC. 3766. The publication must be made once a week for three successive weeks in some newspaper, or supplement thereto, published in the county, and the publication must be contracted for with the lowest bidder, and after ten days' public notice that such will be let. The bidding must be by sealed proposals. If there is no newspaper published in the county, then by posting a copy of the list in three public places in each township.

SEC. 3767. The publication must designate the time and place of sale.

SEC. 3768. The time of sale must not be less than twenty-one nor more than twenty-eight days from the first publication, and the place must be in front of the County Court-house, or, if in the City and County of San Francisco, in or in front of the Tax Collector's office, for all State and county taxes ; and for all other taxes, in front of the Tax Collector's office in their respective towns, cities and local districts.

SEC. 3769. The Collector, as soon as he has made the publication required by Sections 3764, 3765, 3766, and 3767, must file with the County Recorder and County Clerk respectively, a copy of the publication, with an affidavit attached thereto that it is a true copy of the same; that the publication was made in a newspaper or supplement thereto, stating its name and place of publication, and the date of each appearance; and in case there was no newspaper published in his county, that notices were put up in three public places in each of the townships, designating the township and places therein, which affidavit is primary evidence of all facts stated therein.

SEC. 3770. The Collector must collect, in addition to the taxes due on the delinquent list and five per centum added thereto, fifty cents on each lot, piece, or tract of land separately assessed, and on each assessment of personal property, one-half of which must go to the county and the other to the Collector in full for preparing the list.

SEC. 3771. On the day fixed for the sale, or on some subsequent day to which he may have postponed it, of which he must give notice, the Collector, between the hours of ten o'clock A. M. and three P. M., must commence the sale of the property advertised, commencing at the head of the list, and continuing alphabetically or in the numerical order of lots and blocks until completed.

SEC. 3772. He may postpone the day of commencing the sale, or the sale from day to day; but the sale must be completed within three weeks from the day first fixed.

SEC. 3773. The owner or person in possession of any real estate offered for sale for taxes due thereon, may designate, in writing, to the Tax Collector, prior to the sale, what portion of the property he wishes sold, if less than the whole; but if the owner or the possessor does not, then the Collector may designate it, and the person who will take the least quantity of the land, or in case an undivided interest is assessed, then the smallest portion of the interest, and pay the taxes and costs due, including fifty cents to the Collector for the duplicate certificate of sale, is the purchaser. But in case there is no purchaser in good faith for the same, as provided in this chapter, on the first day that the property is offered for sale, then when the property is offered thereafter for sale, and there is no purchaser in good faith of the same, the whole amount of the property assessed shall be struck off to the people of the State as the purchaser, and the duplicate certificate delivered to the County Treasurer, and filed by him in his office. No charge shall be made for the duplicate certificate when the State is a purchaser; and in such case the Tax Collector shall make an entry, " Sold to the State," on the Duplicate Assessment Book opposite the tax, and he shall be credited with the amount thereof in his settlement, made pursuant to sections three thousand seven hundred and ninety-seven, three thousand seven hundred and ninety-eight, and three thousand seven hundred and ninety-nine of this Code.

SEC. 3774. If the purchaser does not pay the taxes and costs before ten o'clock A. M. of the following day, the property, on the next sale day, before the regular sale, must be resold for the taxes and costs.

SEC. 3775. The bid of any person refusing to make the payments for property purchased by him must not be received on the sale of any property advertised in the delinquent list of that year.

SEC. 3776. After receiving the amount of the taxes and costs, the Collector must make out in duplicate a certificate, dated on the day of sale, stating (when known) the name of the person assessed, a description of the land sold, the amount paid therefor, that it was sold for taxes, giving the amount and year of the assessment, and specifying the time when the purchaser will be entitled to a deed.

SEC. 3777. The certificate must be signed by the Collector, and one copy delivered to the purchaser, and the other filed in the office of the County Recorder.

SEC. 3778. The Collector, before delivering any certificate, must in a book enter a description of the land sold corresponding with the description in the certificate, the date of sale, purchaser's name, and amount paid, regularly number the descriptions on the margin of the book, and put a corresponding number on each certificate. Such book must be open to public inspection without fee, during office hours when not in actual use.

SEC. 3779. On filing the certificate with the County Recorder the lien of the State vests in the purchaser, and is only divested by the payment to him, or to the County Treasurer for his use, of the purchase money and fifty per cent. thereon.

SEC. 3780. A redemption of the property sold may be made by the owner or any party in interest within twelve months from the date of the purchase, or at any time prior to the giving of the notice and the application for a deed, as provided for in section thirty-seven hundred and eighty-five of this Code.

SEC. 3781. Redemption must be made in gold or silver coin, and when made to the County Treasurer, he must credit the amount paid to the person named in the Collector's certificate, and pay it on demand to the person or his assignees.

SEC. 3782. In each report the Treasurer makes to the Supervisors he must name the person entitled to redemption money, and the amount due to each.

SEC. 3783. On receiving the certificate of sale the Recorder must file it, and make an entry in a book similar to that required of the Collector.

SEC. 3784. On the presentation of the receipt of the person named in the certificate, or of the County Treasurer for his use, of the total amount of the redemption money, the Recorder must mark the word " Redeemed," the date, and by whom redeemed, on the certificate and in the margin of the book where the entry of the certificate is made.

SEC. 3785. If the property is not redeemed within the time allowed by law for its redemption, the Collector, or his successor in office, must make to the purchaser, or his assignee, a deed of the property, reciting in the deed substantially the matters contained in the certificate, and that no person has redeemed the property during the time allowed for its redemption. In counties where no fee for making said deeds is provided by law, the Collector shall be entitled to receive from the purchaser three dollars for making such deed. No charge must be made by the Collector for the making of any such deed where the State is a purchaser; and the acknowledgment of all said deeds, as provided in section three thousand seven hundred and seventy-three, shall be taken by the County Clerk free of charge; *provided*, however, that the purchaser of property sold for delinquent taxes, or his assignee, must, thirty (30) days previous to the expiration of the time for the redemption, or thirty days before he applies for a deed, serve upon the owner of the property purchased, or upon the person occupying the property, if said property is occupied, a written notice, stating that said property, or a portion thereof, has been sold for delinquent taxes; giving the date of sale, the amount of property sold, the amount for which it was sold, the amount then due, and the time when the right of redemption will expire, or when the purchaser will apply for a deed, and the owner of the property shall have the right of redemption indefinitely until such notice shall have been given and said deed applied for, upon the payment of the fees, percentages, penalties, and costs, required by law. In the case of unoccupied property, a similar notice shall be posted in a conspicuous place upon the property, at least thirty days before the expiration of the time for redemption, or thirty days before the purchaser applies for a deed; and no deed of the property sold at a delinquent tax sale shall be issued by the Tax Collector, or any other officer, to the purchaser of such property, until after such purchaser shall have filed with such Tax Collector, or other officer, an affidavit showing that the notice hereinbefore required to be given, has been given as herein required, which said affidavit shall be filed and preserved by the Tax Collector, as other files, papers, and records, kept by him in his office. Such purchaser shall be entitled to receive the sum of three dollars for the service of said notice and the making of said affidavit; which sum of three dollars shall be paid by the redemptioner at the same time and in the same manner as other costs, percentages, penalties, and fees are paid.

SEC. 3786. The matters recited in the certificate of sale must be recited in the deed, and such deed, duly acknowledged or proved, is primary evidence that:

1. The property was assessed as required by law;

2. The property was equalized as required by law;

3. The taxes were levied in accordance with law;

4. The taxes were not paid;

5. At a proper time and place the property was sold as prescribed by law, and by the proper officer;

6. The property was not redeemed;

7. The person who executed the deed was the proper officer;

8. Where the real estate was sold to pay taxes on personal property, that the real estate belonged to the person liable to pay the tax.

SEC. 3787. Such deed, duly acknowledged or proved, is (except as against actual fraud) conclusive evidence of the regularity of all other proceedings, from the assessment by the Assessor, inclusive, up to the execution of the deed.

SEC. 3788. The deed conveys to the grantee the absolute title to the lands described therein as of the date of the expiration of the period for redemption, free of all incumbrances, except the lien for taxes which may have attached subsequent to the sale, and except when the land is owned by the United States, or this State, in which case it is prima facie evidence of the right of possession, accrued as of the date of the expiration of such period for redemption. Deeds to the State of State lands sold for delinquent taxes shall be recorded by the Recorders of the several counties, as prescribed in section three thousand eight hundred and sixteen of this Code, and a copy of said deeds, duly certified by the County Recorder, and acknowledged before the County Clerk, shall, without delay, be filed in the office of the Surveyor-General, and thereupon the land shall again become subject to entry and sale, in the same manner and subject to the same conditions as apply to other State lands of like character, except that the former possessors of lands thus deeded to the State, their heirs or assigns, shall be preferred purchasers thereof for three months after the deeds are filed with the Surveyor-General, as prescribed in this section; but the Surveyor-General shall not permit an entry, nor make a sale of any lands thus deeded to the State, except, upon the previous payment into the State Treasury, in addition to the price of said lands as compared with the price fixed for other State lands of a like character, by the person or persons proposing to make the entry or purchase, of a sum equal to the delinquent taxes, costs, and penalties, by virtue whereof the State became a purchaser of the lands thus sought to be entered or purchased. The money thus paid into the State Treasury shall be distributed in the manner prescribed in section three thousand eight hundred and sixteen of this Code. In all cases where land has been heretofore sold for delinquent taxes, the deed therefor must be made within one year and three months after this Act takes effect, and unless so made, the purchaser shall be deemed to have relinquished all his rights under such sale.

Sec. 3789. The Assessment Book, Duplicate Assessment Book, or Delinquent List, or a copy thereof certified by the County Auditor, showing unpaid taxes against any person or property, is prima facie evidence of the assessment, the property assessed, the delinquency, the amount of taxes due and unpaid, and that all the forms of law in relation to the assessment and levy of such taxes have been complied with.

Sec. 3790. The Tax Collector may, after the first Monday in February in each year, in each of the counties of this State, except in the City and County of San Francisco, and may, after the first Monday in March in each year, in said City and County of San Francisco, collect the taxes due on personal property, except when real estate is liable therefor, by seizure and sale of any personal property owned by the delinquent.

Sec. 3791. The sale must be at public auction, and of a sufficient amount of the property to pay the taxes, percentage, and costs.

Sec. 3792. The sale must be made after one week's notice of the time and place thereof, given by publication in a newspaper in the county, or by posting in three public places.

Sec. 3793. For seizing or selling personal property, the Tax Collector may charge in each case the sum of three dollars, and the same mileage as is allowed by law to the Sheriff of the county.

Sec. 3794. On payment of the price bid for any property sold, the delivery thereof, with a bill of sale, vests the title thereto in the purchaser.

Sec. 3795. All excess over the taxes, per cent., and costs of the proceeds of any such sale, must be returned to the owner of the property sold, and until claimed must be deposited in the County Treasury, subject to the order of the owner, heirs or assigns.

Sec. 3796. The unsold portion of any property may be left at the place of sale at the risk of the owner.

Sec. 3797. The Tax Collector must, annually, on the third Monday of March, attend at the office of the Auditor with the delinquent list, and the Auditor must then carefully compare the list with the assessments of persons and property not marked " Paid " on the assessment book, and when taxes have been paid, must note the fact in the appropriate column in the assessment book.

Sec. 3798. The Auditor must then administer to the Tax Collector an oath, to be written and subscribed in the delinquent list, that every person and all property assessed in the delinquent list on which taxes have been paid has been credited in the list with such payment.

SEC. 3799. The Auditor must then foot up the amount of taxes remaining unpaid, and credit the Tax Collector with the amount, and have a final settlement with him; and the delinquent list must remain on file in the Auditor's office. In the City and County of San Francisco, the Auditor must charge the Collector with the amount due on such list, and must return to such Collector the copy of the assessment book.

SEC. 3800. At the time mentioned in Section 3797, the Collector must make an affidavit, indorsed on the list, that the taxes not marked "Paid" have not been paid, and that he has not been able to discover any property belonging to, or in possession of, the persons liable to pay the same whereof to collect them.

SEC. 3803. Interest at the rate of two per cent per month must be collected on such delinquent taxes from the time they were first delinquent until paid.

SEC. 3804. Any taxes, per centum, and costs erroneously or illegally collected, may by the order of the Board of Supervisors, be refunded by the County Treasurer.

SEC. 3805. When the Collector discovers that any property has been assessed more than once for the same year, he must collect only the tax justly due, and make return of the facts under affidavit to the County Auditor.

SEC. 3806. If the Collector discovers before the sale that on account of irregular assessment, or of any other error, any land ought not to be sold, he must not offer the same for sale; and the Board of Supervisors must cause the Assessor to enter the uncollected taxes upon the assessment book of the next succeeding year, to be collected as other taxes entered thereon.

SEC. 3807. When land is sold for taxes correctly imposed as the property of a particular person, no misnomer of the owner, or supposed owner, or other mistake relating to the ownership thereof, affects the sale, or renders it void or voidable.

SEC. 3808. If any person removes from one county to another, after being assessed on personal property, the Collector of the county in which he was assessed may employ an attorney to sue for and collect the same in the Assessor's name.

SEC. 3809. On the trial a certified copy of the assessment, signed by the Auditor of the county where the same was made, with the affidavit of the Collector thereto attached, that the tax has not been paid, describing it as on the assessment book or delinquent list, is primary evidence that such tax and the per centum is due, and entitles him to judgment, unless the defendant proves that the tax was paid.

SEC. 3810. The Treasurer and Auditor must allow the expenses of collecting such tax, and permit a deduction thereof from the amount collected, if they do not exceed one-third of the amount of the tax collected.

SEC. 3811. Whenever property is advertised for sale for the non-payment of delinquent taxes, and the assessment is valid in part and void for the excess, the sale shall not for that cause be deemed invalid, nor any grant subsequently made thereunder be held to be insufficient to pass a title to the grantee, unless the owner of the property, or his agent, shall, not less than six days before the time at which the property is advertised to be sold, deliver to the Tax Collector a protest in writing, signed by the respective owner or agent, specifying the portion of the tax which he claims to be invalid, and the grounds upon which such claim is based.

SEC. 3812. In case any owner of property advertised to be sold for delinquent taxes shall, at least six days before the time advertised for the sale to take place, deliver to the Tax Collector his protest in writing against such sale, signed by himself or his agent, claiming that the assessment is void in whole or in part—and if in part only, for what portion, and in either case specifying the grounds upon which such claim is founded—it shall be the duty of the Tax Collector, either:

First—To sell the property assessed for the whole amount appearing upon the duplicate assessment book; or,

Second—Withdraw the property from sale, and report the case to the State Board of Equalization for its direction in the premises; and in such case the Board of Equalization may either direct the foreclosure of the lien of such tax by action, which proceeding is hereby authorized to be had, or direct the Collector to proceed with the sale.

SEC. 3813. In case property assessed for taxes is purchased by the State, pursuant to the provisions of section three thousand seven hundred and seventy-three of this Code, it shall be assessed the next year for taxes in the same manner as if it had not been so purchased. But it shall not be exposed for sale, and the sale thereof, under such assessment, shall be adjourned until the time of redemption, under the previous sale, shall have expired.

SEC. 3814. In case an assessment is made under the provisions of section three thousand eight hundred and thirteen of this Code, and the lands are not redeemed from a previous sale had under section three thousand seven hundred and seventy-three, as provided by law, no sale shall be had under the assessment authorized by said section three thousand eight hundred and thirteen, unless directed by the State Board of Equalization.

SEC. 3815. In case property is sold to the State as purchaser, pursuant to section three thousand seven hundred and seventy-three of this Code, and is subsequently assessed pursuant to section three thousand eight hundred and sixteen of this Code, no person shall be permitted to redeem from such sale, except upon payment also of the amount of such subsequent assessment, costs, fees, and interest.

SEC. 3816. Whenever property sold to the State, pursuant to the provisions of this chapter, shall be redeemed as herein provided, the moneys received on account of such redemption shall be distributed as follows: The original tax and the fifty per cent. paid in redemption shall be apportioned between the State and county in the same proportion that the State tax bears to the county tax; the five per cent. additional, and the money received for delinquent poll tax, shall be paid to the county; the percentage allowed for the collection of the delinquent poll tax shall be paid to the Collector, and the costs to the parties entitled thereto. The County Treasurer shall keep an accurate account of all money paid in redemption of property sold to the State, and shall, on the first Monday of June, in each year, make a detailed report, verified by his affidavit, of each account, year for year, to the Controller of State, in such form as the Controller may desire. Whenever the State shall receive from the Tax Collector any grant of property so sold for taxes, the same shall be recorded, at the request of the County Treasurer, free of charge by the County Recorder, and shall be immediately reported by the County Treasurer to the State Board of Equalization.

Sec. 3817.   In all cases where real estate has been or may hereafter be sold for delinquent taxes, and the State has become the purchaser, and has not disposed of the same, the person whose estate has been or may hereafter be sold, or his heirs, executors, administrators, or other successors in interest, shall at any time after the time of purchase thereof by the State, and before the State shall have disposed of the same, have the right to redeem such real estate by paying to the County Treasurer of the county wherein the real estate is situated the amount of taxes due thereon at the time of said sale, with interest thereon at the rate of seven per cent per annum; and also all taxes that were a lien upon said real estate at the time said taxes became delinquent; and also for each year since the sale for which taxes on said land have not been paid, an amount equal to the percentage of State and county tax for that year, upon the value of said real estate assessed for the year of the sale, with interest from the first day of January of each of said years respectively. at the same rate; and also all costs and expenses, and twenty-five per cent penalty, which may have accrued by reason of such delinquency and sale, and the costs and expenses of such redemption, as hereinafter specified.   The County Auditor shall, on the application of the person desiring to redeem, make an estimate of the amount to be paid, and shall give him triplicate certificates of the amount, specifying the several amounts thereof, which certificates shall be delivered to the County Treasurer. together with the money; and the County Treasurer shall give triplicate receipts, written or indorsed upon said certificates, to the redemptioner, who shall deliver one of said receipts to the State Controller and one to the County Auditor, taking their receipts therefor.   The County Treasurer shall settle for the moneys received as for other State and county moneys.   The County Auditor shall be paid by the redemptioner for making out said estimates the sum of two dollars.   Upon the payment of the money specified in said certificate, and the giving of the receipts aforesaid by the Treasurer, Controller, and Auditor, any deed or certificate of sale that may have been made to the State shall become null and void, and all right, title, and interest acquired by the State under or by virtue of the tax sale shall cease and determine. The receipts of the County Treasurer, Controller, and County Auditor may be recorded in the Recorder's office of the county in which said real estate is situated, in the book of deeds, and the records thereof shall have the same effect as that of a deed of reconveyance of the interest conveyed by said deed or certificate of sale. This act shall not apply to school lands when the full amount of one dollar and twenty-five cents per acre has not been paid to the State therefor.

CHAPTER VIII.

COLLECTION OF TAXES BY THE ASSESSOR ON CERTAIN PERSONAL PROPERTY.

SEC. 3820. The Assessor must collect the taxes on all personal property when, in his opinion, said taxes are not a lien upon real property sufficient to secure the payment of the taxes; *provided*, that in the City and County of San Francisco the Tax Collector shall collect such taxes at any time after the assessment.

SEC. 3821. In the case provided for in the preceding section at the time of making the assessment, or at any time before the first Monday of July, the Asesssor may collect the taxes by seizure and sale of any personal property owned by the person against whom the tax is assessed.

SEC. 3822. The provisions of Sections 3791, 3792, 3793, 3794, 3795 and 3796 apply to such seizure and sale.

SEC. 3823. The Assessor and Collector are governed as to the amount of taxes to be by him collected on personal property, by the State and county rate of the previous year.

SEC. 3824. When the rate is fixed for the year in which such collection is made, then, if a sum in excess of the rate has been collected, such excess shall not be apportioned to the State, but the whole thereof shall remain in the county treasury, and must be repaid by the County Treasurer to the person from whom the collection was made, or to his assignee, on demand therefor.

SEC. 3825. If a sum less than the rate fixed has been collected, the deficiency must be collected as other taxes on personal property are collected.

SEC. 3826. The Assessor, on the first Monday of each month, must make a settlement with the Auditor, and must pay into the County Treasury all moneys collected by him for such taxes during the preceding month, less the compensation allowed him for making such collection.

SEC. 3827. The Auditor must, as soon as the "assessment book" for the year comes into his hands, note opposite the names of each person from whom taxes have been collected the amount thereof.

SEC. 3828. As soon as the rate of taxation for the year is fixed, the Auditor must note, in connection with the entry made under the provisions of the preceding section, the amount of the excess or deficiency.

SEC. 3829. For services rendered in the collection of taxes under section three thousand eight hundred and twenty, the Assessors of the several counties shall receive six per cent on the amount by him collected; *provided*, that all fees or commissions collected under this or any other act by the salaried officers, except in the collection of poll taxes in and for the City and County of San Francisco, shall be by said officers paid into the County Treasury for the use of said city and county.

SEC. 3830. In every county in this State where any officer other than the Assessor is charged with the collection of taxes upon personal property, not a lien upon real property, such officer must, until after the expiration of the term of the present incumbent, discharge the duties cast upon the Assessor under the provisions of this chapter.

CHAPTER IX.

POLL TAXES.

SEC. 3839. Every male inhabitant of this State, over twenty-one and under sixty years of age, except paupers, insane persons, and Indians not taxed, must annually pay a poll tax of two dollars; *provided*, the same be paid between the first Monday in March and the first Monday in July; but if not paid prior to the first Monday in July, then it shall be three dollars; *provided further*, that nothing herein shall affect any laws imposing a greater poll tax upon inhabitants ineligible to citizenship.

SEC. 3840. Poll tax must be collected by the Assessors between the first Monday in March and the second Monday in January of the ensuing year.

SEC. 3841. The County Treasurer must, before the first Monday of March and the first Monday in July of each year, cause to be printed, respectively, of two and three dollars, blank poll tax receipts, a sufficient number for the use of the Assessor.

SEC. 3842. The style of such blanks must be changed every year.

SEC. 3843. The Treasurer must, before the first Monday in March of each year: First—Number and sign the two-dollar blanks, and before the first Monday in July, number and sign the three-dollar blanks. Second—At the time of signing make an entry of the whole number thereof, and of the first and last number placed thereon, in a book kept by him for that purpose. Third—Deliver all such blanks to the Auditor, and charge him therewith.

SEC. 3844. The Auditor upon the receipt thereof must sign the same, and make in a book to be kept by him for that purpose a similar entry to that prescribed in Subdivision 2 of the preceding section.

SEC. 3845. He must, at any time after the first Monday in March and the first Monday in July, upon demand, deliver to the Assessor, in their order, the two and three-dollar blanks, and charge him therewith.

SEC. 3846. The Assessor must demand payment [of] poll tax of every person liable therefor, and on the neglect or refusal of such person to pay the same, he must collect by seizure and sale of any personal property owned by such person.

SEC. 3847. The sale may be made after three hours verbal notice of time and place, and the provisions of sections thirty-seven hundred and ninety-one, thirty-seven hundred and ninety-three, thirty-seven hundred and ninety-four, thirty-seven hundred and ninety five, and thirty seven hundred and ninety-six, apply to such seizure and sale.

SEC. 3848. Every person indebted to one who neglects or refuses, after demand, to pay a poll tax, becomes liable therefor, and must pay the same for such other person after service upon him by the Collector of a notice in writing, stating the name of such person.

SEC. 3849. Every officer authorized to draw the warrants for or to pay the salary or fees of any officer is the debtor of such officer within the meaning of the preceding section.

SEC. 3850. Every person paying the poll tax of another may deduct the same from any indebtedness to such other person.

SEC. 3851. The Assessor must deliver the poll tax receipt, filled out with the name of the person owning the taxes, to the purchaser of property at any such sale; in other cases he must deliver it, filled out in like manner, to the person paying the tax.

SEC. 3852. The receipt so delivered is the only evidence of payment.

SEC. 3853. On the first Monday in each month the Assessor must make oath before the Auditor, of the total amount of poll taxes collected by him during the last preceding month, and must, at the same time, settle with the Auditor for the same, and pay into the County Treasurer's office the total amount of poll taxes collected, less the percentum allowed for fees.

SEC. 3854. On the first Monday in July the Assessor must return to the Auditor all two-dollar blank poll tax receipts received by him and not used, and pay to the Treasurer the total amount collected and not before paid in, less the amount of his fees, and the Auditor must deliver to him the three-dollar receipts; and on the second Monday in January of each year he must return to the Auditor all the three-dollar poll tax receipts received by him and not used, and must make final settlement with the Auditor and Treasurer therefor.

SEC. 3855. The Auditor must, as soon as the settlement is made, return to the Treasurer the receipts not used.

SEC. 3856. The Treasurer must credit the Auditor with the receipts so returned, and must thereupon seal them up securely and deposit and keep them in his office.

SEC. 3857. The Assessor must keep a roll of the names and local residence, or place of business, of all persons subject to or liable for poll tax, and, if paid, date and amount of each payment, and, if not paid, cause of non-payment; *provided*, that no person shall be returned as delinquent on such roll unless a demand has been made upon him in person or through the post-office.

SEC. 3858. On the third Monday in January of each year the Assessor must deliver to the Auditor the roll so made up, and the Auditor must add to the total poll tax delinquent on such roll thirty-three and one-third per centum additional, and without delay deliver such list to the Tax Collector, and charge the Collector therewith.

SEC. 3860. If any person, assessed for a property tax, has not paid to the Assessor the poll tax due from him, or for which he is liable, it, with thirty-three and one-third per cent. in addition thereto, constitutes a lien upon the property assessed to such person, to attach from the first Monday in March in each year, and must be collected in the same manner and at the same time as delinquent taxes are collected.

SEC. 3861. The proceeds of the poll tax must be paid to the County Treasurer, as provided by law, for the exclusive use of the State School Fund, and shall, by such Treasurer, be paid to the State as other moneys belonging to the State.

SEC. 3862. The Assessor, for services rendered in the collection of poll taxes, shall receive the sum of fifteen per cent.; and the Collector, for services rendered in the collection of poll taxes on the delinquent list (including the publication), shall receive the sum of twenty-five per cent. on all delinquent poll tax collected by him.

CHAPTER X.

SETTLEMENTS WITH THE CONTROLLER AND PAYMENTS INTO THE STATE
TREASURY.

SEC. 3865. The Treasurers of the respective counties must at any time upon the order of the Controller and Treasurer of State, settle with the

Controller, and pay over to the Treasurer all moneys in their possession belonging to the State.

SEC. 3866. The Treasurers of the Counties of Alameda, Amador, Contra Costa, Calaveras, El Dorado, Nevada, Placer, Sierra, Solano, Yolo, San Francisco, Sacramento, San Joaquin, Santa Clara, Tuolumne, and Yuba, respectively, must, between the fifteenth and thirtieth days of January, April, July, and October, of each year, and the County Treasurers of the Counties of Humboldt, Del Norte, and Modoc must, between the fifteenth and thirtieth days of October and April, in each year, and the County Treasurers of other counties of this State must, between the fifteenth and thirtieth days of January and June, respectively, in each year, proceed to the State Capital and settle in full with the Controller of State, and pay over in cash to the Treasurer of State, all funds which have come into their hands, as County Treasurers, before the close of business at the end of the previous month. If, in the opinion of the Controller of State, it appears from the report of the County Auditor that sufficient property tax has not been collected to make it for the interest of the State that a settlement should be made, the Controller shall defer the settlement until the next regular settlement. No mileage, fees, or commissions shall be allowed any officer for any deferred settlement; *provided*, that in case any settlement is so deferred that the County Auditor, in his next report to the Controller of State, shall include therein all moneys required to be reported since the date of his last report upon which a settlement was made.

SEC. 3867. Every County Treasurer who neglects or refuses to appear at the office of the Controller or Treasurer at the time specified in this chapter, and then and there to settle and make payment as required by this chapter, forfeits all fees, percentage, and mileage which would have otherwise been due him on such settlement ; and the Controller is required to withhold all such fees, percentage, and mileage, and require the same to be paid into the Treasury for the use and benefit of the State.

SEC. 3868. The Auditor of each county, between the first and tenth day of each month in which the Treasurer of his county is required to settle with the Controller, must make, in duplicate, and verify by his affidavit, a report to the Controller of State, in such form as the Controller may desire, showing specifically the amount due the State from each particular source of revenue at the close of business on the last day of the preceding month.

SEC. 3869. The Auditor must at once transmit by mail or express to the Controller one copy of the report, and must deliver the other copy to the Treasurer of his county.

SEC. 3870. Every Auditor who fails to make and transmit the report required by this chapter, or any report or statement required by this title, forfeits all compensation which would be otherwise due him from the State ; and the Controller is required to withhold such compensation.

26

SEC. 3871.   In the settlement th i C)r troller must deduct the commission; and mileage allowed to the County Treasurer for his services, the State's portion of the repayments made under Section 3834, and any other amount due the county or the officers thereof.

SEC. 3872.   The manner of making payments into the State Treasury is prescribed by Sections 433, 434, 452, and 453 of this Code.

SEC. 3873.   The Controller must, after the Treasurer has made settlement and payment, enter upon each copy of the Au iitor's report a statement show-ing :

1.   The amount of money by the County Treasurer paid into the State Treasury ;

2.   I he amounts deducted for commissions and other allowances ;—

And must then return one copy of the report to the County Treasurer.

SEC. 3874.   The County Treasurer must file with the Auditor of his county the copy returned to him by the Controller.

SEC. 3875.   The Auditor must then make the proper entries in his account with the Treasurer.

SEC. 3876.   The Controller must, in the settlement, allow the Treasurer for mileage at the rate of forty cents per mile from the county seat to the Capital ; such mileage not to exceed at any settlement one hundred dollars.

SEC. 3877.   The Controller may examine the books of any officer charged with the collection and receipt of State taxes.

SEC. 3878.   If he believes any officer has been guilty of defrauding the State of revenue, or has neglected or refused to perform any duty relating to the revenue, he must direct the District Attorney or other counsel to prose-cute the delinquent.

SEC. 3879.   When any law in relation to the revenue of the State has been so far violated as to require the prosecution of the offender for a criminal offense, or proceedings against him by civil action, the Controller may desig-nate the county in which the prosecution or proceedings may be had.

SEC. 3880.   The Controller or Attorney-General may employ other coun-sel than the District Attorney, and the expenses must be audited by the Board of Examiners and be paid out of the State Treasury.

CHAPTER XI.

MISCELLANEOUS PROVISIONS.

SEC. 3881.   Omissions, errors, or defects in form in any original or dupli-cate assessment book, when it can be ascertained therefrom what was in-tended, may, with the written consent of the District Attorney, be supplied or corrected by the Assessor at any time prior to the sale for delinquent taxes, and after the original assessment was made. In the City and County of San Francisco, the written consent of the City and County Attorney shall have the same force and effect as the written consent of the District Attorney.

SEC. 3882. When the omission, error, or defect has been carried into a delinquent list or any publication, the list or publication may be republished as amended, or notice of the correction may be given in a supplementary publication.

SEC. 3883. The publication must be made in the same manner as the original publication, and for not less than one week.

SEC. 3884. In the assessment of land, advertisement, and sale thereof for taxes, initial letters, abbreviations and figures may be used to designate the township, range, section, or parts of section.

SEC. 3885. No assessment or act relating to assessment or collection of taxes is illegal on account of informality, nor because the same was not completed within the time required by law.

SEC. 3886. The fines, forfeitures, and penalties incurred by a violation of any of the provisions of this Title must be paid into the Treasury for the use of the county where the person against whom the recovery is had resides.

SEC. 3888. Taxes must be paid in legal coin of the United States. A tax levied for a special purpose may be paid in such funds as may be directed.

SEC. 3889. Every Assessor, District Attorney, and County Treasurer must annually, on the first Monday of January, make a settlement with the County Auditor of all transactions connected with the revenue for the previous year.

SEC. 3890. The Treasurer, Tax Collector, Assessor, Clerk of the Board of Supervisors, and each member of the Board must separately perform the duties required of him in his office and must not, except in the cases provided by law, perform the duties required of any other officer under this Title.

SEC. 3891. With relation to the Acts passed at the present session of the Legislature, the provisions of this Title must, after this Title takes effect, be construed as though this Code had been passed and approved on the last day of the present session. But the provisions of this section do not apply to any Act expressly amendatory of either of the Codes, or putting into effect any part of either ; nor to an Act approved March sixteenth, eighteen hundred and seventy two, entitled an Act to put into immediate effect certain parts of the Political and Penal Codes ; nor to an Act approved March twenty-second, eighteen hundred and seventy two, entitled an Act to put into effect certain parts of the Codes and provide for their publication.

SEC. 3892. All taxes assessed before this Code takes effect must be collected under the laws in force at the time the assessment was made, and in the same manner as if this Code had not been passed.

Sec. 3893. The Board of Supervisors of each county must make to the Assessor and Auditor thereof a reasonable allowance, not to exceed eight cents per folio, for making the statements required by Sections 3655 and 3728, and for making the duplicate assessment book mentioned in Section 3732 of THE POLITICAL CODE.

Sec. 3894. The Board of Supervisors of each county in this State must allow the Assessor thereof such a number of deputies, to be appointed by him in addition to the number now fixed, or where no deputies are now allowed, so many deputies as will, in the judgment of the Board, enable the Assessor to complete the assessment within the time prescribed by law.

Sec. 3895. The Board must fix the compensation of the deputies so allowed ; and such compensation must be paid out of the General Fund in the County Treasury. The compensation must not exceed five dollars per day for each deputy for the time actually engaged ; nor must any allowance be made but for work done between the first Monday in March and the first Monday in July of each year.

Sec. 3896. The State Board of Equalization may, by an order entered upon its minutes, and certified to the County Auditor of any county in the State, dispense with the duplicate assessment book in such county, in which event the original assessment book shall perform all the offices of such duplicate, and shall have like force and effect.

Sec. 3897. Whenever this State shall become the purchaser of property sold for taxes, and shall receive a grant of the same, the State.Board of Equalization may direct the District Attorney of the county, or the Attorney-General, to bring an action to recover possession of the same. In case of judgment for the recovery of the same, or of any part thereof, the Board of Equalization may order the property so recovered to be sold by the County Treasurer, under such regulations and on such terms as they may prescribe, and a grant from the people of the State, executed by the County Treasurer to the purchaser, reciting the facts necessary to authorize such sale and conveyance, shall convey all the interest of the State in such property, and be prima facie evidence of such facts. But no bid shall be received at such sale for less than twice the amount of all the taxes levied upon such property, and of all interest, costs, and expenses, up to the date of such sale.

Sec. 3898. In case sales are made under the provisions of the next preceding section, the proceeds of such sale shall be paid into the County Treasury. The Treasurer shall retain and distribute to the respective Funds the portion belonging to the county, and shall pay the balance to the State Treasurer, who must place it in the General Fund. The attorney and counsel fees, costs, and expenses of the litigation for the recovery of the property, and of sales by the same, when audited by the Board of Examiners, must be paid out of the General Fund ; *provided*, that the allowances in any one case shall not exceed the amount of said balance in such case.

Sec. 3899. The Controller may, at any time after a delinquent list has been delivered to a Collector, direct such Collector not to proceed in the collection of any tax on said list, amounting to three hundred dollars, further than to offer for sale but once any property upon which such tax is a lien. Upon such direction, the Collector, after offering the property for sale once, and there being no purchaser in good faith, must make out and deliver to the Controller a certified copy of the entries upon the delinquent list relative to such tax ; and the Tax Collector, or the Controller, in case the Tax Collector refuses or neglects for fifteen days after being directed to bring suit for collection by the Controller, may proceed, by civil action in the proper Court, and in the name of the people of the State of California, to collect such tax and costs.

Sec. 3900. In such action, a complaint in the following form is sufficient :

(Title of Court.)

The People of the State of California

vs.

(Naming the defendant.)

Plaintiff avers that the defendant is indebted to plaintiff in the sum of $——, State and county taxes for the fiscal year 18—, with five per cent. added for the non-payment of such taxes, and —— dollars, costs of collection, to date. Plaintiff demands judgment for said several sums, and prays that an attachment may issue in form as prescribed in section five hundred and forty of the Code of Civil Procedure.

(Signed by the Tax Collector, or Controller, or his attorney.)

On the filing of such complaint, the Clerk must issue the writ of attachment prayed for, and such proceedings shall be had thereunder as under writs of attachment issued in civil actions. If, in such action, the plaintiff recover judgment, there shall be included in such judgment an attorney's fee of ten per cent. on the amount of the tax. In such action, the certified copy mentioned in the preceding section, made by the Collector and delivered to the Controller, is prima facie evidence that the person against whose property the tax was levied is indebted to the people of the State of California in the amount of such tax. In case of payment of any such taxes after suit as above mentioned shall have been commenced, or after the recovery of judgment therefor, such payment must be made to the County Treasurer of the county in which such taxes are due, whereupon the Treasurer, after distributing to the several Funds of the county the portions belonging to it, and paying to the Controller or his attorney the portion received as attorney's fees, and other costs, must pay the remainder to the State Treasurer at the times and in the manner prescribed by law for the payment of other State taxes.

STATUTES 1873-4, 447.

An Act in relation to the assessment and collection of taxes upon personal property in the City and County of San Francisco.

[Approved March 18, 1874.]

The People of the State of California, represented in Senate and Assembly, do enact as follows:

SECTION 1.　The City and County of San Francisco is hereby exempted from the provisions of the Political Code relating to the assessment and equalization of personal property for taxation, and the collection of taxes thereon, but only in so far as to give force and effect to the provisions of this Act hereinafter contained.

SEC. 2.　The Assessor of said City and County must complete the assessment of personal property on or before the first Monday in June in each year, and enter the same in a separate assessment book, to be known as "The Assessment Book of Personal Property." As soon as completed, the said assessment book must be delivered to the Clerk of the Board of Supervisors, who must immediately give notice thereof, and of the time the Board will meet to equalize said assessment, by publication in some daily newspaper printed in said City and County; and in the mean time, until the Board meets to equalize said assessments, the assessment book must remain in his office, for the inspection of all persons interested.

SEC. 3.　The Board of Supervisors shall meet on the second Monday in June, and must examine and equalize said assessment, in the same manner as required by the Political Code, and must complete the equalization of said assessment on or before the fourth Monday in June; and the Clerk of the Board must record, in a book to be kept for that purpose, all changes, corrections, and orders made by the Board, and, during its session, must enter in said assessment book all changes and corrections made by the Board, and must deliver the said assessment book, so corrected, to the Auditor of said City and County, on the fourth Monday of June, with an affidavit, in substance the same as that required by section three thousand six hundred and eighty-two of the Political Code.

SEC. 4.　The Board of Supervisors must, on the fourth Monday of June, fix the rate of City and County taxes for the current fiscal year, and the Auditor must, on or before the second Monday of July, prepare and deliver to the Tax Collector a copy of said corrected assessment book, to be styled "Duplicate Assessment Book of Personal Property," in which shall be computed and entered, in separate money columns, the respective sums, in dollars and cents, rejecting the fractions of a cent, to be paid as a tax on the property therein enumerated, and to which must be attached his affi-davit, subscribed and sworn to as follows: " I, ——, Auditor of the City and County of San Francisco, do swear that I received the assessment book of the personal property of the City and County of San Francisco, from the Clerk of the Board of Supervisors, with his affidavit thereto affixed, and that I have corrected it and made it conform to the requirements of the Board of Supervisors; that I have reckoned the respective sums due as taxes, and have added up the columns of valuations and taxes, as required by law, and that the copy to which this affidavit is attached is a true, full, and correct copy thereof." Said duplicate assessment book must contain columns for entry as hereinafter provided, for the State tax upon the property therein assessed.

SEC. 5. The said duplicate assessment book must thereupon be delivered to the Tax Collector; and all the acts required by the Political Code to be performed by the Auditor and Tax Collector in relation to the duplicate assessment book and the taxes therein mentioned, must be performed by said officers, in relation to the assessment book herein provided, so far as the same can be made applicable.

SEC. 6. The Tax Collector, immediately upon receiving said assessment roll, must publish in one or more of the daily newspapers of said City and County that the taxes therein mentioned are due and payable at the office of the Tax Collector of said City and County, and will become delinquent on the first Monday of August, and that unless paid on or before the last men-tioned date five per cent. will be added to the amount thereof. The Tax Collector may, at any time after said taxes become delinquent, collect the same by seizure and sale of any personal property owned by the delinquent, and in proceedings for that purpose must be governed by sections three thousand seven hundred and ninety-one to three thousand seven hundred and ninety-six, inclusive, of the Political Code.

SEC. 7. On the Wednesday following the fourth Monday of September the Tax Collector must return the said duplicate assessment roll to the Au-ditor, who must, at the time provided in the Political Code for computing and entering the State and county taxes, add to or deduct from the valuation of the property enumerated in said assessment book, any per centum which may have been required by the State Board of Equalization, and compute the State taxes to be paid on said personal property, and enter the same, with all delinquent taxes which may appear in said book, in the proper columns. After completing such computations and entries, the Auditor must annex his affidavit to said book, stating that he has truly and correctly made all reduc-tions and additions required by the State Board of Equalization, and com-puted, entered, and added all the State taxes, and all the delinquent City and County taxes, and the per centum due on the property therein enumerated, and return the same to the Tax Collector at the time when the duplicate assessment book of taxes upon real estate is required by law to be delivered.

Sec. 8. The Tax Collector must collect said State taxes, and said delinquent City and County taxes and per centum, at the time and in the same manner as he is by law required to collect other State and county taxes.

Sec. 9. The Assessor may, at any time prior to the fourth Monday in October in each year, specially assess any property which may have been omitted and which shall not be entered upon the regular assessment roll; and, if he makes any such special assessment, he shall forthwith deliver a copy thereof to the Tax Collector, and the original to the Auditor, who shall charge the Tax Collector with the amount of taxes due thereon; and all such special assessments shall be as valid and shall have the same force and effect as regular assessments.

Sec. 10. All the provisions of the Political Code and other laws relating to State and county revenue, except where they are in conflict with, are made part of this Act.

Sec. 11. This Act shall take effect immediately.

SUPPLEMENT CLXIV.

Civil Code, Division 1, Part IV, Title IV.

STREET RAILROAD CORPORATIONS.

Sec. 497. Authority to lay railroad tracks through the streets and public highways of any incorporated city or town may be obtained for a term of years, not exceeding fifty, from the Trustees, Council, or other body to whom is intrusted the government of the city or town, under such restrictions and limitations, and upon such terms, and payment of license tax, as the city or town authority may provide. In no case must permission be granted to propel cars upon such tracks otherwise than by horses, mules, or by wire ropes running under the streets and moved by stationary steam engines, unless for special reasons as hereinafter provided. [*Amended March 3, 1876; Amendments, 1875-76, 76.*]

Sec. 498. The city or town authorities, in granting the right of way to street railroad corporations, in addition to the restrictions which they are authorized to impose, must require a strict compliance with the following conditions, except in the cases of prismoidal or other elevated railways. In such cases, said railway shall be required to be constructed in such a manner as will present the least obstruction to the freedom of the streets on which it may be erected, when allowed by the granting power:

First. To construct their tracks on those portions of streets designated in the ordinance granting the right, which must be as nearly as possible in the middle thereof.

Second. To plank, pave, or macadamize the entire length of the street, used by their track, between the rails, and for two feet on each side thereof, and between the tracks, if there be more than one, and to keep the same constantly in repair, flush with the street, and with good crossings.

Third. That the tracks must not be more than five feet wide within the rails, and must have a space between them sufficient to allow the cars to pass each other freely. [*Amended, April* 3, 1876; *Amendments,* 1875-6, 77.]

SEC. 499. Two corporations may be permitted to use the same street, each paying an equal portion for the construction of the track; but in no case must two railroad corporations occupy and use the same street or track for a distance of more than five blocks.

SEC. 500. Any proposed railroad track may be permitted to cross any track already constructed, the crossing being made as provided in Chapter II, Title III, of this Part. In laying down the tracks and preparing therefor, not more than one block must be obstructed at any one time, nor for a longer period than ten working days.

SEC. 501. The rates of fare on the cars must not exceed ten cents for one fare, for any distance under three miles. The cars must be of the most approved construction for comfort and convenience of passengers, and provided with brakes to stop the same, when required. The rate of speed must not be greater than eight miles per hour. A violation of the provisions of this section subjects the corporation to a fine of one hundred dollars for each offense.

SEC. 502. Work to construct the railroad must be commenced within one year from the date of the ordinance granting the right of way and the filing of articles of incorporation, and the same must be completed within three years thereafter. A failure to comply with these provisions works a forfeiture of the right of way as well as of the franchise, unless the uncompleted portion is abandoned by the corporation, with the consent of the authorities granting the right of way—such abandonment and consent to be in writing.

SEC. 503. Cities and towns in or through which street railroads run may make such further regulations for the government of such street railroads as may be necessary to a full enjoyment of the franchise and the enforcement of the conditions provided herein.

SEC. 504. Any corporation, or agent or employee thereof, demanding or charging a greater sum of money for fare on the cars of such street railroad than that fixed, as provided in this Title, forfeits to the person from whom such sum is received, or who is thus overcharged, the sum of two hundred dollars, to be recovered in a civil action, in any Justice's Court having jurisdiction thereof, against the corporation.

SEC. 505. Every street railroad corporation must provide, and, on request, furnish to all persons desiring a passage on its cars, any required quantity of passenger tickets or checks, each to be good for one ride. Any corporation failing to provide and furnish tickets or checks to any person desiring to purchase the same at not exceeding the rate hereinbefore prescribed, shall forfeit to such person the sum ot two hundred dollars, to be recovered as provided in the preceding section; *provided*, that the provisions of this section shall not apply to such street railroad corporations as charge but five cents fare.

SEC 506. Upon the trial of an action for any of the sums forfeited, as provided in the two preceding sections, proof that the person demanding or receiving the money as fare, or for the sale of the ticket or check, was at the time of making the demand or receiving the money, engaged in an office of the corporation, or vehicle belonging to the corporation, shall be prima facie evidence that such person was the agent, servant or employee of the corporation, to receive the money, and give the ticket or check mentioned.

SEC. 507. In every grant to construct street railroads, the right to grade, sewer, pave, and macadamize or otherwise improve, alter or repair the streets or highways, is reserved to the corporation, and cannot be alienated or impaired; such work to be done so as to obstruct the railroad as little as possible, and, if required, the corporation must shift its rails so as to avoid the obstructions made thereby.

SEC. 508. Each street railroad corporation must pay to the authorities of the city, town, county, or city and county, as a license upon each car, such sum as the authorities may fix, not exceeding fifty dollars per annum in the City of San Francisco, nor more than twenty-five dollars per annum in other cities or towns. Where any street railroad connects or runs through two or more cities or towns, a proportionate or equal share of such license tax must be paid to each of the cities or towns; and no such license tax is due the county authorities where the same is paid to any city or town authority.

SEC. 509. The right to lay down a track for grading purposes, and maintain the same for a period not to exceed three years, may be granted by the corporate authorities of any city or town, or city and county, or Supervisors of any city or county, but no such track must remain more than three years upon any one street; and it must be laid level with the street, and must be operated under such restrictions as not to interfere with the use of the street by the public. The corporate authorities of any city or town, or city and county, may grant the right to use steam or any other motive power in propelling the cars used on such grading tract, when public convenience or utility demands it, but the reasons therefor must be set forth in the ordinance, and the right to rescind the ordinance at any time reserved.

SEC. 510. Street railroads are governed by the provisions of Title Three of this Part, so far as they are applicable, unless such railroads are therein specially excepted.

SEO 511. When a street railroad is constructed, owned or operated by any natural person, this Title is applicable to such person in like manner as it is applicable to corporations.

[For fares on street railroads in cities and towns of more than one hundred thousand inhabitants, see page 276.]

SUPPLEMENT CLXV.

LEGISLATION ON THE PUEBLO LANDS.

1858, 52.

An Act concerning the City of San Francisco, and to ratify and confirm certain Ordinances of the Common Council of said City.

[Approved March 11, 1858.

The People of the State of California, represented in Senate and Assembly, do enact as follows:

SECTION 1.   *Whereas,* The Common Council of the City of San Francisco passed an ordinance, approved by the Mayor on the twentieth day of June, A. D. one thousand eight hundred and fifty-five, which ordinance is in the words and figures following, to wit:

Number eight hundred and twenty-two – Ordinance for the settlement and quieting of the land titles in the City of San Francisco.

The People of the City of San Francisco do ordain as follows:

SEC. 1.   It shall be the duty of the Mayor to enter, at the proper land office of the United States, at the minimum price, all the lands above the natural high-water mark of the Bay of San Francisco, at the time of the admission of California into the Union as a State, situated within the corporate limits of the City of San Francisco, as defined in the Act to i corporate said city, passed April fifteenth, one thousand eight hundred and fifty-one, in trust for the several use, benefit and behoof of the occupants or possessors thereof, according to their respective interests.

SEC. 2.   The City of San Francisco hereby relinquishes and grants all the right and claim of the city to the lands within the corporate limits, to the parties in the actual possession thereof, by themselves or tenants, on or before the first day of January, A. D. one thousand eight hundred and fifty-five, to their heirs and assigns forever; excepting the property known as the slip property, and bounded on the north by Clay street, on the west by Davis street, on the south by Sacramento street, and on the east by the water-lot front.   And excepting, also, any piece or parcel of land situated south, east or north of the water-lot front of the City of San Francisco, as established by an Act of the Legislature of March twenty-sixth, A. D. one thousand eight hundred and fifty-one; *provided*, such possession has been continued up to the time of the introduction of this ordinance in the Common Council; or, if interrupted by any intruder, or trespasser, has been, or may be, recovered by legal process; and it is hereby declared to be the true intent and meaning of this ordinance, that when any of the said lands have been occupied and possessed under and by virtue of a lease or demise, they shall be deemed to have been in the possession of the landlord or lessor under whom they were so occupied or possessed; *provided*, that all persons who hold title to lands within said limits by virtue of any grant made by any ayuntamiento, town council, alcalde or justice of the peace of the former pueblo of San Francisco before the seventh day of July, one thousand eight hundred and forty-six; or grants to lots of land lying east of Larkin street and northeast of Johnston street made by any ayuntamiento, town council, alcalde, of said pueblo, since that date, and before the incorporation of the City of San Francis· o by the State of California; and which grant, or the material portion thereof, was registered or recorded in a proper book of record deposited in the office, or custody, or control of the Recorder of the County of San Francisco, on or before the third day of April, A. D. one thousand eight hundred and fifty; or by virtue of any conveyance duly made by the commissioners of the funded debt of the City of San Francisco, and recorded on or before the first day of January, one thousand eight hundred and fifty-five, shall, for all the purposes contemplated by this ordinance, be deemed to be the possessors of the land so granted, although the said lands may be in the actual occupancy of persons holding the same adverse to the said grantees.

SEC. 3.   The patent issued, or any grant made by the United States to the city, shall inure to the several use, benefit and behoof of the said possessors, their heirs and assigns, mentioned in the preceding section, as fully and effectually, to all intents and purposes, as if it were issued or made directly to them individually and by name.

SEC. 4.   The city, however, as a consideration annexed to the next two preceding sections, reserves to itself all the lots which it now occupies, or has already set apart for public squares, streets, and sites for school houses, city hall, and other buildings belonging to the corporations; and also such lots and lands as may be selected and reserved for streets and other public purposes, under the provisions of the next succeeding sections.

SEC. 5.   The city shall have the right to proceed to lay out and open streets, as soon as the corporation may deem it expedient, in that part of the city west of Larkin street and southwest of Johnston street, and reserves the right to take possession of such lands as it may be necessary to occupy for that purpose, without compensation; and to assess, in the manner provided by the present or any existing charter of the city, upon the lands bounded on such streets, the whole expense of laying out, opening, grading and constructing the same; and payment of the costs of said improvements shall be deemed a charge upon the lands mentioned in this section, to which the City of San Francisco relinquishes her right and title by the second and third sections of this ordinance.

SEC. 6.   The city shall also have the right to select and set apart, from the lands west of Larkin street and southwest of Johnston street, as many lots, not exceeding one hundred and thirty-seven and a half feet square each, as the Mayor and Common Council may, by ordinance, determine to be necessary for sites for school-houses, hospitals, fire-engine-houses, and other public establishments necessary and proper for the use of the corporation; and may lay out and reserve upon the said lands, at convenient and suitable points and distances, public squares, which shall not embrace more than one block, corresponding in size to the adjoining blocks; *provided*, that the selection shall be made within six months from the time of the passage of this ordinance; and that the city shall not, without due compensation, occupy, for the purposes mentioned in this section, after the laying out of the streets aforesaid, more than one-twentieth part of the land in the possession of any one person; and that such possessor shall voluntarily assent thereto; or, refusing to do so, shall not be entitled to the benefit of any concession contained in the second and third sections of this ordinance.

Sec. 7. The lots and lands reserved for the use of the corporation, under the provisions of the next preceding section, shall be selected in localities likely to be most convenient and suitable for their respective uses, and in such proportion to the quantity in the possession of the respective occupants as to make the apportionment as nearly equal as circumstances will admit.

Sec. 8. The selection of said lands and lots shall be made by a commission, to consist of three persons, who shall be chosen by the Common Council, in joint convention, who shall report the same to the Common Council for its approval; and, upon such approval, deeds of release to the corporation for the lands thus selected shall be executed, acknowledged and recorded, in which deeds shall be specified the uses for which they are granted, reserved, and set apart, respectively.

Sec. 9. Although the city hereby renounces in favor of the actual possessors, in accordance with the provisions of section second, any right or claim of its own, nothing in this ordinance is intended to prejudice any other outstanding title to the said lands adverse to the said possessors.

Sec. 10. Application shall be made to the Legislature to confirm and ratify this ordinance, and to Congress to relinquish all the right and title of the United States to the said lands, for the uses and purposes hereinbefore specified.

Sec. 11. Nothing contained in this ordinance shall be construed to prevent the city from continuing to prosecute, to a final determination, her claim now pending before the United States Land Commission, for pueblo lands, for the several use, benefit, and behoof, of the said possessors mentioned in section two, as to the lands by them so possessed, and for the proper use, benefit, and behoof, of the corporation as to all other lands not hereinbefore released and confirmed to the said possessors.

Sec. 12. That all ordinances, or parts of ordinances, conflicting with this ordinance, or any of its provisions, be and the same are hereby repealed.

[Approved June twentieth, one thousand eight hundred and fifty-five.

S. P. WEBB, Mayor.]

And whereas, the said Common Council passed another ordinance, approved by the Mayor of said city, September twenty-seventh, A. D. one thousand eight hundred and fifty-five, which last mentioned ordinance is in the words and figures following, to-wit:

Number eight hundred and forty-five—Ordinance providing for selecting and designating public squares and reservations for hospitals, fire-engines, and school purposes, and for adopting the plan of streets in the western and southwestern portion of the city, according to the provisions of ordinance number eight hundred and twenty-two, and confirmatory of said ordinance number eight hundred and twenty-two.

The People of the City of San Francisco do ordain as follows:

SECTION 1.   Under and by virtue of the provisions of the ordinance of the Common Council number eight hundred and twenty-two, entitled "an ordinance for the settlement and quieting of land titles in the City of San Francisco, approved June twentieth, one thousand eight hundred and fifty-five," the Board of Aldermen and Board of Assistant Aldermen shall meet in joint convention, at their next regular meeting after the passage of this ordinance, and proceed to elect three commissioners, who shall have the powers, and proceed to discharge the duties specified in section eight of said ordinance number eight hundred and twenty-two.

SEC. 2.   It shall be the duty of the City Surveyor, acting in conjunction with the said commissioners, and with their concurrence, to furnish, by way of recommendation to the Common Council, within one month from the date of their appointment, a plan for the location and dimensions of the streets to be laid out within the city limits, west of Larkin, and southwest of Johnston streets, upon which plan shall also be designated the lots and grounds selected by the said commissioners for the use of the city under the provisions of the aforesaid ordinance number eight hundred and twenty-two; *provided*, that the compensation of said commissioners shall not exceed the sum of one hundred dollars each, payable when the Common Council may legally make an appropriation therefor.

SEC. 3.   The said ordinance number eight hundred and twenty-two, referred to in the preceding section one, is hereby re-ordained, ratified, and confirmed in all its parts.

[Approved September twenty-seventh, one thousand eight hundred and fifty-five.   JAMES VAN NESS, Mayor.]

And whereas, in pursuance of the aforesaid ordinance, commissioners were appointed by the Common Council, who in conjunction with the City Surveyor of said city, agreed upon and reported, for the approval of the Common Council, a plan for the location of streets, public squares, and lots for public uses, to be laid out west of Larkin and southwest of Johnston streets, in said city, accompanied by a map of the same, which said plan and map was, by the Justices of the Peace, exercising the powers of a Board of Supervisors of the City and County of San Francisco, adopted, approved, and ratified by an order bearing date the sixteenth day of October, A. D. one thousand eight hundred and fifty-six, which is in the words and figures following, to-wit :

The Board of Supervisors of the City and County of San Francisco do ordain as follows :

SECTION 1.   That the plan or map of the Western Addition, reported by the commission created under an ordinance of the last Common Council of the City of San Francisco, be adopted by this Board, and be declared to be the plan of the city, in respect to the location and establishment of streets and avenues, and the reservation of squares and lots for public purposes in that portion of the then incorporated limits of said city, lying west of Larkin and southwest of Johnston streets.

Be it therefore enacted, that the within and before recited order and ordinances be, and the same are hereby, ratified and confirmed; and all the land entered, or to be entered, in the United States Land Office, in pursuance of section one of the first recited of said ordinances, in trust, shall pass and inure to, and be deemed to have immediately vested in the occupants thereof, for their several use and benefit, according to their respective interests, in execution of the trust designated in an act of Congress, entitled an act for the relief of citizens of towns upon the public lands of the United States, under certain circumstances, approved May twenty-third, one thousand eight hundred and forty-four, as extended and applied by an act of Congress, entitled an act to provide for the survey of the public lands in California, the granting of pre-emption rights therein, and for other purposes, approved March third, one thousand eight hundred and fifty-three; and it shall be the duty of all courts and officers to take judicial notice of the said order and ordinances, as hereinbefore recited, without further proof, as fully and effectually, to all intents and purposes, as if they were public acts of the State Legislature.

SEC. 2.   That the grant or relinquishment of title made by the said city in favor of the several possessors, by sections two and three of the ordinance first above recited, shall take effect as fully and completely, for the purpose of transferring the city's interest, and for all other purposes whatsoever, as if deeds of release and quit-claim had been duly executed and delivered to and in favor of them individually and by name; and no further conveyance or other act shall be necessary to invest the said possessors with all the interest, title, rights, benefits, and advantages, which the said order and ordinances intend or purport to transfer or convey, according to the true intent and meaning thereof ; *provided*, that nothing in this act shall be so construed as to release the City of San Francisco, or City and County of San Francisco, from the payment of any claim or claims due or to become due this State against said City, or City and County, nor to effect or release to said City and County any title this State has or may have to any lands in said City and County of San Francisco.

*An Act to expedite the Settlement of Titles to Lands in the State
of California.*

[Approved July 1, 1864.]

SEC. 1. *Be it enacted by the Senate and House of Representatives of the United
States of America, in Congress assembled,* That whenever the Surveyor-
General of California shall, in compliance with the thirteenth section of an
Act entitled "An Act to ascertain and settle the Private Land Claims in the
State of California," approved March third, eighteen hundred and fifty-one,
have caused any private land claim to be surveyed and a plat to be made
thereof, he shall give notice that the same has been done by a publication,
once a week for four consecutive weeks, in two newspapers, one published
in the City of San Francisco and one published near the land surveyed; and
shall retain in his office, for public inspection, the survey and plat until
ninety days from the date of the first publication in San Francisco shall
have expired; and if no objections are made to said survey, he shall approve
the same, and transmit a copy of the survey and plat thereof to the Commissioner of the General Land Office at Washington, for his examination
and approval; but if objections are made to said survey within the said
ninety days, by any party claiming to have an interest in the tract embraced
by the survey, or in any part thereof, such objections shall be reduced to
writing, stating distinctly the interest of the objector, and signed by him or
his attorney, and filed with the Surveyor-General, together with such affidavits or other proofs as he may produce in support of the objections. At the
expiration of said ninety days, the Surveyor-General shall transmit to the
Commissioner of the General Land Office at Washington a copy of the survey and plat, and objections, and proofs filed with him in support of the objections, and also of any proofs produced by the claimant and filed with him
in support of the survey, together with his opinion thereof; and if the survey
and plat are approved by the said Commissioner, he shall endorse thereon a
certificate of his approval. If disapproved by him, or if, in his opinion, the
ends of justice would be subserved thereby, he may require a further report
from the Surveyor-General of California, touching the matters indicated by
him, or proofs to be taken thereon, or may direct a new survey and plat to
be made. Whenever the objections are disposed of, or the survey and plat
are corrected, or a new survey and plat are made in conformity with his
directions, he shall endorse upon the survey and plat adopted his certificate
of approval. After the survey and plat have been, as hereinbefore provided,
approved by the Commissioner of the General Land Office, it shall be the
duty of the said Commissioner to cause a patent to issue to the claimant as
soon as practicable after such approval.

SEC. 2. *And be it further enacted,* That the provisions of the preceding section shall apply to all surveys and plats by the Surveyor-General of California heretofore made, which have not already been approved by one of the District Courts of the United States for California, or by the Commissioner of the General Land Office; *provided*, that where proceedings for the correction or confirmation of a survey are pending on the passage of this Act in one of the said District Courts, it shall be lawful for such District Court to proceed and complete its examination and determination of the matter, and its decree thereon shall be subject to appeal to the Circuit Court of the United States for the District, in like manner and with like effect as hereafter provided for appeals in other cases to the Circuit Court; and such appeals may be in like manner disposed of by said Circuit Court.

SEC. 3. *And be it further enacted*, That where a plat and survey have already been approved or corrected by one of the Districts Courts of the United States for California, and an appeal from the decree of approval or correction has already been taken to the Supreme Court of the United States, the said Supreme Court shall have jurisdiction to hear and determine the appeal. But where, from such decree of approval or correction, no appeal has been taken to the Supreme Court, no appeal to that Court shall be allowed, but an appeal may be taken within twelve months after this Act shall take effect to the Circuit Court of the United States for California, and said Circuit Court shall proceed to to fully determine the matter. The said Circuit Court shall have power to confirm, or reverse, or modify the action of the District Court, or order the case back to the Surveyor-General for a new survey. When the case is ordered back for a new survey, the subsequent survey of the Surveyor-General shall be under the supervision of the Commissioner of the General Land Office, and not of the District or Circuit Court of the United States.

SEC. 4. *And be it further enacted*, That whenever the District Judge of any one of the District Courts of the United States for California is interested in any land, the claim to which, under the said Act of March third, eighteen hundred and fifty-one, is pending before him, on appeal from the Board of Commissioners created by said Act, the said District Court shall order a case to be transferred to the Circuit Court of the United States for California, which Court shall thereupon take jurisdiction and determine the same. The said District Court may also order a transfer to the said Circuit Court of any other cases arising under said Act, pending before them, affecting the title to lands within the corporate limits of any city or town, and in such cases both the District and Circuit Judges may sit.

SEC. 5. *And be it further enacted*, That all the right and title of the United States to the lands within the corporate limits of the City of San Francisco, as defined in the Act incorporating said City, passed by the Legislature of the State of California, on the fifteenth of April, one thousand eight hundred and fifty-one, are hereby relinquished and granted to the said City and its successors, for the uses and purposes specified in the Ordinances of said.

27

City, ratified by an Act of the Legislature of the said State, approved on the
eleventh of March, eighteen hundred and fifty-eight, entitled " An Act concerning the City of San Francisco, and to ratify and confirm certain Ordinances of the Common Council of the City," there being excepted from
this relinquishment and grant all sites or other parcels of lands which
have been, or now are, occupied by the United States for military, naval, or
other public uses, or such other sites or parcels as may hereafter be designated by the President of the United States, within one year after the rendi-
tion to the General Land Office, by the Surveyor-General, of an approval plat
of the exterior limits of San Francisco, as recognized in this section, in connection with the lines of the public surveys; *and provided*, that the relinquishment and grant by this Act shall in no manner interfere with or prejudice any *bona fide* claims of others, whether asserted adversely under rights
derived from Spain, Mexico, or the laws of the United States, nor preclude
a judicial examination and adjustment thereof.

SEC. 6.   *And be it further enacted*, That it shall be the duty of the Surveyor-
General of California to cause all the private land claims finally confirmed to
be made, whenever requested by the claimants; *provided*, that each claimant
requesting a survey and plat shall first deposit in the District Court of the
District within which the land is situated a sufficient sum of money to pay
the expenses of such survey and plat, and of the publication required by the
first section of this Act. Whenever the survey and plat requested shall have
been completed and forwarded to the Commissioner of· the General Land
Office, as required by this Act, the District Court may direct the application
of the money deposited, or so much thereof as may be necessary, to the
payment of the expenses of said survey and publication.

SEC. 7.   *And be it further enacted*, That it shall be the duty of the Surveyor-
General of California, in making surveys of the private land claims finally
confirmed, to follow the decree of confirmation as closely as practicable whenever such decree designates the specific boundaries of the claim. But when
such decree designates only the out-boundaries within which the quantity
confirmed is to be taken, the location of such quanity shall be made, as near
as practicable, in one tract and in compact form. And if the character of the
land, or intervening grants, be such as to render the location impracticable
in one tract, then each separate location shall be made, as near as practicable, in a compact form. And it shall be the duty of the Commissioner of the
General Land Office to require a substantial compliance with the directions
of this section before approving any survey and plat forwarded to him.

SEC. 8   *A d be it further enacted*, That the Act entitled "An Act to amend
an Act entitled 'An Act to define and regulate the jurisdiction of the District
Courts of the United States in California, in regard to the survey and location
of confirmed Private Land Claims,'" approved June fourteen, eighteen hundred and sixty, and all provisions of law inconsistent with this Act, are hereby repealed

Final Decree confirming the claim of the City of San Francisco to its Pueblo Lands, entered May 18th, 1865.

THE CITY OF SAN FRANCISCO
vs.
THE UNITED STATES.

The appeal in this case taken by the petitioner, the City of San Francisco, from the decree of the Board of Land Commissioners to ascertain and settle private land claims in the State of California, entered on the twenty-first day December, 1854, by which the claim of the petitioner was adjudged to be valid, and confirmed to lands within certain described limits, coming on to be heard upon the transcript of proceedings and decision of said Board, and the papers and evidence upon which said decision was founded, and further evidence taken in the District Court of the United States for the Northern District of California pending said appeal—the said case having been transferred to this Court by order of the said District Court, under the provisions of section four of the Act entitled, "An Act to expedite the settlement of titles to lands in the State of California," approved July 1st, 1864,—and counsel of the United States and for the petitioner having been heard, and due deliberation had, it is ordered, adjudged and decreed that the claim of the petitioner, the City of San Francisco, to the land hereinafter described, is valid, and that the same be confirmed.

The land of which confirmation is made is a tract situated within the County of San Francisco and embracing so much of the extreme upper portion of the peninsula above ordinary high-water mark (as the same existed at the date of the conquest of the country, namely, the seventh of July, A. D. 1846), on which the City of San Francisco is situated, as will contain an area of four square leagues—said tract being bounded on the north and east by the Bay of San Francisco, on the west by the Pacific Ocean, and on the south by a due east and west line drawn so as to include the area aforesaid, subject to the following deductions, namely: such parcels of land as have been heretofore reserved or dedicated to public uses by the United States, and also such parcels of lands as have been by grants from lawful authority vested in private proprietorship, and have been finally confirmed to parties claiming thereunder, by said tribunals, in proceedings now pending therein for that purpose; all of which said excepted parcels of land are included within the area of four square leagues above mentioned, but are excluded from the confirmation to the City. This confirmation is in trust for the benefit of the lot-holders under grants from the Pueblo, Town, or City of San Francisco, or other competent authority, and as to any residue, in trust for the use and benefit of the inhabitants or the City.

FIELD, Circuit Judge.

San Francisco, May 18th, 1865.

SUPPLEMENT CLXVI

1869-70, 353.

An Act to expedite the settlement of land titles in the City and County of San Francisco, and to ratify and confirm the acts and proceedings of certain of the authorities thereof.

[Approved March 14, 1870.]

The People of the State of California, represented in Senate and Assembly, do enact as follows :

SECTION 1. Upon receiving a petition from any person or persons, claiming that they, by themselves, their tenants, or the persons through whom they claim or derive possession, have been, from and including the eighth day of March, Anno Domini eighteen hundred and sixty-six (1866), and still are, in the possession of any of the lands without the corporate limits of the City of San Francisco, as defined in an Act to reincorporate said city, passed by the Legislature of the State of California on the fifteenth day of April, Anno Domini eighteen hundred and fifty-one (1851), and described in the decree of Justice Field, of the United States Circuit Court, confirming the claim of the City and County of San Francisco, entered November second, Anno Domini eighteen hundred and sixty-four (1864), in the Circuit Court of the United States for the Northern District of the State of California, and that they, or the persons through whom they claim or derive possession, have paid to the Tax Collector of the City and County of San Francisco the amount assessed by the Outside Land Committee upon the land described in said petition, to pay for land reserved for public use, provided for in section ten (10) of Order Eight Hundred (800), and also paid the taxes mentioned in section four (4) of said order, and all the taxes levied on said lands for State and municipal purposes now due and remaining unpaid; or, upon receiving a petition from any person or persons, setting forth that said petitioners, by themselves, their tenants, or the persons through whom they claim or derive possession, were, on or before the first (1st) day of January, Anno Domini eighteen hundred and fifty-five (1855), to and including the twentieth (20th) day of June, Anno Domini eighteen hundred and fifty-five (1855), and still are, in possession of the land described in said petition, embraced within the corporate limits of the City of San Francisco, and above high water mark, as defined in the Act to incorporate said city, passed by the Legislature of the State of California, on the fifteenth (15th) day of April, Anno Domini eighteen hundred and fifty-one (1851); and such petition in either case setting forth that such lands have not been sold, leased, dedicated, reserved or conveyed by authority of the said City and County of San Francisco, or the United States, to any one, or for any purpose, and asking for a grant from said city and county, the Board of Supervisors shall proceed to act thereon as hereinafter provided. This petition shall be verified by the oath or affirmation of the party in whose behalf the petition is presented, or by some one acting as his agent, and conversant with the facts detailed in the petition.

SEC. 2. All petitions mentioned in the first section of this Act shall be .referred to the Committee on Outside Lands. The Clerk of the Board of * Supervisors shall be the Clerk of the Outside Land Committee. The party presenting the said petition may appear before said Clerk and make proof, verbal and documentary, of the truth of the matters alleged in his petition. Copies of the documentary evidence shall be filed with said Clerk, and the oral testimony shall be reduced to writing by said Clerk and subscribed by the witness. The proofs of the petitioner being closed, the said committee shall proceed to consider the same, and shall make such report and recommendation thereon as to them shall seem just and proper in the premises. The said committee shall file with the Clerk of the Board of Supervisors the testimony taken as aforesaid, together with the report of the said committee, and said report shall be submitted to the Board of Supervisors for their approval, and if, in their judgment, the claim of the petitioner is well founded, they shall, by an order entered in their minutes, adjudge and award a grant of such lands to the petitioner or petitioners therefor, less the amount reserved for public use. The said Board shall thereupon give public notice of their award by notice, published at least once a week for three successive weeks, in some daily newspaper published in the City and County of San Francisco, which notice shall specify the name of the applicant, the date and filing of his petition, and the tract of land awarded, by a good and sufficient description thereof; proof of publication of such notice shall be made in the manner now or hereafter required by law for the proof of publication in civil process. The Clerk of the said committee shall be allowed compensation, for taking the oath or affirmation of witnesses, twenty-five cents; and for reducing the testimony to writing, twenty cents a folio, which shall be in full for all services rendered by him as Clerk of said committee. The compensation herein allowed to the Clerk of said committee shall be paid to said Clerk by the party presenting the petition.

SEC. 3. Upon receiving proof of the publication of the notice provided for in the second section hereof, and the payment of all necessary expenses for deeds, the Mayor of the City and County of San Francisco is hereby authorized and empowered to execute, acknowledge and deliver to the party or parties presenting the aforesaid petition, a deed of conveyance of the tract or lot of land as aforesaid, adjudged and awarded to the petitioner, and attach thereto the corporate seal of the City and County of San Francisco; *provided*, the petitioner or petitioners shall, before receiving a deed as aforesaid, be required to quit-claim and peaceably deliver the possession

of all land claimed by said petitioner or petitioners, reserved by the Commissioners acting under Ordinance Eight Hundred and Twenty-two (822),
and all those lands reserved by the Committee of the Board on Outside
Lands for the use and benefit of the City and County of San Francisco;
provided, however, that in case a suit shall be pending between the petitioner and some third person, involving the right of possession of the tract,
or some portion thereof, petitioned for, and such third person shall file with
the Clerk of the Board of Supervisors a copy of the complaint filed in such
action, before the deed shall have been executed and delivered to the peti- ʼ
tioner, and also competent proof that such third persons, or the persons
through whom they claim or derive possession, have paid the taxes and
assessments mentioned in the first section of this Act, then and in that case
the deed shall be withheld until such suit shall be finally determined; and
there shall thereafter be executed a deed of conveyance of so much of the
tract of land as shall be involved in the said suit, to the party in whose
favor the said suit shall be finally determined as aforesaid; *provided* further,
that the expenses hereinafter provided for shall be paid before such conveyance shall be delivered.

SEC. 4.   Upon the filing of a petition, as hereinbefore provided, the petitioner shall deposit with the Clerk of the Board of Supervisors a sum of
money sufficient to pay for the publication of the notice hereinbefore provided, and other expenses incident to the granting of the prayer of the
petitioner.   But the Clerk shall not receive on file any petition that shall
not be in conformity with the provisions of this Act.

SEC. 5.   A conveyance executed and delivered in pursuance of the pro-,
visions of this Act shall operate as an acknowledgment on the part of the
said city and county, that the title to the land therein described has passed
under and by virtue of said Order Number Eight Hundred (800), or of said
Ordinance Number Eight Hundred and Twenty-two (822), as the case may
be, and also under and by virtue of the several Acts of Congress and the
Legislature ratifying said order and ordinance, or under the authority of
which the same have been passed; and such conveyance shall likewise operate to grant, convey, remise and release to the party, his heirs and assigns,
named therein, the lands in such conveyance described, and all the estate
and interest, present and future, of the said City and County of San Francisco, in and to such lands.   But no such conveyance shall in any event be
held to import a warranty or covenant of title on the part of, or to bind said
city and county, or any officer thereof.

SEC. 6.   All orders and parts of orders of the Board of Supervisors of the
City and County of San Francisco, conflicting with Order Eight Hundred
and Sixty-six (866) are hereby repealed, but such repeal shall not invalidate
. any of the proceedings instituted under the order of which Order Eight
Hundred and Sixty-six (866) is amendatory, and such proceedings may be
continued under the provisions of said Order Eight Hundred and Sixty-six

(866). Whenever such proceedings have been completed, and the Committee on Outside Lands of said Board of Supervisors, or a majority of them, have executed and delivered a deed or deeds, the person or persons to whom such deed or deeds were executed, may obtain from the Mayor, at his or their own expense, a deed of the same land, executed by him and sealed with the corporate seal of the City and County of San Francisco, without further petition, proof, award or notice; and the Mayor is hereby authorized and empowered to execute such deeds. Any and all such deeds shall have the like force and effect as the conveyances mentioned in section five of this Act; *provided*, that if any grantee in any deed executed by such committee has heretofore sold or conveyed any land included in such deed, or his, her or their interest in such land, by writing recorded in the office of the City and County Recorder of the City and County of San Francisco, the deed executed by the Mayor, and sealed with the aforesaid corporate seal, shall be, as to the lands so sold or conveyed, for, and inure to the benefit of such purchaser or purchasers, grantee or grantees, and their heirs, and the deed executed by the Mayor shall expressly so state.

SEC. 7. Whereas, divers co-owners and tenants in common of certain tracts of land situate in the City and County of San Francisco, and within the limits described in Order Number Eight Hundred (800) of said Board of Supervisors, who are or claim to be in possession thereof as such owners and tenants in common, under and in accordance with the terms and provisions of said Order Number Eight Hundred (800), and as such alleged co-owners and tenants in common, have had said tracts of land delineated by metes and bounds, and as entireties, upon the map mentioned and provided for in said Order Number Eight Hundred (800), and have also severally paid their proportionate share of the taxes upon said tracts of land for the five fiscal years preceding the year beginning July first (1st), eighteen hundred and sixty-six (1866), and all subsequent taxes due thereon, and have filed with said Board their petition, claiming said land under and in accordance with the terms and provisions of said order and Order Number Seven Hundred and Forty-eight (748) of said Board; now, therefore, it shall be lawful for any such alleged co-owners or tenants in common of lands situate within the limits described by said Order Number Eight Hundred (800), or one or more thereof, or his or their successor or successors in interest, who shall have performed the acts and conditions aforesaid, to pay, as such co-owners or tenants in common, his or their proportionate share of the amount of any and all taxes or assessments now levied and due, or which may hereafter (at any time prior to the delivery of a deed from the City and County of San Francisco, for his or their undivided interest in said lands) be levied upon and become due upon the tract or tracts of land, wherein he or they hold as such co-owners or tenants in common; and to facilitate the payment of such proportionate shares, the Tax Collector is hereby authorized to divide into smaller parcels any tract of land claimed

by co-owners, owners in severalty or tenants in common, and to apportion
to each subdivision the ratable proportion, value considered, of the assessment made to the whole tract so divided, and after the payment of the
apportioned assessment upon any one of such subdivisions, no valid objection shall be made by any party to the acts of the Tax Collector in respect
to such division, and the apportioned assessment shall become as valid and
binding upon the respective subdivisions to which they have been so apportioned, as if no division had been made by said Tax Collector.

SEC. 8. All of the acts and proceedings of the Tax Collector of the City and
County of San Francisco, taken or done by him in pursuance of or under
the authority of any order or resolution of the Board of Supervisors of said
city and county, or in pursuance of or under the authority of any Act of the
Legislature of the State of California, in reference to the collection of the
taxes or assessments upon what are commonly designated as the outside
lands of the said city and county, are hereby ratified and confirmed, and
declared to be legal, valid and binding, both upon the lands embraced
within the purview of any such Act of the Legislature of this State, or order
or resolution of said Board of Supervisors of said city and county.

SEC. 9. And whereas, certain lands, known as outside lands of the City
and County of San Francisco, have been advertised for sale by the Tax
Collector of said city and county, for the non-payment of taxes or assessments levied thereon, known as the outside land tax, which sale has been
postponed from time to time by said Tax Collector; and whereas, some of
the parties claiming to be the owners of portions of said lands refuse or
neglect to pay the taxes so levied as aforesaid, and have enjoined the said
Tax Collector from proceeding with said sale; now, therefore, be it enacted,
that all the pieces or parcels of land so advertised by the said Tax Collector
as aforesaid, on which assessments heretofore levied have not been already
paid, or shall not be paid to said Tax Collector within thirty days from and
after the passage of this Act, shall be sold by said Tax Collector, for gold
coin of the United States, as hereinafter provided. Said sales may be adjourned from time to time by said Tax Collector, not exceeding in all sixty
days, and may take place at such place in said city and county as the said
Tax Collector may designate. The time during which any injunction may
be in force restraining the said Tax Collector or other officer of said city and
county from proceeding with said sale shall not be computed as any part of
the periods limited and fixed within which he may perform the acts and
duties herein defined, but shall be excluded therefrom. The said Tax
Collector may retain in his custody so much of the proceeds arising from
said sale as shall be necessary to liquidate and pay off the appraisements
for reserved lands as heretofore made, pursuant to Order Number Eight
Hundred, and all such proper and necessary costs as he may be at in conducting said sale and the collection of such assessments and the overplus
thereof, he shall pay over to the Treasurer of the said city and county; and

said Treasurer shall carry the amount so paid over to him to the credit of the General Fund of said City and County. The amount so retained by the said Tax Collector shall be paid over by him to the parties entitled thereto under section eleven of Order Number Eight Hundred, in discharge of the appraisements for reserved lands; and within thirty days from and after he shall have received a sum from assessments equal to the total amount of appraisements for reserved lands, over and above the expenses and costs of making collections, he shall settle and pay off in full the appraisements made as aforesaid; *provided*, however, when there are conflicting claimants for particular appraisements, said Tax Collector shall not be obliged to make payment in such cases until such conflicting claims shall be determined, amicably or otherwise; and the said Tax Collector is hereby authorized, from time to time, to make distribution on account of said appraisements for reserved lands, pro rata, as often as he shall have on hand fifty per cent. or less thereof.

SEC. 10. Said Tax Collector shall issue to each successful purchaser a receipt, in duplicate, for the amount bid and paid by him, which receipt shall also contain a brief description of the premises sold, and upon its face entitle the bidder, or his assigns, to a deed of conveyance of the premises therein described, at the expiration of twelve months from the date of the sale, unless there shall be a redemption of the premises as hereinafter provided.

SEC. 11. Said lands shall be sold subject to redemption, and such redemption may be made at any time within twelve months from the date of sale, upon paying to the said Tax Collector the amount bid therefor, together with twenty-five per cent. thereon and in addition thereto; and the party redeeming shall also pay such expenses of advertising and other expenses as the said Tax Collector may have incurred in and about the particular tract from the sale of which redemption is sought to be effected; *provided*, that all lands sold for assessment prior to the passage of this Act shall have the same right of redemption as provided for in section eleven of this Act.

SEC. 12. The Tax Collector, after the expiration of twelve months from the date of sale, in which there has been no redemption, shall make a conveyance of the premises sold to the purchaser thereof, or his assigns; and where there has been a redemption, he may make conveyance thereof to the redemptioner. In cases of redemption, the Tax Collector shall pay over to the holders of receipts the amount bid, together with the sum paid by the redemptioner, in addition to the bid.

SEC. 13. This Act shall take effect and be in force from and after its passage.

SUPPLEMENT CLXVII.

1881, 72.

_____

An Act to amend Section 4109 of "An Act to establish a Political Code," approved March 12, 1872, relating to the election and terms of office of county, city and county, and township officers, and to repeal Sections 4024, 4027, and 4111 of said Political Code.

[Approved March 7, 1881.]

The People of the State of California, represented in Senate and Assembly, do enact as follows:

SECTION 1. Section four thousand one hundred and nine of the Political Code is amended to read as follows :

4109. All elective county, city and county, and township officers, except Superior Court Judges, Superintendents of Schools, and Assessors, shall be elected at the general election to be held in the year eighteen hundred and eighty-two, and at the general election to be held every second year thereafter, and shall take office on the first Monday after the first day of January, next succeeding their election, and shall hold office for two years. The years that said officers are to hold office are to be computed respectively from and including the first Monday after the first day of January of any one year to and excluding the first Monday after the first day of January of the next succeeding year; *provided*, that all Supervisors and Justices of the Peace shall take office on the first Monday after the first day of January next succeeding their election, and shall hold office for two years. The years during which a Supervisor and Justice of the Peace is to hold office are to be compu ed respectively from and including the first Monday of January of any one year to and excluding the first Monday of January next succeeding. Assessors of every county, and of every city and county, shall be elected at the general election to be held on the first Tuesday after the first Monday in November, eighteen hundred and eighty-two, and at the general election to be held every four years thereafter, and shall hold office for the term of four years from and after the first Monday after the first day of January next succeeding their election.

SUPPLEMENT CLXVIII.

ARTICLE IV OF THE STATE CONSTITUTION.

LEGISLATIVE DEPARTMENT.

SEC. 30. Neither the legislature, nor any county, city and county, township, school district, or other municipal corporation, shall ever make an appropriation, or pay from any public fund whatever, or grant anything to or in aid of any religious sect, church, creed or sectarian purpose, or help to support or sustain any school, college, university, hospital, or other institution controlled by any religious creed, church, or sectarian denomination whatever; nor shall any grant or donation of personal property or real estate ever be made by the State, or any city, city and county, town, or other municipal corporation for any religious creed, church, or sectarian purpose whatever; *provided*, that nothing in this section shall prevent the Legislature granting aid pursuant to section twenty-two of this article.

ARTICLE IX.

EDUCATION.

SEC. 3. A Superintendent of Schools for each county shall be elected by the qualified electors thereof at each gubernatorial election; *provided*, that the Legislature may authorize two or more counties to unite and elect one Superintendent for the counties so uniting.

SEC. 6. The public school system shall include primary and grammar schools, and such high schools, evening schools, normal schools, and technical schools as may be established by the Legislature, or by municipal or district authority; but the entire revenue derived from the State School Fund, and the State school tax, shall be applied exclusively to the support of primary and grammar schools.

SEC. 7. The Governor, the Superintendent of Public Instruction, and the Principals of the State Normal Schools shall constitute the State Board of Education, and shall compile or cause to be compiled and adopt a uniform series of text books for use in the Common Schools throughout the State. The State Board may cause such text books, when adopted, to be printed and published by the Superintendent of State Printing at the State Printing Office, and when so printed and published, to be sold at the cost price of printing, publishing and distributing the same. The text books so adopted shall continue in use not less than three years; and said State Board shall perform such other duties as may be prescribed by law. The Legislature shall provide for a Board of Education in each county in the State. The County Superintendent and the County Boards of Education shall have control of the examination of teachers and the granting of teachers' certificates within their respective jurisdictions. [Amendment adopted November 4, 1884.]

ARTICLE XI.

RELATING TO CITIES COUNTIES AND TOWNS.

SECTION 1. The several counties, as they now exist, are hereby recognized as legal subdivisions of this State.

SEC. 2. No county seat shall be removed unless two-thirds of the qualified electors of the county, voting on the proposition at a general election, shall vote in favor of such removal. A proposition of removal shall not be submitted in the same county more than once in four years.

SEC. 3. No new county shall be established which shall reduce any county to a population of less than eight thousand; nor shall a new county be formed containing a less population than five thousand; nor shall any line thereof pass within five miles of the county seat of any county proposed to be divided. Every county which shall be enlarged or created from territory taken from any other county or counties, shall be liable for a just proportion of the existing debts and liabilities of the county or counties from which such territory shall be taken.

SEC. 4. The Legislature shall establish a system of county governments which shall be uniform throughout the State; and by general laws shall provide for township organization, under which any county may organize whenever a majority of the qualified electors of such county, voting at a general election, shall so determine; and whenever a county shall adopt township organization, the assessment and collection of the revenue shall be made, and the business of such county and the local affairs of the several townships therein shall be managed and transacted in the manner prescribed by such general laws.

SEC. 5. The Legislature, by general and uniform laws, shall provide for the election or appointment, in the several counties, of Boards of Supervisors, Sheriffs, County Clerks, District Attorneys, and such other county, township, and municipal officers as public convenience may require, and shall prescribe their duties and fix their terms of office. It shall regulate the compensation of all such officers in proportion to duties, and for this purpose may classify the counties by population; and it shall provide for the strict accountability of county and township officers for all fees which may be collected by them, and for all public and municipal moneys which may be paid to them, or officially come into their possession.

SEC. 6. Corporations for municipal purposes shall not be created by special laws; but the Legislature, by general laws, shall provide for the incorporation, organization, and classification, in proportion to population, of cities and towns, which laws may be altered, amended, or repealed. Cities and towns heretofore organized or incorporated may become organized under such general laws whenever a majority of the electors voting at a general election shall so determine, and shall organize in conformity therewith; and cities or towns heretofore or hereafter organized, and all charters thereof framed or adopted by authority of this Constitution, shall be subject to and controlled by general laws.

SEC. 7. City and county governments may be merged and consolidated into one municipal government, with one set of officers, and may be incorporated under general laws providing for the incorporation and organization of corporations for municipal purposes. The provisions of this Constitution applicable to cities and also those applicable to counties, so far as not inconsistent or not prohibited to cities, shall be applicable to such consolidated government. In consolidated city and county governments, of more than one hundred thousand population, there shall be two boards of Supervisors or houses of legislation—one of which, to consist of twelve persons, shall be elected by general ticket from the city and county at large, and shall hold office for the term of four years, but shall be so classified that after the first election only six shall be elected every two years; the other, to consist of twelve persons, shall be elected every two years, and shall hold office for the term of two years. Any vacancy occurring in the office of Supervisor, in either Board, shall be filled by the Mayor or other chief executive officer.

SEC. 8. Any city containing a population of more than one hundred thousand inhabitants may frame a charter for its own government, consistent with and subject to the Constitution and laws of this State, by causing a Board of fifteen freeholders, who shall have been for at least five years qualified electors thereof, to be elected by the qualified voters of such city, at any general or special election, whose duty it shall be, within ninety days after such election, to prepare and propose a charter for such city, which shall be signed in duplicate by the members of such Board, or a majority of them, and returned, one copy thereof to the Mayor, or other chief executive officer of such city, and the other to the Recorder of deeds of the county. Such proposed charter shall then be published in two daily papers of general circulation in such city for at least twenty days, and within not less than thirty days after such publication it shall be submitted to the qualified electors of such city at a general or special election, and if a majority of such qualified electors voting thereat shall ratify the same, it shall thereafter be submitted to the Legislature for its approval or rejection as a whole, without power of alteration or amendment, and if approved by a majority vote of the members elected to each House, it shall become the charter of such city, or if such city be consolidated with a county, then of such city and county, and

shall become the organic law thereof, and supersede any existing charter
and all amendments thereof, and all special laws inconsistent with such
charter. A copy of such charter, certified by the Mayor, or chief executive
officer, and authenticated by the seal of such city, setting forth the submission of such charter to the electors and its ratification by them, shall be
made in duplicate and deposited, one in the office of the Secretary of State,
the other, after being recorded in the office of the Recorder of Deeds of the
county, among the archives of the city; all courts shall take judicial notice
thereof. The charter so ratified may be amended at intervals of not less than
two years, by proposals therefor, submitted by legislative authority of the
city to the qualified voters thereof, at a general or special election held at
least sixty days after the publication of such proposals, and ratified by at
least three-fifths of the qualified electors voting thereat, and approved by the
Legislature, as herein provided for the approval of the charter. In submitting any such charter, or amendment thereto, any alternative article or proposition may be presented for the choice of the voters, and may be voted on
separately without prejudice to others.

SEC. 9.   The compensation of any county, city, town, or municipal officer
shall not be increased after his election or during his term of office; nor shall
his term of any such officer be extended beyond the period for which he is
elected or appointed.

SEC. 10.   No county, city, town, or other public or municipal corporation,
nor the inhabitants thereof, nor the property therein, shall be released or
discharged from its or their proportionate share of taxes to be levied for
State purposes, nor shall commutation for such taxes be authorized in any
form whatsoever.

SEC. 11.   Any county, city, town or township may make and enforce within its limits all such local, police, sanitary, and other regulations as are not
in conflict with general laws.

SEC. 12.   The Legislature shall have no power to impose taxes upon counties, cities, towns, or other public or municipal corporations, or upon the
inhabitants or property thereof, for county, city, town, or other municipal
purposes, but may, by general laws, vest in the corporate authorities thereof
the power to assess and collect taxes for such purposes.

SEC. 13.   The Legislature shall not delegate to any special commission,
private corporation, company, association, or individual, any power to make,
control, or appropriate, supervise, or in any way interfere with, any county,
city, town, or municipal improvement, money, property, or effects, whether
held in trust or otherwise, or to levy taxes or assessments, or perform any
municipal functions whatever.

SEC. 14.   No State office shall be continued or created in any county, city,
town, or other municipality, for the inspection, measurement, or graduation

of any merchandise, manufacture, or commodity; but such county, city, town, or municipality may, when authorized by general law, appoint such officers.

SEC. 15. Private property shall not be taken or sold for the payment of the corporate debt of any political or municipal corporation.

SEC. 16. All moneys, assessments, and taxes belonging to or collected for the use of any county, city, town, or public or municipal corporation, coming into the hands of any officer thereof, shall immediately be deposited with the Treasurer, or other legal depositary, to the credit of such city, town, or other corporation, respectively, for the benefit of the funds to which they respectively belong.

SEC. 17. The making of profit out of county, city, town, or other public money, or using the same for any purpose not authorized by law, by any officer having the possession or control thereof, shall be a felony, and shall be prosecuted and punished as prescribed by law.

SEC. 18. No county, city, town, township, Board of Education, or school district, shall incur any indebtedness or liability in any manner, or for any purpose, exceeding in any year the income and revenue provided for it for such year, without the assent of two-thirds of the qualified electors thereof voting at an election to be held for that purpose, nor unless, before or at the time of incurring such indebtedness, provision shall be made for the collection of an annual tax sufficient to pay the interest on such indebtedness as it falls due, and also to constitute a sinking fund for the payment of the principal thereof within twenty years from the time of contracting the same. Any indebtedness or liability incurred contrary to this provision shall be void.

SEC. 19. In any city where there are no public works owned and controlled by the municipality for supplying the same with water or artificial light, any individual, or any company, duly incorporated for such purpose, under and by authority of the laws of this State, shall, under the direction of the Superintendent of Streets, or other officer in control thereof, and under such general regulations as the municipality may prescribe for damages and indemnity for damages, have the privilege of using the public streets and thoroughfares thereof, and of laying down pipes and conduits therein, and connecting therewith, so far as may be necessary for introducing into and supplying such city and its inhabitants, either with gaslight, or other illuminating light, or with fresh water for domestic and all other purposes, upon the condition that the municipal government shall have the right to regulate the charges thereof. [Amendment adopted November 4, 1884.]

ARTICLE XIV.

WATER AND WATER RIGHTS.

SECTION 1. The use of all water now appropriated, or that may hereafter be appropriated, for sale, rental, or distribution, is hereby declared to be a public use, and subject to the regulation and control of the State, in the manner to be prescribed by law ; provided, that the rates or compensation to be collected by any person, company, or corporation in this State for the use of water supplied to any city and county, or city or town, or the inhabitants thereof, shall be fixed, annually, by the Board of Supervisors, or city and county, or City or Town Council, or other governing body of such city and county, or city or town, by ordinance or otherwise, in the manner that other ordinances or legislative acts or resolutions are passed by such body, and shall continue in force for one year and no longer. Such ordinances or resolutions shall be passed in the month of February of each year, and take effect on the first day of July thereafter. Any Board or body failing to pass the necessary ordinances or resolutions fixing water rates, where necessary, within such time, shall be subject to peremptory process to compel action at the suit of any party interested, and shall be liable to such further processes and penalties as the Legislature may prescribe. Any person, company, or corporation collecting water-rates in any city and county, or city or town in this State, otherwise than as so established, shall forfeit the franchises and water-works of such person, company, or corporation to the city and county, or city or town, where the same are collected, for the public use.

SEC. 2. The right to collect rates or compensation for the use of water supplied to any county, city and county, or town, or the inhabitants thereof· is a franchise, and cannot be exercised except by authority of and in the manner prescribed by law.

ARTICLE XIX.

CHINESE.

SEC. 3. No Chinese shall be employed in any State, county, municipal or other public work, except in punishment for crime.

STATUTES PASSED AT THE SESSION OF THE LEGISLATURE OF 1887.

SUPPLEMENT CLXIX.

1887, 52.

An Act to authorize the Common Councils and Boards of Supervisors of the several cities, counties, and cities and counties in this State to levy taxes for the maintenance of public parks, having an area of over ten acres each, within their respective limits.

[Approved March 8, 1887.]

The People of the State of California, represented in Senate and Assembly, do enact as follows:

SECTION 1. The Common Council and the Board of Supervisors of any city, county, or city and county, of this State, are hereby authorized and empowered to levy a yearly tax of not to exceed three cents upon every one hundred dollars assessed valuation of property, real and personal, in such city, county, or city and county, for the purpose of maintaining and improving any public park or parks, having an area of ten acres each, therein situated.

SEC. 2. All moneys arising from the tax authorized to be levied by the preceding section, shall be collected by the Tax Collector of the city, county, or city and county wherein said park or parks may be situated, and shall be kept by the Treasurer of said city, county, or city and county, subject only to the order of the public officer or officers, or Board or Commissioner, having legal charge and control of the management and maintenance of said park or parks.

SEC. 3. The terms Common Council and Board of Supervisors are hereby declared to include any body or board which, under the law, is the legislative department of the government of any city, county, or city and county.

SEC. 4. This Act shall be enforced from and after its passage.

28

SUPPLEMENT CLXX.

1887, 58.

An Act to amend an Act entitled "An Act to grant to Boards of Health, or Health Officers, in cities, and cities and counties, the power to regulate the plumbing and drainage of buildings, and to provide for the registration of plumbers," approved March 3, 1885, by amending sections one and two thereof.

[Approved March 9, 1887.]

The People of the State of California, represented in Senate and Assembly, do enact as follows:

SECTION 1. Section one of an Act entitled "An Act to grant to Boards of Health, or Health Officers, in cities, and cities and counties, the power to regulate the plumbing and drainage of buildings, and to provide for the registration of plumbers," approved March third, eighteen hundred and eighty-five, is hereby amended so as to read as follows:

Section 1. It shall not be lawful for any person to carry on business, or labor as a master or journeyman plumber, in any incorporated city, or in any city and county, in this State, until he shall have obtained from the Board of Health of said city, or city and county, a license authorizing him to carry on business, or labor as such mechanic. A license so to do shall be issued only after a satisfactory examination by the Board of each applicant upon his qualifications to conduct such business, or to so labor. All applications for license, and all licenses issued, shall state the name in full, age, nativity, and place of residence of the applicant or person so licensed. It shall be the duty of the Secretary of each Board of Health to keep a record of all such licenses issued, together with an alphabetical index to the same.

SEC. 2. Section 2 of said Act is hereby amended so as to read as follows:
Section 2. A list of all licensed plumbers shall be published in the yearly report of the Health Officer or Board of Health.

SEC. 3. This Act shall take effect immediately.

SUPPLEMENT CLXXI.

1887, 95.

An Act to provide for the completion of all unfinished county, city, city and county, towns and townships buildings in the several counties, cities and counties, cities, and towns throughout the State of California.

[Approved March 10, 1887.]

The People of the State of California, represented in Senate and Assembly, do enact as follows:

SECTION 1.   In the event that the Board of Supervisors of the several counties, and cities, cities and counties, of the State of California shall deem it expedient to continue the construction of any unfinished county, or city and coun y, or town, or townships, building or buildings. they are hereby authorized and empowered to express such judgment by resolution or order, in such form as they may deem proper. And for the purpose of raising the money necessary to complete said building or buildings, the Boards of Supervisors of the several counties, cities, and cities and counties of the State of California are hereby authorized and empowered to levy and collect annually for the fiscal year commencing July first, eighteen hundred and eighty-seven, and ending June thirtieth, eighteen hundred and eighty-eight, and each and every fiscal year thereafter during the four fiscal years next ensuing, in the same manner and at the same times as other taxes in said counties, cities, and towns, and townships, and cities and counties, are levied and collected, an ad valorem property tax on real and personal property within the said counties, or cities and counties, cities, towns, and townships, of not to exceed ten cents on each one hundred dollars of value, as shown by the assessment rolls of said counties, and cities and counties, cities, towns, and townships, for the current fiscal year.

SEC. 2.   All laws now in force, except in so far as they relate to the levy and collection of taxes for the completion of any county, or city and county. or city, or towns, or townships building or buildings, are hereby continued in full force and effect.

SUPPLEMENT CLXXII.

1887, 120.

—

An Act authorizing the incurring of indebtedness by cities, towns, or municipal corporations, incorporated under the laws of this State.

[Approved March 15, 1887.]

The People of the State of California, represented in Senate and Assembly, do enact as follows:

SECTION 1. Any city, town, or municipal corporation, incorporated under the laws of this State, may, as hereinafter provided, incur indebtedness to pay the cost of any permanent municipal improvement requiring an expenditure greater than the amount allowed for such improvements by the ordinary annual tax levy.

SEC. 2. Whenever the legislative branch of any city, town, or municipal corporation shall, by ordinance passed by a vote of three fourths of all its members and approved by the Executive of said city, town, or municipal corporation, determine therein that the public interest or necessity demands the acquisition, construction, or completion of any permanent municipal building, work, sewer, property, water rights, bridges, or improvement, the cost of which is too great to be paid out of the ordinary annual income and revenue of the municipality, they may, after publication of such ordinance for at least two weeks in some newspaper published in such city, town, or municipal corporation, and at the next regular meeting after such publication, or at an adjourned meeting thereat, by ordinance, passed by a vote of three fourths of all its members, and also approved by the said Executive, call a special election and submit to the qualified voters of said city, town, or municipal corporation the proposition of incurring a debt for the purpose set forth in the ordinance, and no question other than the incurrence of indebtedness for such purpose shall be submitted. The ordinance of the city calling such special election shall recite the objects and purposes for which the indebtedness is proposed to be incurred; the estimated cost of such improvement; the necessity for such improvement, and that bonds of the city for municipal improvement shall issue for the payment of the cost, as in said ordinance set forth, if the proposition be accepted by the qualified voters of the city, as hereinafter provided, and shall fix the day on which such special election shall be held, the manner of holding such election, and of voting for or against incurring the indebtedness; *provided*, such election shall be held as provided by law for holding elections in such city, town, or municipal corporations.

SEC. 3. Said ordinance shall be published, once each day, for at least ten days, or once a week for two weeks, before the publication of the notice of the special election, in some newspaper published in such city, town, or municipal corporation. After said publication said legislative body shall cause to be published, for not less than two weeks, in at least one each of the newspapers of such city, a notice of such special election, the purposes for which the indebtedness is to be incurred, the amount of the indebtedness to be incurred, the number and character of the bonds to be issued, the rate of interest to be paid, and the amount of tax levy to be made for the payment thereof. It shall require a vote of two thirds of all voters, voting at such special election, to authorize the issuance of the bonds herein provided.

SEC. 4. All bonds of municipality, for permanent improvements, issued under the provisions of this Act, shall be of a character of bonds known as serials, and shall be payable in the manner following: One twentieth part of the whole indebtedness shall be payable each and every year, on a day to be fixed by the legislative branch of the city, together with the annual interest on all sums unpaid at such date; and the bonds shall be issued in such amount as the government of such city may determine, but not less than one hundred dollars each or more than one thousand dollars each, payable on the day fixed in said bond, with interest not to exceed the sum of five per cent per annum. Such bonds may be sold by the said legislative branch of such city, town, or municipal corporation as they may determine, at not less than their face value in gold coin of the United States; and the proceeds of such sale shall be placed in the treasury of such city, town, or municipal corporation, to the credit of the "Municipal Improvement Fund," "No. ——," or other designation, and shall be applied exclusively to the purposes and objects mentioned in the ordinance providing for the issuance of such bonds, until said objects are accomplished; and the residue, if any, shall be transferred to the General Fund of said city, town, or municipal corporation.

SEC. 5. The legislative branch of such city shall, at the time of fixing the general tax levy of said city, and in the manner for such general tax levy provided, levy and collect annually each year for the term of twenty years, a tax sufficient to pay the annual interest on said bonds, and also one twentieth part of the aggregate amount of such indebtedness so incurred. The taxes herein required to be levied and collected shall be in addition to all other taxes levied for city purposes, and shall be collected at the same time and in the same manner as other city taxes are collected.

SEC. 6. Within thirty days after the sale of such bonds, the Executive of said city, town, or municipal corporation shall appoint a Commissioner of such improvement, who shall be confirmed by a vote of not less than three fourths of the members of the legislative branch of said municipal government, and the Commissioner shall have charge of the said improvement and the disbursement of the said funds for such purposes, subject to the conditions of the ordinances of the said city providing for such work or improvement, and such ordinances as may at any time be passed relating thereto; but the Commissioner, when appointed, shall not be removed until the completion of the said improvement, unless by order of the Executive, concurred in by a vote of three fourths of said legislative branch.

Sec. 7.   The compensation of the Commissioner to be appointed under the provisions of this Act shall be fixed by ordinance not to exceed five dollars per day for each day of actual service; said Commissioner shall execute an official bond in the penal sum of ten thousand dollars ($10,000) for the faithful performance of his duties

Sec. 8.   All contracts for the construction or completion of any work, or of improvements, or furnishing of materials for work or improvements, as herein provided for, shall be let to the lowest responsible bidder, who shall furnish such bonds as the legislative branch of said city, town, or municipal corporation may require.

Sec. 9.   Whenever the legislative branch of such city, town, or municipal corporation shall, by resolution, deem it necessary, the Treasurer of such city shall, within ten days after the passage of such resolution, give additional bonds, provided for the proper care and custody of any municipal improvement fund, as in this Act provided.

Sec. 10.   All general and special Acts and parts of such Acts in conflict with this Act, or abridging the rights of cities, towns, or municipal corporations herein, are hereby repealed.

Sec. 11.   This Act shall take effect and be in force from and after its passage.

'SUPPLEMENT CLXXIII.

1887, 148.

———

An Act to amend section thirty-two of an Act entitled "An Act to provide for work upon streets, lanes, alleys, courts, places, and sidewalks, and for the construction of sewers within municipalities," approved March 18, 1885.

[Approved March 15, 1887.]

The People of the State of California, represented in Senate and Assembly, do enact as follows:

Section 1.   Section thirty-two of the Act, the title of which is recited in the title hereof, is hereby amended so as to read as follows:

Section 32.   The proceeds of the sale of the bonds shall be deposited in the City Treasury, to the account of the Sewer Fund, but no payment therefrom shall be made, except to pay for the construction of the sewer or sewers for the construction of which the bonds were issued, and upon the certificate of the Superintendent of Streets and the City Engineer that the work has been done according to the contract; *provided*, that after the completion of the sewers, for the construction of which said bonds were issued, if there be any money of said fund left in the Treasury, the same may be transferred to the General Fund, for general purposes.

Sec. 2.   This Act shall take effect immediately.

SUPPLEMENT CLXXIV.

1887, 149.

An Act to amend section one thousand one hundred and sixty of the Political Code of the State of California, relating to elections.

[Approved March 15, 1887.]

The People of the State of California, represented in Senate and Assembly, do enact as follows:

SECTION 1,   Section one thousand one hundred and sixty of the Political Code is hereby amended to read as follows:

1160.   The polls must be opened at six o'clock on the morning of the day of election, and must be kept open until seven o'clock on the evening of the same day, when the polls shall be closed.

SUPPLEMENT CLXXV.

1887.

SECTION 8 OF ARTICLE IX OF THE STATE CONSTITUTION AS PROPOSED TO BE AMENDED AT THE ELECTION OF APRIL 12, 1887.

SECTION 8.   Any city, or consolidated city and county, containing a population of more than one hundred thousand inhabitants, may frame a charter for its own government, consistent with and subject to the Constitution and laws of the State by causing a Board of fifteen freeholders, who shall have been for at least five years qualified electors thereof, to be elected by the qualified voters of such city, or city and county, at any general or special election, whose duty it shall be, within one hundred days after such election, to prepare and propose a charter for such city, or city and county, which shall be signed in duplicate by the members of such Board, or a majority of them, and returned, one copy thereof to the Mayor, or other chief executive officer of such city, or city and county, and the other to the Recorder of Deeds of the county, or city and county. Such proposed charter shall then be published in two daily papers of general circulation in such city, or city and county, for at least twenty days, and such publication shall be commenced within twenty (20) days after the completion of the charter; and within not less than thirty days after the completion of such publication it shall be submitted by the legislative authority of said city, or city and county, to the qualified electors thereof at a general or special election, and if a majority of such qualified electors voting thereat shall ratify the same, it shall thereafter be submitted to the Legislature for its approval or rejection as a whole, without power of alteration or amendment ; and if approved by a majority vote of the members elected to each House it shall become the charter of such city, or if such city be consolidated with a county, then of such city and county, and shall become the organic law thereof, and supersede any existing charter, and all amendments thereof, and all special laws inconsistent with such charter. A copy of such charter, certified by the Mayor, or other chief executive officer, and authenticated by the seal of such city, or city and county, setting forth the submission of such charter to the electors, and its ratification by them, shall be made in duplicate, and deposited, one in the office of the Secretary of State, the other, after being recorded in the office of the Recorder of Deeds of the county, or city and county, among the archives of the city, or city and county. All Courts shall take judicial notice thereof. The charter so ratified may be amended at intervals of not less than two years, by proposals therefor submitted by legislative authority of the city, or city and county, to the qualified voters thereof, at a general or special election held at least sixty days after the publication of such proposals, and ratified by at least three-fifths of the qualified electors voting thereat, and approved by the Legislature as herein provided for the approval of the charter. In submitting any such charter, or amendment thereto, any alternative article or proposition may be presented for the choice of the voters, and may be voted on separately without prejudice to others. Any city, or consolidated city and county, containing a population of more than ten thousand and not more than one hundred thousand inhabitants, may frame a charter for its own government, consistent with and subject to the Constitution and laws of this State, by causing a Board of fifteen freeholders, who shall have been for at least five years qualified electors thereof, to be elected by the qualified voters of said city, or city and county, at any general or special election, whose duty it shall be, within ninety days after such election, to prepare and propose a charter for such city, or city and county, which shall be signed in duplicate by the members of such Board, or a majority of them, and returned, one copy thereof to the Mayor, or other chief executive officer of said city, or city and county, and the other to the Recorder of the county, or city and county. Such proposed charter shall then be published in two daily papers of general circulation in such city, or city and county, for at least twenty days ; and publication shall be commenced within twenty days after the completion of the charter ; and within not less than thirty days after the completion of such publication it shall be submitted by the legislative authority of said city, or city and county, to the qualified electors of said city, or city and county, at a general or special election, and if a majority of such qualified electors voting thereat shall ratify the same it shall thereafter be submitted to the Legislature for its approval or rejection as a whole, without power of alteration or amendment, and if approved by a majority vote of the members elected to each House it shall become the charter of such city, or if such city be consolidated with a county, then of such city and county, and shall become the organic law thereof, and shall supersede any existing charter, and all amendments thereof, and all special laws inconsistent with such charter. A copy of such charter, certified by the Mayor, or other chief executive officer, and authenticated by the seal of such city, or city and county, setting forth the submission of such charter to the electors, and its ratification by them, shall be made in duplicate, and deposited, one in the office of the Secretary of State, and the other, after being recorded in the office of the Recorder of Deeds of the county, or city and county, among the archives of the city, or city and county ; and thereafter all Courts shall take judicial notice thereof. The charter so ratified may be amended, at intervals of not less than two years, by proposals therefor, submitted by the legislative authority of the city, or city and county, to the qualified electors thereof, at a general or special election held at least sixty days after the publication of such proposals, and ratified by at least three-fifths of the qualified electors voting thereat, and approved by the Legislature as herein provided for the approval of the charter. In submitting any such charter, or amendment thereto, any alternative article or proposition may be presented for the choice of the voters, and may be voted on separately without prejudice to others.

An Act to relinquish the interest of the United States in certain lands to the City and County of San Francisco and their grantees.

[Approved December 20, 1886.]

Be it enacted by the Senate and House of Representatives of the United States of America in Congress assembled, That the right, title, and ownership of the City and County of San Francisco, in the State of California, to the body of land hereinafter described are confirmed, and all the right and title of the United States to said land are hereby granted and relinquished to said city and county, and to those persons, and their successors in interest, to whom portions of said land have been heretofore granted and conveyed by or on behalf of said city and county, to the extent of their interest in said land. Said land hereby granted is described as follows: Situated within the corporate limits of the said city and county; bounded on the north by the southern boundary-line of the land granted by the United States to said city and county by patent dated June twentieth, eighteen hundred and eighty-four; on the west by the Pacific Ocean; on the south by the land surveyed by Deputy United States Surveyor James T. Stratton, in eighteen hundred and sixty-seven and eighteen hundred and sixty-eight, as the southern line of the land granted to said city and county by Act of Congress approved March eighth, eighteen hundred and sixty-six; and also bounded on the south by the northern boundary of the Rancho Laguna de la Merced, granted by the United States to J. de Haro and others, September tenth eighteen hundred and seventy-two, wherever said northern boundary of said rancho is north of said line surveyed by said Stratton; on the east by the western boundary of the Rancho San Miguel, granted by the United States to J. de J. Noe, March thirtieth, eighteen hundred and fifty-seven.

SEC. 2.   That upon the approval of this Act the Commissioner of the General Land Office shall issue a patent for said land to said city and county, and said patent shall inure to said city and county, and the grantees of the same, and their said successors in interest, as a confirmation of said city and county's grants of said land.

SEC. 3.   That all laws in conflict with the provisions of this Act are hereby declared inapplicable to the lands hereby granted and relinquished.

TABLE

HARBOR OF SAN FRANCISCO.

The laws creating a Board of State Harbor Commissioners and regulating the duties thereof are found in the Political Code, Sections 2520 to 2553, inclusive.

The laws regulating Pilots and Pilot Commissioners are found in the Political Code, Sections 2420 to 2491, inclusive.

The laws regulating Port Wardens are found in the Political Code, Sections 2501 to 2511, inclusive.

INDEX.

Page

Board of Election Commissioners............332
Board of Equalization, State and County ...362
Board of Fifteen Freeholders. 429, 439
Board of Fire Commissioners. (See Fire De-
partment.)
Board of Health............................353
   officers of........................... 353
   to regulate plumbing and drainage..308, 309
   to license plumbers.....................432
Board of New City Hall Commissioners.... 196
Board of Park Commissioners. (See Park
Commissioners.)
Board of Supervisors. (See Supervisors.)
Boards of Precinct Registration. 337
Bogus election tickets, in relation to... 350
Bonds—
   all officers must give bonds....... 8
   indebtedness for municipal purposes.....436
Books, blanks, etc., requisitions for......... 51
Boundaries, defined 4
   wards................... 69
   under Charter of 1855, (note)............ 12
Bricks, burning of, regulated 44
Bryant and Brannan streets, grade of 227
Buildings, contracts for.................... 16
   regulations within certain limits......... 20
   repairs of public 254
   fuel for public 144
Burials, regulations for....................357

C

Captains of Police. (See Police.)
Cemetery, appropriation for 144
Cemeteries, regulation as to burials.........358
Certificates for burial......................360
Children, commitments to Industrial School.
....38, 40
   penalty for harboring runaway inmates
   of Industrial School..................... 40
Chinese, removal of, outside cities and towns.279
   Not to be employed on public works.....432
City and County, right to sue and defend, etc. 3
   rights to remain in corporation..........4, 5
   real estate may not be sold 10
   non-liability for accidents on public
   streets......................166, 303, 327
City and County Attorney, salary and duties.
....51, 131
   assistant allowed 103
   clerks of 132
   member of City Hall Commission.......196
   member of Election Commission........332
City Hall. (See New City Hall.)
Clerk of Supervisors, fees for administering
   oaths....................................... 7
   deputy of......... ....80, 144
   salary of 244

Page

Clerk of Supervisors
   duties as Clerk of the Board of Equaliza-
   tion.....................................381
Clerk of Finance Committee............. 35
Clerk of Outside Lands Committee......421
Closing and opening of certain streets at the
   Potrero confirmed........................246
Coal, Supervisors authorized to appoint
   weigher of.............. 67
Collection of personal property tax 393
Columbia Square, gardener for............. 114
Commissioners, New City Hall 196
Congressional Districts......................349
Constitution, provisions
   Article IV (Legislative Department), Sec.
   30....................................... 427
   No appropriation can be made for
   sectarian purposes..................427
   Article IX (Education), Secs. 6, 7 and 8..427
   Election of County Superintendent..427
   The public school system ....
   School text-books.....................427
   Article XI—Relating to cities, counties
   and towns............................423
   Legislature establish system of coun-
   ty governments 428
   Providing for election or appoint-
   ment of county and municipal offi-
   cers.................... 428
   Providing for creating municipal cor-
   porations 429
   Consolidation of city and county governments..........................429
   Framing and adoption of charter prepared by Freeholders..........429, 439
   Compensation of county or municipal
   officers not increased during their
   terms 430
   Counties and municipalities cannot
   be released from State taxation....430
   Legislature no power to impose municipal taxes............... 430
   Special commissions, private companies or individuals not to exercise
   municipal functions.................430
   Private property exempt from seizure
   for corporate debt 431
   No State office can be created for inspection, etc., of merchandise in
   cities or counties...................430
   All county or city moneys must be
   immediately deposited with the
   Treasurer...........................431
   Making a profit of public moneys declared a felony......................431
   How county or municipal indebtedness may be incurred...............431
   Water and artificial light companies
   may lay down mains in cities 431

30

Page

Page

www.ingramcontent.com/pod-product-compliance
Lightning Source LLC
Chambersburg PA
CBHW031813270326
41932CB00008B/411